When should I trav...
Where do I go for ans...
What's the best and easie... ...rip?

frommers.travelocity.c~...

Frommer's, the travel guide leader, has teamed up with **Travelocity.com**, the leader in online travel, to bring you an in-depth, easy-to-use resource designed to help you plan and book your trip online.

At **frommers.travelocity.com**, you'll find free online updates about your destination from the experts at Frommer's plus the outstanding travel planning and purchasing features of Travelocity.com. Travelocity.com provides reservations capabilities for 95 percent of all airline seats sold, more than 47,000 hotels, and over 50 car rental companies. In addition, Travelocity.com offers more than 2,000 exciting vacation and cruise packages. Travelocity.com puts you in complete control of your travel planning with these and other great features:

> **Expert travel guidance from Frommer's** - over 150 writers reporting from around the world!
>
> **Best Fare Finder** - an interactive calendar tells you when to travel to get the best airfare
>
> **Fare Watcher** - we'll track airfare changes to your favorite destinations
>
> **Dream Maps** - a mapping feature that suggests travel opportunities based on your budget
>
> **Shop Safe Guarantee** - 24 hours a day / 7 days a week live customer service, and more!

Whether traveling on a tight budget, looking for a quick weekend getaway, or planning the trip of a lifetime, Frommer's guides and Travelocity.com will make your travel dreams a reality. You've bought the book, now book the trip!

Travelocity.com
A Sabre Company

Frommer's

A New Star-Rating System & Other Exciting News from Frommer's!

In our continuing effort to publish the savviest, most up-to-date, and most appealing travel guides available, we've added some great new features.

Frommer's guides now include a new **star-rating system.** Every hotel, restaurant, and attraction is rated from 0 to 3 stars to help you set priorities and organize your time.

We've also added **seven brand-new features** that point you to the great deals, in-the-know advice, and unique experiences that separate travelers from tourists. Throughout the guide look for:

Finds	Special finds—those places only insiders know about
Fun Fact	Fun facts—details that make travelers more informed and their trips more fun
Kids	Best bets for kids—advice for the whole family
Moments	Special moments—those experiences that memories are made of
Overrated	Places or experiences not worth your time or money
Tips	Insider tips—some great ways to save time and money
Value	Great values—where to get the best deals

We've also added a **"What's New"** section in every guide—a timely crash course in what's hot and what's not in every destination we cover.

Other Great Guides for Your Trip:

Frommer's Canada

Frommer's Vancouver & Victoria

Frommer's Seattle & Portland

Frommer's Washington State

Frommer's Alaska

Frommer's Portable Alaska Cruises & Ports of Call

Frommer's®

British Columbia & the Canadian Rockies

2nd Edition

by Bill McRae

with Shawn Blore

Here's what the critics say about Frommer's:

"Amazingly easy to use. Very portable, very complete."
                                                —*Booklist*

"The only mainstream guide to list specific prices. The Walter Cronkite of guidebooks—with all that implies."
                                                —*Travel & Leisure*

"Complete, concise, and filled with useful information."
                                                —*New York Daily News*

"Hotel information is close to encyclopedic."
                                                —*Des Moines Sunday Register*

"Detailed, accurate, and easy-to-read information for all price ranges."
                                                —*Glamour Magazine*

Hungry Minds™

Best-Selling Books • Digital Downloads • e-Books • Answer Networks
e-Newsletters • Branded Web Sites • e-Learning
New York, NY • Cleveland, OH • Indianapolis, IN

About the Authors

Bill McRae was born and raised in rural eastern Montana, though he spent the better years of his youth attending university in Great Britain, France, and Canada. He has previously written about Montana and Utah for Moon Publications and about the Pacific Northwest and Seattle for Lonely Planet. He has also written for *National Geographic* and Expedia, among others, and is a coauthor of *Frommer's Canada.* He makes his home in Portland, Oregon.

A native of California and resident by turns of Ottawa, Amsterdam, Moscow, and (for the past several years) Vancouver, **Shawn Blore** is an award-winning magazine writer and the best-selling author of *Vancouver: Secrets of the City.* He is also the author of *Frommer's Vancouver & Victoria* and a coauthor of *Frommer's Canada.*

Published by:

Hungry Minds, Inc.

909 Third Ave.
New York, NY 10022

ISBN 0-7645-6599-0
ISSN 1524-1483

Editor: Leslie Shen
Production Editor: M. Faunette Johnston
Photo Editor: Richard Fox
Cartographer: Elizabeth Puhl
Production by Hungry Minds Indianapolis Production Services

Front cover photo: Emerald Lake in Yoho Valley
Back cover photo: Whistler/Blackcomb Mountain Resort

Special Sales

For general information on Hungry Minds' products and services, please contact our Customer Care department; within the U.S. at 800-762-2974, outside the U.S. at 317-572-3993, or fax 317-572-4002. For sales inquiries and reseller information, including discounts, bulk sales, customized editions, and premium sales, please contact our Customer Care department at 800-434-3422.

Manufactured in the United States of America

5 4 3 2 1

Contents

List of Maps

An Invitation to the Reader

In researching this book, we discovered many wonderful places—hotels, restaurants, shops, and more. We're sure you'll find others. Please tell us about them, so we can share the information with your fellow travelers in upcoming editions. If you were disappointed with a recommendation, we'd love to know that, too. Please write to:

Frommer's British Columbia & the Canadian Rockies, 2nd Edition
Hungry Minds, Inc. • 909 Third Avenue • New York, NY 10022

An Additional Note

Please be advised that travel information is subject to change at any time—and this is especially true of prices. We therefore suggest that you write or call ahead for confirmation when making your travel plans. The authors, editors, and publisher cannot be held responsible for the experiences of readers while traveling. Your safety is important to us, however, so we encourage you to stay alert and be aware of your surroundings. Keep a close eye on cameras, purses, and wallets, all favorite targets of thieves and pickpockets.

New! Frommer's Star Ratings & Icons

Every hotel, restaurant, and attraction listing in this guide has been ranked for quality, value, service, amenities, and special features using a star-rating scale. In country, state, and regional guides, we also rate towns and regions to help you narrow down your choices and budget your time accordingly. Hotels and restaurants in the Very Expensive and Expensive categories are rated on a scale of one (highly recommended) to three stars (exceptional). Those in the Moderate and Inexpensive categories rate from zero (recommended) to two stars (very highly recommended). Attractions, towns, and regions are rated according to the following scale: zero stars (recommended), one star (highly recommended), two stars (very highly recommended), and three stars (must-see).

In addition to the rating system, we also use seven icons to highlight insider information, useful tips, special bargains, hidden gems, memorable experiences, kid-friendly venues, places to avoid, and other useful information:

| Finds | Fun Fact | Kids | Moments | Overrated | Tips | Value |

The following abbreviations are used for credit cards:

| AE | American Express | DISC | Discover | V | Visa |
| DC | Diners Club | MC | MasterCard | | |

FROMMERS.COM

Now that you have the guidebook to a great trip, visit our website at **www.frommers.com** for travel information on nearly 2,000 destinations. With features updated regularly, we give you instant access to the most current trip-planning information available. At Frommers.com, you'll also find the best prices on airfares, accommodations, and car rentals—and you can even book travel online through our travel booking partners. At Frommers.com, you'll also find the following:

- Daily Newsletter highlighting the best travel deals
- Hot Spot of the Month/Vacation Sweepstakes & Travel Photo Contest
- More than 200 Travel Message Boards
- Outspoken Newsletters and Feature Articles on travel bargains, vacation ideas, tips & resources, and more!

What's New in British Columbia & the Canadian Rockies

British Columbia and Alberta continue to be the fastest-growing areas in Canada, with an ongoing influx of new immigrants—from overseas and from other parts of Canada—adding to the region's already rich cultural diversity. Few places on earth can match the cosmopolitan atmosphere of Vancouver, and in even far-flung villages you'll find communities of Albanians, Somalis, Cambodians, or Uzbekis. More than ever, Canada is a mosaic of cultures.

While traveling around British Columbia and the Canadian Rockies, we noted that a number of things have changed: Restaurants come and go, B&Bs pop up, new attractions open their doors. Following is a brief overview of a few of these changes.

VANCOUVER Perched on the edge of Coal Harbour, the **Westin Bayshore Resort & Marina,** 1601 Bayshore Dr. (© **800/228-3000**), already had the best location in town. Now, thanks to gobs of money, this icon of 1960s Modernism positively sparkles. It's the perfect spot for those who want to be close to prime recreational areas such as Stanley Park. See chapter 3 for details.

VICTORIA 'Twas a sad day in Victoria when Michael Williams died. The former shepherd turned entrepreneur had single-handedly renovated much of downtown, including the lovely **Swans Suite Hotel,** 506 Pandora Ave. (© **800/668-7926**). Still,

the show must go on, and to ensure it does, Williams donated most of his holdings—Swans included—to the University of Victoria, on condition they continue to operate. It was the largest single bequest to a university in Canadian history. So think of that next time you walk into Swans' brew-pub to hoist a pint. See chapter 4 for details.

VANCOUVER ISLAND Construction is now complete on the **Island Highway** (Hwy. 19), the expressway that runs from the Victoria area to Campbell River. This fast new highway can shear a couple of hours off a road trip between these two hubs. See chapters 5 through 7 for complete coverage of Vancouver Island.

THE GULF ISLANDS BC Ferries is under new management, and these assumedly well-meaning folks have managed to make the already dire state of ferry service to the Gulf Islands even worse. If you're planning to explore these lovely islands, download a copy of the most recent schedules from www.bcferries.com and have a good look. Inter-island ferry service is very infrequent and inconvenient. Before you make reservations at a succession of sumptuous B&Bs, make sure that you can even get between islands within your time frame. See chapter 5 for details.

THE THOMPSON RIVER VALLEY Downtown Kamloops is undergoing a sort of renaissance, and the reopening of the grand **Plaza Heritage Hotel,** 405 Victoria St. (© 877/977-5292), really underscores the point. The fanciest lodging in Kamloops when it was built 80 years ago, it has been completely updated and beautifully decorated. Even if you don't spend the night, it's worth stopping downtown to see how the handsome city center is revitalizing itself with good restaurants and fine shops. See chapter 10 for details.

THE OKANAGAN VALLEY It wasn't that long ago that western Canadian wines were at best a novelty. However, in the past few years, the wine industry—especially in the arid Okanagan Valley—has really taken off. British Columbia wines have come a long way and are ready to step out onto the world stage. In the Okanagan, you will often find only British Columbia wines at high-end restaurants. And, as is often the case, just because you are close to where the wines were produced, don't expect them to be inexpensive.

In Kelowna, a city with a big reputation for fine dining, people notice when someone opens a new restaurant. Especially when that person is Rod Butters, a young chef who previously led the kitchens at such famous hotels as the Chateau Whistler, the Wickaninnish Inn in Tofino, and the Pacific Palisades in Vancouver. **Fresco,** 1560 Water St. (© 250/868-8805), is his first venture as a chef entrepreneur, and the results are stellar. Expect hearty though refined cuisine based on regional meats and produce. See chapter 11 for details.

SOUTHEASTERN BRITISH COLUMBIA The transformation of Golden from sleepy railroad town to international recreation capital fast-forwarded in 2001 with the opening of the **Kicking Horse Mountain Resort** (© 866/754-5425). One of the highest-elevation ski areas in North America, Kicking Horse has downhill runs starting at over 8,000 feet (2,400m). The resort's **Eagle's Eye Restaurant,** located at the top of the gondola at 8,033 feet (2,410m), offers fine dining in a stunning mountain lodge with a view that seems to take in all of the Canadian Rockies. See chapter 12 for details.

CALGARY The rejuvenation of Stephens Street—not so long ago a slightly seedy downtown bowery famous for rowdy bars—continues, and the opening of the **Hyatt Regency Calgary,** 700 Center St. S. (© 800/233-1234), really ought to help boost property values. This high-rise luxury hotel is linked to the new Telus Convention Centre. See chapter 13 for details.

BANFF Why should flash-searing meats at 1,200 degrees bring out the rich flavors of grass-fed beef? Ponder the question at **Saltlik,** 221 Bear St. (© 403/760-2467), one of Banff's newest and most fashionable restaurants. The setting is as cool as the grills are scorching: Industrial chic—concrete and steel—isn't exactly what you expect in an alpine setting, but in summer the glass walls fold back and nearly the entire restaurant turns alfresco. See chapter 14 for details.

The Best of British Columbia & the Canadian Rockies

British Columbia and the Canadian Rockies, which stretch across the provincial border into Alberta, are extravagantly scenic and quietly sophisticated. The diversity of landscapes is astounding: You'll travel from cactus-studded desert to soaring mountaintops and on to wilderness ocean beaches. You can visit traditional Native Canadian villages, thread through market stalls in the largest Chinese community outside of Asia, and cheer on cowboys at an old-fashioned rodeo.

As for creature comforts, British Columbia and the Rockies are famed for their luxury hotels, rustic guest ranches, quiet inns, and B&Bs. And the food? With Alberta beef, Pacific salmon, and some of the world's most fertile farm and orchard land, these two provinces champion excellent regional cuisine.

Finally, there's no better place to get outdoors and enjoy yourself: These areas are flush with ski resorts and golf courses, hiking is a near universal passion, and you'll find no better spot on earth to try your hand at adventure sports like sea kayaking, trail riding, or scuba diving.

This guide is chock-full of recommendations and tips to help you plan and enjoy your trip to western Canada; the following are some places and experiences you won't want to miss.

1 The Best Travel Experiences

- **Wandering Vancouver's West End:** Vancouver is one of the most cosmopolitan cities in the world, and wandering the streets, people-watching, and sipping cappuccinos at street cafes can fill an entire weekend. Stroll up Robson Street with its busy boutique-shopping scene, turn down cafe-lined Denman Street, then stride into 1,000-acre (405-hectare) Stanley Park, a gem of green space with old-growth cedars, miles of walkways, and the city's excellent aquarium. See chapter 3.
- **Taking Tea in Victoria:** Yeah, it's a little corny, but it's also fun—and delicious. Tea, scones, clotted cream—who said the British don't

know good food? The afternoon tea at the Empress is world-renowned, a little stuffy, and very expensive; if that doesn't sound like fun to you, we'll show you other places where tea is more reasonably priced and a lot less formal. See chapter 4.
- **Ferrying through the Gulf Islands:** The Gulf Islands, a huddle of cliff-lined, forested islands between Vancouver Island and the British Columbia mainland, can only be reached via ferry. Hop from island to island, staying at excellent country inns and B&Bs; peddle the quiet farm roads on your bike, stopping to visit artists' studios or to quaff a pint in a cozy

rural pub. The romantic getaway you've been dreaming of starts and ends right here on these idyllic islands. See chapter 5.

- **Traveling the Inside Passage:** The 15-hour Inside Passage ferry cruise aboard the MV *Queen of the North* takes you from Vancouver Island's Port Hardy along an otherwise inaccessible coastline north to Prince Rupert, near the southern tip of the Alaska Panhandle. Orcas swim past the ferry, bald eagles soar overhead, and the dramatic scenery—a narrow channel of water between a series of mountain islands and the craggy mainland—is utterly spectacular. See chapter 9.

- **Wine Tasting in the Okanagan Valley:** The Okanagan Valley in central British Columbia has some of the most arid climatic conditions in Canada, and with irrigation, grape varietals like merlot, cabernet sauvignon, and pinot noir flourish here. Vineyards line the edges of huge, glacier-dug lakes and clamber up the steep desert-valley walls. Taste delicious wines, go for a swim, play some golf, eat at excellent restaurants, and do it all again tomorrow. See chapter 11.

- **Golfing Southeastern British Columbia:** The upper reaches of the mighty Columbia River rise in a verdant, trench-like valley, towered over by the 12,000-foot (3,600m) Canadian Rockies. Nowhere else will you find such a variety of championship golf resorts in such a dramatically beautiful landscape. See chapter 12.

- **Skiing the Canadian Rockies:** You can hit all three ski areas in Banff National Park with a one-price ticket, using the frequent shuttle buses to ferry you and your skis from resort to resort. The skiing is superlative, the scenery astounding, and—best of all—you can stay at Banff's luxury hotels for a fraction of their astronomical summer rates. See chapter 14.

- **Riding Herd at a Guest Ranch:** The edge of the Great Plains nudges up to the face of the Canadian Rockies in Alberta, making this some of the most fertile and beautiful ranching country anywhere. For more than a century, ranches have welcomed guests to their rustic lodges and cabins, offering trail rides, cattle drives, evening barbecues, and barn dances that'll keep you entertained whether you're a greenhorn or an old hand. See chapter 14.

2 The Best Active Vacations

- **Hiking the West Coast Trail:** Hiking the entire length of the rugged 43-mile (69km) West Coast Trail, from Port Renfrew to Bamfield on Vancouver Island, takes 5 to 7 days, but it's truly the hike of a lifetime. This wilderness coastline, edged with old-growth forest and lined with cliffs, is utterly spectacular, and can be reached only on foot. If you're not up for it, consider a 7-mile (11km) day trip on the more easily accessible stretch just south of Bamfield. See chapter 6.

- **Scuba Diving off Vancouver Island:** According to no less an authority than Jacques Cousteau, the waters off Vancouver Island offer some of the best diving in the world. Nanaimo and Port Hardy are popular departure points, with outfitters ready to drop you into the briny world of the wolf eel, yellow-edged cadlina, and giant Pacific octopus. See chapters 6 and 7.

- **Kayaking Clayoquot Sound:** Paddle a kayak for 4 or 5 days through the waters of Clayoquot Sound on Vancouver Island's wilderness west coast, from the funky former fishing village of Tofino to a natural hot-springs bath near an ancient Native village. Along the way, you'll see thousand-year-old trees and glaciers, whales and bald eagles. And if the pocketbook allows, you can stop in at one of two resorts that offer some of the best cuisine in the world. See chapter 6.

- **Salmon Fishing from Campbell River:** Even though salmon fishing is not what it once was, Campbell River is still the "Salmon-Fishing Capital of the World." Join a day trip with an outfitter and fish the waters of Discovery Passage. Get ready to hook the big one! Even if your trophy salmon gets away, you'll see plenty of wildlife: bald eagles, seals, even orcas and porpoises. See chapter 7.

- **Rafting the Chilko-Chilcotin-Fraser Rivers:** This 3-day white-water extravaganza flushes you from the slopes of the glaciered Coast Range down through shadowy canyons to the roiling waters of the mighty Fraser River, second in North America only to the Columbia River in power and size. A number of outfitters in Williams Lake offer river options ranging from half-day thrill rides to multi-day trips with catered camping. See chapter 10.

- **Canoeing Bowron Lakes Provincial Park:** Every summer, canoeists and kayakers set out to navigate a perfect 72-mile (120km) circle of six alpine lakes, with minimal portages in between. There are no roads or other signs of civilization beyond the launch point, except some well-placed cabins, campsites, and shelters. The full circuit is a 7-day trip, but the memories will last a lifetime. See chapter 10.

- **Mountain Biking the Kettle Valley Railway:** This rails-to-trails hiking-and-biking route travels from Lake Okanagan up and over Okanagan Mountain, crossing 17 trestles and traversing two tunnels on its 108-mile (175km) route. The entire circuit, which takes from 3 to 5 days, provides lots of challenging grades and excellent scenery. See chapter 11.

- **Heli-Skiing near Golden:** Helicopters lift adventurous skiers to the tops of the Selkirk and Purcell mountains that rise just west of Golden, accessing acres of virgin powder far from the lift lines and crowds of traditional ski resorts. **CMH Heli-Skiing (© 800/661-0252)** offers a variety of holidays, most based out of its private high-country lodges and reached only by helicopter. See chapter 12.

- **Cross-Country Skiing at Canmore:** The 1988 Olympic cross-country skiing events were held at Canmore, on the edge of Banff National Park. The routes at the Canmore Nordic Centre are now open to the public and offer 44 miles (70km) of world-class skiing. Canmore offers lots of moderately priced lodging, none finer than the **McNeill Heritage Inn (© 877/MCNEILL)**. See chapter 14.

- **Lodge-to-Lodge Trail Riding in Banff National Park:** See the park's backcountry without getting blisters on your feet. Instead, get saddle-sore as you ride horseback on a 3-day excursion, spending the nights in remote but comfortable mountain lodges. **Warner Guiding and Outfitting (© 403/762-4551)** provides all meals and lodging, plus oats for Silver. See chapter 14.

3 The Best Nature- & Wildlife-Viewing

- **Tide Pools at Botanical Beach near Port Renfrew:** Waves have eroded potholes in the thrust of sandstone that juts into the Pacific at Botanical Beach, which remain water-filled when the waves ebb. Alive with starfish, sea anemones, hermit crabs, and hundreds of other sea creatures, these potholes are some of the best places on Vancouver Island to explore the rich intertidal zone. See chapter 5.
- **Bald Eagles near Victoria:** Just a few miles north of Victoria is one of the world's best bald eagle–spotting sites: Goldstream Provincial Park. Recent counts put the number of eagles wintering here at around 4,000. (Jan is the best month for viewing, though there are eagles here year-round.) See chapter 5.
- **Gray Whales at Pacific Rim National Park:** Few sights in nature match observing whales in the wild. March is the prime viewing time, as the whales migrate north from their winter home off Mexico. During March, both Tofino and Ucluelet celebrate the Pacific Rim Whale Festival; outfitters offer whale-watching trips out onto the Pacific. See chapter 6.
- **Orcas at Robson Bight:** From either the northeast shore of Vancouver Island or a whale-watching boat out of Telegraph Cove or Port MacNeill, watch orcas (killer whales) as they glide through the Johnstone Strait in search of salmon, and rub their tummies on the pebbly beaches at Robson Bight. See chapter 7.
- **Spawning Salmon at Adams River:** Every October, the Adams River fills with salmon, returning to their home water to spawn and die. While each autumn produces a large run of salmon, every fourth year (the next are 2002 and 2006), an estimated 1.5 to 2 million sockeye salmon struggle upstream to spawn in the Adams River near Squilax. Roderick Haig-Brown Provincial Park has viewing platforms and interpretive programs. See chapter 10.
- **Songbirds and Waterfowl at the Columbia River Wetlands:** Between Golden and Windermere, the Columbia River flows through a valley filled with fluvial lakes, marshes, and streams—perfect habitat for hundreds of species, including moose and coyotes. Protected as a wildlife refuge, the wetlands are on the migratory flyway that links Central America to the Arctic; in spring and fall, the waterways fill with thousands of birds—over different 270 species. Outfitters in Golden and Invermere operate float trips through the wetlands. See chapter 12.
- **Elk in Banff National Park:** You won't need to mount an expedition to sight elk in Banff: They graze in the city parks and on people's front lawns. To see these animals in their own habitat, take the Fenlands Trail just west of Banff to Vermillion Lakes, another favorite grazing area. See chapter 14.
- **Black Bears in Waterton Lakes National Park:** There are black bears throughout the Canadian west, but chances are good you'll spot a bear or two along the entry road to Waterton Lakes National Park, where the open grasslands of the prairies directly abut the sheer faces of the Rocky Mountains (remember, bears are originally prairie animals). See chapter 14.

4 The Best Family-Vacation Experiences

- **The Beaches near Parksville and Qualicum Beach:** The sandy beaches near these towns warm in the summer sun, then heat the waters of Georgia Strait when the tides return. Some of the warmest ocean waters in the Pacific Northwest are here, making for good swimming and family vacations. See chapter 6.

- **The MV *Lady Rose* (© 800/663-7192):** This packet steamer delivers mail and merchandise to isolated marine communities along the otherwise inaccessible Alberni Inlet, the longest fjord on Vancouver Island's rugged west coast. Along the way, you may spot eagles, bears, and porpoises. The MV *Lady Rose* is large enough to be stable, yet small enough to make this daylong journey from Port Alberni to Bamfield and back seem like a real adventure. See chapter 6.

- **The Okanagan Lakes:** Sunny weather, sandy lake beaches, and miles of clean, clear water: If this sounds like the ideal family vacation, then head to the lake-filled Okanagan Valley. Penticton and Kelowna have dozens of family-friendly hotels, watersports rentals, and lakeside parks and beaches. Mom and Dad can enjoy the golf and wineries as well. See chapter 11.

- **Fort Steele Heritage Town (© 250/489-3351):** In 1864, the frontier community of Fort Steele was a mining boomtown with a population of 4,000. Twenty years later, the town was practically abandoned, soon becoming a ghost town. Now a provincial heritage site, Fort Steele again bustles with life: The town has been largely rebuilt, other historic structures have been moved in, and daily activities with living-history actors give this town a real feel of the Old West. See chapter 12.

- **Fort Calgary Historic Park (© 403/290-1875):** This reconstruction of the Mountie fort on the banks of the Bow River—and the genesis for the city of Calgary—has always been interesting, as volunteers have been in the process of rebuilding the original fort. In the last couple years, critical mass has been reached and new/old Fort Calgary is really taking shape: It's gone from a good idea to a great attraction. But what's really cool is that the labor has been volunteer and that all the work was done using tools and techniques from the 1880s. Take the kids and give them a lesson in history and volunteerism! See chapter 13.

- **West Edmonton Mall (© 800/661-8890):** Okay, so it's a mall. But what a mall! Within its 5.2 million square feet are 800 stores and a mammoth entertainment center that contains a complete amusement park, roller coaster, bungee-jumping platform, and lake-size swimming pool with real sand beaches and rolling waves. You can also ice-skate, watch performing dolphins, ride a submarine, attend movies at 19 theaters—oh, and get your shopping done, too. See chapter 13.

- **The Kicking Horse River:** One of the best white-water rafting trips in the Rockies is on the Kicking Horse River near Golden. While it's the treacherous Class IV rapids that give the river its fame, there are also stretches gentle enough for the entire family. Better yet, most outfitters run simultaneous trips on both sections of the river, so part of your brood can run the rapids while the other enjoys a leisurely float through lovely Rocky Mountain scenery. See chapter 14.

5 The Best Places to Rediscover Native Canadian Culture & History

- **Quw'utsun' Cultural Centre** (Duncan; ✆ **877/746-8119** or **250/746-8119**): North of Victoria, this facility contains a theater, carving shed, ceremonial clan house, restaurant, and art gallery, all dedicated to preserving traditional Cowichan history and culture. Try to visit when the tribe is preparing a traditional salmon bake. See chapter 5.

- **Kwagiulth Museum and Cultural Centre** (Quadra Island; ✆ **250/285-3733**): To the Native Indians along the Northwest coast, the potlatch was one of the most important ceremonies, involving the reenactment of clan myths and ritual gift giving. When Canadian officials banned the potlatch in the 1920s, the centuries-old costumes, masks, and artifacts of the Kwagiulth tribe were confiscated and sent to museums in eastern Canada and England. When the items were repatriated in the early 1990s, the tribe built a handsome museum to showcase this incredible collection of Native art. See chapter 7.

- **Alert Bay** (off Vancouver Island): One of the best-preserved and still vibrant Native villages in western Canada, Alert Bay is a short ferry ride from northern Vancouver Island. Totem poles face the waters, and cedar-pole longhouses are painted with traditional images and symbols. The **U'Mista Cultural Centre** (✆ **250/974-5403**) contains a collection of carved masks, baskets, and potlatch ceremonial objects. See chapter 7.

- **Gwaii Haanas National Park Reserve** (Queen Charlotte Islands): A UNESCO World Heritage Site and a Canadian National Park, this is the ancient homeland of the Haida people. Located on the storm-lashed Queen Charlottes, it isn't easy or cheap to get to: You'll need to kayak, sail, or fly in on a floatplane. But once here, you'll get to visit the prehistoric village of Ninstints, abandoned hundreds of years ago and still shadowed by decaying totem poles. See chapter 9.

- **'Ksan Historical Village** (Hazelton; ✆ **250/842-5544**): The Gitxsan people have lived for millennia at the confluence of the Skeena and Bulkley rivers, hunting and spearing salmon from the waters. On the site of an ancient village near present-day Hazelton, the Gitxsan have built a pre-Contact replica village, complete with longhouses and totem poles. No ordinary tourist gimmick, the village houses a 4-year carving school, Native-art gift shop, traditional-dance performance space, artists' studios, restaurant, and visitor center. See chapter 9.

- **Secwepemc Museum & Heritage Park** (Kamloops; ✆ **250/828-9801**): This heritage preserve contains a Native Secwepemc village archaeological site from 2,400 years ago, plus recreations of village structures from five different eras. It's not all just history here: The Shuswap, as the Secwepemc are now called, also perform traditional songs and dances and sell art objects. See chapter 10.

6 The Best Museums & Historic Sites

- **Museum of Anthropology** (Vancouver; ✆ 604/822-3825): Built to resemble a traditional longhouse, this splendid museum on the University of British Columbia campus contains one of the finest collections of Northwest Native art in the world. Step around back to visit two traditional longhouses. See chapter 3.
- **Royal British Columbia Museum** (Victoria; ✆ 800/661-5411): The human and natural history of coastal British Columbia is the focus of this excellent museum. Visit a frontier main street, view lifelike dioramas of coastal ecosystems, and gaze at ancient artifacts of the First Nations peoples. Outside, gaze upward at the impressive collection of totem poles. See chapter 4.
- **The Museum at Campbell River** (Campbell River; ✆ 250/287-3103): The highlight of this regional museum is a multimedia presentation that retells a Native Indian myth using carved ceremonial masks. Afterwards, explore the extensive collection of contemporary aboriginal carving, then visit a fur trapper's cabin and see tools from a pioneer-era sawmill. See chapter 7.
- **North Pacific Cannery Museum** (Port Edward; ✆ 250/628-3538): Salmon canning was big business in northern British Columbia in the early 20th century. Located on the waters of Inverness Passage, this isolated cannery built an entire working community of 1,200 people—complete with homes, churches, and stores—on boardwalks and piers. Now a national historic site, the mothballed factory is open for tours,

and you can even spend a night at the old hotel. See chapter 9.
- **Fort St. James National Historic Site** (Vanderhoof; ✆ 250/996-7191): In summer, the rebuilt log Fort St. James trading post hums with activity, as actors play the roles of explorers, traders, and craftspeople. This open-air museum of frontier life is a replica of the first non-Native structure in British Columbia, constructed in 1806. See chapter 9.
- **Barkerville** (52 miles/83km east of Quesnel; ✆ 250/994-3302): Once the largest city west of Chicago and north of San Francisco—about 100,000 people passed through during the 1860s—the gold-rush town of Barkerville is one of the best-preserved ghost towns in Canada. Now a provincial park, it comes to life in summer, when costumed "townspeople" go about their frontier way of life amid a completely restored late-Victorian pioneer town. See chapter 10.
- **Glenbow Museum** (Calgary; ✆ 403/268-4100): One of Canada's finest museums, the Glenbow has fascinating displays on the Native and settlement history of the Canadian Great Plains, plus changing art shows and thematic exhibitions. The gift shop is a good place to find local crafts. See chapter 13.
- **Bar U Ranch National Historic Site** (Longview; ✆ 403/395-2212): A working ranch established in the 1880s, the Bar U preserves the artifacts and lifestyles of Alberta's cattle-ranching past. This is still a real ranch: You might catch a rodeo one day, a calf branding the next. See chapter 13.

7 The Most Scenic Views

- **Vancouver from Cloud Nine** (© **604/687-0511**): Situated on the top floor of the tallest building in Vancouver, towering 42 floors above the city, the restaurant/ lounge Cloud Nine has 360-degree views that go on forever. See chapter 3.
- **Genoa Bay from the Deck of the Brigantine Inn** (Vancouver Island; © **250/746-5422**): A gentle bay on Vancouver Island's eastern shores, framed by mesa-like mountains and overlooking Salt Spring Island: This is one of the most enchanting views in all British Columbia. Order a drink at the Brigantine, watch the sun set, and enjoy the moment. See chapter 5.
- **The Canadian Rockies from Eagle's Eye Restaurant** (© **250/ 344-8626**): The Kicking Horse Mountain Resort isn't just the newest skiing area in the Canadian Rockies. This exciting development also boasts the highest-elevation restaurant in all of Canada. The Eagle's Eye sits at the top of the slopes, 8,033 feet (2,410m) above sea level. Ascend the gondola to find eye-popping views of high-flying glaciered crags—and excellent cuisine. See chapter 12.
- **Calgary Tower** (© **403/266-7171**): At 626 feet (191m), this is one landmark that you'll want to get on top of. From the windows of this revolving watchtower, you'll see the face of the Rocky Mountains to the west and the endless prairies to the east. If you like the view, stay for dinner or a drink. See chapter 13.
- **Flightseeing over Banff and Jasper National Parks:** Fly over some of the most dramatic landscapes in North America. **Alpenglow Aviation** (© **888/ 244-7117**) offers flights along the Continental Divide in the Rockies, culminating with views of the Columbia Icefields, the world's largest nonpolar ice cap. See chapter 14.
- **Sulphur Mountain in Banff National Park:** Ride the gondola up to the top of Sulphur Mountain for tremendous views onto the cliff-faced mountains that frame Banff. Hike the ridge-top trails, have lunch in the coffee shop, or run through an entire roll of film. See chapter 14.
- **Moraine Lake in Banff National Park:** Ten snow-clad peaks towering more than 10,000 feet (3,000m) rear up dramatically behind this tiny, eerily green lake. Rent a canoe and paddle to the mountains' base. See chapter 14.
- **Waterton Lakes from the Lounge at the Prince of Wales Hotel** (© **403/226-5551**): There are lots of great views of the Canadian Rockies, but perhaps the most singular is the view from the Prince of Wales Hotel, high above Waterton Lake. With blue-green water stretching back between a series of rugged snowcapped peaks, the view is at once intimate and primeval. See chapter 14.

8 The Most Dramatic Drives

- **The Sea-to-Sky Highway:** Officially Highway 99, this drive is a lesson in geology. Starting in West Vancouver, the amazing route begins at sea level at Howe Sound and the Squamish Cliffs—sheer rock faces rising hundreds of feet—then up a narrowing fjord, climbing up to Whistler, at the crest of the rugged, glacier-clad

Coast Mountains. Continue over the mountains and drop onto Lillooet. Here, on the dry side of the mountains, is an arid plateau trenched by the rushing Fraser River. See chapter 8.

- **The Sunshine Coast:** Highway 101 follows the mainland British Columbia coast from West Vancouver, crossing fjords and inlets three times on ferries on its way to Powell River. On the east side rise the soaring peaks of the Coast Mountains, and to the west lap the waters of the Georgia Strait, with the green bulk of Vancouver Island rising in the middle distance. From Powell River, you can cross over to Vancouver Island on the BC Ferries service to Comox. See chapter 8.

- **Hazelton to Hyder, Alaska:** This trip through the backcountry leads to two of the most isolated communities in North America. Highway 37 departs from the Yellowhead Highway near Hazelton, heading north through forests and climbing up to the Coast Range summit, an alpine wilderness choked with glaciers. The road then drops precipitously down to sea level at Stewart, British Columbia, and its cross-border neighbor, Hyder, Alaska.

These twin towns are at the head of the Portland Canal, one of the longest fjords in the world. See chapter 9.

- **Williams Lake to Bella Coola:** Start at the ranching town of Williams Lake, and turn your car west toward the looming Coast Mountains. Highway 20 crosses the arid Fraser River plateau, famed for its traditional cattle ranches, until reaching the high country near Anaheim Lake. After edging through 5,000-foot (1,500m) Heckman Pass, the route descends what the locals simply call "The Hill": a 20-mile (32km) stretch of road that drops from the pass to sea level with gradients of 18%. The road terminates at Bella Coola on the Pacific, where summer-only ferries depart for Port Hardy on northern Vancouver Island. See chapter 10.

- **The Icefields Parkway** (Hwy. 93 through Banff and Jasper national parks): This is one of the world's grandest mountain drives. Cruising along it is like a trip back to the ice ages. The parkway climbs past glacier-notched peaks to the Columbia Icefields, a sprawling cap of snow, ice, and glacier at the very crest of the Rockies. See chapter 14.

9 The Best Walks & Rambles

- **Vancouver's Stanley Park Seawall:** Stroll, jog, run, blade, bike, skate, ride—whatever your favorite mode of transport is, use it, but by all means get out here and explore this wonderful park. See chapter 3.

- **Victoria's Inner Harbour:** Watch the boats and aquatic wildlife come and go while walking along a pathway that winds past manicured gardens. The best stretch runs south from the Inner Harbour near the Parliament Build-

ings, past the Royal London Wax Museum. See chapter 4.

- **Strathcona Provincial Park:** Buttle Lake, which lies at the center of Strathcona Provincial Park, is the hub of several hiking trails that climb through old-growth forests to misty waterfalls and alpine meadows. Return to the trail head, doff your hiking shorts, and skinny-dip in gem-blue Buttle Lake. See chapter 7.

- **Johnston Canyon in Banff National Park:** Just 15 miles

(24km) west of Banff, Johnston Creek cuts a deep, very narrow canyon through limestone cliffs. The trail winds through tunnels, passes waterfalls, edges by shaded rock faces, and crosses the chasm on footbridges before reaching a series of iridescent pools, formed by springs that bubble up through highly colored rock. See chapter 14.

- **Plain of Six Glaciers Trail in Banff National Park:** From Chateau Lake Louise, a trail rambles along the edge of emerald-green Lake Louise, then climbs up to the base of Victoria Glacier. At a rustic teahouse, you can order a cup of tea and scones—each served up from a wood-fired stove—and gaze up at the rumpled face of the glacier. See chapter 14.

- **Maligne Canyon in Jasper National Park:** As the Maligne River cascades from its high mountain valley to its appointment with the Athabasca River, it carves a narrow, deep chasm in the underlying limestone. Spanned by six footbridges, the canyon is laced with trails and interpretive sites. See chapter 14.

10 The Best Luxury Hotels & Resorts

- **Fairmont Hotel Vancouver** (Vancouver; ✆ **800/866-5577**): Built by the Canadian Pacific Railway on the site of two previous Hotel Vancouvers, this landmark opened in 1929. The château-style exterior, the lobby, and even the guest rooms—now thoroughly restored—are built in a style and on a scale reminiscent of the great European railway hotels. See chapter 3.

- **The Fairmont Empress** (Victoria; ✆ **800/866-5577**): Architect Francis Rattenbury's masterpiece, the Empress has charmed princes (and their princesses), potentates, and movie moguls since 1908. If there's one hotel in Canada that represents a vision of bygone graciousness and class, this is it. See chapter 4.

- **Hastings House** (Salt Spring Island; ✆ **800/661-9255**): This farm matured into a country manor and was then converted into a luxury inn. The manor house is now an acclaimed restaurant; the barn and farmhouse have been remade into opulent suites. You might feel like you've been transported to an idealized English estate, if it weren't for those wonderful views of the Pacific. See chapter 5.

- **Wickaninnish Inn** (Tofino; ✆ **800/333-4604**): Standing stalwart in the forest above the sands of Chesterman Beach, this new log, stone, and glass structure boasts incredible views over the Pacific and extremely comfortable luxury-level guest rooms. The dining room is equally superlative. See chapter 6.

- **Palliser Hotel** (Calgary; ✆ **800/41-1414**): Calgary's landmark historic hotel, the Palliser is permeated with good breeding and high style. The magnificent lobby looks like an Edwardian gentlemen's club, and the guest rooms are large and luxurious. See chapter 13.

- **Fairmont Hotel Macdonald** (Edmonton; ✆ **800/441-1414**): When the Canadian Pacific bought and refurbished this landmark hotel, all of the charming period details were preserved, and the inner workings were modernized and brought up to snuff. The result is an elegant but still-friendly small hotel. From the kilted bellman to the gargoyles on the walls, this is a real class act. See chapter 13.

- **Rimrock Resort Hotel** (Banff; ✆ 800/661-1587): Banff is known for its scenery and its high prices; this is one of the few luxury hotels whose rates are actually justified. New and architecturally dramatic, it steps nine stories down a steep mountain slope. A fantastic marble lobby, great Italian restaurant, and handsomely appointed bedrooms complete the package. See chapter 14.

- **Fairmont Chateau Lake Louise** (Lake Louise; ✆ 800/441-1414): First of all, there's the view: Across a tiny gem-green lake rise massive cliffs, shrouded in glacial ice. And then there's the hotel: Part hunting lodge, part palace, the Chateau is its own community, with sumptuous boutiques, sports-rental facilities, seven dining areas, and beautifully furnished guest rooms. See chapter 14.

- **Post Hotel** (Lake Louise; ✆ 800/661-1586): Quietly gracious hospitality in a dramatic Canadian Rockies setting is the hallmark of this luxurious lodge. The original log-built dining room and bar remain from the 1940s, now joined by a new hotel wing with extremely comfortable and beautifully furnished rooms. The "F" suites are the most desirable. See chapter 14.

11 The Best Bed-and-Breakfasts & Country Inns

- **West End Guest House** (Vancouver; ✆ 604/681-2889): This 1906 heritage home is filled with an impressive collection of Victorian antiques. Fresh-baked brownies accompany evening turndown service, and the staff is thoroughly professional. See chapter 3.

- **Andersen House Bed & Breakfast** (Victoria; ✆ 250/388-4565): Your hosts outfit their venerable 1891 Queen Anne home in only the latest decor, from raku sculptures to carved-wood African masks. Their taste is impeccable—the old place looks great. See chapter 4.

- **The Old Farmhouse B&B** (Salt Spring Island; ✆ 250/537-4113): The Old Farmhouse is an 1894 farmstead with a newly built guesthouse. The welcome you'll get here is as engaging and genuine as you'll ever receive, and the breakfasts are works of art—one of the hosts is a former professional chef. See chapter 5.

- **Oceanwood Country Inn** (Mayne Island; ✆ 250/539-5074): Overlooking Navy Channel, this inn offers top-notch lodgings and fine dining in one of the most extravagantly scenic locations on the west coast. Admirably, the inn maintains an array of prices that range from affordable and cozy garden-view rooms to luxury-level suites that open onto hot-tub decks and hundred-mile views. See chapter 5.

- **Sunset B&B** (Gabriola Island; ✆ 877/247-2032): A stylish modern home overlooking the ferry-churned waters of the Georgia Strait, the Sunset is the place for book and music lovers to enjoy an enchanting getaway. The rooms, especially the wood-paneled Wild Rose Suite, are wonderfully comfortable. See chapter 6.

- **Bahari B&B** (Qualicum Beach; ✆ 877/752-9278): This magnificent modern home is seriously Pacific Rim: The spectacular art and architecture of Bahari is half Asian, half contemporary North American. The rooms are extremely comfortable and beautifully outfitted with pan-Pacific amenities and objects. One of the most stylish B&Bs in western Canada. See chapter 6.

- **Hollyford Guest Cottage** (Qualicum Beach; ℭ 877/ 224-6559): Often, when B&Bs are described in terms of art and antiques, you end up with cloying Victoriana and uncomfortable beds. Not at the Hollyfod: Its fascinating collections range from early Canadian landscape painting to Mountie paraphernalia. The owners share their life-long passion for intriguing objets d'art, and make sure that the guest rooms are modern and comfortable. Admiring the antiques sure beats sleeping in one. See chapter 6.

- **Casa Rio Lakeside B&B** (Kelowna; ℭ 800/313-1033): If you're going to the Okanagan Valley to relax on the beaches, make this your B&B choice. Casa Rio has 150 feet (46m) of private lakeside beach, and it's far from the frenetic pace and traffic of downtown Kelowna. The three-story modern home is beautifully designed and decorated, the rooms very comfortable. See chapter 11.

- **The Cedars, A Garden Inn** (Kelowna; ℭ 800/951-0769): A dream of a quaint English cottage, the Cedars is a handsome Arts and Crafts–style home in a quiet neighborhood, just a block from Okanagan Lake's beaches. The inn has been beautifully restored and thoughtfully decorated to maintain its vintage charm, but updated to provide all the facilities you'd expect at a fine hotel. See chapter 11.

- **Mulvehill Creek Wilderness Inn and Bed & Breakfast** (Revelstoke; ℭ 877/837-8649): Equidistant to a waterfall and Arrow Lake, this remote inn in the forest has everything going for it: nicely decorated rooms with locally made pine furniture, a beautiful lounge with fireplace, decks to observe the hens and the garden (each of which does its bit for breakfast), and gracious hosts who exemplify Swiss hospitality. Swimming, boating, fishing—it's all here. See chapter 12.

- **Union Bank Inn** (Edmonton; ℭ 780/423-3600): Not quite a B&B, not quite a hotel, the absolutely charming Union Bank Inn is something in between. Right downtown, this marble-faced 1910 bank sat vacant for many years before being redeveloped as an inn and restaurant. Each bedroom was individually decorated by one of Edmonton's top interior designers. See chapter 13.

- **McNeill Heritage Inn** (Canmore; ℭ 877/MCNEILL): This inn began its life in 1907 as the home of Canmore Mine's manager, and has passed through several lives since. Thankfully, the gracious building is now a beautifully restored B&B with spacious rooms and beautiful common areas. One of the best. See chapter 14.

- **Thea's House** (Banff; ℭ 403/ 762-2499): A vision of stone, pine, and antique carpets, Thea's is a newly built bed-and-breakfast just 5 minutes from downtown Banff. "Elegant Alpine" is Thea's style, a cross between a log lodge and a vision out of *Architectural Digest*. Perfect for a romantic getaway. See chapter 14.

- **Mountain Home Bed & Breakfast** (Banff; ℭ 403/762-3889): All the comforts of home, plus commodious rooms and thoughtful hospitality. There are bigger and fancier places, but this is one of the best all-in-one B&B packages in the Rockies—and it's just steps from downtown Banff. See chapter 14.

12 The Best Lodges, Wilderness Retreats & Log-Cabin Resorts

- **Tigh-Na-Mara Resort Hotel** (Parksville; ✆ **800/663-7373**): Comfortably rustic log cabins in a forest at beach's edge: Tigh-Na-Mara has been welcoming families for decades, and the new luxury log suites are just right for romantic getaways. See chapter 6.

- **Strathcona Park Lodge** (Strathcona Provincial Park; ✆ **250/286-3122**): A summer camp for the whole family is what you'll find at Strathcona Park Lodge, with rustic lakeside cabins and guided activities that range from sea kayaking and fishing to rock climbing and mountaineering. See chapter 7.

- **Deer Lodge** (Lake Louise; ✆ **800/661-1595**): There are grander and more famous places to stay at Lake Louise, but this lodge has charm and atmosphere to spare without the frantic pace of the nearby Chateau. See chapter 14.

- **Tekarra Lodge** (Jasper; ✆ **888/404-4540**): Quaint little cabins ring a central lodge building at this well-loved getaway. The cabins are atmospherically rustic; best of all, you're a mile distant from Jasper's busy town center. See chapter 14.

- **Becker's Chalets** (Jasper; ✆ **780/852-3779**): These very attractive new cabins are set right along the Athabasca River. Some units are as large as houses. Jasper's best restaurant is here as well. See chapter 14.

- **Overlander Mountain Lodge** (Jasper East; ✆ **780/866-2330**): Forget the wildly overpriced rooms in Jasper Townsite and stay here, just a quarter mile (.5km) outside the park gates. Lovely new cabins plus a handsome older lodge with a good restaurant make this an in-the-know favorite. See chapter 14.

- **Emerald Lake Lodge** (Yoho National Park; ✆ **800/663-6336**): Location, location, location: Sumptuous lakeside cabins at the base of the Continental Divide make this a longtime favorite family-vacation spot. See chapter 14.

13 The Best Restaurants for Northwest Regional Cuisine

See "A Taste of British Columbia & the Canadian Rockies," in the appendix, for more information on the style of cuisine unique to this region.

- **Lumière** (Vancouver; ✆ **604/739-8185**): From its early days, Lumière has been in the running for best restaurant in Vancouver. You won't be disappointed by the French-influenced Pacific Rim cuisine here. See chapter 3.

- **Blue Crab Bar and Grill** (Victoria; ✆ **250/480-1999**): You might think that the food would have a hard time competing with the view at this restaurant in the Coast Hotel, but you'd be wrong. The creative chef serves up the freshest seafood, the presentation is beautiful, and the dishes are outstanding. See chapter 4.

- **Sooke Harbour House** (Sooke; ✆ **250/642-3421**): This small country inn has one of the most noted restaurants in all of Canada. Fresh regional cuisine is the specialty, with an emphasis on local seafood. Views over the Strait of Juan de Fuca to Washington's mighty Olympic Mountains are spectacular. See chapter 5.

- **de Montreuil** (Kelowna; ☎ **250/ 860-5508**): Vivid and earthy flavors dominate at this popular and youthful hangout in the Okanagan Valley. Expect French finesse, exotic tastes, and regional ingredients such as pheasant, local foie gras, and fiddleheads. See chapter 11.
- **Fresco** (Kelowna; ☎ **250/ 868-8805**): Another exciting new restaurant at the epicenter of the fast-growing Okanagan wine district, Fresco brings together fresh local ingredients and sophisticated preparations in a classy but casual dining room. The chef/owner has cooked in the top restaurants in Canada: He came to Kelowna to open his first solo effort. See chapter 11.
- **All Seasons Café** (Nelson; ☎ **250/ 352-0101**): Innovative preparations and rich, hearty flavors are the hallmarks of the cuisine at this superlative restaurant in a downtown Nelson heritage home. Food this stylish and up-to-date would pass muster anywhere; to find it in Nelson is astonishing. See chapter 12.
- **River Café** (Calgary; ☎ **403/ 261-7670**): You'll walk through a quiet, tree-filled park on an island in the Bow River to reach this bustling place. At the restaurant's center, an immense wood-fired oven and grill produce smoky grilled meats and vegetables, all organically grown and freshly harvested. On warm evenings, picnickers loll in the grassy shade. See chapter 13.
- **Brava** (Calgary; ☎ **403/228-1854**): A broad menu with lots of options for snacks or full-on meals makes this a great choice for casual diners. Located in Calgary's hottest neighborhood, Brava features Alberta beef and game dressed in exciting sauces and presented with dazzling architectural élan. See chapter 13.
- **Hardware Grill** (Edmonton; ☎ **780/423-0969**): Although located in one of Edmonton's first hardware stores, there's nothing antique about the food at the Hardware Grill. A very broad selection of inventive appetizers makes it fun to snack your way through dinner. See chapter 13.
- **Saltlik** (Banff; ☎ **403/760-2467**): At first, this high-design steel, concrete, and glass structure seems out of place in alpine Banff. But this contemporary-styled restaurant is very much in place with its menu, featuring an excellent selection of Alberta meats, sear-cooked at a blazing 1,200 degrees. See chapter 14.
- **Sinclair's** (Canmore; ☎ **403/ 678-5370**): Right downtown in Canmore, Sinclair's has some of the finest and most vibrantly flavored food in the Canadian Rockies. The menu reads like an adventure novel: Exotic fruits and berries meet and wed homegrown produce and meats. See chapter 14.

14 The Best Festivals & Special Events

- **Vancouver's Three F Festivals:** The Folk, the Fringe, and the Film are the three F's in question. The Folk Fest brings folk and world-beat music to a waterfront stage in Jericho Park. The setting is gorgeous, the music great, and the crowd something else. Far more urban is the Fringe, a festival of new and original plays that takes place in the arty Commercial Drive area. The plays are wonderfully inventive; better yet, they're short and cheap. In October, the films of the world come to Vancouver. Serious film buffs buy a pass and see all 500 flicks (or as many as they can before their eyeballs fall out). See chapter 3.

- **Celebration of Light** (Vancouver): This 4-night fireworks extravaganza takes place over English Bay in Vancouver. Three of the world's leading fireworks manufacturers are invited to represent their countries in competition against one another, setting their best displays to music. On the fourth night, all three companies launch their finales. See chapter 3.

- **Market in the Park** (Salt Spring Island): The little village of Ganges fills to bursting every Saturday morning, as local farmers, craftspeople, and flea marketers gather to talk, trade, and mill aimlessly. With all ages of hippies, sturdy housewives, fashion-conscious Eurotrash, and rich celebrities all mixed together, the event has the feel of a weird and benevolent ritual. See chapter 5.

- **World Championship Bathtub Race** (Nanaimo): Imagine guiding a claw-foot tub across the 36-mile (58km) Georgia Strait from Nanaimo to Vancouver: That's how this hilarious and goofily competitive boat race began. Nowadays, dozens of tubbers attempt the crossing as part of late July's weeklong Marine Festival, with a street fair, parade, and ritual boat burning and fireworks display. See chapter 6.

- **Calgary Stampede:** In all of North America, there's nothing like the Calgary Stampede. Of course it's the world's largest rodeo, but it's also a series of concerts, an art show, an open-air casino, a carnival, a street dance—you name it, it's undoubtedly going on somewhere here. In July, all of Calgary is a party—and you're invited. See chapter 13.

- **Klondike Days** (Edmonton): July's Klondike Days commemorate the city's key role as a departure point to the Klondike goldfields in the Yukon. The Sourdough River Raft Race pits dozens of homemade boats against the strong currents of the North Saskatchewan River. The whole city gets decked out in its turn-of-the-20th-century finery for the street fairs, music events, parades, and general high jinks. See chapter 13.

2

Planning Your Trip to British Columbia & the Canadian Rockies

Here's where you'll find tips on when to visit, what documents you'll need, and where to get more information. Planning ahead can make all the difference between a smooth trip and a bumpy ride.

1 The Regions in Brief

Canada's westernmost province, British Columbia, and the Canadian Rockies region, which stretches into the province of Alberta, are incredibly diverse, with many distinct regions that vary both in geography and culture.

Vancouver is one of the most beautiful and cosmopolitan cities in the world. While there are certainly good museums and tourist sights, what we love most are the incredible mosaic of people and languages, the bustle of the streets, the mountains reaching down into the sea, and the wonderful food. Kayaking and canoeing are just off your front step in False Creek and the Georgia Strait, and skiing just up the road at **Whistler/Blackcomb Mountain Resorts,** one of the continent's greatest ski areas.

Vancouver Island is a world apart from busy urban Vancouver. At the island's southern tip is the British Columbia capital of **Victoria,** a small, charming city that makes a lot of fuss about its Merry Olde Englishness. In summer, the crowds can be off-putting, the sham Britishness intolerable. But in the off-season, Victoria is just a beautifully preserved frontier town in a magnificently scenic seaside location.

The rest of the mountainous island ranges from rural to wild. It would be easy to spend an entire vacation just on Vancouver Island, especially if you take a few days for **sea kayaking** on the island's wilderness west coast near **Tofino,** or off the east coast in the beautiful **Gulf Islands.** Or you can learn to **scuba dive:** No less an authority than Jacques Cousteau has claimed that these waters are some of the best diving environments in the world. Vancouver Island is also home to dozens of First Nations Canadian bands. If you're shopping for **Native arts,** this is the best single destination in western Canada.

From the northern tip of Vancouver Island, you can board a BC Ferries cruiser and take the 15-hour trip through the famed **Inside Passage** to Prince Rupert, a port town just shy of the Alaska Panhandle. Getting a glimpse of the dramatically scenic Inside Passage is what fuels the Alaska-to-Vancouver cruise-ship industry; by taking this route on BC Ferries, you'll save yourself thousands of dollars and catch the same views. From Prince Rupert, you can journey out to the mystical **Queen Charlotte Islands,** the ancient homeland of the Haida people, or turn inland and drive up the glacier-carved Skeena River valley to **Prince George,** on the Fraser River.

You can also reach the upper reaches of the Fraser River from Vancouver by following Highway 99 north past Whistler and Lillooet to the **Cariboo Country.** This route follows the historic Cariboo Trail, a gold-rush stage-coach road blazed in the 1860s. The road now leads through cattle- and horse-covered grasslands, past 19th-century ranches, and by lakes thick with trout. The gold rush started at **Barkerville,** which is now one of the best-preserved ghost towns in North America. In addition to this great family destination, the Cariboo Country offers the province's best **guest ranches** and rustic lakeside **fishing resorts.**

The Thompson River meets the Fraser River south of Lillooet. This mighty river's southern fork has its headwaters in the **Shuswap Lakes,** a series of interconnected lakes that are favorites of houseboaters. The north fork Thompson River rises in the mountains of **Wells Gray Provincial Park,** one of British Columbia's neglected gems. Hiking and camping are as compelling as in the nearby Canadian Rockies, but without the overwhelming crowds.

One of the best summer family destinations in western Canada is the **Okanagan Valley.** Stretching from the U.S.–Canadian border nearly 120 miles (200km) north to Vernon, this arid canyon is filled with glacier-trenched lakes, which in summer become the playground for all manner of watersports. The summer heat is also good for wine grapes: This is the center for British Columbia's growing wine industry. Add to that a dozen golf courses and excellent lodging and dining in the cities of **Penticton** and **Kelowna,** and you've got the makings for an excellent vacation.

The **Canadian Rockies** are among the most dramatically scenic destinations in the world. Unfortunately, this is hardly a secret—you'll find the entire area dripping with tourists in summer and early fall. **Banff** and **Jasper** national parks in Alberta are especially busy and expensive; however, it's hard to find fault with the sheer beauty of these places. If you don't like the crowds and high prices, we cover several other options as well. The British Columbia side of the Rockies contains much less busy mountain parks, including **Yoho, Glacier,** and **Kootenay** national parks, plus **Mount Robson Provincial Park.** Another spectacular mountain retreat is **Waterton Lakes National Park,** which joins the United States's Glacier National Park. You can also save money by staying outside the parks at Canmore and near Hinton, both in Alberta, or at Golden, British Columbia.

These considerations aside, spending several days in the Rockies should remain a part of any western Canadian itinerary. Despite the crowds, the town of **Banff** is charming and filled with great hotels and fine restaurants; **Lake Louise** is a magical sight; and the **Icefields Parkway,** which joins Banff and Jasper parks, is completely spellbinding. Throughout this area, chances are good you'll see lots of **wildlife,** like black bears, moose, bighorn sheep,

---

Tips **Planning Ahead**

The road trip between Calgary and Vancouver includes the most popular series of destinations in Canada. If you're planning to make this memorable journey, be sure to make lodging reservations as far in advance as possible.

British Columbia

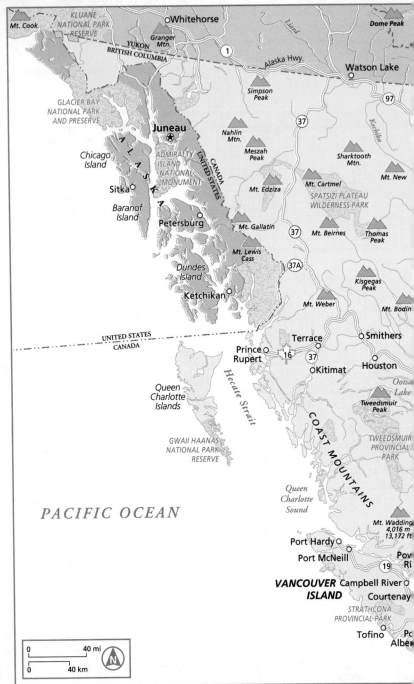

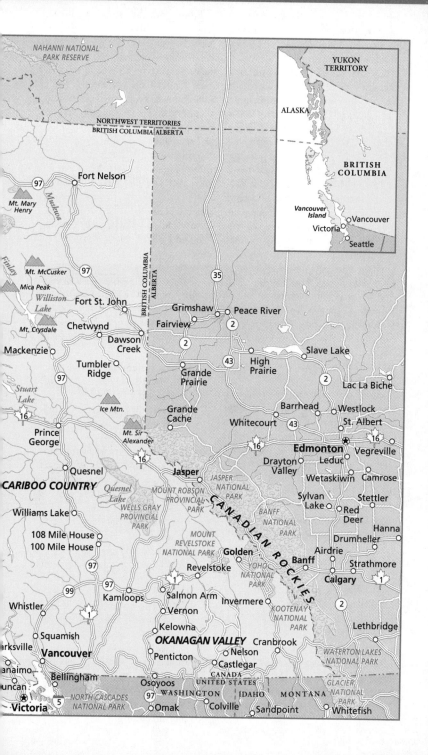

NAHANNI NATIONAL
PARK RESERVE

YUKON
TERRITORY

ALASKA

BRITISH
COLUMBIA

Vancouver
Island

Vancouver

Victoria

Seattle

NORTHWEST TERRITORIES
BRITISH COLUMBIA ALBERTA

97   Fort Nelson

Mt. Mary
Henry

Muskwa

Finlay

Mt. McCusker   97

Mica Peak

Williston
Lake

BRITISH COLUMBIA   ALBERTA

Fort St. John

35

Mt. Crysdale   Chetwynd   Grimshaw   Peace River

Fairview   2

Mackenzie   Dawson
Creek   2

Tumbler
Ridge   Grande
Prairie   43   High
Prairie   Slave Lake

97   2   Lac La Biche

Stuart
Lake   Grande
Cache   Barrhead   Westlock

16   Whitecourt   43   St. Albert

Prince
George   Mt. Sir
Alexander   16   16   Edmonton   Vegreville

16

Jasper   Drayton
Valley   Leduc

Quesnel   JASPER
NATIONAL
PARK   Wetaskiwin   Camrose

CARIBOO COUNTRY   Quesnel
Lake   MOUNT ROBSON
PROVINCIAL
PARK   Sylvan
Lake   Stettler

WELLS GRAY
PROVINCIAL
PARK   BANFF
NATIONAL
PARK   Red
Deer

Williams Lake   Hanna

108 Mile House   MOUNT
REVELSTOKE
NATIONAL PARK   Drumheller

100 Mile House   Golden   Airdrie

97   Revelstoke   YOHO
NATIONAL
PARK   Banff   Strathmore

99   1   Calgary   1

Whistler   Kamloops   Salmon Arm   Invermere   KOOTENAY
NATIONAL
PARK   2

Squamish   Vernon

arksville   Vancouver   Kelowna   Lethbridge

anaimo   Penticton   OKANAGAN VALLEY   Cranbrook   WATERTON LAKES
NATIONAL PARK

uncan   Bellingham   Nelson

Castlegar   CANADA

Victoria   5   Osoyoos   UNITED STATES   GLACIER
NATIONAL
PARK

97   WASHINGTON   IDAHO   MONTANA

NORTH CASCADES
NATIONAL PARK   Omak   Colville   Sandpoint   Whitefish

CANADIAN ROCKIES

mountain goat, and elk. The parks all offer marvelous outdoor recreation, including **hiking, mountain biking, climbing,** and **skiing.**

Calgary, the city that oil built, is a friendly town in the foothills of the Rockies. One of the most prosperous cities in all of Canada, Calgary is still a ranchers' town, and the disparity between its role as a cow town and world oil center is one of its principal charms. The dichotomies are never more apparent than during the **Calgary Stampede,** the world's largest rodeo and an excuse for turning the city into one huge party. You can also thank Calgary's prosperity for its wonderful restaurant scene.

Edmonton, the capital of Alberta, sits high above the North Saskatchewan River at the center of a vast, farm-covered plain. This welcoming city's historic district is great for strolling and eating. While Edmonton lacks the high spirits and urbane attitude of Calgary, it's no slouch when it comes to fine dining and excellent hotels. And if you enjoy shopping—or swimming, carnival rides, or performing dolphins—then you must visit the **West Edmonton Mall,** one of the world's largest shopping centers. Like a cross between Disneyland, Las Vegas, and the Gap, West Ed Mall is unlike any mall you've ever seen.

2 Visitor Information

For advance information on British Columbia, contact **Tourism British Columbia,** P.O. Box 9830, Stn. Prov. Govt., 1803 Douglas St., 3rd Floor, Victoria, BC V8W 9W5 (© **800/ 435-5622** or 250/356-6363; www. hellobc.com).

To request information on Alberta, contact **Alberta Economic Development and Tourism,** Commerce Place, 10155 102nd St., Edmonton, AB T5J 4L6 (© **800/661-8888;** www.travelalberta.com), or **Travel Alberta,** Box 2500, Edmonton, AB T5J 2Z1/Eau Claire Market, 200 Barclay Sq., Calgary, AB T2P 1K1 (© **800/ 661-8888;** www.travelalberta.com).

For information on Canada's national parks, contact **Parks Canada National Office,** 25 Eddy Street Hull, Quebec K1A 0M5 (© **888/ 773-8888;** www.parkscanada.gc.ca), or **Canadian Heritage,** 15 Eddy St., Hull, QC K1A 0M5 (© **819/ 997-0055;** www.pch.gc.ca).

ON THE WEB The excellent travel directories **www.canadatravel.ca** and **www.canada.worldweb.com** have thousands of links to websites for destinations and activities across the country. Also take a look at the official tourism site for Canada at **www. travelcanada.ca.**

Here are some useful provincial and city sites:

- **British Columbia:** www.hellobc. com, www.discoverbc.com, www. travel.bc.ca
- **Alberta:** www.travelalberta.com, www.explorealberta.com, www. discoveralberta.com
- **Vancouver:** www.tourism-vancouver.org, www.vancouver plus.ca, www.vancouverwow.com; also see www.whistler.com (Whistler Resort Guide)
- **Victoria:** www.city.victoria.bc.ca, www.victoriabc.com, www. greater victoria.com/directory.htm
- **Banff:** www.bannflakelouise.com, www.worldweb.com/Parks Canada-Banff, www.banff.com
- **Calgary:** www.visitor.calgary. ab.ca, www.discovercalgary.com, www.calgaryplus.ca, www.calgary wow.com
- **Edmonton:** www.gov.edmonton. ab.ca/enjoying_edmonton.html, www.discoveredmonton.com, www.edmontonplus.ca, www. tourism.ede.org

3 Entry Requirements & Customs

ENTRY REQUIREMENTS

All visitors to Canada must be able to provide proof of citizenship. A passport is not required for U.S. citizens and permanent residents, though it is the easiest method of proving citizenship. If you don't have a passport, you'll need to carry other forms of proof of citizenship, such as a certificate of naturalization, a certificate of citizenship, a birth certificate with photo ID, a certificate of birth abroad with photo ID, or a voter registration card with photo ID or social security card. Some form of photo ID is a good idea. Although officers at border control are allowed to ask for any of these forms of identity, in most cases they request only a U.S. driver's license. Permanent U.S. residents who aren't U.S. citizens must have their Alien Registration Cards (green cards). If you plan to drive into Canada, be sure to bring your car's registration papers.

Citizens of most European countries and of former British colonies and certain other countries (Israel, Korea, and Japan, for instance) do not need visas, but must carry passports. Entry visas are required for citizens of more than 130 countries; these must be applied for and received from the Canadian embassy in your home country. For more information, see http://cicnet.ci.gc.ca/english/visit/index.html.

An important point: Anyone under 18 must have a letter from a parent or guardian granting him or her permission to travel to Canada. The letter must state the traveler's name and the duration of the trip. It's essential that teenagers carry proof of identity, otherwise their letter is useless at the border.

CUSTOMS

WHAT YOU CAN BRING INTO CANADA Customs regulations are generous in most respects, but get complicated when it comes to firearms, plants, meats, and pets. Fishing tackle poses no problems, but the bearer must possess a nonresident license for the province or territory where he or she plans to use it. You can bring in free of duty up to 50 cigars, 200 cigarettes, and about a half-pound of tobacco, providing you're over 18. Those of age (18 or 19, depending on the province) are also allowed about 40 ounces of liquor, 50 ounces of wine, or 24 12-ounce containers of beer or ale. Dogs, cats, and most pets can enter Canada with their owners, though you must have proof of rabies vaccinations within the last 3 years.

For details, contact the **Customs and Revenue Agency,** 1st Floor, 2265 St. Laurent Blvd., Ottawa, ON K1G 4K3 (© **800/461-9999** in Canada, 506/636-5064 in the U.S., or 204/983-3500; www.ccra-adrc.gc.ca).

WHAT YOU CAN BRING HOME
Returning citizens of the **United States** who have been away for 48 hours or more are allowed to bring back, once every 30 days, US$400 worth of merchandise duty-free. You'll be charged a flat rate of 10% duty on the next US$1,000 worth of purchases. Be sure to have your receipts handy. On gifts, the duty-free limit is US$100. You cannot bring fresh foodstuffs into the United States; most tinned foods, however, are allowed. For more information, contact the **U.S. Customs Service,** 1301 Constitution Ave. (P.O. Box 7407), Washington, DC 20044 (© **877/287-8667;** www.customs.gov), and request the free pamphlet *Know Before You Go.* It's also available at www.customs.gov/know.htm.

Citizens of the **United Kingdom** returning from Canada (or from the U.S.) have a customs allowance of: 200 cigarettes; 50 cigars; 250 grams of smoking tobacco; 2 liters of still table wine; 1 liter of spirits or strong liqueurs (over 22% volume); 2 liters of fortified wine, sparkling wine, or other liqueurs; 60 milliliters of perfume; 250 milliliters of toilet water; and £145 worth of all other goods, including gifts and souvenirs. People under 17 cannot have the tobacco or alcohol allowance. For more information, contact **HM Customs & Excise,** Passenger Enquiry Point, 2nd Floor, Wayfarer House, Great South West Road, Feltham, Middlesex TW14 8NP (℗ **020/8910-3744;** www. hmce.gov.uk).

The duty-free allowance in **Australia** is A$400 or, for those under 18, A$200. Citizens can bring in 250 cigarettes or 250 grams of loose tobacco, plus 1,125 milliliters of alcohol. If you're returning with valuable goods you already own, such as foreign-made cameras, you should file form B263. A helpful brochure, available from Australian consulates or Customs offices, is *Know Before You Go* (www.customs. gov.au/bizlink/TRAVEL/know.htm). For more information, contact the

Australian Customs Services, Customs House, 5 Constitution Ave, Canberra ACT 2601/G.P.O. Box 8, Sydney, NSW 2001 (℗ **1300/ 363-263** or 02/6275-6666; www. customs.gov.au).

The duty-free allowance for **New Zealand** citizens is NZ$700. Citizens over 17 can bring in 200 cigarettes or 50 cigars or 250 grams of tobacco (or a combination of all three if their combined weight doesn't exceed 250g); plus 4.5 liters total of wine and/or beer, or 1.125 liters of liquor. Fill out a certificate of export, listing the valuables you are taking out of the country; that way, you can bring them back without paying duty. The free pamphlet *New Zealand Customs Guide for Travellers, Notice No. 4* is available at New Zealand consulates and Customs offices. For more information, contact **New Zealand Customs,** 50 Anzac Ave., P.O. Box 29, Auckland (℗ **0800/428-786** or 09/300-5399; www.customs.govt.nz).

4 Money

CURRENCY Canadians use dollars and cents; at press time, the **Canadian dollar** is worth around US65¢. Most tourist places in Canada will take American cash, but for the best rate you should change your funds into Canadian currency.

The standard paper denominations are $5, $10, $20, $50, and $100. Note that Canada has no $1 bills; single bucks come in brass coins bearing the picture of a loon—hence their nickname, the "loonie." There's also a $2 coin sometimes referred to as a "twoonie."

If you do spend American money at Canadian establishments, you should understand how the conversion is done. Often you'll see a sign reading U.S. CURRENCY X%, with some percentage for the X. This percentage, say 25%, is the "premium"—it means

that for every U.S. greenback you hand over, the cashier will see it as $1.25 Canadian. Shop around to get the best rate. Best of all, exchange your money at a bank.

TRAVELER'S CHECKS **American Express** offers traveler's checks through various banks and its own offices, where fees generally range from 1% to 4%. If you're an Amex cardholder, you can get checks over the phone at ℗ **800/721-9768.** Checks are also available at www.american express.com/tconline/phase2/urls/ BuyTC.asp.

Visa offers its traveler's checks at various banks and other locations. To find an issuer near you, call ℗ **800/ 227-6811.** The service charge ranges from 1.5% to 2%.

Be sure to sign your traveler's checks and keep a record of their serial numbers (separate from the checks).

The Canadian Dollar & the U.S. Dollar

The prices cited in this guide are given first in Canadian dollars (C$), then in U.S. dollars (US$); amounts over $5 have been rounded to the nearest dollar. Note that the Canadian dollar is worth significantly less than the American dollar but buys nearly as much in the way of goods and services. As we go to press, US$1 = C$1.55, or C$1 = US65¢, and those were the equivalencies used to figure the prices in this guide.

Here's a brief table of equivalents:

C$	US$	C$	US$
1	0.65	1.55	1
5	3.25	7.75	5
10	6.50	15.50	10
20	13.00	31.00	20
50	32.50	77.50	50
80	52.00	124.00	80
100	65.00	155.00	100

You'll need the serial numbers in case your checks are lost or stolen.

ATMs   You can generally get the best rate of exchange using a bank card at an ATM. Contact the **Cirrus** (℃ 800/424-7787; www.master card.com/cardholderservices/atm) or **Plus** (℃ 800/843-7587; www.visa. com/pd/atm/main.htm) networks for a list of banks in Canada that will accept your card, or just search out any machine with your network's symbol.

CREDIT CARDS   Credit cards are invaluable when traveling, providing a safe way to carry money. You can also withdraw cash advances from your cards, although you'll start paying hefty interest immediately.

Almost all credit-card companies have emergency toll-free numbers you can call if your wallet is stolen. Call **Visa** at ℃ 800/847-2911, **American Express** at ℃ 800/992-3404, or **MasterCard** at ℃ 800/622-7747.

5 When to Go

THE WEATHER   Canada west of the Rocky Mountains has generally mild winters, with snow mostly at the higher elevations. Even though spring comes early—usually in March—gray clouds can linger through June. Dry summer weather is assured only after July 1, but often continues through October. The Canadian Rockies are often socked in with cloud and rain throughout the summer; plan to spend several days here to assure that you'll catch at least some good weather. In winter, the Rockies fill with snow, but frequently the weather is not as cold as you'd expect. Chinook winds from the prairies can bring warm air systems, boosting temperatures up to early spring levels. On the prairies of Alberta, winters can be fiercely cold and windy. If you plan to travel across the prairies or through the Rockies in winter, be sure to have snow tires and chains.

As a general rule, spring runs from mid-March to mid-May, summer from mid-May to mid-September, fall from mid-September to mid-November, and winter from mid-November to mid-March. Remember that your car should be winterized through March and that snow sometimes falls as late as April.

Evenings tend to be cool everywhere, particularly on or near water. In late spring and early summer, you'll need a supply of insect repellent if you're planning bush travel or camping.

For up-to-date weather conditions, check out **http://weatheroffice.ec.gc.ca**.

HOLIDAYS   Canadian   national holidays include New Year's Day, Good Friday, Easter Monday, Victoria Day (in mid- to late May, the weekend before U.S. Memorial Day), Canada Day (July 1), Labour Day (first Mon in Sept), Thanksgiving (in mid-Oct), Remembrance Day (Nov 11), Christmas Day, and Boxing Day (Dec 26).

British Columbia and Alberta also celebrate a provincial holiday (called British Columbia or Alberta Day), usually on the first Monday of August.

FESTIVALS & SPECIAL EVENTS
Western Canada has some wonderfully unique festivals and events, from the Nanaimo Bathtub Race to the rowdy Calgary Stampede. Each community's special events are listed in the regional chapters that follow.

6 The Active Vacation Planner

See the individual destination chapters for specific details on how and where to enjoy the activities below.

BIKING   Most of western Canada's highways are wide and well maintained, and thus well suited for long-distance bicycle touring. Most resort areas offer rentals (it's a good idea to call ahead and reserve a bike).

While most hiking trails are closed to mountain bikes, other trails are developed specifically for backcountry biking. Ask at national park and national forest information centers for a map of mountain-bike trails.

Probably the most rewarding biking anywhere is in Banff and Jasper national parks. The Icefields Parkway is an eye-popping route that leads past soaring peaks and glaciers.

CANOEING & KAYAKING   Low-lying lakes and rivers form vast waterway systems across the land. Multi-day canoeing trips make popular summer and early fall expeditions; you'll see lots of wildlife and keep as gentle a pace as you like. The Bowron Lakes in the Cariboo Country make an excellent weeklong paddle through wilderness.

DIVING   An amazing array of marine life flourishes amid the 2,000 shipwrecks off the coast of British Columbia. Divers visit the area year-round to see the Pacific Northwest's unique underwater fauna and flora, and to swim among the ghostly remains of 19th-century whaling ships and 20th-century schooners.

The Pacific Rim National Park's Broken Group Islands is home to a multitude of sea life; the waters off the park's West Coast Trail are known as "the graveyard of the Pacific" for the hundreds of shipwrecks. Nanaimo and Campbell River, on Vancouver Island, are both centers for numerous dive outfitters.

FISHING   Angling is enjoyed across western Canada. However, the famed salmon fisheries along the Pacific coast face highly restricted catch limits in most areas, and outright bans on fishing in others. Not all salmon species are threatened, though, and rules governing fishing change quickly, so check locally with outfitters to find out if a season will open while you're visiting. Trout are found throughout the region, some reaching great size in the lakes in the British Columbia interior.

Fishing in Canada is regulated by local governments or tribes, and appropriate licenses are necessary. Angling for some fish is regulated by season; in some areas, catch-and-release fishing is enforced. Be sure to check with local authorities before casting your line.

If you're looking for a great fishing vacation with top-notch accommodations, contact **Oak Bay Marine Group,** 1327 Beach Dr., Victoria (℡ **800/663-7090** or 250/ 598-3366; www.obmg.com), which operates nine different resorts. Three are on Vancouver Island; the other lodges are on remote islands and fjords along the north coast.

HIKING Almost every national and provincial park in Canada is webbed with trails, ranging from easy nature hikes to long-distance backcountry trails. Late summer and early fall are good times to visit, since trails in the high country may be snowbound until July. For many people, the Canadian Rockies, with their abundance of parks and developed trail systems, provide the country's finest hiking. Before setting out, request hiking and trail information from the parks and buy a good map.

HORSEBACK RIDING Holidays on horseback have a long history in western Canada, and most outfitters and guest ranches offer a variety of options. Easiest are half-day rides on an easygoing horse, with sufficient instruction to make you feel comfortable no matter what your previous riding ability. Multi-day pack trips take riders off into the backcountry, with lodging in tents or at rustic camps. These trips are best for those who don't mind roughing it: You'll probably go a day or two without showers and end up saddle sore and sunburned. The Canadian Rockies in Alberta are filled with guest ranches offering a wide range of horseback activities.

SEA KAYAKING One of the best places to practice sea kayaking is in the sheltered bays, islands, and inlets along the coast of British Columbia; kayaks are especially good for wildlife-viewing. Most coastal towns have rentals, instruction, and guided trips. Handling a kayak isn't as easy as it looks, and you'll want to have plenty of experience in sheltered coves before heading out into the surf. Be sure to check the tide schedule and weather forecast before setting out, as well as what the coastal rock formations are. You'll need to be comfortable on the water and ready to get wet, as well as be a strong swimmer.

SKIING Canada, a mountainous country with heavy snowfall, is one of the world's top ski destinations. Both downhill and cross-country skiing are open to all ages, though downhill skiing carries a higher price tag: A day on the slopes, with rental gear and lift ticket, can easily top C$90 (US$59).

For downhill skiing, the Canadian Rockies and the Whistler/Blackcomb resort near Vancouver are the primary destinations. The 1988 Winter Olympics were held at Nakiska, just outside Banff National Park, and the park itself is home to three other ski areas, including Lake Louise, the country's largest. If you're just learning to ski, then the easier slopes at Banff Mount Norquay are made to order. Readers of *Condé Nast Traveler* repeatedly award Whistler/Blackcomb the title of best ski resort in North America.

Almost all downhill areas also offer groomed cross-country ski trails. Canmore Nordic Centre, in Alberta, was the site of the 1988 Olympic cross-country competition, and is now open to the public.

WHITE-WATER   RAFTING Charging down a mountain river in a rubber raft is one of the most popular adventures for many people visiting Canada's western mountains. Trips range from daylong excursions, which demand little of a participant other than sitting tight, to long-distance trips through remote backcountry. Risk doesn't correspond to length of trip: Individual rapids and water conditions can make even a short trip a real adventure. You should be comfortable in water, and a good swimmer if you're floating an adventurous river.

Jasper National Park is a major center for short yet thrilling white-water trips. Another excellent destination is the Kicking Horse River near Golden, British Columbia.

7 Tips for Travelers with Special Needs

FOR TRAVELERS WITH DISABILITIES

For information on disability travel, contact the **BC Accessibility Advisor,** Accessibility Program, Ministry of Municipal Affairs, Box 9490 Stn. Prov. Govt., Victoria, BC V8W 9N7 (✆ **250/387-7908**). In Alberta or British Columbia, the **Canadian Paraplegic Association** (✆ **888/ 654-5444** or 780/424-6312 in Alberta; **877/324-3611** or 604/ 324-3611 in BC; www.canparaplegic. org) can offer advice. The official British Columbia and Alberta accommodations guides provide information about accessibility options at lodgings throughout western Canada.

A World of Options, a 658-page book of resources for travelers with disabilities, covers everything from biking trips to scuba outfitters. It costs $35 and is available from **Mobility International USA,** P.O. Box 10767, Eugene, OR 97440 (✆ **541/ 343-1284** voice and TDD; www. miusa.org). Annual membership for Mobility International is $35, which includes the quarterly newsletter *Over the Rainbow.*

In addition, **Twin Peaks Press,** P.O. Box 129, Vancouver, WA 98666 (✆ **360/694-2462;** home.pacifier. com/~twinpeak), publishes travel-related books for people with disabilities.

You can join the **Society for Accessible Travel & Hospitality (SATH),** 347 Fifth Ave., Suite 610, New York, NY 10016 (✆ **212/447-7284;** fax 212/725-8253; www.sath.org), for $45 annually, $30 for seniors and students, to gain access to its vast network of connections in the travel industry. SATH provides information sheets on travel destinations and referrals to specialized tour operators. Its quarterly magazine is full of good information and resources. A year's subscription is $18.

FOR GAY & LESBIAN TRAVELERS

The larger cities of western Canada— Edmonton, Calgary, Victoria, and especially Vancouver—are generally gay tolerant, though you'll find less openly gay visibility and nonchalance here than in comparably sized U.S. cities. Each of these cities has a number of gay bars and gay-owned businesses, as well as a small gay newspaper. In smaller cities and towns, gay and lesbian travelers are advised to be more cautious about overt displays of affection.

The **International Gay & Lesbian Travel Association,** or **IGLTA** (✆ **800/448-8550** or 954/776-2626; fax 954/776-3303; www.iglta.org), links up travelers with the appropriate gay-friendly organizations. It offers newsletters, marketing mailings, and a membership directory. Membership is open to individuals for $200 yearly. Members are kept informed of gay and gay-friendly hoteliers, tour operators, and airline and cruise-line representatives. Note that travel information is available on the website at no charge.

There are also two good guide-books, both focused on gay men but including information for lesbians as well. You can get the *Spartacus International Gay Guide* or *Odysseus* from most gay and lesbian bookstores, or order them online. Both lesbians and gays might want to pick up a copy of *Gay Travel A to Z.* The **Ferrari Guides** (www.ferrariguides.com) is yet another good gay and lesbian series.

Out and About, 995 Market St., 14th Floor, San Francisco, CA 94103 (© **800/929-2268** or 415/644-8044; www.outandabout.com), offers guidebooks and a newsletter packed with information on the global gay and lesbian scene. A year's subscription to the newsletter costs $49. *Our World,* 1104 North Nova Rd., Suite 251, Daytona Beach, FL 32117 (© **904/441-5367;** www.ourworldpublishing.com), is a slicker monthly magazine highlighting travel bargains and opportunities. Annual subscription rates are $25 (or $12 for online access only).

FOR SENIORS
Don't be shy about asking for discounts, but always carry identification that shows your date of birth. Many hotels offer senior discounts, and in most cities, people over 60 qualify for reduced admission to theaters, museums, and other attractions, as well as discounted fares on public transportation.

A venerable resource for seniors interested in educational travel is **Elderhostel,** 11 Avenue de Lafayette, Boston, MA 02111 (© **877/426-8056;** www.elderhostel.org). It offers numerous programs in Canada, but since the trips are popular, you must enter a lottery well in advance. The monthly newsletter *Mature Traveler* offers tips and news; it's available for $30 annually from G E M Publishing Group, P.O. Box 50400, Reno, NV 89513. Other good information for seniors can be found

at **Arthur Frommer's Budget Travel Online,** starting at the page www.frommers.com/vacations/special_travelers/senior.

FOR FAMILIES
Several books offer tips to help you travel with kids. Most concentrate on the United States, but two, *Family Travel* (Lanier Publishing International; also see www.familytravelguides.com) and *How to Take Great Trips with Your Kids* (Harvard Common Press), are full of good general advice that can apply to travel anywhere. Another reliable tome, with a worldwide focus, is *Adventuring with Children* (Alpenbooks).

Family Travel Times is published by TWYCH (Travel with Your Children; © **888/822-4388** or 212/477-5524; www.familytraveltimes.com) and includes a weekly call-in service for subscribers. Subscriptions are $39. Contact TWYCH for a free publication list and sample issue.

FOR STUDENTS
The best resource for students is the **Council on International Educational Exchange,** or **CIEE (www.ciee.org).** It can set you up with an ID card (see below), and its **Council Travel Service** (© **800/226-8624;** www.counciltravel.com) is the biggest student travel agency in the world. It can get you discounts on plane tickets, rail passes, and the like. Ask for a list of CTS offices in major cities so you can keep the discounts flowing (and aid lines open) as you travel.

CIEE, through Council Travel, offers the **International Student Identity Card (ISIC)** for US$22. It's the only officially acceptable form of student identification, good for cut rates on transportation and attractions. It also provides you with basic health and life insurance and a 24-hour help line. If you're under 26, you can get a GO 25 card, which gets you the insurance and some of the discounts.

In Canada, **Travel CUTS,** 200 Ronson St., Suite 320, Etobicoke, ON, M9W 5Z9 (© **800/667-2887** or 416/614-2887, or 866/246-9762 for reservations; www.travelcuts.com), offers similar services; its offices sell the ISIC card for C$16 (US$10). Worldwide, you can also find student travel options at **STA Travel** (© **800/ 781-4040** in the U.S.; www. statravel.com).

8 Getting There

BY PLANE

THE MAJOR AIRLINES Western Canada is linked with the United States, Europe, and Asia by frequent nonstop flights. Calgary and Vancouver are the major air hubs; regional airlines connect to smaller centers.

Air Canada (© 888/247-2262; www.aircanada.ca), Canada's dominant airline, has by far the most flights between the United States and Canada. Most major U.S. carriers also fly daily between cities in Canada and the States—these include **American Airlines** (© 800/433-7300; www.aa. com), **Continental** (© 800/ 525-0280; www.continental.com), **Delta** (© 800/221-1212; www.delta. com), **Northwest** (© 800/447-4747; www.nwa.com), **United** (© 800/ 241-6522; www.ual.com), and **US Airways** (© 800/428-4322; www. usair.com). Canada's primary discount airline, **Canada 3000** (© 888/ 300-0669 or 416/674-3000; www. canada3000.com), has a more limited number of routes.

Air Canada offers nonstop service to Calgary from London and Frankfurt. It also links Edmonton and London, with connecting flights year-round and direct flights during the summer and into fall. Canada 3000 flies many routes from Europe, usually connecting through Toronto.

International airlines with nonstop service to Vancouver include **British Air** (© 800/247-9297 in the U.S. and Canada, 0845/773-3377 in the U.K.; www.british-airways.com), **KLM** (© 800/447-7747 in the U.S. and Canada for KLM partner Northwest Airlines, or 020/474-7747 in the Netherlands; www.klm.com), **Lufthansa** (© 800/563-5954 in the U.S., 800/581-6400 in Canada, or 0803/803-803 in Germany; www. lufthansa.com), **Qantas** (© 800/ 227-4500 in the U.S. and Canada; www.qantas.com), and **SAS** (© 800/ 221-2350 in the U.S. or Canada; www.scandinavian.net). Asian airlines that fly into Vancouver include **China Airlines** (© 800/227-5118 or 604/682-6777 in Vancouver; www. china-airlines.com), **Cathay Pacific** (© 800/233-2742; www.cathay-usa. com), **Japan Air Lines** (© 800/ 525-3663; www.japanair.com), and **Korean Air** (© 800/438-5000; www. koreanair.com). Additionally, **Air Canada** offers international flights from Mexico, most cities in northern Europe, and many centers in Asia. **Canada 3000** offers flights from Europe and Mexico at considerable discounts, as well as flights from Australia or New Zealand. Canada's **Air Transat** (© 866/847-1112; www. airtransat.com) offers still more options from Europe and Latin America.

Another option is to fly into Seattle, Washington, 2 hours south of Vancouver. Airfares are frequently less expensive to Seattle, and the difference in distance to destinations like the Okanagan, the Canadian Rockies, and Vancouver Island is negligible (driving from Seattle to Vancouver, for instance, takes about 2½ hours). Seattle's **Sea-Tac Airport** has nonstop flights from London, Copenhagen, Frankfurt, Seoul, Tokyo, and Hong Kong, among others. See chapters 4

Flying for Less: How to Find the Best Airfare

- **Take advantage of APEX fares.** Advance-purchase excursion fares are often the key to getting the lowest fare. You generally must be willing to buy your tickets as far ahead as possible: The **21-day APEX** is seconded only by the **14-day APEX,** with a stay of 7 to 30 days. There's often a surcharge for flying on a weekend, and cancellation policies can be strict.
- **Watch for sales.** You'll almost never see them during July and August or the Thanksgiving or Christmas seasons, but at other times, you can get good deals. If you already hold a ticket when a sale breaks, it may even pay to exchange it, which usually incurs a charge of between $50 and $100. Just about all airlines now post sale fares on their websites.
- **Stay an extra day or fly midweek.** If your schedule is flexible, you can often save money this way. Many airlines won't volunteer this information, so be sure to ask.
- **Check with consolidators (a.k.a. bucket shops) .** These buy seats in bulk and sell them to the public at prices below the airlines' published discounted rates. Their small, boxed ads usually run in Sunday newspaper travel sections. Also try the online consolidators **OneTravel** (www.onetravel.com), **CheapTickets** (© 888/922-8849; www.cheaptickets.com), and **Hotwire** (© 877/HOTWIRE; www. hotwire.com). Other options include **FlyCheap** (© 800/FLY-CHEAP; www.flycheap.com) and **TFI Tours International** (© 800/745-8000 or 212/736-1140; www.lowestairprice.com), a clearinghouse for unused seats.
- **Book a seat on a charter flight.** Most charter operators sell their seats through travel agents. Before deciding to take a charter, however, check the ticket restrictions: You may be asked to buy a tour package, pay in advance, be amenable if the departure day is changed, pay a service charge, or pay harsh penalties if you cancel (but be understanding if the charter doesn't fill up and is canceled up to 10 days before departure). Summer charters fill up more quickly than others and are almost sure to fly, but seriously consider cancellation and baggage insurance.

and 5 for information on ferries from Washington to Vancouver Island.

ONLINE RESOURCES Internet users can tap into the same databases that were once accessible only to travel agents. Consumers can comparison shop for airfares, book flights, and learn of last-minute bargains, as well as reserve hotel rooms and rental cars. Be aware, however, that the cheapest options may still be available only through traditional or discounter travel agencies (some of which can also be found on the Internet; see below).

On Wednesdays, **Air Canada** (www.aircanada.ca) announces highly discounted flights, or WebSavers, for the following weekend. Reserve these flights a day in advance to depart anytime Thursday through Saturday and return Monday through Wednesday.

Most major airlines offer similar Internet-only fares, often called E-savers. **Smarter Living** (www.smarterliving. com) will compile comprehensive lists of these discounts and e-mail them to you.

Travelocity (www.travelocity.com or www.frommers.travelocity.com) and **Expedia** (www.expedia.com) are the most longstanding and reputable planning sites. The latest buzz is about **Orbitz** (www.orbitz.com), a site launched by several airlines. It shows all possible fares for your desired trip, offering fares lower than those available through travel agents. (Stay tuned: At press time, travel-agency associations were waging an antitrust battle against this site.) **Qixo** (www.qixo.com) is a powerful search engine that allows you to search for flights on 20 other sites (such as Travelocity) at once.

BY CAR & FERRY

There are nearly two dozen border crossings between the United States and the provinces of Alberta and British Columbia. Ferries link Port Angeles, Seattle, and Anacortes, in Washington, with port facilities in the Victoria area; see chapter 4 for more information. Be sure to bring your car's registration papers.

BY BUS

Greyhound Canada (© 800/661-8747 in Canada; www.greyhound.ca) operates the major intercity bus system in Canada, with frequent links to cities in the U.S. northern tier (many more than what's offered by Greyhound USA). You can also use Greyhound's reservations system to make arrangements on some smaller local carriers, such as Island Coach Lines.

BY TRAIN

Amtrak (© 800/USA-RAIL; www.amtrak.com) can get you into Canada at a few border points, where you can connect with **VIA Rail** (© 888/VIARAIL** in Canada, or 416/236-2029; www.viarail.ca). There are a couple of main routes into Canada from the East Coast, plus one from Chicago, and VIA Rail will then take you west to Alberta and British Columbia. On the West Coast, the *Cascades* runs from Eugene, Oregon, to Vancouver, British Columbia. Round-trip fares are US$66 to US$128 from Portland and US$46 to US$68 from Seattle.

Amtrak and VIA Rail both offer a North American rail pass, which gives you 30 days of unlimited travel. At press time, the cost ranges from US$471 to US$674, with a 10% discount for seniors and students.

PACKAGE TOURS

Escorted tours take care of all the details; independent packages simply give you a package price on the big-ticket items and leave you free to find your own way. Independent tours give you much more flexibility but require more effort on your part. Those who prefer not to drive and don't relish the notion of getting from train or bus stations to hotels on their own might prefer an escorted tour.

INDEPENDENT PACKAGES Air Canada (© 800/254-1000) offers travel bargains ranging from city packages to fly/drive tours, escorted tours, and ski holidays.

World of Vacations (© 800/661-1312; www.wov.com) features an array of independent package tours, including a number of fly/rail deals.

Collette Tours (© 800/340-5158; www.collettevacations.com) offers independent tours that include Victoria, Vancouver, Edmonton, and Calgary, as well as the Rockies and other wilderness destinations.

ESCORTED TOURS Collette Tours (see above) offers a wide variety of escorted trips by bus and train; some combine western Canada with

Alaska. An escorted train tour goes from Vancouver to Banff aboard the *Rocky Mountaineer* (see below).

Brewster Transportation and Tours (✆ 800/661-1152; www.brewster.ca) arranges tours throughout western Canada, both escorted and independent. Its offerings include motorcoach and train excursions, ski vacations, city and resort packages, and independent driving tours. One highlight is a visit to the Columbia Icefield in Jasper National Park. Many packages in the Rockies include stays at guest ranches.

The **Great Canadian Railtour Company** (✆ 800/665-7245; www.rockymountaineer.com) operates the *Rocky Mountaineer* from mid-April to mid-October. The train winds past waterfalls, glaciers, snowcapped peaks, and roaring streams. You can travel east from Vancouver or west from Jasper, Calgary, or Banff. Tours range from 2 to 12 days, with stays in both the mountains and cities.

John Steel Railtours (✆ 800/988-5778; www.johnsteel.com) offers both independent and escorted packages, many through the Rockies, which combine train and other forms of travel. Packages run from 5 to 12 days and include stays in cities and national parks.

9 Getting Around

BY PLANE
Canada's biggest transcontinental airline is **Air Canada** (✆ 800/776-3000; www.aircanada.ca). Most of Canada is also served by the discount airline **Canada 3000** (✆ 888/300-0669 or 416/674-3000; www.canada3000.com). Other carriers include **Air Transat** (✆ 866/847-1112; www.airtransat.com) and **WestJet** (✆ 888/937-8538; www.westjet.com).

Within Canada, Air Canada operates daily service among all major cities and many smaller destinations, and its allied connector carriers, such as Air BC, serve scores of smaller towns. Canada 3000, WestJet, and Air Transat all serve most major Canadian cities, as well as some smaller ones. In general, expect to find the most travel options through Air Canada, but, in some cases, significantly lower fares through its competitors.

BY CAR
Rental-car companies include **Hertz** (✆ 800/654-3131 in the U.S., or 800/263-0600 in Canada; www.hertz.com), **Avis** (✆ 800/331-1212 in the U.S., or 800/331-1084 in Canada; www.avis.com), **Dollar** (✆ 800/800-4000; www.dollar.com), **Thrifty** (✆ 800/THRIFTY; www.thrifty.com), **Budget** (✆ 800/527-0700 in the U.S., or 800/472-3325 in Canada; https://rent.drivebudget.com), **Enterprise** (✆ 800/RENTACAR in the U.S., or 800/268-8900 in Canada; www.enterprise.com), and **National** (✆ 800/CAR-RENT in the U.S., or 800/387-4747 in Canada; www.nationalcar.com). Vehicles tend to get scarce from mid-May to the end of

---

Tips **Sample Distances Between Major Cities**

- From **Vancouver** to: Seattle, 141 miles (227km); Calgary, 604 miles (975km); Edmonton, 718 miles (1,159km)
- From **Victoria** to: Toronto, 2,911 miles (4,687km)
- From **Calgary** to: Edmonton, 182 miles (294km); Montréal, 2,299 miles (3,700km)

summer; reserve as far in advance as possible.

CAA, or **Canadian Automobile Association** (© 800/222-4357; www.caa.ca), extends privileges to AAA members; bring your membership card.

DRIVING RULES Wearing seat belts is compulsory for all passengers. Children under 5 must be in child restraints. Motorcyclists must wear helmets. In British Columbia and Alberta, it's legal to turn right at a red light after you've come to a full stop. Pedestrians have the right of way. The speed limit on express routes (limited-access highways) ranges from 62 to 68 mph (100–110km per hour). Drivers must carry proof of insurance at all times.

BY TRAIN

On **VIA Rail** (© 888/VIARAIL in Canada, or 416/236-2029; www.viarail.ca), you can traverse the continent comfortably in sleeping cars, parlor coaches, bedrooms, and roomettes. Virtually all of Canada's major cities (save Calgary) are connected by rail. Some luxury trains, like the *Canadian*, boast dome cars with panoramic picture windows, hot showers, and elegant dining cars.

Seniors, students, and children receive a 10% discount on all fares. A **Canrailpass,** C$658 (US$428) in high season, gives you 12 days of unlimited travel in one 30-day period.

ⓒ *FAST FACTS:* British Columbia & the Canadian Rockies

American Express There are offices in Vancouver, Victoria, Calgary, and Edmonton; see the regional chapters that follow for addresses and phone numbers. To report lost or stolen traveler's checks, call © 800/221-7282.

Electricity Canada uses the same electrical plug configuration and current as does the United States, 110 to 115 volts, 60 cycles.

Embassies & Consulates All embassies are in Ottawa, the national capital; the U.S. embassy is at 490 Sussex Dr. (© 613/238-5335; www.usembassycanada.gov). You'll find **U.S. consulates** in Alberta at 615 Macleod Trail SE, 10th Floor, Calgary (© 403/266-8962), and in British Columbia at Mezzanine, 1095 W. Pender St., Vancouver (© 604/685-4311). Visit www.amcits.com for further U.S. consular services information.

There's a **British consulate general** at 777 Bay St., Suite 2800, Toronto (© 416/593-1290; for more information, see www.britain-in-canada.org), and an **Australian consulate general** at Suite 316, 175 Bloor St. E., Toronto (© 416/323-1155; for more information, see www.ahc-ottawa.org).

Emergencies In life-threatening situations, call © 911.

Liquor Laws In British Columbia, all beer, wine, and spirits are sold only in government liquor stores, which keep very restricted hours and charge extortionate prices. Alberta's liquor laws more resemble those in the United States. The minimum drinking age there is 18; in all other provinces it's 19. Not too long ago, Alberta privatized its liquor sales to the public. You still need to go to liquor stores for all forms of alcohol, including beer and wine, but there are a lot more stores than in the past, and they keep much longer hours.

Mail Standard mail is carried by **Canada Post** (© **800/267-1177** in Canada, or 416/979-8822; www.canadapost.ca). At press time, it costs C$.47 (US31¢) to send a first-class letter or postcard within Canada, C$.60 (US39¢) from Canada to the United States. Airmail service to other countries is C$1.05 (US68¢). If you put a return address on your letter, make sure it's Canadian, otherwise don't use one.

Maps Both provincial tourist offices (see "Visitor Information," above) produce excellent road maps. The Alberta map is free; the British Columbia map costs C$5 (US$3.25) and must be purchased from **Davenport Maps,** Suite 201, 2610 Douglas St., Victoria (© **250/384-2621;** maps@ davenportmaps.com).

Pets To bring your dog or cat to Canada, carry proof that it has had its rabies shots in the last 3 years.

Pharmacies Drugstores and pharmacies are found throughout western Canada. In fact, many prescription-only drugs in the United States are available over the counter in Canada, and pharmacists are more likely to offer casual medical advice than their counterparts in the States.

Smoking Smoking in restaurants and public places is more prevalent in Canada than in many places in the United States, but less so than in Europe. Most restaurants will have no-smoking sections; hotels will have no-smoking rooms, and many inns and B&Bs don't permit it at all.

Taxes The **goods and service tax (GST)** is a 7% federal tax on virtually all goods and services. Some hotels and shops include the GST in their prices, others add it on separately. Additionally, British Columbia levies a 7% sales tax on purchases and services. Alberta has no provincial sales tax.

Visitors can reclaim the GST portion of hotel bills and the price of goods purchased in Canada. The minimum rebate is C$14 (US$9, the tax on C$200/US$130) and the claim must be filed within a year. The rebate doesn't apply to car rentals or restaurant meals. To obtain refunds, you must submit your original receipts (which will be returned) with an application form. You can get the form in some larger hotels, in some duty-free shops, or by phone at © **800/66-VISIT** in Canada, or 613/991-3346.

Receipts from several trips during the same year may be submitted together. Claims of less than C$500 (US$325) can be made at certain designated duty-free shops at international airports and border crossings. You will need to present your receipts, have your purchases available for inspection, and show proof that you are leaving Canada (such as departing plane tickets). Otherwise, you can mail the forms to **Visitor Rebate Program,** Canada Customs and Revenue Agency, Summerside Tax Centre, 275 Pope Rd., Suite 104, Summerside, PE C1N 6C6.

Telephone The Canadian phone system is the same as the system in the United States. Phone numbers have 10 digits: The first three numbers are the area code, which corresponds to a province or division thereof, plus a seven-digit local number. To call within the same locality, usually all you have to dial is the seven-digit local number. If you're making a long-distance call, precede the local number with "1" plus the area code.

For **directory assistance,** dial © **411.** If that doesn't work, dial 1 + area code + 555-1212. Many public phones are set up to accept phone cards, which are readily available at drugstores, tobacco shops, and other shops.

Time Zone Most of British Columbia is in the Pacific time zone, 8 hours earlier than Greenwich mean time. A sliver of British Columbia, stretching from Golden down to Cranbrook, is on mountain time, an hour later than the rest of the province. All of Alberta is in the mountain time zone. From the first Sunday in April to the last Sunday in October, daylight saving time is in effect in both provinces; clocks are advanced by 1 hour.

Tipping For good service in a restaurant, tip 15% to 20%. Tip hairdressers or taxi drivers 10%. Bellhops get C$1 per bag; for valets who fetch your car, a C$2 tip should suffice.

Water The water in Canada is legendary for its purity. You can drink water directly from the tap anywhere in the country. Bottled water is also widely available.

3

Vancouver

by Shawn Blore

If you really want to understand Vancouver, stand at the edge of the Inner Harbour (the prow of the Canada Place pavilion makes a good vantage point) and look up: past the floatplanes taking off over Stanley Park, around the container terminals, over the tony waterfront high-rises, and then up the steep green slopes of the north-shore mountains to the twin snowy peaks of the Lions. All this—well, 90% of it anyway—is the result of a unique collaboration between God and the Canadian Pacific Railway (CPR).

It was the Almighty—or Nature (depending on your point of view)—who raised up the Coast range and then sent a glacier slicing along its foot, simultaneously carving out a deep trench and piling up a tall moraine of rock and sand. When the ice retreated, water from the Pacific flowed in and the moraine became a peninsula, flanked on one side by a deep natural harbor and on the other by a river of glacial meltwater. Some 10,000 years later, a CPR surveyor came by; took in the peninsula, the harbor, and the river; and decided he'd found the perfect spot for the railway's new Pacific terminus. He kept it quiet until the company had bought up most of the land around town, and then the railway moved in and set up shop. The city of Vancouver was born.

The resulting boom was pretty small. Though the port did a good business shipping out grain, and sawmills and salmon canneries sprang

up, the city was too far from the rest of North America for any serious manufacturing. Vancouver became a town of sailors, lumberjacks, and fishers— until the 1980s, when it decided to host Expo '86, a stunning success. The world came to visit, including many people from the newly emerging tiger economies of Hong Kong, Taiwan, and Malaysia. They looked at the mountains, the ocean, and the price of local real estate and were amazed. Many people moved here and settled new neighborhoods. On the Fraser river delta, the bedroom community of Richmond became a city, with a population more than half Chinese. In older neighborhoods, prices went ballistic, doubling and tripling overnight. And on the railyard-turned-Expo site, 40 new high-rise condo towers began to rise.

Unlike previous immigrants, these newcomers didn't worry about finding work; they made their own, founding financial-services, software, education, engineering, and architectural-consulting businesses. A film industry sprang up. Vancouver became a postmodern town of Jags, Beemers, and cell phones. The steakhouse and ubiquitous "Chinese and Canadian" diner gave way to a thousand little places offering sushi and Szechwan, tapas and bami, and, inevitably, fusion.

Working indoors, Vancouverites fell in love with outdoor activities like mountain biking, windsurfing, kayaking, rock climbing, parasailing, snowboarding, and backcountry skiing.

When they mastered all these, they began experimenting with new sports, and strange summer-winter combinations were born: skiing-kayaking, mountain biking–snowboarding, and snowshoe-paragliding.

Splints and scrapes aside, folks seemed happy with the new state of affairs—and the rest of the world seemed to agree. *Outside* magazine voted Vancouver one of the 10 best cities in the world to live in. *Condé Nast Traveler* called it one of the 10 best cities to visit. And the World Council of Cities ranked it second only to Geneva for quality of life. Heady stuff, particularly for a spot that fewer than 20 years ago was derided as the world's biggest mill town. But then again, God—and the Canadian Pacific Railway—works in mysterious ways.

1 Essentials

GETTING THERE

BY PLANE **Vancouver International Airport** (www.yvr.ca) is 8 miles (13km) south of downtown on uninhabited Sea Island. For airlines that serve Vancouver, see "Getting There" in chapter 2. **Tourist Information Kiosks** on Levels 2 and 3 of the Main and International terminals (© 604/276-6101) are open daily from 6:30am to 11:30pm.

Courtesy buses to airport hotels are available, and a shuttle links the Main and International terminals to the South Terminal, where smaller and private aircraft are docked. The **YVR Airporter** (© 604/946-8866) provides frequent bus service to downtown's major hotels, a 30-minute ride. The one-way fare is C$10 (US$7) for adults, C$8 (US$5) for seniors, and C$5 (US$3.25) for children. The average **taxi** fare from the airport to downtown is C$25 (US$16). Most major **car-rental agencies** have airport counters and shuttles. Drivers heading into Vancouver take the Arthur Laing Bridge, which leads directly into Granville Street, the most direct route to downtown.

BY TRAIN Vancouver is the western terminus of **VIA Rail** (© 800/561-8630; www.viarail.ca), which connects virtually all of Canada's major cities (save Calgary). **Amtrak** (© 800/USA-RAIL; www.amtrak.com) has service from Seattle and points south. **BC Rail,** 1311 W. First St., North Vancouver (© 800/663-8238; www.bcrail.com), connects Vancouver to Whistler and other cities in the province.

The main rail station, **Pacific Central Station,** is at 1150 Station St., near Main Street and Terminal Avenue just south of Chinatown. From here, you can reach downtown Vancouver by cab for about C$5 (US$3.25). A block from the station is the **SkyTrain's Main Street Station,** within minutes of downtown. A one-zone SkyTrain ticket (covering the city of Vancouver) is C$1.75 (US$1.15).

BY BUS **Greyhound Canada** (© 800/661-8747 or 604/482-8747; www.greyhound.ca) and **Pacific Coach Lines** (© 800/661-1725 or 604/662-8074; www.pacificcoach.com) have their terminals at the **Pacific Central Station,** 1150 Station St. Pacific Coach Lines provides daily service between Vancouver and Victoria for C$26 (US$17) one-way, including ferry. **Quick Coach Lines** (© 604/940-4428; www.quickcoach.com) connects Vancouver to the Seattle-Tacoma International Airport. The 4-hour ride costs C$39 (US$25) one-way.

BY CAR From Seattle, the 140-mile (226km) drive along **U.S. Interstate 5** takes about 2½ hours. The road changes into **Highway 99** when you cross the border at the Peace Arch. You'll drive through the cities of White Rock, Delta, and Richmond; pass under the Fraser River through the George Massey Tunnel;

ⓔ Special Events & Festivals

At the New Year's Day **Polar Bear Swim** at English Bay Beach, hardy citizens show up in elaborate costumes to take a dip in the icy waters. Usually in late February, the **Chinese New Year** is celebrated with 2 weeks of firecrackers, dragon parades, and other festivities. In March or April, the **Vancouver Playhouse International Wine Festival** (www. winefest.bc.sympatico.ca) features the latest vintages; April's **Vancouver Sun Run** (www.sunrun.com) is Canada's biggest 10K race, featuring 17,000 runners and walkers who start and finish at B.C. Place Stadium.

The June **VanDusen Flower and Garden Show,** at the VanDusen Botanical Garden, 5251 Oak St. (ⓒ 604/878-9274), is Vancouver's premier floral gala. The late-June **Alcan Dragon Boat Festival** brings more than 150 local and international teams racing huge dragon boats. Music, dance, and Chinese acrobatics also take place as part of the events at the **Plaza of Nations** (ⓒ 604/688-2382).

During the July **Vancouver International Jazz Festival** (ⓒ 604/ 872-5200; www.jazzvancouver.com), more than 800 musicians perform at venues around town. Running July through September, the **Bard on the Beach Shakespeare Festival** (ⓒ 604/739-0559) presents Shakespeare's plays in Vanier Park. On **Canada Day,** July 1, Canada Place Pier hosts an all-day celebration including music, dance, and fireworks. The second or third weekend in July brings the **Vancouver Folk Music Festival** (ⓒ 604/602-9798; www.thefestival.redpoint.ws) at Jericho Beach Park. During the **HSBC Power Smart Celebration of Light** ★★★ (www. celebration-of-light.com), three international fireworks companies compete for a coveted title by launching their best displays, which are programmed to explode in time to accompanying music over English Bay Beach.

From mid-August to Labour Day, the **Pacific National Exhibition** (ⓒ 604/253-2311; www.pne.bc.ca) offers everything from big-name entertainment to a demolition derby, livestock demonstrations, fashion shows, and North America's finest all-wooden roller coaster. On Labour Day weekend, the **Molson Indy** (ⓒ 604/684-4639; www.molson indy.com) roars around the streets of False Creek, attracting more than 500,000 spectators. Later in September, the **Fringe Festival** (ⓒ 604/ 257-0350; www.vancouverfringe.com) highlights the best of Vancouver's independent theater.

Every October, the **Vancouver International Film Festival** (ⓒ 604/ 685-0260; www.viff.org) features 250 new works, revivals, and retrospectives, representing filmmakers from 40 countries. All December, the **Christmas Carol Ship Parade** lights up Vancouver Harbour, as cruise ships decorated with colorful lights sail around English Bay, while onboard guests sip cider and sing carols.

and cross the Oak Street Bridge. The highway ends here and becomes Oak Street, a busy urban thoroughfare. Turn left onto 70th Avenue. (A small sign suspended above the left lane at the intersection of Oak Street and 70th Avenue

Greater Vancouver

CYPRESS PROVINCIAL PARK

99

Capilano Lake

LYNN HEADWATERS REG. PARK

Seymour River

WEST VANCOUVER

Capilano River Reg. Park

Capilano Rd.

DISTRICT OF NORTH VANCOUVER

Marine Dr.

1

CITY OF NORTH VANCOUVER

English Bay

STANLEY PARK

Burrard

Inlet

See "Downtown Vancouver" map

Burrard St.

Hastings St.

University of British Columbia

Broadway

7

Victoria Dr.

BURN

PACIFIC SPIRIT PARK

V A N C O U V E R

Dunbar St.

Arbutus St.

Granville St.

St.

Main St.

99A

1A

Boundary Rd.

99

Marine Dr.

Marine Way

Vancouver International Airport

Sea Island

North Arm Fraser River

99

91

Westminster Hwy.

Strait of Georgia

RICHMOND

River Rd.

Steveston Hwy.

99

Westham Island

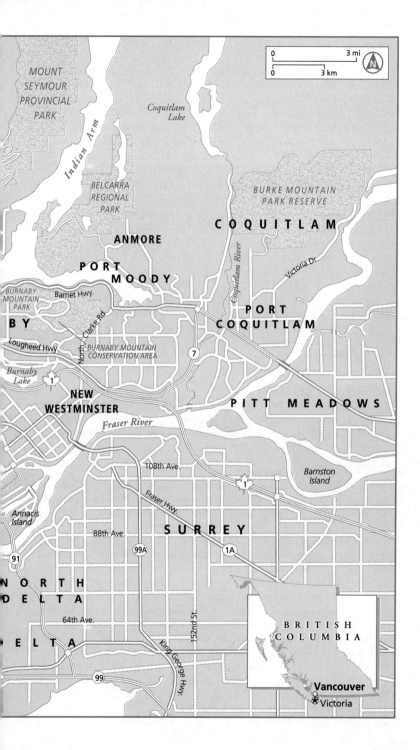

MOUNT
SEYMOUR
PROVINCIAL
PARK

Indian Arm

*Coquitlam
Lake*

BELCARRA
REGIONAL
PARK

BURKE MOUNTAIN
PARK RESERVE

ANMORE

C O Q U I T L A M

P O R T
M O O D Y

*BURNABY
MOUNTAIN
PARK*

Barnet Hwy.

Coquitlam River

Victoria Dr.

P O R T
C O Q U I T L A M

B Y

Lougheed Hwy.

North Clarke Rd.

BURNABY MOUNTAIN
CONSERVATION AREA

7

*Burnaby
Lake*

1

P I T T   M E A D O W S

NEW
WESTMINSTER

Fraser River

108th Ave.

1

*Barnston
Island*

*Annacis
Island*

Fraser Hwy.

88th Ave.

S U R R E Y

99A

1A

91

N O R T H
D E L T A

64th Ave.

152nd St.

B R I T I S H
C O L U M B I A

E L T A

King George Hwy.

99

Vancouver

⊗ Victoria

0 _____ 3 mi
0 _____ 3 km

N

reads CITY CENTRE.) Six blocks later, turn right onto Granville Street. This street heads directly into downtown Vancouver on the Granville Street Bridge.

Trans-Canada Highway 1 is a limited-access freeway running all the way to Vancouver's eastern boundary, where it crosses the Second Narrows bridge to North Vancouver. When coming on Highway 1 from the east, exit at Cassiar Street and turn left at the first light onto Hastings Street (Hwy. 7A), adjacent to Exhibition Park. Follow Hastings Street 4 miles (6.5km) into downtown. When coming to Vancouver from Whistler or parts north, take exit 13 (the sign says TAYLOR WAY, BRIDGE TO VANCOUVER) and cross the Lions Gate Bridge into Vancouver's West End.

BY SHIP & FERRY   The **Canada Place** cruise-ship terminal, at the base of Burrard Street (© **604/665-9085**), is a city landmark. Topped by five eye-catching white Teflon sails, Canada Place Pier juts out into the Burrard Inlet and is at the edge of the downtown financial district. Many cruise ships dock at Canada Place and the nearby Ballantyne Pier to board passengers headed for Alaska via British Columbia's Inside Passage. Buses and taxis greet new arrivals, but you can also easily walk to many major hotels.

BC Ferries (© **888/BCFERRY** in B.C., or 250/386-3431; www.bcferries. bc.ca) has three routes between Vancouver and Vancouver Island. The most direct route to Victoria is the Tsawwassen–Swartz Bay ferry. The Tsawwassen terminal is about 12 miles (19km) south of Vancouver. The Mid-Island Express operates between Tsawwassen and Duke Point, just south of Nanaimo (a 2-hr. crossing). The Horseshoe Bay–Nanaimo ferry leaves Horseshoe Bay near West Vancouver and arrives 95 minutes later in Nanaimo.

VISITOR INFORMATION

The **Vancouver Tourist Info Centre,** 200 Burrard St. (© **604/683-2000;** www. tourism-vancouver.org), is open from May to Labour Day, daily from 8am to 6pm; the rest of the year, Monday through Friday from 8:30am to 5:30pm and Saturday from 9am to 5pm.

CITY LAYOUT

Think of Vancouver's downtown peninsula as being like an upraised thumb on the mitten-shaped Vancouver mainland. Stanley Park, the West End, Yaletown, and Vancouver's business-and-financial center are on the "thumb," bordered to the west by English Bay, to the north by Burrard Inlet, and to the south by False Creek. The mainland part of the city, the "mitten," is mostly residential. Both the mainland and the peninsula are covered by a simple rectilinear street pattern.

On the downtown peninsula are four key east-west streets. **Robson Street** starts at B.C. Place Stadium, flows through the West End's shopping district, and ends at Stanley Park. **Georgia Street**—far more efficient for drivers than the pedestrian-oriented Robson—runs from the Georgia Viaduct on downtown's eastern edge through Vancouver's commercial core and carries on through Stanley Park and over the Lions Gate Bridge to the North Shore. Three blocks north of Georgia is **Hastings Street,** which begins in the West End, runs east through downtown, and skirts Gastown's southern border as it heads east to the Trans-Canada Highway. **Davie Street** starts at Pacific Boulevard near the Cambie Street Bridge, travels through Yaletown into the West End's more residential shopping district, and ends at English Bay Beach.

Three north-south downtown streets will get you everywhere you want to go in and out of downtown. Two blocks east of Stanley Park is **Denman Street,**

> **Tips Finding an Address**
>
> In many Vancouver addresses, the suite or room number precedes the building number. For instance, 100-1250 Robson St. is Suite 100 at 1250 Robson St. In downtown, Chinatown's **Carrall Street** is the east-west axis from which streets are numbered and designated. Westward, numbers increase progressively to Stanley Park; eastward, numbers increase heading toward Commercial Drive. For example, 400 West Pender would be about 4 blocks from Carrall Street heading toward downtown; 400 East Pender would be 4 blocks on the opposite side of Carrall Street. Off the peninsula, the system works the same, but **Ontario Street** is the east-west axis. All east-west roads are avenues (like Fourth Avenue), and streets (Main Street) run exclusively north-south.

which runs from West Georgia Street at Coal Harbour to Beach Avenue at English Bay Beach. This main West End thoroughfare is where the locals go to dine out. It's also the shortest north-south route between the two ends of the Stanley Park Seawall. East of Denman is **Burrard Street,** which starts near the Canada Place Pier, runs south through downtown, crosses the Burrard Street Bridge, and then forks. One branch, still Burrard Street, continues south and intersects **West Fourth Avenue** and **Broadway** before terminating at **West 16th Avenue** on the borders of Shaughnessy. The other branch becomes **Cornwall Avenue,** which heads due west through Kitsilano, changing its name two more times to **Point Grey Road** and then **Northwest Marine Drive** before entering the University of British Columbia campus.

Granville Street starts near the Waterfront Station on Burrard Inlet and runs the entire length of downtown, crosses over the Granville Bridge to Vancouver's West Side, and continues south before crossing the Arthur Laing Bridge to Vancouver International Airport.

On the mainland portion of Vancouver, the city's east-west roads are successively numbered from First Avenue at the downtown bridges to 77th Avenue by the banks of the Fraser River. By far the most important east-west route is **Broadway** (formerly Ninth Ave.), which starts a few blocks from the University of British Columbia and extends across the length of the city to the border with neighboring Burnaby, where it becomes the Lougheed Highway. In Kitsilano, **West Fourth Avenue** is also an important east-west commercial corridor. Intersecting with Broadway at various points are a number of north-south commercial streets, each of which defines a particular neighborhood. The most significant are (west to east) **Macdonald Street** in Kitsilano, then **Granville Street, Cambie Street, Main Street,** and **Commercial Drive.**

NEIGHBORHOODS IN BRIEF

Keep in mind that this is a city where property is king and where the word *west* has such positive connotations, folks have gone to great lengths to associate it with their particular patch of real estate. Thus there's the **West End,** the **West Side,** and **West Vancouver,** which improbably enough is located immediately beside **North Vancouver.** The West End is a high-rise residential neighborhood on the downtown peninsula. The West Side is half of Vancouver, from

Ontario Street west to the University of British Columbia. (The more working-class **East Side** covers the city's mainland portion, from Ontario Street east to Boundary Road.) Tony West Vancouver is a city to itself on the far side of Burrard Inlet. Together with its more middle-class neighbor North Vancouver, it forms an area called the **North Shore.**

Downtown Vancouver's commercial core runs from Nelson Street north to the harbor, with Homer Street as the eastern edge and a more ragged boundary running roughly along Burrard Street forming the western border. The prime office space is on or near Georgia Street. Hotels stick mostly to the northern third of downtown, clustering thickly near the water's edge. Walking is a good bet for getting around, day or night. Lots of people live in and around Vancouver's central business district, so the area is always populated.

The West End A fascinating neighborhood of high-rise condos mixed with Edwardian homes, the West End has all the necessities of life: great cafes and clubs, many and varied bookstores, and some of the city's best restaurants. The Pacific laps against the West End on two sides, in the form of Burrard Inlet to the north and English Bay to the south, and on the western edge spreads Stanley Park. Burrard Street forms the West End's eastern border.

Gastown The city's oldest section, Gastown was rebuilt in brick after the 1886 fire wiped out the original wooden city. Its cobblestone streets and late-Victorian architecture make it well worth a visit, despite an infestation of curio shops and souvenir stands. It lies east of downtown, in the 6 square blocks between Water and Hastings streets and Cambie and Columbia streets.

Chinatown South of Hastings, between Gore and Carrall streets to the east and west and Keefer Street to the south, Chinatown isn't large, but is intense. Fishmongers call out their wares, customers haggle over produce, and, inside any of a dozen restaurants, you'll find an entire extended family sitting at a single big round table, consuming half a dozen plates of succulent Cantonese cooking.

Yaletown The former warehouse district, below Granville Street and above Pacific Boulevard, from Davie Street over to Smithe, has long since been converted to an area of lofts, clubs, restaurants, high-end furniture shops, and a fledgling multimedia biz. In recent years, the neighborhood has finally come into its own.

Granville Island On a peninsula on False Creek, this former industrial site is now a fun mix of urban markets, artisan workshops, theaters, cafes, offices, parks, and restaurants.

Kitsilano In the 1960s, Kitsilano was Canada's Haight-Asbury, a slightly seedy enclave of coffeehouses, head shops, and long-haired hippies. Today, Kits is one of Vancouver's most popular neighborhoods, with a mix of affordable apartments and heritage homes, funky shops, great dining, and pleasant streets. And then there's Kits Beach. Roughly speaking, Alma and Burrard streets form Kitsilano's east and west boundaries, with West 16th Avenue to the south and the ocean to the north.

Richmond Twenty years ago, Richmond was mostly farmland, with a bit of sleepy suburb. Now it has become Asia West, an agglomeration of malls geared to new (read: rich, educated, and successful) Chinese immigrants. Malls like the Aberdeen Mall and Yao Han Centre will make you feel as if you've just stepped into Singapore.

Commercial Drive Every immigrant group that ever passed through the city has left its mark on "The Drive." Combine those influences with the indigenous culture of left-wing activism and ongoing yuppification, and the result is a peculiar but endearing mix: the Italian cafe next to the Marxist bookstore across from the vegetarian deli that has taken to selling really expensive yeast-free Tuscan bread.

Punjabi Market Most of the businesses catering to Vancouver's

sizable Punjabi population are found on a 4-block stretch of Main Street, from 48th up to 52nd avenues. During business hours, the fragrant scent of spices wafts out from food stalls and Hindi pop songs blare from hidden speakers.

The North Shore (North Vancouver & West Vancouver) The most impressive thing about the North Shore is its huge, wild mountain range. The cities themselves, however, aren't without their charms. West Vancouver offers some fine waterfront restaurants, particularly in the Dundarave area. North Vancouver's Lonsdale Quay Market—where the SeaBus docks—makes a pleasant outing.

2 Getting Around

BY PUBLIC TRANSPORTATION The reliable **Translink/BC Transit** (© 604/521-0400; www.translink.bc.ca) system includes electric buses, SeaBus catamaran ferries, and the magnetic-rail SkyTrain. Regular service on the main routes runs daily from 5am to 2am, with less frequent "Owl" service operating on several routes until 4:20am.

Fares are the same for the bus, SeaBus, and SkyTrain. One-way, all-zone fares are C$1.75 (US$1.15) after 6:30pm Monday through Friday and all day on weekends and holidays. At other times, a one-zone fare is C$1.75 (US$1.15) and covers the entire city. A two-zone fare—C$2.50 (US$1.60)—is required to travel to nearby suburbs such as Richmond or North Vancouver. DayPasses, which are good on all public transit, are C$7 (US$4.55) for adults and C$5 (US$3.25) for seniors, students, and children. Passes are available at the visitor center, SeaBus terminals, convenience stores, drugstores, and other outlets displaying the FareDealer symbol.

The **SkyTrain** is a magnetic-rail train serving 20 stations along its 35-minute trip from downtown Vancouver east to Surrey through Burnaby and New Westminster. The **SeaBus** catamarans take passengers and cyclists on a scenic 12-minute commute between downtown's Waterfront Station and North Vancouver's Lonsdale Quay.

BY TAXI Within the downtown area, you can expect to travel for less than C$6 (US$3.90). Cabs are easy to find in front of major hotels, but flagging one can be tricky; most drivers are usually on radio calls. For a pickup, call **Black Top** (© 604/731-1111), **Yellow Cab** (© 604/681-1111), or **MacLure's** (© 604/731-9211).

BY CAR You won't need a car to explore the city, but you may want one to explore the environs. Rental agencies with counters and shuttle service at the airport include **Avis** (© **800/879-2847** or 604/606-2847), **Budget** (© **800/ 527-0700** or 604/668-7000), **Enterprise** (© **800/736-8222** or 604/ 688-5500), **Hertz** (© **800/263-0600** or 604/688-2411), **National/Tilden** (© **800/387-4747** or 604/685-6111), and **Thrifty** (© **800/367-2277** or 604/606-1666).

All major downtown hotels have guest parking; rates vary from free to C$20 (US$13) per day. There's public parking at **Robson Square** (enter at Smithe and Howe sts.), the **Pacific Centre** (Howe and Dunsmuir sts.), and **The Bay** department store (Richards near Dunsmuir St.). You'll also find lots at Thurlow and Georgia streets, Thurlow and Alberni streets, and Robson and Seymour streets. Metered street parking rules are strictly enforced. Unmetered parking is often subject to neighborhood residency requirements; check the signs. If your car is towed or if you need a towing service, call **Unitow** (© **604/251-1255**) or **Busters** (© **604/685-8181**). Members of AAA can get assistance from the **Canadian Automobile Association (CAA),** 999 W. Broadway (© **604/ 268-5600,** or 604/293-2222 for road service).

BY BICYCLE   Vancouver is decidedly bike-friendly. There are plenty of rental places along Robson and Denman streets near Stanley Park. Bike routes are designated throughout the city. Paved paths crisscross though parks and along beaches. Helmets are mandatory, and riding on sidewalks is illegal except on designated paths.

Cycling BC (© **604/737-3034**) accommodates cyclists on the SkyTrain and buses by providing Bike & Ride lockers at all Park & Ride lots. It also dispenses information about events, bike touring, and insurance. Many downtown parking lots and garages have no-fee bike racks.

You can take a bike on the SeaBus for free. All West Vancouver blue buses (including the bus to the Horseshoe Bay ferry terminal) can carry two bikes free, on a first-come, first-served basis. In Vancouver, only a limited number of suburban routes allow bikes on the bus, and space is limited. Bikes aren't allowed on the SkyTrain or in the George Massey Tunnel, but a tunnel shuttle can transport you across the Fraser. It operates four times daily from mid-May to September, and on weekends only from May to Victoria Day (the third weekend in May).

BY FERRY   Crossing False Creek to Vanier Park or Granville Island on one of the blue mini-ferries is cheap and fun. The **Aquabus** docks at the foot of Howe Street. It takes you either to Granville Island's public market or east along False Creek to Science World and Stamps Landing. The **Granville Island ferry** docks at Sunset Beach below the Burrard Street Bridge and the Aquatic Centre and goes to Granville Island and Vanier Park. Ferries to Granville Island leave every 5 minutes from 7am to 10pm; those to Vanier Park, every 15 minutes from 10am to 8pm. One-way fares for both companies on all routes are $2.50 (US$1.60) for adults and C$1.25 (US$.80) for seniors and children.

 FAST FACTS: Vancouver

American Express The office at 666 Burrard St. (© **604/669-2813**) is open Monday through Friday from 8am to 5:30pm and Saturday from 10am to 4pm.

Area Codes The area code for Vancouver and the rest of the British Columbia lower mainland is **604.** Note that 10-digit dialing was recently introduced in the Vancouver area. All calls, whether long-distance or not, must be preceded by the 604 area code. The area code for all other parts of British Columbia, including Victoria, Vancouver Island, and the interior, is **250.**

Consulates The **U.S. Consulate** is at 1095 W. Pender St. (✆ **604/685-4311**). The **British Consulate** is at 800-1111 Melville St. (✆ **604/683-4421**). The **Australian Consulate** is at 1225-888 Dunsmuir St. (✆ **604/684-1177**).

Doctors Hotels usually have a doctor on call. The **Vancouver Medical Clinics,** Bentall Centre, 1055 Dunsmuir St. (✆ **604/683-8138**), takes drop-ins Monday through Friday from 8am to 5pm. **Carepoint Medical Centre,** 1175 Denman St. (✆ **604/681-5338**), is open daily from 9am to 9pm.

Emergencies Dial ✆ **911** for fire, police, ambulance, and poison control.

Hospitals **St. Paul's Hospital,** 1081 Burrard St. (✆ **604/682-2344**), is the closest facility to downtown and the West End. West Side Vancouver hospitals include **Vancouver General Hospital Health and Sciences Centre,** 855 W. 12th Ave. (✆ **604/875-4111**), and **British Columbia's Children's Hospital,** 4480 Oak St. (✆ **604/875-2345**). In North Vancouver, there's **Lions Gate Hospital,** 231 E. 15th St. (✆ **604/988-3131**).

Internet Access There's free Internet access at the **Vancouver Public Library Central Branch,** 350 W. Georgia St. (✆ **604/331-4000**). Downtown, try **Roberto's Internet Café,** 311 West Pender (✆ **604/683-6500**). **Webster's Internet Cafe,** 340 Robson St. (✆ **604/915-9327**), is across from the main library. In Kitsilano, **Dakoda's Internet Cafe,** 1602 Yew St. (✆ **604/731-5616**), is a pleasant cafe in the pub/restaurant zone across from Kits Beach.

Pharmacies **Shopper's Drug Mart,** 1125 Davie St. (✆ **604/685-6445**), is open 24 hours. Several Safeway supermarkets have late-night pharmacies, including the one at the corner of Robson and Denman streets, which is open until midnight.

Police The Vancouver City Police can be reached at ✆ **604/717-3535.**

Post Offices The main post office, 349 W. Georgia St., at Homer Street, is open Monday through Friday from 8am to 5:30pm. Postal outlets are located in souvenir stores and drugstores displaying the red-and-white Canada Post emblem.

Safety Overall, Vancouver is a safe city; violent-crime rates are quite low. However, property crimes and crimes of opportunity (such as items being stolen from unlocked cars) do occur with troubling frequency, particularly downtown. Downtown's East Side, between Gastown and Chinatown, is a troubled neighborhood and should be avoided at night.

3 Where to Stay

Most hotels are in the downtown/Yaletown area, or else in the West End. Both neighborhoods are close to major sights and services. Reservations are highly recommended June through September and over the holidays.

Downtown Vancouver

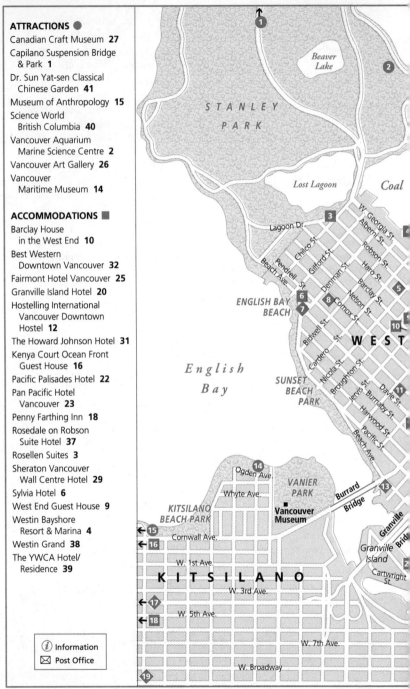

ATTRACTIONS ●

Canadian Craft Museum **27**

Capilano Suspension Bridge
& Park **1**

Dr. Sun Yat-sen Classical
Chinese Garden **41**

Museum of Anthropology **15**

Science World
British Columbia **40**

Vancouver Aquarium
Marine Science Centre **2**

Vancouver Art Gallery **26**

Vancouver
Maritime Museum **14**

ACCOMMODATIONS ■

Barclay House
in the West End **10**

Best Western
Downtown Vancouver **32**

Fairmont Hotel Vancouver **25**

Granville Island Hotel **20**

Hostelling International
Vancouver Downtown
Hostel **12**

The Howard Johnson Hotel **31**

Kenya Court Ocean Front
Guest House **16**

Pacific Palisades Hotel **22**

Pan Pacific Hotel
Vancouver **23**

Penny Farthing Inn **18**

Rosedale on Robson
Suite Hotel **37**

Rosellen Suites **3**

Sheraton Vancouver
Wall Centre Hotel **29**

Sylvia Hotel **6**

West End Guest House **9**

Westin Bayshore
Resort & Marina **4**

Westin Grand **38**

The YWCA Hotel/
Residence **39**

ⓘ Information
✉ Post Office

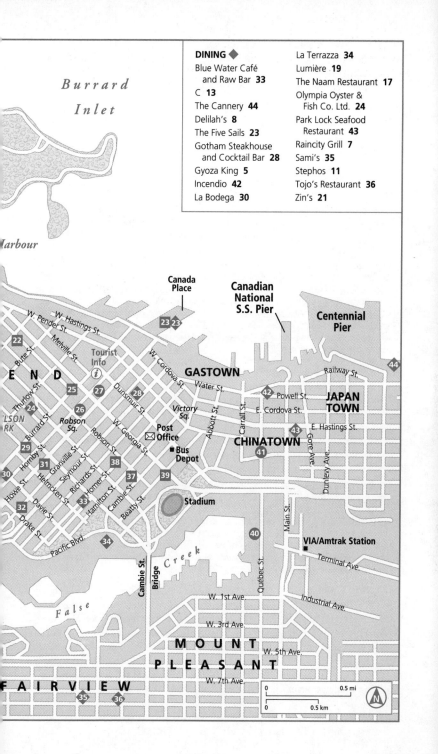

DINING ◆

Blue Water Café and Raw Bar **33**
C **13**
The Cannery **44**
Delilah's **8**
The Five Sails **23**
Gotham Steakhouse and Cocktail Bar **28**
Gyoza King **5**
Incendio **42**
La Bodega **30**

La Terrazza **34**
Lumière **19**
The Naam Restaurant **17**
Olympia Oyster & Fish Co. Ltd. **24**
Park Lock Seafood Restaurant **43**
Raincity Grill **7**
Sami's **35**
Stephos **11**
Tojo's Restaurant **36**
Zin's **21**

Burrard
Inlet

Harbour

Canada Place

Canadian National S.S. Pier

Centennial Pier

W. Pender St.
W. Hastings St.
Melville St.
22
Bute St.
W. Cordova St.
Tourist Info ⓘ
GASTOWN
Water St.
Railway St.
44
Thurlow St.
E N D
25
27
Dunsmuir St.
28
42 Powell St.
Carrall St.
JAPAN TOWN
LSON RK
24
Burrard St.
Robson Sq.
26
Victory Sq.
W. Georgia St.
E. Cordova St.
43
E. Hastings St.
Gore Ave.
Dunlevy Ave.
29
Hornby St.
Robson St.
Post ✉ Office
CHINATOWN
41
30
31
Granville St.
Seymour St.
Richards St.
Homer St.
38
■ Bus Depot
Howe St.
Helmcken St.
33
37
39
Hamilton St.
Cambie St.
Beatty St.
Stadium
32
Davie St.
Drake St.
40
Main St.
VIA/Amtrak Station
■
Terminal Ave.
34
Pacific Blvd.
Cambie St.
Bridge St.
Creek
Quebec St.
Industrial Ave.
False
W. 1st Ave.
W. 3rd Ave.
M O U N T
W. 5th Ave.
P L E A S A N T
F A I R V I E W
W. 7th Ave.
35
36

0   0.5 mi
0   0.5 km

Ⓝ

If you have trouble finding a room, call the hot lines run by **Super Natural British Columbia** (✆ **800/663-6000**) or **Tourism Vancouver** (✆ **604/683-2000**). Both can make last-minute bookings at hotels and B&Bs. **Born Free Bed & Breakfast of B.C.** (✆ **800/488-1941** or 604/298-8815; www.vancouverbandb.bc.ca) can help you find the B&B that best suits your needs.

DOWNTOWN & YALETOWN
EXPENSIVE

Fairmont Hotel Vancouver ★★   Thanks to a recent C$75-million (US$49-million) renovation, the grande dame of Vancouver's hotels has been restored beyond its former glory. A city landmark since it first opened its doors in 1939, the hotel has been completely brought up to 21st-century standards. Rooms are spacious, and bathrooms gleam with marble touches. The decor evokes an elegance of days gone by. A number of wheelchair-accessible units are available. For those who like to be pampered, the hotel has just inaugurated its state-of-the-art spa facilities.

900 W. Georgia St., Vancouver, BC V6C 2W6. ✆ **800/866-5577** or 604/684-3131. Fax 604/662-1929. www.fairmont.com. 556 units. High season C$259–C$489 (US$168–US$318) double; C$419–C$1,899 (US$272–US$1,234) suite. Low season from C$179 (US$116) double; from C$339 (US$220) suite. Children under 18 stay free in parents' room. AE, DC, DISC, MC, V. Parking C$19 (US$12). Small pets allowed for C$25 (US$16). **Amenities:** Two restaurants (brasserie, West Coast grill), bar; indoor pool; health club; excellent spa; Jacuzzi; sauna; concierge; tour desk; car-rental desk; business center; shopping arcade; salon; 24-hr. room service; massage; babysitting; laundry service; same-day dry cleaning. *In room:* A/C, TV w/ pay movies, dataport, minibar, coffeemaker, hair dryer, iron.

Pan Pacific Hotel Vancouver ★★   Since its completion in 1986, this luxury hotel atop the Convention Centre has become perhaps the key landmark on the Vancouver waterfront; Canada Place and the cruise-ship terminal are at its doorstep. If you're taking an Alaskan cruise, this is the place to stay. Superior guest rooms face the city and offer a partial waterfront view. For the best views, book a deluxe room and wake to see the sun glinting on the mountains of the North Shore and the floatplanes drifting in from parts west and north. All units contain elegant maple furniture and huge picture windows.

300–999 Canada Place, Vancouver, BC V6C 3B5. ✆ **800/937-1515** or 604/662-8111. Fax 604/685-8690. www.panpac.com. 504 units. May–Oct C$465–C$545 (US$302–US$354) double. Nov–Apr C$380–C$430 (US$247–US$280) double. C$565–C$3,000 (US$367–US$1,950) suite year-round. AE, DC, DISC, MC, V. Parking C$21 (US$14). **Amenities:** Three restaurants, bar; outdoor heated pool; outstanding health club with universal gym, small indoor track, squash courts, and more (C$15/US$10 user fee); spa; Jacuzzi; sauna; concierge; tour desk; car-rental desk; business center; shopping arcade; 24-hr. room service; massage; babysitting; laundry service; same-day dry cleaning. *In room:* A/C, TV w/ pay movies, dataport, minibar, coffeemaker, hair dryer, iron, safe.

Sheraton Vancouver Wall Centre Hotel ★★★   The tallest and largest hotel in the city, the Wall Centre is hard to miss: Just look for the towering two-tone oval spire. Completed in 2001, this is development mogul Peter Wall's personal tribute to everything he's ever liked in the world's finest accommodations. The opulent decor includes a gold-leaf staircase, custom-designed furniture, handblown glass chandeliers, and a half-dozen peepholes on each bedroom door. All guest rooms are elegantly appointed with blond-wood furnishings, floor-to-ceiling windows, luxury bathrooms, heated floors, down duvets, and Egyptian cotton sheets.

1088 Burrard St., Vancouver, BC V6Z 2R9. ✆ **800/325-3535** or 604/331-1000. Fax 604/331-1000. www.sheratonvancouver.com. 735 units. May 15–Oct 22 C$199–C$399 (US$129–US$259) double; C$249–C$549 (US$162–US$357) suite. Oct 23–May 14 C$129–C$249 (US$84–US$162) double; C$179–C$399

(US$116–US$259) suite. Valet parking C$19 (US$12). **Amenities:** Two restaurants, two bars; indoor pool; state-of-the-art health club; spa; Jacuzzi; sauna; concierge; tour desk; car-rental desk; business center; salon; 24-hr. room service; babysitting; laundry service; same-day dry cleaning. *In room:* A/C, TV w/ pay movies, dataport, minibar, coffeemaker, hair dryer, iron, safe.

The Westin Grand ★★★ The luxurious Westin Grand, shaped to look like a grand piano, opened in 1999 within easy walking distance of Yaletown and the Robson shopping area. The spacious suites are brightened by natural light pouring in through floor-to-ceiling windows, a nice foil to the somber mahogany furniture and earth-toned decor. Rooms for travelers with disabilities are available.

433 Robson St., Vancouver, BC V6B 6L9. © 888/680-9393 or 604/602-1999. Fax 604/647-2502. www.westingrandvancouver.com. 207 units. May 16–Oct 14 C$199–C$429 (US$129–US$279) suite. Oct 15–May 15 C$149–C$299 (US$97–US$194) suite. Children under 17 stay free in parents' room. AE, DC, DISC, MC, V. Self-parking C$15 (US$10); valet parking C$19 (US$12). **Amenities:** Restaurant; outdoor pool; excellent health club; Jacuzzi; sauna; children's programs; concierge; business center; 24-hr. room service; babysitting; laundry service; dry cleaning. *In room:* A/C, TV w/ pay movies, dataport, kitchen, minibar, coffeemaker, hair dryer, iron, safe.

MODERATE

Best Western Downtown Vancouver This Best Western is a 5-block walk from the theater area at the south end of downtown. Some guest rooms have harbor views; 32 have kitchens. The hotel isn't overflowing with facilities, but the rooms are well furnished and the location is convenient.

718 Drake St. (at Granville St.), Vancouver, BC V6Z 2W6. © 888/669-9888 or 604/660-9888. Fax 604/669-3440. www.bestwesterndowntown.com. 143 units. C$139–C$209 (US$90–US$136) double; C$280–C$350 (US$182–US$228) penthouse. Rates include continental breakfast. AE, DC, DISC, MC, V. Parking C$5 (US$3.25). **Amenities:** Restaurant; exercise room; Jacuzzi; sauna; game room; tour desk; shuttle service to downtown; babysitting; laundry service. *In room:* A/C, TV/VCR, dataport, coffeemaker, hair dryer, iron, safe.

Rosedale on Robson Suite Hotel ★★ *Kids* Located across from Library Square, the Rosedale provides excellent value for the money. All units feature sofa beds and kitchenettes. Designated two-bedroom family suites are decorated in either sports or Barbie themes and furnished with bunk beds and toy chests. On Saturday nights, the staff puts on a movie or crafts night to take the little ones off their parents' hands. Even the family dog is welcome.

838 Hamilton St. (at Robson St.), Vancouver, BC V6B 6A2. © 800/661-8870 or 604/689-8033. Fax 604/689-4426. www.rosedaleonrobson.com. 275 units. May–Sept C$205–C$285 (US$133–US$185) suite. Oct–Apr C$125–C$185 (US$81–US$120) suite. Extra person C$20 (US$13). Rates include morning beverages and baked goods. AE, DC, DISC, MC, V. Parking C$8 (US$5). **Amenities:** Restaurant (New York deli); indoor lap pool; exercise room; Jacuzzi; sauna; steam room; concierge; tour desk; car-rental desk; business center; limited room service; massage; babysitting; laundry service; same-day dry cleaning. *In room:* A/C, TV w/ pay movies, fax, dataport, kitchen, coffeemaker, hair dryer, iron.

INEXPENSIVE

The Howard Johnson Hotel *Finds* Yet another sign of south Granville's rapid gentrification, this formerly down-at-the-heels hotel was bought, gutted, renovated, and reopened in 1998 with an eye to the budget-conscious traveler. The rooms are comfortably if simply furnished. Some have kitchenettes, and suites provide sofa beds.

1176 Granville St., Vancouver, BC V6Z 1L8. © 888/654-6336 or 604/688-8701. Fax 604/688-8335. www.hojovancouver.com. May 1–Oct 15 C$129–C$149 (US$84–US$97) double; C$149–C$169 (US$97–US$110) suite. Oct 16–Apr 30 C$69–C$89 (US$45–US$58) double; C$99–C$119 (US$64–US$77) suite. Children under 17 stay free in parents' room. Rates include continental breakfast. AE, DC, MC, V. Parking C$8 (US$5). **Amenities:** Restaurant (Italian), bar; access to nearby health club; concierge; tour desk; babysitting; laundry service; same-day dry cleaning. *In room:* A/C, TV w/ pay movies, dataport, fridge, coffeemaker, hair dryer, iron, safe.

The YWCA Hotel/Residence ★★ *Value* Built in 1995, this attractive residence is an excellent choice for travelers (including families) on a budget. Rooms are simply furnished; some have TVs. A number of small grocery stores and reasonably priced restaurants are nearby.

733 Beatty St., Vancouver, BC V6B 2M4. © 800/663-1424 or 604/895-5830. Fax 604/681-2550. www.ywca hotel.com. 155 units (53 with private bathroom). C$68–C$88 (US$44–US$57) double with shared bathroom, C$74–C$112 (US$48–US$73) double with private bathroom. Weekly, monthly, group, and off-season discounts available. AE, MC, V. Parking C$5 (US$3.25) per day. **Amenities:** Three kitchens; three TV lounges; access to YWCA Fitness Centre (the best gym in town); coin-op laundry. *In room:* A/C, dataport, fridge, hair dryer.

THE WEST END
EXPENSIVE
Pacific Palisades Hotel ★★★ *Finds* You'll see right away that this is not just another boring hotel. Bold and bright colors, whimsical glass chandeliers, and a sleek metal fireplace give the place a contemporary look. Watch your step for Pal the robotic dog, who likes to sniff out newcomers by the check-in desk. Guest rooms, located in two recently renovated towers, are fabulous, with funky colors and wall-to-wall windows.

1277 Robson St., Vancouver, BC V6E 1C4. © 800/663-1815 or 604/688-0461. Fax 604/688-4374. www. pacificpalisadeshotel.com. 233 units. May 1–Oct 15 C$275 (US$179) double; C$325 (US$211) suite. Oct 16–Apr 30 C$200 (US$130) double; C$250 (US$162) suite. Full kitchen C$10 (US$7) extra. Rates include afternoon wine tasting. AE, DC, DISC, MC, V. Parking C$15 (US$10). **Amenities:** Restaurant (see Zin's under "Where to Dine," below), bar; indoor lap pool; basketball court; excellent health club; spa; Jacuzzi; sauna; bike rentals; concierge; tour desk; business center; 24-hr. room service; massage; babysitting; coin-op laundry and laundry service; same-day dry cleaning. *In room:* A/C, TV, dataport, kitchenette, minibar, fridge, coffeemaker, hair dryer, iron.

Westin Bayshore Resort & Marina ★★★ *Kids* Thanks to a C$50-million (US$33-million) renovation, this venerable 1960s resort hotel looks better than ever. Perched on the water's edge overlooking Stanley Park's eastern entrance, the Bayshore is a short stroll from downtown, and the neighborhood just keeps getting better. Rooms in the original building have been completely refurbished. Units in the newer tower are spacious and bright, all with balconies. Children get their own welcome package upon check-in, and Super Saturday—a behind-the-scenes tour and movie night—gives parents the night off.

1601 Bayshore Dr., Vancouver, BC V6G 2V4. © 800/228-3000 or 604/682-3377. Fax 604/687-3102. www. westinbayshore.com. 510 units. Mid-Apr to Oct C$289 (US$188) double; C$450–C$700 (US$293–US$455) suite. Nov to mid-Apr C$195 (US$127) double; C$370–C$420 (US$241–US$273) suite. Children under 19 stay free in parents' room. AE, DC, MC, V. Self-parking C$10 (US$7); valet parking C$15 (US$10). **Amenities:** Two restaurants, bar; indoor and magnificent outdoor pool with mountain view; health club; Jacuzzi; sauna; watersports rentals; children's programs; concierge; tour desk; car-rental desk; business center; shopping arcade; 24-hr. room service; massage; babysitting; laundry service; same-day dry cleaning. *In room:* A/C, TV w/ pay movies, dataport, minibar, coffeemaker, hair dryer, iron.

MODERATE
Barclay House in the West End ★★ *Finds* This beautiful 1904 house is just a block from the heritage Barclay Square, on a quiet, maple-lined street. The elegant parlors are perfect for lounging on a rainy afternoon, sipping a glass of complimentary sherry before venturing out for dinner in the trendy West End. All rooms are furnished in Victorian style. The modern conveniences, such as CD players and luxury bathrooms, blend in perfectly.

1351 Barclay St., Vancouver, BC V6E 1H6. © 800/971-1351 or 604/605-1351. Fax 604/605-1382. www. barclayhouse.com. 5 units. C$145–C$225 (US$94–US$146) double. MC, V. Free parking. **Amenities:** Access to nearby fitness center; extensive video library. *In room:* TV/VCR w/ pay movies, hair dryer.

Rosellen Suites ★★ (Kids)   Staying at the Rosellen is like having your own apartment in the West End. Stanley Park is within a few blocks, and Denman Street's restaurants and shops are just 3 blocks east. The hotel offers a no-frills stay; the lobby is open only during office hours, and guests receive their own key. The largest apartment is the director's suite, with two bedrooms, a dining room, and a spacious kitchen. The one-bedroom suites sleep four people comfortably.

102–2030 Barclay St., Vancouver, BC V6G 1L5. ☎ 888/317-6648 or 604/689-4807. Fax 604/684-3327. www.rosellensuites.com. 30 units. June–Aug C$159–C$199 (US$103–US$129) 1-bedroom apt (for up to 4); C$199–C$299 (US$129–US$194) 2-bedroom apt (for up to 6); C$399 (US$259) penthouse. Sept–May C$105–C$119 (US$68–US$77) 1-bedroom apt; C$125–C$229 (US$81–US$149) 2-bedroom apt; C$325 (US$211) penthouse. 3-night minimum stay. Free cots and cribs. AE, DC, DISC, MC, V. Limited parking C$5 (US$3.25); reserve when booking room. Pets welcome. **Amenities:** Access to nearby health club; coin-op laundry. In room: TV, dataport, kitchen, coffeemaker, hair dryer, iron.

West End Guest House ★★ (Finds)   This 1906 heritage home is a fine example of what the neighborhood looked like up until the 1950s, before the concrete condos replaced the original Edwardian houses. It's a wonderful respite from the hustle and bustle of the West End. The rooms offer the ultimate in bedtime luxury: feather mattresses, down duvets, and your very own resident stuffed animal. Particularly indulgent is the Grand Queen Suite, with skylights, brass bed, fireplace, and claw-foot tub. Owner Evan Penner pampers his guests with a scrumptious breakfast and afternoon drinks. Throughout the day, guests have access to the porch kitchen, stocked with home-baked munchies.

1362 Haro St., Vancouver, BC V6E 1G2. ☎ 604/681-2889. Fax 604/688-8812. www.westendguesthouse.com. 7 units. C$145–C$240 (US$94–US$156) double. Rates include full breakfast. AE, DISC, MC, V. Free valet parking. **Amenities:** Free bikes; concierge; business center; laundry service. In room: TV/VCR, fax, dataport, hair dryer, iron.

INEXPENSIVE

Hostelling International Vancouver Downtown Hostel   Located in a converted nunnery, this modern hostel makes a convenient base. The beach is a few blocks south; downtown is a 10-minute walk north. Most beds are in quad dorms; two rooms have private bathrooms. Guests share common cooking facilities and a patio. In summer, book well ahead.

1114 Burnaby St. (at Thurlow St.), Vancouver, BC V6E 1P1. ☎ 888/203-4302 or 604/684-4565. Fax 604/684-4540. www.hihostels.bc.ca. 239 beds; some double and triple units. C$20 (US$13) per bed IYHA members, C$24 (US$16) nonmembers; doubles C$55 (US$36) members, C$64 (US$42) nonmembers; triples C$70 (US$46) members, C$86 (US$56) nonmembers. Annual membership C$35 (US$23). MC, V. Limited free parking. **Amenities:** Bike rentals; game room; activities desk; free shuttle to bus/train station and Jericho Beach; coin-op laundry. In room: No phone.

Sylvia Hotel   Built in 1912, the gray-stone, ivy-wreathed Sylvia is on the shores of English Bay, a few blocks from Stanley Park. The lobby sets up high expectations with its stained-glass windows and marble staircase. Alas, the elegance does not carry over to the rooms, which are rather plainly furnished. The best units are on the higher floors. Rooms in the annex have individual heating but offer less atmosphere.

1154 Gilford St., Vancouver, BC V6G 2P6. ☎ 604/681-9321. Fax 604/682-3551. www.sylviahotel.com. 118 units. Apr–Sept C$75–C$135 (US$49–US$88) double. Oct–Mar C$75–C$100 (US$49–US$65) double. Children under 18 stay free in parents' room. AE, DC, MC, V. Parking C$7 (US$4.55). **Amenities:** Restaurant, bar; concierge; limited room service; dry cleaning. In room: TV, dataport, hair dryer.

THE WEST SIDE
EXPENSIVE
Granville Island Hotel ✿ *Finds*   The Granville Island Hotel offers a unique waterfront setting in the heart of some of the city's most interesting galleries and theaters, and just a short stroll from the cornucopia that is the Granville Island food market. The rooms are spacious, with large windows, soaker tubs, and marble or slate floors; third-floor units have vaulted ceilings and balconies.

1253 Johnston St., Vancouver, BC V6H 3R9. ✆ **800/663-1840** or 604/683-7373. Fax 604/683-3061. www. granvilleislandhotel.com. 85 units. C$229 (US$149) double. Off-season discounts available. AE, DC, DISC, MC, V. Parking C$6 (US$3.90). Pets welcome. **Amenities:** Restaurant, brewpub; access to nearby health club and tennis courts; small exercise room; Jacuzzi; bike rentals; concierge; tour desk; car-rental desk; business center; limited room service; massage; babysitting; laundry; same-day dry cleaning. *In room:* A/C, TV w/ pay movies, fax, dataport, minibar, coffeemaker, microwave (on request), hair dryer, iron.

MODERATE
Kenya Court Ocean Front Guest House ✿ *Finds*   Each tastefully furnished suite in this architectural landmark at Kitsilano Beach has an unobstructed view of English Bay, downtown, and the Coast Mountains. It's an ideal launching pad for strolls around Granville Island, Vanier Park, and other Kitsilano sights; jogging trails are nearby.

2230 Cornwall Ave., Vancouver, BC V6K 1B5. ✆ **604/738-7085.** H&dwilliams@telus.net. 4 units. C$135–C$165 (US$88–US$107) double. Extra person C$50 (US$33). Rates include full breakfast. No credit cards. Garage or street parking. **Amenities:** Nearby outdoor pool and tennis courts. *In room:* TV, kitchen, fridge, coffeemaker, hair dryer, iron.

INEXPENSIVE
Penny Farthing Inn   This 1912 house is filled with antiques and stained glass; in the backyard is an English country–style garden. All rooms are decorated with lovely pine furniture. Bettina's Room features a fireplace and a small balcony. Sophie's Room, though smaller, has a porch with two wicker chairs. Lucinda's Room—with a private bathroom across the hall—offers the best value. Coffee, tea, and hot chocolate are always on hand; fix a cuppa and watch the resident cats at play while you relax.

2855 W. Sixth Ave., Vancouver, BC V6K 1X2. ✆ **866/739-9002** or 604/739-9002. Fax 604/739-9004. www. pennyfarthinginn.com. 4 units. May–Oct C$115 (US$75) double; C$170 (US$111) suite. Nov–Apr C$95 (US$62) double; C$145 (US$94) suite. Rates include full breakfast. No credit cards. Street parking. **Amenities:** Free bikes; business center. *In room:* TV/VCR, CD player, fax, dataport, fridge, coffeemaker, hair dryer.

THE NORTH SHORE (NORTH VANCOUVER & WEST VANCOUVER)
MODERATE
Beachside Bed & Breakfast ✿✿ *Finds*   The Beachside sits on its own private little beach on the shores of English Bay, with a sweeping view of Stanley Park and the downtown skyline. The common area features wall-to-ceiling windows and binoculars for gazing at the seals and bald eagles. Two beachfront units face the ocean; one has a jetted tub for two, the other has a private Jacuzzi.

4208 Evergreen Ave., West Vancouver, BC V7V 1H1. ✆ **800/563-3311** or 604/922-7773. www.beach.bc.ca. 3 units. C$150–C$250 (US$98–US$163) double. Extra person C$30 (US$20). Rates include full breakfast. MC, V. Free parking. **Amenities:** Jacuzzi. *In room:* TV/VCR, fridge, coffeemaker, hair dryer, iron.

Lonsdale Quay Hotel ✿   Directly across the Burrard Inlet from the Canada Place Pier, this hotel is at the water's edge above the Lonsdale Quay Market at the SeaBus terminal. An escalator rises from the midst of the food and crafts stalls to the front desk on the third floor. The rooms are simply but tastefully decorated, without the grandeur or luxurious touches of comparably priced downtown hotels. Nevertheless, the hotel has unique harbor and city views, and provides easy access to the BC Rail and ferry terminals.

123 Carrie Cates Court, North Vancouver, BC V6M 3K7. © **800/836-6111** or 604/986-6111. Fax 604/986-8782. www.lonsdalequayhotel.com. 83 units. High season C$125–C$225 (US$81–US$146) double, C$350 (US$228) suite. Low season C$90–C$165 (US$59–US$107) double, C$250 (US$163) suite. Extra person C$25 (US$16). Senior discounts available. AE, DC, DISC, MC, V. Parking C$7 (US$4.55); free Sat–Sun and holidays. **Amenities:** Two restaurants; small exercise room; spa; bike rentals; children's play area; concierge; tour desk; shopping arcade; limited room service; massage; babysitting; laundry service; same-day dry cleaning. *In room:* A/C, TV, fax, dataport, minibar, coffeemaker, hair dryer, iron.

4 Where to Dine

Vancouverites seem to dine out more often than residents of any other Canadian city. Outstanding meals are available in many different cuisines, from Caribbean to Mongolian. And although Vancouverites have come to expect top quality, they still refuse to pay the kind of top dollar forked over by diners in New York or San Francisco. For discerning foodies from elsewhere, Vancouver is a steal.

Note: See the "Downtown Vancouver" map (p. 48) to locate most of the restaurants in this section.

DOWNTOWN & YALETOWN
VERY EXPENSIVE

C ✶✶✶ SEAFOOD/WEST COAST   C brings back the conspicuous consumption of the 1980s in a room done up in brilliant shades of Miami white and a little postindustrial decor (bread baskets made from heavy-gauge rubber, footrests upholstered with truck-tire retreads). Beyond the decor, however, C recreates the '80s through the sheer indulgent quality with which it serves fish. The taster box includes gravlax cured in Saskatoon berry tea, artichoke carpaccio, abalone tempura, and grilled garlic squid. For the ultimate experience, order the seven-course sampling menu.

1600 Howe St. © **604/681-1164.** www.crestaurant.com. Reservations recommended. Main courses C$21–C$32 (US$14–US$21). AE, DC, MC, V. Mon–Fri 11:30am–2:30pm; Sun 11am–2:30pm; daily 5:30–11pm. Valet parking C$7 (US$4.55). Bus: 1 or 2.

The Five Sails ✶✶ WEST COAST/FRENCH   The view of Coal Harbour and the Coast Mountains is as spectacular as the food here. Look for appetizers that combine pasta with seafood, like the Dungeness crab ravioli served with a basil flan and tomato emulsion. The Marseille bouillabaisse, thick with seafood, is worth a try, as is the grilled halibut with sautéed morels and shallot confit, finished with a rich veal jus.

In the Pan Pacific Hotel, 999 Canada Place Way. © **604/891-2892.** Reservations recommended. Main courses C$25–C$38 (US$16–US$25); tasting menus C$55–C$65 (US$36–US$42). AE, DC, MC, V. Daily 6–10pm. SkyTrain: Waterfront.

Gotham Steakhouse and Cocktail Bar ✶✶ STEAKHOUSE   A 40-foot (12m) timber ceiling is divided down the middle, with a cocktail bar on one side, a dining room on the other, and a patio with fireplace balancing things out. Furnishings are aggressively masculine. The wine list is encyclopedic. And then there's the food: The deep-fried calamari appetizer is a light and tasty revelation. Jumbo shrimp are sumo-sized. And the steaks—a porterhouse cut the size of a catcher's mitt, a filet mignon as tall as half a bread loaf—just melt away on your tongue. Forget the veggie side dishes entirely and spend the money on another glass of merlot.

615 Seymour St. ⓒ **604/605-8282.** Fax 604/605-8285. www.gothamsteakhouse.com. Reservations recommended. Main courses C$27–C$49 (US$18–US$32). AE, DC, MC, V. Mon–Fri 11:30am–2:30pm; daily 5–11pm (cocktail bar somewhat later). Bus: 4 or 7.

EXPENSIVE

Blue Water Café and Raw Bar ★★★ SEAFOOD   If you had to describe this place in one word, it would be *fresh:* fresh seafood and a fresh concept. The raw bar serves up sushi, oysters, and sashimi. Main courses include seared yellowfin tuna in a citrus-pepper crust. In season, order the diver-caught sea scallops, plainly grilled and served with sautéed zucchini, pancetta, and arugula in a maple chive dressing. Since it opened in 2000, the Blue Water has become one of Vancouver's hottest restaurants. Reservations are recommended, but it's just as much fun to wait at the bar, watching sushi-maestro Max Katsuno at work while you chill your cocktail on the world's only (so far) fully refrigerated bar top.

1095 Hamilton St., Yaletown. ⓒ **604/688-8078.** www.bluewatercafe.net. Reservations recommended. Main courses C$17–C$30 (US$11–US$20). AE, DC, MC, V. Daily 11am–1am (light menu 3–5pm and 11pm–1am). Bus: 2.

La Terrazza ★★ ITALIAN   Located on the edge of Yaletown, La Terrazza's sleek exterior contrasts sharply with the warm, bustling dining room inside. A tasting menu with matching wines highlights a different culinary region of Italy each month. Main courses include various pasta dishes, along with the outstanding duck breast with frangelico brandy. Save room for the white cheesecake baked in phyllo, topped with sour cherries and fruit coulis.

1088 Cambie St. ⓒ **604/899-4449.** www.laterrazza.ca. Reservations recommended. Main courses C$16–C$30 (US$10–US$20). AE, DC, MC, V. Mon–Thurs 5–11pm; Fri–Sat 5pm–midnight; Sun 5–10pm. Bus: 2.

MODERATE

La Bodega ★★ *Value* TAPAS   This warm, dark Spanish bar has a dozen or so tables and some great little romantic corners. Expect authentic tapas—marinated mushrooms, ceviche, pan-fried squid, and good black olives. Specials include *conejo* (rabbit with tomatoes and peppers), quail, and local scallops. La Bodega has a good selection of Portuguese and Spanish wines and the best sangria in town.

1277 Howe St. ⓒ **604/684-8815.** Reservations recommended. Tapas C$3.95–C$7.95 (US$2.55–US$5); main courses C$11–C$18 (US$7–US$12). AE, DC, MC, V. Mon–Fri 4:30pm–midnight; Sat 5pm–midnight; Sun 5–11pm. Bus: 4 or 7.

INEXPENSIVE

Olympia Oyster & Fish Co. Ltd. *Finds* FISH-AND-CHIPS   This hole in the wall, just off Vancouver's trendiest shopping street, serves up the city's best fish-and-chips. The fish is always fresh and flaky, and can be grilled if you prefer. Choose sole, halibut, or cod, which can be combined with oysters or prawns. Smoked salmon can be wrapped up or shipped home.

820 Thurlow St. ⓒ **604/685-0716.** Main courses C$6–C$10 (US$3.90–US$7). AE, MC, V. Mon–Fri 10am–8pm; Sat 10am–7pm; Sun 11am–7pm. Bus: 5.

THE WEST END
EXPENSIVE

Delilah's ★★ CONTINENTAL   This bordello of a dining room features velvet chaise lounges and cherubim cavorting on the ceiling. First order of business is a martini—Delilah's forte, and the fuel firing the laughter and conversation all around. The menu is heavy on seafood, which Delilah's does simply but well. Try seared jumbo scallops with saffron risotto or grilled swordfish with a sun-dried cherry/cranberry compote.

1789 Comox St. © 604/687-3424. Reservations accepted for parties of 6 or more. Fixed-price menu C$23–C$32.50 (US$15–US$21). AE, DC, MC, V. Daily 5:30pm–midnight. Bus: 5 to Denman St.

Raincity Grill WEST COAST Raincity has a prime location by English Bay Beach, a spacious patio, and a long, low dining room that hugs the shoreline. But they do pack 'em in here, making dinner more of a social occasion than you may have wished. Ah, but the view. And the food: an appetizer of barbecued quail with a sage and goat-cheese polenta, a salad of smoked steelhead, and entrees like grilled Fraser Valley free-range chicken. The award-winning wine list sticks pretty close to home.

1193 Denman St. © 604/685-7337. www.raincitygrill.com. Reservations recommended. Main courses C$18–C$34 (US$12–US$22). AE, DC, MC, V. Mon–Fri 11:30am–2:30pm; Sat–Sun 10:30am–2:30pm; daily 5–10:30pm. Bus: 1 or 5.

MODERATE

Zin's GLOBAL Zin's takes you on a food trip around the globe, dish by dish. Unlike fusion, where flavors from all over the world are mushed together on one plate, these dishes arrive chastely one after the other. Start with grilled *naan* and mint tomato chutney, followed by a goat-cheese fondue or Malaysian *laksa* seafood stew in coconut broth. The wine list has close to 50 choices by the glass.

1277 Robson St. © 604/408-1700. www.zin-restaurant.com. Main courses C$11–C$17 (US$7–US$11). AE, DC, MC, V. Mon–Wed 7am–midnight; Thu–Sat 7am–1am; Sun 8am–11pm.

INEXPENSIVE

Gyoza King, 1508 Robson St. (© 604/669-8278), features an entire menu of these succulent dumplings, as well as noodles and staples like *katsu-don* (pork cutlet over rice).

Stephos *Value* GREEK The cuisine here is simple Greek fare at its finest and cheapest. Customers wait 10 to 15 minutes for a seat amid travel posters, potted ivy, and whitewashed walls. Order spicy eggplant dip while you peruse the menu. The lamb, fried calamari, and souvlakis are served with rice, roast potatoes, and Greek salad. The beef, lamb, or chicken pita come with fries and tzatziki.

1124 Davie St. © 604/683-2555. Reservations accepted for parties of 5 or more. Main courses C$4.25–C$10 (US$2.75–US$7). AE, MC, V. Daily 11:30am–11:30pm. Bus: 5.

GASTOWN & CHINATOWN
EXPENSIVE

The Cannery SEAFOOD At least some of the pleasure of a meal here comes from simply finding the place. Hop over the railway tracks and thread your way past container terminals and packing plants until you're sure you're lost, and then you'll see it—a great ex-warehouse of a building, with old nets and seafaring memorabilia, plus one of the best views in Vancouver. Good, traditional seafood is often alder-grilled, with ever-changing specials to complement the salmon and halibut basics. The wine list is stellar.

2205 Commissioner St., near Victoria Dr. © 604/254-9606. www.canneryseafood.com. Reservations recommended. Main courses C$17–C$27 (US$11–US$18). AE, DC, DISC, MC, V. Mon–Fri 11:30am–2:30pm; Mon–Sat 5:30–10:30pm; Sun 5:30–9:30pm. Closed Dec 24–26. Bus: 7 to Victoria Dr. From downtown, head east on Hastings St., turn left on Victoria Dr. (2 blocks past Commercial Dr.), then right on Commissioner St.

MODERATE

Incendio ✦, 103 Columbia St. (© **604/688-8694**), is a sublime Gastown hideaway with wood-fired pizzas and homemade pastas. The wine list is decent, the beer list inspired.

Park Lock Seafood Restaurant *Kids* CHINESE/DIM SUM   If you've never done dim sum, try this traditional dining room in the heart of Chinatown. From 8am to 3pm daily, waitresses wheel around carts loaded with delicacies. When you see something you like, grab it. Choices include *hargow* and *shumai* (steamed shrimp and pork dumplings), prawns wrapped in fresh white noodles, sticky rice cooked in banana leaves, and lots more.

544 Main St. (at E. Pender St.), 2nd Floor. © **604/688-1581.** Reservations recommended. Main courses C$10–C$35 (US$7–US$23); dim sum C$2.50–C$3.25 (US$1.60–US$2.10). AE, MC, V. Daily 8am–3pm; Tues–Sun 5–10pm. Bus: 19 or 22.

THE WEST SIDE
VERY EXPENSIVE

If you don't mind splurging, head to **Tojo's Restaurant** ✦✦, 202–777 W. Broadway (© **604/872-8050**), where the exquisite flavors of the sushi will explode in your mouth.

Lumière ✦✦✦ FRENCH   The success of this dining experiment in the heart of Kitsilano has turned chef Rob Feenie into a hot commodity. Preparation and presentation are immaculately French, and ingredients are resolutely local, which makes for interesting surprises—fresh local ginger with the veal, raspberries in the foie gras. Lumière's tasting menus change with the season: Simply choose one of four options (including a vegetarian menu) and sit back for a culinary journey you won't soon forget.

2551 W. Broadway. © **604/739-8185.** Reservations recommended. Tasting menus C$60–C$100 (US$39–US$65). AE, DC, MC, V. Tues–Sun 5:30–9:30pm. Bus: 9 or 10.

INEXPENSIVE

The Naam Restaurant ✦ *Kids* VEGETARIAN   Back in the 1960s, when Kitsilano was Canada's hippie haven, the Naam was tie-dye central. Things have changed a tad since then, but Vancouver's oldest vegetarian restaurant retains a pleasant granola feel. The decor is simple and welcoming: well-worn wooden tables, local art, a fabulous garden patio. The healthy fare ranges from vegetarian burgers to tofu teriyaki; the sesame spice fries are a Vancouver institution.

2724 W. Fourth Ave. © **604/738-7151.** www.thenaam.com. Reservations not needed. Main courses C$4.95–C$10 (US$3.20–US$7). AE, MC, V. Daily 24 hr. Live music nightly 7–10pm. Bus: 4 or 22.

Sami's ✦✦ *Finds* INDIAN   Always in the running for best Indian in Vancouver, Sami's is still going strong. The food is worth the journey to this strip mall; among the inventive dishes are Mumbai-blackened New York steak atop spiked mashers with blueberry coriander jus. Service is efficient and knowledgeable.

986 W. Broadway. © **604/736-8330.** Reservations not accepted. Main courses C$12 (US$8). DC, MC, V. Mon–Sat 11:30am–2:30pm; daily 5–11pm. Bus: 9.

THE NORTH SHORE
EXPENSIVE

The Beach House at Dundarave Pier ✦✦ WEST COAST   With a dramatic waterfront location, heated patio, and rich interiors, this restored 1912 teahouse serves consistently good, innovative (but not *too* experimental) food. Start with grilled portobello with Okanagan Valley goat cheese, moving on to garlic-crusted rack of lamb with honey balsamic glaze.

150 25th St., West Vancouver. ℭ **604/922-1414.** www.beachhousewestvan.com. Reservations recommended. Main courses C$12–C$16 (US$8–US$10) lunch, C$17–C$29 (US$11–US$19) dinner. AE, DC, MC, V. Mon–Sat 11am–3pm; Sun brunch 10:30am–3pm; Sun–Thurs 5–10pm; Fri–Sat 5–11pm. Light menu 3–5pm. Bus: 255 to Ambleside Pier.

The Salmon House on the Hill ✈ WEST COAST/SEAFOOD   High above West Vancouver, the Salmon House offers spectacular views. Chef Dan Atkinson's menu reflects his extensive research into local ingredients and First Nations cuisine. An alderwood-fired grill dominates the kitchen, lending a delicious flavor to many of the dishes. Try alder-grilled salmon with a Pernod bread stuffing, or perhaps sesame-crusted tuna in a mustard and wasabi sauce. The wine list has earned an award of excellence from *Wine Spectator.*

2229 Folkstone Way, West Vancouver. ℭ **604/926-3212.** www.salmonhouse.com. Reservations recommended for dinner. Main courses C$11–C$15 (US$7–US$10) lunch, C$17–C$30 (US$11–US$20) dinner. AE, DC, MC, V. Mon–Sat 11:30am–2:30pm; Sun brunch 11am–2:30pm; Sun–Thurs 5–10pm; Fri–Sat 5–10:30pm. Bus: 251 to Queens St.

5 Exploring Vancouver

Note: See the "Downtown Vancouver" map (p. 48) to locate most of the sights covered in this section.

THE TOP ATTRACTIONS
DOWNTOWN & THE WEST END

Canadian Craft Museum ✈   Hidden behind the Cathedral Place building at the edge of a beautiful courtyard, this museum presents a small but impressive collection of Canadian and international crafts in glass, wood, metal, clay, and fiber. It will appeal to modern-art lovers and anyone who devours interior-design and architectural magazines.

639 Hornby St. ℭ **604/687-8266.** Craftmus@direct.ca. Admission C$5 (US$3.25) adults; C$3 (US$1.95) seniors and students; free for children under 12. By donation Thurs 5–9pm. Mon–Wed and Fri–Sat 10am–5pm; Thurs 10am–9pm; Sun noon–5pm. Closed Tues Sept–May. SkyTrain: Granville. Bus: 3

Vancouver Aquarium Marine Science Centre ✈✈✈ *Kids*   One of North America's largest and best, the Vancouver Aquarium houses more than 8,000 marine species. In the icy-blue Arctic Canada exhibit, you can see beluga whales whistling and blowing water at unwary onlookers. Human-sized freshwater fish inhabit the Amazon Rain Forest gallery; overhead, an hourly rainstorm is unleashed in an atrium that houses three-toed sloths and piranhas. On the Marine Mammal Deck, there are sea otters, sea lions, and a Pacific white-sided dolphin. During regularly scheduled shows, the staff explain marine mammal behavior while working with these impressive creatures.

Stanley Park. ℭ **604/659-FISH.** www.vanaqua.org. Admission C$14.50 (US$9) adults; C$12 (US$8) seniors, students, and youths 13–18; C$9 (US$6) children 4–12. Late June to Labour Day daily 9:30am–7pm; Labour Day to late June daily 10am–5:30pm. Bus: 135; "Around the Park" shuttle bus June–Sept only. Parking C$5 (US$3.25) summer, C$3 (US$1.95) winter.

Vancouver Art Gallery ✈✈   The VAG shows visitors what sets Canadian and West Coast art apart from the rest of the world. There is an impressive collection of paintings by British Columbia native Emily Carr, as well as contemporary rotating exhibits of sculpture, graphics, photography, and video art.

750 Hornby St. ℭ **604/662-4719** or 604/662-4700. www.vanartgallery.bc.ca. Admission C$10 (US$7) adults, C$6 (US$3.90) students and youths, C$30 (US$20) families, free for children 12 and under. By donation Thurs 5–9pm. Mon–Wed and Fri–Sun 10am–5:30pm; Thurs 10am–9pm. Closed Mon–Tues in fall and winter. SkyTrain: Granville. Bus: 3.

GASTOWN & CHINATOWN

Dr. Sun Yat-sen Classical Chinese Garden ⭐   This garden is truly a remarkable place, but to get the full effect, take the free tour. The engaging guides can explain how the garden is based on the yin-yang principle, or the idea of harmony through dynamic opposition: Soft moving water flows across solid stone, and smooth, swaying bamboo grows around gnarled, immovable rocks. When our guide ended her tour, the entire audience burst into applause.

578 Carrall St. ℂ 604/689-7133. www.vancouverchinesegarden.com. Admission C$7.50 (US$4.90) adults, C$6 (US$3.90) seniors, C$5 (US$3.25) students and children. Daily May 1–June 14 10am–6pm; June 15–Aug 31 9:30am–7pm; Sept 1–Sept 30 10am–6pm; Oct 1–April 30 10am–4:30pm. Bus: 19 or 22.

THE WEST SIDE

Museum of Anthropology ⭐⭐⭐   In 1976, architect Arthur Erickson re-created a Native post-and-beam structure out of modern concrete and glass to house one of the world's finest collections of Native art. Haida artist Bill Reid's masterpiece, *The Raven and the First Men,* is worth the price of admission alone. The huge cedar carving depicts a Haida creation myth, in which Raven—the trickster—coaxes humanity out into the world from its birthplace in a clamshell. Some of Reid's fabulous creations in gold and silver are also on display. The grounds contain 10 hand-carved totem poles.

6393 NW Marine Dr. ℂ 604/822-3825. www.moa.ubc.ca. Admission C$7 (US$4.55) adults, C$5 (US$3.25) seniors, C$4 (US$2.60) students and children 6–18, C$20 (US$13) families. Free Tues after 5pm. Late May to early Sept Wed–Mon 10am–5pm, Tues 10am–9pm; early Sept to late May Wed–Sun 11am–5pm, Tues 11am–9pm. Closed Dec 25–26. Bus: 4, 10, or 99.

Science World British Columbia ⭐ *Kids*   Science World is impossible to miss. It's in the big, blinking geodesic dome on the eastern end of False Creek. At this hands-on scientific discovery center, you can walk through the interior of a camera, create a cyclone, watch a zucchini explode as it's charged with 80,000 volts, and create music with a giant synthesizer. In the OMNIMAX Theatre, take a death-defying flight through the Grand Canyon and perform other spine-tingling feats.

1455 Quebec St. ℂ 604/443-7443. www.scienceworld.bc.ca. Admission C$19.75 (US$13) adults; C$12.25 (US$8) seniors, students, and children. Mon–Fri 10am–5pm; Sat–Sun 10am–6pm. SkyTrain: Main St.–Science World.

Vancouver Museum   Established in 1894, the Vancouver Museum is dedicated to the city's history. Visitors can walk through the steerage deck of a 19th-century passenger ship, peek into a Hudson's Bay Company trading post, or take a seat in an 1880s Canadian-Pacific Railway passenger car. Re-creations of Victorian and Edwardian rooms show how early Vancouverites lived.

1100 Chestnut St., in Vanier Park. ℂ 604/736-4431. www.vanmuseum.bc.ca. Admission C$8 (US$5) adults, C$6 (US$3.90) youths. Group rates available. Fri–Wed 10am–5pm; Thurs 10am–9pm. Closed Mon Sept–June. Bus: 22, then walk 3 blocks south on Cornwall Ave. Boat: Granville Island Ferry to Heritage Harbour.

THE NORTH SHORE

Grouse Mountain Resort ⭐⭐   Once a small, local ski hill, Grouse has been developing into a year-round recreation park. Only a 20-minute drive from downtown, the SkyRide gondola transports you to the 3,700-foot (1,110m) summit, where there's a bar, restaurant, theater, ski and snowboard area, hiking and snowshoeing trails, skating pond, logger sports show, helicopter tours, mountain-bike trails, and Native feast house. Some of these are included in the cost of your SkyRide ticket—most aren't—but the view is free and one of the best around.

6400 Nancy Greene Way, North Vancouver. (✆ **604/984-0661**. www.grousemountain.com. SkyRide C$18.95 (US$12) adults, C$16.95 (US$11) seniors, C$13.95 (US$9) youths, C$7 (US$4.55) children 6–12. Free SkyRide with advance Observatory Restaurant reservations. Daily 9am–10pm. SeaBus: Lonsdale Quay, then transfer to bus 236.

PLAZAS, PARKS & GARDENS

Unlike many a city, Vancouver's great urban gathering places stand not at the center but on the periphery; the two **seawalls,** one at one end of Denman street by **English Bay,** the other at the other end of Denman by **Coal Harbour,** are where Vancouverites go to stroll and be seen.

Stanley Park is a 1,000-acre (405-hectare) rain forest near the busy West End, filled with towering cedar, placid lagoons, trails, lawns, and gardens. It houses the Vancouver Aquarium, a petting zoo, restaurants, cricket greens, a pool, a miniature railway, and a water park. It also boasts abundant wildlife and amazing marine views.

The **Dr. Sun Yat-sen Classical Chinese Garden** is a tranquil oasis in the heart of Chinatown (see "The Top Attractions," above). On the West Side, **Queen Elizabeth Park,** at Cambie Street and West 33rd Avenue, sits atop a 500-foot-high (152m) extinct volcano and is the highest urban vantage point south of downtown, offering panoramic views in all directions. Nearby is the **VanDusen Botanical Garden,** 5251 Oak St., at 37th Avenue (✆ **604/878-9274**), with rolling lawns, lakes, Elizabethan hedge mazes, and sculptures.

Pacific Spirit Park (usually called the Endowment Lands) comprises 1,885 acres (760 hectares) of temperate rain forest, marshes, and beaches; it includes nearly 22 miles (35km) of trails for hiking, riding, and mountain biking. Across the Lions Gate Bridge is **Capilano River Regional Park,** 4500 Capilano Rd. (✆ **604/666-1790**), which surrounds the Capilano Suspension Bridge. Hikers can follow the river for 4½ miles (7km) to the Burrard Inlet and the Lions Gate Bridge.

For general information on Vancouver's parks, call ✆ **604/257-8400.**

6 Outdoor Pursuits

BEACHES   English Bay Beach lies at the end of Davie Street off Denman Street and Beach Avenue. South of English Bay Beach near the Burrard Street Bridge is **Sunset Beach.** On Stanley Park's western rim, **Second Beach** is a quick stroll north from English Bay Beach. A playground, snack bar, and immense heated freshwater pool make it popular with families. Farther along the seawall lies secluded **Third Beach,** due north of Stanley Park Drive.

At **Kitsilano Beach,** along Ogden Street, a heated saltwater pool is open in summer. Farther west along Point Grey Road is **Jericho Beach,** followed by **Locarno Beach** and **Spanish Banks.** Below UBC's Museum of Anthropology, **Wreck Beach** is Vancouver's immensely popular nude beach.

**BIKING   ** Marked bicycle lanes traverse Vancouver, including the cross-town Off-Broadway route, the Adanac route, and the Ontario route. One of the city's most scenic cycle paths has been extended and now runs all the way from Canada Place Pier to Pacific Spirit Park.

Mountain bikers love the cross-country ski trails on **Hollyburn Mountain** in Cypress Provincial Park. Mount Seymour's steep **Good Samaritan Trail** connects to the Baden-Powell Trail and the Bridle Path near Mount Seymour Road. Closer to downtown, both **Pacific Spirit Park** and **Burnaby Mountain** offer excellent beginner and intermediate off-road trails.

Rentals run C$4 to C$10 (US$2.60 to US$7) per hour or C$15 to C$40 (US$10 to US$26) per day. **Spokes Bicycle Rentals & Espresso Bar,** 1798 W. Georgia St. (© **604/688-5141**), rents bikes, helmets, and child trailers. **Bayshore Bicycle and Rollerblade Rentals,** 745 Denman St. (© **604/688-2453**), and 1601 W. Georgia St. (© **604/689-5071**), rents 21-speed mountain bikes, tandems, and kids' bikes.

BOATING You can rent powerboats for a few hours or several weeks at **Stanley Park Boat Rentals, Ltd.,** Coal Harbor Marina (© **604/682-6257**). **Granville Island Boat Rentals, Ltd.,** 1696 Duranleau St., Granville Island (© **604/682-6287**), rents speedboats and offers sportfishing, cruising, and sightseeing charters. Rates begin at C$30 (US$20) per hour or C$135 (US$88) per day.

CANOEING & KAYAKING Both placid, urban False Creek and the incredibly beautiful 19-mile (30km) North Vancouver fjord known as Indian Arm have launching points you can reach by car or bus. Rentals range from C$25 to C$32 (US$16 to US$21) per day. Tours are C$70 to C$110 (US$46 to US$72) per person. **Adventure Fitness,** 1510 Duranleau St., Granville Island (© **604/687-1528**), offers lessons and rentals. In North Vancouver, **Deep Cove Canoe and Kayak Rentals,** Deep Cove (© **604/929-2268**), is an easy starting point for those planning an Indian Arm run. It offers rentals, lessons, and tours. **Lotus Land Tours,** 2005-1251 Cardero St. (© **800/528-3531** or 604/684-4922), runs 1-day kayak tours on Indian Arm for C$130 (US$85), which includes a barbecue salmon lunch.

DIVING British Columbia's underwater scenery is stunning, but the water is chilly. Cates Park in Deep Cove, Whytecliff Park and Porteau Cove near Horseshoe Bay, and Lighthouse Park are nearby dive spots. The **Diving Locker,** 2745 W. Fourth Ave. (© **604/736-2681**), offers rentals (C$50/US$33 per day) and courses. Hiring a dive master to accompany you costs about C$60 (US$39) per dive; a seat on a weekend dive boat runs C$69 (US$45) per dive.

ECOTOURS **Rockwood Adventures,** 1330 Fulton Ave. (© **604/926-7705**), offers guided hikes of the North Shore rain forest, complete with a trained naturalist and a gourmet lunch. Tours cover Capilano Canyon, Bowen Island, or Lighthouse Park and cost C$75 (US$49).

FISHING To fish, you need a nonresident saltwater or freshwater license. **Hanson's Fishing Outfitters,** 102-580 Hornby St. (© **604/684-8988** or 684-8998), and **Granville Island Boat Rentals,** 1696 Duranleau St. (© **604/682-6287**), are outstanding outfitters as well as sources for tackle and licenses. The *Vancouver Sun* prints a daily fishing report that details which fish are in season and where they can be found.

GOLF The **University Golf Club,** 5185 University Blvd. (© **604/224-1818**), is a great 6,560-yard, par-71 course with a clubhouse, pro shop, bar and grill, and sports lounge. Or call **A-1 Last Minute Golf Hotline** (© **800/684-6344** or 604/878-1833) for discounts and short-notice tee times at more than 30 area courses.

HIKING Trail maps are available from the **Greater Vancouver Regional Parks District** (© **604/432-6350**) and from **International Travel Maps and Books,** 552 Seymour St. (© **604/687-3320**). For a challenge without the time commitment, hike the aptly named **Grouse Grind** from the bottom of Grouse Mountain to the top, then buy a one-way ticket down on the SkyRide gondola

(C\$5/US\$3.25). Lynn Canyon Park, Lynn Headwaters Regional Park, Capilano River Regional Park, Mount Seymour Provincial Park, Pacific Spirit Park, and Cypress Provincial Park have good easy-to-challenging trails that wind through stands of Douglas fir and cedar. Pay attention to the trail warnings posted at the parks; some have bear habitats.

IN-LINE SKATING   Locals skate along beach paths, park paths, and promenades. **Bayshore Bicycle and Rollerblade Rentals,** 745 Denman St. (✆ 604/688-2453), charges rental rates of C\$5 (US\$3.25) per hour, with a 2-hour minimum.

JOGGING   You'll find fellow runners traversing Stanley Park's **Seawall Promenade,** where the scenery is spectacular and cars aren't allowed.

SAILING   **Cooper Boating Center,** 1620 Duranleau St. (✆ 604/687-4110), offers cruises, rentals, and instruction. Prices vary widely, from C\$150 (US\$98) for a 3-hour lesson to C\$4,000 (US\$2,600) for a 1-week charter.

SKIING & SNOWBOARDING   It seldom snows in the city's downtown and central areas, but Vancouverites can ski before work and after dinner at the three ski resorts in the North Shore mountains.

   Grouse Mountain Resort, 6400 Nancy Greene Way, North Vancouver (✆ 604/984-0661, or 604/986-6262 for snow report), has four chairs, two beginner tows, two T-bars, and 22 alpine runs, plus a half pipe for snowboarders. Lift tickets cost C\$29 (US\$19) for adults, C\$22 (US\$14) for youths 13 to 18, and C\$16 (US\$10) for children.

   Mount Seymour Provincial Park, 1700 Mt. Seymour Rd., North Vancouver (✆ 604/986-2261, or 604/986-3999 for snow report), has the area's highest base elevation, four chairs, and a tow. Lift tickets are C\$18 (US\$12). A shuttle to Mount Seymour departs several times daily from Rogers Avenue in Lonsdale Quay (accessible via SeaBus). The trip takes about 50 minutes. Round-trip fares are C\$7 (US\$4.55) for adults and C\$5 (US\$3.25) for children.

   Cypress Bowl, 1610 Mt. Seymour Rd. (✆ 604/926-5612, or 604/419-7669 for snow report), has the area's biggest vertical drop at 1,750 feet (533m), challenging ski and snowboard runs, and 10 miles (16km) of track-set cross-country trails. Lift tickets are C\$35 (US\$23) for adults, C\$29 (US\$19) for youths 13 to 18, C\$17 (US\$11) for children 5 to 12, and C\$2 (US\$1.30) for children under 5. A shuttle to Cypress departs several times daily from Lonsdale Quay (accessible via SeaBus). A round-trip costs C\$7 (US\$4.55) for adults and C\$5 (US\$3.25) for children.

SWIMMING   The midsummer saltwater temperature rarely exceeds 65°F (18°C). Some swimmers opt for fresh- and saltwater pools at city beaches (see "Beaches," above). Others take to indoor pools, including the **Vancouver Aquatic Centre,** 1050 Beach Ave. (✆ 604/665-3424), and the **YWCA Fitness Centre,** 535 Hornby St. (✆ 604/895-5777).

WILDLIFE-WATCHING   In winter, thousands of **bald eagles** line the banks of Indian Arm fjord and the Squamish, Cheakamus, and Mamquam rivers to feed on spawning salmon. The summer **salmon runs** attract tourists to coastal streams and rivers to watch the waters turn red with leaping coho and sockeye. The salmon are plentiful at Goldstream Provincial Park (see chapter 5, "Southern Vancouver Island & the Gulf Islands"). Along the Fraser River delta, more than 250 **bird species** migrate to or perennially inhabit the George C. Reifel Sanctuary's wetland reserve. Stanley Park and Pacific Spirit Park are both home to a heron rookery. You can see these large birds nesting just outside the Vancouver Aquarium. Ravens, waterfowl, raccoons, skunks, beavers, and even coyotes are also full-time residents.

WINDSURFING   Windsurfing isn't allowed at the mouth of False Creek near Granville Island, but you can bring a board to Jericho and English Bay beaches. Rentals (from C$17/US$11 per hr.) and instruction can be found at **Windsure Windsurfing School,** 1300 Discovery St., at Jericho Beach (© **604/224-0615**).

7 Shopping

Robson Street is the spot for high-end fashions. Vancouver's old money heads to the 10-block stretch of **Granville Street** from 6th to 16th avenues for classic fashions, housewares, and furniture. **Water Street** in Gastown features antiques, First Nations art, and funky retro shops. **Main Street** from 19th to 27th avenues means antiques, and lots of 'em. **Granville Island,** a rehabilitated industrial site beneath the Granville Street Bridge, is one of the best places to pick up salmon and other seafood, as well as crafts and gifts.

ANTIQUES   The **Vancouver Antique Centre,** 422 Richards St. (© **604/ 669-7444**), has everything from china and jewelry to military objects.

BOOKS   Since 1957, **Duthie Books,** 2239 W. Fourth Ave., Kitsilano (© **604/732-5344**), has been synonymous with good books in Vancouver. **Chapters,** 788 Robson St. (© **604/682-4066**), has pleasant nooks and comfy benches in which to browse at length.

DEPARTMENT STORES & MALLS   Ever since the establishment of its trading posts in the 1670s, **The Bay** (Hudson's Bay Company), 674 Granville St. (© **604/681-6211**), has built its reputation on quality goods. You can still buy a Hudson's Bay woolen point blanket, but you'll also find Tommy Hilfiger and DKNY. The 200-shop **Pacific Centre Mall,** 700 W. Georgia St. (© **604/ 688-7236**), contains Godiva, Benetton, and Eddie Bauer. For more upscale boutiques like Armani, try the **Sinclair Centre,** 757 W. Hastings St. (© **604/ 659-1009**).

FASHION   Designer outlets include **Chanel,** 103-755 Burrard St. (© **604/ 682-0522**); **Salvatore Ferragamo,** 918 Robson St. (© **604/669-4495**); **Gianni Versace,** 757 W. Hastings St. (© **604/683-1131**); and **Polo/Ralph Lauren,** The Landing, 375 Water St. (© **604/682-7656**). For something uniquely West Coast, **Dorothy Grant,** 250-757 W. Hastings St. (© **604/681-0201**), offers gorgeous First Nations designs.

FOOD & WINE   At **Chocolate Arts,** 2037 W. Fourth Ave. (© **604/ 739-0475**), the works are so exquisite that they're sometimes a wrench to eat. **Murchie's Tea & Coffee,** 970 Robson St. (© **604/669-0783**), is a Vancouver institution. The **Lobsterman,** 1807 Mast Tower Rd. (© **604/687-4531**), can pack salmon and other seafood for air travel. **Marquis Wine Cellars,** 1034 Davie St. (© **604/684-0445**), carries a full range of local and international wines.

JEWELRY   Since 1879, **Henry Birk & Sons Ltd.,** 698 W. Hastings St. (© **604/669-3333**), has designed and created beautiful jewelry and watches. On Granville Island, **The Raven and the Bear,** 1528 Duranleau St. (© **604/ 669-3990**), is a great spot for Native jewelry.

NATIVE ART   **Images for a Canadian Heritage,** 164 Water St. (© **604/ 685-7046**), is a government-licensed First Nations gallery, featuring traditional and contemporary works. The **Leona Lattimer Gallery,** 1590 W. Second Ave. (✆ **604/732-4556**), presents museum-quality masks, totem poles, and jewelry, at more affordable prices than galleries downtown.

SPORTING GOODS Everything you'll ever need for the outdoors is at **Mountain Equipment Co-op,** 130 W. Broadway (✆ **604/872-7858**).

8 Vancouver After Dark

Check out the weekly *Georgia Straight, Vancouver* magazine (www.vanmag.com), or *Xtra! West,* the gay-and-lesbian tabloid. The **Vancouver Cultural Alliance Arts Hot Line** (✆ **604/684-2787;** www.allianceforarts.com) is a great source for performing arts, literary events, and art films. **Ticketmaster** (Vancouver Ticket Centre), 1304 Hornby St. (✆ **604/280-3311;** www.ticketmaster.ca), has 40 outlets in the greater Vancouver area.

Three major Vancouver theaters regularly host touring performances: the **Queen Elizabeth Theatre,** 600 Hamilton St., and the **Vancouver Playhouse,** which share a phone number (✆ **604/665-3050**) and website (www.city. vancouver.bc.ca); and the **Orpheum Theatre,** 801 Granville St. (✆ **604/665-3050**).

THE PERFORMING ARTS Every summer brings an outdoor Shakespeare series called **Bard on the Beach,** in Vanier Park (✆ **604/737-0625**). You can also bring a picnic to Stanley Park and watch **Theatre Under the Stars** (✆ **604/687-0174;** www.tuts.bc.ca), which features musicals and comedies. The **Fringe Festival** (✆ **604/257-0350;** www.vancouverfringe.com) offers more than 500 innovative shows each September. The **Arts Club Theatre Company** (✆ **604/687-1644;** www.artsclub.com) performs at the Granville Island Stage at the Arts Club Theatre, 1585 Johnston St., and at the Stanley Theatre, 2750 Granville St.

The extremely active **Vancouver Symphony,** 601 Smithe St. (✆ **604/876-3434;** www.vancouversymphony.ca), presents great classical works, pop and show tunes, and music geared toward children. The traveling summer concert series takes the orchestra from White Rock to the top of Whistler Mountain. The **Vancouver Opera,** 500-845 Cambie St. (✆ **604/683-0222;** www. vanopera.bc.ca), alternates between obscure or new works and more popular favorites.

Ballet British Columbia, 502-68 Water St. (✆ **604/732-5003;** www.ballet bc.com), strives to present innovative works. For information on festivals and other dance companies, call the **Dance Centre** (✆ **604/606-6400**).

BARS, PUBS & LOUNGES **Fred's Tavern,** 1006 Granville St. (✆ **604/605-4350**), features a steady stream of simulcast sports, but for some reason the beautiful young crowd is mostly interested in each other. The **Brickhouse Bar,** 730 Main St. (✆ **604/689-8645**), is a great bar in the slowly gentrifying neighborhood around Main and Terminal. **Steamworks Pub & Brewery,** 375 Water St. (✆ **604/689-2739**), offers a dozen in-house beers, from dark ales to refreshing wheat lagers. View junkies will think they've died and gone to heaven at the rotating **Cloud Nine,** 1400 Robson St., on the 42nd floor of the Empire Landmark Hotel (✆ **604/687-0511**).

LIVE-MUSIC CLUBS Sadly, the functional **Starfish Room,** 1055 Homer St., has closed its doors. For folk, the **WISE Hall,** 1882 Adanac (✆ **604/254-5858**), is the place to be. And for blues, go to the smoky old **Yale Hotel,** 1300 Granville St. (✆ **604/681-9253**).

DANCE CLUBS **Richards on Richards,** 1036 Richards St. (© **604/ 687-6794**), has been packing 'em in for close to 2 decades. **Sonar,** 66 Water St. (© **604/683-6695**), is Vancouver's purest hip-hop house joint, named one of the world's top 20 clubs by Britain's *Ministry* magazine. And at the **Stone Temple Cabaret,** 1082 Granville St. (© **604/488-1333**), it's straight-up disco, with lights, smoke, and an early-20s collegiate crowd.

GAY & LESBIAN BARS **Homers,** 1249 Howe St. (© **604/689-2444**), has a relaxed atmosphere, a few billiards tables, and a great pub menu. The **Dufferin Pub,** 900 Seymour St. (© **604/683-4251**), is home to the city's glitziest drag show. The **Odyssey,** 1251 Howe St. (© **604/689-5256**), is the hippest gay/ mixed dance bar in town. The **Heritage House Hotel,** 455 Abbott St. (© **604/ 685-7777**), is home to two gay bars, **Charlie's Lounge** and the slightly seedy **Chuck's Pub,** and one lesbian locale, the **Lotus Cabaret.** The Lotus crowd is normally mixed, but on Fridays it's women only.

Victoria

by Shawn Blore

Just 90 minutes by ferry from Vancouver's urban bustle is the other Vancouver—Vancouver Island. At its southeastern tip is the province's capital and the island's largest city, Victoria.

Victoria spent the better part of the 20th century in a reverie, looking back to its glorious past as an outpost of England at the height of the Empire. It was a booming colonial city in the 19th century, but Victoria's lot began to fade soon after Vancouver was established in the 1880s. When its economy finally crashed early in the 20th century, shocked Victorians realized they were looking at a future with nothing much to live on but some fabulous Tudor and Victorian architecture, a beautiful natural setting, and a carefully cultivated sense of Englishness. So they decided to market that.

So successful was the sales pitch that the Victorians themselves began to believe they inhabited a little patch of England. They began growing elaborate rose gardens, which flourished in the mild Pacific climate, and cultivated a taste for afternoon tea with jam and scones. For decades, the reverie continued unabated.

But the Victorians proved flexible enough to accommodate some changes as well. City restaurants branched out into seafood and ethnic and fusion cuisines. And as visitors have shown themselves more interested in exploring the natural world, Victoria has quietly added whale-watching and mountain-biking trips to its traditional tours on London-style double-decker buses.

Today, the result is that Victoria is the only city in the world where you can zoom out on a Zodiac in the morning to see a pod of orcas and make it back in time for a lovely afternoon tea with all the trimmings.

1 Essentials

GETTING THERE

BY PLANE   **Victoria International Airport** (© 250/953-7500; www.cyyj.ca) is near the Sidney ferry terminal, 17 miles (27km) north of Victoria off the Patricia Bay Highway (Hwy. 17). **Air Canada** (© 888/247-2262; www.aircanada.ca) offers direct connections from Seattle and Vancouver, among others. Commuter airlines and floatplanes that serve the city include Air Canada affiliate **Air BC** (© 888/247-2262 or 604/688-5515), **Harbour Air Seaplanes** (© 800/665-0212 or 604/688-1277; www.harbour-air.com), **Tofino Air** (formerly Pacific Spirit Air; © 800/665-2359; www.tofinoair.ca) **Kenmore Air** (© 800/543-9595;), and **Helijet Airways** (© 250/382-6222 in Victoria, or 604/273-1414 in Vancouver; www.helijet.com).

The airport bus service, operated by **AKAL Airport** (© 250/386-2526), makes the trip into town in 45 minutes; the fare is C$13 (US$8) one-way. Both

C **Special Events & Festivals**

So many flowers bloom in February that the city holds an annual **Flower Count** (© 250/383-7191). In April, Victoria hosts the **TerrifVic Dixieland Jazz Party** (© 250/953-2011), with bands from around the world playing swing, Dixieland, honky-tonk, and fusion. In May, thousands of yachts sail into the harbor during the **Swiftsure Yacht Race** (© 250/953-2033). June's **Jazz Fest International** (© 250/388-4423) brings jazz, swing, bebop, fusion, and improv artists from around the world. The **Folkfest,** a free 8-day world-beat music festival, takes place at the end of the month.

The provincial capital celebrates **Canada Day** (July 1) with events centered around the Inner Harbour, including music, food, and fireworks. The August **First Peoples Festival** (© 250/384-3211) highlights the culture and heritage of the Pacific Northwest First Nations tribes. In November, the **Great Canadian Beer Festival** (© 250/952-0360) features samples from the province's best microbreweries. And Victoria rings in the New Year with **First Night** (© 250/380-1211), a family-oriented New Year's Eve celebration with free performances at many downtown venues.

Empress Cabs (© 250/381-2222) and **Blue Bird Cabs** (© 250/382-8294) make airport runs; a taxi ride costs about C$40 (US$26). Several car-rental firms have desks at the airport, including **Avis** (© 250/656-6033), **Hertz** (© 250/656-2312), and **Tilden** (© 250/656-2541).

BY TRAIN   Travelers on the Horseshoe Bay–Nanaimo ferry can board a train that winds down the Cowichan River valley through Goldstream Provincial Park into Victoria. **VIA Rail's E&N Railiner,** or the *Malahat,* leaves Courtenay, about 130 miles (210km) northwest of Victoria, at 1:15pm daily, arriving in Nanaimo at 3:07pm and in Victoria at 5:45pm. The **E&N Station,** 450 Pandora Ave. (© 800/561-8630), is near the Johnson Street Bridge. The fare from Nanaimo to Victoria is C$20 (US$13) for adults, C$18 (US$12) for seniors and students, and C$12 (US$8) for children.

BY BUS   Pacific Coach Lines (© 800/661-1725 or 604/662-8074; www. pacificcoach.com) operates service between Vancouver and Victoria. The 4-hour trip from Vancouver to the Victoria Depot, 710 Douglas St., includes passage on the Tsawwassen–Swartz Bay ferry. The adult fare is C$26 (US$17) one-way.

BY SHIP & FERRY   See "Getting There" in chapter 3, "Vancouver," for information on **BC Ferries** (© 888/BCFERRY in B.C., or 250/386-3431; www.bcferries.bc.ca) service between Vancouver and Victoria.

Black Ball Transport (© 250/386-2202 in Victoria, or 360/457-4491 in Port Angeles; www.northolympic.com/coho) operates the **MV *Coho*** between Port Angeles, Washington, and Victoria, with one-way fares at US$8 per adult passenger, US$30 per car. The crossing takes 1½ hours.

Victoria Clipper (© 800/888-2535, or 250/382-8100 in Victoria; www. victoriaclipper.com) runs high-speed, passenger-only catamaran service between Seattle and Victoria, with some sailings stopping in the San Juan Islands. Adult tickets are around US$60 to US$125. Sailing time is about 3 hours

June through October, **Victoria/San Juan Cruises** operates the *Victoria Star* (© **800/443-4552** or 360/738-8099) from Bellingham, Washington, to Victoria. Round-trip adult fares range from US$79 to US$89. It takes about 3 hours.

VISITOR INFORMATION

Across from the Empress hotel is the **Tourism Victoria Visitor Info Centre,** 812 Wharf St. (© **250/953-2033;** www.tourismvictoria.com). If you need to find accommodations, go to this office or call its reservations hot line (© **800/663-3883** or 250/953-2022) for last-minute bookings. The center is open daily from 9am to 5pm (until 8pm in summer).

CITY LAYOUT

Victoria is on the southeastern tip of Vancouver Island, across the Strait of Juan de Fuca from Washington's snow-capped Olympic Peninsula. The areas of most interest to visitors, including **downtown** and **Old Town,** lie along the eastern edge of the **Inner Harbour.** (North of the Johnson Street Bridge is the **Upper Harbour,** which is almost entirely industrial.) A little farther east, the **Ross Bay** and **Oak Bay** residential areas around Dallas Road and Beach Drive reach the beaches along the open waters of the Strait of Juan de Fuca.

Victoria's central landmark is the **Empress** hotel on Government Street, right across from the Inner Harbour wharf. If you turn your back to the hotel, downtown and Old Town will be on your right, and the provincial **Parliament Buildings** and the **Royal B.C. Museum** will be on your immediate left.

Government Street goes through Victoria's main downtown shopping-and-dining district. **Douglas Street,** parallel to Government Street, is the main business thoroughfare as well as the road to Nanaimo and the rest of the island.

2 Getting Around

Strolling along the Inner Harbour's pedestrian walkways and streets can be very pleasant. The terrain is predominantly flat, and with few exceptions, Victoria's points of interest are accessible in less than 30 minutes on foot.

BY BUS   The **Victoria Regional Transit System (BC Transit),** 520 Gorge Rd. (© **250/382-6161;** http://transitbc.com), operates 40 bus routes through greater Victoria and the nearby towns of Sooke and Sidney. Regular service on the main routes runs from 6am to just past midnight. One-way, single-zone fares are C$1.75 (US$1.15) for adults and C$1.10 (US$.70) for seniors and children 5 to 13; two zones are C$2.50 (US$1.60) and C$1.75 (US$1.15), respectively. DayPasses, which cover unlimited travel throughout the day, cost C$5.50 (US$3.60) for adults, C$4 (US$2.60) for seniors and children. You can buy passes at the visitor center, convenience stores, and outlets displaying the Fare-Dealer symbol.

BY FERRY   Crossing the Inner, Upper, and Victoria Harbours on one of the blue 12-passenger **Victoria Harbour Ferries** (© **250/708-0201**) is both cheap and fun. During the summer, ferries to the Empress, Coast Harbourside Hotel, and Ocean Pointe Resort run about every 15 minutes from 9am to 9pm. Off-season, the ferries run only on sunny weekends from 11am to 6pm. The cost is C$3 (US$1.95) for adults and C$1.50 (US$1) for children.

BY TAXI   Within the downtown area, you can expect to travel for less than C$6 (US$3.90). It's best to call for a cab; drivers don't always stop on city streets for flag-downs, especially when it's raining. Call for a pickup from **Empress Cabs** (© **250/381-2222**) or **Blue Bird Cabs** (© **250/382-8294**).

BY CAR   Rental agencies in Victoria include **ABC,** 2507 Government St. (© 800/464-6464 or 250/388-3153); **Avis,** 1001 Douglas St. (© 800/879-2847 or 250/386-8468); **Budget,** 757 Douglas St. (© 800/268-8900 or 250/253-5300); **Hertz,** 102-907 Fort St. (© 800/263-0600 or 250/388-4411); and **Tilden,** 767 Douglas St. (© 800/387-4747 or 250/386-1213).

All major downtown hotels have guest parking; rates vary from free to C$20 (US$13) per day. There are parking lots at **View Street** between Douglas and Blanshard streets; **Johnson Street** off Blanshard Street; **Yates Street** north of Bastion Square; and **The Bay** department store, on Fisgard at Blanshard Street. Metered street parking is hard to come by downtown, and rules are strictly enforced. Unmetered parking on side streets is rare.

BY BICYCLE   There are bike lanes throughout the city, as well as paved paths along parks and beaches. Bikes and child trailers are available by the hour or day at **Cycle BC,** 747 Douglas St. (year-round) or 950 Wharf St. (May–Oct) (© **250/885-2453**). Rentals run C$6 (US$3.90) per hour or C$20 (US$13) per day.

ⓒ FAST FACTS: Victoria

American Express   The office at 1203 Douglas St. (© **250/385-8731**) is open Monday through Friday from 8:30am to 5:30pm and Saturday from 10am to 4pm.

Area Code   The telephone area code for all of Vancouver Island, including Victoria and most of British Columbia, is **250.**

Doctors   Hotels usually have a doctor on call. The **James Bay Treatment Center,** 100-230 Menzies St. (© **250/388-9934**), is open Monday through Friday from 9am to 6pm and Saturday and holidays from 10am to 4pm.

Emergencies   Dial © **911** for fire, police, ambulance, and poison control.

Hospitals   Local hospitals include the **Royal Jubilee Hospital,** 1900 Fort St. (© **250/370-8000,** or 250/370-8212 for emergencies), and **Victoria General Hospital,** 1 Hospital Way (© **250/727-4212,** or 250/727-4181 for emergencies).

Police   The Victoria City Police can also be reached by calling © **250/995-7654.**

Safety   Crime rates are quite low in Victoria, but transients panhandle throughout the downtown and Old Town areas. As in any city, stay alert to prevent crimes of opportunity.

---

3 Where to Stay

Reservations are essential May through September. If you have trouble finding a room, **Tourism Victoria** (© **800/663-3883** or 250/382-1131) can make reservations for you at hotels, inns, and B&Bs.

INNER HARBOUR
VERY EXPENSIVE

Delta Victoria Ocean Pointe Resort and Spa ★★   On the Inner Harbour's north shore, the luxurious OPR offers commanding views of downtown, the

Victoria

ATTRACTIONS ●

Craigdarroch Castle **6**
Fort Rodd Hill &
  Fisgard Lighthouse
  National Historic Site **1**
Maritime Museum
  of British Columbia **5**
Pacific Undersea Gardens **12**
Parliament Buildings **11**
Royal British Columbia
  Museum **10**
Royal London Wax Museum **13**

ACCOMMODATIONS ■

Abigail's Hotel **7**
Admiral Motel **16**
Andersen House
  Bed & Breakfast **15**
Delta Victoria Ocean Pointe
  Resort and Spa **2**
The Empress **9**
The Haterleigh Heritage Inn **14**
Laurel Point Inn **17**
The Magnolia **8**
Swans Suite Hotel **3**
Victoria International
  Youth Hostel **4**

Legislature, and the Empress. Other pluses include the fancy toiletries, fluffy robes, and fine linens. In a city with a fetish for floral prints, the OPR's decor is refreshingly modern—polished woods, muted colors, and not a lot of bric-a-brac. The Inner Harbour units offer the best views, many with floor-to-ceiling windows; rooms facing the Outer Harbour top that with floor-to-ceiling bay windows. Wheelchair-accessible units are available. The spa is one of the best in town.

45 Songhees Rd., Victoria, BC V9A 6T3. ℂ **800/667-4677** or 250/360-2999. Fax 250/360-1041. www.opr hotel.com. 250 units. June–Oct 11 C$448–C$736 (US$291–US$478) double. Oct 12–Dec 31 C$340–C$448 (US$221–US$291) double. Jan–Apr 15 C$295–C$403 (US$192–US$262) double. Apr 16–May 31 C$322–C$574 (US$209–US$373) double. Promotional rates available. Children under 17 stay free in parents' room. AE, DC, MC, V. Underground valet parking C$9 (US$6). Bus: 24 to Colville. Pets under 30 lb. allowed. **Amenities:** Two restaurants (see the Victorian Restaurant under "Where to Dine," below); bar; indoor pool; tennis courts; health club; spa; Jacuzzi; sauna; watersports rentals; bike rentals; concierge; business center; shopping arcade; 24-hr. room service; in-room massage; babysitting; same-day dry cleaning. *In room:* A/C, TV/VCR w/ pay movies, fax, dataport, minibar, coffeemaker, hair dryer, iron, safe.

The Fairmont Empress 👑👑   When you see Francis Rattenbury's 1908 harborside creation, you'll know immediately that you simply *must* stay here. However, be aware that with 90 different configurations, not all rooms are created equal. Some deluxe rooms and all Entree Gold rooms are a dream (or a Merchant Ivory film), with wide windows, high ceilings, and abundant natural light. Entree Gold rooms also include private check-in, concierge service, breakfast in a private lounge, and extras like CD players and bathroom TVs. Many of the other rooms—despite a C$4-million (US$2.6-million) renovation in 1996—are built to the "cozy" standards of 1908. Wheelchair-accessible units are available. If you can afford an Entree Gold or deluxe room, go for it. If not, you may be better off admiring the Empress from afar.

721 Government St., Victoria, BC V8W 1W5. ℂ **800/866-5577** or 250/384-8111. Fax 250/381-4334. www. fairmont.com. 460 units. May–Oct C$295–C$490 (US$192–US$319) double. Nov–Apr C$200–C$395 (US$130–US$257) double. Year-round C$425–C$1,500 (US$276–US$975) suite. AE, DC, DISC, MC, V. Underground valet parking C$17 (US$11). Bus: 5. Small pets allowed for C$50 (US$33). **Amenities:** Three restaurants; bar; indoor pool; health club; Jacuzzi; sauna; concierge; car-rental desk; business center; shopping arcade; 24-hr. room service; in-room massage; babysitting; laundry service; same-day dry cleaning. *In room:* A/C, TV w/ pay movies, dataport, minibar, hair dryer, iron.

EXPENSIVE

The Haterleigh Heritage Inn 👑👑👑   This 1901 home features antique furniture and stunning stained-glass windows, accompanied by attentive personal service. The spacious rooms boast high arched ceilings, sitting areas, and enormous bathrooms, some with Jacuzzi tubs. The Secret Garden room has a small balcony with stunning views of the Olympic Mountains. The Day Dreams room is the dedicated honeymoon suite, but truth be told, all of the suites make for wonderful romantic weekends. Bathrooms come with robes, candles, and plastic champagne flutes. A gourmet, family-style breakfast is served at 8:30am, giving guests a chance to meet and chat. There's complimentary sherry in the drawing room each evening.

243 Kingston St., Victoria, BC V8V 1V5. ℂ **250/384-9995.** Fax 250/384-1935. www.haterleigh.com. 7 units. C$213–C$327 (US$138–US$213) double. Rates include full breakfast. MC, V. Free parking. Bus: 30 to Superior and Montreal sts. **Amenities:** Jacuzzi. *In room:* No phone.

Laurel Point Inn 👑👑   The Laurel's design and lobby reflect Japanese artistic principals: elegant simplicity, blond-wood surfaces, and the subtle integration of light, water, and stone. Wander past the gurgling fountains on your way up to your room, where a crisp cotton kimono has been laid out—something to slip into before stepping out onto the private terrace, with a panoramic view of the harbor and hills. The hotel, occupying most of a promontory jutting out into the Inner Harbour, consists of the original north wing and a new south wing. The south wing is where you want to be: All rooms here are suites, featuring shoji-style sliding doors, Asian art, and deep tubs and floor-to-ceiling glassed-in showers. Wheelchair-accessible units are available. *Note:* Smoking is not permitted.

680 Montreal St., Victoria, BC V8V 1Z8. (C) **800/663-7667** or 250/386-8721. Fax 250/386-9547. www.laurel point.com. 200 units. June–Oct C$259 (US$168) double; C$309 (US$201) junior suite; C$359 (US$233) 1-bedroom suite; C$499 (US$324) full suite. Nov–April C$129 (US$84) double; C$179 (US$116) junior suite; C$229 (US$149) 1-bedroom suite; C$289 (US$188) full suite. May C$239 (US$155) double; C$289 (US$188) junior suite; C$339 (US$220) 1-bedroom suite; C$479 (US$311) full suite. Seasonal discounts available. Children under 12 stay free in parents' room. AE, DC, DISC, MC, V. Valet parking. Bus: 30 to Montreal and Superior sts. Pets accepted for C$25 (US$16). **Amenities:** Restaurant, bar; indoor pool; access to YMCA facilities; Jacuzzi; sauna; concierge; business center; 24-hr. room service; babysitting; same-day dry cleaning. *In room:* A/C, TV w/ pay movies, dataport, coffeemaker, hair dryer, iron.

MODERATE

Admiral Inn 🏨🏨 *Value*   The family-operated Admiral is located near the Washington-bound ferry terminal and close to restaurants and shopping. Its comfortable rooms and reasonable rates attract travelers in search of a harbor view at a price that doesn't break the bank. Rooms are pleasant, with balconies or terraces. The owners provide sightseeing advice as well as extras like an Internet terminal in the lobby.

257 Belleville St., Victoria, BC V8V 1X3. (C) **888/823-6472** or 250/388-6267. Fax 250/388-6267. www.admiral. bc.ca. 29 units. May–Sept C$155–C$199 (US$101–US$129) double; C$169–C$215 (US$110–US$140) suite. Oct–Apr C$99–C$119 (US$64–US$77) double; C$109–C$129 (US$71–US$84) suite. Extra person C$10 (US$7). Children under 12 stay free in parents' room. Rates include continental breakfast. Senior, weekly, and off-season discounts available. AE, DISC, MC, V. Free parking. Bus: 5 to Belleville and Government sts. Pets welcome. **Amenities:** Free bikes; tour desk; business center; coin-op laundry; same-day dry cleaning. *In room:* A/C, TV, kitchenette or kitchen, coffeemaker, hair dryer, iron.

Andersen House Bed & Breakfast 🏨🏨   The 1891 Andersen House has the high ceilings, stained-glass windows, and ornate fireplaces typical of the Queen Anne style, but the art and decor are far more eclectic: hand-knotted Persian rugs, raku sculptures, and carved-wood African masks. All rooms have private entrances; some feature soaker tubs. The sun-drenched Casablanca room boasts a four-poster bed and a lovely boxed window seat. The Andersens also run Baybreeze Manor, a restored 1885 farmhouse a 15-minute drive from downtown. Its three units feature hardwood floors, fireplaces, and Jacuzzi tubs, as well as easy access to Cadboro Beach.

301 Kingston St., Victoria, BC V8V 1V5. (C) **250/388-4565.** Fax 250/721-3938. www.andersenhouse.com. 4 units. June–Sept C$195–C$250 (US$127–US$163) double. Off-season discounts available. Rates include breakfast. MC, V. Some free off-street parking. Bus: 30 to Superior and Oswego sts. Children must be 12 or older. **Amenities:** Jacuzzi. *In room:* TV/VCR, CD player, fridge, coffeemaker, hair dryer, iron.

DOWNTOWN & OLD TOWN
EXPENSIVE

Abigail's Hotel 🏨🏨🏨   The most serious problem you'll face here is determining at exactly what point you slipped from semi-sensuous luxury into decadent indulgence. It could be when you first entered your room and saw the fresh flowers and marble fireplace, with wood in place. More likely, it's when you slipped into the double Jacuzzi in your marble bathroom or nestled into your four-poster canopied bed. In a Tudor mansion just east of downtown, Abigail's began life in the 1920s as a luxury apartment house. Some of the units in the original building are bright and beautifully furnished, with pedestal sinks and down comforters. Others boast soaker tubs and double-sided fireplaces. The six suites in the Coach House addition are the apogee of indulgence. Abigail's chef prepares a gourmet breakfast.

906 McClure St., Victoria, BC V8V 3E7. ✆ 800/561-6565 or 250/388-5363. Fax 250/388-7787. www.abigails hotel.com. 22 units. C$219–C$329 (US$142–US$214) double. Rates include full breakfast. Off-season discounts available. AE, MC, V. Free parking. Bus: 1 to Cook and McClure sts. Children must be 10 or older. **Amenities:** Concierge; tour desk; same-day dry cleaning.

The Magnolia ☆☆   A new boutique hotel in the center of town, the Magnolia offers a taste of luxury at a reasonable price. The tiny lobby, with a fireplace, chandelier, and overstuffed chairs, immediately conveys a sense of quality. Room decor manages to be classic without feeling frumpy, from the two-poster beds with down duvets to the bathrooms with walk-in showers and deep tubs. Some units have excellent harbor views. Business travelers will appreciate the work desks and dual phone lines. The hotel also boasts a microbrewery and full day spa.

623 Courtney St., Victoria, BC V8W 1B8. ✆ 877/624-6654 or 250/381-0999. Fax 250/381-0988. www. magnoliahotel.com. 66 units. June–Oct 15 C$239–C$279 (US$155–US$181) double; C$399–C$419 (US$259–US$272) suite. Oct 16–Apr 15 C$169–C$209 (US$110–US$136) double; C$249–C$269 (US$162– US$175) suite. Apr 16–May 31 C$209–C$229 (US$136–US$149) double; C$289–C$309 (US$188–US$201) suite. Rates include continental breakfast. AE, DC, MC, V. Valet parking C$10 (US$7). Bus: 5 to Courtney St. **Amenities:** Restaurant; bar; access to nearby health club; spa; concierge; salon; limited room service; massage; laundry service; same-day dry cleaning. *In room:* A/C, TV w/ pay movies, dataport, minibar, fridge, coffeemaker, hair dryer, iron.

Swans Suite Hotel ☆☆ *Kids*   This heritage building near the Johnson Street Bridge was abandoned for years, until Victoria renaissance man Michael Williams turned it into an all-in-one hotel, restaurant, brewpub, and nightclub. Many of the spacious suites are split-level, featuring open lofts and huge exposed beams. The two-bedroom units have the feel of little town houses and are great for families. Swans also works for business travelers—it's one of the few hotels in town with dual dataports. *Note:* Smoking is not permitted.

506 Pandora Ave., Victoria, BC V8W 1N6. ✆ 800/668-7926 or 250/361-3310. Fax 250/361-3491. www. swanshotel.com. 30 suites. C$159–C$249 (US$103–US$162) suite. Off-season discounts available. AE, DC, DISC, MC, V. Parking C$8 (US$5). Bus: 23 or 24 to Pandora Ave. **Amenities:** Restaurant; brewpub; limited room service; laundry service; dry cleaning. *In room:* TV, kitchen, coffeemaker, hair dryer, iron.

INEXPENSIVE
Victoria International Youth Hostel   This hostel, right in the heart of Old Town, has all the usual accoutrements. The dorms are on the large side (16 to a room). A couple of family rooms are available, as is one wheelchair-accessible unit. The front door is locked at 2:30am, but you can make arrangements to get in later.

516 Yates St., Victoria, BC V8W 1K8. ✆ 250/385-4511. Fax 250/385-3232. www.hihostels.bc.ca. 104 beds. C$17 (US$11) IYHA members, C$20 (US$13) nonmembers. MC, V. Street parking. Bus: 70 from Swartz Bay ferry terminal. **Amenities:** 2 kitchens; TV lounge; game room; tour desk; laundry; indoor bike lockup. *In room:* No phone.

4 Where to Dine

Victoria is a cornucopia of culinary styles, with something for every taste and budget. Despite all this variety, the one thing you're unlikely to find is a lot of late-night dining. Victorians time their meal to the setting of the sun. Try for a seat at 7pm, and the restaurant will be packed. Try at 9pm, and it'll be empty.

Moments Tea for Two

Afternoon tea at the **Empress,** 721 Government St. (© **250/384-8111**), is undoubtedly the best in town, served in the Palm Court or in the Lobby Lounge, both of which are beautifully ornate and luxurious. Tea runs C$46 (US$30) per person in high season, with seatings at 12:30, 2, 3:30, and 5pm. The **Point Ellice House,** 2616 Pleasant St. (© **250/380-6506**), on the Gorge waterway just outside downtown, also makes a fine destination, especially on a sunny day, when tea is served on the lawn for C$17 (US$11). Seatings are at 12:30, 2, and 3:30pm; reservations are required. With impeccably groomed gardens as a backdrop, the **Butchart Gardens Dining Room Restaurant,** 800 Benvenuto Ave. (© **250/652-4422**), offers a memorable tea experience that runs C$25 (US$16). June through August, seatings are from noon to 7pm; September through May, from noon to 5pm. (See also p. 89.)

Try at 10pm, and it'll be closed, especially on weekdays. Reservations are strongly recommended for prime sunset seating in summer.

EXPENSIVE

The Blue Crab Bar and Grill 🗡🗡 SEAFOOD Victoria's best seafood spot, the Blue Crab combines fresh ingredients, beautiful presentation, and a killer view. Choose from the extensive selection of British Columbia wines, then peruse the chalkboard of daily specials, which are entirely dependent on what came in on the boats or floatplanes that day. The chef is fond of unusual combinations: sea bass with taro root, grapefruit, and blood orange, or foie gras with raspberries. The service is deft, smart, and obliging.

In the Coast Hotel, 146 Kingston St. © **250/480-1999.** Reservations recommended. Main courses C$20–C$30 (US$13–US$20). AE, DC, MC, V. Daily 6:30am–10:30pm. Bus: 30 to Erie St.

The Victorian Restaurant 🗡 WEST COAST One of the only good bets when it comes to waterfront dining in Victoria is this elegant restaurant in the Ocean Pointe Resort. The views are tremendous, and the food has begun to win recognition, including awards from *Wine Spectator* and *Western Living* magazines. The chef takes few culinary risks, sticking to fresh ingredients with a slight emphasis on seafood (but enough lamb, steak, and veggie dishes to cover all the bases).

In the Delta Victoria Ocean Pointe Resort, 45 Songhees Rd. © **250/360-2999.** www.oprhotel.com. Reservations recommended. Main courses C$14–C$29 (US$9–US$19). AE, MC, V. Daily 11am–10:30pm. Bus: 24 to Colville.

MODERATE

Cassis Bistro 🗡🗡 BISTRO This cozy, candlelit bistro features what chef John Hall calls eclectic Italian cuisine, which means dishes from the whole boot plus borrowings here and there from Asia and France. Ingredients are resolutely local, however. Recent highlights have included ling cod filet, lightly seared and served with *shimjii* mushrooms; smoked tuna ravioli in a miso jus; and Fraser Valley duck breast served on a bed of warm goat-cheese crouton. Hall is especially good at pairing his dishes with local British Columbia vintages.

253 Cook St. © **250/384-1932.** Reservations recommended. Main courses C$23–C$27 (US$15–US$18). MC, V. Daily 5:30–9:30pm; Sun brunch 10am–2pm.

Herald Street Caffe ✿ PASTA/WEST COAST   An old warehouse on the far side of Chinatown, this fun cafe sizzles with the sound of diners young and old. The menu lists more than 20 martinis, and the wine list offers a good selection of local reds and whites. The cuisine is sophisticated without going too far over the top. You might start with barbecued duck in phyllo with apple-current chutney. Entrees include many clever seafood dishes as well as free-range chicken, duck and lamb options, and a whole page of pastas.

546 Herald St. ℂ **250/381-1441**. Reservations required. Main courses C$17–C$28 (US$11–US$18). AE, DC, MC, V. Wed–Fri 11:30am–2:30pm; Sat–Sun brunch 11am–3pm; Sun–Thurs 5:30–10pm; Fri–Sat 5:30pm–midnight. Bus: 5.

Millos ✿✿ *(Kids)* GREEK   Millos isn't hard to find—look for the blue-and-white windmill behind the Empress or listen for the hand clapping and plate breaking as diners get into the swing of things. Flaming *saganaki* (a sharp cheese sautéed in olive oil and flambéed with Greek brandy), grilled halibut souvlaki, baby-back ribs, and succulent grilled salmon are a few of the menu items at this lively five-level restaurant. Kids get their own menu. Folk dancers and belly dancers entertain on Friday and Saturday nights.

716 Burdett Ave. ℂ **250/382-4422**. Reservations recommended. Main courses C$10–C$28 (US$7–US$18), with most dishes around C$15 (US$10). AE, DC, MC, V. Mon–Sat 11am–11pm; Sun 4–11pm. Bus: 5.

Pagliacci's ✿✿ ITALIAN   Though the night-owl scene has improved since expatriate New Yorker Howie Siegal opened this restaurant in 1979, Pagliacci's can still boast an un-Victorian kind of big-city buzz. Guests ogle each other's food and eavesdrop on conversations while Howie works the room, dispensing a word or two to long-lost friends, many of whom he's only just met. The menu offers veal parmigiana, tortellini, and 19 or 20 other pastas, many quite inventive and all made by hand. The service isn't fast, but when you're having this much fun, who cares? Grab some wine, munch some focaccia, and enjoy the atmosphere. Sunday through Wednesday nights, there's live jazz, swing, blues, or Celtic music. On Sunday, there's a very good brunch.

1011 Broad St. ℂ **250/386-1662**. Reservations not accepted. Main courses C$11–C$19 (US$7–US$12). AE, MC, V. Sun–Thurs 11:30am–10pm; Fri–Sat 11:30am–midnight (light menu 3–5:30pm).

INEXPENSIVE

Don Mee Restaurant ✿ CHINESE   Since the 1920s, elegant Don Mee's has been serving Victoria's best dim sum, along with piquant Szechwan seafood dishes and delectable Cantonese sizzling platters. You can't miss this second-story restaurant—a huge, neon Chinese lantern looms above the doorway, and a 4-foot-tall, gold-leaf Buddha greets you at the entrance. The dinner specials are particularly good deals if you want to sample lots of everything.

538 Fisgard St. ℂ **250/383-1032**. Reservations not needed. Main courses C$9–C$14 (US$6–US$9); four-course dinner from C$14 (US$9). AE, DC, MC, V. Sun–Thurs 11am–10pm; Fri–Sat 11am–midnight. Bus: 5.

Green Cuisine *(Value)* VEGAN   Victoria's only fully vegan enclave is remarkably tasty, with a salad bar, hot buffet, dessert bar, and bakery. Dishes range from Moroccan chickpea-and-vegetable soup to pumpkin tofu cheesecake, not to mention a wide selection of fresh-baked breads. Wash it all down with fresh-squeezed juices, smoothies, or organic coffees and teas. The atmosphere is casual—bordering on cafeteria—but comfortable. If you like the food, check out the website, which features monthly recipes from the restaurant.

560 Johnson St., in Market Sq. ℂ **250/385-1809**. www.greencuisine.com. Main courses C$3.95–C$10 (US$2.55–US$7). AE, MC, V. Daily 10am–8pm.

Re-bar ★★ *Kids* VEGETARIAN   Even if you're not hungry, it's worth dropping in for one of 80 different juice blends—say, grapefruit, banana, melon, and pear with bee pollen or blue-green algae for added oomph. If you're hungry, then rejoice: Re-bar is the city's premier dispenser of vegetarian comfort food. Disturbingly wholesome as that may sound, Re-bar is not only tasty, but also fun. The room is pastel-tinted funky; service is friendly. Dishes include a vegetable-and-almond patty served with red onions, sprouts, and fresh salsa on a multigrain kaiser roll; quesadillas; and crisp salads with toasted pine nuts, feta, and sun-dried-tomato vinaigrette.

50 Bastion Sq. ℂ 250/361-9223. Main courses C$7–C$14 (US$4.55–US$9). AE, MC, V. Mon–Thurs 8:30am–9pm; Fri–Sat 8:30am–10pm; Sun 8:30am–3:30pm. Bus: 5.

5 Exploring Victoria

Note: See the "Victoria" map (p. 71) to locate most of the sights covered in this section.

THE TOP ATTRACTIONS

Fort Rodd Hill & Fisgard Lighthouse National Historic Site   Perched on an outcrop of volcanic rock, the Fisgard Lighthouse has guided ships toward Victoria's sheltered harbor since 1873. The light no longer has a keeper (the beacon has long been automated), but the site itself has been restored to its original appearance. Exhibits recount stories of the lighthouse and the terrible shipwrecks that gave this coastline its ominous moniker, "the graveyard of the Pacific." Adjoining the lighthouse, Fort Rodd Hill is an 1890s artillery fort that still sports camouflaged searchlights, underground magazines, and its original guns. Check out the artifacts, room re-creations, and audiovisual exhibits with the voices and faces of the men who served here.

603 Fort Rodd Hill Rd. ℂ **250/478-5849.** www.parkscanada.pch.gc.ca. Admission C$3 (US$1.95) adults, C$2.25 (US$1.45) seniors, C$1.50 (US$1) children 6–16, C$7.50 (US$4.90) families. Mar–Oct daily 10am–5:30pm; Nov–Feb daily 9am–4:30pm. No public transit.

Maritime Museum of British Columbia   This museum is dedicated to recalling the province's rich maritime heritage, from the early explorers to the fur-trading and whaling era to the days of grand ocean liners and military conflict. There's also an impressive collection of ship models.

28 Bastion Sq. ℂ **250/385-4222.** www.mmbc.bc.ca. Admission C$6 (US$3.90) adults, C$5 (US$3.25) seniors, C$3 (US$1.95) students, C$2 (US$1.30) children 6–11, C$15 (US$10) families. Daily 9am–4:30pm. Closed Dec 25. Bus: 5 to View St.

Pacific Undersea Gardens *Kids*   A gently sloping stairway leads down to a unique glass-enclosed viewing area, where you can observe the Inner Harbour's marine life up close. Sharks, wolf eels, sea anemones, and salmon are just a few of the organisms that make their homes here. One of the star attractions is a remarkably photogenic octopus (reputedly the largest in captivity). Injured seals and orphaned seal pups are cared for in holding pens alongside the observatory.

490 Belleville St. ℂ **250/382-5717.** www.pacificunderseagardens.com. Admission C$7.50 (US$4.90) adults, C$6.50 (US$4.20) seniors, C$5 (US$3.25) youths 12–17, C$3.50 (US$2.30) children 5–11. MC, V. Sept–June daily 10am–5pm; July–Aug daily 10am–7pm. Bus: 5, 27, 28, or 30.

Parliament Buildings (Provincial Legislature) ★   Designed by 25-year-old Francis Rattenbury, and built between 1893 and 1898 at a cost of nearly C$1 million, the Parliament Buildings (also called the Legislature) are an architectural gem. The 40-minute tour comes across at times like an eighth-grade civics lesson, but it's worth it just to see the fine mosaics, marble, woodwork, and stained glass.

501 Belleville St. (C) 250/387-3046. www.protocol.gov.bc.ca. Free admission. Late May to Labour Day daily 9am–5pm; Sept to late May Mon–Fri 9am–5pm. Tours offered every 20 min. in summer, hourly in winter; check for exact times due to school-group bookings. No tours noon–1pm.

Royal British Columbia Museum ★★★ *Kids*   One of the best regional museums in the world, the Royal B.C. features natural-history dioramas indistinguishable from the real thing. The Natural History Gallery shows coastal flora, fauna, and geography, from the ice age to the present; it includes dioramas of a seacoast, an underground ecology of giant bugs, and a live tidal pool with sea stars and anemones. The Modern History Gallery presents the recent past, including re-creations of Victoria's downtown and Chinatown. The First Peoples Gallery is an incredible showpiece of Native art; it also houses a full-size re-creation of a longhouse. The IMAX theater shows a variety of movies. On the way out, stop by Thunderbird Park, where a cedar longhouse contains a workshop in which Native carvers work on new totem poles.

675 Belleville St. (C) 888/447-7977 or 250/387-3701. www.royalbcmuseum.bc.ca. Admission C$9 (US$6) adults; C$6 (US$3.90) seniors, students, and children; C$24 (US$16) families. Higher rates sometimes in effect for traveling exhibits. Daily 9am–5pm. Closed Dec 25 and Jan 1. Bus: 5, 28, or 30.

Royal London Wax Museum *Overrated*   See the same royal family you already get too much of on TV. See other, older royals of even less significance. See their family pets. All courtesy of Madame Tussaud's 200-year-old wax technology. The chamber of horrors rates well below a *Buffy the Vampire Slayer* episode on the scariness scale. Still not thrilled? The management seems to suspect as much—they've started taking liberties with their wax figures' figures. Look especially for the Princess Diana dummy with the Pamela Anderson implants.

470 Belleville St. (C) 250/388-4461. www.waxworld.com. Admission C$8.50 (US$6) adults, C$7.50 (US$4.90) seniors, C$4 (US$2.60) children. AE, MC, V. Daily June–Sept 9am–7pm; Oct–May 9am–5pm. Bus: 5, 27, 28, or 30.

ARCHITECTURAL HIGHLIGHTS & HISTORIC HOMES

Perhaps the most intriguing downtown edifice isn't a building at all, but a work of art. The walls of **Fort Victoria,** which once covered much of downtown, have been demarcated in the sidewalk with bricks bearing the names of original settlers and fur traders. Look in the sidewalk on Government Street at the corner of Fort Street.

Most of the retail establishments in Old Town are housed in restored 19th-century warehouses. Visitors can take a **self-guided tour** of the buildings, whose history is recounted on outdoor plaques. Most of these buildings are between Douglas and Johnson streets from Wharf to Government streets. The most impressive one once contained shipping offices and warehouses; it's now the home of a 45-shop complex known as **Market Square,** 560 Johnson St./255 Market Sq. (C) 250/386-2441).

What do you do when you're the richest man in British Columbia, when you've clawed, scraped, and bullied your way up from indentured servant to coal baron and merchant prince? You build a castle, of course. In the 1880s, Scottish magnate Robert Dunsmuir built the 39-room, Highland-style **Craigdarroch Castle** ★, 1050 Joan Crescent (C) 250/592-5323), topped with stone turrets and chimneys and filled with the opulent Victorian splendor you read about in romance novels. Admission is C$8 (US$5) for adults, C$5 (US$3.25) for students, and C$2 (US$1.30) for children 6 to 12. It's open daily, mid-June through August from 9am to 7pm and September through mid-June from 10am to 4:30pm.

To get a taste of how upper-middle-class Victorians lived, visit the **Carr House,** 207 Government St. (© **250/383-5843**), where painter Emily Carr was born in 1871. Many of her works depict rugged landscapes or scenes from Native villages along the coast. **Helmcken House,** 675 Belleville St. (© **250/386-0021**), was the residence of a pioneer doctor who settled here in the 1850s; it still contains his medicine chest and original British furniture. **Craigflower Farmhouse,** 110 Island Hwy. (© **250/383-4621**), in the View Royal district, was built in 1856 by a Scottish settler who brought many of his furnishings from the old country. The Carr House, Helmcken House, and Craigflower Farmhouse are open in summer, Thursday through Monday from 11am to 5pm. Admission is C$5 (US$3.25) for adults, C$4 (US$2.60) for students and seniors, and C$3 (US$1.95) for children.

PARKS & GARDENS

Beacon Hill Park stretches from Southgate Street to Dallas Road between Douglas and Cook streets. Stands of indigenous Garry oaks (found only on Vancouver, Hornby, and Salt Spring islands) and manicured lawns are interspersed with gardens and ponds. Hike up Beacon Hill to get a view of the Strait of Georgia, Haro Strait, and Olympic Mountains. The children's farm, aviary, tennis courts, putting green, wading pool, playground, and picnic area make this a wonderful place for families.

Government House, the official residence of the Lieutenant Governor, is at 1401 Rockland Ave., in the Fairfield district. The house itself is closed to the public, but the formal gardens are worth a wander. Round back, the hillside of Garry oaks is one of the last places to see what the area's natural flora would have looked like before European settlers arrived.

Victoria has an indoor garden that first opened as a huge saltwater pool in 1925 (Olympic swimmer and *Tarzan* star Johnny Weismuller competed here) and was converted into a big-band dance hall during World War II. The **Crystal Garden,** 731 Douglas St. (© **250/953-8800**), is filled with rare and exotic flora and fauna. Admission is C$8 (US$5) for adults, C$7 (US$4.55) for seniors, and C$4 (US$2.60) for children 5 to 16. Open daily from 10am to 5:30pm (later in summer).

ORGANIZED TOURS

Gray Line of Victoria (© **250/388-5248;** www.victoriatours.com) conducts bus tours of Victoria and Butchart Gardens. The 1½-hour "Grand City Tour" costs C$18 (US$12) for adults and C$9 (US$6) for children. The same company operates a **trolley service** every 40 minutes from 9:30am to 5:30pm on a circuit of 35 hotels, attractions, shops, and restaurants. A day pass costs C$7 (US$4.55) for adults and C$4 (US$2.60) for children.

For C$12 (US$8), **Victoria Harbour Ferries** (© **250/708-0201**) offers a terrific 45-minute tour of the Inner and Outer Harbours. To get a bird's-eye view, take a 30-minute tour with **Harbour Air Seaplanes** (© **250/361-6786**). Rates are C$72 (US$47) per person.

Tallyho Horse Drawn Tours (© **250/383-5067**) has conducted horse-drawn carriage tours since 1903. Excursions start at the corner of Belleville and Menzies streets; fares are C$14 (US$9) for adults and C$6 (US$3.90) for children.

Discover the Past (✆ **250/384-6698;** www.discoverthepast.com) organizes two year-round walks: "Ghostly Walks" explores Victoria's haunted Old Town, Chinatown, and historic waterfront; the "Neighbourhood Discovery Walk" is a tour through the city's many distinct neighborhoods. The cost is C$10 (US$7) for adults, C$8 (US$5) for seniors and students, and C$6 (US$3.90) for children.

6 Outdoor Pursuits

Specialized outfitters are listed with each activity below. **Sports Rent,** 3084 Blanshard St. (✆ **250/385-7368;** www.sportsrentbc.com), is a general-equipment and watersports rental outlet to keep in mind if you forget to pack something.

BIKING   The 8-mile (13km) **Scenic Marine Drive** bike path begins at Dallas Road and Douglas Street, at the base of Beacon Hill Park. The paved path follows the walkway along the beaches, winds up through the residential district on Beach Drive, and eventually heads south toward downtown on Oak Bay Avenue. The **Inner Harbour pedestrian path** has a bike lane for cyclists who want to take a leisurely ride around the city seawall. The new **Galloping Goose Trail** runs from Victoria west through Colwood and Sooke all the way up to Leechtown. If you don't want to cycle the whole thing, you can find numerous places to park along the way, as well as several places where the trail intersects with public transit. Call **BC Transit** (✆ **250/382-6161**) to find out which bus routes take bikes.

Bikes, helmets, and child trailers are available by the hour or day at **Cycle BC,** 747 Douglas St. (year-round) or 950 Wharf St. (May–Oct) (✆ **250/885-2453**). Rentals run C$6 (US$3.90) per hour and C$20 (US$13) per day.

BOATING   A number of charter companies are docked at the **Oak Bay Marina,** 1327 Beach Dr. (✆ **250/598-3369**), including the **Horizon Yacht Centre** (✆ **250/595-2628**), which offers sailboat charters, lessons, and navigational tips. The **Marine Adventure Centre** (✆ **250/995-2211**), on the floatplane docks in the Inner Harbour, can arrange boat charters and more. Skippered charters in the area run about C$600 (US$390) per day, and boat rentals average C$125 (US$81) for a couple of hours.

CANOEING & KAYAKING   **Ocean River Sports,** 1437 Store St. (✆ **250/ 381-4233;** www.oceanriver.com), can equip you with everything from kayak and canoe rentals to life jackets and tents. Rental for a single kayak is C$14 (US$9) per hour or C$42 (US$27) per day. Ocean River also runs guided tours, which start at C$55 (US$36) for a 3-hour novice lesson and paddle.

FISHING   To fish, you need a nonresident saltwater or freshwater license. **Adam's Fishing Charters** (✆ **250/370-2326**) and the **Marine Adventure Centre** (✆ **250/995-2211**) are good places to look for a charter (see also "Boating," above). **Robinson's Sporting Goods Ltd.,** 1307 Broad St. (✆ **250/385-3429**), is a reliable source for information, lures, licenses, and gear.

GOLF   The **Cedar Hill Municipal Golf Course,** 1400 Derby Rd. (✆ **250/ 595-3103**), is 2 miles (3.5km) from downtown; greens fees are C$26 to C$30 (US$17 to US$20). The Bill Robinson–designed **Cordova Bay Golf Course,** 5333 Cordova Bay Rd. (✆ **250/658-4075**), northeast of downtown, features 66 sand traps and some tight fairways. Greens fees are C$45 to C$48 (US$29 to US$31). The **Olympic View Golf Club,** 643 Latoria Rd. (✆ **250/474-3673;**

www.sunnygolf.com/ov/ov.html), is one of the top 35 courses in Canada, with 12 lakes and a pair of waterfalls; greens fees are C$49 to C$55 (US$32 to US$36). The **A-1 Last Minute Golf Hotline** (© 800/684-6344 or 604/878-1833) can arrange short-notice tee times at area courses.

HIKING   Groups of 10 or more can book a naturalist-guided tour of the island's rain forests and seashore with **Coastal Connections Interpretive Nature Hikes** (© 250/480-9560) or **Nature Calls** (© 877/361-HIKE). Tours cost C$60 to C$110 (US$39 to US$72), transport included, and go to Botanical Beach, East Sooke Park, or the Carmanah Valley.

SWIMMING   The **Crystal Pool & Fitness Centre,** 2275 Quadra St. (© 250/380-7946, or 250/380-4636 for schedule), has a lap pool, children's pool, diving pool, sauna, whirlpool, and steam, weight, and aerobics rooms; open daily from 6am to midnight. Admission is C$4.20 (US$2.75) for adults, C$3.15 (US$2.05) for seniors and students, and C$2.10 (US$1.35) for children 6 to 12. **All Fun Recreation Park,** 650 Hordon Rd. (© 250/474-4546 or 250/474-3184), operates a waterslide complex that's open daily from 11am to 7pm in season. Full-day passes are C$16 (US$10) for sliders over age 6. **Beaver Lake,** in Elk and Beaver Lake Regional Park, has lifeguards on duty.

WHALE-WATCHING   **Victoria Marine Adventures,** 950 Wharf (© 250/995-2211), is one of many outfits offering whale-watching tours in both Zodiacs and covered boats. Fares are C$75 (US$49) for adults and C$49 (US$32) for children. March through October, **Pride of Victoria Cruises,** Oak Bay Beach Hotel, 1175 Beach Dr. (© 250/592-3474), offers 3½-hour whale-watching charters on a 45-foot catamaran. Fares are C$79 (US$51) for adults and C$39 ($25) for children.

WINDSURFING & WATERSPORTS   Windsurfers skim along the Inner Harbour and Elk Lake when the breezes are right. Though there are no specific facilities, French Beach, off Sooke Road on the way to Sooke Harbour, is a popular local spot. **Ocean Wind Water Sports Rentals,** 5411 Hamsterly Rd. (© 250/658-8171), rents nearly every form of watersports gear, including parasails.

7 Shopping

Victoria has dozens of specialty shops that appeal to every taste, and because the city is built to such a pedestrian scale, you can wander from place to place seeking out whatever treasure it is you're after.

ANTIQUES   Many of the best stores are in **Antiques Row,** a 3-block stretch on Fort Street between Blanshard and Cook streets. Though farthest from downtown, **Faith Grant's Connoisseur Shop Ltd.,** 1156 Fort St. (© 250/383-0121), is the best.

BOOKS   **Munro's Book Store,** 1108 Government St. (© 250/382-2464), has a mile-high ceiling, wall murals, and more than 35,000 titles.

DEPARTMENT STORES & MALLS   **The Bay** (Hudson's Bay Company), 1701 Douglas St. (© 250/385-1311), sells Hudson's Bay woolen point blankets along with fashions by Tommy Hilfiger and DKNY. The **Victoria Eaton Centre,** between Government and Douglas streets (© 250/382-7141), is a modern mall disguised as a block of heritage buildings.

FASHION   **A Wear,** 1205 Government St. (© 250/382-9327), sells fashionable threads for younger men and women. More classic lines are to be found at

W. & J. Wilson's Clothiers, 1221 Government St. (© **250/383-7177**), Canada's oldest family-run clothing store. **Prescott & Andrews,** 909 Government St. (© **250/953-7788**), is the place to pick up a sweater.

JEWELRY   Ian MacDonald of **MacDonald Jewelry,** 618 View St. (© **250/382-4113**), designs all of his own interesting creations. At the **Jade Tree,** 606 Humboldt St. (© **250/388-4326**), you'll find British Columbia jade crafted into necklaces, bracelets, and other items.

NATIVE ART   All of the coastal tribes are represented at the **Alcheringa Gallery,** 665 Fort St. (© **250/383-8224**). Presentation is museum quality, with prices to match. **Hill's Indian Crafts,** 1008 Government St. (© **250/385-3911**), features exquisite traditional Native art, including masks and carvings, Haida argillite, and silver jewelry.

8 Victoria After Dark

Monday magazine (www.monday.com) has a near-comprehensive listings section. Get schedules and buy tickets from the **Tourism Victoria Visitor Info Centre,** 812 Wharf St. (© **800/663-3883** or 250/382-1131), open daily from 9am to 5pm (until 9pm in summer).

THE PERFORMING ARTS   The **Royal Theatre,** 805 Broughton St. (© **250/361-0820,** or 250/386-6121 for box office; www.rmts.bc.ca), hosts Victoria Symphony concerts, dance recitals, and touring plays. The box office is at the **McPherson Playhouse,** 3 Centennial Sq., at Pandora Avenue and Government Street (© **250/386-6121**), which is also home to the **Pacific Opera Victoria,** 1316B Government St. (© **250/385-0222,** or 250/386-6121 for box office; www.pov.bc.ca), and the **Victoria Operatic Society,** 798 Fairview Rd. (© **250/381-1021**). The Pacific Opera presents productions in October, February, and April; the Victoria Operatic Society stages old-time musicals and other popular fare year-round.

The **Victoria Symphony Orchestra,** 846 Broughton St. (© **250/385-9771;** www.vos.bc.ca), kicks off its season on the first Sunday of August with Symphony Splash, a free concert performed on a barge in the Inner Harbour. Regular performances run October through May.

The **Belfry Theatre,** 1291 Gladstone St. (© **250/385-6815;** www.belfry.bc.ca), is a nationally acclaimed theatrical group that stages four productions October through April and a summer show in August. The **Fringe Festival** (© **888/FRINGE2** or 250/383-2663; www.victoriafringe.com) presents original fare from late August to mid-September.

BARS, PUBS & LOUNGES   The **Harbour Canoe Club,** 450 Swift St. (© **250/361-1940**), is a pleasant spot to hoist a pint after a long day's sightseeing. Overlooking Victoria Harbour on the west side of the Songhees Point Development, **Spinnaker's Brew Pub,** 308 Catherine St. (© **250/386-BREW** or 250/386-2739), has one of the best views and some of the best beer in town. A truly unique experience, the **Bengal Lounge,** in the Empress, 721 Government St. (© **250/384-8111**), is one of the last outposts of the old empire, except the martinis are ice cold and jazz plays in the background (on weekends, it's live). **Rick's Lounge,** in the Ocean Pointe Resort, 45 Songhees Rd. (© **250/360-2999**), is without doubt the best place to watch the sunset.

LIVE-MUSIC CLUBS   The **Lucky Bar,** 517 Yates St. (© **250/382-5825**), is currently the hottest spot in town. This low, cavernous space has a pleasantly grungy feel, like Seattle's Pioneer Square. It features DJs on Wednesdays, rocka-billy on Thursdays, and good bands (and sometimes DJs) on weekends. **Steam-ers,** 570 Yates St. (© **250/381-4340**), is the city's premier blues bar. **Legends,** 919 Douglas St. (© **250/383-7137**), below street level in the Strathcona Hotel, runs the gamut from blues to zydeco.

DANCE CLUBS   The **Ice House,** in the Horizon West Hotel, 1961 Douglas St. (© **250/382-2111**), is the place if house is your thing. Don't let the name of the **Blues House,** 1417 Government St. (© **250/386-1717**), fool you. It's actu-ally an all-DJ dance spot, featuring everything from house to trip funk to retro-1970s nights. The **One Lounge,** 1318 Broad St. (© **250/384-3557**), spins Top 40 and retro tunes for those in their late 20s to early 30s.

GAY & LESBIAN BARS   **Hush,** 1325 Government St. (© **250/385-0566**), the new gay-yet-straight-friendly space, features top touring DJs. **Friends of Dorothy's Cafe,** 615 Johnson St. (© **250/381-2277**), has a slightly outré staff and a fun-loving crowd. **BJ's Lounge,** 642 Johnson St. (© **250/388-0505**), has a full menu and lounge decor.

5

Southern Vancouver Island & the Gulf Islands

Stretching more than 280 miles (450km) from Victoria to the northwest tip of Cape Scott, Vancouver Island is one of the most fascinating destinations in Canada, a mountainous bulwark of deep-green forests, rocky fjords, and wave-battered headlands. For an area so easily accessible by car, the range of wildlife here is surprising: Bald eagles float above the shorelines, seals and sea lions slumber on rocky islets, and porpoises and orca whales cavort in narrow passes between islands.

The British Columbia capital, Victoria, is the ideal place to begin exploring the entire island; see chapter 4 for complete coverage of the city.

Duncan, the "City of Totem Poles" in the Cowichan Valley north of Victoria, reveals another facet of Vancouver Island culture. This lush green valley is the ancestral home of the Cowichan tribe, famed for crafting hand-knit sweaters; it also contains some of the island's best wineries.

Nestled just off the island's east coast lie the Gulf Islands. The fact that they are only reached by a confusing network of ferries just enhances their sense of remoteness and mystery. Part arty, counterculture enclave, part trophy-home exurb, and part old-fashioned farm and orchard territory, the Gulf Islands are full of contradictions and charm. The largest, Salt Spring Island, is a haven for artists who are attracted to its mild climate and pastoral landscapes.

Running down the spine of Vancouver Island is a lofty chain of mountains that functionally divide the island into west and east. In the west, which receives the full brunt of Pacific storms, vast rain forests grow along inaccessible, steep-sided fjords. Paved roads provide access in only a few places, and boat charters, ferries, and floatplanes are the preferred means of transport.

The east side of Vancouver Island, and in particular the area from Nanaimo southward, is home to the vast majority of the island's population of 750,000. The climate here is drier and warmer than on the storm-tossed west coast, and agriculture is a major industry. Tourism is also key to the local economy: The southeast portion of Vancouver Island has the warmest median temperatures in all of Canada, and tourists and retirees flood the area in search of rain-free summer days.

While the Gulf Islands and the southern portions of Vancouver Island were long ago colonized by European settlers, the original First Nations peoples are very much a part of cultural and political life in the area. Historically, the Pacific coast of British Columbia was one of the greatest centers of art and culture in Native America, and this past is beautifully preserved in many museums and in several villages. Modern-day First Nations artists are very active, and nearly every town has galleries and workshops filled with exquisite carvings, paintings, and sculpture.

This chapter covers the southern portion of Vancouver Island, along with the Gulf Islands. For the area from Nanaimo to Courtenay/Comox and including the West Coast Trail and Pacific Rim National Park, see chapter 6, "Central Vancouver Island." In chapter 7, "Northern Vancouver Island," we discuss the portion of the island from the town of Campbell River northward, including Strathcona Provincial Park.

1 Essentials
GETTING THERE

BY PLANE   **Victoria** is the island's major air hub, with jet, commuter-plane, and floatplane service from Vancouver and Seattle. See chapter 4 for details.

Both standard commuter aircraft and floatplanes provide regularly scheduled service to a number of other island communities. Many towns have regular air service from Vancouver International Airport. All of the southern Gulf Islands, as well as many towns, can be reached by scheduled harbor-to-harbor floatplane service, either from Vancouver International's seaplane terminal or from downtown Vancouver's Coal Harbour terminal. In fact, it's easy to arrange a chartered floatplane for almost any destination along coastal Vancouver Island. Since floatplanes don't require airport facilities, even the most remote fishing camp can be as accessible as a major city.

Commercial airline service is provided by **Air Canada** (© 888/247-2262; www.aircanada.com), **North Vancouver Air** (© 800/228-6608 or 604/278-1608; www.northvanair.com), **Pacific Coastal** (© 800/663-2872; www. pacific-coastal.com), and **WestJet** (© 877/952-4638; www.westjet.com).

Commuter seaplane companies that serve Vancouver Island include **Harbour Air Seaplanes** (© 800/665-0212 or 604/688-1277; www.harbour-air.com), **Tofino Air** (formerly Pacific Spirit Air; © 866/486-3247 for Tofino base, 888/436-7776 for Sechelt base, or 800/665-2359 for Gabriola base; www.tofino air.ca), **Air Rainbow** (© 250/287-8371; www.air-rainbow.com), and **Baxter Aviation** (© 800/661-5599, 604/683-6525, or 250/754-1066; www.baxter air.com).

BY FERRY   **BC Ferries** (© 888/BCFERRY in B.C., or 250/386-3431; www. bcferries.bc.ca) operates an extensive year-round network that links Vancouver Island, the Gulf Islands, and the mainland. Major routes include the crossing from Tsawwassen to Swartz Bay and to Nanaimo, and from Horseshoe Bay (northwest of Vancouver) to Nanaimo. In summer, reserve in advance. Sample fares are included in the regional sections that follow. If you're taking a car, you'll find that ticket prices add up quickly. You may want to leave the car on the mainland and travel by bus, taxi, or air.

Washington State Ferries (© 888/808-7977 in Wash., 206/464-6400 in the rest of the U.S., or 250/381-1551 in Canada; www.wsdot.wa.gov/ferries) has daily service from Anacortes, in Washington, to Sidney, on Vancouver Island. One-way fares for a car and driver are around US$41 in high season.

The year-round passenger ferries run by **Victoria Clipper** (© 800/888-2535 or 206/448-5000; www.victoriaclipper.com) depart from Seattle's Pier 69; adult round-trip tickets range from US$60 to US$125.

From Port Angeles, Washington, the year-round (except for a 2-week maintenance break in January) Black Ball Transport's car ferry **MV Coho** (© 360/457-4491 in Port Angeles, or 250/386-2202 in Victoria; www.northolympic. com/coho) offers service to Victoria for US$8 per adult foot passenger, US$30

Vancouver Island

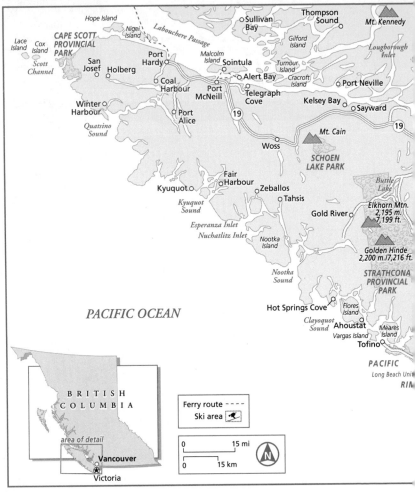

per vehicle. From mid-May to the end of September, foot passengers and bicy-clists can also pay US$25 round-trip to hop on the ***Victoria Express*** (*©* **800/ 633-1589** or 360/452-8088 in the U.S., or 250/361-9144 in Victoria; www. victoriaexpress.com).

In summer only, **Victoria/San Juan Cruises**' daily ***Victoria Star 2*** (*©* **800/ 443-4552;** www.whales.com/dycruise.html) passenger ferry travels between Bellingham and Victoria via the San Juan Islands. Round-trip adult fares range from US$79 to US$89.

BY BUS   One of the easiest ways to get to Vancouver Island destinations is by bus. Conveniently, the bus will start its journey from a city center (like Vancouver), take you directly to the ferry dock and onto the ferry, and then deposit you in another city center (Victoria or Nanaimo). A lot of the hassle of ferry travel is minimized, and the costs are usually lower than other alternatives. (If you're traveling to Vancouver on the VIA Rail system, you'll find bus con-nections simple—the bus and train share the same terminal.)

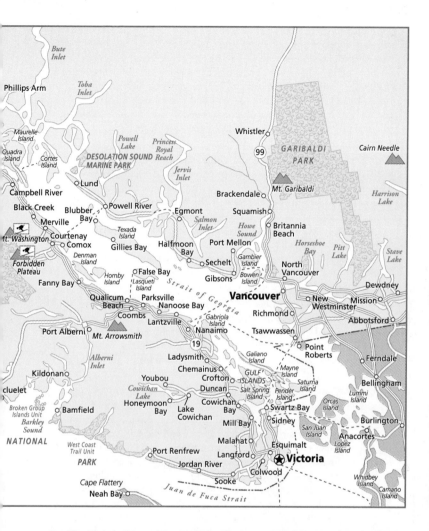

Pacific Coach Lines (℗ **800/661-1725** or 604/662-8074; www.pacific coach.com) offers bus service via BC Ferries from Vancouver to Victoria. The one-way fare is C$28 (US$18) for adults, C$19 (US$12) for seniors, and C$14 (US$9) for children. **Greyhound Canada** (℗ **800/661-8747** or 604/482-8747; www.greyhound.ca) provides eight daily trips between Vancouver and Nanaimo. Fares are C$21 (US$14) one-way.

VISITOR INFORMATION

For general information on Vancouver Island, contact **Tourism Vancouver Island,** Suite 203, 335 Wesley St., Nanaimo (℗ **250/754-3500;** fax 250/ 754-3599; www.islands.bc.ca). Also check out **www.vancouverisland.com.**

GETTING AROUND

While Vancouver Island has an admirable system of public transport, getting to remote sights and destinations is difficult without your own vehicle.

BY FERRY   BC Ferries (© **888/BCFERRY** in B.C., or 250/386-3431; www.bcferries.bc.ca) routes link Vancouver Island ports to many offshore islands, including the southern Gulf Islands of Denman, Gabriola, Galiano, Hornby, Kuper, Mayne, the Penders, Salt Spring, Saturna, and Thetis (see also chapter 6, "Central Vancouver Island"). None of these islands has public transport (although some, like Galiano, have shuttle services), so once there, you'll need to hoof it, hitch it, hire a taxi, or arrange for bike rentals. Most innkeepers will pick you up from the ferry if you've reserved in advance.

BY TRAIN   Another charming way to get around Vancouver Island is on **VIA Rail**'s **E&N Railiner,** also known as the *Malahat* (© **888/VIA-RAIL** or 250/ 383-4324; www.viarail.ca), which makes a daily round-trip run from Victoria to Courtenay in period passenger cars. The *Malahat* passes through some of the most beautiful landscapes on the east coast of Vancouver Island, taking about 4½ hours. Your ticket allows you to get on and off as many times as you'd like: You can stop at Chemainus, Nanaimo, Parksville, or Qualicum Beach and catch the return train back, or take the next day's train north. Prices are very reasonable, especially with 7-day advance purchase. A round-trip between Victoria and Courtenay can cost as little as C$52 (US$34). *Note:* The *Malahat* has no baggage car, and checked-baggage service is not available.

BY BUS   Island Coach Lines (© **800/663-8390** in the U.S., 800/318-0818 in Canada, or 250/388-5248; www.victoriatours.com), run by Laidlaw, operates Vancouver Island's intercity bus service, which runs along the main highway from Victoria to Port Hardy, and from Nanaimo to Tofino. The one-way fare from Victoria to Nanaimo is C$19.25 (US$13), from Nanaimo to Tofino C$33 (US$21), and from Victoria to Port Hardy C$89.50 (US$58).

BY CAR   The southern half of Vancouver Island is well served by paved highways. The trunk road between Victoria and Nanaimo is **Highway 1,** the Trans-Canada. This busy route alternates between four-lane expressway and congested two-lane highway, and requires some patience and vigilance, especially during the summer months. North of Nanaimo, the major road is **Highway 19,** which is now almost all four-lane expressway, a particular improvement being the new 80-mile (128km) **Inland Highway** between Parksville and Campbell River. The older sections of 19, all closer to the island's east coast, are now labeled 19A. North of Campbell River, a long, unimproved section of Highway 19 continues all the way to Port Hardy. The other major paved road system on the island, **Highway 4,** connects Parksville with Port Alberni and on to Ucluelet and Tofino, on the rugged west coast. This road is mostly two-lane, and portions of it are extremely winding and hilly. Access to gasoline and car services is no problem, even in more remote north Vancouver Island.

Rental cars are readily available. Agencies include **Avis** (© **800/272-5871** in Canada, or 800/230-4898 in the U.S.; www.avis.com), **Budget** (© **800/ 268-8900** in Canada, 800/527-0700 in the U.S., or 250/953-5300 in Victoria; https://rent.drivebudget.com), and **National** (© **800/387-4747** or 250/ 386-1213; www.nationalcar.com).

2 The Saanich Peninsula

Sidney is 17 miles (25km) N of Victoria; Swartz Bay is 20 miles (32km) N of Victoria

A long finger of land that extends north from Victoria toward Sidney, the Saanich Peninsula is now largely given over to suburbs of Victoria. Flanked on one side by Saanich Inlet and on the other by the Georgia Strait, the peninsula is dominated by transportation: **Highway 17** is the main vehicle route between Vancouver and Victoria via the Swartz Bay ferries; Washington State Ferries' service to the San Juan Islands and Anacortes travels to and from Sidney; and the Victoria airport is just west of Sidney. The Sidney Harbour area is a pleasant stopover to or from the Swartz Bay ferries.

To get here from Victoria, take Blanchard Street north, which turns into Highway 17. For information, contact the **Saanich Peninsula Visitor Info Centre,** 10382 Patricia Bay Hwy., Sidney (© **250/656-0525**).

Marine Ecology Station ☆ *Kids*   The exhibits in this small, floating-aquarium building are mostly geared toward curious students—touch tanks filled with marine life, as well as microscopes for peering at smaller ocean life. The entire family will enjoy the station's special summer programs, which range from tide-pool exploration to multi-day ecotours and educational camps in the Gulf Islands and on Vancouver Island's west coast; advance registration is required.

Port Sidney Marina, 9835 Seaport Place, Sidney. © 250/655-3711. www.mareco.org. Admission C$4 (US$2.60) adults, C$3 (US$1.95) seniors and children 5–12, C$10 (US$6.50) families. Year-round Sat–Sun and summer Mon–Fri noon–5pm; off-season Mon–Fri 2–5pm.

Butchart Gardens ☆   These internationally acclaimed gardens were born after Robert Butchart exhausted the limestone quarry near his Tod Inlet home. His wife gradually landscaped the deserted eyesore into the resplendent Sunken Garden, opening it for public display in 1904. The 50-acre (20-hectare) gardens now display more than a million plants. Musical entertainment is provided Monday through Saturday evenings June through September; Saturday nights in July and August bring firework displays. A very good lunch, dinner, and afternoon tea are offered in the Dining Room Restaurant. The gift shop sells seeds of some of the plants you'll see.

800 Benvenuto Ave., Brentwood Bay. © 250/652-5256, or 250/652-8222 for dining reservations. Fax 250/652-7751. www.butchartgardens.com. Admission C$19.25 (US$13) adults, C$9.50 (US$6.20) youths 13–17, C$2 (US$1.30) children 5–12. Off-season discounts available. Daily from 9am, Christmas and New Year's Day from 1pm. Take Blanshard St. (Hwy. 17) north toward ferry terminal in Saanich; turn left on Keating Crossroads, which leads directly to the gardens—about 30 min. from downtown Victoria. Bus: 75.

Victoria Butterfly Gardens ☆ *Kids*   Hundreds of exotic species, from the tiny Central American Julia to the Southeast Asian Giant Atlas Moth (with a wingspan approaching 1 ft.), flutter freely through this lush tropical greenhouse. Visitors are provided with an identification chart and set free to roam around. Naturalists are on hand to explain butterfly biology.

1461 Benvenuto Ave., Brentwood Bay. © 877-722-0272 or 250/652-3822. www.butterflygardens.com. Admission C$8 (US$5) adults, C$7 (US$4.55) students and seniors, C$4.50 (US$2.95) children 5–12, 10% discount for families. May 12–Sept daily 9:30am–5pm; Mar–May 11 and Oct daily 9:30am–4:30pm. Closed Nov–Feb. Bus: 75.

3 The Gulf Islands ☆☆

The Gulf Islands are a collection of several dozen mountainous islands that sprawl across the Strait of Georgia between the British Columbia mainland and Vancouver Island. While only a handful of the islands are served by regularly scheduled ferries, this entire area is popular with boaters, cyclists, kayakers, and sailboat enthusiasts. Lying in the rain shadow of Washington State's Olympic Mountains, the Gulf Islands have the most temperate climate in all of Canada, without the heavy rainfall that characterizes much of coastal British Columbia. In fact, the climate here is officially listed as semi-Mediterranean!

The Gulf Islands

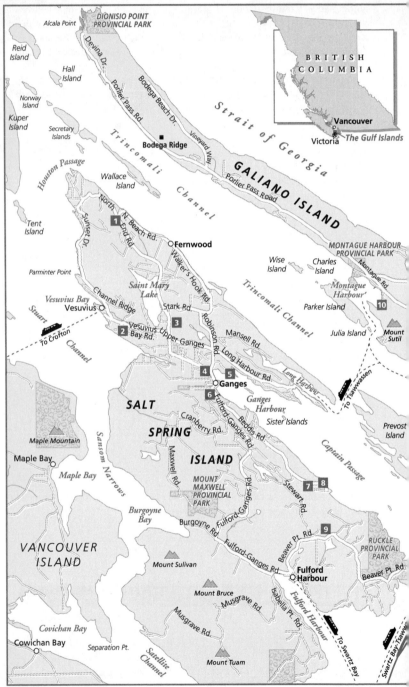

Alcala Point

DIONISIO POINT
PROVINCIAL PARK

Reid
Island

Hall
Island

Norway
Island

Kuper
Island

Secretary
Islands

Devina Dr.

Porlier Pass Rd.

Bodega Beach Dr.

Vineyard Way

Strait of Georgia

BRITISH
COLUMBIA

Vancouver

Victoria

The Gulf Islands

Bodega Ridge

Trincomali Channel

GALIANO ISLAND

Porlier Pass Road

Houston Passage

Wallace
Island

Tent
Island

1

North N. Beach Rd.
End Rd.

Sunset Dr.

Fernwood

Walker's Hook Rd.

Wise
Island

Charles
Island

MONTAGUE HARBOUR
PROVINCIAL PARK

Montague Rd.

Parminter Point

Saint Mary
Lake

Channel Ridge

Stark Rd.

Montague
Harbour

10

Trincomali Channel

Parker Island

Vesuvius Bay

Vesuvius

2 Vesuvius
Bay Rd.

3

Upper Ganges

Robinson Rd.

Mansell Rd.

Julia Island

Mount
Sutil

To Crofton

Stuart Channel

4

5

Long Harbour Rd.

Long Harbour

Ganges

To Tsawwassen

Prevost
Island

6

Ganges
Harbour

Sister Islands

SALT

Cranberry Rd.

Fulford-Ganges Rd.

Beddis Rd.

Captain Passage

SPRING

Maple Mountain

Sansom Narrows

ISLAND

Maxwell Rd.

MOUNT
MAXWELL
PROVINCIAL
PARK

Fulford-Ganges Rd.

Stewart Rd.

7 **8**

Maple Bay

Maple Bay

Burgoyne
Bay

Burgoyne Rd.

Fulford-Ganges Rd.

Beaver Pt. Rd.

9

RUCKLE
PROVINCIAL
PARK

VANCOUVER
ISLAND

Mount Sulivan

Mount Bruce

Musgrave Rd.

Isabella Pt. Rd.

Fulford
Harbour

Beaver Pt. Rd.

Covichan Bay

Musgrave Rd.

Fulford Harbour

Cowichan Bay

Separation Pt.

Satellite Channel

Mount Tuam

To Swartz Bay

To Swartz Bay/Tsawwassen

90

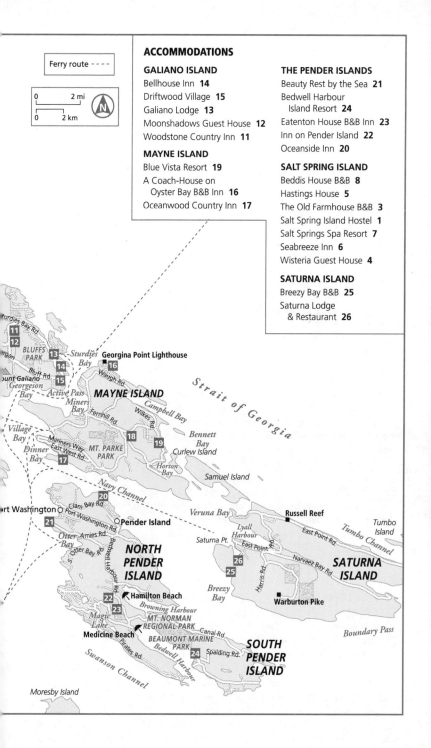

Ferry route - - - -

0   2 mi
0   2 km

ACCOMMODATIONS

GALIANO ISLAND
Bellhouse Inn **14**
Driftwood Village **15**
Galiano Lodge **13**
Moonshadows Guest House **12**
Woodstone Country Inn **11**

MAYNE ISLAND
Blue Vista Resort **19**
A Coach-House on
    Oyster Bay B&B Inn **16**
Oceanwood Country Inn **17**

THE PENDER ISLANDS
Beauty Rest by the Sea **21**
Bedwell Harbour
    Island Resort **24**
Eatenton House B&B Inn **23**
Inn on Pender Island **22**
Oceanside Inn **20**

SALT SPRING ISLAND
Beddis House B&B **8**
Hastings House **5**
The Old Farmhouse B&B **3**
Salt Spring Island Hostel **1**
Salt Springs Spa Resort **7**
Seabreeze Inn **6**
Wisteria Guest House **4**

SATURNA ISLAND
Breezy Bay B&B **25**
Saturna Lodge
    & Restaurant **26**

Sturdies Bay Rd
11
12
organ
BLUFFS
PARK
13 Sturdies Georgina Point Lighthouse
Bay ■ **16**
14 Bluff Rd
Weugh Rd
unt Galiano
15
Georgeson
Bay ~ Active Pass
MAYNE ISLAND
Miners Campbell Bay
Bay Fernhill Rd. Wilkes Rd.
Village
Bay
Mariners Way **18** Bennett
Dinner East West Rd. Bay **19**
Bay MT. PARKE Curlew Island
17 PARK
Horton
Bay
Samuel Island

Strait of Georgia

Navy Channel
20
rt Washington ○ Clam Bay Rd. Veruna Bay Russell Reef Tumbo
21 ○ Port Washington Rd. ○ Pender Island Lyall East Point Rd. Island
Otter Amies Rd. Harbour Tumbo Channel
Bay Otter Bay Rd. Saturna Pt. East Point
NORTH Bedwell Harbour Rd.
PENDER **26** Narvaez Bay Rd. **SATURNA**
ISLAND **25** **ISLAND**

22 ↖ Hamilton Beach *Breezy*
Magic **23** *Browning Harbour* Bay Harris Rd.
Lake MT. NORMAN ■ Warburton Pike
Medicine Beach REGIONAL PARK Canal Rd.
BEAUMONT MARINE Boundary Pass
Pirates Rd. PARK **24** Spalding Rd. **SOUTH**
Bedwell Harbour **PENDER**
Swanson Channel **ISLAND**

Moresby Island

91

Tips   **A Note for Families**

If you're traveling with the kids, you'll find the Gulf Islands a fairly inhos-
pitable place to secure accommodations. Nearly all B&Bs have listed minimum ages for guests (usually 12 or 16), and there are only a few standard
motels or cottage resorts where families are welcome. Note that for all
accommodations, it's mandatory to make reservations well in advance, as
the ferry system doesn't make it exactly easy to just drive on to the next
town to find a place to stay.

The Gulf Islands are the northern extension of Washington's San Juan Islands,
and they share those islands' farming and seafaring past. Agriculture, especially
sheep raising, is still a major industry. However, the past few decades have seen
radical changes in traditional island life: The sheer beauty of the land- and
seascapes, the balmy climate, and relaxed lifestyle have brought in a major influx
of new residents. These islands were a major destination for Vietnam War–era
draft evaders, many of whom set up homes, farms, and businesses here. The
islands quickly developed a reputation as a countercultural hippie enclave, a reputation they still maintain. Even as one generation's radicals gray and become
the islands' business class, younger generations of free spirits have come to grow
organic vegetables, explore an artistic urge, and hang out in the coffee shops.

The 1990s witnessed a parallel but different land-rush. High-tech moguls,
Hollywood stars, and other wealthy refugees from urban centers have been moving to the islands in droves. The quality of facilities has shot up: The islands now
boast fine restaurants, elegant inns, and a multitude of galleries. In fact, the Gulf
Islands are noted across Canada as a major center for crafts and arts.

The population influx is having some unexpected consequences. Groundwater
is a precious commodity on these arid islands, and some inns will ask guests to
monitor their water use. Adding to the problem is that saltwater aquifers underlie
parts of the islands: A well of corrosive saltwater doesn't do anyone much good.

Despite the one-direction migration, the Gulf Islands remain a charming destination. The islands are still underdeveloped, and some of the best restaurants
and lodgings are tucked away in forests down long roads. There's little in the way
of organized activities: no waterslides, theme parks, or major resorts; just incredible scenery, great biking and kayaking, lovely inns, and fine dining.

ESSENTIALS

GETTING THERE   By Ferry   BC Ferries (*©* **888/BCFERRY** in B.C., or
250/386-3431; www.bcferries.bc.ca) operates four different runs to the southern Gulf Islands (five if you count Horseshoe Bay to Bowen Island), from
Tsawwassen on the British Columbia mainland, and from Swartz Bay, Crofton,
and Nanaimo on Vancouver Island. The system was designed primarily to get
commuters to their jobs on the mainland or in Victoria. Getting exactly where
you want to be, exactly when you want to be there, is anything but straightforward (and not always possible). Be aware that the ferries are not particularly
large; to insure that you make the one you want, arrive at least 15 minutes early
(30 min. on summer weekends). You can make reservations on the routes from
Tsawwassen, but not on the other runs.

Ticket pricing is confusing. There are separate fares for drivers, passengers,
and vehicles, plus fees for bikes, kayaks, and canoes on most runs. Tickets from

Vancouver Island (Chemainus, Crofton, Nanaimo, or Swartz Bay) are calculated as return fares. That is, you buy a ticket when you leave from one of these ports, but if you return to the same port, you don't have to buy an additional ticket. However, all fares via Tsawwassen are one-way: You pay going and coming. To make it more puzzling, outward-bound fares from Tsawwassen are more expensive than the same journey to the mainland. Sample peak-season fares: a car and two passengers from Swartz Bay to Salt Spring Island, C$34 (US$22); a single foot passenger, C$6.25 (US$4).

The ferry schedule is also confusing. Pick up a copy and give yourself plenty of time to study it. You can get to any of the major southern Gulf Islands (that is, Gabriola, Galiano, Mayne, the Penders, Salt Spring, and Saturna) from Swartz Bay or Tsawwassen.

By Plane   A number of commuter airlines offer regular floatplane service from either Vancouver Harbour or Vancouver International Airport. One-way tickets to the islands usually cost C$60 to C$70 (US$39 to US$46), not a bad fare when you consider the time and hassle of the ferries. However, floatplanes are small and seats sell out quickly, so reserve ahead of time. Call **Harbour Air Seaplanes** (© 800/665-0212 or 604/688-1277; www.harbour-air.com), **Seair Seaplanes** (© 800/447-3247 or 604/273-8900; www.seairseaplanes.com), or **Tofino Air** (formerly Pacific Spirit Air; © 800/665-2359 for Gabriola base; www.tofinoair.ca).

VISITOR INFORMATION   For general information on the Gulf Islands, contact **Tourism Vancouver Island,** Suite 203, 335 Wesley St., Nanaimo (© **250/754-3500;** fax 250/754-3599; www.islands.bc.ca). A good comprehensive website is **www.gulfislands.com**. A free booking agency, **Canadian Gulf Islands Reservation Service** (© **866/539-3089** or 250/539-3089), can find you a farm vacation, cozy B&B, or cottage on the beach.

GETTING AROUND   Most innkeepers will pick up guests at the ferry or floatplane terminals, if given sufficient notice. There's taxi service on most islands.

By Bicycle   Winding country roads and bucolic landscapes make the Gulf Islands a favorite destination for cyclists. Although the islands' road networks aren't exactly large, it can be great fun to bike the back roads, jump a ferry, and peddle to an outlying inn for lunch. Note that the narrow roads really fill up in summer, making them less than idyllic for cycling. Several parks have designated mountain-bike trails. Bikes can be taken onboard BC Ferries for a small surcharge. Rentals are available on most islands.

By Kayak   The Gulf Islands' lengthy and rugged coastline, plus their proximity to other more remote island groups, make them a good base for kayaking trips. Most of the islands have kayak outfitters; however, not all of them will offer rentals separate from guided tours. If you're an experienced kayaker and just want to rent a kayak, call ahead to inquire. Kayaks and canoes can be taken on the ferries for a small fee.

SALT SPRING ISLAND

The largest of the Gulf Islands, Salt Spring is—to the outside world—a bucolic getaway filled with artists, sheep pastures, and cozy B&Bs. While this image is mostly true, Salt Spring is also a busy cultural crossroads: Movie stars, retirees, high-tech telecommuters, and hippie farmers all rub shoulders here. The hilly terrain and deep forests afford equal privacy for all lifestyles, and that's the way the residents like it.

Salt Spring is divided geographically into three distinct lobes. In fact, the island looks as if it were once three separate islands that somehow got pushed together. Most of the population lives in the area around Ganges and Vesuvius; the rugged lower third of the island is the least developed. Although Salt Spring's configuration makes for a lot of coastline, there are very few beaches; instead, the island's underlying granite forms headlands that drop straight into the sea.

GETTING THERE   Salt Spring Island is served by three different routes on **BC Ferries** (© **888/BCFERRY** in B.C., or 250/381-5452; www.bcferries.bc.ca). From Tsawwassen on the mainland, ferries depart two to four times a day for Long Harbour, on the island's northeast coast. If you're on Vancouver Island, you have a choice of the Crofton–Vesuvius Bay run or the crossing from Swartz Bay to Fulford Harbour, as well as a single Sunday or holiday Monday run from Swartz Bay to Long Harbour via Pender.

Regular floatplane service operates from Vancouver International Airport and Vancouver's Inner Harbour seaplane terminal to Ganges Harbour. See "Essentials," above, for contact information.

VISITOR INFORMATION   The **Salt Spring Chamber of Commerce** operates a visitor center at 121 Lower Ganges Rd. (© **250/537-5252;** www.salt springisland.bc.ca).

GETTING AROUND   If you don't have a car, you will need to rely on a bike or call **Silver Shadow Taxi** (© **250/537-3030**). **Gulf Islands Water Taxi** (© **250/537-2510;** www.saltspring.com/watertaxi) offers speedboat service between Salt Spring, Mayne, and Galiano islands on Wednesdays and Saturdays in summer (June 9–Sept 1), plus Pender and Saturna islands on all school days during the rest of the year. The taxi leaves from Government Dock in Ganges Harbour. Fares are C$10 (US$6.50) from any one point to another. Reservations are recommended; bikes are transported free of charge.

EXPLORING THE ISLAND

With a year-round population of 10,000 residents, Salt Spring is served by three ferries, making it by far the easiest of the Gulf Islands to visit. Not coincidentally, Salt Spring also has the most facilities for visitors. The center of island life is **Ganges,** a little village with gas stations, grocery stores, and banks, all overlooking a busy pleasure-boat harbor. You can easily spend from an hour to most of a day poking around the art galleries, boutiques, and coffee shops here.

In fact, many people visit Salt Spring expressly to see the galleries and studios of local artists and craftspeople: The island is famed across Canada as an artists' colony. Stop by the visitor center for the **Studio Tour Map,** which locates 35 artists—glass blowers, painters, ceramists, weavers, carvers, sculptors—around the island.

Pegasus Gallery, Mouat's Mall, 1-104 Fulford-Ganges Rd. (© **800/ 668-6131** or 250/537-2421; www.pegasusgalleryca.com), displays a mix of contemporary Canadian painting and sculpture as well as Native carving and basketry. The **Vortex Gallery,** 3101 Grace Point Sq., 115 Fulford-Ganges Rd. (© **250/537-4749;** www.vortexgallery.com), features contemporary regional artists, with an emphasis on innovative styles and techniques. The **Stone Walrus Gallery** (© **800/478-6448;** www.stonewalrus.com) has an amazing collection of animal-inspired artwork—paintings, carvings, and ceramics—from around the world. On Fridays from 5 to 9pm, 10 Ganges galleries remain open late for the **Gallery Walk.** From early July to mid-September, **ArtCraft**

> ⌒ **Moments** **The Mother of All Saturday Markets**
>
> Not to be missed is **Market in the Park** ⌖ (www.saltspringmarket.com),
> held April through October, Saturdays from 8am to 4pm, on the water-
> front's Centennial Park. The market brings together a lively mix of crafts-
> people, farmers, musicians, and bakers. It's great fun, and a good chance
> to shop for local products. As you might guess, the people-watching pos-
> sibilities are matchless.

(② **250/537-0899;** www.artcraftgallery.ca) features the work of more than 250
local artists at Mahon Hall, just north of Ganges at Park Drive and Lower
Ganges Road.

BIKING   Although Salt Spring has the best network of paved roads, it's not
the best island for cycling. With ferries unleashing cars throughout the day,
there's a lot more traffic here than you'd think. However, these same ferries—
plus the **Gulf Islands Water Taxi** (see "Getting Around," above)—make Salt
Spring a convenient base for cyclists. For rentals, contact **Salt Spring Kayaking,**
2923 Fulford-Ganges Rd., on the Fulford Harbour wharf (② **250/537-4664;**
www.saltspring.com/sskayak).

BOATING   **Island Escapades,** 118 Natalie Lane (② **888/529-2567** or 250/
537-2537; www.islandescapades.com), offers introductory lake trips starting at
C$35 (US$23), with guided 3-hour ocean tours at C$50 (US$33). **Sea Otter
Kayaking,** 149 Lower Ganges Rd. (② **877/537-5678;** www.saltspring.com/
kayaking), rents kayaks and canoes, starting at C$20 (US$13) an hour. Guided
tours begin at C$35 (US$23) for 2 hours. **Saltspring Kayaking,** 2923 Fulford-
Ganges Rd. (② **250/537-4664;** www.saltspring.com/sskayak), also has guided
tours from C$35 (US$23); its rentals start at C$12 (US$8) per hour. If sailing
is more your style, check out **Welcome Aboard Sailing Charters,** 813 Beaver
Pt. Rd. (② **250/653-4311;** http://saltspring.gulfislands.com/sailing), which
charges C$130 to C$150 (US$85 to US$98) for 3 hours.

HIKING   **Ruckle Provincial Park** (www.elp.gov.bc.ca/bcparks/explore/
parkpgs/ruckle.htm), on the southeast corner of the island, is the largest park in
the Gulf Islands; its entrance is 6 miles (10km) from the Fulford Harbour ferry
terminal on Beaver Point Road. Five miles (8km) of trails wind through forests
to rocky headlands where the tide-pool exploring is excellent; some trails are designated for mountain bikes. Ruckle Park is also the only public campground on
Salt Spring.

WHERE TO STAY

Ruckle Provincial Park, off Beaver Point Road (② **250/391-2300;** www.
elp.gov.bc.ca/bcparks/explore/parkpgs/ruckle.htm), has 70 walk-in sites and
eight reserveable sites for C$12 (US$8). **Salt Spring Island Hostel,** 640
Cusheon Lake Rd. (② **250/537-4149;** www.beacom.com/ssihostel), offers 23
dorm beds, plus a teepee and treehouse. Rates are C$19.50 (US$13) per person
in the dorm, C$15.50 (US$10) per person in a teepee, and C$60 to C$70
(US$39 to US$46) double in a treehouse. It's open March through October.

Beddis House B&B   Perched above a strand of pebble beach, white-clapboard
Beddis House was built as a farmhouse in 1900. The still-producing apple and
plum orchards also date from that period. The owners have built a new beachfront

guesthouse in the style of the original farmhouse. Each bedroom has wonderful views, a patio or balcony, a wood-burning stove, a claw-foot tub, a private entrance, and access to decks and beautifully landscaped gardens.

131 Miles Ave., Salt Spring Island, BC V8K 2E1. (C) 250/537-1028. Fax 250/537-9888. www.saltspring. com/beddishouse. 3 units. Mid-Oct to Apr C$125–C$170 (US$81–US$111) double. May to mid-Oct C$160–C$190 (US$104–US$124) double. Rates include breakfast and afternoon tea. 2-night minimum stay on holiday weekends. Midweek discounts during off-season. MC, V. Closed Dec 15–Feb 1. Children must be 16 or older. **Amenities:** Laundry service. *In room:* Hair dryer, no phone.

Hastings House 🐾🐾 This charming inn is just east of Ganges, in a forested valley that drops directly onto Ganges Harbour. The spot was once the site of a Hudson's Bay Company trading post, and then a late-19th-century farm. In the 1930s, an English couple built an exact replica of a 16th-century Sussex estate, now known as the Manor House. Almost all of the original structures have been converted into beautifully furnished accommodations. The Manor House now serves as the restaurant and library, with two guest suites on the second floor. The farmhouse contains two two-story suites, and the old trading post is now a cottage suite. Architecturally most ingenious are the five suites in the old barn, which offer all of the luxuries you'd expect in a modern five-star hotel. The owners have recently added the three-bedroom Churchill cottage, with excellent views of the grounds and harbor. All units are outfitted with antiques and fireplaces; most have deep soaker tubs.

While the rooms are certainly full of character, what really sets Hastings House apart is its incredible 25-acre (10-hectare) setting. Cheviot ewes trim the meadow grass, the gardens provide vegetables for the excellent restaurant (see "Where to Dine," below), and the old orchard bears sour cherries, apples, and pears. Idyllic only begins to describe this idealized English manor, a member of the exclusive Relais & Châteaux network. Reserve 6 months in advance for summer visits.

160 Upper Ganges Rd., Salt Spring Island, BC V8K 2S2. (C) 800/661-9255 or 250/537-2362. Fax 250/ 537-5333. www.hastingshouse.com. 17 units. Mid-Mar to mid-June and mid-Oct to mid-Nov C$320 (US$208) double, C$385–C$540 (US$250–US$351) suite. Mid-June to mid-Oct C$420 (US$273) double, C$485–C$640 (US$315–US$416) suite. Extra person C$80 (US$52) per night. Rates include full breakfast and tea. Weekly cottage rentals available. AE, MC, V. Closed mid-Nov to Feb. Children must be 16 or older. **Amenities:** Two restaurants; golf course nearby; tennis courts nearby; free bikes; in-room massage; laundry service; same-day dry cleaning. *In room:* Dataport, minibar, hair dryer, iron.

The Old Farmhouse B&B 🐾 One of the best-loved accommodations in the Gulf Islands, the Old Farmhouse combines top-quality lodgings, great food, and two of the friendliest innkeepers you'll ever meet. This Victorian-era homestead was built in 1894 amid 3 acres (1.2 hectares) of meadows and orchards. The bedrooms are in a new, stylistically harmonious guesthouse adjoining the original farmhouse. Each room has a balcony or patio; the decor incorporates just the right country touches—floral wallpaper, wainscoted walls—without lapsing into Laura Ashley excess. The extensive meadows are perfect for lolling with a book or playing a game of croquet. However, the real heart and soul of the place are its proprietors, Karl and Gerti. Previously a chef, Gerti whips out fresh-baked croissants and sticky currant buns as a precursor to the breakfast main course, which might be an unusual fruit omelet or an herb soufflé. *Note:* Smoking is not permitted.

1077 N. End Rd., Salt Spring Island, BC V8K 1L9. (C) 250/537-4113. Fax 250/537-4969. www.bbcanada. com/oldfarmhouse. 5 units. C$170 (US$111) double. Rates include full breakfast. V. Closed Nov–Mar. Children must be 10 or older. **Amenities:** Golf course nearby; lit tennis court; watersports equipment rental; bike rental. *In room:* Hair dryer, no phone.

Salt Springs Spa Resort   Salt Spring's notorious saltwater aquifers are put to good use at this oceanside day spa and chalet on the north end of the island. The center offers a variety of facials, mineral baths utilizing the spa's salt spring water, massage, and aromatherapy. Even if you're not into the spa scene, Salt Springs is worth considering for its new knotty-pine chalets, which face the busy waters of Trincomali Channel and overlook Wallace Island. Each rustic-looking unit has a fireplace, porch, and two tubs: one a therapeutic tub with jetted mineral water, the other a soaker tub. *Note:* Smoking is not permitted.

1460 N. Beach Rd., Salt Spring Island, BC V8K 1J4. © 800/665-0039 or 250/537-4111. Fax 250/537-2939. www.saltspringresort.com. 13 chalets. Mid-June to mid-Sept C$199–C$279 (US$129–US$181) double. Mid-Sept to Oct, Mar to mid-June, and Dec 21–31 C$119–C$239 (US$77–US$155). Nov–Feb except winter holidays C$89–C$179 (US$58–US$116). Extra person C$35 (US$23) per night. 2-night minimum stay in summer, and multiple-night reservations only. Packages available. AE, MC, V. Free parking. Children must be 16 or older. **Amenities:** Golf course nearby; spa; free rowboats and bikes; game room; massage; coin-op laundry. *In room:* Kitchen, fridge, coffeemaker, hair dryer, no phone.

Seabreeze Inn *(Finds) (Kids)*   An alternative to Salt Spring's expensive B&Bs, the Seabreeze is a well-maintained motel just south of Ganges. All rooms are clean and nicely furnished; some have electric fireplaces. Kitchen units are available. Guests can use a large deck with grapevine-covered arbors, picnic tables, and a barbecue.

101 Bittancourt Rd., Salt Spring Island, BC V8K 2K2. © 800/434-4112 or 250/537-4145. Fax 250/537-4323. www.seabreezeinns.com. 29 units. May–Sept C$89–C$179 (US$58–US$116) double; Oct C$79–C$135 (US$51–US$88) double; Nov–Feb C$49–C$99 (US$32–US$64). Extra person C$25 (US$16). 2-night minimum stay on weekends, 3-night minimum stay on holidays. Rates include breakfast. Senior discounts and weekly rates available. Package tours by moped available. Dogs accepted by approval; add C$25 (US$16) per day. AE, DC, DISC, MC, V. **Amenities:** Outdoor pool; golf course nearby; Jacuzzi; sauna; scooter rental; concierge; tour/activities desk; in-room massage; babysitting; coin-op laundry; same-day dry cleaning. *In room:* TV, dataport, coffeemaker, hair dryer, iron.

Wisteria Guest House   This rambling inn, tucked off a side street in Ganges, was once a nursing home. It now offers spacious bedrooms and a cottage at some of the most moderate prices on Salt Spring. The institutional aspect of the building has largely disappeared behind the pleasant furnishings and handsome gardens. One room is wheelchair accessible. *Note:* No smoking is permitted.

268 Park Dr., Salt Spring Island, BC V8K 2S1. © 250/537-5899. www.pixsell.bc.ca/bb/1189.htm. 7 units (1 with private bathroom). C$60–C$90 (US$39–US$59) double. Rates include full breakfast. MC, V. Open in off-season for groups of 4 or more, by reservation only. Closed Oct 15–Mar 15. Children must be 10 or older. **Amenities:** Common room with TV and fireplace; golf course nearby. *In room:* No phone.

WHERE TO DINE

Bouzouki Greek Cafe GREEK   This little cafe looks institutional—metal chairs and laminate tables—but the views over the harbor are lovely, and in summer, there's seating on the waterfront patio. The classic Greek food, ranging from moussaka to lamb kleftiko, is well prepared.

115–2104 Fulford-Ganges Rd., Grace Point Sq., Ganges. © 250/537-4181. Reservations recommended on weekends. Main courses C$8–C$18 (US$5–US$12). MC, V. Daily 9am–9pm. Closed Dec to mid-Feb.

Hastings House *(★★)* PACIFIC NORTHWEST   Easily the most elegant culinary experience on the island, the dining room at Hastings House combines old-world sophistication with the freshest of ingredients. Menus incorporate local produce and fish; many of the herbs and vegetables are grown on the grounds. The rose-covered Manor House is now the inn's restaurant and lounge area. The evening begins with cocktails served by the fireplace. The meal includes an appetizer (perhaps ahi sashimi with black sesame seeds), an excellent soup, a small seafood course (such as gingered scallops with citrus cream), and a choice of four main dishes: Salt Spring lamb is nearly always featured, as is local salmon or other seasonal fish.

Dinner at the Hastings House is for many guests a special occasion. However, if the experience is too formal for your taste, request seating in The Snug, a pleasant room tucked below the main dining room. If you're an aspiring chef, you can also reserve a special table in the kitchen, where you can watch the cooks perform their magic.

160 Upper Ganges Rd. (℧ 250/537-2362. www.hastingshouse.com. Reservations required. Jacket required for men in the formal dining room. Prix-fixe five-course dinner C$85 (US$55). AE, MC, V. Summer (mid-June to mid-Oct) seating at 7:30pm, spring and fall (mid-Mar to mid-June and mid-Oct to mid-Nov) at 7pm. Closed mid-Nov to mid-Mar.

House Piccolo *CONTINENTAL* Located in a heritage home in Ganges, House Piccolo offers excellent food and a good wine list in moderately formal surroundings. The Finnish origins of the chef are reflected in the northern European accents on the unusual menu, particularly the fish specials that feature the best of the local catch. You might see sole in sorrel sauce, or roasted venison with rowan- and juniper-berry-scented demiglace. The dessert menu lists such inspirations as fresh crepes topped with homemade ice cream and lingonberry compote with Finlandia vodka.

108 Hereford Ave., Ganges. (℧ 250/537-1844. Reservations required. Main courses C$18–C$29 (US$12–US$19). AE, DC, MC, V. Daily 5–9pm.

Moby's Marine Pub PUB This airy pub offers the island's best entertainment and is the best spot for a burger and a pint of microbrewed beer. Located just east of Ganges, the dining room overlooks the harbor; in summer, a lively cocktail scene develops on the deck. The menu offers the usual pub grub with twists—lamb burger with chutney, seafood fajitas. Live bands perform on weekends and various weekdays, and Sunday Dinner Jazz is a tradition.

124 Upper Ganges Rd. (℧ 800/334-6629 or 250/537-5559. www.mobyspub.com. Reservations not accepted. Main courses C$8–C$15 (US$5–US$10). MC, V. Mon–Thurs 10am–midnight; Fri–Sat 11am–1am; Sun 10am–midnight. Closed Christmas and Boxing Day.

GALIANO ISLAND

Galiano is a long string bean of an island stretching along the Gulf Islands' eastern flank. On the map, Galiano looks like an attenuated sand spit; it is in fact quite mountainous, with rocky, cliff-faced shorelines and dense forests.

Galiano is the closest Gulf Island to Vancouver, and many of the properties here are the second homes of the city's elite. The rural yet genteel feel of the island is perfect for a romantic getaway or a relaxing break from the hassles of urban life. However, don't come to Galiano looking for high-octane nightlife or boutique shopping. There isn't much of a town on the island, just a few shops and galleries at Sturdies Bay. There are no banks or ATMs, either, though you will find a couple of stores, a pub, a gas station, and—most important—a few unique eateries and many good inns.

GETTING THERE **BC Ferries** serves Sturdies Bay from both Tsawwassen and Swartz Bay. Departures are limited to two per day from Swartz Bay and four from Tsawwassen. Floatplanes serve Galiano Island from the docks at Montague Harbour. **Harbour Air Seaplanes** and **Seair Seaplanes** are your best options here. For contact information, see "Essentials," earlier in this chapter.

VISITOR INFORMATION Contact **Galiano Island Tourist/Visitor Info,** 2590 Sturdies Bay Rd. (℧ 250/539-2233; www.galianoisland.com).

GETTING AROUND   For taxi or bus service, call **Galiano Island Shuttle** (© **250/539-0202**).

EXPLORING THE ISLAND

Galiano is perhaps the most physically striking of the Gulf Islands, particularly the mountainous southern shores. Mount Sutil, Mount Galiano, and the exposed cliffs above Georgeson Bay (simply called the Bluffs) rise above sheep-filled meadows, shadowy forests, and fern-lined ravines. **Active Pass,** the narrow strait that separates Galiano from Mayne Island, is another scenic high spot: All of the pleasure-boat and ferry traffic between Vancouver and Victoria negotiates this turbulent, cliff-lined passage. Watch the bustle of the boats and ferries from **Bellhouse Provincial Park,** a picnicking area at the end of Jack Road, or head to **Montague Harbour Provincial Park,** a beautiful preserve of beach and forest. The new **Dionisio Point Provincial Park,** on the northernmost end of the island, overlooks Porlier Pass, between Galiano and Gabriola. It's accessible only by boat, making it ideal if you want a natural experience without cars and campers around. To get here, use **Dionisio Point Park Water Taxi** (© **250/ 539-3109**), which leaves from Spanish Hills Wharf.

Like Salt Spring Island, Galiano is also a center for artists and craftspeople. **Galiano Art Gallery,** in the Galiano Inn at Sturdies Bay (© **250/539-3539**), displays the work of many Gulf Island painters and sculptors. Also check out the crafts at **Ixchel,** with locations at both Montague Marina (© **250/539-9819;** open mid-Apr to mid-Oct), and 61 Georgeson Bay Rd. (© **250/539-3038;** open Fri–Sun).

BIKING   The farther north you go on Galiano, the more remote the island becomes, making this a favorite of cyclists. While you won't have to worry too much about traffic on the 19-mile-long (30km) paved road that runs up the island's west side, there are enough steep ascents to keep your attention focused. Mountain bikers can follow unmaintained logging roads that skirt the eastern shores. Contact **Galiano Bicycle Rental,** 36 Burrill Rd. (© **250/539-9906**), for rentals.

HIKING   Several short hikes lead to Active Pass overlooks, including the trail to the top of 1,082-foot (330m) Mount Galiano and the cliff-edge path in Bluffs Park. Bodega Ridge is a park about two-thirds of the way up the island, with old-growth forest, wildflowers, and views of the distant Olympic and Cascade mountain ranges.

KAYAKING & BOATING   Home to otters, seals, and bald eagles, the gentle waters of Montague Harbour are a perfect kayaking destination. **Galiano Island Sea Kayaking** (© **888/539-2930** or 250/539-2930; www.galianoislandsea kayak.com) offers guided trips; a 2-hour wildlife-viewing paddle is C$25 (US$16). The 4-hour catamaran cruise sails to a remote island, where your skipper prepares a gourmet meal. The cost is C$39 (US$25) for adults. If you want to really get away, consider one of the multi-day kayaking/camping trips with **Gulf Island Kayaking** (© **250/539-2442;** www.seakayak.bc.ca/tour). Both of the above also offer kayak rentals.

WHERE TO STAY

The only campground is at **Montague Harbour Provincial Marine Park** (© **250/539-2115** for reservations, or 250/391-2300 for information; www. env.gov.bc.ca/bcparks/explore/parkpgs/montague.htm), with 40 sites (15 walk-in and 25 drive-in, a portion of each reserveable) for C$15 (US$10). It offers beach access, but no showers or flush toilets.

Bellhouse Inn ☞ If you're looking for historic charm and a scenic location, the Bellhouse Inn is hard to beat. The 1890 farmhouse sits in a grassy meadow above a private beach. The views of Mayne Island across Active Pass are stunning, and orcas sometimes frolic right in front of you. The 6 acres (2.4 hectares) of grounds retain the feel of the old farm, with fruit trees lining the property and sheep grazing in the fields. Each inn bedroom has a private balcony, and one has a Jacuzzi. The lounge, filled with vintage furniture and period art, is a great spot to curl up with a book. The proprietor also sails a 43-foot boat during the summer months, and for a fee you can take a trip out into the pass.

Bellhouse also offers two modern "cabins." These motel-like units don't share the charm of the original inn, but they do sleep up to six, offer kitchens and TVs, and are available to families with young children or pets. *Note:* Smoking is not permitted in the inn or cabins.

29 Farmhouse Rd., Galiano Island, BC V0N 1P0. ☏ **800/970-7464** or 250/539-5667. Fax 250/539-5316. www.bellhouseinn.com. 5 units. June–Sept C$95–C$195 (US$62–US$127) double, C$125 (US$81) cabin. Oct–May C$85–C$125 (US$55–$81) double, C$90 (US$59) cabin. Extra person in cabin C$10 (US$6.50). Inn rates include breakfast. 2-night minimum stay applies for cabins and on many weekends and holidays for inn. MC, V. Children accepted in cabins; inn guests must be 16 or older. **Amenities:** Golf course nearby; in-room massage. *In room:* Hair dryer, iron, no phone.

Driftwood Village ⬚*Kids* ⬚*Finds* This venerable choice is perfect for a laid-back vacation with the kids and pets in tow. The cottages, of differing vintages and styles, are scattered around a 2-acre (.8-hectare) garden complete with ponds, flowers, and fruit trees. Most have fireplaces and decks with views onto Sturdies Bay. All are decorated with a sense of artful thrift that will instantly bring back youthful memories of idealized lakeside holidays.

205 Bluff Rd. E., Galiano Island, BC V0N 1P0. ☏ **888/240-1466** or 250/539-5457. www.driftwoodcottages. com. 11 units. Dec 28–Jan 1 and late June to mid-Sept C$98 (US$64) studio double, C$115 (US$75) 1-bedroom heritage double, C$135 (US$88) 1- or 2-bedroom luxury double, C$155 (US$101) Jacuzzi suite. Off-season and shoulder-season rates available. Extra person C$10–C$20 (US$6.50–US$13). Rates include ferry pickup. MC, V. Pets accepted for C$10 (US$6.50) per night. **Amenities:** Badminton court; Jacuzzi. *In room:* TV or TV/VCR, kitchen or kitchenette, fridge, coffeemaker, no phone.

Galiano Inn ☞ Formerly the Galiano Lodge and one of the original accommodations on the island, for decades the inn greeted ferry passengers as they arrived in Sturdies Bay. In the 1980s, two new buildings of glass and native wood went up—one for a new lodge and one for a restaurant. The current ownership took over in 1999 and began a massive makeover of the place. This time, things have changed as never before. The new Galiano Inn has a Mediterranean motif and an upscale restaurant, and is completing a full-service spa for 2002. It offers some of the largest rooms and best views on Galiano; unique on the island, guests can simply leave the car at home and walk the 2 minutes from the ferry. Each suite has a fireplace and patio or balcony. Rooms with king beds also have Jacuzzi tubs; all bathrooms have glass-walled shower stalls and fixtures of 24-karat gold. One room is wheelchair accessible.

The Atrevida restaurant sits in an atrium overlooking the water and mountains, and serves fine West Coast cuisine matched by a sizeable wine selection. The inn is also home to the Galiano Art Gallery, featuring local artists. *Note:* Smoking is not permitted.

134 Madrona Dr., Galiano Island, BC V0N 1P0. ☏ **877/530-3939** or 250/539-3388. Fax 250/539-3338. www.galianoinn.com. 10 units. C$185–C$225 (US$120–US$146). Off-season rates available. Rates include full breakfast. MC, V. Free parking. **Amenities:** Restaurant, lounge; golf course nearby; spa; tour/activities desk; courtesy limo; business center; limited room service; massage; laundry service. *In room:* Dataport, hair dryer.

Moonshadows Guest House This B&B stands at the edge of a copse of trees, overlooking meadows and distant Mount Galiano. The architect-designed guesthouse combines the best elements of modern homes—a spacious and airy floor plan filled with flickering sunlight—with the rich stone-and-wood surfaces of a classic older inn. The rooms are nicely decorated with quilts and wicker. The Gardenside Suite has a private deck and massive bathroom with a stationary bike, two-person soaker tub, and walk-in shower. *Note:* Smoking is permitted outdoors only.

771 Georgeson Bay Rd., Galiano Island, BC V0N 1P0. © **888/666-6742** or 250/539-5544. Fax 250/539-5544. www3.telus.net/moonshadowsbb. 3 units. C$90–C$145 (US$59–US$94) double. Rates include full breakfast. 2-night minimum stay on holiday weekends, plus on summer weekends in suite. MC, V. Children must be 12 or older. **Amenities:** Jacuzzi; massage. *In room:* TV/VCR, hair dryer, no phone.

Woodstone Country Inn ✿✿ Spending a few days here is like staying at the home of a favorite friend, a friend who luckily shares your exquisite good taste. The quintessential small country inn, Woodstone is the most refined lodging on Galiano. It sits in a stand of fir trees overlooking a series of meadows, which serve as a de facto bird sanctuary. The entire inn is decorated with restrained but hearty good taste: the owners' collection of folk art and sculpture from their world travels, including marvelous carvings from arctic Canada and southern Africa, plus many quality antiques. The guest rooms are beautifully furnished, with writing tables, upholstered chairs, and intriguing art. All units have fireplaces, some have soaker tubs, and one is wheelchair accessible. Rooms on the main floor have small private patios. The restaurant (see below) serves the island's finest cuisine. *Note:* Smoking is not permitted.

743 Georgeson Bay Rd., RR 1, Galiano Island, BC V0N 1P0. © **888/339-2022** or 250/539-2022. Fax 250/539-5198. www.gulfislands.com/woodstone. 12 units. C$105–C$185 (US$68–US$120) double. Rates include full breakfast and afternoon tea. Packages available. AE, MC, V. Closed Dec–Jan. Children must be 15 or older. **Amenities:** Restaurant, lounge; golf course nearby; concierge; tour/activities desk; business center; in-room massage. *In room:* Hair dryer, no phone.

WHERE TO DINE

The convivial **Daystar Market Café** (© **250/539-2800**) is just north of Sturdies Bay at the intersection of Georgeson Bay and Porlier Pass roads. Part of an organic- and health-food store, it serves mostly vegetarian meals for lunch and dinner daily. **Montague Café,** at the Montague Harbour Marina (© **250/539-5733**), offers light dining right on the water.

La Berengerie Restaurant FRENCH This old farmhouse overlooking a woodland glade could easily be a Breton cottage by a shaded brook. The menu offers a choice of entree—perhaps duck breast with kumquat sauce, or seafood-stuffed sole—plus soup, salad, and dessert. The dining room is simply decorated (pots of flowers, colorful Provençal linens) yet warm and inviting. The food is somewhat inconsistent, although on a good day can be very memorable. In July and August, La Berengerie offers a vegetarian cafe menu on its garden patio.

Montague Rd. © **250/539-5392.** www.gulfislands.com/laberengerie. Reservations recommended. Prix-fixe four-course menu C$27.50 (US$18). V. Daily 5–9pm (10pm in summer).

Woodstone Country Inn ✿✿ INTERNATIONAL The dining room at Woodstone is one of the best restaurants in all of the Gulf Islands. The menu is a compelling blend of classic French cuisine enlivened with vivid international flavors. You might find cedar-plank-baked salmon served with balsamic marinated tomatoes, or perhaps seared duck breast atop wild-rice pancakes. Each day's menu includes a choice of three entrees—meat, fish, or vegetarian—accompanied by homemade bread, soup, and a delightful salad. The wine list is an interesting mix of Okanagan, California, and French vintages. The absolute professionalism combined with a convivial atmosphere make dining here an enchanting experience.

743 Georgeson Bay Rd., RR 1. © **888/339-2022** or 250/539-2022. Reservations required. Four-course dinner C$30–C$35 (US$20–US$23). AE, MC, V. Reservations taken daily for seating from 6–8:30pm.

MAYNE ISLAND

Bucolic Mayne Island is a medley of rock-lined bays, forested hills, and pastureland. Mayne was once a center of Gulf Island agriculture, noted for its apple and tomato production. Many of the island's early farmhouses remain, and a rural, lived-in quality is one of Mayne's most endearing features.

GETTING THERE   **BC Ferries** serves Mayne Island with regularly scheduled runs from both Tsawwassen and Swartz Bay. **Harbour Air, Tofino Air,** and **Seair Seaplanes** all offer floatplane service between Mayne and Vancouver. For contact information, see "Essentials," earlier in this chapter.

VISITOR INFORMATION   Contact the **Mayne Island Community Chamber of Commerce,** Box 2, Mayne Island (no phone; www.mayneisland chamber.ca).

GETTING AROUND   Call **M.I.D.A.S. Taxi** (© **250/539-3132** or 250/ 539-0181) for a ride.

EXPLORING THE ISLAND

Miner's Bay is by default the commercial center of the island, though in most locales this somewhat aimless collection of homes and businesses wouldn't really qualify as a village. However, it's this understated approach to life that provides Mayne Island with its substantial charm. Don't let the rural patina fool you: Some of the lodgings and restaurants are world-class, and even though organized activities are few, it's hard to be bored on such a lovely island.

Mayne doesn't boast the provincial parks and public lands that the other Gulf Islands do, though there are several beach access sites that provide opportunities for swimming in warm weather, and beachcombing during other times of the year. **Bennett Bay,** on the northeast coast, is the best swimming beach. **Campbell Bay,** just northwest, is another favorite pebble beach. **Dinner Bay Park** is lovely for a picnic.

On a sunny day, the grounds of the **Georgina Point Lighthouse** offer dramatic viewpoints. Located on the island's northern tip, this lighthouse juts into Active Pass and overlooks the southern shores of Galiano Island, less than a mile distant.

Mayne Island is home to a number of artists; the widely available map of the island lists more than 20 studios that are open to visitors. The pottery of **John Charowsky,** 490 Fernhill Rd. (© **250/539-3488;** www.gulfislands.com/john charowskystudio), is especially attractive.

BIKING   Mayne is one of the best islands for cyclists. The rolling hills provide plenty of challenges, yet the terrain is considerably less mountainous than that of the other islands. For rentals, contact **Bayview B&B,** 764 Steward Dr. (© **800/376-2115** or 250/539-2924; www.maynebbb.com).

HIKING   The roads on Mayne are usually quiet enough that they can also serve as paths for hikers. Those looking for more solitude should consider

Mounte Parke Regional Park, off Fernhill Road in the center of the island. The park's best views reward those who take the 1-hour hike to Halliday Viewpoint.

KAYAKING & BOATING   Mayne Island Kayak & Canoe Rentals (✆ **250/539-2667**; www.mayneisle.com/kayak), at Seal Beach in Miner's Bay, rents kayaks and canoes for C$20 (US$13) for 2 hours, or C$42 (US$27) for a full day. The company will drop off kayaks at any of six launching points on the island, and if you get stranded, will even pick up kayaks (and too-weary kayakers) from other destinations. If you'd rather let the wind do the work, call **Island Charters** (✆ **250/539-5040**). A half-day excursion (C$135/US$88 for two) lets you explore the coasts of Mayne, Saturna, and the Pender islands, or you can arrange for the sailboat to deliver you to other island destinations (this is the really classy way to get to your country inn).

WHERE TO STAY

Blue Vista Resort _Kids_   This venerable resort is that rare Gulf Island lodging: a place where kids and pets are welcome. Located on the warm eastern side of Mayne Island—close to beaches, kayaking, and hiking—the comfortable cabins are a great value and come with fireplace, deck, and barbecue. One-bedroom cottages have ramps for wheelchair access. Blue Vista also offers boating and biking tours. _Note:_ Smoking is not permitted.

563 Arbutus Dr., Mayne Island, BC V0N 2J0. ✆ **877/535-2424** or 250/539-2463. www.bluevistaresort.com. 8 units. C$50–C$80 (US$33–US$52) 1-bedroom cottage; C$80–C$95 (US$52–US$62) 2-bedroom cottage. Extra person C$10 (US$6.50). Off-season and weekly rates available. MC, V. Pets accepted in two cottages for C$6 (US$3.90) per night. **Amenities:** Kayak and canoe rentals; bike rentals; laundry service. _In room:_ TV, kitchen, fridge, coffeemaker, no phone.

A Coach-House on Oyster Bay B&B Inn 🐦   This modern home on a private bay (2 miles/3km from the ferry terminal) was designed to look like one of Mayne Island's old heritage farm homes, but with up-to-date comforts. Each unit has a gas fireplace, patio or balcony, and private entrance, plus luxury touches like robes and complimentary sherry. A path from the inn leads to a hot tub and gazebo, perched just 10 feet from the tide line on a rock ledge. From here, the views toward Tsawwassen across the Strait of Georgia are magnificent. Otters frequently come into the bay, and orcas gather just offshore. Deer feel so at home that they sometimes sleep right in the garden. The Couch-House is convenient to the Georgina Point Lighthouse. In summer, the water along the small private beach is warm enough for swimming. _Note:_ Smoking is not permitted.

511 Bayview Dr., Mayne Island, BC V0N 2J0. ✆ **888/629-6322** or 250/539-3368. Fax 250/539-2236. www. acoachhouse.com. 3 units. C$130–C$150 (US$85–US$98) double. Off-season rates available. Rates include breakfast. 2-night minimum stay in summer and on holidays. MC, V. **Amenities:** Jacuzzi; free bikes and tennis rackets; kayak and canoe rentals. _In room:_ Hair dryer, no phone.

Oceanwood Country Inn 🐦🐦🐦   Of all the great places to stay in the Gulf Islands, perhaps the best is this luxury lodging with an excellent restaurant, attentive staff, and spacious rooms with sumptuous furnishings. It's a gem of understated elegance, with just the right blend of comfortable formality and relaxed hospitality. All but one of the rooms have magnificent views of Navy Channel and Saturna Island. The original inn's charming rooms are less expensive, yet still good-sized and beautifully outfitted; two have balconies. The rooms in the new wing are truly large, with private decks, two-person tubs, and fireplaces. The Wisteria Suite is a three-tiered unit with two baths, multiple decks, and an outdoor soaker tub.

The inn's public rooms are equally impressive. Facing the gardens are a comfortable living room and library, separated by a double-sided fireplace. The dining room is one of the most sophisticated places to eat in British Columbia (see "Where to Dine," below). *Note:* Smoking is permitted outdoors only.

630 Dinner Bay Rd., Mayne Island, BC V0N 2J0. *©* **250/539-5074.** Fax 250/539-3002. www.oceanwood. com. 12 units. Mid-June to mid-Sept C$159–C$329 (US$103–US$214). Mid-Sept to Dec 2 and Mar 2 to mid-June C$119–C$279 (US$77–US$181). Extra person C$25 (US$16). Rates include full breakfast and afternoon tea. MC, V. Closed Dec 3–Mar 1. **Amenities:** Restaurant, bar; golf course nearby; Jacuzzi; sauna; free bikes; in-room massage. *In room:* Hair dryer, no phone.

WHERE TO DINE

Manna Bakery Café, on Fernhill Road in Miner's Bay's tiny strip mall (*©* **250/ 539-2323**), is the place to go for a cappuccino and fresh-baked cinnamon roll. Just above the marina in Miner's Bay, the **Springwater Lodge** (*©* **250/ 539-5521**) is a comfortably ramshackle pub/restaurant with great views; try the fish-and-chips.

Oceanwood Country Inn ✶✶ PACIFIC NORTHWEST   Refined yet robust, the cuisine at Oceanwood is one of the best expressions of up-to-date, full-flavored cooking in the Gulf Islands. The chef brings together the rich bounty of Northwest fish, meat, game, and produce in a daily changing tableau of vivid tastes and textures. The fish selection might be local paupiettes of sole with herb gnocchi and blackberry vinaigrette, and the meat entree could be grilled duck breast with cranberry demiglace served on foie-gras–stuffed ravioli. The dining room overlooks a lily pond and garden; the decor is handsome but unfussy.

630 Dinner Bay Rd. *©* **250/539-5074.** www.oceanwood.com. Reservations required. Four-course prix-fixe menu C$44 (US$29). MC, V. Daily, most sittings 6–8pm. Closed Dec–Feb.

THE PENDER ISLANDS

The Penders consists of North and South Pender islands, separated by a very narrow channel that's spanned by a one-lane bridge. North Pender is much more developed, though that's all relative out in the Gulf Islands. It has a rather startling housing development on its southwest side, a 1970s suburb plopped down on an otherwise rural island. Neither of the Penders seems to share the long-standing farming background of the other Gulf Islands, so forests are thick and all-encompassing. The Penders do have some lovely beaches and public parks with good hiking trails. Toss in a handful of local artists, and you have the recipe for a tranquil island retreat.

GETTING THERE   **BC Ferries** serves Pender Island with regularly scheduled runs from both Tsawwassen and Swartz Bay. The commuter airlines mentioned in previous sections also offer floatplane service to and from Vancouver. For more information, see "Essentials," earlier in this chapter.

VISITOR INFORMATION   The **Pender Island Visitor Info Centre,** 2332 Otter Bay Rd. (*©* and fax **250/629-6541**), is open from May 15 to September 2.

EXPLORING THE ISLANDS

Mount Norman Regional Park, which encompasses the northwest corner of South Pender Island, features hiking trails through old-growth forest to wilderness beaches and ridge-top vistas. Access to trails is just across the Pender Island bridge.

The extensive network of roads makes these islands good destinations for cyclists. Rentals are available at **Otter Bay Marina,** 2311 McKinnon Rd.

(© **250/629-3579**), where you'll also find **Mouat Point Kayaks,** 1615 Storm Crescent (© **250/629-6767**). If beachcombing or sunning are more your style, try **Hamilton Beach** on the east side of North Pender, or **Medicine Beach** and the beaches along **Beaumont Marine Park,** both of which flank Bedwell Harbour.

WHERE TO STAY

Beauty Rest by the Sea   An uncommonly dramatic setting—acres of rocky headland overlooking the channel between North Pender and Prevost islands—provides the Beauty Rest with physical charms that other B&Bs can only dream of. The grounds—basically all of a small cliff-sided peninsula—have been in the family for generations. The attractive ranch-style home has three well-appointed guest rooms, two with private entrances. Guests are free to watch boats and whales in the channel, sun on the small pebble beach, or read on the deck or in the solarium. *Note:* Smoking is not permitted.

1301 Mackinnon Rd., N. Pender Island, BC V0N 2M1. © 250/629-3855. Fax 250/629-3856. www.pender isle.com. 3 units. Mid-May to Sept C$130–C$135 (US$85–US$88) double. Oct to mid-May C$110–C$115 (US$72–US$75). Extra person C$25 (US$16). Rates include breakfast. MC, V. Not suitable for children. *In room:* Fridge, coffeemaker, no phone.

Bedwell Harbour Island Resort ✴ (*Kids*)   Bedwell Harbour is the most active place in all South Pender Island. This sprawling complex, with cabins, motel rooms, condo town houses, and a marina, is also the Canadian Customs House for vessels coming in from Washington's San Juan Islands. In summer, this is a busy spot; you can easily spend an afternoon at a wharf-side table with your favorite drink, watching a parade of boats pass by. The resort is very attractive, particularly the newer condo units with balconies and decks. Families will like the cabins, and the motel rooms offer good value. Luxury villa apartments with fireplaces were added recently. An on-site store sells provisions and some outdoor gear.

9801 Spalding Rd., S. Pender Island, BC V0N 2M3. © **800/663-2899** or 250/629-3212. Fax 250/629-6777. www.bedwell-harbour.com. 24 units. C$119–C$339 (US$77–US$220) double. Mar to mid-May and Sept 4–30 C$79–C$239 (US$51–US$155) double. Extra person C$12 (US$8). Rates for units without kitchens include breakfast. Children under 16 stay free in parents' room. AE, MC, V. Closed Oct–Mar. Pets allowed. **Amenities:** Restaurant; bar; golf course nearby; outdoor pool; tennis courts; canoe rentals; bike rentals; children's center; activities desk; babysitting. *In room:* Fridge.

Eatenton House B&B Inn   This contemporary B&B offers wonderful gardens and views of forest and the sparkling waters of Browning Harbour. The spacious rooms are great for groups; the largest is essentially a suite with two bedrooms. A fireplace commands the dining area and antiques-filled sitting room. On nice afternoons, the deck is where you'll be spending most of your time. *Note:* Smoking is not permitted.

4705 Scarff Rd., Pender Island, BC V0N 2M1. © **888/780-9994** or 250/629-8355. Fax 250/629-8375. www. penderislands.com. 3 units. C$95–C$135 (US$62–US$88) double. Extra person C$20 (US$13). Rates include full breakfast. Honeymoon, off-season, and anniversary packages available. MC, V. Children must be 15 or older. **Amenities:** Golf course nearby; Jacuzzi. *In room:* Teakettle, hair dryer, no phone.

Inn on Pender Island (*Kids*)   The Inn on Pender Island is the name given to an enterprising complex at the center of North Pender. Nine large, unfussy units are in a modern motel building and come with TVs and fridges. Pets and kids are welcome, and breakfast is delivered to your door. These basic rooms are a real deal in the otherwise expensive Gulf Islands. Also part of the complex are three new log cabins. Each has a kitchenette and deck; two also have hot tubs. These, too, are a great value when you consider the sky's-the-limit prices of comparable lodgings. Likewise, the restaurant is a just-fine place to eat, with good pizza and Northwest cuisine.

4709 Canal Rd., N. Pender Island, BC V0N 2M0. (C) **800/550-0172** or 250/629-3353. Fax 250/629-3167. www.innonpender.com. 12 units. C$79–C$89 (US$51–US$58) lodge double; C$130 (US$85) cabin. Extra person C$10 (US$6.50). Lodge rates include breakfast. MC, V. Small pets allowed for C$2 (US$1.30). **Amenities:** Restaurant; Jacuzzi; business center. *In room:* TV/VCR, coffeemaker.

Oceanside Inn ♠ The Oceanside Inn ranks among the most private getaways on the Penders, cantilevered above a rocky cliff overlooking Navy Channel and Mayne Island. The arbutus trees that line the shore are home to bald eagles and turkey buzzards. The dramatic setting alone strongly recommends the place; the fact that it has been recently renovated, and is operated by a charming host, makes it even more of a find. Three suites have private decks and hot tubs; two rooms have fireplaces. All units have private entrances. Weekend packages include one dinner for two (from C$299/US$194). *Note:* No smoking is permitted.

4230 Armadale Rd., N. Pender Island, BC V0N 2M3. (C) **250/629-6691.** www.penderisland.com. 4 units. C$129–C$225 (US$84–US$146) double. Rates include full breakfast. Off-season rates and 2-day escape and honeymoon packages available. V. Children must be 15 or older. Pets allowed with prior arrangement for C$25 (US$16). **Amenities:** Restaurant (guests only); golf course nearby; health club; spa; tour/activities desk; in-room massage; coin-op laundry; laundry service. *In room:* Fax, minibar, hair dryer, iron, no phone.

WHERE TO DINE

One of the Penders' drawbacks is its lack of dining options. Your best bet is the **Bedwell Harbour Island Resort** (see "Where to Stay," above). Its dining room has an excellent reputation. **Memories,** at the Inn on Pender Island ((C) **250/ 629-3353**), is the only other real choice. Don't let the rather plain exterior of this family restaurant put you off. The food—ranging from pizza to ribs to fresh fish—is quite tasty. It's open for dinner only.

SATURNA ISLAND

The most remote of the southern Gulf Islands, Saturna is both pristine and, compared with its neighbors, mostly vacant—it has only about 300 residents. Whereas other islands are best described as rural, Saturna is truly wild. Served by direct ferries from Swartz Bay and a few indirect sailings from Tsawwassen, Saturna is hard to get to. You'll find it's easiest to ferry to Vancouver Island and then back out, or over to Mayne Island, which has direct sailings to Saturna.

Its remoteness makes Saturna a favorite destination of outdoorsy types. The island boasts nice beaches, including Russell Reef, Veruna Bay, and Shell Beach at **East Point Park.** This park, with its still-active lighthouse, is a good spot to watch for orcas. Hikers can drive to **Mount Warburton Pike** and follow the **Brown Ridge Nature Trail.** Kayakers can explore the rocky islets surrounding Tumbo Island, just offshore Saturna's eastern peninsula. Facilities are few and far between, though in several cases, exemplary. For more information, check out **www.saturnatourism.bc.ca**.

WHERE TO STAY & DINE

Breezy Bay B&B Fifty acres (20 hectares) of farmland surround this 1890s farmhouse, which overlooks sheep and llama pastures and cliff-lined Breezy Bay. The interior of the house is lined with wainscot and period moldings, and a stone fireplace dominates the lounge and library. The cozy bedrooms share two bathrooms. Paths lead to the beach, with access for swimming and kayaking. Children are welcome.

131 Payne Rd., Saturna Island, BC V0N 2Y0. ☎ **250/539-5957.** Fax 250/539-3339. www.gulfislands.com/
saturna/breezybay. 4 units. C$65–C$85 (US$42–US$55) double. Extra person C$25 (US$16). Rates include full
breakfast. No credit cards. Closed Oct–Mar. *In room:* No phone.

Saturna Lodge & Restaurant ★★   This well-established resort has in recent
years been revamped into an upscale country inn. Between 1995 and 2000, the
lodge's proprietors planted 60 acres (24 hectares) of wine grapes and opened the
region's first major vineyard, marking a new direction for the Gulf Islands. Now
the lodge has taken on a winery theme—each guest room is named for a grape
varietal. One room has a soaker tub; all have either ocean or garden views. The
attractive lounge overlooks the gardens and has a fireplace, small library, and tel-
evision. *Note:* Smoking is not permitted.

For most guests, the highlight of a stay here is a meal at the restaurant. The
menu features Saturna Island lamb, local seafood, and organic produce. Dishes
might include seared halibut with a sesame, soy, and tomato coulis. In good
weather, the menu offers barbecued meats and fish from the outdoor grill.
There's an extensive wine list, of course, featuring the Saturna vineyard's wines
as well as others from around British Columbia. The restaurant is accessible by
boat, if that's your style.

130 Payne Rd., Saturna Island, BC V0N 2Y0. ☎ **888/539-8800** or 250/539-2254. Fax 250/539-3091. www.
saturna-island.bc.ca. 7 units. June–Sept C$135–C$195 (US$88–US$127) double. Apr–May and Oct
C$120–C$175 (US$78–US$114) double. Rates include three-course breakfast. Special packages available.
MC, V. Closed Nov–Feb. Pets allowed for C$10 (US$6.50) per night. **Amenities:** Restaurant, bar; Jacuzzi; free
bikes; tour/activities desk; business center. *In room:* Hair dryer, no phone.

4 West of Victoria: Sooke Harbour & Port Renfrew

Port Renfrew: 63 miles (102km) W of Victoria

Following Highway 14 west from Victoria, the suburbs eventually thin; by the
time you reach Sooke, the vistas open up to the south, where Washington's
Olympic Mountains prop up the horizon. There are several reasons to explore
this part of the island, though the motivations basically boil down to the wild
and the civilized.

Highway 14 gives access to a number of beaches and parks with good swimming and recreation, finally leading to Port Renfrew, the southern trail head for
the famous West Coast Trail (see chapter 6, "Central Vancouver Island").

Ambitious backcountry drivers can make a loop journey from Highway 14.
From Port Renfrew, a good logging road leads up the San Juan River valley, connecting to the southern shores of Cowichan Lake just west of Duncan. You can
make this drive in one very long day, or divide the trip up by planning to spend
the night camping at Cowichan Lake or at one of Duncan's moderately priced
hotels.

The civilized reason to make the journey west from Victoria is the superlative
Sooke Harbour House, one of the most renowned small inns in all of Canada.

IN & AROUND SOOKE

The little town of Sooke doesn't offer a lot to divert the visitor, but there are a
number of recreation areas nearby that warrant a stop. **Sooke Potholes Provincial Park** preserves a curious geologic formation. The Sooke River flows down
a series of rock ledges, pooling in waist-deep swimming holes before dropping
in waterfalls to another series of pools and waterfalls. In July and August, the
normally chilly river water warms up. The trails that link the pools are nice for
a casual hike. There are more trails in adjacent **Sooke Mount Provincial Park.**

To reach these parks, drive west on Route 14 almost to the town of Sooke; turn right on Sooke River Road. Nine miles (15km) west of Sooke is **French Beach Park**, a sand-and-gravel beach that's one of the best places to watch for gray whales. The park has 69 campsites.

WHERE TO STAY

Markham House B&B and Honeysuckle Cottage 🖈🖈

On the outskirts of Sooke, nestled in the woods, sits this admirably well executed Tudor-style home on 10 acres (4 hectares) of landscaped grounds. The rooms are outfitted with antiques, featherbeds, and duvets. The cottage has its own kitchenette, woodstove, and hot tub. The main house features an elegant parlor with fireplace. Breakfasts are sumptuous and healthy. Outside, you can sit by the trout pond, play bocce, or practice your golf swing on the mini-fairway and green. Of course, you may also want to head out to the water or explore the region's parks, and your gracious hosts will help you make plans. The proprietors also own a condo in Victoria, and packages for stays at both properties are available. *Note:* Smoking is permitted outdoors only.

1853 Connie Rd., Victoria, BC V9C 4C2. 📞 **888/256-6888** or 250/642-7542. Fax 250/642-7538. www.markhamhouse.com. 4 units. July–Sept and mid-Dec to Jan 3 C$105–C$195 (US$68–US$127) double. Oct to mid-Dec and Jan 4–June C$95–C$169 (US$62–US$110) double. Rates include full breakfast and tea. AE, DC, DISC, MC, V. Take Sooke Rd. (Hwy. 14) west from Victoria 15 miles (25km); turn left on Connie Rd. Pets allowed; outdoor accommodations can be provided. Not suitable for children. **Amenities:** Golf course nearby; croquet; badminton; concierge; room service; laundry service. *In room:* TV/VCR.

Point-No-Point Resort 🖈

Get away from it all in your own little cabin on the ocean, with 40 acres (16 hectares) of wilderness around you, a wide, rugged beach in front of you, and nothing to do but laze the day away in your hot tub. This resort has been welcoming guests since 1950. All cabins have fireplaces; newer ones have hot tubs and decks, and two are wheelchair accessible. Lunch and dinner can be had in the sunny dining room; its tables are conveniently equipped with binoculars, so you won't miss a bald eagle as you eat. In summer, the resort runs a fishing boat charter.

1505 West Coast Hwy. (Hwy. 14), Sooke, BC V0S 1N0. 📞 **250/646-2020.** Fax 250/646-2294. www.pointnopointresort.com. 25 units. C$130–C$220 (US$85–US$143) cabin double. 2- or 3- night minimum stay on weekends and holidays. Off-season rates available. Summer fishing packages available. AE, MC, V. Free parking. Pets allowed for C$10 (US$6.50) per night and C$100 (US$65) refundable dog deposit. No children in cabins with hot tubs. **Amenities:** Restaurant/teahouse; in-room massage; laundry service. *In room:* Kitchen, fridge, coffeemaker, no phone.

Sooke Harbour House 🖈🖈🖈

This little inn at the foot of a beautiful pebble-and-sand spit, 18½ miles (30km) west of Victoria, has earned an international reputation. Each handsomely decorated suite boasts a fireplace, fresh flowers, and views of the water. All but one have decks, and many have Jacuzzis. Extras include in-room breakfast, optional in-room dinner, and massages by appointment. A nice perk to staying here is easy access to the spit, a public park that juts out into the mouth of Sooke Harbour, breaking the rougher waters of the Strait of San Juan de Fuca. It's a nice stroll out and back—perfect for watching the sunset, as well as seals, otters, and birds. Sooke Harbour House has one of the best restaurants in Canada (see "Where to Dine," below).

1528 Whiffen Spit Rd., Sooke, BC V0S 1N0. 📞 **800/889-9688** or 250/642-3421. Fax 250/642-6988. www.sookeharbourhouse.com. 28 units. July to mid-Sept C$299–C$555 (US$194–US$361) double. May–Oct and winter holidays C$280–C$490 (US$182–US$319). Nov–Apr C$230–C$355 (US$150–US$231). Rates include breakfast and lunch. Dinner C$65 (US$42) extra. Off-season discounts available. Children 12 and under stay free in parents' room. DC, MC, V. Free parking. Closed Mon–Wed Dec 3–20 and Jan 7–Feb 6. Take the Island Hwy. (Hwy. 1) to the Sooke/Colwood turnoff (Junction Hwy. 14). Follow Hwy. 14 to Sooke. About 1 mile (1.6km) past the town's only traffic light, turn left onto Whiffen Spit Rd. Pets allowed for C$20 (US$13) per night. **Amenities:** Restaurant; golf course nearby; spa; Jacuzzi; bike rentals; concierge; tour/activities desk; car-rental desk; room service; in-room massage; babysitting; laundry service. *In room:* TV or TV/VCR, fridge, coffeemaker, hair dryer, iron.

WHERE TO DINE

17-Mile House PUB   For inexpensive but reliable fare, the 17-Mile House has the most character in the area. Built in the late 1800s, this establishment became a regional hub in the 1920s when it installed the only phone around. Today, you can sup on a nice salad, burger, or one of many pasta, meat, or seafood entrees while admiring the old wood, brick, and tile interior. You might tap out a tune on the pub's 150-year-old piano or settle for a game of billiards; Saturdays feature live music. If you want to spend the night, rooms go for C$20 to C$50 (US$13 to US$33).

5126 Sooke Rd. © 250/642-5942. http://members.home.net/17milehouse. Main courses C$8–C$24 (US$5–US$16). Sun–Thurs 11am–11pm; Fri–Sat 11am–midnight. MC, V. On Sooke Rd. (Hwy. 14) between Connie and Gillespie rds. Victoria bus no. 61.

Sooke Harbour House ★★★ NORTHWEST COAST   Regarded as one of the best restaurants in Canada, Sooke Harbour House treats you to a sensual culinary experience using almost all local ingredients, with an emphasis on the foods of West Coast Native peoples and the produce of the inn's own gardens. The restaurant is situated at the rear of the inn, a rambling white house on a bluff, and offers spectacular views and a quiet atmosphere. A sample fall menu features seared weathervane scallops with a wild mushroom ragout, or cumin and coarse salt roasted lamb loin served with a black currant, Grand Fir scented lamb stock reduction, potato pavé, braised leeks, and Ladybird Farm carrots. A la carte selections are available on weekends only, and with advance notice, the kitchen will prepare a seven- to nine-course gastronomical adventure for C$99 (US$64). If you really want to splurge, the sommelier will pick a match for each dish from one of the top wine lists in the world, according to *Wine Spectator.*

1528 Whiffen Spit Rd., Sooke. © 250/642-3421. www.sookeharbourhouse.com. Reservations required. Main courses C$29–C$38 (US$19–US$25). Sun–Thurs prix-fixe four-course menu C$65 (US$42). Prices may be higher in summer and on holidays. AE, DC, MC, V. Daily 5–9pm. Take the Island Hwy. to the Sooke/Colwood turnoff (Junction Hwy. 14). Continue on Hwy. 14 to Sooke. About a mile (1.5km) past the town's only traffic light, turn left onto Whiffen Spit Rd.

IN & AROUND PORT RENFREW

Port Renfrew is a seaside village whose main claim to fame is as one of the termini of the West Coast Trail. Day-trippers from Vancouver also come out to visit **Botanical Beach Provincial Park** ★, an area with spectacular tide-pool formations, unique geology, and one of the richest intertidal zones on the entire North American west coast. About 2½ miles (4km) south of Port Renfrew, Botanical Beach is a ledge of sandstone that juts out into the churning waters of the Strait of Juan de Fuca. Over the millennia, tidal action has carved out pits and pools, which you'll find filled with sea urchins, clams, periwinkles, giant anemones, and chitons and sea stars. In spring and fall, watch for gray whales. Check local tide tables to maximize opportunities for wildlife-viewing and tide-pool exploration: A low tide of 4 feet (1.2m) or less is best. Picnic facilities and toilets are available.

Hiking the Juan de Fuca Marine Trail

This long-distance hiking trail links China Beach Park, just past the town of Jordan River, to Botanical Beach Provincial Park, near Port Renfrew, along a stretch of near-wilderness coastline. Similar to the famed West Coast Trail but less extreme, the rugged 29-mile (47km) trail offers scenic beauty, spectacular hiking, wildlife-viewing, and roaring surf in its course along the Pacific coastline of the Strait of Juan de Fuca. Most of the trail is designed for strenuous day or multi-day hiking. Unlike the West Coast Trail, it can be easily broken down into daylong segments between trail heads accessed along Highway 14: China Beach, Sombrio Beach, Parkinson Creek, and Botanical Beach. Plan on 3 days to hike the entire thing; campsites are regularly spaced along the trail.

Conditions are always changing, so before proceeding, obtain up-to-date information by checking the trail head information shelters. If you're camping, keep a tide chart handy and refer to trail head postings about points that will be impassable at high tide. Wear proper footwear—the trail gets very muddy—and appropriate clothing, plus raingear if you're going to camp. And leave a plan of your trip (including which trail you're hiking), with arrival and departure times, with a friend or relative. Also, don't leave a car full of valuables in the trail head parking lots—break-ins are common.

For information on Juan de Fuca Marine Park, contact **BC Parks,** South Vancouver Island District, 2930 Trans-Canada Hwy., Victoria (© **250/391-2300;** fax 250/478-9211; www.elp.gov.bc.ca/bcparks). Another good website is **www.sookenet.com/sooke/activity/trails/ jdftrail.html**.

WHERE TO STAY & DINE

Port Renfrew lodgings are mostly geared to the long-distance backpacking set coming to or from the West Coast Trail. The **West Coast Trail Motel,** Parkinson Road (© **877/299-2288** or 250/647-5565), has simple rooms from C$69 (US$45). The **Trailhead Resort,** at the end of Highway 14 by Snuggery Cove, across the port from the trail head (© **250/647-5468**), offers motel suites for C$90 (US$59).

Arbutus Beach Lodge   Right on the beach of Port San Juan, the Arbutus offers some of the best accommodations in Port Renfrew. Rooms are clean and nicely decorated. Guests can use a reading room with fireplace, a lounge with pool table, and a hot tub overlooking the water. A small cabin next to the lodge features a full kitchen. Breakfasts and optional dinners are served in a restaurant-like atrium. Your hosts can help arrange all sorts of activities. *Note:* Smoking is not permitted in the lodge.

5 Queesto Dr., Port Renfrew, BC V0S 1K0. © **250/647-5458.** Fax 250/647-5552. www.sookenet.com/ arbutus. 5 units. C$65–C$95 (US$42–US$62). Extra person C$15 (US$10) per night. Rates include continental breakfast. Off-season and weekly discounts available. MC, V. Children must be 16 or older. **Amenities:** Restaurant (guests only); Jacuzzi; free bikes. *In room:* TV, no phone.

5 North of Victoria: Goldstream Provincial Park ⟨★⟩

North of Victoria, the Island Highway climbs up over the high mountain ridge called the Malahat, shedding the suburbs as it climbs. Goldstream Provincial Park is a tranquil arboreal setting that overflowed with prospectors during the 1860s gold-rush days, hence its name. Today, its natural beauty attracts hikers, campers, and birders who stop to spend a few hours or days in the beautiful temperate rain forest.

Hiking trails take you past abandoned mine shafts and tunnels as well as stands of Douglas fir, lodgepole pine, red cedar, indigenous yew, and arbutus trees. The **Gold Mine Trail** leads to Niagara Creek and the abandoned mine. The **Goldstream Trail** goes to the salmon-spawning areas (you might also catch sight of mink and river otters racing along this path).

Three species of salmon make **annual salmon runs** up the Goldstream River during the months of October, November, December, and February. Visitors can easily observe this natural wonder along the riverbanks. Goldstream is also a major attraction for bird-watchers, as numerous bald eagles winter here each year. January is the best month for spotting these majestic creatures.

For information on all provincial parks on the South Island, contact **BC Parks** (📞 **250/391-2300;** www.env.gov.bc.ca/bcparks). Goldstream Park's **Freeman King Visitor Centre** (📞 **250/478-9414**) offers guided walks, talks, and programs geared towards kids throughout the year. It's open daily from 9:30am to 6pm. Take Highway 1 about 20 minutes north of Victoria.

WHERE TO STAY

The Aerie ★   Safe to say, there's nothing else on Vancouver Island like the Aerie. This Mediterranean-inspired villa was designed and decorated by an Austrian hotelier with gobs of money and unlimited self-confidence. For some, it's the very picture of paradise. For others, the result is a tad over the top. The setting—on the forested slopes of the Malahat—is certainly spectacular, and the view out over Finlayson Inlet is unsurpassed. Inside, no expense has been spared. Dior duvets sit atop gargantuan four-poster beds, and king-bed suites have balconies, fireplaces, and Jacuzzi or soaker tubs. Extras include fresh-cut flowers and chocolate truffles, a helipad, spa treatments, and an outdoor wedding chapel. Most guests also sample the excellent cuisine in the dining room (see below). *Note:* Smoking is not permitted.

600 Ebedora Lane, P.O. Box 108, Malahat, BC V0R 2L0. 📞 **800/518-1933** or 250/743-7115. Fax 250/743-4766. www.aerie.bc.ca. 29 units. May 18–Oct 13 C$285–C$325 (US$185–US$211) double, C$375–C$465 (US$244–US$302) suite. Mar 28–May 17 and Oct 14–Nov 25 C$225–C$295 (US$146–US$192) double, C$345–C$525 (US$224–US$341) suite. Nov 26–Mar 27 C$185–C$230 (US$120–US$150) double, C$285–C$425 (US$185–US$276) suite. Rates include a 7am breakfast hamper at your door and full breakfast later on. Packages available. AE, DC, MC, V. Free parking. Take Hwy. 1 north to the Spectacle Lake turnoff; take the first right and follow the winding driveway up. **Amenities:** Restaurant, lounge; golf courses nearby; indoor pool; tennis court; spa; Jacuzzi; sauna; concierge; limited room service; in-room massage; laundry service; same-day dry cleaning. *In room:* A/C, TV (VCRs available), dataport, minibar, fridge, coffeemaker, hair dryer, iron.

WHERE TO DINE

The Aerie ★★ FRENCH/NORTHWEST   Ornate. Overwhelming. Over the top? Depends on your tastes. The dining room of this villa boasts panoramic views, a gold-leaf ceiling, chandeliers, and faux-marble columns. When it comes to the cooking, over-the-top might be a good thing. Consider, for example, an appetizer of venison-and-pistachio paté with dried-fruit compote, juniper-and-port glaze, and herbed sunflower croutons. Entrees include beef tenderloin with a caramelized shallot crust in a red-wine-and-rosemary reduction. An excellent selection of brandies and coffee will take you over the peak and down the far side.

600 Ebedora Lane, Malahat. ℂ 250/743-7115. www.aerie.bc.ca. Reservations required. Main courses C$35–C$42 (US$23–US$27); five- to eight-course set menu C$65–C$95 (US$42–US$62). AE, DC, MC, V. Daily 6–10pm. Free parking. Take Hwy. 1 to the Spectacle Lake turnoff; take the first right and follow the winding driveway.

Six Mile Pub PUB   The Six Mile was popular with sailors when the Esquimalt Naval Base opened nearby in 1864, then became the hub for provincial boot-leggers during prohibition. With a lively bar and intimate dining rooms, it has broad appeal. You can enjoy the ambience of the fireside room, which has an oak bar with stained glass, or the beautiful scenery from the patio. The food is sea-soned with fresh herbs from the garden. Start with one of the house brews, then move on to a juicy prime rib or tasty veggie burger.

494 Island Hwy., View Royal. ℂ 250/474-3663. www.sixmilepub.com. Main courses C$7–C$16 (US$4.50–US$10). AE, DC, MC, V. Daily 11am–12:30am; Sun 10am–12:30am.

6 Duncan & the Cowichan Valley

Duncan: 36 miles (57km) N of Victoria

The Cowichan Valley is one of the richest agricultural areas on Vancouver Island. The Cowichan Indians have lived in the valley for millennia, and today the band's reservation spreads immediately to the south of the town of Duncan. European settlers, drawn by the valley's deep soil and warm temperatures, estab-lished farms here in the 1870s. Although the orchards and sheep pastures of yore remain, the valley's providential location also makes it one of the few sites in western British Columbia for vineyards, a new and booming crop.

For visitors, the town of Duncan, at the center of the valley, may seem a pretty low-key place, but its centrality to excellent recreation and cultural sights makes it a comfortable hub for exploring this part of Vancouver Island. Cowichan Lake is a popular summertime getaway, with swimming beaches and boating. Maple Bay and Cowichan Bay are marina-dominated harbor towns with good pubs and restaurants, plus enchanting views. And don't forget those wineries: Cowichan Valley is home to several good ones, most with tasting rooms open to the public.

ESSENTIALS

GETTING THERE   Duncan is 36 miles (57km) north of Victoria on High-way 1. It's also a stop on the **E&N Railiner.** For information, contact **VIA Rail** (ℂ **888/VIA-RAIL** or 250/383-4324; www.viarail.ca). **Island Coach Lines** (ℂ **800/663-8390,** 250/388-5248, or 250/385-4411; www.victoriatours.com) passes through Duncan on its Victoria/Nanaimo service.

VISITOR INFORMATION   The **Duncan Visitor Information Centre,** 381A Trans-Canada Hwy. (ℂ **250/746-4636**), is open from April 15 to Octo-ber 15. Online, go to **www.city.duncan.bc.ca.** For year-round information on the entire valley, contact the **Cowichan Tourism Association,** 25 Canada Ave., Duncan (ℂ **250/715-0709;** www.cowichan.bc.ca).

EXPLORING THE AREA
DUNCAN: THE CITY OF TOTEM POLES

Duncan is a welcoming city of 5,330, with a mix of First Nations peoples and descendants of European settlers. Congested Highway 1 runs to the east of the old town center, and you'll miss Duncan's old-fashioned charm if you don't get off the main drag (follow signs for Old Town Duncan).

Downtown Duncan still bustles with stationers, dress shops, bakeries, haber-dasheries, cafes, candy shops—it's the quintessential small and friendly Cana-dian town. The main reason to make a detour downtown is to see the city's impressive collection of modern **totem poles.** The First Nations peoples of this region are famed for their carving skills. However, most historic totem poles are now in museums or are rotting in front of abandoned villages, and for a long time few Native Canadians had any reason to keep the old skills and traditions alive. In the 1980s, the mayor of Duncan began an ambitious project of com-missioning local First Nations artists to carve new totem poles, which were then erected around the city. Today, with more than 80 totem poles rising above the downtown area, Duncan's public art is one of the world's largest collections of modern totem carving, a wonderful assemblage that represents the continuation of an ancient art form unique to the Northwest coast.

The totem poles are scattered around the city, mostly in the pedestrian-friendly downtown area: Simply follow the yellow shoeprints on the pavement. You can also take a free guided tour, which starts from in front of the Cowichan Valley Museum, at the E&N Railway station, Station Street and Canada Avenue. The tours are given from May to mid-September, Tuesday through Sat-urday from 10am to 4pm. Reserve for groups of five or more by calling the **Duncan Business Improvement Area Society** (© 250/715-1700).

The B.C. Forest Discovery Centre *Kids*   This 100-acre (40.5-hectare) site explores the history of the logging industry. In recent years, the focus of the exhibits has shifted from an unreflective paean to tree cutting to a more thought-ful examination of sustainable forestry practices, woodland ecosystems, and the role (sometimes surprising) of wood products in our lives. No matter what you may think of logging as a practice, the history of forestry in British Columbia is fascinating, and this museum does a good job of presenting both the high and low points. Kids will love the vintage steam train, which circles the grounds on narrow-gauge rails.

2892 Drinkwater Rd., 1¼ miles (2km) north of Duncan on Hwy. 1 (near Somenos Lake). © 250/715-1113. www.bcforestmuseum.com. Admission C$8 (US$5.20) adults, C$7 (US$4.55) seniors and students 13–18, C$4.50 (US$2.95) children 5–12. May 12–Labour Day daily 10am–6pm; Apr 13–May 11 and Sept 4–Oct 8 daily 10am–4pm.

Quw'utsun' Cultural Centre   The Cowichan (Quw'utsun') people were the original inhabitants of this valley, and the tribes' cultural history and tradi-tional way of life are the focus of Quw'utsun' Centre, on the southern edge of downtown Duncan ("Quw'utsun'" means "warming your back in the sun"). The parklike enclosure along the Cowichan River contains several modern longhouse structures flanked by totem poles. Join a guided tour of the village, or take a seat in the theater to watch the excellent presentation *The Great Deeds,* a retelling of Cowichan myth and history. At the building devoted to traditional carving, you can talk to carvers as they work, and even take up a chisel yourself. In fall, the center hosts interpretive cultural/ecological tours of the Cowichan River and the life cycle of its salmon.

The Cowichan tribes are famous for their bulky sweaters, knit with bold motifs from hand-spun raw wool. The gallery at Quw'utsun' is the best place in the valley to buy these hand-knit sweaters (expect to pay around C$250/ US$163), as well as carvings, prints, jewelry, and books. In summer, the cafe serves traditional foods. On Sundays in July and August, there's a midday alder-planked salmon barbecue feast with drumming and storytelling. Call ahead for details.

200 Cowichan Way. © 877/746-8119 or 250/746-8119. www.quwutsun.ca. Admission C$10 (US$6.50) adults, C$8 (US$5.20) seniors and students 13–17, C$6 (US$3.90) children 12 and under and First Nations individuals, C$25 (US$16.25) families. May–Sept daily 9am–6pm; Oct–Apr daily 10am–5pm.

COWICHAN BAY
This small but busy port town edges along the mouth of the Cowichan River. Just 4¼ miles (7km) southeast of Duncan, many visitors come to walk the board-walks and admire the boats amid the sounds, smells, and sights of a working har-borside village. The **Cowichan Bay Maritime Centre,** 1761 Cowichan Bay Rd. (© 250/746-4955; www.classicboats.org), tells the story of the clash of Native and European cultures in the Cowichan Valley. It also serves as a workshop for the building of wooden boats. Admission is C$1 (US$.65); hours are daily from 9am to dusk between April and October.

MAPLE BAY & GENOA BAY
Maple Bay is a lovely harbor town 4¼ miles (7km) northeast of Duncan. Take Tzouhalem Road east to Maple Bay Road, then head northeast. Although not a major destination, it's worth the short drive just to take in the view—a placid bay of water beneath steep-sloped mountains. Ponder the vista at the **Brigan-tine Inn** ★, on Beaumont Avenue (© 250/746-5422), a friendly pub with local brews and a bayside deck. If you're into **diving,** Maple Bay is said to have been one of Jacques Cousteau's favorite spots in the world!

Genoa Bay is directly south of Maple Bay. This tiny harbor is actually on Cowichan Bay, though the mountainous terrain mandates that overland trans-port make a circuitous route around Mount Tzouhalem. Again, the point of the journey is the charm of the location. Enjoy a drink at the **Grapevine Cafe** (see "Where to Dine," below), which also operates **Genoa Bay Charters** (© 250/746-0797; www.cowichan.com/business/grapevine). If you're traveling with a group, consider a day of Gulf Island sightseeing on the MV *Rendezvous,* com-plete with catered meals from the Grapevine.

COWICHAN VALLEY VINEYARDS
The warm summers and mild winters of the Cowichan Valley make this one of the few areas in western British Columbia where wine grapes flourish. Pinot noir, pinot gris, Marechale Foch, and Gewürztraminer are popular varietals. The following wineries welcome guests, and most will arrange tours with sufficient notice. For more information, see **www.islandwineries.ca**.

Blue Grouse Vineyards and Winery, 4365 Blue Grouse Rd., south of Dun-can, off Lakeside Road near Koksilah Road (© 250/743-3834; www.bluegrouse vineyards.com), is open for tastings from 11am to 5pm, Wednesday through Saturday year-round (and Sun Apr–Sept).

Alderlea Vineyards, 1751 Stamps Rd., near Maple Bay (© 250/746-7122; www.islandwineries.ca/alderlea.htm), is open Thursday through Sunday from 1 to 5pm.

Cherry Point Vineyards, 840 Cherry Point Rd., near Telegraph Road southeast of Cowichan Bay in eastern Cobble Hill (© 250/743-1272; www. cherrypointvineyards.com), is one of the most prominent Cowichan Valley wineries, with national awards to prove it. The tasting room is open daily from 10am to 6pm.

Vigneti Zanatta Winery and Vineyards, 5039 Marshall Rd., south of Duncan near Glenora (℮ **250/748-2338;** www.zanatta.ca), is open March through December, Wednesday through Sunday from noon to 5pm. Its restaurant, Vinoteca, is one of the best places to eat in the area (see "Where to Dine," below).

Venturi-Schulze Vineyards, 4235 Trans-Canada Hwy., Cobble Hill (℮ **250/ 743-5630;** www.venturischulze.com), is a must for oenophiles, with some of the most outstanding wines in Canada. However, it is open for tours by appointment only. Venturi-Schulze offers frequent intimate winemaker dinners served in a 100-year-old farmhouse; call ahead for the schedule.

A newer vineyard in the region is **Godfrey-Brownell,** west of Duncan at 4911 Marshall Rd. (℮ **250/748-4889;** www.gbvineyards.com). Call for information on tastings.

Another twist on the local scene is **Merridale Cider,** 1230 Merridale Rd., Cobble Hill, west of Highway 1 (℮ **800/998-9908** or 250/743-4293; www. merridalecider.com), which produces both apple and pear cider. Call to inquire about a visit.

COWICHAN LAKE, COWICHAN RIVER & THE BACKCOUNTRY

Cowichan Lake, 17 miles (28km) west of Duncan on Highway 18, is a long, narrow lake nestled between mountain slopes. With a population of about 3,000, it's one of the primary summer playgrounds for valley residents. A number of provincial parks provide access to swimming beaches, boat landings, and campsites; **Gordon Provincial Park,** on the lake's south shore, is the most convenient for Duncan-based travelers.

Backcountry explorers can follow the roads along both sides of 19-mile-long (30km) **Cowichan Lake** to access remote areas of Vancouver Island's wilderness west coast. Well-maintained forestry roads from Cayuse and Honeymoon Bay, on the south side of the lake, lead to **Port Renfrew,** one of the starting points of Pacific Rim National Park's famed West Coast Trail (see "West of Victoria: Sooke Harbour & Port Renfrew," above, as well as chapter 6, "Central Vancouver Island"). From here, paved roads connect to Sooke and Victoria. From the west end of Cowichan Lake, gravel roads lead to **Nitinat Lake,** renowned for its windsurfing, and **Carmanah/Walbran Provincial Park,** a vast preserve of misty old-growth forests.

The Cowichan River flows east out of Cowichan Lake. The **Cowichan River Trail,** which passes through fern glades and forests, provides excellent access to the beautiful jade-green waters. The 12-mile (20km) trail begins just east of Cowichan Lake (follow signs from Hwy. 18 for Skutz Falls Trailhead) and follows the river to Glenora, southeast of Duncan. The river is popular for steelhead and trout fishing, as well as kayaking. Some canyon rapids are considered too dangerous for passage; inquire locally before setting out.

WHERE TO STAY
IN & AROUND DUNCAN

Best Western Cowichan Valley Inn   This is Duncan's most comfortable full-service lodging, conveniently located for visiting the B.C. Forestry Centre. Its handsomely furnished guest rooms come with numerous amenities. A wheelchair-accessible room is available. Choices is one of the best family restaurants in Duncan, and the hotel's beer-and-wine shop is one of the best places in town to purchase local wines.

6474 Trans-Canada Hwy., Duncan, BC V9L 6C6. ℂ **800/927-6199** or 250/748-2722. Fax 250/748-2207. 42 units. C$91–C$125 (US$59–US$81) double. Extra person C$6 (US$3.90). Senior and AAA discounts available. Children 16 and under stay free in parents' room. Pets allowed with approval. AE, DC, DISC, MC, V. Free parking. Located 1¼ miles (2km) north of Duncan. **Amenities:** Restaurant, pub; small heated outdoor pool; golf course nearby; exercise room; volleyball court; tour/activities desk; beer-and-wine store. *In room:* A/C, TV, dataport, fridge, coffeemaker, hair dryer, iron.

Fairburn Farm Country Manor ⚡ If you dream of an idealized farm vacation, this is your B&B. You'll feel instantly at home, even if the closest you've ever come to rural living is mowing your lawn. Fairburn Farm has been in existence since the 1880s. The beautifully preserved farmhouse boasts high ceilings, antique moldings, tiled fireplaces, and a broad porch. A farm manager's cottage—with two bedrooms and kitchen—is available in summer for three or more people staying 6 days. This is one of the few B&Bs that welcomes families.

The farm consists of 130 working acres (53 hectares) plus forested areas with trails. Guests are welcome—but not obliged—to join in farm activities: This is a real working farm, with chickens, cattle, orchards, and a new enterprise—a water-buffalo dairy for the production of authentic mozzarella. You can commune with the friendly sheepdogs, or watch the cycles of rural life from a distance by relaxing with a glass of wine in the gazebo. The friendly proprietors serve breakfasts of homemade baked goods, fresh eggs, and orchard fruit. *Note:* Smoking is not permitted.

3310 Jackson Rd., Duncan, BC V9L 6N7. ℂ **250/746-4637.** Fax 250/746-4317. www.fairburnfarm.bc.ca. 7 units. Mid-Apr to mid-Oct C$110–C$150 (US$72–US$98) double. Extra person C$20 (US$13). July–Aug C$850 (US$553) cottage for 3 or more people for 6 days. MC, V. Closed Oct 15–Mar 31. Free parking. **Amenities:** In-room massage; babysitting. *In room:* No phone.

Travelodge Silver Bridge Inn Its reasonably priced, well-maintained rooms make the Silver Bridge a good choice. King-bed units have fridges; honeymoon suites boast gas fireplaces and double Jacuzzis. Located next to the Cowichan River, the motel is within walking distance of the Quw'utsun' Cultural Centre. The pub, with an attractive shaded deck, is in a converted century-old house.

140 Trans-Canada Hwy., Duncan, BC V9L 3P7. ℂ **888/858-2200** or 250/748-4311. Fax 250/748-1774. www. travelodgeduncan.com. 34 units. C$82–C$169 (US$53–US$110) double. Extra person C$10 (US$6.50). AAA, senior, weekly, group, corporate, and sports-team rates available. AE, DC, MC, V. Free parking. Pets allowed for C$10 (US$6.50) per night. **Amenities:** Restaurant (Cantonese and Canadian buffets), pub; golf course nearby; limited room service; laundry service; same-day dry cleaning. *In room:* A/C, TV, dataport, coffeemaker, hair dryer.

Village Green Inn Situated on the Island Highway (Trans-Canada Highway) near the Quw'utsun' Cultural Centre, this inn contains tastefully decorated rooms in muted tones, all offering ample amounts of peace and quiet.

141 Trans-Canada Hwy., Duncan, BC V9L 3P8. ℂ **800/665-3989** or 250/746-5126. Fax 250/746-5126. www. bctravel.com/si/villagegreen.html. 80 units. C$64–C$90 (US$42–US$59) double; C$79–C$105 (US$51–US$68) suite. Kitchenette C$5 (US$3.25) extra. Senior discounts available. Children under 12 stay free in parents' room. Small pets allowed with approval. AE, DC, MC, V. Free parking. **Amenities:** Restaurant; bar; heated indoor pool; golf course nearby; tennis court; sauna; limited room service; laundry service; same-day dry cleaning; beer-and-wine store. *In room:* A/C, TV, coffeemaker.

IN COWICHAN BAY

Old Farm B&B This B&B's history dates back to 1908, when an English sea captain built his dream home on the Cowichan River estuary. The handsome main house has three second-floor guest rooms with brass beds, luxury linens, and imported toiletries; one unit has a private deck. There are two additional rooms on the third floor, each with two twin beds, which can be rented in combination with one of the other guest rooms. (This option is popular with families and groups.) The Robert Service Suite—named for the poet laureate of the Klondike, who hailed from near here—has a private entrance, kitchen, deck, and Jacuzzi. Breakfasts feature homegrown fruits and local farm ingredients. *Note:* Smoking is not permitted.

2075 Cowichan Bay Rd., Cowichan Bay, BC V0R 1N0. ✆ **888/240-1482** or 250/748-6410. Fax 250/ 748-6410. www.oldfarminncowichan.com. 4 units. C$75–C$125 (US$49–US$81) double. Extra person C$25 (US$16). Rates include breakfast. MC, V. Free parking. Children must be 12 or older. **Amenities:** Golf course nearby; historic grass tennis courts nearby; badminton court; Jacuzzi; kayak rentals nearby; laundry service. *In room:* Hair dryer, no phone.

WHERE TO DINE
IN & AROUND DUNCAN

Just Jakes BURGERS/LIGHT DINING   This laid-back, funky restaurant is a cross between a fern bar and a soda fountain, and the staff is young and engaging. The menu offers a wide selection of burgers, salads, steaks, and pasta: pleasantly passé food that perfectly mirrors Duncan's attractively slow-paced downtown.

45 Craig St. ✆ **250/746-5622.** www.justjakes.bc.ca. Reservations recommended. Main courses C$6–C$22 (US$4–US$14). AE, MC, V. Mon–Thurs 11am–9pm; Fri–Sat 11am–10pm.

Vinoteca ✦ *Finds* FRESH LOCAL/COUNTRY ITALIAN   A combination wine-tasting room and country-style restaurant, Vinoteca is located in a historic farmhouse at the Vigneti Zanatta vineyards (see "Cowichan Valley Vineyards," above). The menu plays counterpoint to the wines produced here. The dishes are based on hearty country fare—you might choose oven-roasted Cornish hen stuffed with figs and apples, with rosemary mustard and citrus jus, or lemon risotto cakes with seafood, fresh tomatoes, and tarragon. As much as possible, the ingredients used at Vinoteca are grown on the farm or nearby.

At Vigneti Zanatta Winery, 5039 Marshall Rd., near Glenora south of Duncan (call for directions). ✆ **250/ 709-2279.** www.zanatta.ca/vinoteca.htm. Reservations recommended. Main courses C$12–C$25 (US$7.80–US$16). MC, V. Mar–Dec Wed–Sun seatings noon–3:30pm and from 6pm. Other nights possible by reservation. Closed Jan–Feb.

IN COWICHAN BAY

Masthead Restaurant ✦ WEST COAST   The building that now houses the Masthead was the town's original hotel. Its dining room now serves the area's finest Northwest cuisine. Appetizers include succulent crab cakes, sauced with a jalapeño lime aioli. Salmon is served two ways: grilled with citrus cream sauce, or baked in parchment with white wine and dill. A real showstopper is the halibut, pan-fried with a hazelnut crust and served with an orange ginger butter sauce. The rack of lamb with a minted blueberry sauce is another standout. The airy dining room manages to seem nicely traditional without being cloying. In good weather, sit out on the deck.

1705 Cowichan Bay Rd., Cowichan Bay. ✆ **250/748-3714.** Reservations recommended. Main courses C$15–C$21 (US$10–US$14). MC, V. June–Sept Mon–Sat and Oct–May Tues–Sat seatings 5:30–8pm.

Rock Cod Café SEAFOOD   Rock Cod Café has the best fish-and-chips in the area. From the deck, you can watch the fish coming in off the boats. The chalk-board menu is crammed with whatever else is fresh. Since the cafe has a liquor license—something most British fish-and-chip shops can't boast—you can turn a humble meal of halibut and fries into an afternoon's worth of pleasure.

4-1759 Cowichan Bay Rd., Cowichan Bay. ✆ **250/746-1550.** Reservations recommended in summer. Main courses C$6–C$14 (US$4–US$9). MC, V. Daily 11am–9pm.

IN GENOA BAY

The Grapevine Café ★★ PACIFIC NORTHWEST   One of the most delightful dining experiences in the Duncan area is found at the relaxed yet stylish Grapevine. From the dining room or the deck, you can follow the to-ing and fro-ing of pleasure boats and see towering forested bluffs reflected in the waters of the bay. Appetizer favorites include Cajun-spiced fried oysters with the house-secret spicy cream sauce. The prime rib is legendary, as are the baby-back ribs. Each day's menu also includes four seafood specials, perhaps an arctic char with champagne caviar cream. What makes a meal here so satisfying—besides the dramatic scenery and peaceful atmosphere—is the food's perfect blend of restaurant sophistication and hearty home cooking.

5100 Genoa Bay Rd., Genoa Bay Marina, Genoa Bay. (℃ 250/746-0797. Reservations recommended. Main courses C$17–C$20 (US$11–US$13). MC, V. Mar Sat–Sun, Apr and Oct Wed–Sun seatings 11:30am–2:30pm and 5:30–8:30pm. June–Sept daily seatings 5:30–9pm. Closed mid-Oct to Feb.

7 En Route to Nanaimo

CHEMAINUS: THE CITY OF MURALS

Settled in the 1850s by European farmers, Chemainus quickly became a major timber-milling and -shipment point, due to the town's Horseshoe Bay, the oldest deepwater port on the Canadian west coast. Prosperity saw the building of handsome homes and a solid commercial district. By the mid–20th century, the sawmills here were among the largest in the world, fed by the seemingly unending supply of wood from Vancouver Island's vast old-growth forests.

When the mills closed in 1983, the town slid into decline. Economic prospects for Chemainus seemed dim until someone had the bright idea of hiring an artist to paint a mural depicting the town's history. Tourists took notice, and soon mural painting became the raison d'être of this town of only slightly more than 3,500 residents. Chemainus claims to be Canada's largest permanent outdoor art gallery. Much of downtown is now covered with murals, most dealing with area history and local events.

Stop by the **Chemainus Visitor Info Centre,** 9758 Chemainus Rd. (℃ 250/ 246-3944; ccoc@tourism.chemainus.bc.ca), open from May to early September, for a walking-tour map of the murals, or go to **www.northcowichan.bc. ca/muralmap.htm** or **www.muraltown.com** for an online map. Across the street from the visitor center in Heritage Park is an informational kiosk where you can join a horse-drawn wagon tour of the murals for C$4 (US$2.60) for adults, C$2 (US$1.30) for kids. Or simply follow the yellow shoeprints painted on the sidewalks.

Much of the town is quiet and pedestrian-oriented, making it a pleasant place for a stroll and a good spot for lunch. **Old Town Chemainus,** along Willow and Maple streets, is filled with Victorian cottages converted into shops and cafes. The **Chemainus Theatre,** 9737 Chemainus Rd. (℃ **800/565-7738** or 250/ 246-9820; www.ctheatre.bc.ca), is a late-19th-century opera house that now serves as a popular dinner theater. The season runs February through December; call ahead to reserve.

WHERE TO STAY

Birdsong Cottage Bed & Breakfast ★   Filled with Victorian bric-a-brac and unusual objets d'art, Birdsong is an enchanting, English-style garden cottage. The owners, both professional musicians, admit to being "a bit theatrical." Rather an understatement: Whimsy pervades the place, from the extensive ugglers, dancers and an assortment of acrobats fill the street.

he shoots you a wide-eyed look as a seven-foot cartoon character approaches.

hat brought you here was wanting the kids

see something magical while they still believed in magic.

merica Online Keyword: Travel

th 700 airlines, 50,000 hotels and over 5,000 cruise and vaca-

n getaways, you can now go places you've dreamed of.

Travelocity.com
A Sabre Company
Go Virtually Anywhere.

RLD'S LEADING TRAVEL WEB SITE, 5 YEARS IN A ROW" WORLD TRAVEL AWARDS

collection of Victorian hats (which guests are encouraged to try on) to the grand piano and Celtic harp. The exterior continues the theme, with a wraparound porch and turreted veranda, burbling fountains, and loads of architectural gingerbread. Everything here is over the top, but lovingly so. The guest rooms are beautifully outfitted, with quality linens and fresh flowers. Two units have TV/VCRs. Breakfasts are elaborate affairs.

9909 Maple St., Chemainus, BC V0R 1K0. (℄ **250/246-9910.** Fax 250/246-2909. www.romanticbb.com. 3 units. C$105 (US$68) double. Extra person C$20 (US$13). Rates include breakfast and evening tea. Extended-stay, group, and wedding packages available. MC, V. **Amenities:** Golf course nearby; courtesy limo. *In room:* hair dryer, iron, no phone.

Castlebury Cottage ✰   The proprietors of Birdsong also operate this cottage designed as a "folly"—a small, whimsical, European-style castle. The upstairs suite has a fireplace, canopy bed, and two-person soaker tub. The style is thoroughly baroque, with lots of ornate flourishes and rough frescoed walls. The downstairs "dungeon" is smaller but similarly appointed, and available only to groups also taking the upstairs. To complete the experience, you can order a five-course "medieval" meal accompanied by live harp music for C$180 (US$117). *Note:* Smoking is not permitted.

9910 Croft St., Chemainus, BC V0R 1K0. (℄ **250/246-9228.** Fax 250/246-2909. www.castleburycottage.com. 2 units. May–Sept C$285–C$325 (US$185–US$211) suite, C$145 (US$94) dungeon. Oct–Apr C$190–C$250 (US$124–US$163) suite, C$125 (US$81) dungeon. Rates include breakfast basket. 2-night minimum on weekends and holidays. MC, V. Not suitable for children. **Amenities:** Golf course nearby; in-room massage; laundry service; dry cleaning. *In room:* A/C, TV/VCR, kitchen or kitchenette, fridge, coffeemaker, hair dryer, iron.

WHERE TO DINE
Willow Street Café, 9749 Willow St. (℄ **250/246-2434**), is a hip eatery serving up sandwiches, wraps, and salads; the deck is the best people-watching perch in town. Open daily from 9am to 5pm.

The Waterford Restaurant ✰ NORTHWEST   Located in the heart of historic Old Town, the Waterford is Chemainus's best choice for intimate fine dining. The antiques-filled room is in a Victorian-era storefront that has been extended to include a lovely garden deck—an especially charming spot for lunch. Meat dishes include a rack of lamb melding the flavors of Dijon mustard, mint, and rosemary. Seafood options include poached sole stuffed with crab and shrimp in a white wine sauce. The proprietors provide excellent service and innovative cuisine.

9875 Maple St. (℄ **250/246-1046.** Reservations recommended. Main courses C$13–C$20 (US$8–US$13). AE, MC, V. Tues–Sun 11:30am–2:30pm and Wed–Sun seatings 5–8:30pm. Also open for dinner Tues in summer.

CEDAR & YELLOW POINT
South of Nanaimo, a forested peninsula juts out into the waters of the Georgia Strait. The land is rural and mostly undeveloped. The little community of Cedar is as close as the area comes to a town; this wouldn't qualify as much of a destination if it weren't for the fact that one of Vancouver Island's most popular lodges and one of its best restaurants are located here. It's a short drive from Nanaimo, and a detour through the forests and farmland makes for a pleasant break from Highway 1.

WHERE TO STAY
Yellow Point Lodge ✰✰   Beloved Yellow Point Lodge is located on 180 acres (73 hectares) of forested waterfront, with over 1½ miles (2.5km) of rocky beach and secluded coves. This family-operated resort was established in the 1930s.

The three-story log-and-stone building has an enormous lobby, a huge fireplace, and a dining room with communal tables, all with wondrous views of Vancouver Island and the southern Gulf Islands. Inside the lodge are a number of comfortable hotel-like rooms, all with ocean views; scattered around the woods are cabins and cottages in a wide range of styles. Most basic are the beach cabins and the rustic Beach Barracks with communal washhouses. Some of the more luxurious one-, two-, and three-bedroom cottages have fireplaces. One room is appointed for those with disabilities.

Hiking trails are on the property and in nearby provincial parks. Meals are served in the dining room, where a real sense of camaraderie develops among the guests. The good, home-style cooking features standards like roast beef and grilled salmon. If this unique blend of summer camp and luxury resort appeals to you, be sure to reserve well ahead. The lodge is a summer tradition for many people, and not just for the wealthy. Part of the charm of Yellow Point is that there are affordable lodging options here for almost everyone, and everyone gets the same friendly service. *Note:* Smoking is not permitted.

3700 Yellow Point Rd., Ladysmith, BC V9G 1E8. © **250/245-7422.** Fax 250/245-7411. www.yellowpoint lodge.com. 53 units (27 with private bathroom, most with shower only). C$115–C$190 (US$75–US$124) double. Rates include all meals. AE, MC, V. Ferry, bus, train, or airport shuttle available for small fee. Children must be 14 or older. **Amenities:** Outdoor saltwater pool; golf course nearby; tennis courts; volleyball and badminton courts; Jacuzzi; sauna; free bikes; free kayaks and canoes; massage. *In room:* No phone.

WHERE TO DINE

The Crow & Gate *Finds* PUB This Tudor-style pub on a 10-acre (4-hectare) farm is a friendly haven of English style. It looks straight out of the Cotswolds, with low ceilings, handcrafted beams, and gleaming brass accents complemented by a brick fireplace and leaded-glass windows. The menu offers roast beef and Yorkshire pudding, shepherd's pie, and roasted Cornish game hen. In summer, sit out on the flower-decked patio.

2313 Yellow Point Rd. © **250/722-3731.** www.shift.to/crowandgate. Reservations recommended. Main courses C$8–C$13 (US$5–US$8). MC, V. Daily 11am–midnight; closes early when not busy and on some holidays (call ahead). Take the old Island Hwy. (Hwy. 19) north past Cassidy, or exit Island Hwy. 1 at Hwy. 19 to Cedar and Harmac. Cross the Nanaimo River, then turn right on Cedar Rd., which leads onto Yellow Point Rd. Continue for 1 mile (1.6km).

The Mahle House ★★ PACIFIC NORTHWEST The Mahle (pronounced "Molly") House is located in a tiny country town, in a salmon-pink heritage home overlooking a park. From this unlikely address, it has developed a huge reputation for excellent regional cuisine emphasizing locally grown, mostly organic produce and meats. You might choose duck breast with ginger, orange, and triple sec sauce; venison with a chanterelle sauce; or Chinook salmon, scallops, and porcupine prawns with saffron aioli and lemon oil. The award-wining wine list is extensive. The restaurant also offers two bargain nights: a Wednesday five-course dinner for C$29 (US$19) and a Thursday tapas-like "grazing platter" for C$40 (US$26) for two.

At Cedar and Hemer rds., Cedar. © **250/722-3621.** www.mahlehouse.com. Reservations highly recommended. Main courses C$14–C$32 (US$9–US$21). AE, MC, V. Wed–Sun from 5pm. Closed Dec 21–29 and Jan 1–15.

Central Vancouver Island

Central Vancouver Island's major population center is Nanaimo, the arrival point for visitors taking ferries from the mainland and the site of a major 19th-century coal-mining operation. In recent years the city has moved away from its dependence upon resource extraction and is now sparkling with redevelopment, taking advantage of its scenic location—overlooking a bay full of islands, the choppy waters of Georgia Strait, and the glaciated peaks of the mainland.

In sharp contrast to the serenity of the east-coast islands, the wild, raging beauty of the Pacific Ocean on Vancouver Island's west coast entices photographers, hikers, kayakers, and divers to explore Pacific Rim National Park, Long Beach, and the neighboring towns of Ucluelet, Tofino, and Bamfield. Thousands of visitors arrive between March and May to see Pacific gray whales pass close to shore as they migrate north to their summer feeding grounds. More than 200 shipwrecks have occurred off the shores in the past two centuries, luring even more travelers to this eerily beautiful underwater world. And the park's world-famous West Coast Trail beckons intrepid backpackers to brave the 5- to 7-day hike over the rugged rescue trail—established after the survivors of a shipwreck in the early 1900s died from exposure because there was no land-access route for the rescuers.

On east-central Vancouver Island, the towns of Parksville, Qualicum Beach, Courtenay, and Comox are famous for their warm, sandy beaches and numerous golf courses.

Note: See the "Vancouver Island" map (p. 86) to locate areas covered in this chapter.

1 Essentials

GETTING THERE
BY PLANE   See chapter 4 for details on flights to **Victoria,** the main air hub for all of Vancouver Island.

Nanaimo and Comox/Courtenay have regular air service from Vancouver. Other towns can be reached via floatplane, either from Vancouver International's seaplane terminal or from downtown Vancouver's Coal Harbour terminal. Since floatplanes don't require airport facilities, even the most remote fishing camp can be as accessible as a major city.

Air Canada (© **888/247-2262;** www.aircanada.com), which hosts flights by subsidiary Air BC, offers service to Comox/Courtenay, Nanaimo, and Victoria. **Pacific Coastal Airlines** (© **800/663-2872;** www.pacific-coastal.com) also serves these destinations, and **WestJet** (© **877/952-4638;** www.westjet.com) serves all but Nanaimo.

Commuter seaplane companies include **Harbour Air Seaplanes** (© **800/ 665-0212** or 604/688-1277; www.harbour-air.com), **Tofino Air** (formerly Pacific Spirit Air; © **866/486-3247** for Tofino base, 888/436-7776 for Sechelt base, or 800/665-2359 for Gabriola base; www.tofinoair.ca), **Air Rainbow** (© **250/287-8371;** www.air-rainbow.com), and **Baxter Aviation** (© **800/ 661-5599,** 604/683-6525, or 250/754-1066; www.baxterair.com).

BY FERRY   BC Ferries (© **888/BCFERRY** in B.C., or 250/386-3431; www. bcferries.bc.ca) operates an extensive year-round network that links Vancouver Island, the Gulf Islands, and the mainland. Major routes include the crossing from Tsawwassen to Swartz Bay and to Nanaimo, and from Horseshoe Bay (northwest of Vancouver) to Nanaimo. In summer, reserve in advance. Sample fares are included in the regional sections that follow.

BY BUS   One of the easiest ways to get to and from Vancouver Island desti- nations is by bus. Conveniently, the bus will start its journey from a city center (like Vancouver), take you directly to the ferry dock and onto the ferry, and then deposit you in another city center (Victoria or Nanaimo). A lot of the hassle of ferry travel is minimized, and the costs are usually lower than other alternatives. (If you're traveling to Vancouver on the VIA Rail system, you'll find bus con- nections simple, as the buses and trains share the same terminal.)

Pacific Coach Lines (© **800/661-1725** or 604/662-8074; www.pacific coach.com) offers bus service via BC Ferries from Vancouver to Victoria. One- way fare is C$28 (US$18) for adults, C$19 (US$12) for seniors, and C$14 (US$9) for children. **Greyhound Canada** (© **800/661-8747** or 604/482-8747; www.greyhound.ca) provides eight daily trips between Vancouver and Nanaimo. Fares are C$21 (US$14) one-way.

VISITOR INFORMATION
For information on Vancouver Island, contact **Tourism Vancouver Island,** Suite 203, 335 Wesley St., Nanaimo (© **250/754-3500;** fax 250/754-3599; www. islands.bc.ca). Also check out **www.vancouverisland.com**.

GETTING AROUND
While Vancouver Island has an admirable system of public transport, getting to remote sights and destinations is difficult without your own vehicle.

BY FERRY   BC Ferries (© **888/BCFERRY** in B.C., or 250/386-3431; www. bcferries.bc.ca) routes link Vancouver Island ports to many offshore islands.

BY TRAIN   A scenic way to travel is on **VIA Rail's E&N Railiner,** the *Mala- hat* (© **888/VIA-RAIL** or 250/383-4324; www.viarail.ca), which runs from Victoria to Courtenay. See p. 88 for details.

BY BUS   Island Coach Lines (© **800/663-8390** in the U.S., 800/318-0818 in Canada, or 250/388-5248; www.victoriatours.com) runs along the main highway from Victoria to Port Hardy, and from Nanaimo to Tofino. The fare from Victoria to Nanaimo is C$19.25 (US$13), from Nanaimo to Tofino C$33 (US$21), and from Victoria to Courtenay C$38.50 (US$25).

BY CAR   The southern half of Vancouver Island is well served by paved high- ways. The trunk road between Victoria and Nanaimo is **Highway 1,** the Trans- Canada. This busy route alternates between four-lane expressway and congested two-lane highway, and requires some patience and vigilance, especially during the busy summer months. North of Nanaimo, the major road is **Highway 19,** which is now almost all four-lane expressway; a particular improvement being the new 80-mile (128km) **Inland Highway** between Parksville and Campbell River. The older sections of 19, all closer to the island's east coast, are now labeled 19A. The other major paved road system on the island, **Highway 4,** connects Parksville with Port Alberni and on to Ucluelet and Tofino, on the rugged west coast. This road is mostly a two-lane, and portions of it are extremely winding and hilly. Access to gasoline is no problem on the island, but don't head out on a long stretch of unpaved road without filling up.

Rental-car agencies include **Avis** (© **800/272-5871** in Canada, or 800/230-4898 in the U.S.; www.avis.com), **Budget** (© **800/268-8900** in Canada, 800/527-0700 in the U.S., or 250/953-5300 in Victoria; https://rent.drivebudget.com), and **National** (© **800/387-4747** or 250/386-1213; www.nationalcar.com).

2 Nanaimo & Gabriola Island

Nanaimo: 70 miles (113km) N of Victoria

For over a century, Vancouver Island's second-largest city (pop. 77,000) was the center of vast coal-mining operations, without much in the way of cultural niceties. In the last 20 years, however, Nanaimo has undergone quite a change. With its newly redeveloped waterfront, scenic surroundings, good restaurants, and a location central to many other Vancouver Island destinations, there's plenty here for several days of exploration. Note, however, that Nanaimo is a fairly large city, complete with lots of suburban strip malls and plenty of traffic. It may not hold the same charm as the island's less populous destinations, but those who enjoy Victoria may well take a liking to its smaller cousin.

Just a 20-minute ferry ride from Nanaimo Harbour is Gabriola Island, though it feels a world away. Gabriola makes a marvelous day trip, providing a little of everything—sandy beaches, fine restaurants, galleries, petroglyph sites, and tide pools—without surrendering its sense of wooded serenity.

ESSENTIALS

GETTING THERE By Plane   Regular service between Vancouver and Nanaimo Airport, 15 miles (24km) south of the city, is offered by **Air BC** through **Air Canada** (© **888/247-2262;** www.aircanada.com).

Harbour Air Seaplanes (© **800/665-0212** or 604/688-1277; www.harbourair.com) and **Baxter Aviation** (© **800/661-5599,** 604/683-6525, or 250/754-1066; www.baxterair.com) offer floatplane flights from Vancouver to Nanaimo Harbour.

By Car   Nanaimo is 70 miles (113km) from Victoria via Highway 1, the Trans-Canada Highway. At Nanaimo, the Trans-Canada crosses Georgia Strait via the Horseshoe Bay ferry. North of Nanaimo, the main trunk road becomes Highway 19. It's 99 miles (161km) from Nanaimo to Campbell River, 128 miles (206km) to Tofino.

By Ferry   BC Ferries (© **888/BCFERRY** in B.C., or 250/386-3431; www.bcferries.bc.ca) operates two major runs to Nanaimo. The crossing from Horseshoe Bay in West Vancouver to Nanaimo's Departure Bay terminal is one of the busiest in the system; expect delays. New PacifiCat Ferries cut the normal 1½-hour crossing down to just over an hour. The Tsawwassen ferry arrives and departs at Nanaimo's Duke Point terminal, just south of town off Highway 1. Tickets for both ferries are C$9 (US$6) per passenger and C$30 (US$20) per car, with slightly higher prices on weekends.

By Train   The **E&N Railiner** operates daily service between Victoria and Courtenay. For information, contact **VIA Rail** (© **888/VIA-RAIL** or 250/383-4324; www.viarail.ca).

Nanaimo

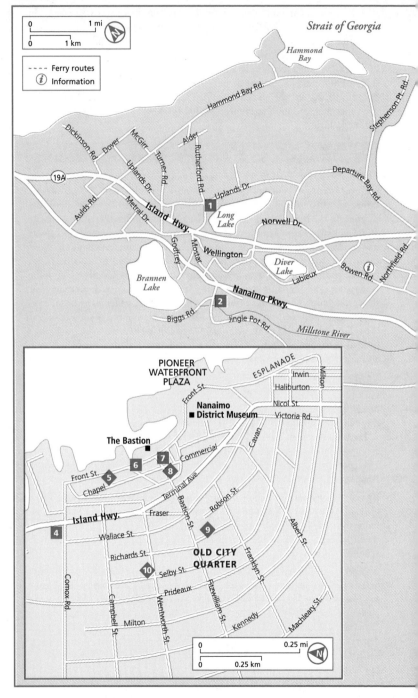

0   1 mi
0   1 km

---- Ferry routes
(i) Information

Strait of Georgia

Hammond
Bay

Dickinson Rd.

Dover

McGirr

Turner Rd.

Alder

Rutherford Rd.

Hammond Bay Rd.

Stephenson Pt. Rd.

19A

Uplands Dr.

Island Hwy.

Uplands Dr.

Departure Bay Rd.

Aulds Rd.

Metral Dr.

Long
Lake

Norwell Dr.

Godfrey

Mostar

Wellington

Diver
Lake

Labieux

Bowen Rd.

Northfield Rd.

(i)

Brannen
Lake

Nanaimo Pkwy.

Biggs Rd.

Jingle Pot Rd.

Millstone River

PIONEER
WATERFRONT
PLAZA

ESPLANADE

Irwin

Milton

Haliburton

Front St.

Nicol St.

Nanaimo
■ District Museum

Victoria Rd.

The Bastion ■

Cavan

7

Commercial

6

8

Front St.

5

Chapel

Terminal Ave.

Bastion St.

Robson St.

Island Hwy.

Fraser

9

Albert St.

4

Wallace St.

OLD CITY
QUARTER

Richards St.

Comox Rd.

10

Selby St.

Franklyn St.

Prideaux

Fitzwilliam St.

Campbell St.

Wentworth St.

Milton

Kennedy

Machleary St.

0   0.25 mi
0   0.25 km

N

124

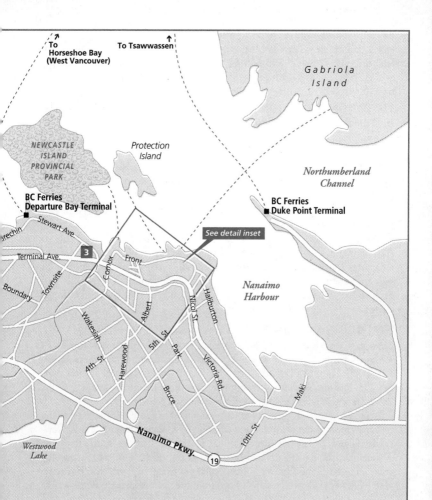

To
Horseshoe Bay
(West Vancouver)

To Tsawwassen

*Gabriola
Island*

*NEWCASTLE
ISLAND
PROVINCIAL
PARK*

*Protection
Island*

*Northumberland
Channel*

**BC Ferries
Departure Bay Terminal**

**BC Ferries
Duke Point Terminal**

rechin

Stewart Ave.

Terminal Ave.

3

Comox

Front

See detail inset

Nicol St.

Haliburton

*Nanaimo
Harbour*

Boundary

Townsite

Albert

5th St.

Park

Victoria Rd.

Maki

Wakesiah

Harewood

4th St.

Bruce

10th St.

*Westwood
Lake*

Nanaimo Pkwy.

19

ACCOMMODATIONS ■

Best Western Dorchester Hotel **6**
Coast Bastion Inn **7**
Howard Johnson Harbourside Hotel **4**
Pepper Muffin Country Inn **2**
Sheraton Four Points Hotel **1**
Travelodge Nanaimo **3**

DINING ◆

Flo's Diner **8**
The Globe Bar & Grill **5**
Maffeo's **10**
Wesley Street Café **9**

*PACIFIC
OCEAN*

**BRITISH
COLUMBIA**

*Vancouver
Island*

Nanaimo
○ ○ **Vancouver**
Victoria ✪
○ Seattle

By Bus Greyhound Canada (© **800/661-8747** or 604/482-8747; www.
greyhound.ca) provides eight daily trips between Vancouver and Nanaimo.
Island Coach Lines (© **800/663-8390** in the U.S., 800/318-0818 in Canada,
or 250/388-5248 in Victoria; www.victoriatours.com) can take you from Victoria to Nanaimo.

VISITOR INFORMATION Contact **Tourism Nanaimo,** Beban House,
2290 Bowen Rd. (© **800/663-7337** or 250/756-0106; fax 250/756-0075;
www.tourismnanaimo.com). In summer, an **Info Centre** operates out of the
Bastion, at Pioneer Waterfront Plaza.

GETTING AROUND Nanaimo Regional Transit System (© **250/
390-4531;** www.rdn.bc.ca) provides public transport in the Nanaimo area. Fares
are C$1.75 (US$1.15) for adults and C$1.25 (US$.80) for seniors and youths.
For a cab, call **AC Taxi** (© **800/753-1231** or 250/753-1231) or **Swiftsure Taxi**
(© **250/753-8911**).

The **BC Ferries** route to Gabriola Island leaves from behind the Harbour
Park Shopping Centre on Front Street (note that this is not the same dock as
either the Tsawwassen- or Horseshoe Bay–bound ferries), roughly every hour
between 7am and 11pm. In summer, the round-trip fare is C$5.25 (US$3.40)
per person, plus C$13.50 (US$9) for a car. You can bring your bike free of
charge.

EXPLORING NANAIMO

Nanaimo's steep-faced waterfront has been recently restructured with tiers of
walkways, banks of flowers, marina boardwalks, and floating restaurants. Called
Pioneer Waterfront Plaza, the area fills on Fridays with the local farmers' market. The **Bastion,** a white fortified tower, rises above the harbor as a relic of the
1850s (it now holds a summer tourist information center).

Nanaimo's busy natural port has ferry links to Vancouver's Horseshoe Bay and
to Tsawwassen to the south, as well as to lovely **Gabriola Island** and to **Newcastle Island,** a car-free provincial park on the harbor's northern flank.
Throughout the day, floatplanes buzz in and out of the boat basin, shuttling
commuters back and forth to Vancouver. If you're up for a run, the **Harbourside Walkway** stretches 2½ miles (4km) from the heart of the city all the way to
Departure Bay.

The old downtown, centered on Commercial, Front, and Bastion streets, is a
series of pleasant winding streets behind the harbor. The long-established
Scotch Bakery, 87 Commercial St. (© **250/753-3521**), is the place to sample
the delicious Nanaimo Bar, created as a treat for 19th-century coal miners. **Artisan's Studio,** 70 Bastion St. (© **250/753-6151**), is a co-op gallery that displays
the work of local artists and craftspeople.

Another good strolling destination is the **Old City Quarter,** an uptown section of the city center that was severed from the harbor-front area when the
Island Highway cut through downtown. Now reached from the harbor by walking up the Bastion Street overpass, the 3-block area has been redeveloped into
upscale housing, boutiques, and fine restaurants.

Nanaimo District Museum Nanaimo's regional museum is a worthwhile
introduction to the area's past, first as a home for the Snunéymuxw (the name
from which Nanaimo derives) people and then as an industrial boomtown. An
intriguing exhibit links painted dioramas of traditional Snunéymuxw life with a
simulation of an archaeological dig near Discovery Bay in 1992. In drawers

---

(Moments   **Only in Nanaimo: The World Championship Bathtub Race**

From its beginnings in 1967, Nanaimo's signature summer draw has grown into a weeklong series of events that shows off the city's good-natured spirit. Fewer than half of the original racing vessels—old claw-foot tubs fitted with engines—completed the crossing of 36-mile (58km) Georgia Strait from Nanaimo Harbour to Vancouver's Fisherman's Cove. Most capsized at Nanaimo—in fact, the first tub to sink now receives the coveted Silver Plunger Award. These days, most contestants race in specially designed tubs that look like single-person speedboats. The race is the climax of Marine Festival, which includes a street fair, parade, and traditional "Sacrifice to the Bathtub Gods." For information, go to http://bathtub.island.net.

---

beneath the dioramas are the actual artifacts found at the site and pictured in the paintings. You'll also see an exhibit documenting the history and cultural importance of Chinatowns in Nanaimo's past—the last burned down in 1960 and was never rebuilt. A gift shop sells wooden carvings from the local Snunéymuxw.

100 Cameron Rd. (*C*) 250/753-1821. www.nanaimo.museum.bc.ca/ndm. Admission C$2 (US$1.30) adults, C$1.75 (US$1.15) seniors, C$.75 (US$.50) children 6–12. May 24 to Labour Day daily 9am–5pm; day after Labour Day to May 23 Tues–Sat 9am–5pm. From Front St., head up Museum Way, then left on Gordon St. and left again on Cameron Rd.

FERRYING TO NEWCASTLE ISLAND

Just off the coastline, **Newcastle Island Provincial Park** (*C* 250/391-2300 for BC Parks, South Vancouver Island District) is an ideal destination for hikers, cyclists, and campers. Two Salish Indian villages were established here before British settlers discovered coal on the island in 1849. The Canadian-Pacific Steamship Company purchased the island in 1931, creating a resort with a dance pavilion, teahouse, and floating hotel. The island now attracts outdoorsy types to its many trails; selected walks range from 1¼ to 2½ miles (2–4km). The popular **Mallard Lake Trail** leads through the wooded interior toward a freshwater lake; the **Shoreline Trail** runs across steep cliffs, onto sand and gravel beaches suitable for swimming, and up to a great eagle-spotting perch. The park maintains 18 **campsites,** with toilets, wood, fire pits, and water. Rates are C$12 (US$8).

From April to Canadian Thanksgiving (early Oct), the **Scenic Ferries** (*C* 250/753-5141; www.scenicferries.com) run leaves daily between 10am and early evening from the wharf at the peninsula tip of **Maffeo-Sutton Park** (just north of downtown). The round-trip fare for the 10-minute crossing is C$5 (US$3.25) for adults and C$4 (US$2.60) for seniors and children; bikes are C$2 (US$1.30).

EXPLORING GABRIOLA ISLAND

Much of Gabriola (pop. 4,000) is reached along North Road and South Road, two country lanes that provide a loop route around the island. A third road, Taylor Bay Road, departs from the ferry dock to access Gabriola's rocky northern reaches. It takes about half an hour to drive from one end of the island to the other.

The main commercial center is just up the hill from the ferry terminal and is often referred to as **Folklife Village.** The moniker seems a little precious until you learn that the log structure was originally constructed as the Folklife Pavilion for Vancouver's Expo '86. Stop by **Gabriola Artworks,** 575 North Rd. (© **250/247-7412**), an excellent gallery of local arts and crafts.

Sandwell Provincial Park is one of Gabriola's nicest beaches and picnic areas, with paths leading through old-growth forests and to views of the Entrance Island lighthouse. Turn off North Road onto Barrett Road and follow the signs.

At the southern end of Gabriola is Silva Bay, a marina resort featuring an ambitious new restaurant and pub (see "Where to Dine," below). Nearby is **FOGO Folk Art Studio** ☆, 3065 Commodore Way (© **250/247-8082;** www.fogo art.com). The Lauders' intricately carved characters perfectly capture the quirks of human nature. Wandering around the studio grounds is a true delight. Just south of Silva Bay is **Drumbeg Provincial Park,** which has a good swimming beach.

Gabriola Island and the area around Nanaimo are rich in prehistoric **petroglyph rock carvings.** On the South Road, near the United Church (about 6 miles/10km from the ferry terminal), a short path leads to a mix of fantastical creatures and abstract shapes scratched in sandstone. Park in the church lot and follow the signs. Note that the Snunéymuxw regard these petroglyphs as sacred, and frown on people taking pictures or rubbings of them.

Taylor Bay Road leads to more parks and beaches on the north end of the island. **Gabriola Sands Provincial Park** protects two of the island's best beaches, at Taylor Bay and Pilot Bay. Toward the end of the road (now called Berry Point Rd.) is the **Surf Lodge,** 885 Berry Point Rd. (© **250/247-9231**), with a pub and restaurant overlooking the Georgia Strait, and the superlative **Sunset B&B** (see "Where to Stay," below).

OUTDOOR PURSUITS

BUNGEE JUMPING The **Bungy Zone** (© **888/668-7771,** 800/668-7874, or 250/753-5867; www.bungyzone.com), off the Island Highway 15 minutes south of Nanaimo, is North America's only legal bridge jump, sending you over the Nanaimo River for C$95 (US$62).

DIVING ☆☆ All of the waters off Vancouver Island are known for their superior diving opportunities. One of the single best dives in the Northwest is at **Dodds Narrows,** between Vancouver Island and Mudge Island. It boasts outstanding visibility, a high concentration of wildlife, and dramatic rock formations. Other area dives include **Snake Island Wall,** with a drop-off that seems to extend into the abyss, and the wreck of the **HMCS Saskatchewan,** sunk off Snake Island in 1997 as part of Canada's artificial reef project.

Ocean Explorers Diving, 1956 Zorkin Rd., near Departure Bay (© **800/ 233-4145** or 250/753-2055; www.oceanexplorersdiving.com), offers charter dives and packages that include 2 nights' accommodation and five boat dives, with prices ranging from C$290 to C$350 (US$189 to US$228).

Two live-aboard dive outfitters offer charters to many destinations around Vancouver Island. **Mamro Adventures,** 1-5765 Turner Rd., Suite 203 (© **250/ 756-8872;** www.mamro.com/index.html), can accommodate six passengers on trips of 1 to 10 days. Popular excursions include Port Hardy, famed for its dense marine-mammal population, and the Gulf Islands, Sunshine Coast, and Georgia Strait. **Sea Experience,** 1956 Zorkin Rd., at Departure Bay (© **250/ 756-8895;** www.seaventurer.com), offers trips on the west side of the island for up to 10 people.

WHERE TO STAY
IN NANAIMO

Best Western Dorchester Hotel ⭐ The Dorchester stands on the most venerable spot in Nanaimo: the site of the Hudson's Bay Company trading post in the 1850s, and then of the city's old opera house. Reminders of the opera-house days remain: The handsome chandeliers are all original, as are the ornate columns flanking the dining room. For a historic hotel, the guest rooms are quite large; ask for a bay-side unit. Rooms for those with disabilities are available. *Note:* Smoking is not permitted in two-thirds of the hotel.

70 Church St., Nanaimo, BC V9R 5H4. © 800/661-2449 or 250/754-6835. Fax 250/754-2638. www. dorchesternanaimo.com. 65 units. C$80 (US$52) double. Extra person C$10 (US$7) per night. Senior and AAA discounts and corporate and off-season rates available. AE, DISC, DC, MC, V. Free parking. Pets accommodated for C$20 (US$13) per night. **Amenities:** Restaurant, lounge; golf course nearby; laundry service; same-day dry cleaning. *In room:* TV, dataport, coffeemaker, hair dryer, iron.

Coast Bastion Inn At this modern high-rise hotel, every room boasts a waterfront view, and the Harbourside Walkway scene is just seconds away. It's worth the splurge for a superior room, with upgraded amenities and views from two sides. Two wheelchair-accessible rooms are available. The hotel connects to the new Port Theatre complex.

11 Bastion St., Nanaimo, BC V9R 6E4. © 800/663-1144 or 250/753-6601. Fax 250/753-4155. www. coasthotels.com. 179 units. High season C$145–C$179 (US$94–US$116) double; C$215–C$250 (US$140–US$163) suite. Extra person C$10 (US$7). Senior and AAA discounts, theater packages, and off-season rates available. AE, DC, DISC, MC, V. Pets allowed for C$10 (US$7) per day. Valet parking C$9 (US$5.85); self-parking C$4.50 (US$2.95). **Amenities:** Restaurant, lounge; exercise room; Jacuzzi; sauna; concierge; 24-hr. room service; in-room massage; babysitting; laundry service; same-day dry cleaning. *In room:* A/C, TV w/ pay movies, dataport, coffeemaker, hair dryer, iron.

Howard Johnson Harbourside Hotel This motel complex is within easy walking distance of downtown, with direct access to the Harbourside Walkway and to lovely Bowen Park via trails that flank the Millstone River. The rooms are clean, good-size, and nicely furnished. Executive-level units have dataports and kitchenettes.

1 Terminal Ave., Nanaimo, BC V9R 5R4. © 800/663-7322 or 250/753-2241. Fax 250/753-6522. www.hojo nanaimo.com. 101 units. C$109–C$129 (US$71–US$84) double. Extra person C$10 (US$7). Off-season rates and senior and AAA discounts available. Pets allowed for C$10 (US$7) per day. Children under 12 stay free in parents' room. AE, DC, DISC, MC, V. Free parking. **Amenities:** Restaurant, lounge (Hemingway's Cigar and Martini Bar); heated outdoor pool; golf courses nearby; guest passes for nearby gym; tour desk; Budget car-rental office next door; limited room service; laundry service; same-day dry cleaning; beer-and-wine store. *In room:* A/C, TV, coffeemaker, hair dryer.

Pepper Muffin Country Inn ⭐ *Kids* This country B&B offers a rural get-away just minutes from downtown. Kids will enjoy exploring the 6-acre (2.4-hectare) farm with sheep, llamas, chickens, and a friendly poodle. A stream plays host to beaver, otter, and trout. Although newly constructed as an inn, the building was designed with quirky angles and rooflines, and is tastefully furnished with antiques. Each bedroom has a balcony. At breakfast, you'll learn what Pepper Muffin refers to: savory corn muffins flecked with jalapeño pepper. *Note:* Smoking is not permitted.

3718 Jingle Pot Rd., Nanaimo, BC V9R 6X4. © 250/756-0473. Fax 250/756-0421. www.peppermuffin.com. 3 units. C$89–C$99 (US$58–US$64) double. Rates include breakfast. AE, MC, V. **Amenities:** Golf course nearby; outdoor Jacuzzi; video library. *In room:* TV/VCR, hair dryer, no phone.

Sheraton Four Points Hotel Completed in 1998, the Sheraton is the area's most luxurious lodging. Each 600-square-foot Arbutus Suite has two TVs, a kitchenette, and a king bed. The Maple Suites are smaller but equally pleasing, and the standard rooms are a good value for the money. There are two wheelchair-accessible units. The public areas are handsome, particularly the lobby with its soaring ceilings and chandelier.

4898 Rutherford Rd., Nanaimo, BC V9T 4Z4. ℂ 800/325-3535 or 250/758-3000. Fax 250/729-2808. www. starwood.com/fourpoints. 72 units. C$99–C$209 (US$64–US$136) double; C$209–C$319 (US$136–US$207) suite. Fridge or microwave C$10 (US$7) per day. Extra person C$10 (US$7) per day. Senior and AAA discounts available. AE, DC, DISC, MC, V. **Amenities:** Restaurant, lounge; indoor pool; golf course nearby; exercise room; limited room service; laundry service; same-day dry cleaning. *In room:* A/C, TV, dataport, coffeemaker, hair dryer, iron.

Travelodge Nanaimo   A midprice motel with a great location, this Travelodge is just 2 blocks from the Vancouver ferry, and a short walk to downtown. All of the clean, comfortable rooms have balconies or patios. The front desk can help you arrange activities around Nanaimo.

96 Terminal Ave. N., Nanaimo, BC V9S 4J2. ℂ 800/667-0598 or 250/754-6355. Fax 250/754-1301. www. vquest.com/travelodgena. 78 units. July–Aug C$91–C$113 (US$59–US$73) double. June and Sept C$88–C$111 (US$57–US$72) double. Oct–May C$74–C$90 (US$48–US$59) double. Extra person C$6 (US$3.90). Rates include continental breakfast. Senior and AAA discounts available. AE, DISC, MC, V. Free parking. Pets allowed for C$10 (US$7) per night. **Amenities:** Golf course nearby; exercise room; sauna; coin-op laundry; dry cleaning. *In room:* TV, dataport, coffeemaker, hair dryer.

ON GABRIOLA ISLAND
Sunset B&B ⍟   This B&B on the rugged eastern shores of Gabriola Island overlooks rocky Orlobar Point and the Georgia Strait; paths lead to protected coves and tidal basins. The modern home is designed around a spacious open plan with vaulted ceilings and picture windows. The Wild Rose Suite is an amazing series of rooms that extends the entire length of the B&B. It consists of a sitting room with fireplace, bedroom, and enormous bathroom. Two other rooms overlook the side gardens. As lovely as they are, the real treasures here are the knowledgeable hosts. Once a Vienna Boys Choir singer, Gottfried brings a passion for music to the B&B, and Trudy contributes her love for reading. Guests are encouraged to listen to CDs or linger in the library. Breakfasts feature fruits, muffins, and—if you're lucky—Gottfried's Viennese scrambled eggs.

969 Berry Point Rd., Gabriola Island, BC V0R 1X0. ℂ 877/247-2032 or 250/247-2032. Fax 250/247-2036. www.sunsetcl.com. 3 units. High season C$75–C$150 (US$49–US$98) double. Rates include ferry pickup and full breakfast. MC, V. Children must be 14 or older. **Amenities:** Access to home computer. *In room:* Dataport, hair dryer.

WHERE TO DINE
IN NANAIMO
Flo's Diner DINER   Regulars—from businessmen to arty young things—come to Flo's for a sandwich or brunch, served up with attitude. This campy diner is probably the most colorful (in both senses of the word) place in the city, with mannequins and movie-star memorabilia for decor. The food is standard diner fare, though prepared with zest.

187 Commercial St. ℂ 250/753-2148. Reservations recommended on Sun. Main courses C$4.50–C$8 (US$2.95–US$5). V. Mon–Fri 8:30am–5:30pm; Sat 9am–5:30pm; Sun brunch 9am–3pm. Open later in summer.

The Globe Bar & Grill PUB   The pick of Nanaimo's many good pubs, the Globe is housed in an 1889 hotel with exposed brick and towering ceilings. Choices range from burgers, pasta, and pizza to steaks and fish, better prepared

---

Tips Two Popular Pubs

In summer, for a pint of ale and a burger, take the 10-minute Protection Connection ferry ride to the **Dinghy Dock Floating Marine Pub,** on Protection Island (🕐 **250/753-2373**). It's exactly what its name says—a floating pub—and boasts spectacular sunset views of Nanaimo and the Vancouver Island mountains. The ferry leaves on the hour from the Commercial Inlet boat basin, below Pioneer Waterfront Plaza. You'll get a wonderful view of the harbor from the **Lighthouse Bistro,** off Harbourside Walkway at 50 Anchor Way (🕐 **250/754-3212;** http://nanaimo.ark.com/~litehse). Open daily from 11am to midnight and until 1am in summer (the restaurant closes earlier), this floating pub also serves as the city's floatplane base—watch these flying boats take off and arrive from just beside your table.

---

than at most pubs. The selection of local beers is daunting. Add a game room, patio, and cigar room, and you've got something for everyone.

25 Front St. 🕐 **250/754-4910.** www.globebar.net. Main courses C$7–C$15 (US$4.55–US$9.75). AE, DC, MC, V. Free parking on street after 5pm and on weekends; validated parking for private lot. Daily 11am–midnight.

Maffeo's ITALIAN   This converted home in the Old Town Quarter offers richly authentic Italian dishes. The pasta-and-risotto sheet numbers nearly 25 choices. The meat and fish entrees are likewise classics, with osso buco, veal parmegiano, and other favorites. The atmosphere is warm and homey; in summer, you can dine in the garden.

538 Wentworth St. 🕐 **250/753-0377.** www.maffeos.com. Reservations recommended. Main courses C$12–C$22 (US$8–US$14). AE, MC, V. Daily seatings begin at 4:30pm.

Wesley Street Café ★★ WEST COAST CONTEMPORARY   Nanaimo's premier fine-dining restaurant serves the most up-to-date food in the city in a comfortably formal Old Town Quarter room. The cuisine pairs European preparations with flavors from the Far East, utilizing the stellar produce, seafood, and meats of western Canada. Starters include seared ahi tuna with curry butter, scallion aioli, and flying-fish roe. Entrees include seared Chilean sea bass with sweet parsnip, wilted spinach, and a vanilla bean sauce, and duck confit with ginger pear chutney. Live jazz is featured every Saturday night.

321 Wesley St. 🕐 **250/753-6057.** www.wesleycafe.com. Reservations required. Main courses C$14–C$26 (US$9–US$17). AE, MC, V. Mon–Fri 11:30am–2:30pm and 5:30–10pm; Sat–Sun noon–2:30pm.

ON GABRIOLA ISLAND

Silva Bay Bar and Grill SEAFOOD/GRILL BISTRO   Take the 20-minute Gabriola ferry and drive to the island's southern tip to find the Silva Bay Bar and Grill, formerly the Latitudes restaurant. It's a more casual place than its predecessor, catering to boaters fresh off the water as well as island families. The restaurant still has excellent views and offers dining out on the deck. Choose from baby-back ribs, fajitas, or a platter of grilled halibut, scallops, prawns, and green mussels in a white wine lemon pepper sauce. Sunday brunch is served from 11am to 1pm.

3383 South Rd., in the Silva Bay Resort and Marina. 🕐 **250/247-8662.** Reservations recommended. Main courses C$7–C$23 (US$4.50–US$15). MC, V. Daily 11am–10pm (call ahead for off-season hr.).

3 Parksville & Qualicum Beach

23 miles (37km) N of Nanaimo

These twin resort towns are near the most popular beaches on Vancouver Island. Spending a week here is a family tradition for many residents of British Columbia. With miles of sand and six golf courses, it's the perfect base for a relaxing vacation. Parksville (pop. 10,500) and Qualicum Beach (pop. 7,500) are also good stopping-off points for travelers making the trip to or from Victoria and Tofino.

ESSENTIALS

GETTING THERE **Island Coach Lines** (© **800/663-8390** in the U.S., 800/318-0818 in Canada, or 250/388-5248 in Victoria; www.victoriatours. com) offers bus transport to the Parksville and Qualicum area along the Highway 1/Highway 19 corridor; one-way fare from Victoria is C$27.50 (US$18). **VIA Rail's E&N Railiner,** or the *Malahat* (© **888/VIA-RAIL** or 250/ 383-4324; www.viarail.ca), stops in both towns on its daily trip from Victoria to Courtenay. **KD Air** (© **800/665-4244,** 604/688-9957, or 250/752-5884; www.kdair.com) flies daily from Vancouver to the Qualicum Beach Airport for C$183 (US$119) round-trip. The closest other air service is at Nanaimo; for details, see "Nanaimo & Gabriola Island," above.

VISITOR INFORMATION Contact the **Qualicum Beach Visitor Information Centre,** 2711 W. Island Hwy. (© **250/752-9532;** fax 250/752-2923; www.qualicum.bc.ca), or **Parksville Visitor Information Centre,** 1275 E. Island Hwy. (© **250/248-3613;** fax 250/248-5210; www.chamber.parksville. bc.ca). For information on this part of Vancouver Island, contact the **Oceanside Tourism Association,** 174 Railway St., Qualicum Beach (© **888/799-3222** or 250/752-2388; fax 250/752-2392; www.oceanside-bc.com).

EXPLORING THE AREA

While these towns share similar beaches and are all but connected by country-club developments and marinas, there are differences between the two. Parksville has several large resorts and beachfront hotels, and is more of a long developed strip without much of a town center. In contrast, Qualicum Beach accommodations are largely B&Bs, and there is a more traditional town center with shopping and cafes—but this part of town is a couple miles inland, away from the beach.

In Qualicum Beach, you can access the beach from many points along Highway 19A, the old Island Highway. Likewise, in Parksville, the beach is accessible downtown from the old Island Highway, near the junction of Highway 4A, and at the adjacent Parksville Community Beach and Playground. However, the best beaches are preserved in **Rathtrevor Beach Provincial Park,** just east of Parksville's town center. The 860-acre (348-hectare) park offers trails, bird-watching sites, and a campground.

Note: If you're looking for miles of broad, white-sand strands lapped by azure water, you may be surprised. The sea is quite shallow here, with a very gentle slope. When the tide goes out, it exposes hundreds of acres of gray-sand flats. When the tide is in, the beach disappears beneath the shallow waters. There are benefits to this: The summer sun bakes the sand while the tide is out, so when the tide comes back in, the shallow water is warmed by the sand, thus making the water agreeable for swimming.

When you're not on the beach, one particularly good place to stop in Qualicum Beach is the **Old School House,** 122 Fern Rd. W. (© **250/752-8133**), which now houses galleries, studios, and a gift shop.

HORNE LAKE CAVES PROVINCIAL PARK

West of Qualicum Beach, **Horne Lake Caves Provincial Park** (© 250/ **954-4600** for Strathcona Park District) offers access to a lakeside park area, with camping and canoeing, and a system of caves on the slopes of the Beaufort Range. Two caves are open for self-exploration, though you must bring at least two sources of light, and helmets are recommended (in summer, rent one from the park office). From mid-June to Labour Day, the park offers a variety of guided tours, starting with the family-oriented Riverbend Cave Interpretive Program. For more adventure, contact **Island Pacific Adventures/Horne Lake Adventures** (© **250/757-8687**; www.hornelake.com) to reserve for its 5-hour Riverbend Expedition (C$79/US$51), which culminates in roping up a seven-story waterfall. No prior climbing experience is necessary.

HITTING THE LINKS

There are six golf courses in the Parksville–Qualicum Beach area, and over a dozen within an hour's drive. **Eagle Crest Golf Club,** 2035 Island Hwy., Qualicum Beach (© **800/567-1320** or 250/752-9744; www.eaglecrest.bc.ca), is an 18-hole, par-71 course with an emphasis on shot making and accuracy. **Glengarry Golf Links,** 1025 Qualicum Rd., Qualicum Beach (© **250/752-8786**; www.glengarrygolf.com), has nine links-style holes, plus a forested and scenic back nine. **Qualicum Beach Memorial,** 115 Crescent Rd. W. (© **250/ 752-6312**), has nine holes, stunning ocean views, and a restaurant. **Arrowsmith Golf and Country Club,** north of Qualicum Beach at 2250 Fowler Rd. (© **250/752-9727**; www.golfarrowsmith.com), is a family-oriented course with 18 holes and a par-61 rating.

Fairwinds, east of Parksville at 3730 Fairwinds Dr., Nanoose Bay (© **250/ 468-7666**; www.fairwinds.bc.ca/golf.html), is a challenging 18-hole, par-71 course with ocean views and lots of trees. **Morningstar Golf Club** ☆, 525 Lowry's Rd., Parksville (© **250/248-2244**; www.morningstar.bc.ca), is an 18-hole, par-72 championship course with a 74 rating. Designed by Les Furber, it has seaside links and fairways that run in and out of the woods. Each of the above has a driving range, clubhouse, and pro shop.

WHERE TO STAY

Campsites at **Rathtrevor Beach Provincial Park** (© **800/689-9025** for reservations, or 250/248-9449 in off-season) go for C$12 to C$19 (US$8 to US$12); open in July and August.

Ambleside Cottage B&B   This 1929 English-style cottage is actually a large estate-style home with handsomely furnished bedrooms. The living room features a massive granite fireplace. There's also a cottage that sleeps up to six. A private path leads down to the beach. *Note:* Smoking is not allowed on the premises.

395 Burnham Rd., Qualicum Beach, BC V9K 1G5. © **877/752-2930** or 250/752-2930. Fax 250/752-2987. www.amblesidecottage.com. 6 units. May–Sept C$90–C$145 (US$59–US$94) double; Oct–Apr C$75–C$95 (US$49–US$62) double. Extra person C$10–C$20 (US$7–US$13). Cottage C$800 (US$520) per week. Rates include full breakfast. MC, V. Closed mid-Oct to mid-Feb; call to check. Children must be 15 or older. Pets allowed in cottage only. **Amenities:** Outdoor pool; golf courses nearby; tennis court; courtesy limo; laundry service. *In room:* No phone.

Bahari B&B ☆   Bed-and-breakfasts come in all shapes and styles, but Bahari is unique for its artistically exquisite sure-handedness. Decorated with an Asian influence that's more elegant than the clutter typical of many B&Bs, this property could easily take pride of place in *Architectural Digest.* All units have balconies, robes, and quality linens. Even the bathrooms contain one-of-a-kind fixtures, like room 2's incredible custom-made counter of slumped glass. Guests are welcome in the sitting room and TV room, with leather couches and fireplace. Follow the paths to the beach, frequented by seals and eagles, or watch ships ply the waters of the Georgia Strait. Kids are allowed in a separate apartment with fireplace and kitchen.

5101 Island Hwy., Qualicum Beach, BC V9K 1Z1. ☎ **877/752-9278** or 250/752-9278. Fax 250/752-9038. www.baharibandb.com. 5 units. Feb–May and Oct–Nov C$85–C$135 (US$55–US$88) double, C$120–C$190 (US$78–US$124) 2-bedroom apt; June–Sept C$125–C$185 (US$81–US$120) double, C$180–C$260 (US$117–US$169) apt. 2-night minimum stay in apt June–Sept. Rates include breakfast. Weekly rates and packages available. AE, MC, V. Children accepted in apt; B&B guests must be 16 or older. **Amenities:** Golf course nearby; Jacuzzi; free laundry facilities. *In room:* TV, hair dryer.

Best Western Bayside Inn   Perched right above the sands in central Parksville, this resort offers bounteous amenities at moderate prices. Half of the rooms face the beach, and the other half look onto the mountains of Vancouver Island. Heron's offers Mediterranean seafood cuisine, with summer seating on the deck. The bar features darts, pool, and satellite sports broadcasts. *Note:* Smoking is not permitted in most rooms.

240 Dogwood St., Parksville, BC V9P 2H5. ☎ **800/663-4232** or 250/248-8333. Fax 250/248-4689. www. bwbayside.com. 59 units. Oct–Mar C$89–C$109 (US$58–US$71) double; Apr–June C$99–C$129 (US$64–US$84) double. July–Sept C$119–C$179 (US$77–US$116) double. Extra person C$10 (US$7). AE, DC, DISC, MC, V. Free parking. Pets allowed for C$15 (US$10). **Amenities:** Restaurant, bar; indoor pool; golf course nearby; full-service health club and spa; Jacuzzi; sauna; bike rentals; tour/activities desk; business center; limited room service; in-room massage; babysitting; laundry service; same-day dry cleaning. *In room:* TV, dataport, coffeemaker, hair dryer, iron.

Hollyford Guest Cottage 🌟🌟   The rooms are stylish and the hosts charming, but what really makes this place stand out is its collection of antiques and Canadiana. The lounge's carved black-walnut sideboard—rumored to have been designed for the Banff Springs Hotel—is simply amazing. You'll also see Native jewelry, Inuit art, and an homage to the Mounties. Lest this sound like a museum, let us assure you that the proprietors have that rare knack for presenting objects as art, not clutter. Each guest room has heated floors, a fireplace, and a soaker tub. At breakfast, your hosts will bring out the antique china, Waterford crystal, and silver from the glory days of the Canadian Pacific Railway. *Note:* Smoking is not permitted.

106 Hoylake Rd. E. (at Memorial Ave.), Qualicum Beach, BC V9K 1L7. ☎ **877/224-6559** or 250/752-8101. Fax 250/752-8102. www.hollyford.ca. 3 units. June–Sept C$165 (US$107) double; Oct–May C$135 (US$88) double. Rates include full breakfast and refreshment sideboard. Off-season rates may vary. MC, V. Children must be 12 or older. **Amenities:** Golf course nearby; free loaner bikes; laundry service; same-day dry cleaning. *In room:* TV/VCR, CD player, hair dryer.

Maclure House B&B Inn   This ivy-covered, half-timbered 1921 mansion was modeled after a Scottish hunting lodge. You'll see expanses of leaded glass, 30-foot (9m) ceilings, and ornate moldings. Bedrooms are decorated according to British Empire themes, but with restraint applied. Two units face the ocean and share a balcony. The Ocean Suite boasts a fireplace and an incredible bathroom with original fixtures.

1015 E. Island Hwy., Parksville, BC V9P 2E4. ☎ **250/248-3470.** Fax 250/248-5162. www.maclurehouse.com. 4 units. Mid-June to mid-Sept C$95–C$140 (US$62–US$91) double. Mid-Sept to mid-June C$80–C$115 (US$52–US$75) double. Extra person C$12–C$21 (US$8–US$14). Rates include three-course breakfast and afternoon treats. Special packages available. AE, MC, V. **Amenities:** Restaurant (see "Where to Dine," below); lounge; golf courses nearby; tennis court; concierge; coin-op laundry; laundry service; dry cleaning. *In room:* Hair dryer, no phone.

Pacific Shores Nature Resort 🐾   Pacific Shores is a large time-share development integrated into the landscape; it sits above a half mile of waterfront, tucked into a grove of arbutus and fir trees. Trails lead across the property, and the resort even has its own fish hatchery. Most impressive are the extensive gardens—if you see a plant you like, you may be able to purchase a cutting from the nursery.

The array of accommodations is not easily summarized. The handsomely decorated standard suites have two bedrooms, a kitchen, fireplaces, a balcony, and two bathrooms, one with a jetted tub. It's a good idea to call and discuss the various floor-plan options with the reservations staff. Families are welcome and minimum stays of a week are preferred in summer. But you usually also have the option to rent a hotel-style room for shorter stays. Several rooms have wheelchair access. As of 2002, Pacific Shores will have a new restaurant, pub, and full-service spa. Resort staff can help you book activities with local outfitters.

1–1600 Stroulger Rd., Nanoose Bay, BC V9P 9B7. ℂ **866/986-2222** or 250/468-7121. Fax 250/468-2001. www.pacific-shores.com. Up to 132 units. C$80–C$280 (US$52–US$182) 1- or 2-bedroom condo. AE, DISC, MC, V. Free parking. **Amenities:** Convenience store and deli; large indoor pool with "ozonated" water; health club with full weight room; Jacuzzis; sauna; free kayaks, canoe, and rowboat; outdoor children's play area; use of two computers with Internet access; massage; laundry service. *In room:* TV/VCR, dataport, fridge, coffeemaker, iron.

Tigh-Na-Mara Resort Hotel 🐾🐾 *Kids*   This time-honored log-cabin resort just keeps getting better. Established in the 1940s, Tigh-Na-Mara has expanded over the years: more cottages, lodge rooms, and condo suites, all with fireplaces and most with kitchens. The cottages are comfortably lived-in, and the oceanside condos are new and lavish. Families will appreciate the lengthy list of supervised activities, plus amenities like video rentals and babysitting. The restaurant has a full children's menu, plus Friday barbecues and dances in summer. At press time, the resort was adding a new spa and health club.

1095 E. Island Hwy., Parksville, BC V9P 2E5. ℂ **800/663-7373** or 250/248-2072. Fax 250/248-4140. www. tigh-na-mara.com. 210 units. July–Aug C$109–C$249 (US$71–US$162) double. Rates vary throughout the year. Extra person C$5–C$10 (US$3.25–US$7). Weekly rates available. Varying minimum stays apply in summer, on holidays, and on weekends. AE, DC, MC, V. Free parking. One pet allowed per cottage Sept–June for C$2 (US$1.30) per day. **Amenities:** Restaurant (Northwest); bar; indoor pool; golf courses nearby; tennis court; access to health club; sauna; paddle boats; bike rentals; children's programs; concierge; tour/activities desk (in summer); car-rental desk; business center; in-room massage; babysitting; coin-op laundry; laundry service; dry cleaning. *In room:* TV, fridge, coffeemaker.

WHERE TO DINE

Beach House Café INTERNATIONAL   The flavors of the Orient and Austria blend together at this popular beachside restaurant. An outstanding choice is the Madras shrimp and fruit coconut milk curry, also available as a vegetarian dish by request. On the European side of the menu, the Jagerschnitzel (veal medallions with wild-mushroom sauce) is a standout. The dining room is comfortable, filled with sun and views.

2775 W. Island Hwy., Qualicum Beach. ℂ **250/752-9626.** Reservations suggested. Main courses C$10–C$18.50 (US$7–US$12). MC, V. Daily 11am–2:30pm and 5–10pm.

Cola Diner BURGERS   We've all been to retro 1950s-style restaurants; this roadhouse, however, is the real thing, with both a soda fountain and a jukebox. The menu is filled with burgers, gravity-defying Dagwood sandwiches, and side dishes like onion rings and fries. The owners are native Germans, so dishes from the homeland also work their way onto the menu. The diner is fully licensed.

6060 W. Island Hwy., Qualicum Bay. (© 250/757-2029. www.colaland.com/diner.html. Reservations recommended. Main courses C$4.95–C$20 (US$3.20–US$13). MC, V. Wed–Mon 10am–10pm.

Kalvas Restaurant SEAFOOD   Kalvas is the locals' special-occasion restaurant, a rustic-looking lodge with a bustling dining room. The specialties are steaks and seafood prepared in traditional supper-club style: sole amandine, New York steak, steamed Dungeness crab served with drawn butter, and nine preparations of Fanny Bay oysters.

180 Molliet St., Parksville. (© **250/248-6933.** Reservations recommended. Main courses C$12–C$60 (US$8–US$39). MC, V. Sun–Fri 5–10pm; Sat 5–11pm.

Lefty's Fresh Foods HEALTHY/INTERNATIONAL   Lefty's began as a mostly vegetarian eatery, but over the years has added more chicken and meat dishes. The emphasis remains on healthy cooking, with a menu that borrows from ethnic cuisines and up-to-date comfort food: salads, sandwiches, burgers, pasta, stir-fries, and focaccia pizzas.

710 Memorial St., Qualicum Beach, and 101-280 E. Island Hwy., Parksville. (© **250/752-7530** (Qualicum) and **250/954-3886** (Parksville). www.leftys.tv. Main courses C$8–C$20 (US$5–US$13). AE, DC, MC, V. Thurs–Sat 8am–10pm (to 9pm off-season); Sun–Wed 8am–8pm.

Maclure House Restaurant ☆ INTERNATIONAL   This Tudor-style mansion is perfect for a romantic meal. Guests are seated in the wood-paneled dining room, library, or music room, each with a fireplace and garden views. The snug lounge is a wonderful spot for a drink. In summer, tables spill out onto the flagstone veranda. The menu has a good selection of salads and pastas, plus Indian curries. The specialty is rack of lamb, crusted with Dijon mustard and pecans. An inexpensive three-course dinner (C$16/US$10) offers entree choices such as fish-and-chips, shepherd's pie, and seafood lasagna.

1015 E. Island Hwy., Parksville. (© **250/248-3470.** www.maclurehouse.com. Reservations recommended. Main courses C$13–C$29 (US$8.50–US$19). AE, MC, V. Daily 8:30–2:30pm and seatings 5–8pm.

Red Pepper Grill INTERNATIONAL   Located on a quiet block off the busy Island Highway strip, the Red Pepper Grill features up-to-date pasta and seafood preparations, plus standards such as steak and ribs. There's also a children's menu. The patio is one of downtown's nicest spots on a sunny day.

193 Memorial Ave., Parksville. (© **250/248-2364.** www.redpeppergrill.com. Reservations recommended. Main courses C$6–C$16 (US$4–US$10). MC, V. Tues–Fri 11:30am–2pm; Tues–Sun 5–9pm.

Saigon Garden VIETNAMESE   Vietnamese food isn't as common in Canada as in the United States, making this excellent outpost even more of a treat. Order favorites like pho (noodle soup) and specialties like *com tay cam do bien,* a seafood hot pot with prawns, scallops, squid, royal mushrooms, and lily flowers in a delicate fish broth.

118 Craig St., Parksville. (© **250/248-5667.** Reservations not needed. Main courses C$6–C$10 (US$3.90–US$7). V. Mon–Sat 11am–9pm. Free delivery after 3pm in the Parksville area.

Shady Rest Waterfront Pub & Restaurant CANADIAN   Both the restaurant and the pub here have outdoor seating, and both serve the same Qualicum Beach–style comfort food. The appetizer menu is extensive, making this a convenient choice if you're not hungry enough for a full-on meal. Entrees range from stir-fries to burgers, plus the freshest local seafood.

3109 W. Island Hwy., Qualicum Beach. (© **250/752-9111.** Reservations recommended for the restaurant. Main courses C$10–C$18 (US$7–US$12). MC, V. Restaurant daily 8am–9pm; pub food service Sun–Thurs 11am–9pm and Fri–Sat 11am–10pm. Pub open until 1am Fri–Sat.

4 En Route to Vancouver Island's Wild West Coast

From Parksville, Highway 4 cuts due west, climbing up over the mountainous spine of Vancouver Island before dropping into Port Alberni, at the head of the Pacific's Alberni Inlet. From here, you can join the mail boats **MV *Lady Rose*** and **MV *Frances Barkley*** as they ply the inlet's narrow waters, delivering mail, supplies, and passengers to isolated communities. Bamfield, the southern terminus of the mail-boat run, is one of the two departure points for the West Coast Trail. Mail boats from Port Alberni also negotiate the waters of Barkley Sound and the Broken Group Islands before arriving at Ucluelet, a gentrifying resort town.

THE DRIVE TO PORT ALBERNI

Just west of Parksville is the **North Island Wildlife Recovery Centre,** 1240 Leffler Rd., Errington (© **250/248-8534;** http://nanaimo.ark.com/~niwra), which takes in injured and orphaned wildlife. Its eagle flight cage is the largest in Canada. Open April through October, daily from 10am to 4pm. Take a left from Highway 4 onto Bellevue Road; turn right onto Ruffels Road and then left onto Leffler.

Just 1½ miles (3km) west of the junction with Highway 19, turn south to **Englishman's Falls Provincial Park.** Easy trails lead to both the upper and lower falls. Picnic tables and a basic campground are available.

Below the cliffs of 5,963-foot (1,818m) Mount Arrowsmith, Highway 4 passes along the shores of **Cameron Lake.** The western end of the lake is preserved as **MacMillan Provincial Park,** a magnificent stand of old-growth forest.

Finally, you'll reach **Port Alberni,** a hard-working town of nearly 20,000. The busy port is home to a number of fishing charters and boat-tour companies, as well as the mail boats that offer day trips to Bamfield and Ucluelet. If you need a hotel, consider the **Coast Hospitality Inn,** 3835 Redford St. (© **800/663-1144** or 250/723-8111; www.alberni.net/coasthi), with doubles from C$140 (US$91); or the **Best Western Barclay,** 4277 Stamp Ave. (© **800/563-6590** or 250/724-7171; www.bestwesternbarclay.com), with rooms from C$109 (US$71) in high season.

MV *LADY ROSE* & MV *FRANCES BARKLEY*

Lady Rose Marine Services operates two packet freighters that deliver mail and supplies to communities along the Alberni Inlet and Barkley Sound. In addition, the boats take sightseers to the wild outback of Vancouver Island, offering a fascinating glimpse into the daily life of remote fishing and logging communities. You'll likely see bald eagles and probably bears, and, if you're lucky, orcas or porpoises. The freighters also convey kayakers bound for the Broken Group Islands. The company operates a lodge at Sechart as well.

Year-round, the freighters depart from the north side of Harbour Quay at 8am on Tuesday, Thursday, and Saturday. They head to Bamfield via Kildonan, with an hour-long layover before returning to Port Alberni at 5:30pm. From the first Friday in July to the first Friday in September, there's an additional 8am Friday sailing from Port Alberni to Bamfield.

June through September, freighters also depart at 8am on Monday, Wednesday, and Friday for Ucluelet via Sechart near the Broken Group Islands, arriving back in Port Alberni at 7pm (the freighters are no longer allowed to land in the Broken Group, but between October and May they will drop kayakers at the islands with advance notice). From the first Sunday in July to the first Sunday in September, there's an additional 8am Sunday sailing to Bamfield via Sechart, which arrives back in Port Alberni at 6:15pm.

One-way fare to Bamfield is C$23 (US$15); the return is C$45 (US$29). One-way fare to Ucluelet is C$25 (US$16); the return is C$50 (US$33). You can go to Kildonan only for C$12 (US$8) each way, or to Sechart—and the lodge—for C$20 to C$30 (US$13 to US$20), depending on the season. On all journeys, children 8 to 17 pay half. Bring windproof jackets and hats, as the weather can change dramatically during the course of the trip. Reservations are required. For freighter ticket information and lodge reservations, contact **Lady Rose Marine Services** (© **800/663-7192** Apr–Sept, or 250/723-8313; fax 250/723-8314; www.ladyrosemarine.com).

5 The West Coast Trail ✦ & Pacific Rim National Park ✦

The west coast of Vancouver Island is a magnificent area of old-growth forests, stunning fjords (called "sounds" in local parlance), rocky coasts, and sandy beaches. And although Pacific Rim National Park was established in 1971, it wasn't until 1993 that the area really exploded into the consciousness of people outside the immediate area. That was when thousands of environmentalists from around the world gathered to protest the clear-cutting of old-growth forests in Clayoquot Sound. When footage of the protests ran on the evening news, people who saw the landscape for the first time were moved to come experience it firsthand. Tourism in the area has never looked back.

There are three units to Pacific Rim National Park (http://parkscan.harbour. com/pacrim). Along the southwest coast is a strip of land that contains the 46-mile (75km) **West Coast Trail,** which runs between Port Renfrew (covered in chapter 5, "Southern Vancouver Island & the Gulf Islands") and Bamfield (see above). It's considered one of the world's great hikes, but the grueling 5- to 7-day journey—with frequent dangerous river crossings and rocky scrambles—is not for the inexperienced. The **Broken Group Islands** unit is a wilderness archipelago in the mouth of Barkley Sound, and a popular destination for divers and sea kayakers. The **Long Beach** unit fronts onto the Pacific between the towns of Ucluelet and Tofino. Long Beach is more than 19 miles (30km) long, broken here and there by rocky headlands and bordered by tremendous groves of cedar and Sitka spruce. The beach is popular with birds and marine life.

The town of **Ucluelet** (pronounced You-*clue*-let, meaning "safe harbor") sits on the southern end of the Long Beach peninsula, on the edge of Barkley Sound. Though it has a winter population of only 1,800, thousands of visitors arrive between March and May to see the Pacific gray whales.

At the far northern tip of the peninsula, **Tofino** (pop. 1,500) borders beautiful Clayoquot Sound. It's the center of the local ecotourism business, though it's

---

Tips **Special Events**

About 20,000 Pacific gray whales migrate here annually. During the second week of March, the **Pacific Rim Whale Festival** ✦ (© **250/726-7742** or 250/725-3414; www.island.net/~whalef) is held in Tofino and Ucluelet. The annual whale migration is celebrated with guided whale-watching hikes; First Nations' storytelling, music, dancing, and art; children's activities; and contests.

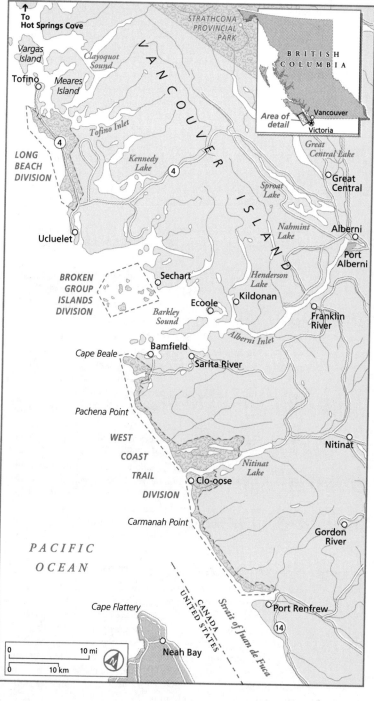

↑
To
Hot Springs Cove

STRATHCONA
PROVINCIAL
PARK

Vargas
Island

Clayoquot
Sound

Tofino

Meares
Island

Tofino Inlet

BRITISH
COLUMBIA

Area of
detail

Vancouver

Victoria

LONG
BEACH
DIVISION

4

Kennedy
Lake

4

VANCOUVER ISLAND

Great
Central Lake

Great
Central

Sproat
Lake

Nahmini
Lake

Alberni

Port
Alberni

Ucluelet

BROKEN
GROUP
ISLANDS
DIVISION

Sechart

Barkley
Sound

Ecoole

Henderson
Lake

Kildonan

Franklin
River

Cape Beale

Bamfield

Sarita River

Alberni Inlet

Pachena Point

WEST

COAST

TRAIL

DIVISION

Nitinat
Lake

Clo-oose

Nitinat

Carmanah Point

Gordon
River

PACIFIC

OCEAN

Cape Flattery

CANADA
UNITED STATES

Strait of Juan de Fuca

Port Renfrew

14

0   10 mi

0   10 km

Neah Bay

still relatively small. Hikers and beachcombers come to Tofino simply for the scenery; others use it as a base from which to explore the sound.

ESSENTIALS

GETTING THERE **By Plane** May through September, **North Vancouver Air** (© 800/228-6608 or 604/278-1608; www.northvanair.com) operates twin-engine, turbo-prop planes daily to Tofino from Vancouver or Seattle's Boeing Field; October through April, flights run three or four times a week. The fare from Vancouver is C$270 (US$176) round-trip; flying time is 45 minutes. **Northwest Seaplanes** (© 800/690-0086; www.nwseaplanes.com) and **Sound Flight** (© 800/825-0722; www.soundflight.com) offer floatplane service between Renton, Washington (outside of Seattle), and Tofino from mid-June to late September. One-way fares run around US$195.

By Car From Nanaimo, take the Island Highway (Hwy. 19) north for 31 miles (52km). Just before Parksville, there's a turnoff for Highway 4, which leads first to the mid-island town of Port Alberni (about 23 miles/38.3km west) and then the coastal towns of Ucluelet (62 miles/103.3km west) and Tofino (81 miles/135km west of Port Alberni). The road is well paved, but gets winding and hilly after Port Alberni.

By Ferry A 4½-hour ride aboard the **Lady Rose Marine Services** (© 800/663-7192 Apr–Sept, or 250/723-8313; fax 250/723-8314; www.ladyrose marine.com) MV *Lady Rose* takes you from Port Alberni to Ucluelet. See p. 137 for more information.

By Bus **Island Coach Lines** (© 800/663-8390 in the U.S., 800/318-0818 in Canada, or 250/385-4411 in Victoria; www.victoriatours.com) operates daily service. The fare for the 7-hour trip from Victoria is C$49.50 (US$32) to Ucluelet and C$52.25 (US$34) to Tofino. The bus also stops in Nanaimo and picks up passengers arriving from Vancouver on the ferry.

VISITOR INFORMATION The **Ucluelet Visitor Info Centre,** 100 Main St., by Government Wharf on Ucluelet Harbour (© 250/726-4641; www. uclueletinfo.com), is open July through September, Monday through Friday from 11am to 5pm. Also check out **www.ucluelet.com**. The **Long Beach Visitor Information Centre** (© 250/726-4212)—about a mile (1.6km) from the Highway 4 junction to Tofino; off to the right as you head to Tofino, before the entrance to the Gold Mine Trail—is open from mid-March to September, daily from 10am to 6pm. The **Tofino Visitor Info Centre,** 380 Campbell St. (© 250/725-3414; www.tofinobc.org), is open March through September, Monday through Friday from 11am to 5pm. Also see **www.island.net/~tofino/ insiders**.

THE HIKE OF A LIFETIME: THE WEST COAST TRAIL

After the SS *Valencia* ran aground in 1906 and most of the survivors died of exposure on the beach, the government built a rescue trail between Bamfield and Port Renfrew. The trail follows a rugged shoreline where approximately 66 ships have met their demise along this stretch of "the graveyard of the Pacific." Upgraded in the 1970s as part of the new Pacific Rim National Park, the West Coast Trail has gained a reputation as one of the world's greatest extreme hiking adventures. Each year, about 9,000 people tackle the entire challenging 46-mile (75km) route, and thousands more hike the very accessible **7-mile (11km) oceanfront stretch** at the northern trail head near Bamfield.

⌒Moments   Diving the Graveyard of the Pacific

The waters off the park's West Coast Trail are known throughout the world as "the graveyard of the Pacific." Hundreds of 19th- and 20th-century ship-wrecks silently attest to the hazards of sailing without an experienced guide in these unforgiving waters. The Cousteau Society rates this area one of the world's best. There are even underwater interpretive trails that nar-rate the area's unique history. For an index of diving outfitters, check out **www.3routes.com/na/can/bc/09/index.html** and **http://bamfield.sd70.bc.ca/guide/diving.html**.

The West Coast Trail land is temperate coastal rain forest dominated by old-growth spruce, hemlock, and cedar. The topography ranges from sandy beaches to rocky headlands and wide sandstone ledges. Caves, arches, tidal pools, and waterfalls add variety to the shoreline.

Imperative for the full hike are: planning ahead (get a topographic map and tidal table), stamina (train for rock climbing as well as hiking), and experience (advanced wilderness-survival and minimum-impact camping knowledge). Vet-erans recommend going with at least two companions, packing weatherproof gear, and bringing about 50 feet (15m) of climbing rope per person. Only 52 people per day are allowed to enter the main trail (26 from Port Renfrew, 26 from Bamfield), and registration with the park office is mandatory. Most people make the hike in 5 to 7 days.

Call **Discover BC** (✆ **800/663-6000**) after March 1 to schedule your entry reservation for the coming May-through-September season. In summer, you can also contact the **parks service** (✆ **250/728-3234** or 250/647-5434) for infor-mation. Good websites include **http://parkscan.harbour.com/pacrim** and **www.boreasbackcountry.com/polaris/hiking/wct.htm**.

Make your reservations as early as possible. There's a C$25 (US$16) booking fee and C$70 (US$46) trail-use fee. If you want to try your luck, there are six daily first-come, first-served waitlist openings at each trail head information center—Gordon River at the south end and Pachena Bay at the north end. The park service says you'll probably wait 1 to 3 days for an opening.

UCLUELET

When fishing was the major industry on the coast, Ucluelet was the big town. It was here that most of the ships docked, and here that the processing and pack-ing plants were located. With the recent boom in ecotourism, however, Ucluelet is scrambling to catch up. At the moment, it offers a couple of fine B&Bs, but has yet to develop the same range of restaurants and activities as Tofino. Things are changing fast, however, and Ucluelet is still cheaper, just as close to Long Beach, and more likely to have vacancies in the high season.

Fishing, kayaking, and whale-watching are the big attractions. While the eco-tourism draws are gaining in popularity, fishing is still quite popular here, much more so than in Tofino. Charter companies include **Quest Charters,** in the boat basin (✆ **250/726-7532;** www.ucluelet.com/questcharters). If you want to combine lodging with your fishing expedition, check out **Island West Resort,** 1990 Bay St. (✆ **250/726-7515;** www.islandwestresort.com), or, for more lux-ury, Oak Bay Marine Group's **Canadian Princess Resort,** 1943 Peninsula Rd. (✆ **800/663-7090;** www.canadianprincess.com).

Subtidal Adventures, 1950 Peninsula Rd., in the West Ucluelet Mall (© 877/444-1134 or 250/726-7336; www3.telus.net/subtidaladventures), offers whale-watching trips, kayaking expeditions out to the Broken Group Islands, and even an archaeological tour. **Aqua Marine Adventures,** 1932 Peninsula Rd. (© 866/726-7727 or 250/726-7727; www.westcoastwhales. com), operates whale-watching tours that let passengers listen to whales through the boat's hydrophone system. **Majestic Ocean Kayaking,** 125 Garden St., off Helen Road (© 800/889-7644 or 250/726-2868; www.majestic.bc.ca), runs kayak trips to Ucluelet Sound, Barkley Sound, Broken Group Islands, and Clayoquot Sound.

Pristine Adventures (© 250/726-4477; www.alberni.net/pristine) can arrange a guided canoe trip that lets you see wildlife up close, in particular black bears. The standard 3-hour harbor tour has averaged 500 bear sightings per season. Canoeing lessons are included.

For a short hike, set out on the 1¾-mile (3km) **Wild Pacific Trail,** which takes you out to the Amphitrite Lighthouse, a prime whale-watching spot. The trail is a work in progress, and should be a full 10 miles (16km) long when completed. See also "Outdoor Pursuits" under "Tofino," below, for information on guided walks offered by **Long Beach Nature Tour Company** ★.

WHERE TO STAY

Ocean's Edge B&B ★ *Finds* This is *the* place to stay for nature lovers, considering that its hosts are some of the most knowledgeable naturalists around. The B&B sits on a tiny peninsula, with only a thicket of hemlocks sheltering it from the wind and surf of the ocean. The rooms are pleasant, but the real attraction is the scenery and abundant wildlife. Owners Bill and Susan McIntyre have installed a skylight in the kitchen so that breakfasting guests can keep an eye on a pair of bald eagles, which nest in a Sitka spruce in the driveway. The former chief naturalist of Pacific Rim National Park, Bill is a fount of information. See "Outdoor Pursuits" under "Tofino," below, for information on his guided walks. *Note:* Smoking is not permitted.

855 Barkley Crescent, Box 557, Ucluelet, BC V0R 3A0. © 250/726-7099. Fax 250/726-7090. www. oceansedge.bc.ca. 3 units. C$120 (US$78) double. Rates include full breakfast. Off-season rates available. 2-night minimum stay may apply. MC, V. Not suitable for children. *In room:* No phone.

A Snug Harbour Inn ★ This clifftop B&B overlooking its own little bay makes the most of its location. Guests can use a monster-size telescope to watch the sea lions on the reef offshore. Inside, the spacious bedrooms have fireplaces and opulent bathrooms. The heart-shaped tub in the master suite may be a bit over the top, but who's complaining? Two new units will be pet-friendly and accessible for those with disabilities. Gourmet breakfasts include homemade baked goods and imaginative hot dishes. *Note:* Smoking is permitted outside only.

460 Marine Dr., Box 318, Ucluelet, BC V0R 3A0. © 888/936-5222 or 250/726-2686. Fax 250/726-2685. www.awesomeview.com. 4 units. June–Sept C$230–C$290 (US$150–US$189) double; Nov–Feb C$180– C$200 (US$117–US$130); Oct and Mar–May C$200–C$250 (US$117–US$163). Rates include full breakfast. Various multi-day packages available. MC, V. Children not accepted. **Amenities:** Jacuzzi; access to kitchen and TV. *In room:* Hair dryer, no phone (except for master suite).

WHERE TO DINE

Fine dining is only just beginning to have a presence here, as urban refugees with a flair for cooking try to make a go of it. The **Matterson Teahouse and Garden,** 1682 Peninsula Rd. (© 250/726-2200), specializes in seafood. Daily hours are 7:30am to 9pm in summer (until 8pm in winter). The **Rusty Anchor,** 168 Fraser

ⓒ Broken Group Islands

Lying off the coast of Ucluelet are the Broken Group Islands, an archipelago of about 300 islands and islets in Barkley Sound that are part of Pacific Rim National Park. Due to the relatively calm waters, abundant wildlife, and dramatic seascapes, these islands are popular destinations for experienced sea kayakers and ocean canoeists.

Divers can explore historic shipwrecks as well as reefs teeming with marine life (dive outfitters operate out of Bamfield, described above). The underwater drop-offs shelter large populations of feather stars, rockfish, and wolf eels that grow as long as 7 feet (2m) and occasionally poke their heads out of their caves.

Access to the Broken Group Islands is limited. In both Bamfield and Ucluelet, you'll find a number of operators who can arrange a trip, or you can take a packet freighter from Port Alberni. Lady Rose Marine Services drops off kayakers at Sechart, on a spur of Vancouver Island across from the islands themselves; kayakers then make the crossing on their own.

Sechart is also the site of the **Sechart Whaling Station Lodge,** another operation of Lady Rose Marine Services. It primarily serves the needs of kayakers, though it's open to anyone who wants a unique wilderness experience. Rates are C$115 to C$130 (US$75 to US$85), including three family-style meals a day, or C$65 (US$42) without meals. The only ways to get to the lodge are via one of the company freighters, on a **Toquart Connector Water Taxi** (ⓒ **250/720-7358)** from Bamfield, or on your own vessel. Kayak rentals are available. For reservations, contact **Lady Rose Marine Services** (ⓒ **800/663-7192** Apr–Sept, or 250/723-8313; fax 250/723-8314; www.ladyrosemarine.com).

Lane (ⓒ **250/726-3463**), focuses on seafood spring through fall, and steaks in winter. March through September, it's open daily from 11am to 10pm; October through February, Monday through Friday from 11:30am to 2:30pm and 5 to 8pm. There are also many good options up toward Tofino.

TOFINO

Not long ago the center of massive environmental protests—and a center of the ecotourism business ever since—Tofino remains a rather schizophrenic town. Part of it is composed of ecotourism outfitters, activists, and serious granolas; another part is comprised of loggers (not so many anymore) and fishermen; and then there's a third contingent of Tla-o-qui-aht and Ahousaht peoples, who live mostly outside the town. Conflict was common in the early years, but recently all parties seem to have learned to get along. For a hilarious take on the culture clash between incoming eco-freaks and long-term rednecks during the 1993 summer of discontent, pick up *The Green Shadow,* by local eco-freak (and closet redneck) Andrew Struthers.

Tofino is becoming more crowded and subject to a particular brand of gentrification. On the beaches south of town, a few luxury inns have gone up. Upscale restaurants and boutiques have opened, too. It can be difficult at times to find solitude in what's still an amazingly beautiful and wild place. Accordingly, more people may decide to avoid the crowds and visit Tofino in winter, to watch dramatic storms roll in over the coast. In summer, book accommodations well in advance.

OUTDOOR PURSUITS

FISHING Sportfishing is excellent off the west coast. Long Beach is also great for bottom fishing. You'll need a nonresident saltwater or freshwater license. Tackle shops sell licenses and often carry the publications *BC Tidal Waters Sport Fishing Guide* and *BC Sport Fishing Regulations Synopsis for Non-tidal Waters*. Independent anglers should also pick up the *BC Fishing Directory and Atlas*.

Chinook Charters, 450 Campbell St. (© **800/665-3646** or 250/725-3431; www.chinookcharters.com), runs charters starting at C$85 (US$55) per hour, with a minimum of 5 hours. It also offers whale-watching and wildlife-viewing tours. **Ospray Charters,** 350 Main St. (© **888/286-3466** or 250/725-2133; www.ospray.com), offers packages starting at C$199 (US$129) per day, and also charters boats for C$100 (US$65) per hour, with a minimum of 6 hours. **Jay's Clayoquot Ventures,** 564 Campbell St. (© **888/534-7422** or 250/725-2700; www.steelheadsalmonhalibut.com), offers saltwater fly-fishing, freshwater expeditions by plane, and helicopter expeditions.

GUIDED NATURE HIKES Bill McIntyre, former chief naturalist of Pacific Rim National Park, runs the **Long Beach Nature Tour Company** ✦ (© **250/ 726-7099;** www.oceansedge.bc.ca/LBNT.html), which offers highly recommended beach walks, storm-watching, land-based whale-watching, and rain-forest tours. Also excellent are the tours offered by naturalist Adrienne Mason of **Raincoast Communications** (© **250/725-2878;** amason@port.island.net). She will greatly enhance your knowledge of the local flora and fauna and ecology.

HIKING The 7-mile (12km) stretch of rocky headlands, sand, and surf along the coast of the **Long Beach Unit** is the most accessible section of Pacific Rim National Park. Numerous trails from a half mile to 2 miles (0.8km–3km) long take you through the temperate rain forest that edges the shore. The **Gold Mine Trail** (about 2 miles/3km), near Florencia Bay, still has a few artifacts from the days when a gold-mining operation flourished amid the trees.

The **Big Cedar Trail** (© **250/725-3233**), on Meares Island, is a 2-mile (3km) boardwalked path that was built to protect the old-growth forest. Maintained by the Tla-o-qui-aht band, the trail has a long staircase leading up to the Hanging Garden Tree, which is said to be between 1,000 and 1,500 years old.

In town, the paths in 12-acre (5-hectare) **Tofino Botanical Gardens,** 1084 Pacific Rim Hwy. (© **250/725-1220;** www.tofinobotanicalgardens.com), meander past theme gardens and old-growth forest and wind down to Tofino Inlet. Admission is C$8 (US$5) for adults, C$6 (US$3.25) for students, and C$2 (US$1.30) for children. Open daily from 9am to dusk.

KAYAKING For beginners, half-day tours to Meares Island (usually with the opportunity to do a little hiking) are a good bet. For rentals, lessons, and tours, contact **Pacific Kayak,** 606 Campbell St. (© **250/725-3232;** www.tofino-bc. com/pacifickayak). Its 4-hour Meares Island tour runs C$47 (US$31). The **Tofino Sea-Kayaking Company,** 320 Main St. (© **800/863-4664** or 250/ 725-4222; www.island.net/~paddlers), also offers courses, rentals, and tours.

WHALE-WATCHING, NATURE TOURS & BIRDING This region is inhabited by gray whales, bald eagles, porpoises, orcas, seals, and sea lions.

> ⌒*Tips* **Hot Springs Cove**
>
> Hot Springs Cove is a natural hot spring located about 40 miles (67km) north of Tofino; it's accessible only by water. Take a water taxi, canoe, or kayak up to Clayoquot Sound to enjoy a swim in the steaming pools and bracing waterfalls. A number of kayak outfitters and boat charters offer trips here (see "Whale-Watching, Nature Tours & Birding," above). On the way, guides generally try to take some time for whale-watching as well.

Chinook Charters, 450 Campbell St. (© **800/665-3646** or 250/725-3431; www.chinookcharters.com), offers whale-watching trips on 25-foot Zodiac (inflatable, rigid-bottom) boats or its 32-foot Chinook Key (C$50/US$33). It also conducts trips to Hot Springs Cove (C$75/US$49). **Jamie's Whaling Station,** 606 Campbell St. (© **800/667-9913,** 877/470-7444, or 250/725-3919; www.jamies.com), uses a glass-bottomed, 65-foot power cruiser as well as Zodiacs for whale-watching tours from mid-February to October, starting at C$59 (US$38). A Hot Springs Cove trip is C$89 (US$58). For an interesting combination, try the Sea-to-Sky tour, which starts out with a boat ride, then a hike through the rain forest to the Hot Springs, and finally a return to Tofino by floatplane (C$139/US$90). March through November, **Remote Passages,** 71 Wharf St. (© **800/666-9833** or 250/725-3330; www.remotepassages.com), runs whale-watching tours on Zodiacs (C$59/US$38). A Hot Springs trip costs C$89 (US$59).

Reservations are recommended for all outfitters. Young children, pregnant women, and those with health problems are advised to avoid Zodiac tours, as they jolt you around pretty well. The outfitters mentioned above also offer other nature-viewing tours, particularly for black bears, and may offer special packages. For land-based bird-watching, contact **Raincoast Communications** (see "Guided Nature Hikes," above).

RAINY-DAY ACTIVITIES: SHOPPING, STORM-WATCHING & MORE

Studios and galleries are springing up around Campbell and Main streets. Take a peek at the **Eagle Aerie Gallery,** 350 Campbell St. (© **604/725-3235;** www.royhenryvickers.com), which is constructed in the style of an Indian longhouse. It features the sculpture and carvings of Roy Henry Vickers, a hereditary chief and son of a Tsimshian fisherman. The **House of Himwitsa Native Art Gallery,** 300 Main St. (© **250/725-2017;** www.himwitsa.com), owned by First Nations members, has quality masks, totems, jewelry, and apparel.

When you're done gallery-hopping, grab a steaming latte at the **Wildside Booksellers and Espresso Bar,** 320 Main St. (© **250/745-4222**), or pamper yourself with a massage at the **Ancient Cedars Spa,** at the Wickaninnish Inn (© **800/333-4604** or 250/725-3100; www.wickinn.com/Frames/SPfrm.htm).

Watching the winter storms from behind big glass windows has become very popular in Tofino. For a slight twist on this, try the outdoor storm-watching tours offered by the **Long Beach Nature Tour Company** (© **250/726-7099;** www.oceansedge.bc.ca/LBNT.html). Bill McIntyre, former chief naturalist of Pacific Rim National Park, will explain how storms work—as well as where to stand so you can get close without getting swept away.

WHERE TO STAY

There are easily 100 or more places to stay in Tofino; the **Tofino Visitor Info Centre,** 380 Campbell St. (© **250/725-3414;** www.tofinobc.org), open March through September, Monday through Friday from 11am to 5pm, keeps a helpful list of vacancies. In addition to the luxury inns listed below, the **Long Beach Lodge Resort** (© **250/725-2442;** fax 250/725-2402; www.longbeachisland resort.com) is being completed as this book goes to press. It promises to be a choice place to stay.

The Clayoquot Wilderness Resort ★★

The latest in absolute luxury in the area, the Clayoquot Wilderness Resort (CWS) floats alone in splendid isolation on Quait Bay, about a half-hour boat ride from Tofino. Guests are encouraged to use the lodge as a base camp for exploring the sound. The CWS offers trips to Hot Springs Cove as well as horseback-riding and mountain-biking excursions. The spacious guest rooms offer down duvets, private decks, and robes. Meals are prepared by noted West Coast chef Timothy May.

CWS also has an "outpost camp" at Bedwell River, at the edge of Strathcona Park. Billed as a 21st-century safari-style enclave of ultra-luxurious sleeping and dining tents—with wind-powered air-conditioning, hot and cold water, flush toilets, king beds, and epicurean meals—this is the epitome of camping without roughing it. The price of admission is a little rough, however: C$1,150 (US$748) for two.

P.O. Box 728, Tofino, BC V0R 2Z0. © **888/333-5405** or 250/725-2688. Fax 250/725-2689. www.wildretreat. com. 16 units. June 29–Sept 3 C$978 (US$636) double. May 18–June 28 and Sept 4–Oct 7 C$738 (US$480) double. Mar 16–May 17 and Oct 8–Nov 30 C$538 (US$350) double. Rates include all meals, plus transfer to and from Tofino. Spa and fishing packages available. AE, MC, V. Parking provided in Tofino. **Amenities:** Restaurant; health club; spa; Jacuzzi; sauna; watersports equipment rentals; bike rentals; tour/activities desk; massage.

House of Himwitsa

Overlooking the government dock in the center of town, the House of Himwitsa offers spacious units with gas fireplaces, sofa beds, and water views; three rooms have hot tubs out on a private deck. The proprietors can help arrange tours. *Note:* Smoking is not permitted.

300 Main St., P.O. Box 176, Tofino, BC V0R 2Z0. © **800/899-1947** or 250/725-2017. Fax 250/725-2361. www.himwitsa.com. 4 units. Mid-June to mid-Sept C$160–C$225 (US$104–US$146) double. Mid-Sept to mid-June C$135–C$185 (US$88–US$120) double. Extra person C$20 (US$13). Children under 2 stay free in parents' room. AE, MC, V. **Amenities:** Restaurant (closed off-season); art gallery. *In room:* TV/VCR, dataport, kitchenette, coffeemaker.

The Inn at Tough City ★★

This is possibly the nicest small inn in Tofino, and certainly the quirkiest. Built from salvaged and recycled material, the inn is chock-full of thoughtfully arranged antiques and bric-a-brac. The colorful guest rooms are decorated to feel rather like a young city hipster's apartment. Several feature soaker tubs or fireplaces; two rooms are wheelchair accessible. *Note:* Smoking is not permitted.

Tough City Sushi is worth a meal for the decor alone—this is where the proprietors' fondness for memorabilia dominates just about every inch of wall and ceiling space. The menu offers standard sushi fare (and you can be sure the seafood's as fresh as can be), as well as Japanese steakhouse dishes.

350 Main St., P.O. Box 8, Tofino, BC V0R 2Z0. © **250/725-2021.** Fax 250/725-2088. www.toughcity.com. 8 units. Mid-May to mid-Oct C$140–C$175 (US$91–US$114) double. Mid-Mar to mid-May C$90–C$130 (US$59–US$85). Mid-Oct to mid-Mar C$75–C$120 (US$49–US$78). MC, V. Pets allowed for C$10 (US$7). **Amenities:** Restaurant; in-room massage available; babysitting available. *In room:* TV, dataport, coffeemaker, hair dryer.

Middle Beach Lodge ★★   This beautiful complex is comprised of two adjacent locations, directly on Middle Beach and on a headland overlooking the ocean. The rustic look was accomplished by using recycled beams from old buildings in Victoria, with very pleasing results. Accommodations range from simple lodge rooms to cabins with decks, soaker tubs, and fireplaces. The beach lodge is adult-oriented, and its cozy rooms have no TVs or phones—all other accommodations do. Children are allowed in some cabins and have access to the dining area in the headland lodge. Wheelchair-accessible rooms are available. *Note:* Smoking is not permitted.

400 MacKenzie Beach Rd., P.O. Box 100, Tofino, BC V0R 2Z0. ✆ 250/725-2900. Fax 250/725-2901. www.middlebeach.com. 64 units. C$90–C$195 (US$59–US$127) double; C$175–C$295 (US$114–US$192) suite; C$185–C$395 (US$120–US$257) single cabin; C$170–C$325 (US$111–US$211) duplex cabin; C$110–C$210 (US$72–US$137) triplex cabin; C$80–C$200 (US$52–US$130) standard sixplex suite; C$200–C$325 (US$130–US$211) deluxe sixplex suite. AE, MC, V. **Amenities:** Restaurant (dinners served on a variable schedule); golf course nearby; exercise room; coin-op laundry.

Red Crow Guest House   Whereas the Wickaninnish and other lodges show you the wild, stormy side of the coast, the Red Crow displays a gentler beauty. Located by the sheltered waters of Clayoquot Sound, this Cape Cod house offers pleasant bedrooms, outfitted with 1920s-style furnishings, and an eclectic cottage with kitchen. The Red Crow sits on a protected sanctuary that hosts up to 150 avian species, so birders should bring binoculars. *Note:* Smoking is not permitted.

1084 Pacific Rim Hwy. (Box 37), Tofino, BC V0R 2Z0. ✆ 250/725-2275. Fax 250/725-3214. www.tofinoredcrow.com. 3 units. Double C$140–C$165 (US$91–US$107) mid-June to early Oct; C$120–C$140 (US$78–US$91) mid-Mar to mid-June; C$90–C$100 (US$59–US$65) early Oct to mid-Mar. Cottage C$125–C$195 (US$81–US$127). Room rates include full breakfast. Extra person C$20 (US$13). MC, V. **Amenities:** Golf course nearby; free canoe and rowboat; laundry service. *In room:* Fridge, coffeemaker, hair dryer, no phone.

The Tides Inn on Duffin Cove   This inn's bedrooms all have private entrances and spectacular views of Clayoquot Sound. One room features a Jacuzzi tub and another a steam bath, and one has a fireplace. A wooden stairway leads down to a semiprivate beach. The proprietors also rent a nice condo unit in town. *Note:* Smoking is not permitted.

160 Arnet Rd. (Box 325), Tofino, BC V0R 2Z0. ✆ 250/725-3765. Fax 250/725-3325. www.tidesinntofino.com. 3 units. Summer C$95–C$125 (US$62–US$81) B&B double, C$135–C$145 (US$88–US$94) condo double; fall/winter C$80–C$100 (US$52–US$65) B&B double, C$85–C$105 (US$55–US$68) condo double. Rates include full breakfast. 2-night minimum stay. No credit cards. Children must be 12 or older. **Amenities:** Pool table; Jacuzzi. *In room:* TV/VCR, fridge, coffeemaker, hair dryer, iron, no phone.

Tin-Wis Best Western Resort   The Tla-o-qui-aht First Nations band run this large, hotel-like lodge on MacKenzie Beach. All rooms are spacious, with oceanfront views, although more pedestrian than you'll find at most other beachfront lodges. Options include queen loft units and deluxe king rooms with fireplaces and kitchenettes. Most units have sofa beds, making them a good choice for families.

1119 Pacific Rim Hwy., Box 380, Tofino, BC V0R 2Z0. ✆ 800/661-9995 or 250/725-4445. Fax 250/725-4447. www.tinwis.com. 86 units. C$110–C$195 (US$72–US$127) standard double; C$150–C$225 (US$98–US$146) queen loft or king; C$225–C$300 (US$146–US$195) executive king. Senior, AAA, and group discounts available. AE, DC, DISC, MC, V. **Amenities:** Restaurant, lounge; well-equipped exercise room; large Jacuzzi. *In room:* TV, fridge, coffeemaker, hair dryer.

Whalers on the Point Guesthouse   This modern hostel is one way to save money in an increasingly expensive town. Located downtown, with views of

Clayoquot Sound, it offers both shared and private rooms. The hostel offers discounts on a variety of activities, arranged through local outfitters.

81 West St., Box 296, Tofino, BC V0R 2Z0. © **250/725-3443.** Fax 250/725-3463. www.tofinohostel.com. 55 beds. Double C$70–C$109 (US$46–US$71) May–Sept, from C$50 (from US$33) Oct–Apr. Shared C$22–C$24 (US$14–US$16) per person. Hostelling International member, off-season, multi-day, and family discounts available. MC, V. **Amenities:** Kitchen; sauna; bike rentals; game room; TV room; Internet kiosk; coin-op laundry. *In room:* No phone.

The Wickaninnish Inn ★★★   No matter which room you book in this beautiful cedar, stone, and glass lodge, you'll wake to a magnificent view of the untamed Pacific. The inn is on a rocky promontory, surrounded by old-growth forest and the sands of Chesterman Beach. The spacious guest rooms contain fireplaces, soaker tubs, and balconies. Two units are appointed for those with disabilities. Storm-watching packages have become so popular that the inn is as busy in winter as it is in summer.

Osprey Lane at Chesterman Beach (P.O. Box 250), Tofino, BC V0R 2Z0. © **800/333-4604** or 250/725-3100. Fax 250/725-3110. www.wickinn.com. 46 units. Mar–May C$230–C$350 (US$150–US$228); June–Sept C$360–C$480 (US$234–US$312); Oct C$260–C$380 (US$169–US$247); Nov–Feb C$210–C$330 (US$137–US$215). Premier rooms add C$60 (US$39). Whale-watching, golfing, fishing, and diving packages available; No-Stress Express packages include air transport and accommodations. AE, DC, MC, V. Free valet parking. Located 3 miles (5km) south of central Tofino. Pets accepted for C$20 (US$13). **Amenities:** Restaurant (see review of the Pointe Restaurant, below); bar; spa; concierge; activities desk; car-rental desk; limited room service; massage; babysitting; laundry service. *In room:* TV, dataport, minibar, coffeemaker, hair dryer, iron.

CAMPING

The 94 campsites at **Green Point** are maintained by **Pacific Rim National Park** (© **250/726-7721** or 250/726-4212 in summer; for reservations, call 800/689-9025 and specify Campground No. 50; http://parkscan.harbour.com/pacrim). The grounds are full every day in July and August, and the average wait for a site is 1 to 2 days. When you arrive in the area, leave your name at the ranger station to be placed on the list. Sites cost C$10 to C$20 (US$6.50 to US$13). You'll be rewarded for your patience with a magnificent view, pit toilets, fire pits, pumped well water, and free firewood. Closed November through March.

Bella Pacifica Resort & Campground, 2 miles (3km) south of Tofino on the Pacific Rim Highway (© **250/725-3400;** www.bellapacifica.com), has 165 sites, from which you can walk to MacKenzie Beach or take the resort's trails to Templar Beach. Flush toilets, hot showers, water, laundry, ice, fire pits, firewood, and full and partial hookups are available. Rates are C$17 to C$34 (US$11 to US$22). Reserve at least a month in advance for summer weekends. Open midMarch to mid-November.

WHERE TO DINE

See the Inn at Tough City under "Where to Stay," above, for a description of **Tough City Sushi.**

The Common Loaf Bake Shop ★ BAKERY/CAFE   Locally famous as the gathering place for granolas and lefty rabble-rousers back when they amassed in Tofino to take their stand, the Loaf has expanded in recent years, which just goes to show you can make money selling idealism along with your muffins. Located at the "far" end of town, the Common Loaf does baked goods really well: muffins, cookies, whole-grain breads, and sticky cinnamon buns. It also serves lunches of soups, curry, and pizza.

180 First St. © **250/725-3915.** Reservations not accepted. Main courses C$4–C$10 (US$2.60–US$7). No credit cards. Summer daily 8am–9pm; winter daily 8am–6pm.

The Pointe Restaurant ★★ PACIFIC NORTHWEST   Views of the roaring ocean serve as the backdrop to an experience that can only be described as pure Pacific Northwest. The chef applies his talents to an array of local ingredients, including Dungeness crab, halibut, salmon, and lamb. Signature main courses include Fraser Valley duck breast in a maple butter sauce, served with cabbage and pecan gnocchi.

The Wickaninnish Inn, Osprey Lane at Chesterman Beach. ✆ 250/725-3106. www.wickinn.com. Reservations recommended. Three- to five-course prix-fixe menus C$60–C$85 (US$39–US$55). AE, DC, MC, V. Daily 8–11am, 11:30am–2pm, 2:30–9pm (light menu in lounge), and 5–9pm.

The RainCoast Café ★ WEST COAST/VEGETARIAN   This cozy restaurant has developed a deserved reputation for some of the best—and best value— seafood and vegetarian dishes in town. To start, try the RainCoast salad— smoked salmon, sautéed mushrooms, and chèvre cheese on a bed of greens, served with maple-balsamic vinaigrette. You'll find many Asian-inspired dishes, such as clams, scallops, and tiger prawns over soba noodles with a lime-miso sauce. Wild salmon is always on the menu in some form—perhaps in a spring roll wrapper with caramelized mango and a hoisin-lime-ginger sauce.

101-120 Fourth St., off Campbell St. ✆ 250/725-2215. www.raincoastcafe.com. Main courses C$13–C$24 (US$8–US$16). AE, MC, V. Daily 5–9pm (until 10:30pm July–Sept).

6 Courtenay & Comox

37 miles (62km) N of Qualicum Beach

Facing each other across the Courtenay Estuary, Comox (pop. 12,500) and Courtenay (pop. 20,000) are twin towns that provide a bit of urban polish to a region rich in outdoor recreation. Because they're north of the Victoria-to-Tofino circuit that defines much of the tourism on Vancouver Island, these towns are refreshingly untouristy. Comox has a working harbor with a fishing fleet; Courtenay, a lumber-milling center, has an old downtown core where the shops haven't yet completely transformed into boutiques. Which isn't to say that these towns lack sophistication: You'll find excellent lodging and restaurants, as well as the new and opulent Crown Isle Golf Resort. Depend on the pace of change to quicken even further: The Comox Valley is the fastest-growing region of Vancouver Island.

Courtenay and Comox are also stepping-off points for adventures in the Beaufort Mountains, just to the west. From Mount Washington Alpine Resort, trails lead into the southeast corner of Strathcona Provincial Park. There are also adventures to be had at sea level: The shallow Courtenay Estuary is home to abundant wildlife, particularly birds and sea mammals.

ESSENTIALS

GETTING THERE   By Plane   Comox Valley Regional Airport, north of Comox, has daily flights from Vancouver. The airport is served by **Air BC,** a subsidiary of **Air Canada** (✆ **888/247-2262;** www.aircanada.com); **Pacific Coastal Airlines** (✆ **800/663-2872;** www.pacific-coastal.com); and **WestJet** (✆ **877/952-4638;** www.westjet.com).

By Ferry   BC Ferries (✆ **888/BCFERRY** in B.C., or 250/386-3431; www. bcferries.bc.ca) crosses from Powell River on the mainland to Little River, just north of Comox. Nanaimo's Duke Point and Departure Bay are the closest terminals with connections to the Vancouver area. If you'd like to see the Sunshine Coast on your way to Comox/Courtenay—and stay overnight to make it possible

---

(Tips Special Events

The **Filberg Festival** attracts over 140 artists and craftspeople from across the province. It takes place at Filberg Park, with some events in the lodge and others in tents and booths. The festival includes musical entertainment and theater. It's held the first weekend of August; admission is C$8 (US$5) for adults, C$2 (US$1.30) for children 6 to 12. Tickets can be purchased at **www.sidwilliamstheatre.com** or by calling (© **866/898-8499** or 250/338-2420, ext. 3. For information, contact the park (see below) or the festival coordinator (© **250/334-9242;** www.filbergfestival.com).

---

and worthwhile—cross from Horseshoe Bay to Langdale in Gibsons, then drive along Highway 101 to Earl's Cove in Sechelt, crossing again to Saltery Bay in Powell River, finally ferrying from Westview in Powell River to Comox.

By Train & Bus   Courtenay, which is 90 minutes north of Nanaimo on Highway 19, is also the terminus for **VIA Rail**'s **E&N Railiner,** or *Malahat* (© **888/VIA-RAIL** or 250/383-4324; www.viarail.ca), which offers daily service from Victoria. **Island Coach Lines** (© **800/663-8390** in the U.S., 800/318-0818 in Canada, or 250/388-5248 in Victoria; www.victoriatours.com) provides daily service from Nanaimo and points south. One-way fare to Courtenay from Victoria is C$38.50 (US$25).

VISITOR INFORMATION   Contact the **Comox Valley Visitor Info Centre,** 2040 Cliffe Ave., Courtenay (© **888/357-4471** or 250/334-3234; www.tourism-comox-valley.bc.ca).

EXPLORING THE AREA

Highway 19A becomes Cliffe Avenue as it enters Courtenay. It then crosses the Courtenay River and continues north toward Campbell River, bypassing the old town centers of both Courtenay and Comox. This is a comparative blessing, as it allows these commercial districts to quietly gentrify without four lanes of traffic shooting past. The new Inland Highway 19 bypasses the towns altogether; the Comox Valley Parkway exit will take you from the highway over to Cliffe Avenue.

COURTENAY

Courtenay's town center revolves around Fourth, Fifth, and Sixth streets just west of the Courtenay River. It's a pleasant place for a stroll, with a number of shops to browse. The **Artisans Courtyard,** 180B Fifth St. (© **250/338-6564;** www.artinglass.org), is a co-op with more than 60 members. Next door is the **Potter's Place,** 180A Fifth St. (© **250/334-4613**), which offers the works of 29 potters, ranging from porcelain to raku.

The **Courtenay District Museum & Paleontology Centre,** 207 Fourth St. (© **250/334-0686;** www.courtenaymuseum.ca), tells the story of the region's First Nations peoples with a good collection of masks, basketry, and carvings. The museum's highlight is a 40-foot (12m) cast skeleton of an elasmosaur, a Cretaceous-era marine reptile. (The Comox Valley was once covered by a tropical sea, and the area now yields a wealth of marine fossils.) **Fossil tours** of the exhibits and paleontology lab, culminating in a trip to a local dig, are offered daily in July and August and on a more limited basis April through June. Tickets are C$15 (US$10) for adults, C$12 (US$8) for seniors and students, and

C$7.50 (US$5) for children; call ahead for reservations. Admission to the museum alone is C$3 (US$1.95) for adults and C$2.50 (US$1.65) for seniors and children. Summer hours are Monday through Saturday from 10am to 5pm and Sunday from noon to 4pm. Winter hours are Tuesday through Saturday from 10am to 5pm.

COMOX

The old center of Comox is small, with just a few shops and cafes to tempt travelers. What's definitely worth exploring, however, is the **marina area** in Comox Harbour. Walkways offer views of the boats and the bay; rising above it all are the jagged peaks of Strathcona Park. Another excellent place for a stroll is **Filberg Lodge and Park,** 61 Filberg Rd. (© **250/334-9242;** www.filbergfestival.com/lodge.html). Nine acres (3.6 hectares) of lawn and forest, plus a petting zoo, surround a handsome Arts and Crafts–style home. Once a private residence, the lodge is now open for tours from 11am to 5pm on Easter weekend plus weekends in May and September, and daily from July to Labour Day.

PARKS & BEACHES

Continue past the marina on Comox Road to **Gooseneck Park,** a local favorite. **Saratoga Beach** and **Miracle Beach Provincial Park** are about a half-hour drive north of Courtenay on Highway 19. **Seal Bay Regional Nature Park and Forest,** 15 miles (24km) north of Courtenay off Highway 19, is a 1,764-acre (714-hectare) preserve laced with hiking and mountain-biking trails. Hours are from 6:30am to 11pm.

OUTDOOR PURSUITS

GOLF   One of the finest courses on Vancouver Island is **Crown Isle Resort & Golf Community** ✯, 399 Clubhouse Dr., Courtenay (© **888/338-8439** or 250/703-5050; www.crownisle.com). This 18-hole links-style championship course has already hosted the Canadian Tour. Facilities are lavish, including an eye-popping clubhouse, steam rooms, and a hotel and villas (see "Where to Stay," below).

KAYAKING   With the Courtenay Estuary and Hornby, Tree, and Denman islands an easy paddle away, sea kayaking is very popular. **Comox Valley Kayaks,** 2020 Cliffe Ave., Courtenay (© **888/545-5595** or 250/334-2628; www.comox valleykayaks.com), offers rentals, lessons, and tours. Rentals start at C$20 (US$13) for 2 hours.

SKIING   Mount Washington Alpine Resort ✯ (© **800/231-1499** or 250/338-1386, or 250/338-1515 for snow report; www.mtwashington.bc.ca) is British Columbia's third-largest ski area, a 5-hour drive from Victoria and open year-round (for hiking or skiing, depending on the season). The summit reaches 5,215 feet (1,588m), and the mountain averages 350 inches (860cm) of snow per year. A 1,600-foot (488m) vertical drop and 50 groomed runs are served by six lifts and a beginners' tow. Thirty-four miles (55km) of Nordic track-set and skating trails connect to Strathcona Provincial Park. The new **Raven Lodge** has restaurants, equipment rentals, and locker rooms. Lift rates are C$45 (US$29) for adults, C$37 (US$24) for seniors and students, and C$24 (US$16) for kids 7 to 12. Take the Strathcona Parkway 23 miles (37km) to Mount Washington, or use turnoff 130 from Inland Highway 19.

The condos and lodges at Mount Washington remain open year-round. For information, contact **Alpine Accommodations** (© **888/837-4663;** www.alpinechalets.com) or **Peak Accommodations** (© **866/826-7325** or

250/897-3851; www.peakaccom.com). Summer rates for a two-bedroom condo are around C$75 (US$49); winter rates range from C$115 to C$175 (US$75 to US$114).

WHERE TO STAY

The **Travelodge Courtenay,** 2605 Island Hwy. (© **800/795-9486** or 250/334-4491; www.travelodgecourtenay.com), offers extras at a relatively modest cost. The clean, unfussy rooms start at C$76 (US$49).

Coast Westerly Hotel   The Coast Westerly presents a rather off-putting visage: The three-story slant-fronted wall of glass that encases the lobby probably seemed like a stylish idea when the hotel was first built. But once you get past it, you'll discover that the guest rooms are spacious and nicely furnished. For the kids, there's even a Nintendo game console in every room. The wing in back offers rooms with balconies, some overlooking the river.

1590 Cliffe Ave., Courtenay, BC V9N 2K4. © **800/668-7797** or 250/338-7741. Fax 250/338-5442. www.coastwesterlyhotel.com. 108 units. C$139–C$159 (US$90–US$103) double. Extra person C$10 (US$7). Off-season and senior rates available. AE, MC, V. Ski and golf packages available. Pets accepted. **Amenities:** Restaurant, pub, lounge; indoor pool; golf course nearby; exercise room; Jacuzzi; sauna; limited room service. *In room:* A/C, TV w/ pay movies, dataport, coffeemaker.

Greystone Manor B&B   For many guests, the high point of a stay here is a chance to wander the lush 1½-acre (.6-hectare) gardens. The charming innkeepers claim that gardening wasn't even a particular passion in their lives until they bought this property. But a passion it has now become: Every year, they put in more than 3,500 bedding plants. The house itself is a handsome 1918 Tudor-style Craftsman. Guests share a magnificent wood-paneled sitting room with loads of unpainted moldings, a grand piano, and comfy couches. *Note:* Smoking is not permitted.

4014 Haas Rd., Courtenay, BC V9N 9T4. © **250/338-1422.** www.bbcanada.com/1334.html. 3 units. C$85 (US$55) double. Rates include full breakfast. MC, V. Children must be 13 or older. *In room:* Hair dryer, no phone.

Kingfisher Oceanside Resort and Spa ★★   This long-established resort has modernized with an added bank of beachfront suites and a classy spa. The older motel units are nicely furnished with balconies or patios. The newer suites are splendid, each with a kitchen, VCR, fireplace, balcony, and heated bathroom floors. Our favorite is room 401, with windows on two sides. Two accessible units are available. The restaurant is one of the best in town (see "Where to Dine," below). The spa offers a wide selection of treatments and body work. *Note:* Smoking is not permitted.

4330 Island Hwy. S., Courtenay, BC V9N 9R9. © **800/663-7929** or 250/338-1323. Fax 250/338-0058. www.kingfisherspa.com. 64 units. C$129 (US$84) double; C$170 (US$111) suite. Extra person C$10 (US$7). Golf, ski, fishing, spa, and women's wellness packages available. Senior discounts available. AE, DC, DISC, MC, V. Free parking. Pets allowed in 3 rooms for C$7 (US$4.55). Located 4½ miles (7km) south of Courtenay. **Amenities:** Restaurant; outdoor pool; golf course nearby; tennis court; exercise room; spa; Jacuzzi; sauna; canoe and kayak rentals; activities desk; courtesy limo; business center; 24-hr. room service; massage; babysitting; coin-op laundry; laundry service; dry cleaning. *In room:* TV, dataport, fridge, coffeemaker, hair dryer.

The Villas at Crown Isle Resort ★★ Value   For the money, these villas are an incredible deal. Located at Crown Isle Golf Resort, they overlook the first fairway and are just yards from the spectacular clubhouse. The suites are truly large and filled with luxury touches: Many have gourmet kitchens, Jacuzzis, fireplaces, VCRs, and balconies. A newer building has well-appointed hotel-style rooms. Villa guests have access to the fitness equipment in the resort club-house, a full spa is opening in 2002, and, of course, there's that golf course.

399 Clubhouse Dr., Courtenay, BC V9N 9G3. ☎ 888/338-8439 or 250/703-5000. Fax 250/703-5035. www.crownisle.com/villa.html. 54 units. Nov–Apr from C$119 (US$77) fairway room; from C$149 (US$97) villa. Oct from C$129 (US$84) fairway room; from C$179 (US$116) villa. May–Sept from C$149 (US$97) fairway room; from C$229 (US$149) villa. Extra person C$15 (US$10). Golf and ski packages available. AE, MC, V. Free parking. **Amenities:** Two restaurants; golf course; health club; spa; business center; limited room service; laundry service; same-day dry cleaning. *In room:* TV, coffeemaker.

WHERE TO DINE

Atlas Café INTERNATIONAL   This cafe serves up affordable, flavorful variations on global cuisine; many of the dishes are vegetarian. Popular choices include a platter of spanakopita, hummus, tzatziki, Greek salad, and pita bread, or a stir-fry of fresh vegetables with tofu or chicken in a spicy peanut sauce over brown rice. Weekend brunch is served until 2pm. In nice weather, sit out on the garden patio. For 2002, Atlas is adding a tapas and martini bar.

250 Sixth St., Courtenay. ☎ 250/338-9838. www.comoxvalleyrestaurants.com/atlas_cafe.htm. Reservations accepted for parties of 6 or more only. Main courses C$7–C$19 (US$4.55–US$12). MC, V. Daily 8:45am–10pm. May close in midwinter; call ahead.

Bar None Café VEGETARIAN   This friendly restaurant specializes in international dishes made from organic ingredients. The buffet features salads, soups, and hot entrees. The chalkboard menu offers pastas, pizzas, curries, and sandwiches. Bar None also has a juice bar and bakery, and serves omelets, tofu scrambles, and waffles at breakfast. On a sunny day, grab a smoothie and take a seat on the patio. Note that the Bar None does not serve alcohol.

244 Fourth St., Courtenay. ☎ 250/334-3112. www.island.net/~barnone. Reservations not needed. Main courses C$5–C$10 (US$3.25–US$10). Buffet C$2 (US$1.30) per 100 grams (3.5 oz.). AE, MC, V. Mon–Sat 7:30am–7:30pm.

The Black Fin Pub PUB/CANADIAN   On the short walk from downtown Comox to the marina, you'll pass this hospitable pub overlooking the harbor. The menu is large and, for a pub, quite interesting; some of the appetizers feature Thai and Chinese flavors. Entrees range from schnitzel to curry chicken. The usual burgers and sandwiches are also in abundance. Sunday brunch is served until 2pm, and there's an afternoon tea on Monday and Thursday. The entire pub is smoke-free.

132 Port Augusta St., Comox. ☎ 250/339-5030. Reservations accepted for parties of 4 or more in early evening. Main courses C$8–C$15 (US$5–US$10). AE, MC, V. Food service daily 11am–10pm; Fri–Sat until 10:30pm. Hours may be extended in summer.

Kingfisher Oceanside Restaurant ⭐ SEAFOOD/CONTINENTAL   The dining room at this resort brings together waterfront views with high-quality cuisine. If you're staying at the Kingfisher to partake of the new spa services, you'll be pleased with the spa menu, which features low-fat, low-calorie entrees such as poached halibut jardiniere. On the regular menu, one popular entree is cedar-plank-baked salmon with a chutney of sage and blackberries. Also listed are steaks, schnitzels, and lamb dishes.

4330 Island Hwy. S., 4½ miles (7km) south of Courtenay. ☎ 250/338-1323. www.kingfisherspa.com. Reservations advised. Main courses C$12–C$23 (US$8–US$15). AE, DC, DISC, MC, V. Daily 7–10:30am, 11:30am–2pm, and 5–10pm.

Old House Restaurant STEAK/SEAFOOD   As you might suspect, the Old House is located in a heritage home along the banks of the Courtenay River. With four fireplaces and rough-hewn timbers, it feels like a country lodge. This is where locals come for special occasions, and if you're looking for steaks, prime rib, or relatively straightforward preparations of seafood, then it's a good if bustling choice. The patio is a wonderful place for a drink.

1760 Riverside Lane, Courtenay. ✆ **250/338-5406**. www.comoxvalleyrestaurants.ca/old_house.htm. Reservations recommended. Main courses C$11–C$25 (US$7–US$16). AE, MC, V. Sun–Thurs 11am–9pm; Fri–Sat 11am–9:30pm.

Otters Bistro SEAFOOD/STEAK/PASTA   Otters offers inventive cuisine in a stunning setting, just above the marina in Comox, with a spectacular vista across Courtenay Bay. Request a table on the deck if the weather's nice. Seafood dominates the entrees—try a bouillabaisse of shellfish with onions and tomatoes, in a hearty broth of white wine, garlic, saffron, and herbs. For meat lovers, there's rack of lamb rubbed with garlic, rosemary, and Dijon mustard. The substantial wine list focuses on B.C. selections. If you want just a drink and a simple bite, stop by the lounge and order some fresh Fanny Bay oysters.

1805 Beaufort Ave., Comox. ✆ **250/339-6150**. Edgewater Pub ✆ 250/339-6151. Reservations recommended in summer. Main courses C$13–C$17 (US$8–US$10.50). Mon–Thurs early-bird (5–7pm) three-course menu C$16 (US$10). MC, V. Free parking in marina parking lot. Daily 11:30am–2:30pm and 5–9:30pm.

Toscanos ITALIAN   Toscanos is a cheerful restaurant located between downtown Comox and Comox Harbor, with a million-dollar view of the bay and distant Beaufort Mountains. The dining room is rather minimalist, lacking the rustic clutter that passes for decor in many Italian restaurants. The menu is divided between pasta dishes and chicken, veal, and seafood entrees. Desserts include classics like tiramisu and profiteroles.

140 Port Augusta, Comox. ✆ **250/890-7575**. www.comoxvalleyrestaurants.ca/Toscanos.htm. Reservations recommended. Main courses C$11–C$20 (US$7–US$13). MC, V. Mon–Sat 11am–2pm and 5–9pm. Closed holidays.

Northern Vancouver Island

In this chapter, we cover the portion of Vancouver Island from the town of Campbell River—the "Salmon-Fishing Capital of the World"—northward. A quick ferry ride from Campbell River brings you to the ancient First Nations culture of Quadra Island. West of Campbell River lies Strathcona Provincial Park, the oldest provincial park in British Columbia and the largest on Vancouver Island.

The waters along the island's northeast coast near Port McNeill are home to both resident and transient orca whales; the latter move annually from Johnstone Strait to the open Pacific. In this vicinity are also two tiny

unique communities: the First Nations town of Alert Bay, on Cormorant Island, and Telegraph Cove, a boardwalk community on pilings above the rocky shore.

The Island Highway's final port of call, Port Hardy is the starting point for the Inside Passage ferry cruise up the northern coast. It carries passengers bound for Prince Rupert, where it meets the ferries to the Queen Charlotte Islands (see chapter 9, "Northern British Columbia," for complete coverage of these destinations).

Note: See the "Vancouver Island" map (p. 86) to locate areas covered in this chapter.

1 Essentials

GETTING THERE

BY PLANE   See chapter 4 for information on Vancouver Island's major air hub, **Victoria.**

Campbell River and Port Hardy are both served by regular flights from Vancouver. Other towns can be reached by scheduled harbor-to-harbor floatplane service, from Vancouver International's seaplane terminal, from downtown Vancouver's Coal Harbour terminal, or from various harbors in and around Seattle, Washington.

Air Canada (© 888/247-2262; www.aircanada.com), through its subsidiary Air BC, offers service to Campbell River and Victoria. **Pacific Coastal Airlines** (© 800/663-2872; www.pacific-coastal.com) serves these destinations as well as Port Hardy.

Commuter seaplane companies include **Air Rainbow** (© 250/287-8371; www.air-rainbow.com), operating out of Campbell River with service from Vancouver, and **Kenmore Air** (© 800/543-9595; www.kenmoreair.com), departing from Seattle's Lake Union or Lake Washington and flying to Campbell River/Quadra Island and Port McNeill.

BY FERRY   BC Ferries (© 888/BCFERRY in B.C., or 250/386-3431; www.bcferries.bc.ca) operates a route linking Powell River to Comox, not too far south of Campbell River, but reaching Powell River from other points on the mainland requires taking two other ferries—a daunting and costly prospect for one day's travel (see p. 149 for details). Nanaimo's Duke Point and Departure Bay are the closest terminals with connections to the Vancouver area. Port Hardy also connects with Prince Rupert via a 15-hour journey that winds through the Inland Passage. Sample fares are included in the regional sections that follow.

If you're traveling with a car, you'll find that ticket prices add up quickly. You may want to consider leaving the car on the mainland and traveling by bus, taxi, or air; or go to Campbell River by car ferry and bring or rent bikes or kayaks to get around.

Washington State Ferries (© **888/808-7977** in Wash., 206/464-6400 in the rest of the U.S., or 250/381-1551 in Canada; www.wsdot.wa.gov/ferries) has daily service from Anacortes, in Washington, to Sidney, on Vancouver Island. One-way fares for a car and driver cost around US$41 in high season. The 165-mile (266km) drive from Victoria to Campbell River takes 3½ hours. For other ferry options from Washington to Vancouver Island, see p. 85.

BY BUS **Greyhound Canada** (© **800/661-8747** or 604/482-8747; www.greyhound.ca) provides eight daily trips between Vancouver and Nanaimo. Fares are C$21 (US$14) one-way. **Island Coach Lines,** run by Laidlaw (© **800/663-8390** in the U.S., 800/318-0818 in Canada, or 250/388-5248 in Victoria; www.victoriatours.com) operates Vancouver Island's intercity bus service, which runs along the main highway from Victoria to Port Hardy. Sample fares from Victoria are C$44 (US$29) to Campbell River and C$101.75 (US$66) to Port Hardy.

VISITOR INFORMATION

For information on Vancouver Island, contact **Tourism Vancouver Island,** Suite 203, 335 Wesley St., Nanaimo (© **250/754-3500;** fax 250/754-3599; www.islands.bc.ca). Also check out **www.vancouverisland.com**.

GETTING AROUND

While Vancouver Island has an admirable system of public transport, getting to remote sights and destinations is difficult without your own vehicle.

BY FERRY **BC Ferries** (© **888/BCFERRY** in B.C., or 250/386-3431; www.bcferries.bc.ca) links Vancouver Island ports to many offshore islands, including Quadra, Alert Bay, and Sointula. None of these islands has public transport, so once there you'll need to hoof it, hitch it, hire a taxi, or arrange for bike rentals. Most innkeepers will pick you up if you've reserved in advance.

BY BUS See "Getting There," above, for information on **Island Coach Lines.**

BY CAR The southern half of Vancouver Island is well served by paved highways. The trunk road between Victoria and Nanaimo is **Highway 1,** the Trans-Canada. This busy route alternates between four-lane expressway and congested two-lane highway, and requires some patience and vigilance, especially during the busy summer months. North of Nanaimo, the major road is **Highway 19,** which is now almost all four-lane expressway; a particular improvement being the new 80-mile (128km) **Inland Highway** between Parksville and Campbell River. The older sections of 19, all closer to the island's east coast, are now labeled 19A. North of Campbell River, a long, unimproved section of Highway 19 continues all the way to Port Hardy. Access to gasoline is no problem, even in more remote northern areas, but don't head out on a long stretch of unpaved road without filling up.

Rental-car agencies include **Avis** (© **800/272-5871** in Canada, or 800/230-4898 in the U.S.; www.avis.com), **Budget** (© **800/268-8900** in Canada,

800/527-0700 in the U.S., or 250/953-5300 in Victoria; https://rent.drive budget.com), and **National** (© **800/387-4747** or 250/386-1213; www. nationalcar.com).

2 Campbell River & Quadra Island

Campbell River: 28 miles (45km) N of Courtenay, 165 miles (266km) N of Victoria

Busy and utilitarian, Campbell River (pop. 33,000) gives the impression of a town that works for a living. For years, it has been known as the "Salmon-Fishing Capital of the World," but it is also home to a large pulp and paper mill. Between Quadra Island and Campbell River, the broad Strait of Georgia squeezes down to a narrow mile-wide channel called Discovery Passage. All of the salmon that enter the Strait of Juan de Fuca near Victoria to spawn in northerly rivers funnel down into this tight constriction, a churning waterway with 13-foot (4m) tides. Historically, vast hauls of incredibly large fish have been pulled from these waters; fishing lodges have lined these shores for decades. However, salmon numbers at Campbell River have fallen drastically in recent years, and the days of pulling 60-pound Chinooks from the turbulent waters are largely over. Today, you're as likely to take a wildlife-viewing trip on the sound as go fishing for salmon—and if you do fish, there are plenty of restrictions on what you can keep and strong encouragements to practice catch-and-release.

Salmon or no salmon, there are plenty of other attractions in and around Campbell River. Two excellent museums with world-class collections of Native artifacts head the list, and hiking on Quadra Island and in Strathcona Provincial Park appeals to outdoorsy types.

ESSENTIALS

GETTING THERE   By Plane   The **Campbell River and District Regional Airport,** south of Campbell River off Jubilee Parkway, has regular flights on commuter planes from Vancouver and Seattle. **Air Canada** (© **888/247-2262;** www. aircanada.com), through its subsidiary Air BC, offers flights from Vancouver, as does **Pacific Coastal Airlines** (© **800/663-2872;** www.pacific-coastal.com).

Harbor-to-harbor service between Vancouver and Campbell River is available from late June to Labour Day via **Air Rainbow** (© **250/287-8371;** www.air-rainbow.com). You can also fly from Seattle's Lake Washington or Lake Union from mid-May to late September on **Kenmore Air** (© **800/543-9595;** www. kenmoreair.com).

By Car   On the new four-lane Inland Highway (Hwy. 19), Campbell River is 28 miles (45km) north of Courtenay and 165 miles (266km) north of Victoria. Campbell River is the end of this newly improved stretch of roadway. The old Island Highway, 19A, also runs into the center of Campbell River, right along the water as you approach town.

By Bus   Island Coach Lines (© **800/663-8390** in the U.S., 800/318-0818 in Canada, or 250/388-5248 in Victoria; www.victoriatours.com) operates daily service between Victoria and Port Hardy, with stops in Campbell River. The fare to Campbell River is C$44 (US$29) from Victoria, and C$30.25 (US$20) from Nanaimo (the closest ferry from Vancouver).

VISITOR INFORMATION   The **Campbell River Visitor Info Centre,** 1235 Shoppers Row (© **250/287-4636;** www.campbellriverchamber.ca/vic. html), is open from 9am to 5pm (later in summer), daily from late July to Labour Day, Monday through Saturday in shoulder seasons, and Monday

Campbell River

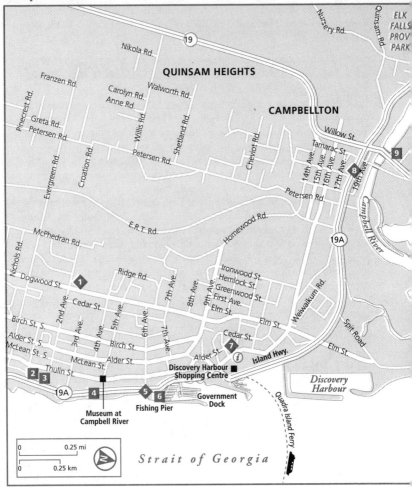

through Friday from October to early May. Another good resource is **Campbell River Tourism** (☎ **800/463-4386** or 250/286-1616; www.campbellrivertourism.com). For information on wildlife-related activities in the area, contact **Wonders of the Wild** (☎ **250/287-2374**; www.wondersofthewild.com).

CAMPBELL RIVER

Downtown Campbell River won't win any awards for quaintness. Busy Island Highway whizzes through town, and the commercial district is dominated by strip malls. One stop of interest is **Wei Wai Kum House of Treasures,** Discovery Harbour Shopping Centre, 1370 Island Hwy. (☎ **250/286-1440**; www.houseoftreasures.com), which sells carvings, totem poles, and clothing from the local Laichwiltach (a.k.a. Ligwitdaxw or Lekwiltok) tribes of the Kwakwaka'wakw First Nations people. Wei Wai Kum is also home to the **Gildas Box of Treasures Theatre,** a facsimile of a Laichwiltach Big House in which members of the band perform traditional dances, songs, and stories.

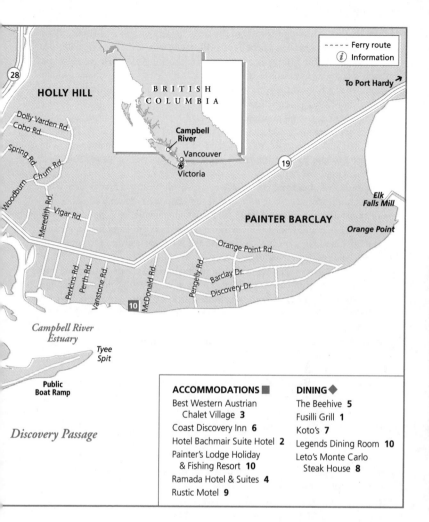

Ferry route
(i) Information

28

HOLLY HILL

Dolly Varden Rd.
Coho Rd.
Spring Rd.
Chum Rd.
Woodburn
Meredith Rd.
Vigar Rd.

BRITISH
COLUMBIA

**Campbell
River**

Vancouver
Victoria

To Port Hardy ↗

19

*Elk
Falls Mill*

PAINTER BARCLAY

Orange Point

Orange Point Rd.

Perkins Rd.
Perth Rd.
Vanstone Rd.
McDonald Rd.
Pengelly Rd.
Barclay Dr.
Discovery Dr.

10

*Campbell River
Estuary*

*Tyee
Spit*

**Public
Boat Ramp**

Discovery Passage

ACCOMMODATIONS ■

Best Western Austrian
  Chalet Village **3**
Coast Discovery Inn **6**
Hotel Bachmair Suite Hotel **2**
Painter's Lodge Holiday
  & Fishing Resort **10**
Ramada Hotel & Suites **4**
Rustic Motel **9**

DINING ◆

The Beehive **5**
Fusilli Grill **1**
Koto's **7**
Legends Dining Room **10**
Leto's Monte Carlo
  Steak House **8**

The Museum at Campbell River ⭐ *Kids* Campbell River's captivating museum is worth seeking out for the carvings and artifacts from local First Nations tribes; especially fine are the contemporary carved masks. Also compelling is the sound-and-light presentation *The Treasures of Siwidi,* which retells an ancient Indian myth. You can see a replica of a pioneer-era cabin, tools from the early days of logging, and, in the theater, a 1914 documentary called *War of the Land Canoes.* The gift shop is one of the best places to buy Native art and jewelry.

470 Island Hwy. ℂ **250/287-3103.** www.crmuseum.ca. Admission C$5 (US$3.25) adults, C$3.75 (US$2.45) seniors and students, C$12 (US$7.80) families, free for children under 6. Mid-May to Sept daily 10am–5pm; Oct to mid-May Tues–Sun noon–5pm.

OUTDOOR PURSUITS

DIVING Beaver Aquatics, 760 Island Hwy. (ℂ **250/287-7652;** www. connected.bc.ca/~baquatics), rents equipment for C$55 (US$36) per day and can provide lessons and information.

FISHING ✦   The Coho salmon in these waters weigh up to 20 pounds (9kg), and even these are dwarfed by the Tyee—30-pound-plus (13.5kg-plus) Chinook (King) salmon. But fishing isn't what it once was in Campbell River. Some salmon runs are now catch-and-release only, and others are open for limited catches; many fishing trips are now billed more as wildlife adventures than hunting-and-gathering expeditions.

To fish here, you need nonresident saltwater and freshwater licenses, available at outdoor-recreation stores throughout Campbell River, including **Painter's Lodge,** 1625 McDonald Rd. (© **250/286-1102;** www.painterslodge.com). The staff here can also provide information on guided boats and fishing rules (see "Where to Stay," below).

Be sure to call ahead and talk to an outfitter or the visitor center to learn what fish are running during your visit, and if the seasons have been opened. Don't be disappointed if there's no salmon fishing when you visit, or if the salmon you do hook is catch-and-release only. For one thing, there are other fish in the sea. And if all you really want is to get out on the water for a little adventure, consider a wildlife-viewing boat tour.

There are dozens of guides in the area, with services that extend from basic to extravagant. Expect to pay C$70 (US$46) per hour for 4 to 5 hours of fishing with a no-frills outfitter. A flashier trip on a luxury cruiser can cost more than C$120 (US$78) per hour. The most famous guides are associated with the Painter's Lodge and its sister property, April Point Lodge (see "Where to Stay," below). A few smaller operations include **Destiny Sportfishing,** 2653 Vargo Rd. (© **250/286-9610;** www.destinyguide.bc.ca); **CR Fishing Village,** 260 Island Hwy. (© **250/287-3630**); and **Larry Craig Salmon Charters,** 47 S. McLean St. (© **250/287-2592**). Also check out **www.campbellrivertourism. bc.ca/member/fishi.html.** Most hotels in Campbell River also offer fishing/lodging packages; ask when you reserve.

GOLF   The Les Furber–designed, 18-hole, par-72 **Morningstar,** 525 Lowry's Rd., Parksville (© **250/248-2244;** www.morningstar.bc.ca), has seaside links and fairways that run in and out of the woods. Because it was carved out of a dense forest, you may see wildlife grazing on the fairway at **Storey Creek Golf Club,** Campbell River (© **250/923-3673;** www.storeycreek.bc.ca).

HIKING   For day hikes, drive to Strathcona Provincial Park (see below) or explore Quadra Island's Mount Seymour or Morte Lake parks. For a pleasant hike closer to Campbell River, drive west 3¾ miles (6km) on Highway 28 to **Elk Falls Provincial Park.** Easy 1- to 2-hour hikes lead to a fish hatchery and let you explore a stream with beaver ponds. From the park, you can also join the **Canyon View Trail,** a loop hike that follows the banks of the Campbell River.

WILDLIFE TOURS   **Eagle Eye Adventures** (© **250/286-0809** or 250/890-0464; www.img.ca/eagle-eye) offers a range of excursions via Zodiac and floatplane. A 6-hour whale- and bear-watching excursion begins by boating to Johnstone Strait to view orcas and black bears. At Port Neville, a floatplane whisks you away for an eagle's-eye view of the Inside Passage (see chapter 9, "Northern British Columbia"). The cost is C$225 (US$146) for adults. **Painter's Lodge** (see "Fishing," above) also offers wildlife-watching trips. See **www.campbellrivertourism.bc.ca/member/adven.html** for a full listing of adventure- and wildlife-tour operators in the area.

WHERE TO STAY

The 122 campsites at **Elk Falls Provincial Park** (© **250/954-4600**) go for C$12 (US$8) in summer (see also "Hiking," above).

Best Western Austrian Chalet Village   Overlooking Discovery Passage, this recently renovated oceanfront hotel offers a choice of regular or housekeeping units (with kitchenettes); some rooms are in loft chalets. Most units have a fridge, and some have VCRs. The staff can arrange whale-watching, fishing, or golfing trips.

462 S. Island Hwy., Campbell River, BC V9W 1A5. © **800/667-7207** or 250/923-4231. Fax 250/923-2840. www.vquest.com/austrian. 56 units. May–Sept C$109 (US$71) double; C$119 (US$77) kitchenette unit, loft chalet, or mini-suite; C$139 (US$90) loft chalet with kitchenette. Oct–Apr C$82–C$95 (US$53–US$62) all units. Extra person C$10 (US$7). Senior and AAA discounts available. AE, DC, DISC, MC, V. Pets allowed in smoking rooms only for C$6 (US$3.90) per night. **Amenities:** Restaurant, pub; indoor pool; golf course nearby; miniature putting green; Jacuzzi; sauna; table tennis; babysitting; coin-op laundry; same-day dry cleaning. *In room:* TV, dataport, fridge, coffeemaker, hair dryer, iron.

Coast Discovery Inn   Part of the sprawling Discovery Harbour Marina and Shopping Centre, the Coast is right downtown and offers dramatic views from its upper stories. The accommodations are spacious and nicely furnished. Kids will be happy to find rooms with computer game consoles. One wheelchair-accessible unit is available.

975 Shoppers Row, Campbell River, BC V9W 2C4. © **800/663-1144** or 250/287-7155. Fax 250/287-2213. www.coasthotels.com. 90 units. C$110–C$170 (US$72–US$111) double. Extra person C$10 (US$7). Family plan, senior and AAA discounts, and corporate rates available. AE, DC, DISC, MC, V. Pets allowed for C$10 (US$7) per night. **Amenities:** Restaurant, pub; golf course nearby; exercise room; Jacuzzi; 24-hr. room service; same-day dry cleaning. *In room:* TV w/ pay movies, dataport, coffeemaker, hair dryer, iron.

Hotel Bachmair Suite Hotel ★ *Value*   This hotel on the southern edge of town offers beautifully outfitted rooms and suites. Furnishings are exquisite: leather couches, fine carpeting, and hand-painted armoires. Kitchens are fully equipped with china, utensils, and appliances. Most units have balconies and views of Discovery Passage. The hotel itself—wrapped in carved-wooden-rail balconies lined by flower boxes—is handsome in the Bavarian style so favored in Canada.

492 S. Island Hwy., Campbell River, BC V9W 1A5. © **888/923-2849** or 250/923-2848. Fax 250/923-2849. www.hotelbachmair.com. 23 units. C$89–C$140 (US$58–US$91) double. Extra person C$10 (US$7). Off-season rates available. Fishing charters arranged. AE, DC, MC, V. Free parking. Pets allowed for C$5 (US$3.25) per night. **Amenities:** Restaurant and bar next door; golf course nearby; in-room massage; babysitting; coin-op laundry; laundry service. *In room:* TV, dataport, kitchen, fridge, coffeemaker, hair dryer.

Painter's Lodge Holiday & Fishing Resort ★   This resort has been a favorite hideaway for stars such as John Wayne, Bob Hope, and Goldie Hawn. Once you see the awe-inspiring location, you'll understand why. Built in 1924 on a point overlooking Discovery Passage, the lodge retains a rustic grandeur, with spacious rooms decorated in natural woods. Four cottages are also available, as are wheelchair-accessible rooms. Guests can enjoy all three meals in the Legends Dining Room (see "Where to Dine," below). Guided fishing trips are available, and hiking trails run through the grounds. *Note:* Smoking is permitted outdoors only.

1625 McDonald Rd., Box 460, Campbell River, BC V9W 5C1. © **800/663-7090** or 250/286-1102. Fax 250/286-0158. www.painterslodge.com. 94 units. C$184–C$479 (US$119–US$309) double; C$152–C$363 (US$98–US$234) cottage. Extra person C$15 (US$10). Off-season discounts available. AE, DC, MC, V. Closed

Nov–Mar. **Amenities:** Restaurant, pub, lounge; heated outdoor pool; golf course nearby; tennis courts; exercise room; Jacuzzi; bike, scooter, and kayak rentals; children's center; tour/activities desk; car-rental desk; courtesy limo; airport shuttle; in-room massage; babysitting; laundry service; same-day dry cleaning. *In room:* TV, coffeemaker, hair dryer.

Ramada Hotel & Suites

Each spacious room here has a balcony and ocean view. Best of all, the Ramada is on the ocean side of busy Island Highway, so you won't have to look over the traffic to see the water. The hotel is adding theme suites—African, Arabian, Igloo, Space, and others. *Note:* One room has a shower only, for travelers with disabilities.

261 Island Hwy., Campbell River, BC V9W 2B3. ℂ **800/663-7227** or 250/286-1131. Fax 250/287-4055. www.ramadacr.ca. 76 units. C$94–C$179 (US$61–US$116) double. Extra person C$10 (US$6.50). Theme, honeymoon, golf, and fishing packages available. AE, MC, V. Free parking. **Amenities:** Two restaurants (fine dining, Japanese), lounge; indoor pool; golf course nearby; exercise room; Jacuzzi; business center; in-room massage; babysitting; coin-op laundry; laundry service; dry cleaning. *In room:* TV w/ pay movies, dataport, coffeemaker, hair dryer, iron.

Rustic Motel

Located on 2 acres (.8 hectare) of parkland beside the river, the Rustic offers moderately priced rooms with everything you'll need for a comfortable stay. There are three two-bedroom suites and a three-bedroom cabin. The Rustic is decked out in summer with baskets of flowers.

2140 N. Island Hwy., Campbell River, BC V9W 2G7. ℂ **800/567-2007** or 250/286-6295. Fax 250/286-9692. www.rusticmotel.com. 42 units. C$80 (US$52) double. Extra person C$10 (US$7). Kitchen C$10 (US$7) extra. Rates include continental breakfast. AE, DC, MC, V. Free parking. Pets allowed for C$5 (US$3.25) per night. **Amenities:** Jacuzzi; sauna; coin-op laundry. *In room:* A/C, TV, dataport, fridge, coffeemaker.

WHERE TO DINE

In addition to the restaurants listed below, try **Koto's,** 80 10th Ave. (ℂ **250/ 286-1422**), an excellent sushi bar, open Tuesday through Friday from 11am to 2pm and Tuesday through Saturday from 5:30 to 9pm.

The Beehive CANADIAN

A family dining institution dating back to 1929 (but not in the current location), the Beehive offers good eggy breakfasts, moving on to a menu of burgers, fish-and-chips, and sandwiches during the day. The dinner offerings expand to include steak, pasta, and seafood dishes. A new patio overlooks the water.

921 Island Hwy. ℂ **250/286-6812.** Reservations recommended in summer. Dinner main courses C$7–C$22 (US$4–US$14). AE, MC, V. Mid-June to Labour Day daily 6:30am–10pm; Labour Day to mid-June daily 7am–8pm.

Fusilli Grill ITALIAN

A good, casual Italian restaurant located in the suburbs southwest of downtown, Fusilli Grill makes almost all of its own pasta and utilizes local produce, meats, and seafood as much as possible. Lunch features a variety of sandwiches on fresh-baked focaccia. At dinner, there's a choice of steak, fish, and chicken dishes, plus a few Mexican and Asian options for variety.

220 Dogwood St., #4. ℂ **250/830-0090.** www.fusilligrill.bc.ca. Reservations recommended. Main courses C$8–C$23 (US$5–US$15). Evening take-out specials C$8 (US$5). AE, DC, MC, V. Mon–Fri 11am–9:30pm; Sat–Sun 4:30–9:30pm.

Harbour Grill 🌟 CONTINENTAL/SEAFOOD

Owned by the proprietors of the respected establishment Le Chateaubriand—now closed—Harbour Grill features much of the same quality menu in an attractive new location, complete with views of Discovery Passage. The dinner menu features many worthy relics of mid-20th-century fine dining. Yes, you can actually order a real Chateaubriand here, an arm-size roast of beef tenderloin drizzled with béarnaise and topped with asparagus. Other classics of Kennedy-era cuisine include duck with orange sauce and veal Oscar. In summer, fresh seafood specials receive more contemporary preparations. The Harbour Grill isn't exactly a food museum—for one thing, the new location is too bright and modern—it's more like time-travel cuisine, and great fun at that.

112–1334 Island Hwy., in the Discovery Harbour Mall. ℂ **250/287-4143.** www.harbourgrill.com. Reservations recommended. Main courses C$19–C$24 (US$12–US$16) and up. AE, DC, MC, V. Mon–Fri 11:30am–2pm; daily from 5:30pm.

Legends Dining Room ⋆ INTERNATIONAL   The dining room at Painter's Lodge is entirely flanked by windows, affording every table a view of busy Discovery Passage and the free speedboat taxi that runs between the hotel and April Point Lodge, on Quadra Island. If you're having dinner here, consider hopping that water taxi to April Point for a cocktail or pre-dinner appetizer at its sushi bar. Return with salt spray in your hair, ready for a great meal at Legends. Start off with the excellent smoked-salmon–stuffed mushroom caps. The entrees have regional flair—you might choose jambalaya or Cuban-style pork chops, marinated in rum and tandoori spices and served with apple and sun-dried cranberry chutney. As you'd expect at a fishing resort, fish and seafood are menu favorites.

At Painter's Lodge, 1625 McDonald Rd. ℂ **250/286-1102.** Reservations recommended. Main courses C$12–C$25 (US$8–US$16). AE, DC, MC, V. Daily 7am–10pm. Closed Nov–Mar.

Leto's Monte Carlo Steak House GREEK/STEAKHOUSE   It's not clear why Greek immigrants run the best steakhouses in Canada, but they do. It's easier to comprehend why they run the best Greek restaurants. Put the two together, and you get Leto's, which brings together souvlaki, dolmades, and moussaka with perfectly grilled AAA-certified Alberta beef. The calamari served with zesty tzatziki makes a great appetizer course for a 10-ounce New York steak.

1850 Island Hwy. ℂ **250/287-9969.** Reservations recommended. Main courses C$10–C$39 (US$7–US$25). AE, MC, V. Daily 4–10pm (Fri–Sat until 11pm).

QUADRA ISLAND

The **Kwagiulth Museum and Cultural Centre** ⋆, 34 WeWay Rd., Cape Mudge Village (ℂ **250/285-3733;** www.island.net/~kmccchin), boasts one of the world's best collections of artifacts, ceremonial masks, and tribal costumes once used by the Cape Mudge Band of the Ligwitdaxw Kwakwaka'wakw (a.k.a. Kwagiulth) First Nation in elaborate potlatch ceremonies conducted to celebrate births, deaths, marriages, and other important occasions. Potlatches became more and more ostentatious as the centuries went by: Bands and villages spent months, even years, planning feasts and performances, carving totem poles, and amassing literally tons of gifts for their guests. The Canadian government outlawed the practice in 1884 as part of a forced-assimilation policy, and only lifted the ban—which was difficult to enforce—in 1951.

Behind the museum is K'ik'ikg'illas, "The House of Eagles," a recently built longhouse-like structure used to teach carving, dancing, and other traditional ways of life. Ask at the museum to tour the building, which contains an especially impressive totem pole. Across from the museum is a park where a series of petroglyphs document ancient legends.

June through September, the museum is open Monday through Saturday from 10am to 4:30pm and Sunday from noon to 4:30pm; the rest of the year, Tuesday through Saturday from 10am to 4:30pm. Admission is C$3 (US$1.95) for adults, C$2 (US$1.30) for seniors and students, and C$1 (US$.65) for children

6 to 12. From the ferry, take Cape Mudge Road south about 3 miles (5km); watch for signs for WeWay Road and a hand-painted sign saying MUSEUM.

A 10-minute ferry runs between Campbell River and Quathiaski Cove, on Quadra Island. There are trips on the hour from about 6am to 10pm (no Sunday 7am sailing). The round-trip fares are C$4.75 (US$3.10) per person and C$12 (US$8) per vehicle in summer; you can bring a bike for free.

WHERE TO STAY & DINE

April Point Lodge & Fishing Resort ✿ The secluded April Point Lodge, world-famous for its saltwater fishing charters, has magnificent views of the Discovery Passage. This luxury fishing resort and Painter's Lodge, just across the channel, are under the same ownership; there's free boat-taxi service between the two properties, which makes coming for drinks or dinner here easy from Campbell River. The guesthouses are tastefully furnished, with hot tubs, fireplaces, and kitchens. The lodge suites are also nicely appointed. Facilities include helicopter access and seaplane service to Vancouver and Seattle, as well as a marina. See the amenities listed below for the other extras available to April Point guests at Painter's Lodge. *Note:* Smoking is permitted outside only.

The restaurant features Northwest cuisine. To start, try pan-seared Fanny Bay oysters with chili and lime crème fraîche, or choose from the menu of the adjoining sushi bar. For an entree, opt for a daily seafood special or, if you're not in the mood for fish, filet mignon with crisp latkes and caramelized red-onion glaze.

April Point Rd., Quadra Island. c/o Box 1, Campbell River, BC V9W 4Z9. ☎ **800/663-7090** or 250/285-2222. www.aprilpoint.com. 36 units. C$162–C$330 (US$105–US$215) lodge; C$240–C$364 (US$155–US$235) guesthouse. Extra person C$20 (US$13) in lodge, C$30 in guesthouse (US$20). AE, DC, MC, V. **Amenities:** Restaurant, sushi bar, lounge; tennis courts; heated outdoor pool; exercise room; Jacuzzi; bike, scooter, and kayak rentals; children's center; tour/activities desk; car-rental desk; courtesy limo; in-room massage; babysitting; laundry service; same-day dry cleaning. *In room:* TV, coffeemaker, hair dryer.

Tsa-Kwa-Luten Lodge ✿ Owned by the Laichwiltach Cape Mudge Band, this is a modern luxury resort designed to resemble a Native Big House. Overlooking the Discovery Passage, it offers both lodge suites and waterfront cabins. Some suites have lofts, Jacuzzis, or fireplaces. The cabins contain full kitchens; some have fireplaces and hot tubs. All units are beautifully decorated with contemporary Native art. Accommodations for travelers with disabilities are available. The staff can arrange fishing trips and heli-fishing charters.

The restaurant features fresh seafood and steaks prepared with Continental finesse and an eye toward Native traditions. Standouts include the venison Bourguignon, with wild mushrooms and traditional bannock bread, and cedar-plank baked salmon accompanied by a fresh local blackberry butter. Native dancing and entertainment are offered.

Lighthouse Rd., Box 460, Quathiaski Cove, Quadra Island, BC V0P 1N0. ☎ **800/665-7745** or 250/285-2042. Fax 250/285-2532. www.capemudgeresort.bc.ca. 34 units. C$60–C$125 (US$39–US$81) suite; C$100–C$350 (US$65–US$228) cabin. Meal plans available. AE, DC, MC, V. Free parking. Small pets allowed in cabins for C$10 (US$6.50) per day. **Amenities:** Restaurant, bar; lit tennis courts nearby; exercise room; Jacuzzi; sauna; boat, bike, and moped rentals; massage; laundry service. *In room:* Coffeemaker, hair dryer.

3 Strathcona Provincial Park ✿

24 miles (38km) W of Campbell River

British Columbia's oldest provincial park, and the largest on Vancouver Island at 617,500 acres (250,000 hectares), **Strathcona Park** is located west of Campbell River and Courtenay. Mountain peaks, many glaciated or mantled with snow, dominate the park, and lakes and alpine meadows dot the landscape. Roosevelt elk, Vancouver Island marmot and wolf, and black-tailed deer have evolved into distinct species, due to Vancouver Island's separation from the mainland. **Buttle Lake** is the major body of water in the park. It and many other lakes and waterways provide good fishing for cutthroat and rainbow trout and Dolly Varden.

Summers in Strathcona are usually pleasantly warm; evenings can be cool. Winters are fairly mild except at higher elevations, where heavy snowfall is common. Snow remains year-round on the mountain peaks and may linger into July at higher elevations. Rain can be expected at any time of year.

ESSENTIALS

GETTING THERE   Campbell River and Courtenay are the primary access points for the park. Highway 28 passes through the northern section of the park and provides access to Buttle Lake, 30 miles (48km) west of Campbell River. There are two access routes to the Forbidden Plateau area from Courtenay. To reach Paradise Meadows from Courtenay and Highway 19, follow signs to Mount Washington Resort via the Strathcona Parkway. Fifteen miles (25km) up the parkway, you'll come to the resort's Nordic Lodge road on the left. Turn onto this road and go another mile (1.6km) to the Paradise Meadows parking lot. To reach Forbidden Plateau, follow the signs on the Forbidden Plateau road from Highway 19 and Courtenay. It's 12 miles (19km) to the former Forbidden Plateau ski area (now closed) and the trail head.

VISITOR INFORMATION   Contact **BC Parks District Manager,** Box 1479, Parksville (✆ **250/954-4600;** www.env.gov.bc.ca/bcparks).

SEEING THE HIGHLIGHTS

The Buttle Lake area (off Hwy. 28) and the Forbidden Plateau area (accessed through Courtenay) both have some visitor-oriented developments. Just outside the park boundaries, **Strathcona Park Lodge** (see "Where to Stay," below) offers lodging, dining, and a variety of activities. The rest of the park is largely undeveloped and appeals primarily to those seeking wilderness surroundings. To see and enjoy much of the park's scenic splendor requires hiking or backpacking into the alpine wilderness.

A paved road joins **Highway 28** (the Gold River Hwy.) near the outlet of **Buttle Lake** and winds its way southward, hugging the shoreline. Along this scenic road are numerous cataracts and creeks that rush and tumble into the lake.

Some of the more prominent peaks include Mount McBride, Marble Peak, Mount Phillips, and Mount Myra. **Elkhorn Mountain,** at 7,190 feet (2,192m), is the second-highest mountain in the park. Elkhorn, along with Mount Flannigan and Kings Peak, can be seen from Highway 28. The highest point on Vancouver Island at 7,216 feet (2,200m), the **Golden Hinde** stands almost in the center of the park to the west of Buttle Lake.

A second area of the park, **Forbidden Plateau,** is accessed by gravel road from Courtenay. Those who hike into the plateau are rewarded with an area of subalpine beauty and views that extend from the surrounding glaciers and mountains to farmlands and forest.

The 1,443-foot (440m) **Della Falls,** one of the 10 highest waterfalls in the world, is located in the southern section of the park, and is reached by a rugged multi-day hike (see "Hiking," below).

HIKING

FROM THE BUTTLE LAKE AREA   The 1.9-mile (3km) **Upper Myra Falls Trail** starts just past the Westmin mine operation. This 2-hour hike leads through old-growth forests and past waterfalls. The 4.1-mile (6.6km) **Marble Meadows Trail** starts at Phillips Creek Marine Campsite on Buttle Lake. It features alpine meadows and limestone formations; allow 6 hours round-trip. The 2,952-foot (900m) **Lady Falls Trail,** which begins at the Highway 28 viewing platform, takes about 20 minutes and leads to a picturesque waterfall.

FROM THE PARADISE MEADOWS TRAIL HEAD (MOUNT WASHINGTON)   The 1.4-mile (2.2km) **Paradise Meadows Loop Trail** is an easy walk through subalpine meadows, taking about 45 minutes. The 8.6-mile (14km) **Helen McKenzie–Kwai Lake–Croteau Lake Loop Trail** takes 6 hours and offers access to beautiful lakes and mountain vistas. There's designated camping at Kwai Lake. From Lake Helen McKenzie, the trail follows forested slopes over rougher terrain before rising to a rolling subalpine area to Circlet Lake, which offers designated camping. Allow 4 hours.

FROM FORBIDDEN PLATEAU   The 3.1-mile (5km), 2-hour **Mount Becher Summit Trail** starts at the former ski lodge and goes up one of the runs to the trail head near the T-bar. It provides excellent views of the valley and Strait of Georgia.

OTHER TRAILS IN STRATHCONA PARK   The **Della Falls Trail** is 20 miles (32km) round-trip. It starts at the west end of Great Central Lake (between Port Alberni and Tofino on Hwy. 4) and follows the old railway grade up the Drinkwater Valley. You must take a boat across the lake to get to the trail head. At **Ark Resort,** 11000 Great Central Lake Rd. (© **250/723-2657;** www.arkresort.com), you can take a high-speed water taxi or rent a motorboat or canoe. The whole trip will take 3 to 6 days. The trail passes historic railroad logging sites and accesses Love Lake and Della Lake. Some unbridged river crossings can be hazardous.

CAMPING

Buttle Lake, with 85 sites, and **Ralph River,** with 76 sites, are both located on Buttle Lake, accessible via Highway 28 (the Gold River Hwy.) west of Campbell River. Sites go for C$15 (US$10). The campgrounds have water, toilets, and firewood.

WHERE TO STAY

Strathcona Park Lodge ★★   This rustic lodge, north of Strathcona Park along upper Campbell Lake, is far more than just a place to stay in the woods. With a wide variety of programs appealing to everyone from families to Golden Agers, the lodge has something to offer everyone who loves the outdoors. Activities include climbing and rappelling, along with gentler pursuits such as canoeing, fishing, and swimming. Because the package options are numerous, it's a good idea to call to discuss your interests. The popular 4-day Adventure Sampler includes lodging, meals, and activities (climbing, kayaking, orienteering, hiking, and more) for C$795 (US$517) per person, based on booking for two. Even if you choose not to participate in any of the adventure programs, the lodge is a lovely place to hang out and use as a base for exploring the park. All accommodations are sparely yet comfortably furnished. Some chalet units have shared bathrooms; all other rooms have private bathrooms. The lakefront cabins with kitchens are the most charming, though you must reserve well in advance. In summer, the Whale Room serves three buffet-style meals daily. Guests sit at long communal tables. *Note:* Smoking is not permitted.

25 miles (40km) west of Campbell River on Hwy. 28. Mailing address: Box 2160, Campbell River, BC V9W 5C5. (C) 250/286-3122. 250/286-6010. www.strathcona.bc.ca. 39 units. C$50–C$88 (US$33–US$57) chalet double with shared bathroom; C$88–C$144 (US$57–US$94) double with private bathroom; C$149–C$295 (US$97–US$192) cabin. 2- or 3-night minimum stays in cabins. Off-season discounts available. MC, V. **Amenities:** Exercise room; sauna; canoe and kayak rentals; children's programs; massage; babysitting; coin-op laundry. *In room:* No phone.

4 West to Gold River & Nootka Sound

Highway 28 continues past Strathcona Park another 6 miles (9km) to **Gold River** (pop. 2,049), a logging port and mill town just to the east of the Muchalet Inlet, and the only major northwestern island community accessible by paved road. The wild coastline around the **Nootka Sound,** to the west of Gold River, was the site of the first European settlement in the northwest. The tiny coastal communities here are almost completely isolated from roads, and rely on the **MV** *Uchuck III* for public transport and movement of goods. Passengers are welcome to join the MV *Uchuck III* as it goes between Gold River, Nootka Sound, and Kyuquot Sound.

January through June, the Tahsis day trip leaves on Tuesdays at 9am, traveling into Nootka Sound and up the Tahsis Inlet between Vancouver and Nootka islands to the village of Tahsis. The 9-hour round-trip costs C$45 (US$29) for adults, C$41 (US$27) for seniors, and C$23 (US$15) for children 7 to 12.

From July 4 to mid-September, the MV *Uchuck III* runs a day trip on Wednesdays and Saturdays from Gold River to Friendly Cove, or Yuquot, the ancestral home of the Mowachaht people. The return trip runs 6 to 7½ hours and costs C$40 (US$26) for adults, C$37 (US$24) for seniors, and C$20 (US$13) for kids.

On Thursdays year-round, the boat departs for Kyuquot Sound, to the north. This 2-day trip goes up the Tahsis and Esperanza inlets to the open sea and eventually the village of Kyuquot, where passengers stay overnight before returning the following day. The cost, which includes lodging, is C$310 (US$185) for two. A similar trip departs Mondays for Zeballos, a former gold-mining town and good wildlife-viewing spot just a way from Tahsis. This trip costs C$250 (US$163) for two, including lodging.

For more information or to make reservations, contact **Nootka Sound Service Ltd.** ((C) **250/283-2515** or 250/283-2325; www.mvuchuck.com). The MV *Uchuck III* will also take kayakers to various destinations on its routes; inquire for details.

If you need accommodations in Gold River, contact the **Tourist Info Centre** ((C) **250/283-2202;** www.village.goldriver.bc.ca) or try the **Ridgeview Motor Inn,** 395 Donner Ct. ((C) **800/989-3393** or 250/283-2277; www.ccr-biz.com/ridgeviewmotorinn), where doubles range from C$79 to C$125 (US$51 to US$81) in high season.

5 Telegraph Cove, Port McNeill, Alert Bay & Port Hardy

Telegraph Cove: 123 miles (198km) N of Campbell River

It's a winding 123-mile (198km) drive through forested mountains along the Island Highway (Hwy. 19) from Campbell River to **Port McNeill,** on northern Vancouver Island. But the majestic scenery, crystal-clear lakes, and unique wilderness along the way make it worthwhile.

The highway rejoins the coast along **Johnstone Strait,** home to a number of orca (killer whale) pods, which migrate annually from the Queen Charlotte Strait south to these salmon-rich waters. Whale-watching trips out of Port McNeill and Telegraph Cove are the principal recreational activities; this is one of the most noted whale-watching areas in British Columbia.

Also worth a visit is the island community of **Alert Bay,** a traditional First Nations town site festooned with totem poles and carvings. The museum houses a famous collection of ceremonial masks and other artifacts.

The Island Highway's terminus, **Port Hardy,** is 32 miles (52km) north of Port McNeill. Although it's a remote community of only 5,470, Port Hardy is the starting point for three unique experiences: the Inside Passage ferry cruise (see chapter 9, "Northern British Columbia") to Prince Rupert, the Discovery Coast ferry cruise (see chapter 9), and the untamed rain forest and coastline of Cape Scott Provincial Park (see section 6, later in this chapter).

ESSENTIALS

GETTING THERE   There are three principal ways to get to Vancouver Island's northernmost towns and islands: by car, bus, and plane. You can also reach Port Hardy from the north via the Inside Passage ferry from Prince Rupert (see chapter 9, "Northern British Columbia").

By Plane   **Pacific Coastal Airlines** (© 800/663-2872; www.pacific-coastal. com) flies daily from Vancouver to Port Hardy Airport. From late May to late September, **Kenmore Air** (© 800/543-9595; www.kenmoreair.com) flies sea-planes from Seattle's Lake Union or Lake Washington to Port McNeill.

By Car   Telegraph Cove is 123 miles (198km) north of Campbell River along the Island Highway (Hwy. 19). Port McNeill is another 5 miles (9km) north. Port Hardy is 148 miles (238km) north of Campbell River.

By Bus   **Island Coach Lines** (© 800/663-8390 in the U.S., 800/318-0818 in Canada, 250/388-5248 in Victoria; www.victoriatours.com) operates daily service between Nanaimo and Port McNeill and Port Hardy. The fare from Nanaimo to Port Hardy is C$82.50 (US$54).

VISITOR INFORMATION   Although there's no official visitor center in Telegraph Cove, you can call **Information for Tourists** (Stubbs Island Whale Watching; see below) at © 250/928-3185. The **Port McNeill Visitor Info Centre,** 351 Shelley Crescent (© 250/956-3131; www.portmcneill.net), is open year-round, and daily in summer from 10am to 6pm. The **Alert Bay Visitor Info Centre,** 116 Fir St. (© 250/974-5213; www.village.alertbay.bc.ca), is open in summer, daily from 9am to 6pm, and the rest of the year, Monday through Friday from 9am to 5pm. The **Port Hardy Visitor Info Centre,** 7250 Market St. (© 250/949-7622; www.ph-chamber.bc.ca), is open June through September, daily from 8:30am to 7pm, and October through May, Monday through Friday from 8:30am to 5pm. For additional information on northern island destinations, contact the **Vancouver Island North Visitors' Association** (© 800/903-6660 or 250/949-9094; www.vinva.bc.ca).

TELEGRAPH COVE

Telegraph Cove, 13⅗ driving miles (22km) southeast of Port McNeill—by way of the Island Highway and then a stretch of paved and gravel road—offers an unusual story. The town's handful of permanent residents lives in one of the few remaining elevated-boardwalk villages on Vancouver Island, overlooking Johnstone Strait.

This postcard-perfect fishing village's buildings are perched on stilts over the water, making it an entertaining destination for a stroll.

First a sawmill and fishing port, then an army camp, now a resort, Telegraph Cove's once isolated charm is quickly changing. The town is largely dominated by comfortably rustic **Telegraph Cove Resort,** which offers many historic boardwalk homes as rental units. With a good restaurant, busy boat basin, and wonderful bay and island views, the resort village is a longtime family favorite.

WHALE-WATCHING & OTHER OUTDOOR PURSUITS

Telegraph Cove is right on the Johnstone Strait, a narrow passage that serves as the summer home to hundreds of orcas as well as dolphins, porpoises, and seals. Bald eagles also patrol the waterway, and more unusual birds pass through the area, an important stop on the Pacific Flyway.

Ten miles (17km) south of Telegraph Cove and somewhat accessible—though not inside its proper boundaries—by boat charter, the **Robson Bight Ecological Reserve** provides some of the most fascinating whale-watching in the province. Orcas regularly beach themselves in the shallow waters of the Bight's pebbly "rubbing beaches" to remove the barnacles from their tummies. Boaters are not allowed to enter the reserve itself, but you can visit nearby areas and watch from afar.

Stubbs Island Whale-Watching, at the end of the Telegraph Cove boardwalk (© **800/665-3066** or 250/928-3185; www.stubbs-island.com), offers whale-watching tours in boats equipped with hydrophones, so you can hear the whales' underwater communication. These 3½-hour cruises cost around C$68 (US$44) for adults.

From May to mid-October, **Tide Rip Tours**, 28 Boardwalk (© **888/643-9319** or 250/339-5320; www.tiderip.com), offers excursions in covered water taxis to watch grizzly bears for C$289 (US$188).

For kayaking tours, contact **Telegraph Cove Sea Kayaking** (© **888/756-0099** or 250/756-0094; www.tckayaks.com). Half-day rental rates for a single start at C$35 (US$23).

WHERE TO STAY & DINE

Although both of the following establishments have mailing addresses in Port McNeill, they are located in or near Telegraph Cove.

Hidden Cove Lodge   Built years before a road reached this isolated harbor, Hidden Cove was meant to be approached by boat, and it still saves its best face for those who arrive this way. The handsome lodge, with a cathedral-ceilinged great room, is nestled beside a secluded cove. The guest rooms are clean and simply decorated. Three new cabins have efficiency kitchens and decks. There's also a floating guesthouse with five rooms that share bathrooms. Hidden Cove's easygoing, unaffected atmosphere belies the fact that it attracts the rich and famous. The restaurant, open to nonguests by reservation only, serves quality international dishes. Whale-watching, birding, heli-fishing, kayaking, and hiking tours can be arranged. *Note:* Smoking is not permitted.

Lewis Point, 1 Hidden Cove Rd., Box 258, Port McNeill, BC V0N 2R0. © and fax **250/956-3916.** www.hiddencovelodge.com. 15 units (8 with private bathroom). C$130–C$150 (US$85–US$98) lodge double; C$100–C$125 (US$65–US$81) guesthouse double; C$299 (US$194) cottage. Extra person C$25 (US$16). Lodge rates include full breakfast. Off-season rates available. MC, V. Free parking. Take the Island Hwy. (Hwy. 19) to turnoff for Telegraph Cove/Beaver Cove; turn right and follow signs. The lodge is 4 miles (6.5km) from Telegraph Cove. **Amenities:** Restaurant; golf course nearby; Jacuzzi; in-room massage available; babysitting available; coin-op laundry. *In room:* No phone.

Telegraph Cove Resorts Most of the accommodations offered by Telegraph Cove Resorts are refurbished homes from the early 20th century, scattered along the boardwalk. They range from small rooms in a former fishermen's boardinghouse to three-bedroom homes that sleep up to nine. All have bathrooms and kitchens, but no phones or TVs. There are also hotel-style rooms (no kitchens) at the Wastell Manor, a large home built in 1912. Although none of the historic properties are exactly fancy, they are clean, simply furnished, and make for a unique experience. In addition, 121 campsites are a short walk from the boardwalk. Open May through October, the campground provides hot showers, laundry, toilets, fire pits, and water. Sites are C$23 (US$15). On Sunday, the resort encourages guests to join the afternoon potluck. Amenities include moorage and fishing charters.

Box 1, Telegraph Cove, BC V0N 3J0. © 800/200-HOOK or 250/928-3131. Fax250/928-3105. www.telegraph coveresort.com. 21 units. Mid-June to mid-Oct C$89–C$225 (US$58–US$146) cabin; C$145–C$175 (US$94–US$114) suite. Mid-Oct to mid-June C$49–C$125 (US$32–US$81) cabin; C$80–C$130 (US$52–US$85) suite. Extra person C$10 (US$6.50). Packages available. MC, V. Located 16 miles (26km) south of Port McNeill. Pets allowed in some cabins for C$5 (US$3.25) per night. **Amenities:** Restaurant (Canadian/seafood), pub; kayak rentals; coin-op laundry. *In room:* Coffeemaker, no phone.

PORT MCNEILL & ALERT BAY

Port McNeill (pop. 3,000) is a logging and mill town—not particularly quaint—that serves as an access point for whale-watching and other wildlife tours, numerous outdoor-recreation opportunities, and the ferry to Alert Bay. Alert Bay (pop. 1,000) is a fascinating destination for anyone interested in First Nations culture. It has a wonderful collection of totem carvings and wall murals, as well as historic buildings.

During the second week of June, the Nimpkish Reserve hosts **June Sports & Indian Celebrations** (© **250/974-5556,** the 'Namgis First Nation office) on the soccer field in Alert Bay. Traditional tests of strength and agility are demonstrated by the island's tribal members.

BC Ferries (© **888/BCFERRY** in B.C., or 250/386-3431; www.bcferries. bc.ca) runs daily service between Port McNeill and Alert Bay. The crossing takes about 45 minutes; peak fares are C$5.75 (US$3.75) per passenger, C$14.50 (US$9) per vehicle.

EXPLORING ALERT BAY

Alert Bay has a rich First Nations heritage that can be seen in its proudly preserved architecture and artifacts. It has been a Kwakwaka'wakw (Kwagiulth) village for thousands of years. The integration of Scottish immigrants into the area during the 19th and 20th centuries is clearly depicted in the design of the **Anglican Church,** on Front Street (© **250/974-5401**). The cedar building was erected in 1881; its stained-glass window designs reflect a fusion of Kwakwaka'wakw and Scottish motifs. It's open in summer, Monday through Saturday from 8am to 5pm.

Walk a mile (1.6km) from the ferry terminal along Front Street to the island's two most interesting attractions. A 173-foot (53m) **totem pole**—the world's highest—stands next to the **Big House,** the tribal community center. The cedar totem pole features 22 figures of bears, orcas, and ravens. The Big House is usually closed to the public, but visitors are welcome to enter the grounds to get a closer look at the building, which is covered with traditional painted figures. In July and August, the **T'sasala Cultural Group** (© **250/974-5475**) presents dance performances in the Big House, usually Wednesday through Saturday. The cost is C$12 (US$8) for adults and C$5 (US$3.25) for children.

A few yards down the road from the Big House is the **U'Mista Cultural Centre** ⋆, Front Street (⟡ **250/974-5403;** www.umista.org), which displays carved masks, cedar baskets, copper jewelry, and other potlatch artifacts that were confiscated by the Canadian government in 1921. Admission is C$5 (US$3.25) for adults, C$4 (US$2.60) for seniors and students, and C$1 (US$.65) for children 12 and under. The museum is open in summer, daily from 9am to 5pm, and in winter, Monday through Friday from 9am to 5pm.

WHALE-WATCHING & OTHER OUTDOOR PURSUITS

Orcas, dolphins, and eagles all gather along Johnstone Strait to snack on fish that converge at this narrows between Vancouver Island and a series of tightly clustered islands. For more information on tour providers, as well as other businesses and attractions in Alert Bay, contact **Alert Bay Adventures,** 62c Fir St. (⟡ **877/974-9911** or 250/974-9911; www.alertbay.com).

From Port McNeill, **Mackay Whale Watching Ltd.,** 1514 Broughton Blvd. (⟡ **877/663-6722** or 250/956-9865; www.whaletime.com), offers daily tours to Johnstone Strait on a 55-foot passenger cruiser with hydrophone. A 4-hour trip costs C$65 (US$42).

Seasmoke Tours/Sea Orca Expeditions (⟡ **800/668-6722** in B.C., or 250/974-5225; www.seaorca.com) offers whale-watching sailing trips from June to mid-October. Excursions aboard a 44-foot, hydrophone-equipped sailboat include baked goods and Devonshire tea. Half-day tours cost C$70 (US$46). Seasmoke also offers tour/lodging packages at a bungalow on Alert Bay.

WHERE TO STAY & DINE

If you can't get into the recommended Telegraph Cove–area resorts and don't want to continue on to Port Hardy or Campbell River, try the **Dalewood Inn,** 1703 Broughton Blvd. (⟡ **877/956-3304** or 250/956-3304; www.dalewood inn.com), a motor inn with decent rooms starting at C$66 (US$43) in high season. Also try the **Haida-Way Motor Inn,** 1817 Campbell Way (⟡ **800/ 956-3373** or 250/956-3373; www.pmhotels.com), which has 62 units for C$96 (US$62) in summer.

Oceanview Camping & Trailer Park, Alder Road, Alert Bay (⟡ **250/ 974-5213;** fax 250/974-5470), has a great view of the Johnstone Strait and nature trails that fan out from the 23 sites. Rates are C$10 to C$15 (US$7 to US$10). Full hookups, flush toilets, hot showers, a free boat launch, and boat tours make this a great deal. The 'Namgis Nation runs the **Gwakawe Campground,** Alert Bay (⟡ **250/974-5274;** www.namgis.bc.ca/camping), where C$13 (US$8) gets you a beachfront site and access to showers, laundry, water, and firewood.

Sportsman's Steak & Pizza, on Beach Drive, Port McNeill (⟡ **250/ 956-4113**), offers a hearty menu of basics such as roast chicken, steaks, burgers, and pizzas. Beach Drive has a number of other restaurants as well.

Oceanview Cabins   Overlooking Mitchell Bay and only a mile from the ferry terminal, this quiet waterfront resort is Alert Bay's best value. Simply furnished, comfortable cabins contain queen beds and kitchens; two have shower-only bathrooms. Reserve a few months in advance for summer.

390 Poplar St., Alert Bay, BC V0N 1A0. ⟡ 250/974-5457. Fax 250/974-2275. www.alertbay.com/oceanview. 12 units. C$50–C$65 (US$33–US$42) double. Extra person C$5 (US$3.25). MC, V. *In room:* TV, no phone.

PORT HARDY

Port Hardy is the final stop on the Island Highway. This sizeable community is slowly moving away from a resource-based economy: Fishing, forestry, and mining have waned—though not disappeared—and the town is gradually developing an economy based on tourism.

A principal reason to venture here is the ferry to **Prince Rupert**—in fact, the ferry is a mainstay of the local tourism industry. The night before the 15-hour Inside Passage ferry runs, the town is booked up and reservations are needed at most restaurants. Port Hardy is also the point of departure for the Discovery Coast ferry cruise (see chapter 9, "Northern British Columbia").

People also visit for the diving, hiking, and excellent halibut and salmon fishing. Sportfishing is very good here, as the runs of salmon in local rivers continue to be strong and are therefore open to more fishing than at threatened runs elsewhere. Port Hardy is also the launching point for a land-based journey to **Cape Scott,** a wilderness park at the northern tip of Vancouver Island, and planning has begun to create an 81-mile (130km) hiking and multi-use trail along the island's northeastern coast from Shushartie Bay, just west of Port Hardy, to Cape Scott.

The **Port Hardy Museum,** 7110 Market St. (© **250/949-8143**), holds relics from early Danish settlers, plus a collection of stone tools from about 8000 B.C. found just east of town. Admission is by donation. The gift shop is one of the few places in town where you can find local carving and artwork. Hours are from mid-May to mid-October, Tuesday through Saturday from 11:30am to 5:30pm, and from mid-October to mid-May, Wednesday through Saturday from noon to 5pm.

OUTDOOR PURSUITS

DIVING ❧ Diving is excellent in the Port Hardy area. **North Island Diving and Water Sports,** at Market and Hastings (© **250/949-2664**), is a full-service dive store; rentals and instruction are available. For an entire vacation's worth of diving, contact **God's Pocket Resort** (© **888/534-8322** or 250/949-9221; www.godspocket.com). Located on Hurst Island, 12 miles (19km) north of Port Hardy in Queen Charlotte Strait, the resort offers complete diving and fishing packages. A 3-day package goes for C$660 (US$429) and includes all boat transport between the resort and Port Hardy, meals, lodging, and two boat dives per day. For more information on diving in the region, go to **www.3routes. com/scuba/na/can/bc/08/index.html**.

FISHING From Port Hardy, you can arrange day charter trips with local outfitters. **Catala Charters and Lodge** (© **800/515-5511** or 250/949-7560; www. catalacharters.net) offers guided fishing trips and operates the C-View B&B. **Codfather Charters** (© **250/949-6696;** www.fishingbc.com/Codfather) offers year-round fishing and accommodations in a waterfront lodge.

To simply rent a boat, contact **Hardy Bay Boat Rental,** 6555 Hardy Bay Rd. (© **250/949-7048** or 250/949-0155; www.hardybayfishing.com). Rates start at C$22 (US$14) per hour or C$190 (US$124) per day.

Port Hardy is the stepping-off point for trips to remote **fishing camps,** many with long pedigrees and well-to-do clientele. One of the most famous is **Nimmo Bay Resort** (© **800/837-HELI** or 250/949-2549; www.helifish.com), a full-service resort where a week's fishing with transportation by helicopter will run you around C$4,995 (US$3,247). Access is by floatplane or boat.

One of the only camps directly accessed from Port Hardy is **Duval Point Lodge** (© **250/949-6667;** www.island.net/~duval), which offers multi-day packages from its base camp about 5 miles (8km) north of town (accessed by boat). Guests receive a short training session; groups are then given their own boat and pointed to the channel. From here on, you keep your own schedule and run expeditions as you see fit. Guests stay in two two-story floating lodges, each with four bedrooms, a mix of private and shared bathrooms, and full kitchen. The outfitter provides rod and reel, bait, boat, cleaning area, and freezers. Guests do their own cooking. Guides are available, though part of the fun here is the satisfaction of running your own boat and interacting with other guests. The lodge also has two land-based log cabins, each with three bedrooms. Anyone who comes in their own boat can stay in these cabins; rates start at C$195 (US$127), with a 4-night minimum. Boat/lodging packages start at C$640 (US$416) per night, with a 4-night minimum. The lodge is closed October through May. Duval Point is not for those looking for five-star comforts and pampering. But if you want access to excellent fishing and adventure with congenial hospitality, it's a great value.

HIKING   For serious hikers, the best destination is **Cape Scott Provincial Park,** at the island's northwest point (see below).

KAYAKING   The dozens of uninhabited islands in the Goletas Channel directly offshore from the **Duval Point Lodge** (see "Fishing," above) are excellent for exploration by kayak, as is the coastline west of Duval Point. Experienced kayakers can base themselves at the lodge and explore on their own with a 4-day package (C$580/US$377). If you'd rather have some guidance, join a 5-day supported kayak/camping trip that takes in several islands and remote beach campsites (C$780/US$507).

North Island Kayak (© 877/949-7707 or 250/949-7707; www.island. net/~nikayak) offers rentals, instruction, and tours. It has locations both in Port Hardy and on the Johnstone Strait, and offers a number of tours to view orcas. A daylong instruction course on calm waters is C$69 (US$45). Half-day rentals start at C$20 (US$13) for a single.

WHERE TO STAY

Port Hardy has several well-worn hotel complexes. Reserve well in advance, especially on days when the ferries run. The **Wild Woods Campsite,** Forestry Road (© **250/949-6753;** ranger@island.net), is off the road to the ferry terminal. The 60 sites are a great value, offering fire pits, hot showers, toilets, beach access, and moorage for C$7 to C$20 (US$4.55 to US$13).

Airport Inn   Although this motel is 8 miles (13km) from downtown, it deserves mention because it's the best maintained of Port Hardy's many older motor inns. Rooms are large and furnished with all of the basics; some have kitchenettes. The hotel is within walking distance of the airport.

4030 Byng Rd., Box 2039, Port Hardy, BC V0N 2P0. © **888/218-2224** or 250/949-9434. Fax 250/949-6533. www.porthardy-airportinn.com. 45 units. C$85–C$95 (US$55–US$62) double. Extra person C$10 (US$7). Kitchen C$15 (US$10) extra. Senior and AAA discounts available. AE, MC, V. Free parking. Pets allowed. **Amenities:** Restaurant, pub, coffee shop; golf course nearby; limited room service; babysitting available; coin-op laundry. *In room:* TV, dataport, coffeemaker, hair dryer.

Kay's Bed & Breakfast   This conveniently located B&B has a lovely ocean view and offers free pickup service from the ferry terminal. Breakfast features fresh baked goods. For travelers with disabilities, a ground-floor room is available with in-room breakfast. *Note:* Smoking is not permitted.

7605 Carnarvon Rd., Box 257, Port Hardy, BC V0N 2P0. ✆ **800/829-0963** or 250/949-6776. www.bbcanada. com/4737.html. 3 units (2 with shared bathroom). C$65–C$75 (US$42–US$49) double. Extra person C$15 (US$10). Rates include continental breakfast. Off-season rates available. No credit cards. *In room:* TV, kitchen, fridge, coffeemaker, hair dryer, no phone.

Oceanview B&B Perched on a bluff overlooking Port Hardy Bay, Oceanview is a comfortably furnished, spotless modern home. A large room with two queen beds and a bathroom overlooks the cul-de-sac and gardens, and another spacious unit offers views of the bay. The hostess offers a friendly welcome and advice on local travel.

7735 Cedar Place, Box 1837, Port Hardy, BC V0N 2P0. ✆ and fax **250/949-8302.** www.island.net/~ocean vue. 3 units (2 with shared bathroom). C$85–C$100 (US$55–US$65) double. Rates include continental breakfast. No credit cards. Children must be 12 or older. *In room:* TV, hair dryer, no phone.

Pioneer Inn (Port Hardy) Pioneer Inn is located in a parklike setting on the banks of the Quatse River, 5 miles (8km) south of Port Hardy. There are often vacancies here on the nights before the ferry departs, when the downtown motels fill up. The rooms are basic but well maintained. Some units contain kitchens; there's one wheelchair-accessible room. Amenities include a campground, picnic area, and ferry shuttle service (for a fee).

4965 Byng Rd., Box 699, Port Hardy, BC V0N 2P0. ✆ **800/663-8744** or 250/949-7271. Fax 250/949-7334. 36 units. Mid-May to mid-Oct C$85–C$99 (US$55–US$64) double. Mid-Oct to mid-May C$54–C$74 (US$35–US$48) double. Extra person C$10 (US$7). 25 RV sites. C$21 (US$14) per vehicle. Electricity, sewer, and water included; cable TV and telephone hookup extra. Off-season and senior discounts available. AE, MC, V. Pets allowed for C$10 (US$7). **Amenities:** Restaurant, coffee shop; golf course nearby; playground; room service available; coin-op laundry. *In room:* TV, coffeemaker.

Quarterdeck Inn Opened in 1999, the Quarterdeck has more going for it than just its comparative youth. Perched directly above a busy marina, all units have great views onto a fishing and pleasure-boat port. The spacious rooms are outfitted with quality furniture; some contain kitchenettes and VCRs. Dataports and irons are also available. The hosts can arrange all sorts of outdoor and cultural activities, including whale-watching and fishing charters. The Quarterdeck also has an RV park (C$20/US$13 full hookup).

6555 Hardy Bay Rd., P.O. Box 910, Port Hardy, BC V0N 2P0. ✆ **877/902-0459** or 250/902-0455. Fax 250/ 902-0454. www.quarterdeckresort.net. 40 units. C$110 (US$72) double. Rates include continental breakfast. AE, DC, DISC, MC, V. Free parking. Small pets allowed for C$10 (US$6.50) per day. **Amenities:** Restaurant; golf course nearby; Jacuzzi; tour/activities desk; massage; coin-op laundry. *In room:* TV, coffeemaker, hair dryer.

WHERE TO DINE

For a simple meal or snack, or to get picnic provisions, stop by the **Fresh Connection,** 8950 Granville St. #115 (✆ **250/949-8117**), a small bakery that also offers lunchtime soups and sandwiches.

IV's Quarterdeck Pub PUB/CANADIAN This friendly pub and dining room, right above the marina, offers a large menu of appetizers, salads, sandwiches, burgers, and standards like steaks, ribs, and chicken. Locals will be quick to tell you that this is the best casual dining in Port Hardy; the clientele is a friendly mix of fishermen, tradesmen, and travelers.

6555 Hardy Bay Rd. ✆ **250/949-6922.** www.quarterdeckresort.net. Reservations not accepted. Main courses C$7–C$16 (US$4.55–US$10). AE, MC, V. Daily 11am–midnight.

Sam's Place GREEK/CANADIAN   It doesn't look like much from the outside, but this cozy restaurant on the south side of town offers some of Port Hardy's best dining. The broad menu encompasses excellent Greek cooking (such as seafood souvlaki), pizza, steak and seafood combos, Continental-style chicken and veal entrees, and lighter pasta dishes. The house specialty is Yani's Veal, with peppercorn sauce and tiger shrimp.

North Island Mall, Trustee Rd., off Hwy. 19. ℂ 250/949-9733. Reservations recommended in summer. Main courses C$8–C$18 (US$5–US$12). AE, DC, MC, V. Summer daily 11am–9pm; call in off-season.

6 Cape Scott Provincial Park

42 miles (68km) W of Port Hardy

Cape Scott Provincial Park is a 54,000-acre (21,870-hectare) coastal wilderness at the northwest tip of Vancouver Island. The park is characterized by 40 miles (64km) of spectacular ocean frontage, including about 14 miles (23km) of wide, sandy beaches, running from Nissen Bight in the north to San Josef Bay in the south and interspersed with rocky promontories and headlands. **Nels Bight,** midway between the eastern boundary of the park near Nissen Bight and the Cape Scott Lighthouse, is a 1½-mile-long (3km), white-sand beach; it's considered the most impressive of the nine beaches in the park.

Hansen Lagoon is a stopping place for Canada geese and a variety of waterfowl traveling the Pacific Flyway. Deer, elk, black bear, otter, cougars, and wolves are in evidence in the forested and open uplands, and seals and sea lions inhabit offshore islands.

The heavy rainfalls and violent windstorms of the Cape Scott area have shaped its history. Annual precipitation is nearly 200 inches. Even in summer, prolonged sunny periods are a rarity. High winds, rain, and generally stormy conditions can be expected at any time of the year.

Cape Scott Provincial Park is true wilderness, preserving magnificent areas of coastal British Columbia. Visitors can expect to find little development other than trails. Anyone contemplating a visit should be prepared for adverse weather conditions. There is no best time to visit the park, although midsummer is generally preferred.

ESSENTIALS

GETTING THERE   Hiking trails provide the only access to the park. The trail head for all park trails, in the extreme southeast corner of the park, is reached by a 42-mile (67km) part-paved, part-gravel road. From Port Hardy, follow signs for Winter Harbour or Holberg, and take the road for the park from Holberg. At some point in the not-too-distant future, a **North Coast Trail,** running 81 miles (130km) around the coast from Shushartie Bay, just west of Port Hardy, may connect hikers with the park.

VISITOR INFORMATION   Contact **BC Parks District Manager,** Box 1479, Parksville (ℂ **250/954-4600;** www.elp.gov.bc.ca/bcparks/explore/parkpgs/cape.htm).

HIKING

The easiest and most popular hike in the park is the 1½-mile (2.5km) one-way from the trail head to **San Josef Bay.** The trail leads through forest along the San Josef River, reaching the beach in about 45 minutes. Once at the beach, you can explore the ruins of the Henry Ohlsen home and post office, a relic of the Danish settlements of the early 1900s. The first section of beach is wide and white, flanked by rocky cliffs, and makes a great spot for a picnic. San Josef Bay is a good place to explore by kayak; surfers ride the high waves here as well.

The highlight of the park is the 14.6-mile (23.6km) one-way trail out to **Cape Scott.** This involves hiking along trails that are frequently very muddy. Most hikers manage it in 3 days, with 2 nights spent at Nels Bight—which means you won't be carrying your gear on the final leg to Cape Scott. Nels Bight is a spectacular coastline of sand and rocky beaches, and is a popular place to camp; fresh water is available. After one inland portion just past Nels Bight, the rest of the trail to Cape Scott and its lighthouse basically follows the beach. Note that access to the cape itself is restricted due to liability issues. You can easily see the cape from the lighthouse, however.

Facilities in the park are minimal. There are a few wilderness campgrounds with dry toilets, notably at San Josef Bay's second beach, Nels Bight, and at Eric Lake. Be sure to wear waterproof boots, and if you're spending the night, be prepared for sudden and extreme changes of weather.

8

The Sunshine Coast & Whistler

One of British Columbia's most scenic drives and the province's most celebrated year-round recreation center are both just north of Vancouver, making great destinations for a weekend away or a short road trip. The Sunshine Coast Highway is the name given to Highway 101 as it skirts the islands, fjords, and peninsulas of the mainland's Strait of Georgia coast. The scenery is spectacular, and the fishing and logging communities along the route offer friendly hospitality. No small part of the charm of this drive are the ferry rides: To reach road's end at Lund, you'll need to take two ferries, both offering jaw-dropping vistas of glaciered peaks floating above deep-blue waters. To make this route into a full loop trip, catch a third ferry from Powell River across the Strait of Georgia to Comox, and begin your exploration of Vancouver Island (covered in chapters 5 through 7).

The road to Whistler is equally spectacular, as it follows fjordlike Howe Sound, flanked by cliffs and towering peaks. But there's more to do here than gawk at the landscape: Whistler is Canada's premier skiing destination in winter, and a hiking and white-water rafting mecca in summer. Accommodations, dining, and recreational facilities are first-class, and the well-planned lodging developments have yet to overwhelm the natural beauty of the valley.

1 The Sunshine Coast

Powell River: 88 miles (142km) N of Vancouver

It's a travel writer's truism that the "getting there" part of a trip is half the fun. In the case of the Sunshine Coast—that strip of wildly scenic waterfront real estate north of Vancouver, along the mainland Strait of Georgia coast—the "getting there" is practically the entire reason for making the journey. But what a journey!

Backed up against the high peaks of the glaciated Coastal Mountain range, overlooking the tempestuous waters of the Strait of Georgia and onto the rolling mountains of Vancouver Island, this maritime-intensive trip involves two ferry rides and a lovely canoodling drive between slumbering fishing villages, eventually terminating at Lund, the end of the road for the Pacific Coast's Highway 101.

Powell River is the only town of any size along this route. Long a major lumber-milling center, Powell River is beginning to focus on tourism as a supplement to its resource-based economy. Diving in the sea life–rich waters of the Georgia Strait is a particularly popular activity along the Sunshine Coast.

ESSENTIALS

GETTING THERE   By Car & Ferry   Getting to Powell River and the Sunshine Coast requires taking a couple of ferries. From West Vancouver's Horseshoe Bay **BC Ferries** (© **888/223-3779**) terminal, ferries embark for Langdale, a 40-minute crossing. Driving north along Highway 101, the road hugs the coast along the Sechelt Peninsula, terminating 50 miles (81km) later at Earls Cove, where another ferry departs for a 50-minute crossing to Saltery Bay. The fare for each ferry is C$8 (US$5) per passenger, C$28 (US$18) per car. From Saltery Bay, Powell River is another 19 miles (31km). Lund, the terminus of Highway 101, is another 17 miles (28km).

You can also cross to Comox/Courtenay, on central Vancouver Island, from Powell River. This popular 75-minute crossing makes for a scenic loop tour of British Columbia's rugged coast and islands. The fare is C$8 (US$5) per passenger, C$25 (US$16) per vehicle. (See chapter 6, "Central Vancouver Island," for coverage of Comox and Courtenay.)

By Bus **Malaspina Coach Lines** (© **604/682-6511** in Vancouver, or 604/485-5030 in Powell River) offers service from Vancouver to Powell River via Highway 101 and the Sechelt Peninsula.

By Plane **Pacific Coastal Airlines** (© **800/663-2872** or 604/273-8666) flies from Vancouver to Powell River.

VISITOR INFORMATION Contact the **Powell River Visitors Bureau,** 4690 Marine Ave. (© **604/485-4701;** www.prcn.org).

EXPLORING THE AREA

Although Powell River is only 88 miles (142km) north of Vancouver, it feels light-years removed from the urban sprawl. It's probably because of the ferries: Commuting from the Sunshine Coast—the name given to the rocky, mountain-edged coastline that lies in the rain shadow of Vancouver Island—wouldn't make sense if you worked in Vancouver's financial district.

Highway 101 is a very scenic route, with soaring 10,000-foot (3,048m) peaks to the east and the swelling blue waters of the Strait of Georgia to the west. The first town north of the Horseshoe Bay–Langdale Ferry is **Gibsons** (pop. 3,732), a bucolic seaside community that served as the setting for the 1980s TV series *The Beachcombers.* Much of the action took place in **Molly's Reach Café,** 647 School Rd. (© **604/886-9710**), which has evolved from a film set of a restaurant into a real eatery with fine home-style cooking. Wander along the Gibsons Seawalk, which leads from the Government Wharf to Gibsons Marina, and watch fishing boats unload their catch. **Roberts Creek Provincial Park,** 5½ miles (9km) north of town, has a great tide-pool area that's perfect for picnicking.

Seventeen miles (28km) north of Gibsons is **Sechelt** (pop. 7,545), an arty little town on a sandy finger of land—all that connects the Sechelt Peninsula to mainland British Columbia. The town is a delightful clutter of galleries and cafes. The **Sechelt Indian Nation** is headquartered here; the imposing House of Hewhiwus contains a cultural center, museum, and gift shop. A couple miles north of Sechelt is **Porpoise Bay Provincial Park,** with a nice beach and riverside trail.

Continue north along Highway 101, admiring views of Vancouver Island. Drive past the Earls Cove ferry terminal to **Skookumchuk Narrows Provincial Park.** All of the seawater that lies behind 25-mile-long (40km) Sechelt Peninsula—which includes three major ocean inlets—churns back and forth through this passage in an amazing display of tidal fury. It's about an hour's walk to the park's viewing area. Tides are so fierce, they actually roar, causing boiling whirlpools and eddies.

Southwestern British Columbia

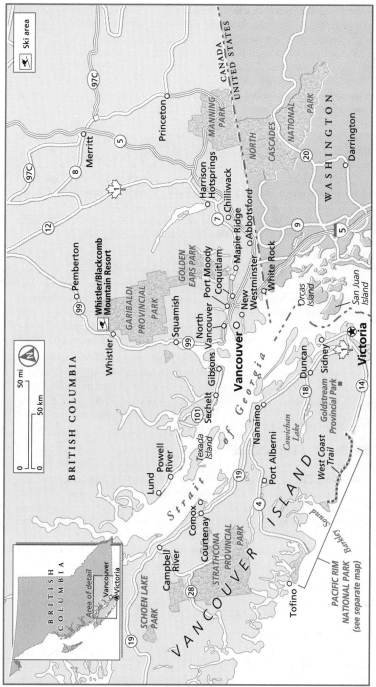

Powell River (pop. 14,143) is dominated by one of the world's largest pulp and paper mills. That said, the town sits on a lovely location, and if you're feeling adventurous, it's a major center for diving and kayaking.

The old portion of town is called the **Homesite,** a company town that grew up alongside the original lumber mill near the harbor. The only designated National Historic Region in British Columbia, the Homesite contains more than 30 commercial buildings and about 400 residential buildings, all in late Victorian style. Ask at the visitor center for the heritage walking-tour brochure. The **Powell River Historic Museum,** 4800 Marine Dr. (© 604/485-2222), has one of the largest archives of historic photos in the province, along with artifacts from the Native Sechelt. It's open Monday through Friday from 10am to 5pm, plus weekends from mid-May to Labour Day. Admission is C$3 (US$1.95).

From Powell River, many travelers take the ferry over to Comox/Courtenay on Vancouver Island and continue the loop back south. However, Powell River isn't the end of the road. That honor goes to tiny **Lund,** 17 miles (28km) north on Highway 101. The main reason to make the trip is to say you did it, and to pop into the century-old Lund Hotel for a drink or a meal.

OUTDOOR PURSUITS

CANOEING & KAYAKING   The Sunshine Coast, with its fjord-notch coastline, myriad islands, and protected waters, makes for excellent kayaking. The **Desolation Sound** area, north of Lund, is especially popular. The **Powell Forest Canoe Route,** a 4- to 8-day backcountry paddle, links four lakes in a 50-mile (81km) circuit. **Powell River Sea Kayaks,** 6812E Alberni St. (© 866/617-4444 or 604/483-2160; www.bcseakayak.com), offers rentals and tours.

DIVING   The center for diving along the Sunshine Coast, Powell River boasts visibility of 100-plus feet (30m) in winter, lots of sea life, and varied terrain. Area dive spots include five shipwrecks and several boats sunk as artificial reefs. **Don's Dive Shop,** 4552 Willingdon Ave. (© 604/485-6969; www.donsdive shop.com), is one of the area's leading outfitters, with a variety of dives starting at C$90 (US$59) an hour.

WHERE TO STAY & DINE
IN SECHELT
Four Winds B&B ⭐   It's hard to imagine a more compelling site: a thrust of bare rock stretching out into the Strait of Georgia, backed up against a grove of fir and spruce. This modern home is lined with picture windows, all the better to capture the astonishing view of islands and sea, frequently visited by whales, herons, and seals. Guest rooms are beautifully decorated. Most notably, one of the owners is a licensed massage therapist, and will schedule sessions utilizing craniosacral therapy and neuromuscular techniques. *Note:* Smoking is not permitted.

5482 Hill Rd., Sechelt, BC V0N 3A8. © 800/543-2989, 604/885-3144, or 604/740-1905. Fax 604/885-3182. www.sunshine.net/fourwinds. 3 units. C$145–C$165 double (US$94–US$107). Rates include full breakfast and afternoon tea. Golf packages available. MC, V. **Amenities:** Golf course nearby; spa; Jacuzzi; massage; limited laundry service. *In room:* A/C, hair dryer, no phone.

IN POWELL RIVER
Beach Gardens Motel   Popular with divers and kayakers, the Beach Gardens has comfortable rooms and a handsome location overlooking Malaspina Strait; most units have views. Twelve cottages are available. Amenities include a marina and a beer-and-wine store.

7074 Westminster Ave., Powell River, BC V8A 1C5. (℃ **800/663-7070** or 604/485-6267. Fax 604/485-2343. www.beachgardens.com. 66 units. C$84 (US$55) double, C$64 (US$42) cottage. Off-season rates available. AE, MC, V. Free parking. Pets allowed in ground-floor rooms. **Amenities:** Golf course nearby; exercise room; watersports-equipment rentals; babysitting; coin-op laundry; beer-and-wine store. *In room:* TV, coffeemaker, iron.

Coast Town Centre Hotel Right downtown, Powell River's newest hotel offers well-appointed guest rooms and a full health club. All-inclusive fishing and golf packages are available.

4660 Joyce Ave., Powell River, BC V8A 3B6. (℃ **800/663-1144** or 604/485-3000. Fax 604/485-3031. www. coasthotels.com. 71 units. C$99–C$169 (US$64–US$110) double. AE, DC, DISC, MC, V. Free parking. Pets allowed for C$10 (US$7) per day. **Amenities:** Restaurant; pub; golf course nearby; exercise room; Jacuzzi; carrental desk; business center; 24-hr. room service; babysitting; laundry service; same-day dry cleaning. *In room:* AC, TV w/ pay movies, dataport, coffeemaker, hair dryer.

Desolation Resort (★ Twenty minutes north of Powell River is Desolation Resort, which offers luxury and a wilderness experience rolled into one. Guests stay in suites in attractive log structures built by local craftspeople. These are fully modern spaces, with cedar interiors, hardwood floors, and tasteful decor. The resort sits above Okeover Inlet, just a matter of feet from your balcony. Chartered boating or diving trips can be arranged.

2694 Dawson Rd, Okeover Inlet, Powell River, BC V8A 4Z3. (℃ **604/483-3592.** Fax 604/483-7942. www. desolationresort.com. 7 units. July–Sept C$120–C$190 (US$78–US$124) double; C$210–C$230 (US$137–US$150) chalet. May–June and Dec 23–Jan 3 C$110–C$170 (US$72–US$111) double; C$190–C$210 (US$124–US$137) chalet. Oct–April except winter holidays C$95–C$120 (US$62–US$78) double; C$130–C$150 (US$85–US$98) chalet. Extra person C$20 (US$13) per night. Discounts for stays over 2 nights. Packages available. AE, MC, V. Pets allowed in off-season for additional charge. **Amenities:** Watersports equipment; boat, kayak, and canoe rentals. *In room:* Kitchen, no phone.

2 Whistler: North America's Premier Ski Resort (★

74 miles (120km) N of Vancouver

The premier ski resort in North America, according to *Ski* and *Snow Country* magazines, the **Whistler/Blackcomb** complex boasts more vertical, more lifts, and more ski terrain than any other ski resort in North America. And it isn't all just downhill skiing: There's also backcountry, cross-country, snowboarding, snowmobiling, heli-skiing, and sleigh riding. In summer, there's rafting, hiking, golfing, and horseback riding.

And then there's **Whistler Village.** Back in the 1970s, the city fathers, having made a conscious decision to build a resort town, looked to their minions in the planning department and ordered them to make it so. The results are impressive—a resort town of 40,000 beds, arranged around a central village street in a compact-enough fashion that you can park your car and remain a pedestrian for the duration of your stay.

What was sacrificed in this drive to become the perfectly planned community was space for the odd, the funky, the quaint, and the nonconforming. Whistler has none of the strip malls, cheap motels, and gas stations that mar some resort towns—but neither will you run across that quaint little restaurant run by an old Tyrolean couple, tucked away on an out-of-the-way hillside. So it goes.

The towns north of Whistler, **Pemberton** and **Mount Currie,** are refreshment stops for cyclists and hikers and the gateway to the icy alpine waters of **Birkenhead Lake Provincial Park** (see "Fishing," below) and the majestic **Cayoosh Valley,** which winds through the glacier-topped mountains to the Cariboo town of Lillooet.

ESSENTIALS

GETTING THERE   By Car   Whistler is a 2-hour drive from Vancouver along Highway 99, also called the **Sea-to-Sky Highway.** The drive is spectacular, winding first along the edge of Howe Sound before climbing through the mountains. Parking at the mountain is free for day skiers. For overnight visitors, most hotels charge about C$7 (US$4.55).

By Bus   The **Whistler Express,** 8695 Barnard St., Vancouver (© **604/266-5386,** or 604/905-0041 in Whistler; www.perimeterbus.com), operates bus service from Vancouver International Airport to the Whistler Bus Loop, as well as drop-off service at many hotels. The trip takes 2½ to 3 hours; round-trip adult fares are C$100 (US$65) in summer and C$110 (US$72) in winter. Reservations are required.

   Greyhound, Pacific Central Station, 1150 Station St., Vancouver (© **604/662-8051,** or 604/932-5031 in Whistler), operates service from Vancouver to the Whistler Bus Loop. The trip takes about 2½ hours; one-way fares are C$20 (US$13) for adults and C$10 (US$7) for children.

By Train   BC Rail (© **800/663-8238** or 604/984-5246; www.bcrail.com) operates the *Cariboo Prospector.* It leaves North Vancouver daily at 7am and chugs up the Howe Sound coastline through the scenic Cheakamus River Canyon and Garibaldi Provincial Park until it reaches the Whistler train station at 9:35am. The same train leaves Whistler at 6:20pm and arrives in North Vancouver at 9pm. The 2½-hour trip costs C$39 (US$25) for adults, C$35 (US$23) for seniors, C$23 (US$15) for children 2 to 12, and C$8 (US$5) for children under 2.

VISITOR INFORMATION   The **Whistler Visitor Info Centre,** 2097 Lake Placid Rd. (© **604/932-5528**), is open daily from 9am to 5pm. **Information kiosks** on Village Gate Boulevard at the entry to Whistler Village, at the main bus stop, and at other locations are open from mid-May to early September during the same hours. **Tourism Whistler,** Whistler Conference Centre, 4010 Whistler Way (© **604/932-3928;** www.tourismwhistler.com), is open daily from 9am to 5pm to provide information and assist with event tickets and last-minute accommodations bookings.

GETTING AROUND   Compact and pedestrian-oriented, Whistler Village has signed trails and paths linking together all shops and restaurants. If you're staying in the Village, you can park your car and leave it for the duration of your stay. The walk between the Whistler Mountain (Whistler Village) and Blackcomb Mountain (Upper Village) resorts takes about 5 minutes.

By Bus   A year-round **public transit service** (© **604/932-4020**) operates frequently from the Tamarisk district and the BC Rail station to the neighboring districts of Nester's Village, Alpine Meadows, and Emerald Estates. Bus service from the Village to Village North and Upper Village accommodations is free. For other routes, one-way fares are C$1.50 (US$1) for adults.

By Taxi   The Village's taxis operate around the clock. Taxi tours, golf-course transfers, and airport transport are also offered by **Airport Limousine Service** (© **800/278-8742** or 604/273-1331), **Whistler Taxi** (© **604/938-3333**), and **Sea-to-Sky Taxi** (© **604/932-3333**).

By Car   Rental cars are available from **Budget,** Holiday Inn Sunspree, 4295 Blackcomb Way (© **604/932-1236**); and **Thrifty,** Listel Whistler Hotel, 4121 Village Green (© **604/938-0302**).

CENTRAL AMERICA   MIDDLE AMERICA

AT&T Direct® Service

The easy way to call home from anywhere.

Global
connection
with the AT&T
Network

AT&T
direct
service

the easy way to call home, take the attached wallet guide.

SPECIAL EVENTS   Dozens of downhill **ski competitions** are held December through May. They include the Owens-Corning World Freestyle Competition (Jan), Power Bar Peak to Valley Race (Feb), Kokanee Fantastic Downhill Race (Mar), and Whistler Snowboard World Cup and World Cup Freestyle (Dec).

During the third week in July, **Whistler's Roots Weekend** (*©* **604/ 932-2394**) brings the sounds of Celtic, zydeco, bluegrass, Delta blues, Latin, folk, and world-beat music down to the villages and up to the mountains. The **Whistler Summit Concert Series** (*©* **604/932-3434**) is held on August weekends, with the mountains providing a stunning backdrop for performers such as the Barenaked Ladies, Amanda Marshall, and Blue Rodeo.

The **Alpine Wine Festival** (*©* **604/932-3434**) on the mountaintop during the first weekend in September, features tastings, a winemaker's dinner, and other events highlighting North America's finest vintages. Also in September, mountain bikers compete in the **Power Bar Garibaldi Gruel** and the **Cheaka- mus Challenge Fall Classic Mountain Bike Race.** The second weekend of the month ushers in the **Whistler Jazz & Blues Festival** (*©* **604/932-2394**), a great opportunity to see jazz, gospel, R&B, and blues.

Cornucopia (*©* **604/932-3434**), held in early November, is Whistler's premier wine-and-food festival. The opening gala showcases 50 top wineries from the Pacific region. Other events include a celebrity chef competition and wine tastings.

HITTING THE SLOPES

Whistler/Blackcomb Mountain   Now that both mountain resorts are jointly operated by Intrawest, your pass gives you access to both ski areas. Locals have their preferences, but the truth is that both offer great skiing. **Whistler Mountain** has 5,006 feet (1,502m) of vertical and over 100 marked runs that are serviced by a high-speed gondola and eight high-speed chairlifts, plus four other lifts and tows. Helicopter service from the top of the mountain makes another 100-plus runs on nearby glaciers accessible. There are cafeterias and gift shops on the peak as well as a licensed restaurant. **Blackcomb Mountain** has 5,280 feet (1,584m) of vertical and over 100 marked runs that are serviced by nine high-speed chairlifts, plus three other lifts and tows. The cafeteria and gift shop aren't far from the peak, and the licensed restaurant is worth the gondola trip even if you're not skiing. The view is spectacular, the food decent. Both mountains also have bowls and glade skiing, with Blackcomb offering glacier skiing well into August.

4545 Blackcomb Way, Whistler. *©* 604/932-3434, or snow report 604/687-7507 in Vancouver, 604/ 932-4211 in Whistler. www.whistler-blackcomb.com. Winter lift tickets C$61–C$63 (US$40–US$41) adults, C$53–C$55 (US$34–US$36) youths and seniors, C$31–C$32 (US$20–US$21) children. Lifts open daily 8:30am–3:30pm (to 4:30pm mid-Mar until closing, depending on weather and conditions).

LESSONS & PROGRAMS   Whistler/Blackcomb offers **ski lessons** and **ski guides** for all levels and interests. (For skiers looking to try snowboarding, a rental package and a half-day lesson are particularly attractive options.) Phone **Guest Relations** (*©* **604/932-3434**) for details. You can rent ski and snowboard gear at the base of both Whistler and Blackcomb Villages, just prior to purchasing your lift pass. **Summit Ski** (*©* **604/938-6225** or 604/932-6225), at various locations, including the Delta Whistler Resort and Market Pavilion, rents high-performance and regular skis, snowboards, telemark and cross-country skis, and snowshoes.

The *Whistler Explorer*

If you have only a day to explore the backcountry of southern British Columbia, don't miss the *Whistler Explorer*. For centuries, the arid canyons, alpine meadows, and crystal-clear lakes of the area between Whistler and Kelly Lake were inaccessible to all but the most experienced hikers. Now, **BC Rail** (© 800/339-8752 or 604/984-5246; www.bcrail.com) operates the *Whistler Explorer*, offering a leisurely way to see the remote landscape. Departing from the Whistler train station on Lake Placid Road at 8am, the *Explorer* takes an 8½-hour round-trip ramble through the spectacular Pemberton Valley and past Seton Lake and Anderson Lake. After leaving the historic town of Lillooet, the train follows the Fraser River, climbing high above the canyon and offering breathtaking views before arriving at Kelly Lake, which is adjacent to the historic Cariboo Gold Rush Trail. After a 1-hour break, passengers reboard the train, returning to Whistler at 5:30pm. It's the ideal way to discover the backcountry without braving an overnight camping-and-hiking expedition into this stretch of pristine wilderness. The round-trip fare is C$139 (US$90) for adults and seniors, C$99 (US$64) for children 2 to 12.

BACKCOUNTRY SKIING   The **Spearhead Traverse,** which starts at Whistler and finishes at Blackcomb, is a well-marked backcountry route that has become extremely popular. **Garibaldi Provincial Park** (© 604/898-3678) maintains marked backcountry trails at **Diamond Head, Singing Pass,** and **Cheakamus Lake.** These are ungroomed and unpatrolled trails, and you have to be self-reliant—you should be at least an intermediate skier, bring appropriate clothing and avalanche gear, and know how to use it. There are several access points along Highway 99 between Squamish and Whistler.

HELI-SKIING   Intermediate and advanced skiers who can't get enough fresh powder on the regular slopes can call **Whistler Heli-Skiing** (© 888/HELISKI or 604/932-4105; www.heliskiwhistler.com), one of the more established operators. A three-run day, with 4,500 to 6,000 feet (1,400–1,800m) of vertical helicopter lift, costs C$560 (US$364).

CROSS-COUNTRY SKIING   The 18 miles (30km) of easy to very difficult trails at **Lost Lake** start a block away from the Blackcomb Mountain parking lot. They're groomed for track skiing and ski-skating; they're also patrolled. Passes are C$10 (US$7); a 1-hour lesson runs C$69 (US$45). The **Valley Trail System** in the Village becomes a well-marked ski trail in winter. Contact the **Whistler Nordic Centre** (© 888/771-2382 or 604/905-6936; www.whistlernordiccentre.com) for more information.

OTHER WINTER PURSUITS

SNOWMOBILING & ATVing   The year-round ATV and snowmobile tours offered by **Canadian Snowmobile Adventures Ltd.,** Carleton Lodge, 4290 Mountain Sq., Whistler Village (© 604/938-1616; www.canadiansnowmobile.com), are a unique way to take to the trails. A 1-hour tour costs C$69 (US$45) for a driver and C$59 (US$38) for a passenger. Drivers must have a valid driver's license. Backcountry and dinner excursions are also available.

SNOWSHOEING   Snowshoeing is the world's easiest form of snow locomotion; it requires none of the training and motor skills of skiing or boarding. You can wear your own shoes or boots, provided they're warm and waterproof, strap on your snowshoes, and off you go! **Outdoor Adventures@Whistler** (© 604/932-0647; www.adventureswhistler.com) has guided tours for novices at C$39 (US$25) for 1½ hours. Rentals are C$15 (US$10) per day. **Cougar Mountain at Whistler,** 36-4314 Main St. (© 888/297-2222 or 604/932-4086; www.whistlerbackcountry.com), has guided tours to the Cougar Mountain area at C$49 (US$32) for 2 hours.

SLEIGHING & DOG SLEDDING   Call **Whistler Backcountry Adventures** (offered through Cougar Mountain at Whistler, above) to have a musher and his team of Inuit sled dogs take you for a backcountry ride, for C$249 (US$162) per sled, with a maximum of two people or 400 pounds. In winter, **Blackcomb Horsedrawn Sleigh Rides,** 103-4338 Main St. (© 604/932-7631; www.whistlerweb.net/resort/sleighrides), conducts nightly tours priced at C$45 (US$29) for adults and C$25 (US$16) for children. The tour will take you up past the ski trails and onto a wooded trail with a magnificent view of the lights at Whistler Village.

WARM-WEATHER PURSUITS

BIKING   Some of the best mountain-bike trails are on Whistler and Blackcomb mountains. Some of the backcountry trails at Lost Lake are marked for mountain biking as well. Lift tickets at both mountains are C$19 to C$30 (US$12 to US$20). You can rent a bike from **Trax & Trails,** Chateau Whistler Resort, 4599 Chateau Blvd., Upper Village (© 604/938-2017), or the **Whistler Bike Company,** Delta Whistler Resort, 4050 Whistler Way, Whistler Village (© 604/938-9511). Prices run C$10 (US$7) per hour to C$30 (US$20) per day.

CANOEING & KAYAKING   The 3-hour kayak and canoe tour offered by **Whistler Sailing & Water Sports Center Ltd.** (© 604/932-7245) is a great way for novices, intermediates, and experts to get acquainted with an exhilarating stretch of racing glacial water between Green Lake and Alta Lake. Packages begin at C$35 (US$23) unguided and include gear and transportation. Also available are lessons, clinics, and sailboat rentals.

FISHING   Anglers from around the world are drawn to the area's many glacier-fed lakes and rivers and to **Birkenhead Lake Provincial Park,** 40 miles (67km)

Tips   A Worthwhile Museum

To learn more about Whistler's unique heritage, flora, and fauna, visit the **Whistler Museum & Archives Society,** 4329 Main St., off Northlands Boulevard (© 604/932-2019). Interesting exhibits reveal the life and culture of the Native Indian tribes that have lived in the lush Whistler and Pemberton valleys for thousands of years. There are also re-creations of the village's early settlement by British immigrants during the late 1800s and early 1900s. Admission is by donation. Open mid-May to Labour Day, daily from 10am to 4pm; call for off-season hours.

north of Pemberton. Buy a fishing license when you arrive at **Whistler Back-country Adventures,** 36-4314 Main St. (© **604/932-3474;** www.whistler backcountry.com). **Whistler River Adventures** (see "Jet-Boating," below) and **Sea-to-Sky Reel Adventures** (© **604/894-6928**) offer catch-and-release fishing trips in the surrounding rivers. Rates are C$139 to C$190 (US$90 to US$124) per person, based on two people.

GOLF   Robert Trent Jones's **Chateau Whistler Golf Club,** at the base of Blackcomb (© **604/938-2092,** or 604/938-2095 for pro shop), is an 18-hole, par-72 course. With an elevation gain of more than 400 feet (120m), this course traverses mountain ledges and crosses cascading creeks. Greens fees are C$130 to C$205 (US$85 to US$133), which includes cart rental.

The award-winning, par-71 **Nicklaus North at Whistler** (© **604/938-9898**) is a 5-minute drive north of the Village on the shores of Green Lake. The mountain views are spectacular. This is just the second Canadian course designed by Nicklaus and, of all the courses he's designed worldwide, the only one to bear his name. Greens fees are C$125 to C$205 (US$81 to US$133).

Whistler Golf Club (© **800/376-1777** or 604/932-4544), designed by Arnold Palmer, features nine lakes, two creeks, and magnificent vistas. This 18-hole, par-72 course offers a driving range, putting green, sand bunker, and pitching area. Greens fees range from C$69 to C$149 (US$45 to US$97).

A-1 Last Minute Golf Hotline (© **800/684-6344** or 604/878-1833) can arrange next-day tee times with savings of as much as 40%. Call between 3 and 9pm for the next day or before noon for the same day.

HIKING   There are numerous easy trails in and around Whistler. Besides taking a lift up to the Whistler and Blackcomb mountain trails in summer, you have a number of choices. **Lost Lake Trail** starts at the northern end of the day-skier parking lot at Blackcomb. The lake is less than a mile from the entry. The 18 miles (30km) of marked trails that wind around creeks, beaver dams, blueberry patches, and cedar groves are ideal for biking, cross-country skiing, or strolling. The **Valley Trail System** is a paved trail that connects parts of Whistler. It starts on the west side of Highway 99 adjacent to the Whistler Golf Course and winds through residential areas and parks. The **Singing Pass Trail** in Garibaldi Provincial Park is a 4-hour hike of moderate difficulty. Take the Whistler Mountain gondola to the top and walk down the path that ends in the Village on an access road. Winding down from above the tree line, the trail takes you through stunted alpine forest into Fitzsimmons Valley. There are several access points into the park along Highway 99 between Squamish and Whistler.

Nairn Falls Provincial Park, about 20 miles (33km) north of Whistler on Highway 99, features a 1-mile (1.6km) trail that leads to a stupendous view of the icy Green River as it plunges over a rocky cliff into a narrow gorge. **Joffre Lakes Provincial Park,** on Highway 99 north of Mount Currie, is an intermediate-level hike that leads past brilliant-blue glacial lakes up to the foot of a glacier. The **Ancient Cedars** area of Cougar Mountain is an awe-inspiring grove of towering cedar and Douglas fir. Some of the trees are over 1,000 years old. They're reached by a moderate 2½-mile (4km) trail.

HORSEBACK RIDING   **Whistler River Adventures** (see "Jet-Boating," below) offers 2-hour trail rides along the Green River, through the forest, and across the Pemberton Valley from its facility in Pemberton, a 35-minute drive north of Whistler. The cost is C$59 (US$38).

> ⌒Tips   **A Day at the Spa**
>
> That resort lifestyle can be hard on the body, so why not relax at one of Whistler's outstanding spas? The **Spa at Chateau Whistler Resort** (℮ **604/ 938-2086**) is the best in town, offering massages, aromatherapy, body wraps, steam baths, and more. **Whistler Body Wrap,** 210 St. Andrews House (℮ **604/932-4710**), can nurture you with an array of services, such as shiatsu, facials, pedicures, and aromatherapy.

JET-BOATING   Whistler River Adventures, Whistler Mountain Village Gondola Base (℮ **888/932-3532** or 604/932-3532; www.whistlerriver.com), takes guests up the Green River just below Nairn Falls, where moose, deer, and bear sightings are common. The Lillooet River tour goes past ancient petroglyphs, fishing sites, and the tiny Native village of Skookumchuk. **Whistler Jet Boating Company Ltd.** (℮ **604/894-5200**) runs sightseers down the icy Green River or takes them speed cruising through the Lillooet River valley in summer. Tours by both companies range from 1-hour trips for C$82 (US$53) to 4-hour cruises for C$139 (US$90).

RAFTING   Whistler River Adventures (see "Jet-Boating," above) offers runs down the Green, Elaho, and Squamish rivers. They include equipment and transportation for C$63 to C$139 (US$41 to US$90). Novices are taken to the Green River, where small rapids and snowcapped mountain views highlight a half-day trip. Experts get a full day of Class IV excitement on the Elaho or Squamish, including a salmon barbecue lunch. Trips depart daily May through August. **Wedge Rafting,** Carleton Lodge, Whistler Village (℮ **604/932-7171;** www.wedgerafting.com), takes first-timers to its wilderness launch area for briefing and equipping, then an exciting hour or more on the icy Green River. Tours cost C$61 (US$40).

TENNIS   The Whistler Racquet & Golf Resort, 4500 Northland Blvd. (℮ **604/932-1991;** www.whistlertennis.com), has three covered courts, seven outdoor courts, and a practice cage, all open to drop-in visitors. Indoor courts are C$28 (US$18) per hour and outdoor courts C$12 (US$8) per hour. In summer, adult tennis camps are C$250 to C$364 (US$163 to US$237) for 3 days. Kids' camps cost C$40 (US$26) per day drop-in, or C$150 (US$98) for a 5-day camp. Book early for camps.

The **Mountain Spa & Tennis Club,** Delta Whistler Resort, Whistler Village (℮ **604/938-2044**), and the **Chateau Whistler Resort,** Upper Village (℮ **604/ 938-8000**), offer courts to drop-ins for about C$12 (US$8) per hour. There are free **public courts** (℮ **604/938-PARK**) at Myrtle Public School, Alpha Lake Park, Meadow Park, Millar's Pond, Brio, Blackcomb Benchlands, White Gold, and Emerald Park.

SHOPPING

The **Whistler Marketplace** (in the center of Whistler Village) and the area surrounding the **Blackcomb Mountain lift** brim with clothing, jewelry, crafts, gift, and equipment shops that are generally open daily from 10am to 6pm.

The **Horstman Trading Company,** beside the Chateau Whistler Resort at the base of Blackcomb (℮ **604/938-7725**), carries men's and women's casual

---

(Kids **Especially for Kids**

Near the base of the mountains, Whistler Village and the Upper Village sponsor daily activities for active kids of all ages. Offerings include an in-line skating park; trapeze, trampoline, and climbing lessons; summer skiing; and snowboarding. There's even a first-run multiplex movie theater.

The **Dave Murray Summer Ski and Snowboard Camp** (✆ **604/932-5765;** www.skiandsnowboard.com) is North America's longest-running summer ski camp. Junior programs cost about C$1,675 (US$1,089) per week, including food, lodging, and lift passes. Mornings and early afternoons are spent skiing, boarding, or free-riding. The rest of the day is occupied by a range of other outdoor activities. The comprehensive instruction and adult supervision are excellent. *Note:* This camp is not for beginners; it caters to youths 10 to 18.

---

wear, from swimwear to fleece vests. **Escape Route,** Whistler Marketplace (✆ **604/938-3228**), has a great line of outdoor clothing and gear.

Gallery Row, in the Delta Whistler Resort, consists of three of Whistler's top galleries: **Whistler Village Art Gallery** (✆ **604/938-3001**), **Northern Lights Gallery** (✆ **604/932-2890**), and **Adele Campbell Gallery** (✆ **604/ 938-0887**). Their collections include fine art, sculpture, and glass. The fascinating **Whistler Inuit Gallery,** Chateau Whistler Resort (✆ **604/938-3366**), specializes in Inuit, West Coast, and contemporary Indian artists.

WHERE TO STAY

There are over 40,000 guest beds in Whistler Valley, but the biggest decision you'll make is whether to stay in or out of Whistler Village. Staying in the Village, you can forget your car for the duration of your visit and walk along cobblestone pathways from hotel to ski lift to restaurant to pub. Visitors from around the world stroll from shop to shop and sit at outdoor cafes. The Village is thus a lively place, but is never completely quiet. Staying outside the Village, you'll have a short drive to the lifts or restaurants (though many places offer shuttle service), but you'll also have a touch more of that mountain tranquillity.

All the studios, condos, and hotel suites in the Village are top-quality. By the same token, there's little to choose from in terms of room quality between a midrange hotel like the Holiday Inn and a higher-end hotel like the Pan Pacific. In both you can expect a gas fireplace, kitchenette, small balcony, sofa bed, and one or two bedrooms. (The price difference normally pays for extra amenities: The Pan has a heated pool and hot tubs on a deck overlooking Whistler Mountain.) Outside the Village, there is a bit more variety, including a fine Austrian-style inn reviewed below.

Whether you decide to stay in or out of town, the best thing to do is simply decide on your price point and call one of the central booking agencies. The studios, condos, town houses, and chalets are available year-round. Prices run from C$90 to C$1,400 (US$59 to US$910). **Whistler Central Reservations** (✆ **800/944-7853** or 604/664-5625; fax 604/938-5758; www.whistler-resort. com) has over 2,000 rental units and can book a wide range of accommodations, from B&Bs to hotel rooms and condos. Furthermore, it can provide a customized package with lift tickets and air or ground transportation to and from Vancouver.

Other booking agencies, including **Whistler Chalets and Accommodations Ltd.** (© **800/663-7711** in Canada, or 604/932-6699; www.whistlerchalets. com) and **Rainbow Retreats Accommodations Ltd.** (© **604/932-2343;** www. rainbowretreats.com), have many properties to suit every budget and group size.

Reservations for peak winter periods should be made by September at the latest.

IN THE VILLAGE

Fairmont Chateau Whistler Resort ✰✰   The one exception to the everything's-the-same-in-Whistler rule, the Chateau Whistler is outstanding. Little expense was spared in re-creating the look and feel of an old-time country retreat at the foot of Blackcomb Mountain. In the lobby, massive wooden beams support an airy peaked roof; in the Mallard Bar, double-sided stone fireplaces cast a cozy glow on the leather armchairs. The rooms feature duvets, robes, and soaker tubs. Wheelchair-accessible units are available. Gold-service guests can have breakfast or relax après-ski in a private lounge with the feel of a Victorian library. The hot tubs look out over the base of the ski hill.

4599 Chateau Blvd., Whistler, BC V0N 1B4. © **800/441-1414** in the U.S., 800/606-8244 in Canada, or 604/ 938-8000. www.fairmont.com. Fax 604/938-2099. 558 units. Winter C$399–C$435 (US$259–US$283) double, C$570–C$1,399 (US$371–US$909) suite; summer C$299–C$335 (US$194–US$218) double, C$425–C$1,000 (US$276–US$650) suite. AE, MC, V. Underground valet parking C$25 (US$16). **Amenities:** Two restaurants (see review of the Wildflower under "Where to Dine," below), Mallard Bar; heated indoor/outdoor pool; 18-hole golf course; tennis courts; health club with massage therapy; sauna; whirlpool; steam room; weight room; full-service spa; concierge; room service; ski and bike storage. *In room:* A/C, TV, dataport, minibar, coffeemaker, hair dryer, iron.

The Pan Pacific Lodge Whistler ✰   The Pan Pacific's appointments are topnotch, and the kitchens (in all suites) contain everything required to whip up a gourmet meal. With sofa beds and Murphy beds, the studios are fine for couples; the one- and two-bedroom suites allow a bit more space for larger groups or families. Wheelchair-accessible units are available as well. Comfortable as the rooms are, however, the true advantage to the Pan Pacific is its location at the foot of the Whistler Mountain gondola. Not only can you ski right to the hotel, but thanks to a heated outdoor pool and Jacuzzi deck, you can also sit at the end of the day sipping a glass of wine, gazing up at the slopes, and marveling at the ameliorative effects of warm water on aching muscles.

4320 Sundial Crescent, Whistler, BC V0N 1B4. © **888/905-9955** or 604/905-2999. Fax 604/905-2995. www. panpac.com. 121 units. Nov 22–Dec 21 C$259–C$309 (US$168–US$201) studio, C$359–C$409 (US$233–US$266) 1-bedroom suite, C$559–C$609 (US$363–US$396) 2-bedroom suite; Dec 22–Jan 1 C$559–C$649 (US$363–US$422) studio, C$759–C$809 (US$493–US$526) 1-bedroom, C$959–C$1,009 (US$623–US$656) 2-bedroom; Jan 2–Apr 15 C$409–C$459 (US$266–US$298) studio, C$559–C$609 (US$363–US$393) 1-bedroom, C$759ndC$809 (US$493–US$526) 2-bedroom; May 1–Nov 21 C$149–C$229 (US$97–US$149) studio, C$199–C$279 (US$129–US$181) 1-bedroom, C$249–C$329 (US$162–US$214) 2-bedroom. AE, MC, V. Underground valet parking C$15 (US$10). **Amenities:** Restaurant (fine dining), pub (see review of Dubh Linn under "Where to Dine," below); heated outdoor pool; Jacuzzis; fitness center; steam room; concierge; 24-hr. room service; coin-op laundry; ski, bike, and golf bag storage. *In room:* A/C, TV, dataport, fridge, coffeemaker, hair dryer, iron.

OUTSIDE THE VILLAGE

Cedar Springs Bed & Breakfast Lodge ✰   This charming lodge is comfortably modern yet understated. The honeymoon suite boasts a fireplace and balcony. The sitting room has a TV and video library. Gourmet breakfasts are served by the fireplace in the dining room, and guests are welcome to enjoy an afternoon tea. The owners can provide box lunches and special-occasion dinners. A complimentary Alpine Meadows bus provides transportation to and from the Village.

8106 Cedar Springs Rd., Whistler, BC V0N 1B8. ✆ **800/727-7547** or 604/938-8007. Fax 604/938-8023. www.whistlerbb.com. 8 units (6 with private bathroom). C$109–C$245 (US$71–US$159) double; C$165–C$279 (US$107–US$181) suite. Rates include full breakfast. MC, V. Free parking. Take Hwy. 99 north toward Pemberton 2½ miles (4km) past Whistler Village. Turn left onto Alpine Way, go a block to Rainbow Dr. and turn left, go a block to Camino St. and turn left. The lodge is a block down at the corner of Camino and Cedar Springs Rd. **Amenities:** Jacuzzi; sauna; bike rentals. *In room:* No phone.

Durlacher Hof Pension Inn ★★   This lovely inn has an authentic Austrian feel and a sociable atmosphere. Both are the result of the exceptional care shown by owners Peter and Erika Durlacher. Guests are greeted by name at the entranceway, provided with slippers, and then given a tour of the chalet-style property. The rooms, one of which is wheelchair accessible, come with duvets, robes, bathrooms (some with jetted tubs), and incredible views from private balconies. Better still is the lounge, with a welcoming fireplace and delectable après-ski appetizers baked by Erika.

7055 Nester's Rd. (P.O. Box 1125), Whistler, BC V0N 1B0. ✆ **604/932-1924.** Fax 604/938-1980. www.durlacherhof.com. 8 units. Dec 18–Mar 31 C$179–C$259 (US$116–US$168) double; June 19–Sept 30 C$120–C$199 (US$78–US$129) double. Extra person C$30 (US$20). Spring and fall discounts available. Rates include full breakfast and afternoon tea. MC, V. Free parking. Take Hwy. 99 about half a mile (1km) north of Whistler Village to Nester's Rd. Turn left; the inn is immediately on the right. **Amenities:** Licensed lounge (guests only); Jacuzzi; sauna; bike and ski storage. *In room:* TV.

Hostelling International Whistler *Value*   One of the few inexpensive options in Whistler, this place also happens to have one of the nicest locations: on the south edge of Alta Lake, with a deck and lawn looking toward Whistler Mountain. Inside, the hostel is extremely pleasant.

5678 Alta Lake Rd., Whistler, BC V0N 1B0. ✆ **604/932-5492.** Fax 604/932-4687. www.hihostels.ca. 33 beds in 4- to 6-bed dorms (with shared bathrooms). C$19.50 (US$13) IYHA members, C$23.50 (US$15) nonmembers; annual membership C$35 (US$23). Family and group memberships available. MC, V. Free parking. **Amenities:** Kitchen; sauna; bike rentals; free canoe and rowboat (in summer); ping-pong tables; bike, ski, and board storage; drying room for ski gear. *In room:* No phone.

CAMPING

Reservations at the following parks are available through **Discover Camping** (✆ **800/689-9025**); rates are C$12 to C$15 (US$8 to US$10). South of Whistler on the Sea-to-Sky corridor is the popular **Alice Lake Provincial Park,** often jammed with hikers and bikers. Twenty-seven kilometers (16 miles) north of Whistler, the more adult-oriented campground at **Nairn Falls,** on Highway 99 (✆ **604/898-3678**), has pit toilets, pumped well water, fire pits, and firewood, but no showers. Its proximity to the roaring Green River and the town of Pemberton makes it appealing to many hikers. The 85 sites at **Birkenhead Lake Provincial Park,** off Portage Road, Birken (✆ **604/898-3678**), fill up quickly in summer. Boat launches, great fishing, and well-maintained tent and RV sites make this an angler's paradise and one of the province's top 10 camping destinations. Facilities include fire pits, firewood, pumped well water, and pit toilets.

WHERE TO DINE

Whistler literally overflows with dining choices: A stroll through the Village will take you past 25 to 30 restaurants. Gourmets on the go can find soups, salads, and an incredible fried meatloaf sandwich at **Chef Bernard's,** 4573 Chateau Blvd. (✆ **604/932-7051**), open daily from 7am to 9pm.

Araxi Restaurant & Bar ★★ ITALIAN/WEST COAST   Consistently winning awards for its wine list, as well as repeatedly voted best restaurant in Whistler by *Vancouver* magazine, this is one of the top places to dine. Outside, the heated patio seats 80 amid barrels of flowers; inside, the antiques and terra-cotta tiles give it a subtle Italian ambience. The menu, however, is more West Coast, with an emphasis on regional products. Soups and salads are made with fresh ingredients like Pemberton sheep cheese and Okanagan tomatoes. The locally caught trout is smoked in the Araxi kitchen. Main courses include seafood like ahi tuna and scallops and, for meat lovers, alder-smoked pork loin.

4222 Village Sq. ✆ **604/932-4540.** Main courses C$11–C$40 (US$7–US$26). AE, MC, V. Daily 11am–10:30pm.

Caramba! Restaurant MEDITERRANEAN   The dining room here is bright and filled with the pleasant buzz of nattering diners. From the open kitchen, smells wafting out hint tantalizingly of fennel and artichoke. Caramba! may be casual dining, but its menu offers fresh ingredients prepared with pizzazz. Try the pasta, free-range chicken, or grilled calamari.

12-4314 Main St., Whistler Town Plaza. ✆ **604/938-1879.** Main courses C$11–C$17 (US$7–US$11). AE, MC, V. Daily 11:30am–10:30pm.

Citta Bistro ★ INTERNATIONAL   Citta's is a favorite restaurant and nightspot, serving thin-crust pizzas, gourmet burgers, and delicious finger foods like bruschetta, spring rolls, and nachos. Its terrace is the best people-watching corner in town.

In Whistler Village Sq. ✆ **604/932-4177.** Reservations suggested. Main courses C$7–C$11 (US$4.55–US$7). AE, MC, V. Daily 11am–1am.

Dubh Linn Gate Irish Lounge PUB   The Gate is a convincing re-creation of a Dublin pub, with good-quality pub food, excellent beer, and, more often than not, a balladeer singing a song or two about the auld sod.

In the Pan Pacific Lodge Whistler, 4320 Sundial Crescent. ✆ **604/905-2999.** Reservations not accepted. Main courses C$11–C$17 (US$7–US$11). AE, MC, V. Mon–Sat 7am–1am; Sun 7am–midnight.

Rimrock Cafe and Oyster Bar ★ SEAFOOD   Rimrock is like a Viking mead hall of old, with a high ceiling and grand stone fireplace. But it's the food, not the atmosphere, that inspires people to hop in a cab and make the C$5 (US$3.25) journey from Whistler Village. The first order of business should be a plate of oysters, served up half a dozen ways, from raw to cooked in hell (broiled with fresh chilies). The signature Rimrock oyster is still the best: broiled with béchamel sauce and smoked salmon. Main courses are equally inventive. Look for lobster and scallops in light tarragon sauce on a bed of capellini or swordfish broiled with pecans, almonds, pistachios, and a mild red Thai curry.

2117 Whistler Rd. ✆ **604/932-5565.** www.rimrockwhistler.com. Main courses C$13–C$30 (US$8–US$20). AE, MC, V. Daily 11:30am–11:30pm.

Uli's Flipside *Finds* ITALIAN   One Whistler resident threatened dire, if unspecified, consequences if we told readers about this local favorite. It's not that Uli's is the best restaurant in town or even the best pasta place (though it's certainly in the running); it's just that few other spots offer the same combination of excellent pasta, a good wine list, and a pleasant room, all at moderate prices. Given that Whistler shares the West Coast affliction of early dining, Uli's is also your best bet for late-night bites.

Moments **Après-Ski**

"Après-ski" refers to that delicious hour after a hard day on the slopes, when you sit back with a cold drink, nurse the sore spots, and savor the glow that comes from a day well skied. On the Blackcomb side, **Merlin's Bar,** at the base ((C) **604/938-7735**), is the most obvious spot, but hidden away inside the Chateau Whistler Resort is something better: the **Mallard Bar** ((C) **604/938-8000**), one of the most civilized après-ski bars on earth.

4433 Sundial Place, upstairs. (C) 604/935-1107. Main courses C$11–C$17 (US$7–US$11). AE, DC, MC, V. Mon–Sat 3pm–1am; Sun 3pm–midnight.

Val d'Isère FRENCH   The elegant Val d'Isère offers a taste of Alsace, a hearty regional cuisine that will warm you even on the coldest of days. Start with the goat-cheese soufflé, followed by braised duck on a bed of figs, red cabbage, and polenta with port-wine reduction. For lighter fare—perhaps on a summer day on the patio—consider seared scallops with candied lemon/ginger sauce, accompanied by a glass of Riesling. The desserts are luscious: Try the profiteroles with vanilla ice cream.

4314 Main St., Whistler Town Plaza. (C) 604/932-4666. www.valdisere-restaurant.com. Main courses C$22–C$34 (US$14–US$22). AE, MC, V. June–Oct daily 11:30am–11pm; Nov–May daily 5–10pm.

The Wildflower ✿ PACIFIC NORTHWEST   Over by the Blackcomb lifts, the Wildflower serves innovative cuisine in a civilized dining room. The seasonal menu features fresh Pacific seafood—the pine-roasted salmon is a specialty—as well as delicious local meats from the British Columbia interior. On weekends, the Flavours of the Pacific Northwest dinner buffet (C$40/US$26) is like a greatest hits of regional fine dining.

In the Fairmont Chateau Whistler Resort, 4599 Chateau Blvd. (C) 604/938-8000. Reservations required. Main courses C$18–C$40 (US$12–US$26). AE, MC, V. Daily 6–10pm.

WHISTLER AFTER DARK

For a town of just 8,000, Whistler has a more than respectable nightlife scene. Bands touring through Vancouver regularly make the trip up the Sea-to-Sky. Concert listings can be found in the *Pique,* a free local paper.

The popular **Tommy Africa's,** beneath the Pharmasave at the entrance to the Main Village ((C) **604/932-6090**), caters to the 18-to-22 crowd—that's half of Whistler on weekends. Dark and cavernous, **Maxx Fish,** in the Village Square below the Amsterdam Café ((C) **604/932-1904**), provides refuge to 20-somethings who like their music with lots of beat and not much light. **Garfinkel's,** at the entrance to Village North ((C) **604/932-2323**), draws a slightly older crowd, though you'll feel old if you're much over 30.

At the **Boot Pub,** on Nancy Green Drive off Highway 99 ((C) **604/932-3338**), throngs of young Australian lift operators cram the room, bouncing to the band or DJ and spilling draft beer over the floor and their mostly unwashed clothes. **Buffalo Bills,** across from the Whistler Gondola ((C) **604/932-6613**), provides alternative entertainment in the form of a pool table, video ski machine, and 1980s music. The **Savage Beagle,** Village Square ((C) **604/938-3337**), caters to the 30-something crowd with a fabulous selection of beers and bar drinks. It has a pleasant little pub upstairs and house-oriented dance floor below.

9

Northern British Columbia

When you begin talking about the "north" in Canada, you have to be careful. Although the following destinations are certainly northerly—reached by at least one day's very long drive from Vancouver, or by a 15-hour ferry trip from Vancouver Island—most of this chapter's towns and sights are geographically in British Columbia's midsection. However, by the time you reach Prince George or Prince Rupert, you'll feel the palpable sense of being in the north: The days are long in summer and short in winter, and the spruce forestlands have a primordial character, as if they had just recently been released from the grip of the ice age. First Nations peoples make up a greater percentage of the population here than in more southerly areas, and Native communities and heritage sites are common.

One of the most dramatic ways to reach northern British Columbia is by ferry. The BC Ferries Inside Passage route operates between Port Hardy, on Vancouver Island, and Prince Rupert, on the mainland; this full-day ferry run passes through mystical land- and seascapes, with excellent wildlife-viewing opportunities. From Prince Rupert—a fishing town with an excellent Native-arts museum—you can catch another ferry to the Queen Charlotte Islands, which lie truly on the backside of beyond. A part of these islands is preserved as Gwaii Haanas National Park Reserve, a refuge of rare flora and fauna, and the ancient homeland of the Haida people.

Inland from Prince Rupert, the Yellowhead Highway (Hwy. 16) follows the mighty Skeena and Bulkley rivers past First Nations villages and isolated ranches, finally reaching Prince George, the largest city in northern British Columbia. Prince George is also a transportation gateway. Whether you're coming west from Edmonton, east from Prince Rupert, north from Vancouver, or south from Alaska, you'll pass through this city at the junction of the Fraser and Nechako rivers.

From Highway 16, there are two options for travelers who wish to explore realms even farther north. The famed 1,413-mile (2,280km) Alaska Highway—the only overland route to the 49th state—begins at Dawson Creek. More than 600 miles (960km) of the route wind across northern British Columbia, through black-spruce forest and over the Continental Divide. The Alaska Highway exercises an irresistible attraction to die-hard road-trippers, many of them retirees with RVs. Another route north, the Stewart-Cassiar Highway, also labeled Highway 37, leaves the Yellowhead Highway west of the Hazeltons, cutting behind the towering Coast Mountains to eventually join the Alaska Highway in the Yukon.

While all the major highways in northern British Columbia remain open year-round, frigid weather and short daylight hours make winter travel difficult; it's far better to see this beautiful wilderness landscape under the glow of the summer's midnight sun.

1 The Inside Passage ⚓ & Discovery Coast

The ferry cruise along British Columbia's Inside Passage combines the best scenic elements of Norway's rocky fjords, Chile's Patagonian range, and Nova Scotia's wild coastline. Less than half a century ago, there was only one way to explore this rugged coastline: by booking the 4-day passage on an Alaska-bound cruise ship or freighter.

Since 1966, **BC Ferries** (✆ **888/BCFERRY** in B.C., or 250/386-3431; www. bcferries.bc.ca) has operated the **Inside Passage ferry** between Port Hardy (discussed in chapter 7, "Northern Vancouver Island") and Prince Rupert (on the mainland, discussed below), with stops at the small Discovery Coast communities of Bella Coola, Ocean Falls, Shearwater, McLoughlin Bay, and Klemtu. These stopovers became so popular that in 1994, the company added the **Discovery Coast ferry** to its schedule. The ferry system also connects Prince Rupert to the remote **Queen Charlotte Islands,** the ancestral home of the Haida tribe (see below).

For information on the region, contact the **Northern BC Tourism Association,** 850 River Rd., Prince George (✆ **800/663-8843** or 250/561-0432; www. nbctourism.com).

THE INSIDE PASSAGE ⚓

Fifteen hours may seem like a long time to be on a ferry. But you'll never get bored as the *Queen of the North* ⚓ noses its way through an incredibly scenic series of channels and calm inlets, flanked by green forested islands. Whales, porpoises, salmon, bald eagles, and sea lions line the route past the mostly uninhabited coastline. This 304-mile (491km) BC Ferries run between Port Hardy and Prince Rupert follows the same route as expensive Alaska-bound cruise ships, but at a fraction of the cost. And in midsummer, with the north's long days, the trip is made almost entirely in daylight.

The ferry from Port Hardy initially crosses a couple hours' worth of open sea—where waters can be rough—before ducking behind Calvert Island. Except for a brief patch of open sea in the Milbanke Sound north of Bella Bella, the rest of the trip follows a narrow, protected channel between the mainland and a series of islands.

The actual Inside Passage begins north of Bella Bella, as the ferry ducks behind mountainous Princess Royal and Pitt islands. The passage between these islands and the mainland is very narrow—often less than a mile (1.6km) wide. The scenery is extraordinarily dramatic: Black cliffs drop thousands of feet directly into the channel, notched with hanging glacial valleys and fringed with forests. Powerful waterfalls shoot from dizzying heights into the sea. Eagles float along thermal drafts, and porpoises cavort in the ferry's wake. Even in poor conditions (the weather is very changeable here), this is an amazing trip.

The 410-foot *Queen of the North* carries up to 750 passengers and 157 vehicles. Onboard, you'll find a cafeteria, snack bar, buffet-style dining, playroom, business center, and gift shop. From mid-May to early October, the ferry makes the journey north one day, returning south the next. The rest of the year, service gradually drops to about one ferry per week each way. Midsummer one-way fares are C$99 (US$64) per passenger, C$233 (US$151) per car. Reservations are mandatory. The ship's cabins rent for C$50 to C$60 (US$33 to US$39), for day use. In summer, the ferry leaves both Prince Rupert and Port Hardy at 7:30am, so under normal circumstances, you'll arrive at your destination at 10:30pm—thus you probably won't need a sleeping berth. You will, however, want to have lodging reservations at your destination; by the time the ship docks and you wait to drive your car off, it can be close to midnight.

At Prince Rupert, you can also catch an **Alaska Marine Highway ferry** (© **800/642-0066;** www.dot.state.ak.us/amhs), which stops here on its run between Bellingham, Washington, and Skagway, Alaska. Passenger fare from Prince Rupert to Skagway is C$214/US$143; a car costs C$471/US$314. The trip can range anywhere from 30 to 50 hours, depending on the number of stops.

THE DISCOVERY COAST PASSAGE

Also departing from Port Hardy, the Discovery Coast's *Queen of Chilliwack* connects small, mostly First Nations communities along the fjords and islands of the northern coast, including Namu, Bella Bella, Shearwater, Ocean Falls, and Klemtu. The most popular part of this run is the summer-only service to Bella Coola, which links to Highway 20, a paved and gravel road that's a day's drive from Williams Lake, in central British Columbia's Fraser Valley (see "Williams Lake," in chapter 10).

In summer, a direct ferry runs on Thursday to Bella Coola, a Tuesday circular run goes north to McLoughlin Bay and Shearwater before returning to Port Hardy via Bella Coola, and a Saturday circular run goes to the above ports as well as Klemtu and Ocean Falls before returning via Bella Coola. The Tuesday and Saturday departures require a night on the boat. In high season, fares between Port Hardy and Bella Coola are C$102.50 (US$67) per passenger and C$205 (US$133) per car. For sleeping, you might snag one of 110 extra-wide reclining seats. Otherwise, BC Ferries recommends bringing a tent or cot, which you can set up on the leeward side of the boat. You can rent pillows and blankets for C$5 (US$3.25); lockers and showers are available. Pets are allowed onboard, but must remain in vehicles on the car deck; owners may go down to tend to their needs.

2 Prince Rupert

304 miles (491km) N of Port Hardy, 470 miles (756km) W of Prince George

British Columbia's most northerly coastal city, Prince Rupert (pop. 17,000) is a city in transition. For years a major fishing and timber port, it is now turning to tourism to bolster its economy. Although scarcely a fancy place, Prince Rupert has much to offer travelers. Ecotourism has taken off, sportfishing is excellent in local rivers and in the protected waters of Chatham Sound, and the town is a convenient hub for exploring the sights of the Pacific Northwest. From here, ferries go north to Alaska, west to the Queen Charlotte Islands, and south to Vancouver Island and Bellingham, Washington.

Prince Rupert exudes a hard-working, good-natured vigor, and the population is a well-integrated mix of First Nations and European-heritage Canadians. You'll experience the palpable sense of being on the northern edge of the world, which gives the city—situated on a series of rock ledges above the broad expanse of the Pacific—a sense of purpose and vitality.

ESSENTIALS

GETTING THERE   By Ferry   For information on BC Ferries service from Port Hardy and Alaska Marine Highway service between southeast Alaska and Washington, see "The Inside Passage," above. For information on BC Ferries service to the Queen Charlottes, see below.

⌒Tips   Special Events

During the second week in June, Prince Rupert hosts **Seafest** (☎ 250/ 624-9118), which features a fishing derby, parades, games, food booths, bathtub races, and the annual blessing of the fleet.

By Train   A **VIA Rail** (☎ 888/VIA-RAIL or 800/561-8630; www.viarail.ca) train, the *Skeena*, departs from Prince Rupert on Wednesday, Friday, and Sunday at 8am and arrives in Prince George at 8:10pm. One-way fares start at C$71 (US$46). The train follows the same route as the Yellowhead Highway along the scenic Skeena River valley. At Prince George, travelers can continue east into Alberta or southwest to Vancouver on VIA Rail's Western Transcontinental rail service, the *Canadian*.

By Plane   **Air Canada** (☎ 888/247-2262; www.aircanada.com), through its regional subsidiaries, provides service between Vancouver and Prince Rupert. **Hawk Air** (☎ 866/429-5247 or 800/487-1216; www.hawkair.net) also offers daily service from Vancouver. **Harbour Air** (☎ 800/689-4234, or 250/ 627-1341 in Prince Rupert; www.harbour-air.com) departs from the seaplane base at Seal Cove with scheduled service to the Queen Charlotte Islands, as well as flights to many communities along the coast. Harbour Air also offers flight-seeing tours of the region.

By Car   Prince Rupert is the terminus of the Yellowhead Highway, Canada's most northerly transcontinental roadway. Between Prince Rupert and Prince George, the route is 450 miles (724km) of extraordinary scenery. For car rentals, call **National** (☎ 800/CAR-RENT or 250/624-5318; www.nationalcar.com).

By Bus   **Greyhound Canada** (☎ 800/661-8747 or 604/482-8747; www.greyhound.ca) serves Prince Rupert and Prince George with two buses daily each way. The fare is about C$96 (US$62).

VISITOR INFORMATION   The **Prince Rupert Visitor Info Centre,** Suite 215, Cow Bay Road (☎ 800/667-1994 in Canada, or 250/624-5637; fax 250/ 627-0992; www.tourismprincerupert.com), is on the waterfront about 1¼ miles (2km) from Highway 16, now the pickup and drop-off point for the airport. It's open year-round, Monday through Saturday from 8am to 4pm, Monday through Friday from 5:30 to 9pm, and Sunday from 8 to 11am and 5:30 to 9pm (all day in summer).

EXPLORING THE AREA

Prince Rupert gets more than 18 hours of sunlight a day in summer. And despite its far-north location, this coastal city enjoys a mild climate most of the year. Mountain biking, cross-country skiing, fishing, kayaking, hiking, and camping are just a few of the region's popular activities.

Northern British Columbia's rich Native Indian heritage has been preserved in Prince Rupert's museums and archaeological sites. But you don't need to visit a museum to get a sense of the community's history. Relics of the city's early days are apparent in its old storefronts, miners' shacks, and churches. Built on a series of rocky escarpments, the city rises ledge by ledge, starting at the harbor with a well-established train station and the **Kwinitsa Railway Museum** (☎ 250/ 627-1915 or 250/627-3207). This area is overlooked by the old commercial

Prince Rupert

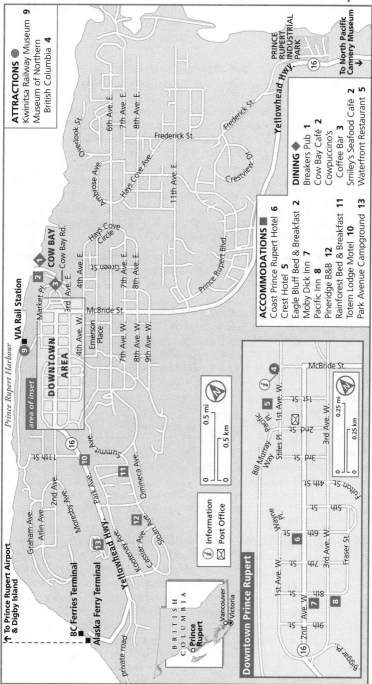

↖ To Prince Rupert Airport & Digby Island

Prince Rupert Harbour

VIA Rail Station

ATTRACTIONS ●
Kwinitsa Railway Museum **9**
Museum of Northern
British Columbia **4**

COW BAY

Frederick St.

Overlook St.

Ambrose Ave.

Hays Cove Ave.

6th Ave. E.
7th Ave. E.
8th Ave. E.

11th Ave. E.

Crestview Dr.

PRINCE
RUPERT
INDUSTRIAL
PARK

Yellowhead Hwy.

16

To North Pacific
Cannery Museum
→

DINING ◆
Breakers Pub **1**
Cow Bay Café **2**
Cowpuccino's
Coffee Bar **3**
Smiley's Seafood Café **2**
Waterfront Restaurant **5**

Hays Cove
Circle

Green St.

4th Ave. E.
7th Ave. E.
8th Ave. E.

Prince Rupert Blvd.

Market Pl.
3rd Ave. E.
4th Ave. E.

McBride St.

Emerson
Place

4th Ave. W.
7th Ave. W.
8th Ave. W.
9th Ave. W.

DOWNTOWN
AREA

area of inset

11th St.

16

Summit Ave.

Park Ave.

Omineca Ave.

Moresby Ave.

Graham Ave.
Atlin Ave.
2nd Ave.

Kootenay Ave.
Cassiar Ave.
Spear Ave.

Yellowhead Hwy.

10

11

12

13

BC Ferries Terminal

Alaska Ferry Terminal

private road

ACCOMMODATIONS ■
Coast Prince Rupert Hotel **6**
Crest Hotel **5**
Eagle Bluff Bed & Breakfast **2**
Moby Dick Inn **7**
Pacific Inn **8**
Pineridge B&B **12**
Rainforest Bed & Breakfast **11**
Totem Lodge Motel **10**
Park Avenue Campground **13**

ⓘ Information
☒ Post Office

0   0.5 mi
0   0.5 km

BRITISH
COLUMBIA

Vancouver
○ Prince
Rupert
✱ Victoria

Downtown Prince Rupert

McBride St.

4
ⓘ

5
Bill Murray Way

1st Ave. W.

Stiles Pl.

1st St.
2nd St.
3rd Ave. W.

3rd St.
4th St.
Fulton St.

5th St.

Wayne Pl.

6
6th St.
3rd Ave. W.

Fraser St.

1st Ave. W.

7th St.
8th St.

7
8
9th St.

16 2nd Ave. W.

Briggar Pl.

0   0.25 mi
0   0.25 km

center, which itself is overlooked by the historic residential area, dominated by massive stone churches. The historic **Cow Bay** district on the north waterfront, with galleries, restaurants, and the visitor center, is Prince Rupert's major center for tourist activity.

Museum of Northern British Columbia   This museum displays artifacts of the Tsimshian, Nisga'a, and Haida First Nations, who have inhabited this area for more than 10,000 years. There are also artifacts and photographs from Prince Rupert's 19th-century European settlement. In summer, the museum sponsors a number of special programs, including 2-hour archaeological boat tours of the harbor (which allow you to see active dig sites at ancestral villages that date back more than 5,000 years). The gift shop is one of the best places in town to buy Native art. Also sponsored by the museum is the **Carving Shed,** a working studio located a block away on Market Place. Visitors are welcome, but are encouraged to be discreet while the carvers concentrate.

100 First Ave. ✆ **250/624-3207.** Fax 250/627-8009. www.museumofnorthernbc.com. Admission C$5 (US$3.25) adults, C$2 (US$1.30) students, C$1 (US$.65) children 6–11, C$10 (US$7) families. MC, V. Summer Mon–Sat 9am–8pm, Sun 9am–5pm; winter Mon–Sat 10am–5pm.

North Pacific Cannery Museum ⭐   The province's oldest working salmon-cannery village, built on Inverness Passage in 1889, was home to hundreds of First Nations, Japanese, Chinese, and European workers and their families. This company-owned community reached its apex from 1910 to 1950, when the work force numbered 400 and the community grew to about 1,200; the cannery has been closed since 1968. Now a National Historic Site, the complex includes the cannery building, residences, the company store, a hotel, and a dining hall—a total of over 25 structures linked by a boardwalk (the land is so steep here that most of the houses were built on wharves). Workers were segregated by race: the Chinese, Japanese, and Native Canadian workers had their own micro-neighborhoods, all overseen by the European bosses. Guided tours provide an interesting glimpse into a forgotten way of life.

The boardinghouse is now open for B&B accommodations as the **Waterfront Inn,** with doubles going for C$45 (US$29). The **Cannery Café** and **Forge Broiler Bar** are open during museum hours, and the **Salmon House Restaurant** (✆ **250/628-3273**) is open from 11am to 7pm, year-round.

12 miles (20km) south of Prince Rupert, in Port Edward. ✆ **250/628-3538.** http://district.portedward.bc. ca/northpacific. Admission C$8 (US$5) adults, C$7.50 (US$4.90) seniors and students, C$5.50 (US$3.60) children 6 and over. May 1–Sept 30 daily 9am–6pm. Call for off-season hr. Take the Port Edward turnoff on Hwy. 16 and drive 3 miles (6km) past Port Edward on Skeena Dr.

ARCHAEOLOGICAL, WILDLIFE & ADVENTURE TOURS

Prince Rupert is at the center of an amazingly scenic area, but unless you have your own boat, you'll find it hard to get around. A good option is to sign on with a local tour operator. One of the most unique excursions is the **Pike Island Archaeological Tour,** operated by the Metlakatla band of the Tsimshian First Nation. Tiny Pike Island (Laxspa'aws) is 5½ miles (9km) from Prince Rupert in Venn Passage, and is at the center of a rich archaeological area that was once one of the most densely populated regions in pre-Contact Native America. The island has three village sites, which were abandoned 18 to 20 centuries ago. Although none have been excavated, guides point out the house depressions in the forest floor and discuss the midden deposits, the shellfish and bone piles that were essentially the garbage pits of these prehistoric people. Tours are offered daily from July to Labour Day, starting at 11:30am and returning to Prince Rupert at

4pm. The trails on the island are not difficult, but are not wheelchair accessible. Tickets are C$45 (US$29) and can be purchased at the museum or reserved by calling © **250/628-3201.** For more information, see **www.pikeisland.ca**.

If you want to see wildlife in pristine landscapes, consider a sailing expedition into the **Khutzeymateen Grizzly Bear Preserve.** Offered by **Sunchaser Charters** (© **250/624-5472;** www.citytel.net/sunchaser), the trip involves sailing up the Khutzeymateen Inlet, northwest of Prince Rupert. There's no other access to the preserve—the first bear sanctuary in the world—except by boat or floatplane, and humans are forbidden to actually land. The 4-day trip, offered May through September, costs C$1,300 (US$845).

A handy place to sign up for a variety of tours is **Seashore Charters** (© **800/ 667-4393** or 250/624-5645; www.seashorecharter.com), which has a trailer office at First Avenue East and McBride Street. Among the options are harbor tours by boat and city tours by bus, each costing C$20 (US$13), and whale-watching tours for C$75 (US$49).

West Coast Launch Ltd., at the cruise-ship dock in Cow Bay (© **800/ 201-8377** or 250/624-3151; www.westcoastlaunch.com), offers whale-watching tours, grizzly-bear tours in the Khutzeymateen from mid-May to mid-July (C$140/US$91), and kayak drop-off and pickup.

For a historical 2-hour walking tour of the city, contact **Heritage Walking Tour** (© **250/624-3207** or 250/624-5637). It leaves daily May through August from the Museum of Northern British Columbia (see above) and is free with museum admission. A self-guided walking-tour booklet is also available for C$2 (US$1.30).

OTHER OUTDOOR PURSUITS

FISHING Prince Rupert is famed for its excellent sportfishing. There are dozens of charter operators based in town. The **Visitor Info Centre,** in Cow Bay (© **800/667-1994** in Canada, or 250/624-5637; www.tourismprincerupert. com), or **Seashore Charters** (© **800/667-4393** or 250/624-5645; www. seashorecharter.com) can steer you to the one that best serves your needs.

Fishing charters can range in length from a half-day to weeklong trip, and range in facilities from rough-and-ready boats to luxury cruisers. Expect a guided trip to cost from C$450 (US$293) for a half day. Long-established companies include **Frohlich's Fish Guiding** (© **250/627-8443;** www.fishing-charter.net) and **Predator Fishing Charters** (© **250/627-1993;** www.citytel. net/~predator), which also provides charters for diving. **Pacific Northwest BC Sea Tours and Charters' New Pacifica Charters** (© **250/624-3272** or 250/ 624-1964; www.citytel.net/seatours) offers outings for fishing, diving, wildlife-viewing, and photography.

At the floating **Palmverville Lodge,** east of Prince Rupert (© **250/624-8243** or 250/624-1803; www.palmerville.bc.ca), half-day fishing charters are C$400 (US$260). A package that includes a charter, meals, and lodging for two goes for C$450 (US$293) per person, per night. The lodge is also open to B&B guests at a rate of C$55 (US$36) per person.

HIKING **Far West Sports,** 212 Third Ave. W. (© **250/624-2568**), is one of the best sources of information about hiking and mountain-biking trails. The area experiences annual as well as seasonal changes in trail conditions, and some hiking and backcountry ski areas are too challenging for beginners.

There are a number of good hiking options right in Prince Rupert. One trail follows Hays Creek from McBride Street down to the harbor. Just 4 miles

(6.4km) east on Highway 16 is a trail head for three more wilderness hikes. The 2½-mile (4km) loop **Butze Rapids Trail** winds through wetlands to Grassy Bay and to Butze Rapids, a series of tidal cataracts. The sometimes-steep trail to the **Tall Trees** grove of old-growth cedars and to the viewpoint on **Mount Oldfield** requires more stamina. Check with the visitor center or the **North Coast Forest District Office,** 125 Market Place (© **250/624-7460;** www.for.gov.bc.ca/prupert/district/ncoast), for more information.

KAYAKING & CANOEING The waters surrounding Prince Rupert are tricky, and rough tidal swells and strong currents are common. **Eco Trek Adventures** (© **250/624-8311;** www.citytel.net/ecotreks) offers guided half-day trips (C$47/US$31) and 2-day expeditions to the grizzly sanctuary (C$595/US$387). Single kayak rentals start at C$25 (US$16) for 2 hours.

WHERE TO STAY

The **Totem Lodge Motel,** 1335 Park Ave. (© **800/550-0178** or 250/624-6761; fax 250/624-3831), is the closest lodging to the Alaska and BC Ferries terminal. Its simple rooms start at C$82 (US$53).

A mile (1.6km) from the ferry terminal, **Park Avenue Campground,** 1750 Park Ave. (© **800/667-1994** or 250/624-5861; fax 250/627-8009), has 77 full-hookup and 10 unserviced sites, plus open areas for tent camping. Facilities include laundry, showers, toilets, playground, and phones. Reserve in advance in summer. Rates are C$14 to C$19 (US$9 to US$12).

Coast Prince Rupert Hotel Right downtown, the Coast offers views of the harbor and mountains from just about every spacious room. Friendly service and good dining options make this a fine lodging choice. You can bet on the races in the Turf Lounge, or dance at Bogey's Cabaret. Guided fishing charters can be arranged in summer.

118 Sixth St., Prince Rupert, BC V8J 3L7. © **800/663-1144** or 250/624-6711. Fax 250/624-3288. www.coasthotels.com. 92 units. C$105–C$110 (US$68–US$72) double. Extra person C$10 (US$7). Family plan, corporate and off-season rates, and senior and AAA discounts available. AE, DC, DISC, MC, V. **Amenities:** Restaurant, lounge, club; golf course nearby; guest passes to full-service health club; limited room service; laundry service; same-day dry cleaning; beer-and-wine store. *In room:* A/C, TV, dataport, fridge (on request), coffeemaker, hair dryer, iron.

Crest Hotel ☆ The Crest offers the best views, good dining, and beautifully furnished rooms. Situated on the bluff's edge overlooking Tuck Inlet, Metlakata Pass, and the harbor, this is one of the finest hotels in northern British Columbia. The rooms are nicely furnished, though in a style more beholden to the 1980s than the 21st century. The wood-paneled lobby and common rooms are opulent. The staff will happily set you up with fishing charters and wildlife-viewing trips. The Waterfront Restaurant is the best in town (see "Where to Dine," below), and Charley's Lounge, with a heated deck, has the city's best year-round view from a bar stool.

222 First Ave. W., Prince Rupert, BC V8J 3P6. © **800/663-8150** or 250/624-6771. Fax 250/627-7666. www.cresthotel.bc.ca. 102 units. C$145–C$165 (US$94–US$107) double; C$179–C$249 (US$116–US$162) suite. AE, MC, V. Free parking. Small pets allowed for C$10 (US$7). **Amenities:** Restaurant, coffee shop, bar; golf course nearby; health club; Jacuzzi; sauna; limited room service; dry cleaning. *In room:* TV w/ pay movies, dataport, coffeemaker, hair dryer, iron.

Eagle Bluff Bed & Breakfast One of the best-located B&Bs in the city—at least if you like Prince Rupert's bustling maritime ambience—the Eagle Bluff sits right on the wharf at Cow Bay. Accommodations include single, double, and family units; the lower level is wheelchair accessible. The Cow Bay Café (see "Where to Dine," below) is just a few doors away.

201 Cow Bay Rd., Prince Rupert, BC V8J 1A2. **②** **800/833-1550** in Canada, or 250/627-4955. Fax 250/627-7945. www.citytel.net/eaglebluff. 7 units (2 with shared bathroom). C$55–C$90 (US$36–US$59) double. Rates include full or continental breakfast. MC, V. **Amenities:** Laundry service. *In room:* TV.

Moby Dick Inn   Well established and serviceable, the Moby Dick is a clean, unfussy choice. It has a central location between downtown and the ferry docks. Rooms are nicely outfitted; most have coffeemakers and hair dryers. Wheelchair-accessible units are available.

935 Second Ave. W., Prince Rupert, BC V8J 1H8. **②** **800/663-0822** or 250/624-6961. Fax 250/624-3760. www.mobydickinn.com. C$79–C$89 (US$51–US$58) double. Children under 12 stay free in parents' room. AE, DC, DISC, MC, V. Small pets allowed. **Amenities:** Restaurant, bar; golf course nearby; Jacuzzi; sauna; limited room service; coin-op laundry. *In room:* TV, dataport, fridge.

Pacific Inn   Recently renovated, this motor lodge is a good value for its large, clean rooms in a convenient location, midway between downtown and the ferry docks. The owners take pride in the place, and it shows. The front desk will arrange local tours and activities.

909 Third Ave. W., Prince Rupert, BC V8J 1M9. **②** **888/663-1999** or 250/627-1711. Fax 250/627-4212. www.pacificinn.bc.ca. 77 units. C$75–C$85 (US$49–US$55) double. Rates include continental breakfast. Off-season rates and senior discounts available. AE, MC, V. Pets allowed for C$10 (US$7). **Amenities:** Restaurant (seafood); golf course nearby; coin-op laundry across street. *In room:* TV, dataport, fridge (on request), coffeemaker, hair dryer.

Pineridge B&B ✿   This attractive B&B is near downtown and the ferry terminals. The bedrooms come with nice touches like robes and down duvets. Two sitting rooms contain a TV, fireplace, library, and games. The entire house is tastefully decorated with mostly clean-lined, modern furnishings and local art and crafts. The friendly hosts will help you plan activities and arrange charters. *Note:* Smoking is not permitted.

1714 Sloan Ave., Prince Rupert, BC V8J 3Z9. **②** **888/733-6733** or 250/627-4419. Fax 250/624-2366. www.pineridge.bc.ca. 3 units. Summer C$90 (US$59) double; off-season C$70 (US$46) double. Rates include full breakfast. Not suitable for children. MC, V. Follow signs to ferry terminal, turn left (or from ferry turn right) onto Smithers St., go 2 blocks, and turn right onto Sloan Ave. *In room:* No phone.

Rainforest Bed & Breakfast   Located in a quiet, residential section of Prince Rupert, this cozy B&B offers guests a shared kitchenette and a sitting room with TV and phone. Breakfast includes fresh-squeezed juices and delicious homemade cinnamon rolls. Your hosts offer free ferry and airport pickup and drop-off.

706 Ritchie St., Prince Rupert, BC V8J 3N5. **②** **888/923-9993** or 250/624-9742. Fax 250/627-5551. www.citytel.net/rainforest. 3 units. C$65–C$75 (US$42–US$49) double. Rates include full breakfast. Children 8–13 stay in parents' room for C$5 (US$3.25) per night. No credit cards. Free parking and short-term vehicle storage. From the ferry terminal, drive 3 min. on Hwy. 16 (also called Park Ave. on the coastal side of town). Turn right on Smithers St., left on Kootenay, then right on Ritchie. **Amenities:** Courtesy limo. *In room:* No phone.

WHERE TO DINE

Cowpuccino's Coffee Bar, 25 Cow Bay Rd. (**②** **250/627-1395**), is a friendly, slightly funky coffee shop with good homemade muffins.

Breakers Pub ✿ PUB   Breakers is a popular pub with a harbor view and well-prepared international food. The offerings range from salads and wraps to pasta, pizza, and grilled local fish. This is a hopping social spot, with a new game room and dance floor; the young and prosperous of Prince Rupert gather here to get happy with a microbrew or two.

117 George Hills Way (on the Cow Bay Wharf). 🕐 **250/624-5990.** Reservations not needed. Main courses C$6–C$21 (US$3.90–US$14). AE, DC, MC, V. Mon–Thurs 11:30am–midnight; Fri–Sat 11:30am–1am; Sun noon–midnight.

Cow Bay Café 🕵 PACIFIC NORTHWEST   This homey place is like a little Vancouver street cafe plunked down on the edge of a dock. The casual, slightly hippie atmosphere feels refreshing so far north, and is nicely matched by the menu, which features lots of vegetarian options. Choices include salads, pastas, soups, and sandwiches; at night, there's always fresh fish prepared with zest. If you see an appealing dessert on the menu, order it when you order dinner, because popular items often sell out by the end of the evening.

205 Cow Bay Rd. 🕐 **250/627-1212.** Reservations recommended. Main courses C$11–C$17 (US$7–US$11). AE, MC, V. Tues noon–2:30pm; Wed–Sat noon–2:30pm and 6–8:30pm.

Smile's Seafood Café SEAFOOD   Open since 1922, Smile's serves seafood in every shape and form, from oyster burgers to heaping platters of fried fish. Located on the waterfront in the historic Cow Bay district, Smile's is essentially an old-fashioned, vinyl-seated diner whose base clientele are the town's fishermen and -women.

113 Cow Bay Rd. 🕐 **250/624-3072.** www.mapchannel.com/smiles. Reservations recommended. Main courses C$7–C$40 (US$4.55–US$26). MC, V. Daily 11am–10pm. Often open from 9am in summer; call ahead.

Waterfront Restaurant 🕵 PACIFIC NORTHWEST   Easily Prince Rupert's most sophisticated restaurant, the Waterfront is flanked by banks of windows that overlook the busy harbor. The white-linen-and-crystal elegance of the dining room is matched by the inventiveness of the cuisine. Understandably, much of the menu is devoted to local seafood; Skeena River salmon, for example, is baked with sun-dried cranberries and served with honey lemon butter. A full page of "casual plates" feature smaller portions, salads, and tempting appetizers such as a seafood club sandwich.

In the Crest Hotel, 222 First Ave. W. 🕐 **250/624-6771.** www.cresthotel.bc.ca. Reservations suggested. Main courses C$8–C$32 (US$5–US$21). AE, DC, MC, V. Daily 6:30am–10pm.

3 The Queen Charlotte Islands

The misty and mysterious Queen Charlotte Islands provided inspiration for 19th-century painter Emily Carr, who documented her impressions of the towering totem poles and longhouses at the abandoned village of Ninstints, on Anthony Island. The islands still lure artists, writers, and photographers wishing to experience their haunting beauty.

The Queen Charlottes—also called by their Native name, Haida Gwaii—are the homeland of the Haida people. Sometimes referred to as the Vikings of the Pacific, the Haida were mighty seafarers, and during raiding forays, ranged as far south along the Pacific Coast as Oregon. The Haida were also excellent artists, carvers of both totems and argillite, a slatelike rock that they transformed into tiny totemic sculptures and pendants. The Haida today make up about half of the islands' population of 6,000.

The Queen Charlottes have a reputation as the "Canadian Galapagos," as these islands—ranging between 32 and 85 miles (51 and 136km) from the mainland—have evolved their own endemic species and subspecies of flora and fauna. In recognition of the islands' unique natural and human history, the Canadian government preserved the southern portion of Moresby Island as

Gwaii Haanas National Park Reserve and Haida Heritage Site ⭐. UNESCO followed suit by naming the islands a World Heritage Site.

The islands are primordial and beautiful, but visiting them requires some planning. In fact, if you're reading this in Prince Rupert and thinking about a spur-of-the-moment trip to the Charlottes, you may want to reconsider. Lodging on the islands is limited, and reservations are necessary year-round. The most interesting areas—the abandoned Haida villages—are accessible only by boat, and the Gwaii Haanas National Park limits the number of people who can daily access the archaeological sites. There are only 78 miles (125km) of paved roads, and none of them even come close to the park or the islands' wild western coastline. In short, simply showing up on the Queen Charlottes is not a good idea. The best way to visit is by arranging, in advance, to join a guide or outfitter on a kayaking, flightseeing, sailing, or boating excursion.

ESSENTIALS

GETTING THERE   By Ferry   BC Ferries (✆ **888/BCFERRY** in B.C., or 250/386-3431; www.bcferries.bc.ca) crosses between Prince Rupert and Skidegate, on northerly Graham Island. The 6½- to 7-hour crossing can be quite rough; take precautions if you're prone to seasickness. Ferries run daily in summer; call ahead to reserve. High-season tickets are C$25 (US$16) per passenger and C$93 (US$60) per vehicle.

By Plane   Air Canada (✆ **888/247-2262;** www.aircanada.com) provides daily flights to Sandspit Airport on northern Moresby Island. **Montair** (✆ **888/ 666-8247** or 604/946-6688) flies several days a week from Vancouver to Masset, on Graham Island. **Harbour Air** (✆ **800/689-4234** or 250/627-1341; www. harbour-air.com) has seaplane flights daily from Prince Rupert to Masset and a few times weekly to Sandspit and Queen Charlotte City; it also offers charters and flightseeing tours. Many other charter companies offer transport around the islands as well as flightseeing trips (see below).

VISITOR INFORMATION   The Queen Charlotte Islands Visitor Info Centre, 3220 Wharf St., Queen Charlotte (✆ **250/559-8316;** www.qcinfo. com), is open May through September, daily from 8am to 8pm. On Graham Island, the **Masset Visitor Info Centre,** 1455 Old Beach Rd., Masset (✆ **888/ 352-9292** or 250/626-3982; www.massetbc.com), is open in July and August, daily from 11am to 5pm. Also check out **www.qcislands.net/tourism**.

GETTING AROUND   The Graham Island–to–Moresby Island Skidegate– Alliford Bay ferry operates 12 daily sailings. Peak fares are C$4.75 (US$3.10) per passenger, C$12 (US$8) per car.

With so few roads on the islands, it's fair to ask if it even makes sense to take a car on a short trip. Rentals are available from **Budget,** at the Sandspit Airport, 3113 Third Ave., Queen Charlotte, or 1400 Christie St., Masset (✆ **800/ 268-8900** in Canada, or 800/527-0700 in the U.S.; https://rent.drivebudget.com); **Rustic Car Rentals,** 605 Hwy. 33, Queen Charlotte (✆ **877/559-4641** or 250/ 559-4641); **National,** 1504 Old Beach Rd., Masset (✆ **800/387-4747** or 250/626-3318; www.nationalcar.com); and **Thrifty,** at the Sandspit Airport (✆ **800/THRIFTY** or 250/637-2299; www.thrifty.com).

Bike rentals are available from **Premier Creek Lodging,** in Queen Charlotte City (✆ **888/322-3388** or 250/559-8415; www.qcislands.net/premier). For weeklong bike tours, contact **Wings on Wheels** (✆ **877/626-6049;** www.wings onwheels.com).

EXPLORING THE ISLANDS

Most visitors come to the Charlottes to view its abundant and unusual wildlife, and to visit the ancient Haida villages. In both cases, you'll need to either have your own boat or arrange for a guide to get you from the islands' small settlements to the even more remote areas. The islands provide superlative wilderness adventures—camping, hiking, diving, sailing, kayaking, and fishing—although due to their isolation and sometimes extreme weather, you'll need to plan ahead and know what you're getting into before setting out.

Graham Island is the more populous of the two major islands. **Queen Charlotte City** is a fishing and logging town with a population of about 1,200, sitting above the scenic waters of Beaverskin Bay. QCC, as the village is sometimes dubbed, has the majority of lodgings and facilities for travelers, as well as the administrative headquarters for **Gwaii Haanas National Park Reserve** (see below).

Skidegate Village, just east of the Skidegate ferry terminal, is home to the **Haida Gwaii Museum at Quay 'Ilnagaay** (✆ 250/559-4643), which houses the world's largest collection of argillite carvings, made from the slatelike stone found only in the Queen Charlottes. Admission is C$3 (US$1.95) for adults; the museum is open Monday through Friday from 10am to 5pm and Saturday and Sunday from 1 to 5pm (closed Sun Sept–May, and closed Tues Dec–May). Next to the museum is the longhouse-style office of the **Haida Gwaii Watchmen,** the Native guardians of the islands' Haida villages and heritage sites. Ask here for information on visiting these sites.

Heading north from Skidegate on Highway 16, **Tlell** is an old agricultural community and now somewhat of an artists' colony; watch for signs pointing to studios. Past the logging town of Port Clements, the highway ends at **Masset,** the island's largest town with a population pushing 1,500. **Old Massett,** just north of Masset, is one of the largest Haida settlements on the island, and a good place to shop for carvings and jewelry. Just north of the Masset town center, trails lead through the **Delkatla Wildlife Sanctuary,** one of the first southerly landfalls on the Pacific Flyway.

From Masset, continue north and then east on Tow Hill Road to **Naikoon Provincial Park,** where whales can be spotted from the beaches and peregrine falcons fly overhead. The **Agate Beach Campground** (✆ **250/847-7320**) is a popular place to camp (C$12/US$8).

On **Moresby Island,** the principal center of population is **Sandspit** (pop. 500–700). In summer, Parks Canada operates an information center for visitors headed to the wilderness **Gwaii Haanas National Park Reserve and Haida Heritage Site** 𝕽. There are no roads or shore facilities in the park, and access is by boat or floatplane only. Although there are many amazing sights in this part of the Queen Charlottes, you'll need to be committed to the journey to get here: The distances are great and the costs high. If you're a dedicated wildlife-watcher, it may be worth it to see the rare fauna and flora. Perhaps the most famous site in the park is **SGang Gwaay 'Ilnagaay,** or **Ninstints,** on Anthony Island, an ancient Native village revered as sacred ground by the modern-day Haida. Centuries-old totem poles and longhouses proudly stand in testimony to the culture's 10,000-year heritage.

You must attend a mandatory orientation session before entering Gwaii Haanas National Park, and reservations are required; call ✆ **800/HELLOBC** or 250/387-1642. (Six standby places are also available daily on a first-come, first-served basis.) The **Haida Gwaii Watchmen** (✆ **250/559-8225**) control access to **SGang** Gwaay 'Ilnagaay and other ancient villages in the park, and watchmen members will explain the history and cultural significance of the sites you may visit. For more information, contact **Gwaii Haanas,** Box 37, Queen Charlotte City, BC V0T 1S0 (© **250/559-8818;** http://parkscan.harbour.com/gwaii), or the **Queen Charlotte Islands Visitor Info Centre** (© **250/559-8316;** www. qcinfo.com).

TOURS & EXCURSIONS TO GWAII HAANAS NATIONAL PARK RESERVE

Outfitters must be registered with park officials; the list of authorized tour operators is the best place to start shopping for expeditions into the park. The park entry fees range from C$10 to C$80 (US$7 to US$52)—depending on the number of days you'll be there—and may or may not be included in the cost of tour packages.

Many outfitters, such as **Butterfly Tours Great Expeditions** (© **604/ 740-7018;** www.butterflytours.bc.ca)—alternately booked through **Great Expeditions** (© **800/663-3364** or 604/257-2040; www.greatexpeditions.com)— offer kayaking packages that suit every age and experience level; Butterfly's tours start at C$1,690 (US$1,099). Longtime outfitter **Ecosummer Expeditions** (© **800/465-8884** or 250/674-0102; www.ecosummer.com) offers 1- and 2- week trips to Gwaii Haanas, with prices starting at C$1,495 (US$972). **Pacific Rim Paddling Company** (© **250/384-6103;** www.islandnet.com/~prp) has 7- and 14-day kayak trips to the park, with prices from C$1,395 (US$907). **Queen Charlotte Adventures** (© **250/559-8990;** www.qcislands.net/qciadven) offers a 6-day trip to **SGang** Gwaay 'Ilnagaay for C$1,392 (US$905), plus daylong powerboat tours of the park.

Sailing into Gwaii Haanas is another popular option, and most sailboat operators also have kayaks aboard for guests' use. **Bluewater Adventures** (© **888/ 877-1770** or 604/980-3800; www.bluewateradventures.ca) offers 10-day tours starting at C$2,500 (US$1,625). **Ocean Light II Adventures** (© **604/328-5339;** www.oceanlight2.bc.ca) offers 8-day sailings for C$2,560 (US$1,664). **Takuli III Sailing Adventures** (© **250/559-8667;** www.qcislands.net/takuli) has 4- and 7- day trips to many destinations in Gwaii Haanas; the shorter trip runs C$850 (US$553).

South Moresby Air Charters (© **888/551-4222** or 250/559-4222; www. qcislands.net/smoresby) offers sightseeing seaplane flights to Hot Springs Island and **SGang** Gwaay 'Ilnagaay. The latter trip includes a landing at Rose Bay and a 40-minute boat ride to the ancient village, plus a guided tour. It costs C$1,217 (US$791) for two.

Diving charters around the islands, but not in Gwaii Haanas, can be arranged through **Emerald Sea Sail and Scuba** (© **250/635-5818;** www3.sympatico.bc. ca/emeraldsea).

FISHING

Langara Fishing Adventures (© **800/668-7544** or 604/232-5532; www. langara.com) offers fishing packages with accommodations at one of the most beautiful lodges in western Canada. Geared toward those who want to be pampered, the outfitter picks up guests at Vancouver Airport and delivers them to Langara Island, just north of Graham Island. The rooms at the Langara Island Lodge are luxurious, and the dining room serves expertly prepared Pacific Northwest dishes. Packages include air transport, lodging, meals, boats, tackle, weather gear, and freezing, canning, and taxidermy services. Guided fishing costs extra, as do whale-watching and heli-touring. Rates start at C$3,775 (US$2,454) for a 4-day trip; packages are offered April to October.

For something more low-key, **Naden Lodge,** 1496 Kelkatla St., Masset (© **800/771-8933** or 250/626-3322; www.nadenlodge.bc.ca), offers B&B accommodations and guided fishing from a lovely location right above Masset's boat basin. Numerous charter operators can be found in Masset, Queen Charlotte, and Skidegate. Contact the **Queen Charlotte Islands Visitor Info Centre** (© **250/559-8316;** www.qcinfo.com) for suggestions. **Haida Gwaii Charters,** in Skidegate (© **250/559-8808;** www.haidagwaiicharters.com) has the distinction of being run by local Haida guides.

WHERE TO STAY & DINE

Food on these remote islands is pretty perfunctory. Stop in at **Daddy Cool's Neighbourhood Pub,** Collison Avenue at Main Street, Masset (© **250/626-3210**), for a pint and pub food. It's open daily year-round, from noon to 2am Monday through Saturday, and to midnight on Sunday. The **Sandpiper Restaurant,** Collison Avenue at Orr Street, Masset (© **250/626-3672**), serves hearty portions of seafood, steaks, pasta, sandwiches, and salads. **Oceana,** 3119 Third Ave., Queen Charlotte City (© **250/559-8683**), offers Chinese and Continental cuisine at lunch and dinner.

Dorothy & Mike's Guest House
The atmosphere here has an island flavor: A large deck overlooks the Skidegate Inlet, and a serene garden surrounds the house. The cozy bedrooms are filled with local art and antiques. A common area has an entertainment center and library. The inn is within walking distance of the ocean, restaurants, and shopping. *Note:* Smoking is permitted outdoors only.

3127 Second Ave. (Box 595), Queen Charlotte City, BC V0T 1S0. © 250/559-8439. Fax 250/559-8439. www. qcislands.net/doromike. 8 units (4 with shared bathroom). May–Sept C$60 (US$39) double with shared bathroom; C$75 (US$49) double with private bathroom. Rates include breakfast. Off-season rates available. MC, V. Drive 2 miles (3.5km) away from the Skidegate ferry terminal on Second Ave. *In room:* TV, no phone.

Premier Creek Lodging
Great for the budget-conscious, this heritage lodge dates back to 1910. Many rooms have great views over gardens to Bearskin Bay. There's a range of accommodations, from small, single units with shared bathrooms to suites with kitchens. There's also a full-fledged hostel in a separate building; rates there are C$19 (US$12).

3101 Third Ave. (Box 268), Queen Charlotte City, BC V0T 1S0. © 888/322-3388 or 250/559-8415. Fax 250/559-8198. www.qcislands.net/premier. 12 units. C$55–C$70 (US$36–US$46) double. AE, MC, V. **Amenities:** Restaurant; bike rentals. *In room:* TV, no phone (except in larger rooms).

Sea Raven Motel
The largest lodging in the Queen Charlottes, the Sea Raven is a comfortable motel with many room types, ranging from simple single units to deluxe accommodations with decks; many have ocean views. The rooms are simply furnished, but very clean.

3301 Third Ave. (Box 519), Queen Charlotte City, BC V0T 1S0. © 800/665-9606 or 250/559-4423. Fax 250/559-8617. www.searaven.com. 29 units. C$60–C$90 (US$39–US$59). AE, DC, MC, V. Limited street parking available. Pets allowed for C$10 (US$7). **Amenities:** Restaurant; golf course nearby; kayak and bike rentals; tour/activities desk; car-rental desk; laundry service. *In room:* TV, coffeemaker.

Spruce Point Lodging
This rustic inn, overlooking the Hecate Strait, features rooms with private entrances and excellent views. Each unit has a private bathroom with either shower or tub; some rooms have kitchens. Your friendly hosts can arrange kayaking packages to the surrounding islands. *Note:* Smoking is permitted on outside decks only.

609 Sixth Ave., Queen Charlotte City, BC V0T 1S0. ℂ 250/559-8234. www.qcislands.net/sprpoint. 7 units. C$65 (US$42) double. Kitchen C$10 (US$7) extra. Rates include full breakfast. MC, V. Drive 15 min. west on the main road away from the Skidegate ferry terminal, then turn left at Sam & Shirley's Grocery. *In room:* TV, fridge, coffeemaker.

4 The Yellowhead Highway: From Prince Rupert to Prince George

It's a long 447 miles (715km) from Prince Rupert to Prince George. Even though it's possible to make the journey in one long day's drive, it's far more pleasant to take it slowly, enjoy the scenery, and stop at some of the cultural sights along the way.

The route initially follows the glacier-carved Skeena River valley inland, through the industrial city of **Terrace** and to the **Hazeltons,** twin towns with a lovely river setting and an excellent First Nations cultural center. **Smithers,** cradled in a rich agricultural valley, is another scenic spot, and the most pleasant place along the route to spend a night. Between Burns Lake and Fort Fraser is a series of long, thin lakes, famed for trout angling and rustic fishing resorts.

ESSENTIALS

GETTING THERE   By Car   Terrace is 91 miles (152km) east of Prince Rupert on the Yellowhead Highway (Hwy. 16). From Terrace to Prince George, it's another 357 miles (571km).

By Train   VIA Rail (ℂ 888/VIA-RAIL or 800/561-8630; www.viarail.ca) operates three-times-weekly service between Prince George and Prince Rupert, with stops including Smithers, New Hazelton, and Terrace. The train follows the same route as the Yellowhead Highway.

By Bus   Greyhound Canada (ℂ 800/661-8747 or 604/482-8747; www. greyhound.ca) travels twice daily between Prince Rupert and Prince George. One-way fare from Prince Rupert to Terrace is about C$23 (US$15).

VISITOR INFORMATION   The **Northern BC Tourism Association,** 850 River Rd., Prince George (ℂ 800/663-8843 or 250/561-0432; www. nbctourism.com), provides extensive information on the area.

TERRACE & NISGA'A MEMORIAL LAVA BEDS PROVINCIAL PARK

The Yellowhead Highway (Hwy. 16) follows the lush Skeena River valley from Prince Rupert, on the coast of the Inside Passage, to the province's interior. It's the gateway to the land-based return route from the Inside Passage ferry cruise. The long, winding valley is home to a diverse community of fishers, loggers, and aluminum and paper-mill workers in Terrace, and is the ancestral home of the Gitxsan, Haisla, Tshimshian, and Nisga'a First Nations.

If you want to understand glacial geology, this drive will provide instant illumination. It's easy to picture the steep-sided valley choked with a bulldozer of ice, grinding the walls into sheer cliffs. Streams drop thousands of feet in a series of waterfalls. There are many small picnic areas along this route; plan on stopping beside the Skeena to admire the view.

Terrace is an industrial town of about 14,000, and has only just begun to develop itself for tourists. Stop by the store at the **House of Sim-oi-Ghets,** off Highway 16 (ℂ 250/638-1629; www.kitsumkalum.bc.ca/house.html), a cedar longhouse owned by the Kitsumkalum tribal band of the Tsimshian Nation. It offers jewelry, carvings, bead and leather work, and moccasins.

Twenty-five miles (40km) northwest of town, the **Khutzeymateen Grizzly Bear Preserve** is the province's first official sanctuary of its kind. You must be part of an authorized group or accompanied by a ranger to observe these amazing creatures (see "Archaeological, Wildlife & Adventure Tours" in the Prince Rupert section, above).

North America's rarest subspecies of black bear, the **kermodei,** also makes its home in the valley. The kermodei is unique, a non-albino black bear born with white fur. Its teddy-bear face and round ears are endearing, but the kermodei is even larger than the impressive Queen Charlotte Islands black bear.

At the **Nisga'a Memorial Lava Beds Provincial Park,** vegetation has only recently begun to reappear on the lava plain created by a volcanic eruption and subsequent lava flow in 1750, which consumed this area and nearly all of its inhabitants.

The route to the park's near-lunar landscape begins in Terrace at the intersection of the Yellowhead Highway (Hwy. 16) and Kalum Lake Drive (Nisga'a Hwy.). Follow the mostly paved highway north along the Kalum River past Kalum Lake. Just past Rosswood is **Lava Lake** (where the park boundary begins). A road off to the right, next to Ross Lake, leads to the short **Volcanic Cone Trail,** which will take you to the old volcanic crater. A guide and reservations are mandatory (C$12/US$8), so contact the **Nisga'a Visitor Centre** (© 250/638-9589) or the Terrace office for **BC Parks** (© 250/798-2277), or see **http://members.tripod.com/~hgtours**. As you continue on Nisga'a Highway, you'll go by the town of **New Aiyansh** (the valley's largest Nisga'a village) and finally enter the heart of the park. Veer to the left to go to the visitor center. The entire trip is 48 miles (80km); allow at least 2 hours.

In winter, **Shames Mountain,** 22 miles (35km) west of town (© 877/898-4754 or 250/635-3773; www.shamesmountain.com), is known for its small crowds and huge quantities of snow. Open mid-December to mid-April, it has one double chair and one T-bar lift, along with 20 groomed trails. Lift tickets are C$32 (US$21) for adults, C$21 (US$14) for seniors and youths 13 to 18, and C$16 (US$10) for children 7 to 12. Facilities include a rental and repair shop, store, cafeteria, and pub.

For area information, stop by the **Terrace Visitor Info Centre,** 4511 Keith Ave. (© **250/635-2063;** chamber@kermode.net), open from June 1 to September 1, daily from 8:30am to 6pm; and September 2 to May 31, Monday through Friday from 8:30am to 4:30pm. You can also call the **Terrace Tourism Council** (© 800/499-1639 or 250/635-0832; www.terracetourism.bc.ca).

WHERE TO STAY & DINE

Best Western Terrace Inn Overlooking the surrounding mountains, these well-appointed rooms feature a number of little touches not normally found this far into the backcountry. Facilities include a piano bar and lounge, plus a pub with live entertainment. Lava-bed tours are available upon request.

4553 Greig Ave., Terrace, BC V8G 1M7. © **800/488-1898** or 250/635-0083. Fax 250/635-0092. www.bestwestern.com/ca/terraceinn. 62 units. C$79–C$179 (US$51–US$116) double. Group, corporate, senior, and weekend discounts available. AE, DC, DISC, MC, V. Free parking. Small pets accepted for C$10 (US$7). **Amenities:** Restaurant, bar, lounge; well-equipped exercise room; Jacuzzi; room service; laundry service; dry cleaning. *In room:* A/C, TV, dataport, coffeemaker, hair dryer.

Coast Inn of the West This high-rise hotel dominates downtown Terrace, and is within easy walking distance of the two shopping malls that constitute the city center. It's also close to a fitness and swimming center. The guest rooms are spacious and attractively furnished.

4620 Lakelse Ave., Terrace, BC V8G 1R1. $\mathcal{C}$ **800/663-1144** or 250/638-8141. Fax 250/638-8999. www.
coasthotels.com. 58 units. C$120–C$165 (US$78–US$107) double. Senior and AAA rates available. AE, DISC,
DC, MC, V. **Amenities:** Restaurant, bar, lounge; golf course nearby; limited room service; laundry service;
same-day dry cleaning. *In room:* A/C, TV, dataport, coffeemaker, hair dryer.

Miles Inn on the T'seax   Overlooking the Nisga'a Memorial Lava Beds
Provincial Park, this beautiful lodge is nestled in the Nass River valley. A hot tub
is available for relaxing tired muscles after a day of hiking, climbing, kayaking
the Nass River, or fishing the T'seax River. Home-cooked dinners are available
for an extra charge. *Note:* Smoking is not permitted.

Nass Valley (Box 230), New Aiyansh, BC V0J 1A0. $\mathcal{C}$ and fax **250/633-2636.** www.kermode.net/milesinn. 4
units (2 with private bathroom). C$80 (US$52) double. Rates include breakfast. No credit cards. **Amenities:**
Jacuzzi. *In room:* No phone.

THE STEWART-CASSIAR HIGHWAY: NORTH TO ALASKA

Forty-seven miles (75km) east of Terrace (30 miles/48km west of the Hazeltons)
is the junction of Highway 16 and the Stewart-Cassiar Highway (also labeled as
Hwy. 37), one of two roads leading to the far north of British Columbia, eventually to join the famed Alaska Highway in the Yukon. This route is not as popular as the Alaska Highway, which begins farther east in Dawson Creek, though
the scenery is more spectacular and the road conditions about the same. The
route is now mostly paved, with a few gravel sections; you can depend on delays
due to road construction (see www.th.gov.bc.ca/roadreports.htm for updates).
It's a total of 446 miles (714km) between the Yellowhead Highway and the junction of the Alaska Highway near Watson Lake, the Yukon.

After turning north at the Highway 16 junction, stop in the Native village of
Gitwangak to view the historic totem poles, some more than 100 years old.
Similar totem poles can also be seen 15 miles (24km) farther up the Stewart-
Cassiar Highway at **Kitwancool.**

Even if you don't want to drive all the way to the Yukon or Alaska, consider
a side trip to the twin communities of Stewart, British Columbia, and Hyder,
Alaska, found at the end of Highway 37A, which splits off from the Stewart-
Cassiar at Meziadin Junction, 96 miles (154km) north of the Yellowhead. From
the junction it's just 40 miles (64km) to Stewart, but what a 40 miles! The road
arches up immediately to cross the mighty Coast Mountains before plunging
down to sea level at Stewart. Stop at the Bear Glacier Rest Area, where massive
Bear Glacier—glowing an eerie aqua blue—descends into Strohn Lake, frequently bobbing with icebergs. The boundary-straddling villages of Stewart and
Hyder lie at the head of the Portland Canal, a very long and narrow fjord. The
setting alone—the two ports huddle below high-flying peaks and massive
glaciers—is worth the drive.

Stewart (pop. 700–800) is Canada's most northerly ice-free port. The tidy little town contrasts vividly with Hyder (pop. about 80), its miniscule and isolated
Alaskan cousin. Facilities are basic but serviceable. The best place to stay is the
King Edward Hotel and Motel, on Fifth Avenue ($\mathcal{C}$ **800/663-3126** in B.C.,
or 250/636-2244).

From Hyder, continue along graveled Fish Creek Road for 5 miles (8km) to
Fish Creek, where in July, black and grizzly bears gather to fish for spawning
chum salmon. Follow the road another 20 miles (32km) to an astonishing vista
of Salmon Glacier gouging its steep-sided valley.

Continuing north from Meziadin Junction, the route follows rushing rivers
in narrow valleys. Facilities are very limited; there are 50 campsites available for

C$12 (US$8) mid-May through September at **Kinaskan Lake Provincial Park,** 130 miles (208km) north of Meziadin Junction (℃ **800/689-9025** for reservations; www.discovercamping.ca). Seventeen miles (27km) farther north you can stay at the **Tatogga Lake Resort** (℃ **250/234-3526**), with rustic cabins (C$55/US$36), a woodsy restaurant, and campsites.

The town of **Dease Lake** (pop. 700) will seem like a metropolis by the time you reach it. Since it's about midway on the Stewart-Cassiar Highway, it's a natural place to spend the night. The **Northway Motor Inn,** on Boulder Street (℃ **250/771-5341**), is a standard motel complex. There are a number of campgrounds along Dease Lake itself.

If you think Dease Lake is isolated, consider a side trip to **Telegraph Creek** (pop. 450), 70 miles (112km) west on a gravel road. The road parallels the powerful Stikine River as it trenches a precipitous canyon on its way to the Pacific. Don't even think of driving this road if you have vertigo! The scenery is absolutely compelling, and Telegraph Creek, with both a Native village and frontier-era town, is friendly and welcoming. Just about the only place to stay is the **RiverSong Lodge** (℃ **250/235-3196;** www.stikineriversong.com), formerly the Hudson's Bay Company trading post; camping is also available.

Back on the Stewart-Cassiar Highway, from Dease Lake it's a straightforward 145 miles (232km) of mountains and forests to the junction with the Alaska Highway, 13 miles (21km) east of Watson Lake.

THE HAZELTONS

The Skeena and Bulkley rivers join at the Hazeltons (pop. 2,000). Straddling two river canyons and set below the rugged Rocher de Boule mountains, the Hazeltons are actually three separate towns: **Hazelton** itself, **South Hazelton,** and **New Hazelton,** all in a 5-mile (8km) stretch. The junction of these two mighty rivers was home to the Gitxsan and Wet'suwet'en peoples, for whom the rivers provided both transport and a wealth of salmon. In the 1860s, it became the upriver terminus for riverboat traffic on the Skeena, and Hazelton became a commercial hub for miners, ranchers, and other frontier settlers farther inland.

Both the First Nations and the frontier history are still on view. The old town center of Hazelton, though small, has the feel of a pioneer settlement. And you can get a sense of the Gitxsan culture by visiting **'Ksan Historical Village** ✮, off Highway 62 (℃ **877/842-5518** or 250/842-5544; www.ksan.org), a re-creation of a traditional village. Some of the vividly painted longhouses serve as studios, where you can watch artists carve masks and hammer silver jewelry. If possible, plan your visit to coincide with a performance by the **'Ksan Performing Arts Group,** a troupe of singers and dancers who entertain visitors with music, masks, costumes, and pageantry. The shop here is a great source for Native art and gifts, and the Wilp Tokx, or the House of Eating, is a good place to try Native cooking. There's a C$2 (US$1.30) admission for the grounds themselves. To see the interior of the longhouses, you'll need to join a guided tour, which costs C$8 (US$5) for adults, C$6.50 (US$4.20) for seniors and youths. If you take the tour, you don't have to pay the grounds fee. 'Ksan is open from April 15 to October 15, daily from 9am to 6pm. The rest of the year, only the museum and shop are open, Monday through Friday from 10am to 5pm.

There aren't many lodging choices, but the **28 Inn,** 4545 Yellowhead Hwy. 16, New Hazelton (℃ **877/842-2828** or 250/842-6006; www.28inn.com) is clearly the best, with rooms for C$60 (US$39). The **'Ksan Historical Village** (see above) and **Seeley Lake Provincial Park,** 6 miles (9.5km) west of New

Hazelton (℗ **250/847-7320**), have campgrounds. For advance information on the area, call the **Hazeltons Travel Info Centre** (℗ **250/842-6071** in summer, 250/842-6571 Oct–May). The summer-only **visitor center** is at the junction of Highways 16 and 62 (Main St.).

SMITHERS & THE BULKLEY VALLEY

Smithers (pop. 6,200) is located in a stunningly beautiful valley, flanked on three sides by vast ranges of glaciated peaks and cut through by the fast-flowing Bulkley River. While many communities in North America boast of being Bavarian look-alikes, the countryside around here truly does look like the northern Alps, except for the cattle and horse ranches.

The heart of Smithers is the old commercial strip on **Main Street,** which is perpendicular to the current fast-food–and-motel-laden Highway 16. This attractive area is lined with Bavarian-theme storefronts that offer outdoor gear, gifts, and local crafts.

What Smithers really has to offer is its gorgeous mountain backdrop. With 8,600-foot (2,621m) **Hudson Bay Mountain** rising directly behind the town, snowcapped ranges ringing the valley, and the area's fast-flowing rivers and streams, you'll feel the urge to get outdoors.

Driftwood Canyon Provincial Park, 7 miles (11km) northeast of Smithers, preserves fossil-bearing formations laid down 50 million years ago. Considered one of the world's richest fossil beds, the park has interpretive trails leading through a section of exposed creek bed, which was carved by an ice-age glacier. To get here, drive 2 miles (3km) east of Smithers and turn east on Babine Lake Road.

Additional information on this region can be obtained from the **Smithers Visitor Info Centre,** 1411 Court St. (℗ **800/542-6673** or 250/847-3337; www.bulkley.net/~smicham).

OUTDOOR PURSUITS

HIKING   The 5½-mile (9km) **Perimeter Trail** rings the town, linking parks, golf courses, and residential areas. It's a good place to jog; one especially lovely stretch is along the Bulkley River in Riverside Park. Two excellent hikes are on **Hudson Bay Mountain.** Two miles (3km) west of Smithers, take Kathlyn Lake Road 6½ miles (10.4km) to the trail head. It's an easy half-mile (0.8km) stroll to view the impressive **Twin Falls.** From the same trail head, climb up to Glacier Gulch to get close to the toe of **Kathlyn Glacier.** This strenuous hike is just under 4 miles (6.4km) one-way, but allow at least 3 hours to make the climb.

Follow Hudson Bay Mountain Road west out of Smithers for 6½ miles (10.4km) to **Smithers Community Forest,** with an extensive trail system. The easy 2½-mile (4km) Interpretive Nature Trail makes a loop through the forest. For more rugged hiking, **Babine Mountains Recreation Area** protects 80,000 acres (32,400 hectares) of subalpine meadows, lakes, and craggy peaks. This roadless area is accessible only on foot, but many sights are within the range of day hikers. The **Silver King Basin Trail** passes through subalpine forest before reaching an alpine meadow that explodes with wildflowers in July. To reach the Babine Mountains, go 2 miles (3km) east of Smithers and take Babine Lake Road.

FISHING   The Bulkley River has excellent fishing for steelhead, Chinook, and Coho salmon, though restrictions apply. The best fishing areas on the Bulkley are from the confluence of the Morice River south of Smithers to the town of Telkwa.

WHERE TO STAY

The well-maintained **Aspen Motor Inn,** 4268 Hwy. 16 (© **800/663-7676** or 250/847-4551; www.hiway16.com/aspen), offers large rooms from C$75 (US$49). **Riverside Park Municipal Campsite,** 1600 Main St. N. (© **250/ 847-1600**), has 40 sites with dry toilets, fire pits, and water.

Hudson Bay Lodge   The largest and most comfortable hotel in Smithers, this is a popular stop for the tour-bus crowds making their way to and from the Prince Rupert ferries. The crowds notwithstanding, the facilities here are high quality. See the description of Pepper Jack's Grill under "Where to Dine," below.

3251 Hwy. 16 E. (Box 3636), Smithers, BC V0J 2N0. © **800/663-5040** or 250/847-4581. Fax 250/847-4878. www.hblodge.com. 99 units. C$98–C$118 (US$64–US$77) double. AE, DC, MC, V. Pets allowed for C$5 (US$3.25). **Amenities:** Restaurant, coffee shop, lounge; Jacuzzi; courtesy limo. *In room:* A/C, TV w/ pay movies, coffeemaker, hair dryer.

Stork Nest Inn (Value)   Billing itself as a European-style hotel, the Stork Nest does more than most Smithers lodgings to look Bavarian, with gables, flowers, and a corbeled roofline. But what really makes the place such a prize is the value it offers. The rooms aren't the largest in the province, but they are clean, pleasant, and nicely furnished. Accessible rooms are available.

1485 Main St. (Box 2049), Smithers, BC V0J 2N0. © **250/847-3831**. Fax 250/847-3852. www.storknest inn.com. 23 units. C$65 (US$42) double. Rates include full breakfast. AE, MC, V. Free parking. **Amenities:** Golf course nearby; lit tennis courts; sauna. *In room:* A/C, TV, dataport, fridge.

WHERE TO DINE

Pepper Jack's Grill, in the Hudson Bay Lodge (see above), serves pasta, gourmet pizza, and other international cuisine. Fresh seafood is a highlight, but the stock in trade is beef. Open daily from 5 to 10pm. The **Alpenhorn Pub and Bistro,** 1261 Main St. (© **250/847-5366**), is a pleasant, sports-bar type of pub with gourmet burgers, pastas, sandwiches, and ribs. Open daily from 11am to midnight.

THE LAKES DISTRICT

Between Smithers and Prince George lies a vast basin filled with glacier-gouged lakes, dense forests, and rolling mountains. There are over 300 lakes, whose combined shorelines add up to more than 3,000 miles (4,800km). Not surprisingly, sportfishing is the main draw here, and rustic fishing lodges are scattered along the lake shores.

However, this isn't an easy place to plan a casual visit. Many of the lodges are fly-in or boat-in, and offer only weeklong fishing packages. Most are very rustic indeed. If this is what you're looking for, contact the Burns Lake Chamber of Commerce (see below), which can connect you with the lodge or outfitter that suits your needs.

If you have a day to spare and want to explore the region, there's a paved loop starting in Burns Lake that explores the shores of four of the lakes. Take Highway 35 south from Burns Lake, past Tchesinkut Lake to Northbank on François Lake. From here, take the free half-hour ferry across François Lake and continue south to Ootsa Lake. Here, the road turns west, eventually returning to François Lake, Highway 16 at Houston, and then back east to Burns Lake.

Burns Lake is nominally the center of the Lakes District, and if you end up here needing a place to stay, try the **Burns Lake Motor Inn,** on Highway 16 West (© **800/663-2968** or 250/692-7545). For information on the region, contact the **Burns Lake Chamber of Commerce,** 540 Yellowhead Hwy. 16

(© **250/692-3773**), open in July and August daily and year-round at varying times; call for hours. Also check out **www.hiway16.com**.

At Vanderhoof, 83 miles (133km) east of Burns Lake, take Highway 27 north 37 miles (59km) to **Fort St. James National Historic Site** ⚑ (© **250/ 996-7191;** http://parkscan.harbour.com/fsj), one of the most interesting historic sites in northern British Columbia. Fort St. James was the earliest non-Native settlement in the province, a fur-trading fort established in 1806. In summer, costumed docents act out the roles of traders, craftsmen, and explorers. The park is open mid-May through September, daily from 9am to 5pm. Summer admission is C$4 (US$2.60) for adults, C$2 (US$1.30) for youths 12 to 16, and C$12 (US$8) for families. Free audio-guided tours of the grounds are available in winter; call ahead to request one.

5 Prince George

246 miles (396km) W of Jasper, Alberta; 470 miles (756km) E of Prince Rupert

The largest city in northern British Columbia, Prince George (pop. 82,000) makes a natural base for exploring the sights and recreational opportunities of the province's north-central region, which is filled with forested mountains, lakes, and mighty rivers.

There has been settlement at the junction of the Fraser and Nechako rivers for millennia; the two river systems were as much a transportation corridor for the early First Nations people as for the European settlers who came later. A trading post was established in the early 1800s; the Grand Trunk Railroad, which passed through here in 1914, put Prince George on the map.

What makes the city's economic heart beat is lumber—and lots of it. Prince George is at the center of vast softwood forests, and three major mills here turn trees into pulp, and pulp into paper. The economic boom that these mills introduced has brought a degree of sophistication to the lumber town—there's a civic art gallery, good restaurants, and the University of Northern British Columbia—but not so much that you're likely to forget that you're in the north.

ESSENTIALS

GETTING THERE   By Plane   Air Canada (© **888/247-2262;** www.air canada.com), through regional subsidiaries, provides daily service to Prince George.

By Train   The **BC Rail** (© **800/663-8238** or 604/984-5246; www.bcrail. com) *Cariboo Prospector* departs North Vancouver three times a week at 7am with stops at Whistler, Lillooet, 100 Mile House, Williams Lake, and Quesnel, arriving in Prince George at 9:25pm. The fare is C$212 (US$138).

By Bus   Greyhound Canada (© **800/661-8747** or 604/482-8747; www. greyhound.ca) serves Prince George with daily buses from Vancouver. The fare is about C$128 (US$83). Greyhound also has daily buses between Prince George, Jasper, and Edmonton.

By Car   Prince George is about a third of the way across the province on the east-west Yellowhead Highway (Hwy. 16). South from Prince George, Highway 97 drops through the Cariboo District on its way to Kelowna (445 miles/712km) and Vancouver (via Hwy. 1, 505 miles/808km). From Prince George, you can also follow Highway 97 north to join the Alaska Highway at Dawson Creek (263 miles/421km).

> **Tips   Special Events**
>
> The Ol' Sawmill Bluegrass Jamboree (© 250/564-8573), held 16 miles (26km) up North Nechako Road in mid-August, is a musical event for the whole family, with weekend camping, music workshops, arts and crafts, play areas for the kids, and many talented bluegrass performers.

VISITOR INFORMATION   Contact the **Prince George Visitor Info Centre,** 1198 Victoria St. (© **800/668-7646** or 250/562-3700; fax 250/563-3584; www.tourismpg.bc.ca).

GETTING AROUND   The local bus system is operated by **Prince George Transit** (© 250/563-0011). For a cab, call **Emerald Taxi** (© 250/563-3333) or **Price George Taxi Holdings** (© 250/564-4444). Car-rental agencies include **Avis** (© 800/272-5871 or 250/562-2847; www.avis.com), **Budget** (© 800/268-8900 in Canada, 800/527-0700 in the U.S., or 250/563-9669; https://rent.drivebudget.com), **Hertz** (© 800/263-0600 or 250/963-7454; www.hertz.com), **National** (© 800/CAR-RENT or 250/963-7473; www.nationalcar.com), and **Thrifty** (© 800/THRIFTY or 250/963-8711; www.thrifty.com).

EXPLORING THE AREA

Downtown Prince George is located on a spur of land at the confluence of the Fraser and Nechako rivers. The old commercial district at first seems a bit forlorn, but a stroll around the city center—concentrated around Third Avenue and George Street—reveals a down-and-dirty charm that's reminiscent of towns in the Yukon or Northwest Territories. And the prevalence of tattoo parlors, pawn shops, and old-fashioned coffee shops enhances the impression that this is at heart a rough-and-ready frontier community.

The **Two Rivers Gallery** (© **888/221-1155** or 250/614-7800; www.tworiversartgallery.com) occupies a stylish space in the Civic Centre Plaza, at Patricia Boulevard and Dominion Street. This architecturally innovative, C$5-million (US$3.25-million) structure houses a collection of works by mostly local artists. There's also a sculpture garden, gift shop, and cafe. Hours are Tuesday through Saturday from 10am to 5pm, Sunday from noon to 5pm. Between May and September, it's also open Monday from 10am to 5pm. Admission is C$4.50 (US$2.90) for adults, C$3.75 (US$2.45) for seniors and students, and C$2 (US$1.30) for children 5 to 12. After viewing the gallery, cross Patricia Street and wander the trails in **Connaught Hill Park.** From the top of the hill are good views of the Fraser River and downtown.

At the **Prince George Native Art Gallery,** 1600 Third Ave. (© **250/614-7726;** www.pgnfc.com/gallery), you can see birch-bark biting art, cedar-wood carvings, beadwork, and limited-edition prints by regional Native artists. It's open Tuesday through Friday from 9am to 5pm and Saturday from 10am to 4pm, with extended summer hours possible.

There are more than 120 parks within the city limits, many of them linked by the Heritage River Trails system. The best is 89-acre (36-hectare) **Fort George Park,** on the site of the original fur-trading post. On the grounds are a First Nations burial ground, a miniature railway, a one-room schoolhouse, and the outstanding **Fraser Fort George Regional Museum** ✴ (© **250/562-1612;** www.museum.princegeorge.com), which details the region's ecology, prehistory, and history, starting with exhibits on dinosaurs, moving through the customs of the region's Native Carrier people, and on to the fur-trading and logging past. There are also numerous interactive science exhibits; an Internet cafe; and a SimEx theater, in which viewers' seats move in tandem with motions in films. Admission is C$7.95 (US$5) for adults, C$5.95 (US$3.90) for seniors and students, C$4.95 (US$3.20) for children 2 to 12, or C$19.95 (US$13) per family. Open Wednesday through Sunday from 10am to 5pm. The park is on the Fraser River end of 20th Avenue; from downtown, take Queensway Street south, then turn east on 20th Avenue.

The **Heritage River Trails** take you on a 7-mile (11km) circuit covering the historic sights of town. The loop starts at Fort George Park, goes along the Fraser River, passes through Cottonwood Island Park and along the Nechako River to the Cameron Street bridge, and leads through town and back to Fort George Park.

WHERE TO STAY

If you're looking for a bed-and-breakfast, try the **Prince George B&B Hotline** (© **877/562-2626** or 250/562-2222; www.pgonline.com/bnb/hotline.html).

Coast Inn of the North ⚮   One of the best of British Columbia's Coast hotel chain is right in the thick of things in downtown Prince George. The guest rooms are nicely furnished; ask for a corner room and you'll get a balcony. Among the numerous facilities are a gift shop, travel agency, and florist.

770 Brunswick St., Prince George, BC V2L 2C2. © **800/663-1144** or 250/563-0121. Fax 250/563-1948. www.coasthotels.com. 155 units. C$89–C$165 (US$58–US$107) double. Extra person C$10 (US$7). Family plan, corporate and off-season rates, and senior and AAA discounts available. AE, MC, V. Free parking with engine heater plug-ins. **Amenities:** Three restaurants (Japanese, Continental/Canadian), pub, dance club; indoor pool; fitness center; Jacuzzis; saunas; salon; 24-hr. room service. *In room:* A/C, TV, dataport, minibar.

Connaught Motor Inn   A rambling motor-court lodging just south of downtown, the Connaught is an easy-in, easy-out kind of place with clean, large guest rooms and lots of extras. Most units have dataports.

1550 Victoria St., Prince George, BC V2L 2L3. © **800/663-6620** or 250/562-4441. Fax 250/562-4441. 98 units. C$65–C$75 (US$42–US$49) double. Extra person C$5–C$10 (US$3.25–US$7). Kitchen C$10 (US$7) extra. Senior and AAA discounts and off-season and weekly rates available. AE, DC, MC, V. Pets accepted for C$5 (US$3.25). **Amenities:** Indoor pool; Jacuzzi. *In room:* A/C, TV, fridge.

Econo Lodge *Value*   If you're looking for value, it's hard to beat the clean, unfussy rooms at the Econo Lodge, right downtown. Some larger units have Jacuzzi tubs; wheelchair-accessible rooms are available as well.

1915 Third Ave., Prince George, BC V2M 1G6. © **888/566-6333** or 250/563-7106. Fax 250/561-7216. 30 units. C$67–C$97 (US$44–US$63) double. Extra person C$10 (US$7). Rates include continental breakfast. Off-season rates and senior discounts available. MC, V. Free parking with engine heater plug-ins. Pets allowed for C$10 (US$7). **Amenities:** Exercise room; Jacuzzi; babysitting. *In room:* A/C, TV, dataport, coffeemaker.

Ramada Hotel (Downtown Prince George) ⚮   The grandest of hotels in Prince George, the Ramada offers a variety of rooms—from standard to presidential—right in the center of the city. Some units have Jacuzzis, heated bathroom floors, and full wet bars. Three rooms are wheelchair accessible. The Ramada has the only casino in Prince George, so this is a very busy place, in many ways the focal point of downtown.

444 George St., Prince George, BC V2L 1R6. © **800/830-8833** or 250/563-0055. Fax 250/563-6042. www.ramadaprincegeorge.com. 200 units. C$79–C$180 (US$51–US$117) double. Extra person C$20 (US$13). Senior discounts available. AE, DC, DISC, MC, V. Free covered parking. **Amenities:** Restaurant, bar; large indoor pool; golf course nearby; access to nearby health club; Jacuzzi; sauna; business center; limited room service; same-day dry cleaning. *In room:* A/C, TV w/ pay movies, dataport, coffeemaker.

Sandman Inn The recently built Sandman, along the Highway 97 strip west of downtown, offers large, comfortable guest rooms. Kitchenettes, suites, and wheelchair-accessible units are available.

1650 Central St., Prince George, BC V2M 3C2. © **800/SANDMAN** or 250/563-8131. Fax 250/563-8613. www.sandmanhotels.com/hotels/bc/prince_george.htm. 144 units. C$81–C$133 (US$53–US$86) double. Senior and AAA discounts available. AE, DC, DISC, MC, V. Small pets allowed for C$5 (US$3.25) per day. **Amenities:** Restaurant; indoor pool; golf course nearby; sauna; limited room service from on-site Denny's; laundry service; coin-op laundry; same-day dry cleaning. *In room:* A/C, TV, dataport, coffeemaker, hair dryer.

A Tangled Garden B&B This comfortable, centrally located home has two guest rooms. One unit has a kitchenette, private entrance, queen bed, and phone. A resident cat may keep you company. The hosts will pick up guests by request. *Note:* Smoking is permitted outdoors only.

2957 Sullivan Crescent, Prince George, BC V2N 5H6. © **250/964-3265.** Fax 250/964-3248. www.pgonline. com/bnb/tangledgarden.html. 2 units. C$60–C$70 (US$39–US$46) double. Extra person C$10 (US$7). Rates include full breakfast. No credit cards. Free parking with engine heater plug-ins. **Amenities:** Jacuzzi; courtesy limo. *In room:* TV/VCR.

WHERE TO DINE

For a light meal, head to **Java Mugga Mocha,** 304 George St. (© **250/ 562-3338**), a fun hangout for espresso drinks, sandwiches, and baked goods.

Da Moreno ✿ ITALIAN This coolly elegant space is easily the best choice in town. This restaurant would pass muster in Chicago or New York, which makes its presence in Prince George's ramshackle downtown seem an anomaly—and makes it all the more special. The menu offers a selection of antipasti, pasta, meat, and fish dishes, but the real soul of the place is the list of daily specials— perhaps rack of lamb crusted with mustard and goat cheese, or halibut with braised fennel root. A bar and lounge were recently added.

1493 Third Ave. © **250/564-7922.** Reservations recommended. Main courses C$16–C$30 (US$10–US$20); five-course tasting menu C$47 (US$31). AE, DC, MC, V. Mon–Sat 5–10pm.

Kelly O'Bryan's PUB It's hard to imagine a more ambitious pub menu: Weighing in at 16 pages, it's more like a novel, and it comes complete with answers to pertinent questions like what men wear under their kilts (or just ask your be-kilted waiter). This lively spot covers almost every food group, from "pachos"—lattice fried potatoes topped with melted cheese and green onions— to steaks and lobster, to stir-fries and pasta.

1375 Second Ave. © **250/563-8999.** www.kellyobryans.com. Reservations recommended. Main courses C$7–C$35 (US$4.55–US$23). AE, MC, V. Sun–Thurs 11am–11pm; Fri–Sat 11am–midnight.

Royal Bavarian Restaurant BAVARIAN/GERMAN Hearty meals are the rule here: The menu features spaetzle, schnitzels, and specialties like country pike of beef or pork, spit grilled with a spicy sauce. Seafood and meat dishes generally come in creamy white-wine, hollandaise, or mushroom sauces. Strudel or crepes round out your Bavarian experience.

1205 Third Ave. © **250/564-1051.** Main courses C$8–C$22 (US$5–US$14). AE, MC, V. Mon–Sat 11am–9pm. Closed Jan.

6 The Alaska Highway

Constructed as a military freight road during World War II to link Alaska to the Lower 48, the Alaska Highway—also known as the Alcan Highway, and Highway 97 in British Columbia—has become something of a pilgrimage route. The vast majority of people who make the trip are recent retirees, who take their newly purchased RVs and head up north; it's a rite of passage.

Strictly speaking, the Alaska Highway starts at the Mile 1 marker in **Dawson Creek,** on the eastern edge of British Columbia, and travels north and west for 1,390 miles (2,242km) to **Delta Junction,** in Alaska, passing through the Yukon along the way. The **Richardson Highway** (Alaska Route 4) covers the additional 98 miles (158km) from Delta Junction to **Fairbanks.** As recently as 15 years ago, much of the talk of the Alaska Highway had to do with conditions of the road itself, the freak rain and snowstorms, and the far-flung gas pumps. However, for the road's 50th anniversary in 1992, the final stretches of the road were paved.

While the days of tire-eating gravel roads and extra gas cans are largely past, there are several things to consider before setting out. First, this is a very *long* road. Popular wisdom states that if you drive straight out, it takes 3 days between Dawson Creek and Fairbanks. But much of the road is very winding, slow-moving RV traffic is heavy, and considerable portions are under recon-struction every summer. If you try to keep yourself to a 3-day schedule, you'll have a miserable time.

WHAT TO EXPECT

Summer is the only opportunity to repair the road, so construction crews really go to it; depend on lengthy delays and some very rugged detours. Visitor cen-ters along the way get faxes of daily construction schedules and conditions, so stop for updates, or check out **www.themilepost.com/road_report.html**. You can also call (**867/456-7623** for 24-hour highway information.

While availability of gasoline isn't the problem that it once was, there are a couple of things to remember. Gas prices can be substantially higher than in, say, Edmonton or Calgary. Although there's gas at most of the communities that appear on the road map, most close up early in the evening. You'll find 24-hour gas stations and plenty of motel rooms in the towns of Dawson City, Fort St. John, Fort Nelson, Watson Lake, and Whitehorse.

Try to be patient when driving the Alaska Highway. In high season, the entire route, from Edmonton to Fairbanks, is one long caravan of RVs. Many people have their car in tow, a boat on the roof, and several bicycles chained to the spare tire. Thus encumbered, they lumber up the highway; loath (or unable) to pass one another, convoys of RVs stretch on forever, the slowest of the party setting the pace for all.

DRIVING THE ALASKA HIGHWAY

The route begins (or ends) at Dawson Creek, in British Columbia. Depending on where you start from, Dawson Creek is a long 365-mile (590km) drive from Edmonton or a comparatively short 252 miles (406km) from Prince George on Highway 97. Dawson Creek is a natural place to break up the journey, with ample tourist facilities. If you want to call ahead to ensure a room, try the **Trail Inn,** 1748 Alaska Ave. ((**800/663-2749** or 250/782-8595).

From Dawson Creek, the Alaska Highway soon crosses the Peace River and passes through **Fort St. John,** in the heart of British Columbia's far-north ranch country. The highway continues north, parallel to the Rockies. First the ranches thin, and then the forests thin. Moose are often seen from the road.

From Fort St. John to **Fort Nelson,** you'll find gas stations and cafes every 40 to 50 miles (65 to 81km), though lodging options are pretty dubious. At Fort

Nelson, the Alaska Highway turns west and heads into the Rockies; from here, too, graveled **Liard Highway** (B.C. Hwy. 77; Northern Territories Hwy. 7) continues north to Fort Liard and Fort Simpson, the gateway to **Nahanni National Park.** Fort Nelson is thick with motels and gas stations; because it's hours from any other major service center, this is a good place to spend the night. Try the **Travelodge Fort Nelson,** 4711 50th Ave. S. (© **888/515-6375** or 250/774-3911; www.travelodgefortnelson.com).

The road through the Rockies is mostly narrow and winding; you can depend on finding a construction crew working along this stretch. The Rockies are relatively modest mountains in this area, not as rugged or scenic as they are farther south in Jasper National Park. Once over the Continental Divide, the Alaska Highway follows tributaries of the Liard River through **Stone Mountain** and **Muncho Lake** provincial parks. Rustic lodges are scattered along the road. The lovely log **Northern Rockies Lodge** ⚡, at Muncho Lake (© **800/663-5269** or 250/776-3481; www.northern-rockies-lodge.com), offers lodge rooms for C$55 to C$99 (US$36 to US$64), lakeshore chalets for C$150 to C$300 (US$98 to US$195), and campsites for C$17 to C$27 (US$11 to US$18).

At the town of **Liard River,** stop and stretch your legs or go for a soak at **Liard Hot Springs.** The provincial parks department maintains two nice soaking pools in the deep forest; the boardwalk out into the mineral-water marsh is pleasant even if you don't have time for a dip.

As you get closer to **Watson Lake** in the Yukon, you'll notice that mom-and-pop gas stations along the road will advertise that they have cheaper gas than at Watson Lake. Believe them, and fill up: Watson Lake is an unappealing town whose extortionately priced gas is probably its only memorable feature.

The long road between Watson Lake and **Whitehorse** travels through rolling hills and forest to Teslin and Atlin lakes, where the landscape becomes more mountainous and the gray clouds of the Gulf of Alaska's weather systems hang menacingly on the horizon. Whitehorse is the largest town along the route of the Alaska Highway, and unless you're in a great hurry, plan to spend at least a day here. The **Westmark Whitehorse,** 201 Wood St. (© **800/544-0970** or 867/668-4700; www.westmarkhotels.com), is one of the city's best lodgings, with doubles for C$125 (US$81).

Hope for good weather as you leave Whitehorse, since the trip past **Kluane National Park** is one the most beautiful parts of the entire route. The two highest peaks of Canada straddle the horizon, and glaciers push down mountain valleys. The road edges by lovely Kluane Lake before passing Beaver Creek and crossing over into Alaska. From the border crossing to Fairbanks, it's another 298 miles (481km).

A number of guidebooks deal exhaustively with the Alaska Highway drive; particularly good is the mile-by-mile classic, the annual *Alaska Milepost* (www.themilepost.com).

10

The Cariboo Country & the Thompson River Valley

South of Prince George along Highway 97 and beyond into British Columbia's interior, the Canadian Wild West hasn't changed much in the past century. This is Cariboo Country, a vast landscape that changes from alpine meadows and thick forests to rolling prairies and arid canyons before it encounters the gigantic glacial peaks of the Coast Mountains. The Cariboo's history is synonymous with the word *gold*.

From Vancouver, the Sea-to-Sky Highway (Hwy. 99) passes through Whistler and the Cayoosh Valley, eventually descending into the town of Lillooet, which was Mile 0 of the Old Cariboo Highway during the gold-rush days of the 1860s. Prospectors and settlers made their way north up what's now called the Cariboo Gold Rush Trail (Hwys. 99 and 97).

Highway 97 follows the gold-rush trail through 70 Mile House, 100 Mile House, 108 Mile House, and 150 Mile House. The towns were named after the mile-marking roadhouses patronized by prospectors and settlers headed north to the goldfields.

The gold-rich town of Barkerville sprang up in the 1860s after a British prospector named Billy Barker struck it rich on Williams Creek. Completely restored, the town brings the rough gold-rush days to life. The streets are only 18 feet (5.5m) wide, thanks to a drunken surveyor. Nowadays, you can try your hand at panning for the shiny gold flakes and nuggets that still lie deep within Williams Creek.

Gold isn't the only thing that attracts thousands of visitors to this area. Cross-country skiers and snowmobilers take to the creekside paths in winter; canoeists head a few miles north of Barkerville to a 72-mile (120km) circular route called Bowron Lakes.

From Williams Lake, back-roads enthusiasts can also drive Highway 20 west to the Pacific coastal community of Bella Coola, which in the early days of European exploration was one of the most important First Nations communities on the coast. From Bella Coola, you can catch the Discovery Coast ferry to Port Hardy on the northern tip of Vancouver Island (see chapter 7).

Due east, on the opposite side of Cariboo Country, the Thompson River valley's arid lowlands attract fishers and boaters to the shores of the lower Thompson River and the Shuswap Lakes. Heading north from this dry terrain, you'll reach a majestic 3.2-million-acre (1.3-million-hectare) forested mountain wilderness formed by glaciers and volcanoes—Wells Gray Provincial Park.

1 Cariboo Country Essentials

GETTING THERE

Whether you travel by train or by car, the trip from Whistler to Cariboo Country is a visually exhilarating experience.

BY CAR   The shortest and most scenic route from Vancouver is along Highway 99 past Whistler to Lillooet, continuing to Highway 97 and turning north to 100 Mile House and points north. From Vancouver to Quesnel, it's 360 miles (600km). If you want to bypass the dramatic but slow Highway 99 and head straight up to the central Cariboo district, you can take the Highway 1 expressway east from Vancouver, then jump onto Highway 97 at Merritt.

BY TRAIN   The **BC Rail** (© 800/663-8238 or 604/984-5246; www.bcrail.com) *Cariboo Prospector* departs North Vancouver three times a week. The first part of the route, from Vancouver to Lillooet, is extraordinarily scenic. The train continues north to 100 Mile House, Williams Lake, and Quesnel, and terminates in Prince George. Reserve at least 48 hours in advance.

BY BUS   **Greyhound Canada** (© 800/661-8747; www.greyhound.ca) travels from Vancouver through the Cariboo to Prince George via Highways 1 and 97, passing through 100 Mile House, Williams Lake, and Quesnel. Note that this route does not pass through Lillooet, which has no bus service.

BY PLANE   **Air BC** (© 800/776-3000 in the U.S., 800/663-3721 in B.C., or 250/360-9074) offers daily service between Quesnel and Vancouver. It also offers daily flights between Williams Lake and Vancouver.

VISITOR INFORMATION

Contact the **Cariboo Chilcotin Coast Tourist Association,** 266 Oliver St., Williams Lake (© **800/663-5885** or 250/392-2226; www.cariboocountry.org).

2 Lillooet

84 miles (135km) NE of Whistler

There's nothing subtle about the physical setting of Lillooet (pop. 2,058). To the west, the soaring glaciated peaks of the Coast Mountains are *right there,* filling up half the sky. To the east rise the steep desert walls of the Fountain Range, stained a rusty red and ochre. And cleaving the two mountain ranges is the massive and roaring **Fraser River.** From the Coast Range peaks immediately behind Lillooet to the surging river, it's a drop of nearly 9,000 feet (2,743m), making an incredibly dramatic backdrop.

The entire 1½-hour drive up Highway 99 from Whistler is extravagantly scenic, and it's fair to say that getting to Lillooet is at least as exciting as actually being there. From Whistler, drive north on Highway 99 through Pemberton and Mount Currie. About 4 miles (6.5km) later, you begin your ascent up a number of switchbacks into the spectacular Cayoosh Valley. For 60 miles (100km), this portion of Highway 99 winds through rolling alpine meadows. The scenery then shifts to stark granite walls and cavernous canyons. Suddenly, you'll find yourself in a mountainous antelope-brush desert in the rain shadow of the looming Coast Mountains. Lillooet is nestled in this valley, where the muddy Fraser River is fed by the crystal-clear waters of the Cayoosh Valley creeks.

In town, the **Lillooet Pioneer Museum,** 790 Main St. (© 250/256-4308), is housed in a former Anglican church. It contains an eclectic collection, including Indian artifacts, farming tools, and mining implements. Hours are daily from 9am to 5pm; admission is by donation.

Lillooet was Mile 0 of the 1860s **Cariboo Gold Rush Trail.** In 1858, a trail was established from the Fraser Valley goldfields in the south to the town of Lillooet. At the big bend on Main Street, a cairn marks "Mile 0" of the original Cariboo Wagon Road, cut in 1861 as an access route to the gold-rich creeks of

The Cariboo Country & the Thompson River Valley

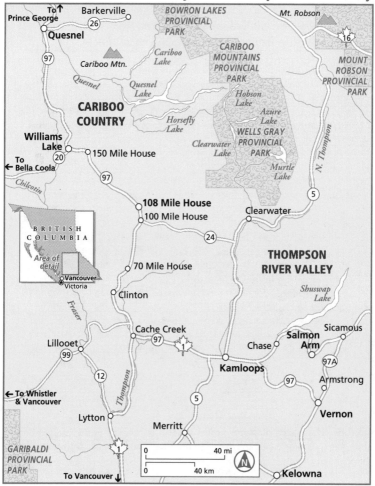

Barkerville. The towns along this road (now Hwy. 97) are named after the roadhouses along the way: 70 Mile House, 100 Mile House, 108 Mile House, and 150 Mile House. Visitors still try their luck here, panning a few shovelfuls of gold along the river's edge.

For information on the region, contact the **Lillooet Visitor Info Centre,** in the Lillooet Pioneer Museum (© **250/256-4308**). It's open from May 24 to October 31, daily from 10am to 6pm.

OUTDOOR PURSUITS

CROSS-COUNTRY SKIING   Miles of cross-country ski trails weave around near Gold Bridge and Bralorne above Lillooet; try the trail that encircles Tyaughton Lake.

FISHING   Anglers hit the surrounding lakes, rivers, and creeks for rainbow and lake trout at places like Tyaughton Lake, Hat Creek, and Turquoise Lake.

Rafting the Fraser & Thompson Rivers: A Side Trip to the Fraser River Canyon

South from Lillooet, Highway 12 edges along the Fraser River valley's precipitous canyon walls. The vistas are astonishing as the raging river trenches its way beneath the horizon-filling peaks of the Coast Range. Although the road is perfectly safe, there are frequent cliff-edge areas that are prone to landslides. In spring, ask in Lillooet about road conditions.

Forty-two miles (67km) from Lillooet, Highway 12 joins Highway 1 at **Lytton,** a small community at the confluence of the Thompson and Fraser rivers. In pre-Contact times, this was one of the most densely populated areas in Native America, as these two mighty rivers each supported vast runs of wild salmon, which provided the primary food source for area Natives.

Nowadays, Lytton is known as a white-water rafting capital. **Hyak Wilderness Adventures** (℃ 800/663-7238; www.hyak.com) offers a day trip that drops through 19 named rapids on the Thompson River for C$105 (US$68), plus a weekend trip that travels 52 miles (83km) and includes a night of camping on an island, meals, gear, and ground transport for C$249 (US$162).

Kumsheen Raft Adventures (℃ 800/663-6667; www.kumsheen.com) offers a number of trips, ranging from the 3-hour "Whitewater Quickie" for C$95 (US$62) to a 2-day adventure on both the Fraser and Thompson rivers. The latter typically includes a night of camping, meals, and ground transport for C$309 (US$201).

GOLF   The **Sheep Pasture Golf Course,** just outside Lillooet (℃ 250/256-4484), is a nine-hole course with a pro shop, clubhouse, driving range, and sheep. That's right, loads of sheep: The course is located on a working sheep ranch that was established in 1858. Tee times are not required.

WHERE TO STAY & DINE

The 26 campsites at **Marble Canyon Provincial Park,** Highway 99, between Lillooet and Highway 97 (℃ 250/851-3000), are open April through November, offering canoeing, fishing, kayaking, and swimming, but minimum facilities (pit toilets, fire pits, and pumped well water). Sites are $12 (US$8). See also the campsites at Tyax Mountain Lake Resort, below.

Don't expect fine dining in Lillooet. You can catch some local color at the **Hotel Victoria Dining Room,** 667 Main St. (℃ 250/256-4112), or get Greek fare at **Dina's Place Restaurant,** 690 Main St. (℃ 250/256-4264).

Tyax Mountain Lake Resort   Just outside the town of Gold Bridge, Tyaughton Lake is the perfect alpine setting for a romantic vacation. On its shores stands this huge log lodge, which offers guests luxurious accommodations and a host of activities, ranging from heli-skiing to barbecues. Fly-out fishing charters, floatplane sightseeing, horseback riding, and cross-country ski trails are available as well.

Tyaughton Lake Rd., Gold Bridge, BC V0K 1P0. ✆ **250/238-2221.** Fax 250/238-2528. www.tyax.com. 34 units, 18 campsites. May and Oct–Dec C$124 (US$81) lodge double; C$258 (US$168) chalet quad. July–Sept C$144 (US$94) lodge double, C$298 (US$194) chalet quad, C$28 (US$18) campsite double. Extra person C$20 (US$13) per night in lodge and chalet; C$9 (US$6) per night at campsite. AE, MC, V. Free parking. Drive 2 hr. (57 miles/92km) from Lillooet on Hwy. 40 to Tyaughton Lake Rd. Pets allowed in chalets and campground. **Amenities:** Restaurant (Pacific Northwest), bar; golf course nearby; tennis court; exercise room; Jacuzzi; sauna; watersports-equipment rentals; bike and canoe rentals; children's programs; tour/activities desk; business center; shopping arcade; coin-op laundry. *In room:* TV, dataport, hair dryer.

3 En Route to 100 Mile House

From Lillooet, Highway 99 heads north along the Fraser River Canyon, affording many dramatic vistas before turning east to its junction with Highway 97. Nineteen miles (30km) north on Highway 97 is **Clinton,** the self-avowed "guest-ranch capital of British Columbia." This is certainly handsome ranch country, with broad cattle- and horse-filled valleys rolling between dry mountain walls.

Hat Creek Ranch   Now a provincial heritage site, Hat Creek House was built in 1861 and served as a stagecoach inn for miners. This open-air museum of frontier life has more than 20 period buildings, including a blacksmith shop, barn, and stable. There's also a good exhibit on the culture of the region's First Nations Shuswap tribe. In summer, concessionaires operate horse-drawn wagon and horseback rides. You can stroll the grounds year-round; however, regular visitor services and guided tours are offered only from mid-May to the end of September.

At junction of Hwys. 99 and 97. ✆ **800/782-0922** or 250/457-9722. Admission C$11 (US$7) adults, C$4.50 (US$2.90) seniors, C$2.50 (US$1.60) children, C$11 (US$7) families. Mid-May to Sept 30 daily 9am–6pm.

WHERE TO STAY

Big Bar Guest Ranch *Kids*   A longtime favorite for horse-focused family vacations, the Big Bar is a comfortable destination with lots of recreational and lodging options. Summer activities include riding and pack trips, or you can canoe, fish, pan for gold, bike, and go for buggy rides. In winter, the ranch remains open for cross-country skiing, snowshoeing, snowmobiling, ice fishing, and dog sledding. The centerpiece of the property is the hand-hewn log Harrison House, built in the early 1900s. In addition to the comfortable, no-fuss lodge rooms and cabins (with fireplaces), there are teepees, a six-bedroom lodge, and campsites.

35 miles (54km) northwest of Clinton off Hwy. 97. Mailing address: P.O. Box 27, Jesmond, BC V0K 1K0. ✆ **250/459-2333.** Fax 250/459-2400. www.bigbarranch.com. 17 units. C$214 (US$139) lodge, including meals; C$149 (US$97) cabin; C$81 (US$53) teepee, including meals. Extra person in lodge C$97 (US$63) adult, C$64 (US$42) child. MC, V. **Amenities:** Restaurant, lounge; Jacuzzi; game room; playground. *In room:* No phone.

Cariboo Lodge Resort   There's been a log lodge on this site for well over a century—the original was built to serve frontier trappers and miners. Times have changed, and so has the Cariboo Lodge. This modern resort hotel, with comfortable rooms and good facilities, makes a perfect base for exploring central British Columbia. The proprietors will organize horseback rides, rafting and mountain-biking tours, and cross-country ski trips. Rooms are large and simply furnished—without the Old West clutter you'd normally expect in such a place.

Box 459, Clinton, BC V0K 1K0. ✆ **877/459-7992** or 250/459-7992. www.cariboolodgebc.com. 23 units. C$80 (US$52) double. MC, V. **Amenities:** Restaurant, pub. *In room:* A/C, TV, fridge, coffeemaker.

Echo Valley Ranch Resort This is as much a western-themed spa as an upscale guest ranch. Both the central Dove Lodge and the Look-out Lodge have sitting rooms with stone fireplaces. Also available are three cabins, one with hot tub. The ranch raises its own beef, chicken, and turkey, and has an organic garden that supplies the excellent restaurant. The full-service spa offers beauty treatments and massage. Activities include riding, fishing, and rafting, plus unusual options like watching falcons being trained and visiting a remote Native village where tribe members net fish in the Fraser River.

31 miles (50km) northeast of Clinton. Mailing address: P.O. Box 16, Jesmond, BC V0K 1K0. ℭ 800/253-8831 or 250/459-2386. www.evranch.com. 15 units. From C$1,680 (US$1,092) per person per week. 3-night minimum stay in high season. Rates include all meals and access to all facilities; horseback riding and guided activities are extra. Packages available. Children must be 13 or older. MC, V. **Amenities:** Restaurant, lounge; indoor pool; Jacuzzi; sauna; spa; exercise room; game room; laundry service. *In room:* TV, dataport, fridge, coffeemaker, hair dryer.

4 100 Mile House & the South Cariboo District

100 Mile House: 109 miles (174km) N of Lillooet, 200 miles (320km) S of Prince George

Named for the roadhouse inn that marked the hundredth mile north of Lillooet in the days of the Cariboo gold rush, 100 Mile House (pop. 1,978) is an attractive ranching community at the heart of a vast recreational paradise. There are thousands of lakes in the valleys that ring the town, making canoeing, fishing, and boating popular activities. In winter, the gently rolling landscape, combined with heavy snowfalls, make 100 Mile House a major cross-country ski destination.

Eight miles (13km) north is 108 Mile House, another frontier-era community now famed for its golf course and **108 Mile House Heritage Site** (ℭ 250/791-5288). This collection of ranch buildings includes an enormous log barn built to stable 200 Clydesdales, the horsepower that drove the stagecoaches.

For information on this region, contact the **South Cariboo Visitor Info Centre,** 422 Hwy. 97 S., 100 Mile House (ℭ 250/395-5353; fax 250/395-4085; www.tourism.100mile.com).

FISHING & WATERSPORTS

100 Mile House is a pleasant enough little town, but it's the outdoor recreation in the surrounding South Cariboo Lakes District that brings most people here. There are dozens of lakes, nearly all with rustic fishing resorts as well as provincial parks offering campgrounds and public boat launches. Be sure to pick up the *Cariboo-Chilcotin Fishing Guide* at the visitor center. For tackle, licenses, and advice, head to **Donex Pharmacy,** 145 Birch St. (ℭ 250/395-4004).

One lake-filled area lies southeast of 100 Mile House along Highway 24, which connects Highway 97 with Highway 5 at Little Fort, on the Thompson River. This scenic drive climbs up along a high plateau between the watersheds of the Fraser and Thompson rivers. The road leads to so many excellent fishing lakes that it's often referred to as the "Fishing Highway."

On Sheridan Lake, the **Loon Bay Resort,** 25 miles (40km) southeast of 100 Mile House (ℭ 250/593-4431; www.loonlakeresort.com), rents tackle, canoes, and motorboats; sells licenses; and maintains cabins (from C$70/US$46) and campsites.

Forty miles (64km) east of 100 Mile House, **Bridge Lake Provincial Park** offers campsites as well as fishing access. The **Nature Hills Resort** (ℭ 250/593-4659) has guided fishing plus boat and tackle rentals. Cabins are C$70 to C$80 (US$46 to US$52).

Perhaps the most beautiful of all these lakes is **Lac des Roches,** 55 miles (88km) east of 100 Mile House. The handsome **Lac Des Roches Resort** (✆ **250/593-4141;** www.lacdesroches.bc.ca) offers boat rentals, campsites (C$16/US$10), and lakeside cabins (from C$79/US$51).

Northeast of 100 Mile House is another lake-filled valley. **Canim Lake** is the most developed, with good swimming beaches. The venerable **Ponderosa Resort** (✆ **250/397-2243;** www.ponderosaresort.com) offers boat rentals, guided fishing, and horseback riding. Cabins are C$85 to C$130 (US$55 to US$85); campsites are around C$20 (US$13). At **Canim Beach Provincial Park,** 28 miles (45km) from 100 Mile House, campsites are C$12 (US$8).

If you're looking for a wilderness canoeing experience, **Moose Valley Provincial Park** preserves a series of small glacial lakes that are linked by short portage trails. The most popular route begins at Marks Lake and links with 11 other lakes, making for a leisurely 2-day loop paddle. For more information, contact **BC Parks,** Cariboo District (✆ **250/398-4414**).

OTHER OUTDOOR PURSUITS

CROSS-COUNTRY SKIING   In February, the town hosts the **Cariboo Marathon,** a 32-mile (50km) race that draws more than 1,000 contestants. There's an extensive public trail system with 125 miles (200km) of groomed trails in the area, with some parts lit at night. Many resorts and guest ranches also have groomed trails. For rentals, try **100 Mile Sport Shop,** 409 Hwy. 97 (✆ **250/395-9812**).

GOLF   The region's finest course is undoubtedly at **108 Ranch Resort,** in 108 Mile House (✆ **800/667-5233** or 250/791-5211). The 18-hole championship course has undulating fairways and fast putting greens. The resort offers a driving range, a pro shop, and lessons.

WHERE TO STAY & DINE

The shipshape **Red Coach Inn,** 170 Hwy. 97 N., 100 Mile House (✆ **800/663-8422** or 250/395-2266), offers rooms from C$79 (US$51), just a short walk from downtown.

Best Western 108 Resort ✆   This upscale hotel, 8 miles (13km) north of 100 Mile House, centers on its fantastic golf course, although even if you're not a duffer, there's a lot to like here. Other activities include horseback riding, mountain biking, and canoeing. In winter, the golf course is transformed into a vast cross-country center. Guest rooms are beautifully furnished, all with balconies. The restaurant serves good Northwest cuisine.

4618 Telqua Dr., Box 2, 108 Mile Ranch, BC V0K 2Z0. ✆ 800/667-5233 or 250/791-5211. Fax 250/791-6537. www.108resort.com. 62 units, 11 campsites. C$130–C$160 (US$85–US$104) double. Extra person C$10 (US$7). Campsites C$20 (US$13) per vehicle with a C$5 (US$3.25) electricity charge. Off-season rates available. Golf, cross-country skiing, and horseback-riding packages available. AE, MC, V. **Amenities:** Restaurant; bar; indoor pool; Jacuzzi; sauna; bike and canoe rentals; stables. *In room:* A/C, TV, dataport, coffeemaker, hair dryer.

Hills Health & Guest Ranch   This spa and guest ranch offers a full complement of beauty treatments as well as activities such as horseback riding, mountain biking, hayrides, downhill skiing on the ranch's own ski area, and cross-country skiing on more than 100 miles (167km) of private trails. The spa has a variety of offerings, including massage, facials, and reflexology. Within the vast spa building are hydrotherapy pools, an aerobics gym, dry saunas, and 15 treatment rooms. The guest rooms feature ranch-style natural pine decor; also available are three-bedroom chalets with kitchens, plus 10 campsites (C$20/ US$13). The restaurant serves a unique blend of cowboy favorites and spa cuisine, specializing in fondue and hot-rock cooking.

Hwy. 97, 108 Mile Ranch, P.O. Box 26, BC V0K 2Z0 ✆ 250/791-5225. Fax 250/791-6384. www.grt-net. com/thehills. 46 units. C$119–C$160 (US$77–US$104) double. All-inclusive packages available. AE, DISC, MC, V. **Amenities:** Two restaurants, lounge; indoor pool; nearby golf course; full-service spa; exercise room; bike and ski rentals; game room; salon; massage. In room: A/C, TV, dataport.

Ramada Limited (Value)   The area's newest lodging, the Ramada has well-furnished accommodations in a variety of configurations—from standard hotel rooms to suites with Jacuzzis and fireplaces to family units with kitchens. All in all, a very good value.

917 Alder Rd. (Hwy. 97), 100 Mile House, BC V0K 2E0. ✆ **877/395-2777** or 250/395-2777. Fax 250/ 395-2037. 36 units. From C$79 (US$51) double. Kitchen C$10 (US$7) extra. Rates include continental breakfast. AE, MC, V. **Amenities:** Jacuzzi; sauna; coin-op laundry. In room: A/C, TV, dataport, coffeemaker.

5 Williams Lake

56 miles (90km) N of 100 Mile House, 337 miles (539km) N of Vancouver

Unabashedly a ranch town, Williams Lake (pop. 11,398) is known across the West for its large, hell's-a-poppin' rodeo, the **Williams Lake Stampede,** held the first weekend of July. It's also the gateway to the Chilcotin, the coastal mountainous area to the west. As the trade center for a large agricultural area, the little lakeside town bustles with activity.

The downtown area is west of the Highway 97 strip, centered on Oliver Street. The **Cariboo Friendship Society Native Arts and Crafts Shop,** 99 S. Third Ave. (✆ **250/398-6831**), sells the work of local Native artists. The building that houses the shop was constructed to resemble a Shuswap pit-house dwelling. The old train depot has been in part converted into **Station House Gallery,** 1 MacKenzie Ave. N. (✆ **250/392-6113**), with local arts and crafts.

The **Museum of the Cariboo Chilcotin,** 113 N. Fourth Ave. (✆ **250/ 392-7404**), contains an exhibit on ranching women, Native arrowheads, and a replica blacksmith shop. Open Tuesday through Saturday from 10am to 4pm, plus Mondays June to August.

For information, contact the **Williams Lake Visitor Centre,** 1148 Broadway S. (✆ **250/392-5025;** wldc@stardate.bc.ca).

OUTDOOR PURSUITS

Red Shreds Bike and Board Shop, 95 S. First Ave. (✆ **250/398-7873**), offers a bounty of information on local hiking, mountain biking, and kayaking; bike and kayak rentals; and a number of specialty trail maps.

FISHING   There are more than 8,000 lakes in the area, and as many streams and rivers. Stop by **Harry's Sporting Supply,** 615 Oliver St. (✆ **250/398-5959**), to find out where the fish are biting.

WHITE-WATER RAFTING   The Chilko-Chilcotin-Fraser river system that runs from the Coast Mountains east is a major rafting destination, though not for the faint of heart or the unguided novice. Inquire at **Red Shreds** (see above) for information and rentals. **Chilko River Expeditions** (✆ **800/967-7238** or 250/398-6711; www.pennywiser.com/chilko) offers a day trip on the Chilcotin for C$93 (US$60).

The Williams Lake Stampede

The Williams Lake Stampede is one of Canada's top rodeos, and is the only British Columbia rodeo on the Canadian Professional Rodeo Association circuit. Begun in the 1920s, the Stampede has grown into a 4-day festival held over the first weekend in July. Rodeo cowboys from across Canada and the western United States gather here to compete for prizes in excess of C$80,000 (US$52,000).

What makes the Stampede so popular is that in addition to the usual rodeo events—barrel racing, bareback and saddle bronco riding, calf roping, bull riding—there are a number of unusual competitions that provide lots of laughs and action. The Ranch Challenge pits real working cowboys from area ranches in a pouch-passing pony express race, a hilarious wild cow–milking contest, and a cattle-penning contest. There are also chariot races with two-horse teams and a chuckwagon race with four-horse teams. In a variation on British sheepdog trials, the Top Dog Competition pits a cowboy and his ranch dog against three unruly cows. The dog puts the cows through a course of barrels, then into a pen; the fastest dog wins.

Other Old West events, like barn dances, a parade, midway rides, and grandstand entertainment, add to the fun. Because the Stampede is very popular, accommodations go fast—make plans well ahead. For information, contact the **Williams Lake Stampede** (© **250/398-8388;** www.imagehouse.com/rodeo). For tickets, call © **800/717-6336.** Reserved seats are C$13 (US$8) for adults, C$8 (US$5) for children and seniors.

WHERE TO STAY

Caesar Inn   If you want a clean, no-fuss place, the Caesar Inn is a good choice. It's right downtown, service is friendly, and the restaurant Giorgio's (see "Where to Dine," below) is one of the best in town.

55 Sixth Ave. S., Williams Lake, BC V2J 1K8. © **800/663-6893** or 250/392-7747. Fax 250/392-4852. 100 units. C$70 (US$46) double. Kitchen C$10 (US$7) extra. Extra person C$4 (US$2.60). Monthly rates available. AE, MC, V. Small pets accepted. **Amenities:** Restaurant, pub; sauna; coin-op laundry. In room: A/C, TV, fridge.

Fraser Inn   The Fraser Inn overlooks Williams Lake from its hillside perch north of town along Highway 97. Large and modern, it offers a level of facilities not usually found in small ranch towns, plus a good restaurant, the Great Cariboo Steak Company (see "Where to Dine," below). Most rooms have great views.

285 Donald Rd., Williams Lake, BC V2G 4K4. © **888/452-6789,** 888/331-8863 in the U.S., or 250/398-7055. Fax 250/398-8269. www.fraserinn.com. 75 units. C$69–C$95 (US$45–US$62) double. Kitchen C$10 (US$7) extra. Extra person C$7–C$10 (US$4.55–US$7). AE, MC, V. Pets accepted. **Amenities:** Restaurant, bar; Jacuzzi; sauna; exercise room; beer-and-wine store. In room: A/C, TV, minibar, coffeemaker.

Sandman Inn   Just 2 blocks from downtown, the Sandman has a newly constructed wing of large one-bedroom suites, plus an older wing with regular motel units. You'll find the place clean, friendly, and close to everything you'll want to do in Williams Lake.

664 Oliver St., Williams Lake, BC V2G 1M6. © **800/726-3626** or 250/392-6557. Fax 250/392-6242. www.sandman.ca. 59 units. C$69–C$85 (US$43–US$55) double. Senior discounts offered. AE, MC, V. Small pets

allowed for C$5 (US$3.25) per day. **Amenities:** Restaurant (a 24-hr. Denny's); indoor pool; sauna; room service from Denny's; coin-op laundry. *In room:* A/C, TV, dataport, coffeemaker.

WHERE TO DINE

Georgio's ⚛ GREEK/STEAKHOUSE   This Greek/Canadian restaurant is
far better than the dingy cafes usually found in motels. As much as possible,
meats and produce are sourced locally from area ranchers and farmers. The main
focus is on steaks, such as the house-specialty garlic tenderloin. Other choices
include Bella Coola salmon with honey lime glaze, plus a complete selection of
well-prepared Greek dishes.

In the Caesar Inn, 55 Sixth Ave. S. ℂ **250/392-7747.** Reservations recommended. Main courses C$8–C$19
(US$5–US$12). AE, MC, V. Daily 7am–10pm.

Great Cariboo Steak Company STEAKHOUSE   This hilltop restaurant is
the town's leading place for steaks and prime rib served in the sizes preferred by
ranchers. It also offers grilled chicken, fish, and pasta dishes. At lunch, the soup-
and-salad bar is a great deal at C$8 (US$5.20).

In the Fraser Inn, 285 Donald Rd. ℂ **250/398-7055.** Reservations recommended. Main courses C$11–C$22
(US$7–US$14). AE, MC, V. Daily 7am–10pm.

6 West on Highway 20 to Bella Coola

285 miles (456km) W of Williams Lake

Highway 20 cuts through a rugged land of lakes and mountains on its way to Bella
Coola, a Native village on a Pacific inlet. This journey takes the adventurous driver
from Williams Lake and the desert canyons of the Fraser River to glaciated peaks
and finally to the shores of a narrow fjord. It's an amazingly scenic trip, but be
ready for lots of gravel roads and steep grades. There aren't a lot of facilities along
the way, so start out with a full tank of gas. You can easily make this trip in a day,
especially in summer, but leave plenty of time to stop and explore.

After climbing up out of the Fraser Canyon, Highway 20 winds along the
Chilcotin Plateau, miles of spacious grasslands that are home to some of the
largest ranches in North America. At Hanceville, the route drops onto the
Chilcotin River, famed for its white-water rafting and kayaking. The **Chilcotin
Hotel,** in Alexis Creek (ℂ **250/394-4214**), is a popular place to stop for a
home-style meal. You can camp right on the river at **Bull Canyon Provincial
Parks,** with 20 sites at C$12 (US$8). The park is 6 miles (10km) west of Alexis
Creek, 79 miles (126km) west of Williams Lake.

Just past Redstone, Highway 20 leaves the Chilcotin River and climbs up the
valley. **Puntzi Lake** is home to a number of old-time fishing resorts. The **Poplar
Grove Resort** (ℂ **800/578-6804** or 250/481-1186) has boat and tackle rentals,
as well as campsites from C$12 (US$8) and cabins from C$45 (US$29).

As Highway 20 presses closer to the Coast Mountains, the landscape is
increasingly dotted with lakes and marshes. At the wee community of **Tatla
Lake,** the pavement ends and the gravel begins. **Anahim Lake,** 205 miles
(328km) west of Williams Lake and the largest settlement on the Chilcotin
Plateau (pop. 522), is noted for its fishing and outdoor recreation. The **Escott
Bay Resort** (ℂ **888/380-8802** or 250/742-3233; www.escottbay.com) has
cabins starting at C$60 (US$39). The general store in Anahim Lake is over a
century old, and its coffeepot is always on. The enormous glaciated peak that
dominates the southern skyline is **Mount Waddington,** which at 13,175 feet
(4,016m) is the highest point in the Coast Mountains.

As you begin the final ascent up to 4,900-foot (1,494m) **Heckman Pass,** note the **Rainbow Range,** 8,000-foot-plus (2,400m-plus) peaks that are brilliantly colored by purple, red, and yellow mineralization.

Nineteen miles (30km) from Anahim Lake, Highway 20 crests Heckman Pass, and then begins **"The Hill."** Bella Coola residents had long dreamed of a road connection to the rest of the province, and a succession of provincial governments promised to build one from the Chilcotin Plateau down to the Pacific. When years went by and nothing happened—civil engineers doubted that a safe road could be made down the steep western face of the Coast Mountains—the locals took matters in their own hands. In 1953, two men in bulldozers set out, one from Heckman Pass, the other from the end of the road at the base of the Coast Mountains. In just 3 months, the two bulldozers kissed blades at the middle of the mountain, and Highway 20 was born. You'll feel your heart in your mouth on a number of occasions as you corkscrew your way down the road. The most notorious portion is 6 miles (10km) of gravel switchbacks, with gradients up to 18%, that drop 4,600 feet (1,402m).

This part of Highway 20 passes through **Tweedsmuir Provincial Park,** British Columbia's second-largest park at 2.5 million acres (1 million hectares). This vast wilderness park of soaring mountains, interlocking lakes, and abundant wildlife is accessible by long-distance hiking trails, floatplane, and canoe. In fact, the Eutsuk Lake–Whitesail Lake circuit provides more than 200 miles (320km) of canoeing waters with just one portage. For information, contact **BC Parks,** 281 First Ave. N., Williams Lake (℃ **250/398-4414**).

The town at the end of the road, **Bella Coola** (pop. 992), is a disorganized little burg in a green glacier-carved valley. Ancestral home to the Bella Coola tribe, Bella Coola once held a Hudson's Bay Company trading fort, then became a fishing center for Norwegian settlers. The waterfront is a busy place in summer, but there's not a lot to do here now.

Besides the lure of the end of the road, the main reason to drive to Bella Coola is to catch the **BC Ferries Discovery Coast** service (see chapter 9, "Northern British Columbia"). This summer-only ferry connects Bella Coola with other even more isolated coastal communities. The ferry terminates at Port Hardy, on Vancouver Island, making this an increasingly popular loop trip. The journey lasts 12 to 13½ hours. In high season, fares are C$102 (US$66) per adult, C$205 (US$133) for a car.

WHERE TO STAY & DINE

There are basic campsites (pump your own water, pit toilets) at **Bailey Bridge Campsite** (℃ **250/982-2342**). See also the Bella Coola Motel, below.

Bella Coola Motel   Located right downtown, this motel occupies the site of the old Hudson's Bay Company trading post on the waterfront. Guest rooms are spacious. RV and tent sites go for C$5 to C$12 (US$3.25 to US$8).

Clayton St., Box 188, Bella Coola, BC V0T 1C0. ℃ **250/799-5323.** Fax 250/799-5323. www.bcadventure. com/bellacoolamotel. 10 units. C$65–C$90 (US$42–US$59) double. Extra person C$10 (US$7). Senior and AAA discounts available. AE, DC, MC, V. Free parking. Pets conditionally accepted with deposit. **Amenities:** Canoe, bike, and scooter rentals; tour/activities desk; shuttle service; laundry service. *In room:* TV, kitchen, fridge, coffeemaker.

Bella Coola Valley Inn   This is the closest lodging to the ferry terminal, with standard motel-style units. Extras include a BC Ferries ticket agency and the popular Smuggler's Cove Restaurant.

MacKenzie St., Box 183, Bella Coola, BC V0T 1C0. (📞 888/799-5316 or 250/799-5316. Fax 250/799-5610. 20 units. C$76–C$95 (US$49–US$62) double. Extra person C$10–C$15 (US$7–US$10). AE, MC, V. **Amenities:** Restaurant, pub; airport and ferry shuttle service. *In room:* TV, fridge, coffeemaker.

7 Quesnel

75 miles (120km) N of Williams Lake, 409 miles (654km) N of Vancouver, 63 miles (101km) S of Prince George

Like most other towns in the Cariboo District, Quesnel (pop. 8,588) was founded during the gold-rush years. Now mostly a logging center, Quesnel serves as gateway to the ghost town of Barkerville and to the canoe paddler's paradise, the Bowron Lakes.

Quesnel is located on a jut of land at the confluence of the Fraser and Quesnel rivers. The small downtown is almost completely surrounded by these rivers. **Ceal Tingley Park,** on the Fraser side, is a pleasant place for a stroll, and it's one of the few spots where you can get right down to the huge and powerful Fraser. Directly across the street is a Hudson's Bay Company trading post built in 1882; it currently houses a restaurant (see Heritage House under "Where to Dine," below).

The main commercial strip is **Reid Street,** a block east of Highway 97. A walk along Reid Street reveals the kinds of old-fashioned shops and services that have been gobbled up by behemoths like Wal-Mart in the United States.

Over on the Quesnel River side of downtown is **LeBourdais Park,** which contains the visitor center and the **Quesnel and District Museum and Archives,** 405 Barlow Ave. (📞 250/992-9580), which tells the story of the gold rush and has good exhibits on the Chinese who worked in the camps. It's open daily May to October; the rest of the year, Monday through Friday afternoons only.

A rodeo, river-raft races, and more than 100 other events attract thousands to Quesnel during the second week of July for **Bill Barker Days** (📞 800/992-4922 in Canada, or 250/992-8716). For general information, contact the **Quesnel Visitor Info Centre,** in Le Bourdais Park, 705 Carson Ave. (📞 800/992-4922 or 250/992-8716; fax 250/992-2181; visitorinfo@cityquesnel.bc.ca), open March through October.

WHERE TO STAY

Ten Mile Lake Provincial Park, 7 miles (11km) north of Quesnel off Highway 97 (📞 250/398-4414), has 141 campsites from C$12 (US$8). Open May through October, the park has flush toilets and showers.

Ramada Limited This well-equipped hotel is in the center of Quesnel, and while that's not promising a lot, it's more interesting than staying at a freeway exit. Next door is the city government and civic center, with a fitness center and skating rink. For the price, rooms are nicely furnished, and there's a pool area for the kids.

383 St. Laurent Ave., Quesnel, BC V2J 2E1. (📞 800/992-1581 or 250/992-5575. Fax 250/995-2254. 46 units. C$55–C$75 (US$36–US$49). Rates include continental breakfast. AE, MC, V. **Amenities:** Indoor pool; Jacuzzi; laundry service. *In room:* A/C, TV, dataport, coffeemaker, hair dryer.

Talisman Inn A well-maintained older motel close to downtown, the Talisman has large, light-filled rooms that overlook a grassy courtyard. Kitchen units and executive suites are available. Some rooms have Jacuzzis, and several are equipped for those with disabilities.

753 Front St., Quesnel, BC V2J 2L2. (📞 800/663-8090 or 250/992-7247. Fax 250/992-3126. www.talisman inn.bc.ca. 87 units. C$63–C$81 (US$41–US$53) double; C$80–C$93 (US$52–US$60) suite; C$105 (US$68) executive suite. Extra person C$5 (US$3.25). Rates include continental breakfast. Corporate and senior rates

available. AE, DC, DISC, MC, V. Free parking. Pets allowed in some units. **Amenities:** Golf course nearby; exercise room; spa; coin-op laundry; laundry service; same-day dry cleaning. *In room:* A/C, TV w/ pay movies, kitchenette, fridge, coffeemaker, iron.

Tower Inn Right downtown, though off the busy main thoroughfare, the Tower Inn offers clean, crisp new guest rooms. Begbie's Bar and Bistro is a popular eatery and hangout.

500 Reid St., Quesnel, BC V2J 2M9. © **800/663-2009** or 250/992-2201. Fax 250/992-5201. 64 units. C$70 (US$45) double. Extra person C$5 (US$3.25). AE, MC, V. **Amenities:** Restaurant, bar. *In room:* A/C, TV/VCR w/ pay movies, hair dryer.

WHERE TO DINE

Heritage House CANADIAN The Heritage House is just that—a historic structure built in 1882 that once housed a Hudson's Bay Company trading post. Although there's plenty of standard Canadian fare on the menu, the restaurant also offers a number of dishes, such as Veal Voyageur and Hudson Bay Stew, that hearken back to Quesnel's frontier past. This is also the place for big, old-fashioned breakfasts.

102 Carson Ave. © **250/992-2700.** Reservations not needed. Main courses C$7–C$15 (US$4.55–US$10). MC, V. Daily 7am–9pm.

Mr. Mike's Steakhouse CANADIAN Mr. Mike's is probably the hippest place in Quesnel, with a cocktail menu that would make a Yaletown club in Vancouver proud. The dining room serves up eclectic fare that focuses on steaks, but includes grilled salmon and boutique burgers. A few Mexican- and Thai-influenced dishes also make their way onto the menu.

450 Reid St. © **250/992-8181.** Reservations recommended. Main courses C$8–C$22 (US$5–US$14). AE, MC, V. Daily 10am–midnight.

8 East to Barkerville 🖈 & Bowron Lakes 🖈

Barkerville: 52 miles (83km) E of Quesnel

Barkerville is one of the premier tourist destinations in interior British Columbia, as well as one of the most intact ghost towns in Canada. However, what lures paddlers and campers to the Cariboo Mountains today isn't a flash of gold, but the splash of water at the Bowron Lakes. These are a chain of six major and a number of smaller interconnecting lakes that attract canoeists and kayakers who paddle and portage around the entire 72-mile (115km) circuit.

Follow the signs in Quesnel to Highway 26 east. The 52-mile (87km) drive to Barkerville takes you deep into the forests of the Cariboo Mountains, where moose and deer are often spotted from the road. The paved highway ends at Barkerville. Bowron Lakes is another 18 miles (30km) northeast on a gravel road.

EXPLORING BARKERVILLE: AN OLD WEST GHOST TOWN

The 1860 Cariboo gold rush was the reason thousands of miners made their way north from the played-out Fraser River gold deposits to Williams Creek, east of Quesnel. **Barkerville** was founded on its shore after Billy Barker discovered one of the region's richest gold deposits in 1862. The town sprang up practically overnight; that year, it was reputedly the largest city west of Chicago and north of San Francisco. Many of the claims continued to produce well into the 1930s, but Barkerville's population moved on, leaving behind an intact ghost town that was designated a historic park in the 1950s.

The original 1869 **Anglican church** and 125 other buildings have been lovingly reconstructed or restored. The **Richland courthouse** stages trials from the
town's past. From May to Labour Day, "townspeople" dress in period costumes.
Visitors can pan for gold, dine in the Chinatown section, or take a stagecoach
ride. In winter, the town becomes a haven for **cross-country skiers.** During the
holidays, Barkerville hosts a special **Victorian Christmas** celebration.

   Barkerville Historic Town (© **250/994-3332;** www.heritage.gov.bc.ca/bark/
bark.htm) is open year-round, daily from dawn to dusk. Two-day admission is
C$8 (US$5) for adults, C$6.25 (US$4.05) for seniors, C$4.75 (US$3.10) for
youths 13 to 17, and C$2.25 (US$1.45) for kids.

WHERE TO STAY & DINE
There are three campgrounds in **Barkerville Provincial Park,** Highway 26
(© **250/398-1414**), open year-round. Sites go for C$12 to C$15 (US$8 to
US$10). **Lowhee Campground** is the best and closest to the park entrance,
with both tent and RV sites, plus showers, flush toilets, pumped well water, and
a sani-station.

The Wells Hotel   Established in 1933, this restored hotel offers amenities that
you'll appreciate after a day of hiking, canoeing, or skiing: fine dining in the
Pooley Street Café, a frothy cappuccino, and a soothing hot tub. The 15 historic
guest rooms are tastefully decorated with antiques; some units have fireplaces.
Another 23 rooms were added in a new wing in 1999; these preserve the flavor
of the older hotel but allow for more space and modern luxuries.

Pooley St. (Box 39), Wells, BC V0K 2R0. © 800/860-2299 in Canada, or 250/994-3427. Fax 250/994-3494.
www.wellshotel.com. 40 units (24 with private bathroom). C$70–C$120 (US$46–US$78) double. Rates
include continental breakfast. AE, MC, V. **Amenities:** Restaurant, espresso shop; pub; Jacuzzi; bike rentals;
massage. *In room:* A/C, TV, dataport, hair dryer.

PADDLING BOWRON LAKES: A CANOEIST'S PARADISE
Eighteen miles (30km) northeast of Barkerville over an unpaved road, there's
access to a circle of lakes that attracts canoeists and kayakers from around the
world. The 304,000-acre (123,120-hectare) **Bowron Lakes Provincial Park** is
a majestic paddler's paradise set against a backdrop of glacial peaks.

   The 7-day circular route is 72 miles (120km) of unbroken wilderness. It
begins at Kibbee Creek and Kibbee Lake, flows into Indianpoint Lake, Isaac
Lake, and the Isaac River, and continues to McCleary, Lanezi, Sandy, and Una
lakes before entering the final stretch: Babcock Lake, Skoi Lake, the Spectacle
Lakes, Swan Lake, and finally Bowron Lake. The long, narrow lakes afford visitors a close look at both shores. You'll catch sight of moose, mountain goats,
beavers, black bears, and grizzly bears. Be prepared to portage for a total of
5 miles (8.5km) between some of the creeks that connect the lakes. The longest
single portage is 1¾ miles (3km). You must pack everything in and out of the
wilderness camps.

   The number of canoes and people allowed to enter the park per day is
restricted in summer. Permit bookings are handled by **Super Natural British
Columbia** (© **800/663-6000** or 250/387-1642). Fees for a full circuit are
C$50 (US$33) per person per one-person canoe/kayak, or C$100 (US$65) per
two-person canoe/kayak. There's a reservation fee of C$19 (US$13). After
September 15, permits can purchased at the **Bowron Lakes Park office,** at the
start of the circuit (© **250/398-4414**). The park does not close in winter, but
there are no rangers in the park after mid-October, so extreme caution must be
used. For information on the park, contact the **District Manager,** Suite 301,

640 Borland St., Williams Lake (© **250/398-4414**; www.env.gov.bc.ca/bcparks/explore/parkpgs/bowron.htm).

You don't have to make the entire journey to enjoy this incredible setting. Open May through October, the **campground** at the park's entrance is a relaxing spot to camp, fish, boat, or simply observe the abundant flora and fauna.

WHERE TO STAY

Bowron Lake Lodge & Resorts   This rustic resort provides all the creature comforts you could ask for in a wilderness setting. Guests can choose from comfortable lodge rooms, cabins, or campsites. There are 3 miles (5km) of trails, 2,000 feet (610m) of private beach, and an airstrip. Views across the lake and onto the forested craggy peaks are extremely dramatic.

Bowron Lake, 672 Walkem St., Quesnel, BC V2J 2J7. © **250/992-2733.** 14 units, 50 campsites. C$60–C$150 (US$39–US$98) double; C$16–C$20 (US$10–US$13) campsite. MC, V. Closed Nov–Apr. **Amenities:** Restaurant, lounge; bike, canoe, and motorboat rentals. *In room:* No phone.

9 The Thompson River Valley

Kamloops: 220 miles (356km) NE of Vancouver, 135 miles (218km) W of Revelstoke

From its juncture with the Fraser River at Lytton, the Thompson River cuts north, then east through an arid countryside grazed by cattle. **Kamloops,** a major trade center for this agricultural region, is increasingly a retirement center for refugees from the gloom of the Pacific coast. In the South Thompson River valley, the **Shuswap Lakes** are popular with houseboaters. It's easy to rent a houseboat in **Salmon Arm** and navigate the 620 miles (1,000km) of waterways, landing at campsites and beaches along the way.

Rising up from the dry terrain of Kamloops, heading north along Highway 5, the road enters the cool forests of the High Country. High above the town of **Clearwater** is the pristine wilderness of **Wells Gray Provincial Park.**

KAMLOOPS

At the confluence of the north and south forks of the Thompson River, Kamloops (pop. 79,566) is the province's fifth-largest city. The forest-products industry is the city's primary economic force, although Kamloops is also a major service center for ranchers and farmers.

ESSENTIALS

GETTING THERE   You can fly into Kamloops on **Air BC** (© **800/247-2262** or 250/376-7222), which operates daily 50-minute flights from Vancouver, and rent a car at the airport from **Budget** (© **250/374-7368**), **Discount** (© **250/372-7170**), or **Hertz** (© **250/376-3022**).

Kamloops is a junction point of many provincial roads, including the Trans-Canada and Coquihalla highways. The fastest route from Vancouver is the Coquihalla (Hwy. 5).

There are eight daily **Greyhound Canada** (© **800/661-8747;** www.greyhound.ca) buses from Vancouver; the fare is C$51 (US$33). **VIA Rail** (© **888/VIA-RAIL;** www.viarail.ca) passes through on the main transnational route. Kamloops is also the overnight stop for the luxury **Rocky Mountaineer Railtour** (© **800/665-7245**).

VISITOR INFORMATION   Contact the **Kamloops Visitor Info Centre,** 1290 W. Trans-Canada Hwy., at exit 368 (© **800/662-1994** or 250/347-3377; www.venturekamloops.com).

EXPLORING THE AREA

Kamloops is a sprawling city in a wide river valley flanked by high desert mountains. A major service center for agricultural industries, Kamloops isn't exactly a tourist town. However, the downtown core centered around **Victoria Street** is a pleasant, tree-lined area. North of downtown along the Thompson is **Riverfront Park,** a lovely expanse of green in an otherwise arid landscape. The sternwheeler *Wanda-Sue* (© **250/374-7447** or 250/374-1505) plies the river waters, providing narrated sightseeing tours.

Kamloops Art Gallery   This is the only public art museum in the Thompson region and the largest in the province's interior, with a collection of more than 1,200 works by Canadian artists. The gallery also mounts changing exhibits of international works.

101-465 Victoria St. © **250/828-3543.** www.galleries.bc.ca/kamloops. Admission C$3 (US$1.95) adult and senior couples, C$2 (US$1.30) seniors and students, C$5 (US$3.25) families; "pay what you can" Thurs 5–9pm. Tues–Sat 10am–5pm (until 9pm Thurs); Sun noon–4pm.

Kamloops Museum & Archives   This museum tells the story of human history in the valley, from the arrival of the Shuswap people through the frontier era and up to World War II, when Kamloops served as a principal ammunition depot for Canada. It preserves a fur trader's cabin, livery stable, and blacksmith shop.

207 Seymour St. © **250/828-3576.** www.city.kamloops.bc.ca/parks/museum.html. Admission by donation. Tues–Sat 9:30am–4:30pm.

Kamloops Wildlife Park *Kids*   This zoological park is home to more than 65 endangered species. Most popular is the grizzly exhibit; you'll also see Siberian tigers, cougars, pygmy owls, and wolves. On the grounds are a miniature railroad, cafe, and playground.

11 miles (17km) east of Kamloops on Hwy. 1. © **250/573-3242.** www.kamloopswildlife.com. Admission C$7 (US$4.55) adults, C$5 (US$3.25) seniors and youths 13–16, C$4 (US$2.60) children 3–12. Daily 8am–4:30pm; check for extended hr. in summer and during holidays.

Secwepemc Museum & Heritage Park ★   The Secwepemc (pronounced *She*-whep-m, anglicized as Shuswap) people have lived along the Thompson River for thousands of years. This heritage park contains an actual archaeological site inhabited 1,200 to 2,400 years ago, plus reconstructions of traditional villages from five different eras. Also featured are song-and-dance performances; displays of native plants and their traditional uses; and a replica of a salmon-netting station.

355 Yellowhead Hwy. © **250/828-9801.** www.secwepemc.org/museum.html. Admission C$6 (US$3.90) adults, C$4 (US$2.60) children 7–17 and seniors. June 1–Labour Day Mon–Fri 8:30am–8pm, Sat–Sun 10am–6pm. Labour Day–May 31 Mon–Fri 8:30am–4:30pm. Summer admission includes performances.

OUTDOOR PURSUITS

FISHING   There are more than 200 lakes within a 2-hour drive of Kamloops. For licenses, equipment, and advice, try **Wilderness Outfitters,** 1304 Battle St. (© **250/372-3311**), an authorized Orvis shop.

GOLF   Aberdeen Hills Golf Links, 1185 Links Way (© **205/828-1149** or 250/828-1143; www.come.to/aberdeenhills), is an 18-hole course with panoramic views. **The Dunes,** 652 Dunes Dr. (© **888/881-4653** or 250/579-3300), is a Graham Cooke–designed 18-hole championship course. **Kamloops Golf & Country Club,** 3125 Tranquille Rd. (© **250/376-8020**), is an

---

Tips **Special Events**

Departing from a different ranch each year, the **Kamloops Cattle Drive** 🐎 (© **800/288-5850** or 250/372-7075; www.cattledrive.bc.ca) has grown immensely popular over the past decade, attracting over 1,000 partici- pants. Cattle, cowboys, and visitors from around the world ride through the High Country's rolling prairies for 5 days in mid-July, finishing with a grand arrival and party in Kamloops. Horses, gear, and even seats on the chuck wagons are available for rent.

18-hole semi-private championship course. **Pineridge Golf Course,** 4725 E. Trans-Canada Hwy. (© **250/573-4333**), is an 18-hole course designed to be "the best short course ever built."

Rivershore Estates and Golf Links 🐎 (© **250/573-4622**) is an award- winning Robert Trent Jones design and has been host to the Canadian National Championships. **Sun Peaks Resort and Golf Course,** 280 Alpine Rd. (© **877/ 828-9989** or 250/578-7222), is a Graham Cooke course adjacent to the ski- resort village at Sun Peaks. Horseback riding, shopping, and six resort hotels are close to the first tee. For family-friendly golf, **McArthur Island Golf Centre** (© **250/553-4211**) offers a nine-hole course, driving range, miniature golf, pro shop, and restaurant.

SKIING   **Sun Peaks Resort** 🐎, Tod Mountain Road, Heffley Creek (© **250/ 578-7232,** or 250/578-7232 for snow report; www.sunpeaksresort.com), is a great powder-skiing and open-run area with a vertical rise of 2,854 feet (870m). The 85 runs are serviced by a high-speed quad, fixed-grip quad, triple chair, double chair, T-bar, and beginner platter. Snowboarders have a choice of two half pipes, one with a super-large boarder-cross. At the bottom of this 3,000- foot (914m) run are handrails, cars, a fun box, hips, quarter pipes, transfers, and fat gaps that were designed by Ecosign Mountain Planners and some of Canada's top amateur riders. Lift tickets are C$49 (US$32) for adults, C$43 (US$28) for children over 12, and C$27 (US$18) for children 12 and under. The resort also offers dog sledding, snowshoeing, and cross-country and snowmobile trails.

WHERE TO STAY

In addition to the following lodgings, most of which are downtown, you'll find a phalanx of easy-in, easy-out motels at Highway 1, exit 368, south and west of the city center.

Best Western Kamloops   New and attractive, this large complex offers lots of facilities and nicely furnished rooms. The lobby is a three-story courtyard filled with tropical plants and an indoor pool. See "Where to Dine," below, for Forsters Restaurant.

1250 Rogers Way, Kamloops, BC V1S 1N5. © 800/665-6674 or 250/828-6660. Fax 250/828-6698. www. kamloops.com/bestwestern. 203 units. C$122–C$159 (US$79–US$103) double. Extra person C$10–C$15 (US$7–US$10). AE, DC, DISC, MC, V. Free parking. Take Hwy. 1, exit 368. **Amenities:** Restaurant, bar; indoor pool; exercise room; Jacuzzi; sauna; business center; room service; laundry service; dry cleaning; beer-and- wine store. *In room:* A/C, TV w/ pay movies, dataport, fridge, coffeemaker, hair dryer, iron.

Coast Canadian Inn 🐎   Right downtown, the Coast Canadian is one of the top hotels in Kamloops, with spacious guest rooms and lots of extras, like com- plimentary passes to a full health club. The Pronto Restaurant is one of the best in the city (see "Where to Dine," below).

339 St. Paul St., Kamloops, BC V2C 2J5. © **800/663-1144** or 250/372-5201. Fax 250/372-9363. www.
coasthotels.com. 94 units. C$112–C$135 (US$72–US$88) double. Extra person C$10 (US$7). Family plan, corporate and off-season rates, and senior discounts available. AE, DC, MC, V. **Amenities:** Restaurant, pub; outdoor pool; exercise room; Jacuzzi; sauna; 24-hr. room service; laundry service; beer-and-wine store. *In room:*
A/C, TV w/ movie channels, dataport, coffeemaker, hair dryer.

Executive Inn Kamloops   Smack-dab in the center of downtown, the Executive Inn (formerly the Stockman's) is the one hotel everyone knows about in
Kamloops, and with good reason: Service is commendable, rooms are good-size,
and you can walk everywhere you need to go. On the property are the Black Jack
Lounge and a casino.

540 Victoria St., Kamloops, BC V2C 2B2. © **888/388-3932** or 250/372-2281. Fax 250/372-1125. www.
executiveinnhotels.com/kamloops/kamloops.html. 150 units. C$99–C$149 (US$64–US$97) double. Extra person C$15 (US$10). Family plan and off-season rates available. AE, DC, DISC, MC, V. Free parking. **Amenities:**
Restaurant, bar, casino; access to health club; exercise room; business center; room service; dry cleaning.
In room: A/C, TV w/ pay movies, dataport, coffeemaker, hair dryer.

Hostelling International–Kamloops   This is one of the grandest hostels in
all of Canada, located in the old 1909 district courthouse. The stone-and-brick
structure has been modernized, but still retains its stained-glass windows and
Gothic arches. The old courtroom is now a sitting room, and the old jail cells
now serve as bathrooms.

7 W. Seymour St., Kamloops, BC V2C 1E4. © **250/828-7991.** Fax 250/828-2442. www.hihostels.bc.ca/main
kamloops.htm. 70 beds. C$16 (US$10) members, C$20 (US$13) nonmembers. Private rooms available. Group
and off-season rates available. MC, V. **Amenities:** Game room; Internet access; laundry; bike and ski storage.
In room: No phone.

Plaza Heritage Hotel ✦   The Plaza began its life as *the* downtown hotel in
Kamloops. A masterful renovation of this 1920s luxury lodging allows it to once
again reclaim that title. There's no mistaking the careful details that preserve the
vintage feel of the decor, but each room has been updated with modern niceties.
Expect quality furniture, luxurious upholstery, and nice touches like old-style
alarm clocks to heighten the period feel.

405 Victoria St., Kamloops, BC V2C 2A9. © **877/977-5292** or 250/377-8075. Fax 250/377-8076. www.plaza
heritagehotel.com. 65 units. From C$119 (US$77) double. Rates include breakfast. AE, MC V. **Amenities:**
Restaurant, coffee shop, pub; beer-and-wine store. *In room:* A/C, TV, dataport, coffeemaker.

Scott's Inn–Downtown *Value*   A standard motel with clean, comfortable
rooms and many extra features, Scott's is located in a quiet residential neighborhood within easy walking distance of downtown. Some units have kitchenettes. Save some money here without taking a cut in quality.

551 11th Ave., Kamloops, BC V2C 3Y1. © **800/665-3343** or 250/372-8221. Fax 250/372-9444. www.
scottsinn.kamloops.com. 51 units. C$60–C$70 (US$39–US$45) double. Kitchen C$10 (US$7) extra. Extra
person C$6–C$10 (US$3.90–US$7). Rates include continental breakfast. Group, senior, corporate, and off-
season discounts available. AE, MC, V. **Amenities:** Restaurant; indoor pool; Jacuzzi; coin-op laundry. *In room:*
A/C, TV w/ pay movies, coffeemaker.

WHERE TO DINE

Chapters Viewpoint Restaurant   INTERNATIONAL/MEXICAN
Perched on a hill above Kamloops, Chapters offers a great view over the city; the
terrace is the place to be for summer drinks. The menu, which features steaks,
prime rib, and classic Continental specialties, also has a marked New Mexican
flavor. A local favorite is the Steak Ranchero, a red-pepper-marinated New York
strip that's grilled and served with a topping of cheese.

In the Howard Johnson Inn & Suites, 610 Columbia St. ✆ **250/374-3224.** Reservations recommended. Main courses C$11–C$24 (US$7–US$16). AE, MC, V. Daily 11:30am–2:30pm and 5–10pm.

Forsters Restaurant CANADIAN   If you don't want to negotiate down-town Kamloops, try this bright and lively restaurant for good food. The house specialty is prime rib in a variety of sizes. There's also a selection of pasta, chicken, and seafood dishes.

In the Best Western Kamloops, 1250 Rogers Way. ✆ **250/372-5312.** Reservations recommended. Main courses C$14–C$24 (US$9–US$16). AE, MC, V. Daily 7–10:30am, 11:30am–2:30pm, and 5–10pm. Take Hwy. 1, exit 368.

Pronto Restaurant CONTINENTAL/SEAFOOD   One of Kamloops's finest restaurants, Pronto is a favorite for special occasions. About half of the menu is devoted to seafood; grilled steelhead trout is dusted with lemon pepper and served with tomato sherry sauce. The meat dishes have a European flavor, ranging from pork schnitzel to rack of lamb with mint and merlot.

In the Coast Canadian Inn, 339 St. Paul St. ✆ **250/372-5201.** Reservations suggested. Main courses C$14–C$33 (US$9–US$21). AE, MC, V. Daily 5–10pm.

Ric's Mediterranean Grill ★★ GRILL   Ric's has done more to revitalize the downtown dining scene than any other restaurant. Out in Kamloops, nobody cares if you mix cuisines, so you'll find a wide-ranging menu—among the lighter fare, selections such as a Thai sirloin steak salad; and from the dinner menu, chutney prawns and scallops, Tequila lime barbecued ribs, or citrus/chili glazed swordfish. Ric's is a handsome place with warm wood furnishings and dramatic black and gold accents.

227 Victoria St. ✆ **250/372-7771.** Main courses C$10–C$30 (US$7–US$20). AE, MC, V. Mon–Fri 11am–10pm; Sat–Sun 4:30–10pm.

THE SHUSWAP LAKES

From Kamloops, the South Thompson River valley extends east to the Shuswap Lakes, a series of waterways that is an extremely popular summer destination for family houseboating parties. With more than 620 miles (1,000km) of shoreline, these long, interconnected lakes provide good fishing, water-skiing, and other boating fun.

The main commercial center for the Shuswap Lakes is **Salmon Arm** (pop. 15,034), 67 miles (108km) east of Kamloops on Highway 1. While the town has plenty of facilities for the traveler, there's not much in the way of sights. The **Salmon Arm Visitor Info Centre,** 751 Marine Park Dr. NE (✆ **250/ 832-2230;** www.sachamber.bc.ca), is open Monday through Friday from 9am to 5pm, plus weekends June through August.

The other sizable commercial center on the lakes is **Sicamous** (pop. 3,088), which has the largest number of houseboat-rental agencies.

OUTDOOR PURSUITS

With a shoreline filled with sandy beaches, coves, and narrow channels, fishing and houseboating are the area's biggest lures.

BOAT RENTALS   Sicamous Creek Marina (✆ **250/836-4611**) rents ski boats, fishing boats, and other power watercraft, as well as kayaks and canoes.

FISHING   To fish here, you need a nonresident freshwater license. Pick up copies of *BC Tidal Waters Sport Fishing Guide* and *BC Sport Fishing Regulations Synopsis for Non-Tidal Waters.* Independent anglers should also get a copy of the *BC Fishing Directory and Atlas.*

Tips   The Salmon Run & Other Special Events

In January, the **Reino Keski-Salmi Loppet** (© 250/832-7740) attracts cross-country skiers from across North America to the Larch Hills Cross-Country Ski Hill in Salmon Arm.

The annual **Salmon Arm Bluegrass Festival** (© 250/832-3258), held in Salmon Arm's R. J. Haney Heritage Park on the first weekend in July, features performers from Canada, the United States, and Europe.

One of nature's most amazing phenomena, the **Adams River Salmon Run**, takes place in late October. Every 4 years, 1.5 to 2 million sockeye salmon struggle upstream to spawn in the Adams River. Trails provide riverside viewing, with trained staff ready to interpret the spectacle. Take the Trans-Canada Highway (Hwy. 1) to Squilax, about 6 miles (10km) east of Chase. Follow the signs north to Roderick Haig-Brown Provincial Park.

GOLF   There are 15 golf courses in the area, making this heaven for golfers. One of the best is the **Salmon Arm Golf Club**, 3641 Hwy. 97B SE (© 250/832-4727; www.salmonarmgolf.com), an 18-hole, par-72 course that's rated among the province's top 20. Rentals and lessons are offered. Greens fees start at C$49 (US$32). Also tops is the **Shuswap Lakes Estate Golf & Country Club**, 2404 Centennial Rd., Sorrento (© 800/661-3955 in Canada, or 250/675-2315), offering an 18-hole, par-71 course with four lakes. Greens fees start at C$52 (US$34). Facilities include a driving range, practice greens, and a pro shop with rentals and lessons.

HIKING   On the northern shore of Shuswap Lake near Squilax, **Shuswap Lake Provincial Park** (© 250/851-3000) offers wonderful strolling, with abundant old-growth ponderosa pines. About a mile (1.6km) offshore, the park's **Copper Island** has a pleasant trail that leads to a high point, where boaters looking for a dry-land hike can survey the lake and surrounding countryside.

WHERE TO STAY & DINE

Many visitors hire a houseboat and cruise the lakes in a leisurely fashion (see "Houseboating on the Shuswap Lakes," below). You'll also find good land-based accommodations, though some of the lower-priced motels see pretty hard use in summer—and it shows. Because most people use the kitchens on their boats, notable restaurants haven't really taken hold here.

The 280 campsites at **Shuswap Lake Provincial Park** (© 250/851-3000), 19 miles (32km) northeast of Highway 1 at Squilax, cost C$19 (US$12). Facilities include hot showers and flush toilets. The 35 sites at **Silver Beach Provincial Park** (© 250/851-3000), with pit toilets and fire pits, are accessible by unpaved road from Anglemount, by ferry from Sicamous, or by boating to the north end of Seymour Arm. Rates are C$8 (US$5). There are 51 sites at **Herald Provincial Park** (© 250/851-3000), 9 miles (15km) northeast of Highway 1 at Tappen, plus hot showers, pit toilets, a sani-station, and a boat launch. Sites are C$19 (US$12).

Best Western Villager West Motor Inn   This Best Western offers good value and is within easy walking distance of central Salmon Arm and the wharf. The hotel is adjacent to two restaurants, a waterslide complex, and the bus station. Lake tours can be arranged.

61 10th St. SW, Salmon Arm, BC V1E 1E4. ✆ **800/528-1234** or 250/832-9793. Fax 250/832-5595. 78 units. C$70–C$90 (US$46–US$59) double. Kitchen C$7 (US$4.55) extra. Extra person C$7 (US$4.55). Commercial and off-season discounts available. AE, MC, V. **Amenities:** Indoor pool; Jacuzzi. *In room:* A/C, TV, dataport.

Coast Shuswap Lodge   At the very center of Salmon Arm, this new hotel offers the most comfortable accommodations in town, with beautifully furnished guest rooms accompanied by friendly service.

200 Trans-Canada Hwy., Box 1540, Salmon Arm, BC V1E 4N3. ✆ **800/663-1144** or 250/832-7081. Fax 250/832-6753. www.coasthotels.com. 40 units. C$140–C$150 (US$91–US$98) double. Extra person C$10 (US$7). Family plan, corporate and off-season discounts, and senior rates available. AE, MC, V. **Amenities:** Restaurant, lounge; outdoor heated pool; Jacuzzi; beer-and-wine store. *In room:* A/C, TV, dataport, coffeemaker.

Holiday Inn Salmon Arm   This hotel opened in 2001 and promises to be the premier place to stay in the Salmon Arm area. Although it's not on the water, you can certainly see it from here: From this hilltop, the entire valley lies before you. Fireplace, kitchen, and Jacuzzi suites are available.

2090 22nd St. NE, Salmon Arm, BC V1E 1E4. ✆ **250/832-7711.** 116 units. C$99–C$119 (US$64–US$77). AE, MC, V. **Amenities:** Restaurant; indoor pool with waterslide; fitness center; business center. *In room:* A/C, TV, dataport, coffeemaker, hair dryer.

Quaaout Lodge   This handsome resort draws heavily on Native tradition in its decor. Set on the shores of Little Shuswap Lake, it's owned by the Shuswap band of the Secwepemc tribe. In addition to standard rooms, there are six units containing fireplaces and Jacuzzis. The excellent restaurant offers many traditional dishes, including alder-smoked salmon, venison, and fried bannock bread. There's easy access to hiking and biking trails; other activities include fishing, cross-country skiing, and canoeing. Adventurous kids can spend a night in a teepee.

Little Shuswap Lake Rd. (Box 1215), Chase, BC V0E 1M0. ✆ **800/663-4303** or 250/679-3090. Fax 250/679-3039. www.quaaout.com. 72 units. C$119–C$180 (US$77–US$117) double. AE, MC, V. Free parking. Take the Trans-Canada Hwy. (Hwy. 1) through the town of Chase. About 10 miles (16km) east, turn left at the Squilax Bridge underpass. Take the overpass; the lodge is on the first road on the left. **Amenities:** Restaurant; indoor pool; Jacuzzi; sauna; exercise room; limited room service; playground. *In room:* A/C, TV, coffeemaker, hair dryer.

THE UPPER THOMPSON RIVER VALLEY

From Kamloops, the North Thompson River flows north into increasingly rugged terrain. The little town of **Clearwater** is the gateway to **Wells Gray Provincial Park,** increasingly the mountain wilderness park of choice for purist hikers and outdoor adventurers as the nearby Canadian Rockies become increasingly crowded and commercialized.

Although **Greyhound** offers bus service daily between Vancouver and Clearwater, you'll need a car to explore the best areas of the High Country. Clearwater is 62 miles (103km) north of Kamloops on Highway 5.

The **Clearwater–Wells Gray Info Centre,** 425 E. Yellowhead Hwy. 5 (✆ **250/674-2646;** clwcofc@mail.wellsgray.net), is at Highway 5 and Wells Gray Park Road. From October 16 to April 14, it's open Monday through Saturday from 9am to 5pm; April 15 to June 30 and September 1 to October 15, daily from 9am to 6pm; July 1 to August 31, daily from 8am to 8pm.

EXPLORING WELLS GRAY PROVINCIAL PARK

Wells Gray Provincial Park (✆ **604/371-6400;** www.env.gov.bc.ca/bcparks/explore/parkpgs/wells.htm) is British Columbia's third-largest park, encompassing more than 1.3 million acres (526,500 hectares) of mountains, rivers, lakes,

Houseboating on the Shuswap Lakes

The best way to see the lakes is to rent a houseboat; after all, Shuswap is the "Houseboating Capital of Canada." Houseboats come equipped with staterooms, bathrooms, and kitchens. All you need to bring is your bedding and food. Reserve well in advance; by late spring, all boats are usually rented for the high season, from mid-June to Labour Day. Low-season rates are up to half off the prices below. Of the numerous rental operations along the Shuswap Lakes, the following are two of the largest.

Admiral House Boats, Sicamous Creek Marina (RR 1, Site 6, Comp 30), Sicamous (© 250/836-4611; www.shuswap.bc.ca/sunny/admiral.htm), rents houseboats April to October. The Admiral boats, which sleep up to eight, have two private staterooms and 1½ bathrooms; the Super Admirals sleep up to 10, with three bedrooms and 1½ bathrooms. Rentals are available in 3-, 4-, and 7-day increments. In high season, a week on an Admiral houseboat goes for C$2,795 (US$1,817), and a week on a Super Admiral costs C$3,055 (US$1,986).

Twin Anchors Houseboat Vacations (www.twinanchors.com) has two locations, one in Salmon Arm at 750 Marine Park Dr. (© 800/665-7782 or 250/832-2745), and the other in Sicamous at 101 Martin St. (© 800/663-4026 or 250/836-2450). It offers three types of boats, including a Cruisecraft that sleeps 15 and costs C$4,495 (US$2,922). Rentals are available in 3-, 4-, 5-, and 7-day increments.

volcanic formations, glaciers, forests, and alpine meadows. Wildlife abounds, including mule deer, moose, bears, beaver, timber wolves, mink, and golden eagles.

Wells Gray has something to offer everyone: birding and wildlife-viewing, hiking, boating, canoeing, and kayaking. Guide operations offer horseback riding, canoeing, rafting, fishing, and hiking. The history enthusiast can learn about the early homesteaders, trappers, and prospectors, or about the natural forces that produced Wells Gray's many volcanoes, mineral springs, and glaciers.

Most of Wells Gray is remote wilderness that can only be viewed after a vigorous hike or canoe excursion. However, in the southern quarter of the park, a road runs 21 miles (34km) from the park entrance to Clearwater Lake. Called simply the **Corridor,** it provides access to many of the park's features as well as its campgrounds and many of its trail heads.

Twice as tall as Niagara Falls, the park's **Helmcken Falls** is an awesome sight easily reached by paved road. Boating, canoeing, kayaking, and fishing are popular pastimes on **Clearwater, Azure, Mahood,** and **Murtle lakes.** The wilderness campgrounds along these lakes make perfect destinations for overnight canoe or fishing trips.

Multi-day hiking destinations include the area around Ray Farm Homestead, Rays Mineral Spring, and the thickly forested **Murtle River Trail** that leads to **Majerus Falls, Horseshoe Falls,** and **Pyramid Mountain,** a volcanic upgrowth that was shaped when it erupted beneath miles of glacial ice that covered the park millions of years ago.

GUIDED TOURS & EXCURSIONS

Besides excellent accommodations, **Trophy Mountain Buffalo Ranch** and **Helmcken Falls Lodge** (see "Where to Stay," below) offer horseback-riding, canoeing and kayaking, cross-country skiing, and hiking trips.

Wells Gray Guest Ranch, Wells Gray Road (✆ **250/674-2792** or 250/674-2774; www.wellsgrayranch.com), offers packages that include hiking, canoeing, rafting, fishing, biking, and motorboating in summer; and dog sledding, cross-country and downhill skiing, snowshoeing, snowmobiling, and ice fishing in winter.

Interior Whitewater Expeditions (✆ **800/661-7238** in Canada, or 250/674-3727; www.interiorwhitewater.bc.ca) offers half- to 5-day rafting and kayaking trips. Consider a 3-hour white-water screamer on the Clearwater River for C$78 (US$51), or a more leisurely 3-hour float down the North Thompson for C$55 (US$36).

Wells Gray Chalets & Wilderness Adventures (✆ **888/SKI-TREK** or 250/587-6444; www.skihike.com) offers backcountry hut-to-hut hiking and cross-country ski trips. Ian Eakins and Tay Briggs run this family-owned company that maintains three chalets nestled deep in the park. Each sleeps up to 12 and is equipped with a kitchen, bedding, sauna, and propane lighting and heat. It's the best of both worlds: You can experience untrammeled wilderness and great rural hospitality. Two of the nicest people you could hope to have as guides, Ian and Tay are extremely knowledgeable about the wildlife and history of the park. They offer guided or self-catered hiking and cross-country ski packages as well as guided 3- and 6-day canoe trips that are custom-designed for families. Summer hikes are C$125 (US$81) per person per day; winter cross-country ski trips are C$140 (US$91) per person per day.

WHERE TO STAY

Most campers head to Wells Gray Provincial Park's **Spahats, Clearwater,** and **Dawson Falls campgrounds** ⚡ (✆ **250/851-3000**), which offer fire pits, firewood, pumped well water, pit toilets, and boat launches. The 88 sites go for C$12 (US$8) per night; check the sign outside the Clearwater visitor center to make sure the grounds aren't full before driving all the way up to the park.

Dutch Lake Motel and Campground   The nicest lodging in the town of Clearwater itself, the Dutch Lake Motel overlooks its namesake lake in a quiet setting away from the highway. All guest rooms have balconies; some have kitchenettes. Canoe rentals can be arranged.

333 Roy Rd. (RR 2, Box 5116), Clearwater, BC V0E 1N0. ✆ **877/674-3325** or 250/674-3325. Fax 250/674-2916. www.dutchlakemotel.com. 27 units. C$80 (US$52) double. Campsites C$20 (US$13). AE, MC, V. **Amenities:** Restaurant, bar; tennis courts. *In room:* A/C, TV, dataport, fridge, coffeemaker, hair dryer, iron.

Helmcken Falls Lodge   Established in the 1920s as a humble trapper's camp, this venerable property has grown into a handsome complex of buildings that includes a 1940s hand-hewn log lodge. Accommodations are located in four-plex lodges, a chalet building, and the original trapper's log cabin. Helmcken Falls Lodge is noted for its recreational activities; affiliated outfitters offer half- and full-day hikes and canoeing trips through the park and environs.

Wells Gray Park Rd., Box 239, Clearwater, BC V0E 1N0. ✆ **250/674-3657.** Fax 250/674-2971. www.helmcken falls.com. 21 units. C$116–C$143 (US$75–US$93). Rafting and kayaking packages available. AE, MC, V. Located 22 miles (35km) north of Clearwater. **Amenities:** Restaurant. *In room:* No phone.

Nakiska Ranch   Gorgeous log cabins, acres of mowed meadows, and Wells Gray's majestic forests and mountains surround the main lodge on this working ranch. The immaculate interiors are straight out of the pages of *House Beautiful,* featuring open kitchens, hardwood floors, and Scandinavian-style wood furnishings. The two-story cabins are pristine hideaways that can sleep up to six. The lodge has a TV lounge with video library; phones and fax machine are also available. Pack lunches go for C$10 (US$7); you must bring your own groceries for dinners or drive into Clearwater.

Trout Creek Rd. (off Wells Gray Park Rd.), Clearwater, BC V0E 1N0. ⓒ 250/674-3655. Fax 250/674-3387. www.nakiskaranch.bc.ca. 8 units. Summer C$105 (US$68) double; C$115–C$135 (US$75–US$88) cabin. Winter C$80 (US$52) double; C$89–C$95 (US$58–US$62) cabin. Swiss-style breakfast buffet available for C$12 (US$8). MC, V. Drive up Wells Gray Park Rd. for 25 miles (42km); it will take about 40 min. Turn right at the ranch sign onto Trout Creek Rd. The ranch is a 10-min. drive from the park entrance. Small pets accepted. *In room:* Fridge, coffeemaker, hair dryer, no phone.

Trophy Mountain Buffalo Ranch Bed & Breakfast and Campground You can't miss the small buffalo herd grazing in a pasture as you drive up the Wells Gray Park Road. Beyond this pastoral setting stand a log lodge, campsites, and cabins. The lodge rooms are cozy and clean. The cabins, tent sites, and RV sites are extremely well kept. Dishwashing sinks are set up on the deck of the shower house, where hot water flows liberally. Hiking and horseback-riding trails surround the ranch, and guided rides run to the cliffs overlooking the Clearwater River valley and to the base of a secluded waterfall (C$45/US$29 for a 2½-hr. trip). If you get a sudden urge to venture deep into the woods near Trophy Mountain, your hosts can outfit you with rental gear, from canoes to cookware.

RR 1 (P.O. Box 1768), Clearwater, BC V0E 1N0. ⓒ 250/674-3095. Fax 250/674-3131. www.buffaloranch.ca. 4 units, 15 campsites, 4 camping cabins. C$50–C$65 (US$32–US$42) double; C$14–C$17 (US$9–US$11) campsite; C$11 (US$7) cabin. Lodge room rates include full breakfast. MC, V. Drive up Wells Gray Park Rd. for 13 miles (20km); it will take about 20 min. Turn left at the ranch sign. *In room:* No phone.

WHERE TO DINE

The **Clearwater Country Inn,** 449 Yellowhead Hwy. E. (ⓒ **250/674-3121**), has good home-style cooking; it's open from 4am to 9pm. **Helmcken Falls Lodge** (ⓒ **250/674-3657**), described above, and **Wells Gray Guest Ranch,** Wells Gray Road (ⓒ **250/674-2774**), offer buffet-style dinners; reservations are required. The friendly **River Café,** 73 Old N. Thompson Hwy. (ⓒ **250/674-0088**), offers salads, espresso drinks, and fresh-baked snacks.

The Okanagan Valley

Just south of the High Country on Highway 97, the arid Okanagan Valley, with its long chain of crystal-blue lakes, is the ideal destination for fresh-water-sports enthusiasts, golfers, skiers, and wine lovers. Ranches and small towns have flourished here for more than a century; the region's fruit orchards and vineyards will make you feel as if you've been transported to the Spanish countryside. Summer visitors get the pick of the crop—at insider prices—from the many fruit stands that line Highway 97. Be sure to stop for a pint of cherries, home-made jams, and other goodies.

An Okanagan-region chardonnay won gold medals in 1994 at international competitions held in London and Paris. And more than three dozen other wineries produce vintages that are following right on its heels. Despite this coveted honor, the valley has received little international publicity. Most visitors are Canadian, and the valley is not yet a major tour-bus destination. Get here before they do.

Many retirees have chosen the Okanagan Valley as their home for its relatively mild winters and dry, desert-like summers. It's also a favorite destination for younger visitors, drawn by boating, water-skiing, sportfishing, and windsurfing on 80-mile-long (128km) Okanagan Lake. In high season, the valley's population increases five-fold from its winter average of about 35,000.

The town of Kelowna in the central valley is the hub of the province's winemaking industry and the area's largest city.

1 Essentials

GETTING THERE

BY CAR   The 242-mile (387km) drive from Vancouver via the Trans-Canada Highway (Hwy. 1) and Highway 3 rambles through rich delta farmlands and the forested mountains of Manning Provincial Park and the Similkameen River region before descending into the Okanagan Valley's antelope-brush and sage-brush desert. For a more direct route to Kelowna, take the Trans-Canada Highway to the Coquihalla Toll Highway, which eliminates more than an hour's driving time. The 126-mile (203km) route runs from Hope through Merritt over the Coquihalla Pass into Kamloops.

BY BUS   Greyhound Canada (© 800/661-8747; www.greyhound.ca) runs daily buses from Vancouver to Penticton and Kelowna, with service continuing on to Banff and Calgary. The one-way fare to Penticton is C$54 (US$35).

BY PLANE   Air Canada, through its affiliate **Air BC** (© 800/667-3721), offers frequent daily commuter flights from Calgary and Vancouver to Penticton and Kelowna.

VISITOR INFORMATION

Contact the **Okanagan Similkameen Tourism Association,** 1332 Water St., Kelowna (© **800/860-5999** or 250/860-5999; info@thompsonokanagan.com), open daily from 9am to 6pm.

2 Touring the Wineries

British Columbia has a long history of producing wines, ranging from mediocre to truly bad. In 1859, missionary Father Pandosy planted apple trees and vineyards and produced sacramental wines for the valley's mission. Other monastery wineries cropped up, but none worried about the quality of their bottlings. After all, the Canadian government had a reputation for subsidizing domestic industries, such as book publishing and cleric wineries, to promote entrepreneurial growth.

In the 1980s, the government threatened to pull its support of the industry unless it could produce an internationally competitive product. The vintners listened. Rootstock was imported from France and Germany, and European-trained master vintners were hired to oversee the development of the vines and the winemaking process. The climate and soil conditions turned out to be some of the best in the world for winemaking, and today, British Columbia wines are winning international gold medals. Competitively priced, in the C$7-to-C$50 (US$4.55-to-US$33) range, they represent some great bargains in well-balanced chardonnays, pinot blancs, and Gewürztraminers; full-bodied merlots, pinot noirs, and cabernets; and dessert ice wines that surpass the best muscat d'or.

The valley's more than three dozen vineyards and wineries conduct free tours and tastings throughout the year. The **Okanagan Wine Festival** (© **250/ 861-6654;** www.owfs.com), an annual celebration of wine and food, is held at area vineyards and restaurants. Contact local visitor centers for information. We recommend specific wineries in the following sections on Oliver, Penticton, and Kelowna.

3 Oliver

32 miles (52km) S of Penticton

The absolute center of the Okanagan fruit-growing orchards is Oliver (pop. 4,285). What makes the area interesting to travelers, however, is its many wineries. Scarcely a tourist town, Oliver exists to serve the needs of local farmers, orchardists, and winemakers. It makes a reasonable stop if you're not obsessed with the resort and watersports lifestyle prevalent in the rest of the Okanagan Valley.

Many of the long-established wineries that put the region's name on the wine-producing map are within a short drive of Oliver. Especially proud of their location are the wineries along the "Golden Mile," situated on the slopes of the mountains west of Oliver along Road 8. **Festival of the Grape** (© **250/ 498-6321;** www.oliverchamber.bc.ca) occurs on the first weekend of October, and is part of the larger Okanagan Wine Festival.

Notable wineries that welcome visitors include **Domaine Combret Estate Winery,** on Road 13 (© **866/837-7647;** www.combretwine.com), which has won medals at the annual Chardonnay du Monde competition in Burgundy.

Gehringer Brothers Estate Winery, Road 8 (© **250/498-3537**), offers German-style wines, including Riesling, pinot gris, pinot noir, and pinot blanc. Try the crisp Ehrenfelser white wine, which carries intense flavors of apricot and almond. The tasting room is open June through October daily.

Hester Creek Estate Winery, Road 8 (℗ 250/498-4435; www.hestercreek. com), has a boutique that's open daily, plus tours by appointment. Especially nice is the patio, an inviting spot for picnickers. Superior growing conditions found at Hester Creek produce intense fruit flavors.

Inniskillin Okanagan, Road 11 (℗ 250/498-6663), offers daily tours and tastings. This winery produces a distinct selection of red wines such as cabernet sauvignon, merlot, and pinot noir.

Tinhorn Creek Vineyards, Road 7 (℗ 888/846-4676; www.tinhorn.com), is one of the top Okanagan wineries. Self-guided tours allow you to linger; guided tours can be arranged by appointment. Specialties include Gewürztraminer, pinot gris, chardonnay, pinot noir, cabernet franc, merlot, and ice wine.

Adjacent to a wilderness area and bird sanctuary overlooking Vaseaux Lake, Blue Mountain Vineyards & Cellars, Allendale Road (℗ 250/497-8244; www.bluemountainwinery.com), has tours and tastings by appointment only. Due to its small output, Blue Mountain wines are available only from the winery and at fine restaurants.

The nicest place to stay in Oliver is the Southwind Inn, 34017 Hwy. 97 S. (℗ 800/661-9922 or 250/498-3442; www.winecountry.com), with doubles for C$75 to C$96 (US$49 to US$62). Amenities include a fine restaurant with patio, pub, and outdoor pool.

For more information on the region, contact the Oliver Visitor Info Centre, 36205 93rd St. (℗ 250/498-6321; fax 250/498-3156; www.oliverchamber. bc.ca).

4 Penticton

50 miles (80km) N of Oliver, 37 miles (60km) S of Kelowna, 245 miles (396km) W of Vancouver via the Coquihalla Hwy.

One of the belles of the Okanagan, Penticton (pop. 32,219) is a lovely midsize city with two entirely different lakefronts. Above the town is the toe-end of vast Okanagan Lake, to the south is Lake Skaha. It's a lovely setting, and a peach of a place for a recreation-dominated holiday. "Peach" has additional significance here, as Penticton is also the center for apple, peach, cherry, and grape production. But there's a lot more to Penticton than agriculture: Facilities range from hostels to world-class resorts, and the restaurants are among the best in this part of British Columbia.

The Penticton Visitor Info Centre is at 888 Westminster Ave. W. (℗ 800/ 663-5052 or 250/493-4055; www.penticton.org). It also houses the British Columbia Wine Information Centre and a good wine shop with all sorts of local vintages.

EXPLORING THE TOWN

It's hard to beat Penticton's location. With Okanagan Lake lapping at the northern edge of town, Lake Skaha's beaches forming the town's southern boundary, and the Okanagan River cutting between the two, Penticton has the feel of a real oasis. Hemmed in by lakes and desert valley walls, Penticton is pleasantly compact and in summer fairly hums with activity. As elsewhere in the Okanagan Valley, watersports are the main preoccupation, but Penticton also has an air of gentility that suggests there's a little more going on than just jet-skiing.

The old commercial center is along Main Street toward the north end of town; there's also a lot of activity along Lakeshore Drive, the boulevard that parallels the beachfront of Okanagan Lake. Lined with hotels and restaurants on

---

> ⌒ *Tips* **Special Events**
>
> The town's big summer celebration is the **Penticton Peach Festival,** held
> the first week of August. It includes parades, watersports competitions,
> live entertainment, street dances, midway rides, and a general and perva-
> sive air of fun. Be the first to taste the valley's best chardonnay, pinot noir,
> merlot, and ice wine at the **Okanagan Wine Festival (© 250/861-6654),**
> held the first and second weeks in October at Penticton wineries and
> restaurants.

---

one side, clogged with sun worshippers on the other, Lakeshore Drive is a very
busy place in summer.

Right on the lakefront is the **SS *Sicamous,*** a sternwheeler that plied the waters
of Okanagan Lake from 1914 to 1935. There are plans to restore it as an operating tour boat, but meanwhile, it's beached in the sand, and currently houses a
scale model of the Kettle Valley Railway. It's open in summer, daily from 9am to
9pm; the rest of the year, Monday through Friday from 9am to 4pm.

Even if you're not into sunbathing, a saunter along the **beachfront promenade** is called for. Beach volleyball, sand castles, and a drinks kiosk in the shape
of a giant peach are just the beginning of what you'll encounter along this long,
broad strand: It's prime people-watching territory.

At the eastern end of the beachfront is the **Art Gallery of the South Okanagan,** 199 Front St. (© **250/493-2928**), a showcase for local artists. The gift shop
is a good spot to pick up a souvenir. Just beyond the gallery is the **Marina on Lake
Okanagan** (© **250/770-2000**), where you can rent all manner of watercraft.

The beach along Skaha Lake is usually more laid-back than the Okanagan
Lake front. The relatively more secluded nature of this beach, plus a large water
park for the kids, makes it a good destination for families. **Skaha Lake Marina**
(© **250/492-7368**) is at the east edge of the beach.

TOURING THE WINERIES

The two main wine-producing areas near Penticton are north along the east
slopes of Okanagan Lake near the community of Naramata, and north along the
west lake slopes near Summerland. From Penticton, follow Upper Bench Road,
which turns into Naramata Road and leads to **Naramata,** 9 miles (14km) north
and one of the first wine-growing regions in British Columbia.

Lang Vineyard, 2493 Gammon Rd. (© **250/496-5987**), was one of the first
small wineries in the province. It's open for tastings and sales daily from May to
October 15.

Hillside Estate, 1350 Naramata Rd. (© **250/493-6274;** www.hillsideestate.
com), is open daily (call ahead in midwinter). From Easter weekend until the
Okanagan Wine Festival, it operates a patio restaurant at the winery.

Lake Breeze Vineyards, 930 Sammet Rd. (© **250/496-5659;** lakebreeze@
telus.net), opens its tasting room from May 1 to October 15, daily from 10am
to 5pm. Its restaurant is open for lunch from May 1 to September 30.

North of Penticton along Highway 97 is another wine-producing area.
Sumac Ridge Estate Winery, 17403 Hwy. 97 (© **250/494-0451;** www.sumac
ridge.com), offers tours daily from May to mid-October. Besides operating a
shop and tasting room, the winery runs the fine Cellar Door Bistro (see "Where
to Dine," below).

Located 26 miles (43km) north of Penticton is the **Hainle Vineyards Estate Winery,** 5355 Trepanier Bench Rd. (📞 250/767-2525; www.hainle.com). Hainle was the first Okanagan winery to produce ice wine. The shop is open May through October, Tuesday through Sunday. November through April, it's open for tastings Thursday through Sunday. The bistro Amphora is open Tuesday through Sunday.

THE KETTLE VALLEY STEAM RAILWAY

The Kettle Valley Railway was completed in 1914 to link coastal communities to the burgeoning mining camps in Kettle River valley, one valley east of the Okanagan Valley. Laying rails through this extreme landscape was quite a feat, as the grade climbed from sea level to 4,000 feet (1,219m) and crossed 18 trestle bridges. Many portions of this highly scenic railway have been converted into rails-to-trails pathways for hikers and mountain bikers, but one section remains in use by original steam trains.

The **Kettle Valley Railway Society,** 18404 Bathville Rd., Summerland (📞 877/494-8424 in B.C., or 250/494-8422; www.kettlevalleyrail.org), offers a 2-hour journey on a 6-mile (10km) section of the original track west of Summerland, 10 miles (16km) north of Penticton. From July 1 to Labour Day, the train runs Thursday through Monday at 10:30am and 1:30pm, departing from the Prairie Valley Station off Bathville Road; from late May to June and from Labour Day to mid-October, the train runs at the same times Saturday through Monday only. Fares are C$14 (US$9) for adults, C$13 (US$8) for seniors and youths, C$10 (US$7) for children 4 to 12, and C$49 (US$32) for families.

OUTDOOR PURSUITS

BIKING   The best Okanagan Valley off-road bike trail is the old **Kettle Valley Railway** ⭐ route. The most scenic and challenging section is from Naramata, north of Penticton along the east side of Okanagan Lake. The rails-to-trails route climbs up steep switchbacks to Chute Lake and then across 17 trestles as it traverses Myra Canyon. The entire mountain-bike route from Naramata to Westbridge in the Kettle River valley is 108 miles (175km) and can take from 3 to 5 days. For information, contact the visitor center (📞 250/493-4055) or check out **www.kettlevalleytrail.com**. Rentals and friendly advice are available at **Sun Country Cycle,** 533 Main St. (📞 250/493-0686).

BOATING & WATERSPORTS   **Okanagan Boat Charters,** 291 Front St. (📞 250/492-5099), rents houseboats that can accommodate up to 10, from C$1,295 (US$842) for 1 week. The **Marina on Okanagan Lake,** 291 Front St. (📞 250/492-2628), rents ski boats, fishing boats, and tackle. If you have a hankering to parasail, contact **Okanagan Parasailing,** on Okanagan Lake just west of the art museum (📞 250/492-2242).

A popular activity is renting a rubber raft from **Coyote Cruises,** in the blue building along the river at Riverside Drive (📞 205/492-2115), then floating from Okanagan Lake down to Skaha Lake, which takes about 2 hours. On a hot day, you'll be joined by hundreds of other people in rafts, inner tubes, and rubber dinghies; the water fight of your life is almost guaranteed.

GOLF   **Penticton Golf & Country Club** (📞 250/492-8727) is an 18-hole, par-70 course just west of downtown on the Okanagan River, with rentals, a driving range, and a clubhouse. Greens fees are C$35 to C$45 (US$23 to US$29). **Twin Lakes Golf Resort,** 11 miles (18km) south of Penticton off Highway 97 (📞 250/497-5359), is an 18-hole course located in a steep-walled canyon; greens fees start at C$37 (US$24).

SKIING Intermediate and expert downhill skiers frequent the **Apex Resort,** Green Mountain Road ((C) **800/387-2739,** 250/492-2880, or 250/492-2929 for snow report), where 56 runs are serviced by a quad chair, a triple chair, a T-bar, and a beginner tow/platter. The 31 miles (52km) of cross-country ski trails are well marked and groomed. Facilities include an ice rink, snow golf, and sleigh rides.

WHERE TO STAY

There are three major lodging areas: the northern lakefront on Okanagan Lake, the southern lakefront on Lake Skaha, and the Main Street strip that connects the two. Penticton has a lot of older motels, many of which have seen years of hard use.

Bear's Den B&B This B&B is 10 minutes south of Penticton in the small village of Kaleden. Perched high above Skaha Lake, views from the patio and balconies are expansive, from the orchards to the glittering lake and mountain slopes beyond. There are four guest rooms, each with whimsical decor. The Bear's Den is a master suite with canopy bed, soaker tub, and that million-dollar view. The teddy-bear theme might not be to everyone's taste, but there's no denying the first-rate quality of the rooms, the gracious welcome, and the wonderful breakfast.

189 Linden Ave., P.O. Box 172, Kaleden, BC V0H 1K0. (C) **866/232-7722** or 250/497-6721. Fax 250/497-6453. www.bearsdenbb.com. 4 units. C$100–C$135 (US$65–US$88) double. Rates include full breakfast. AE, DC, MC, V. Pets accepted for C$10 (US$7) per day. **Amenities:** Nearby golf course; assistance arranging tours and activities; laundry service. *In room:* A/C, TV/VCR, fridge, hair dryer, iron, no phone.

Bel Air Motel This older motor-court motel is just the ticket if you don't want to spend a fortune. Guest rooms are large and stylish, and the balconies decked with flowers. You'll need to drive to get to the beaches, but otherwise it's a good, inexpensive choice, near both restaurants and shopping.

2670 Skaha Lake Rd., Penticton, BC V2A 6G1. (C) **800/766-5770** or 250/492-6111. Fax 250/492-8035. www. belairmotel.bc.ca. 42 units. High season C$69 (US$45) double. Kitchen C$16 (US$10) extra. AE, MC, V. **Amenities:** Outdoor heated pool; Jacuzzi; sauna; playground; coin-op laundry. *In room:* A/C, TV, dataport, coffeemaker.

Best Western Inn at Penticton Roughly midway between the two lake beaches, this Best Western is a short drive from the beach scene, but it's a hand-some hotel with well-furnished rooms and especially nice facilities, such as the beautifully landscaped courtyard and banks of flowers everywhere.

3180 Skaha Lake Rd., Penticton, BC V2A 6G4. (C) **800/668-6746** or 250/493-0311. Fax 250/493-5556. www. bestwestern.bc.ca. 67 units. High season C$109–C$119 (US$71–US$77) double. Kitchen C$20 (US$13) extra. AE, DISC, MC, V. **Amenities:** Restaurant; indoor and outdoor pools with waterslide; Jacuzzi; playground. *In room:* A/C, TV, dataport, fridge, coffeemaker.

Hostelling International–Penticton Right in the heart of downtown, this hostel is in a historic home once owned by a pioneer banker. Private rooms are available.

464 Ellis St., Penticton, BC V2A 4M2. (C) **250/492-3992.** Fax 250/492-8755. www.hihostels.bc.ca. 50 beds. High season C$16–C$20 (US$10–US$13) dorm bed; C$36–C$40 (US$23–US$26) private unit. MC, V. **Amenities:** Kitchen; bike rentals; tour desk; Internet access; coin-op laundry.

Penticton Lakeside Resort Convention Centre & Casino Set on the water's edge, the Penticton Lakeside Resort has its own stretch of sandy Okanagan Lake beachfront. All rooms are smartly outfitted with quality furniture and bal-conies; deluxe suites feature Jacuzzis, and lakeside units are highly recommended for their view. The restaurant menu features locally grown ingredients.

21 W. Lakeshore Dr., Penticton, BC V2A 7M5. ℂ **800/663-9400** or 250/493-8221. Fax 250/493-0607. www. rpbhotels.com. 204 units. C$155 (US$101) double; C$159–C$205 (US$103–US$133) suite. AE, DC, DISC, MC, V. Free parking. In town, follow signs to Main St.; Lakeshore Dr. is at the north end of Main St. Pets accepted for C$20 (US$13). **Amenities:** Restaurant, lounge, casino; indoor pool; tennis courts; extensive health club; Jacuzzi; sauna; watersports-equipment rentals; volleyball; children's center; concierge; tour desk; business center; 24-hr. room service; babysitting; same-day dry cleaning. *In room:* A/C, TV/VCR w/ pay movies, dataport, coffeemaker, hair dryer, iron.

Spanish Villa Resort   Of the many motels that line Lakeshore Drive, the Spanish Villa, directly across the street from the Okanagan Lake beaches, is the most attractive and best maintained. Rooms are furnished with a Mediterranean flair; the most expensive units boast great views. The Villa is close to dozens of restaurants and shops, right in the thick of things.

890 Lakeshore Dr., Penticton, BC V2A 1C1. ℂ **800/552-9199** or 250/492-2922. Fax 250/492-2922. www. spanishvillaresort.com. 60 units. High season C$98–C$128 (US$64–US$83) double. Kitchen C$20 (US$13) extra. AE, DISC, MC, V. **Amenities:** Indoor pool; coin-op laundry. *In room:* A/C, TV, dataport, kitchenette, fridge, coffeemaker, hair dryer.

Travelodge Penticton (Value)   A moderately priced motel within walking distance of Okanagan Lake and next door to the convention center, the Travelodge offers clean, unfussy rooms with lots of extras. All in all, one of the best values in Penticton.

950 Westminster Ave., Penticton, BC V2A 1L2. ℂ **800/578-7878** or 250/492-0225. Fax 250/493-8340. www. travelodge.penticton.com. 34 units. C$80–C$95 (US$52–US$62) double. Kitchen C$10 (US$7) extra. AE, MC, V. **Amenities:** Restaurant; outdoor and indoor pools with waterslide; Jacuzzi; sauna; coin-op laundry. *In room:* A/C, TV, fridge, coffeemaker.

Waterfront Inn   This older, standard-issue motel is right across from a park with beach access to Lake Skaha. The rooms are clean and basic, but if you're here for the lakefront action, you'll enjoy the relative quiet of this location and the fact that you won't have to cross four lanes of traffic to get to the water.

3688 Parkview St., Penticton, BC V2A 6H1. ℂ **800/563-6006** or 250/492-8228. Fax 250/492-8228. www. waterfrontinn.net. 21 units. High season C$60–C$95 (US$39–US$62) double. Kitchen C$10 (US$7) extra. AE, MC, V. **Amenities:** Splash pool and playground; coin-op laundry. *In room:* A/C, TV, fridge.

WHERE TO DINE

Cellar Door Bistro ♠ CONTINENTAL   This attractive choice is hidden inside the Sumac Ridge Estate Winery in Summerland, just north of Penticton. The menu, which changes monthly, has a hearty country French finesse, as in the savory mushroom tart, roast duck breast with chanterelle-studded potatoes, and chardonnay-poached salmon. The dishes are paired with wines from Sumac Ridge.

17403 Hwy. 97, Summerland, 10 miles (17km) north of Penticton. ℂ **250/494-3316.** www.cellardoorbistro. com. Reservations recommended. Main courses C$16–C$26 (US$10–US$17). AE, MC, V. Tues–Sat 11:30–2:30pm and 5–9pm.

Granny Bogners CONTINENTAL   Granny Bogners, in a shake-sided heritage home in a quiet residential area, tops the list when it comes to locals' favorite special-occasion restaurant. The menu is slightly old-fashioned: Choices include chicken cordon bleu, filet mignon with béarnaise sauce, grilled salmon, and veal medaillons in port-and-mushroom sauce. Despite the white linen and crystal, the dining room retains a kind of rustic nonchalance. In summer, dine out on the lovely garden patio.

302 W. Eckhardt. ℂ **250/493-2711.** Reservations required. Main courses C$16–C$25 (US$10–US$16). AE, MC, V. Tues–Sun 5:30–9:30pm.

Historic 1912 Restaurant CONTINENTAL   This romantic hideaway is at the end of a long, winding road, in a lakeside stone building that once served as a general store. The decor is Victorian, featuring dark-wood paneling and white linens. The menu offers seafood specialties like lemon vodka prawns, steak and rack of lamb, pasta dishes, and rich desserts. Special four-course, prix-fixe dinners for two feature table-side cooking and carving.

Lakehill Rd., Kaleden. ✆ **250/497-6868.** Reservations recommended. Main courses C$18–C$36 (US$12–US$23). Four-course, prix-fixe dinners C$65–C$125 (US$42–US$81). MC, V. Tues–Sun 5:30–10pm. Drive 10 min. south of Penticton on Hwy. 97; take the second left after the Okanagan Game Farm onto Lakehill Rd.

Jillo's Upstairs WESTERN CANADIAN   Jillo's has a great location right on Lakeshore Drive, across from the Okanagan Lake beachfront. Guests dine in either the casual main room or on the large patio with views. The menu focuses on local meats and fish, cooked up with a minimum of fuss but with plenty of care. Steaks and grilled beef are central, featuring hand-cut tenderloin. Local fish also get respect: The campfire trout is grilled and served with homemade corn relish; grilled salmon is accompanied by local peach salsa. Lighter appetites will enjoy the salads and pastas.

274 W. Lakeshore Dr. ✆ **250/492-3663.** Reservations suggested. Main courses C$10–C$15 (US$7–US$10). AE, MC, V. Daily 11am–2pm and 5–10pm.

Theo's Greek Restaurant GREEK   Don't be surprised if previous visitors to Penticton immediately offer testimonials about Theo's, a popular place with excellent, highly flavored cooking. The taverna-style dining room has whitewashed walls, a stone floor, and lush greenery. The menu features delectable calamari, succulent marinated lamb, and favorites like dolmades and moussaka. Even the requisite local salmon is baked with an oregano-and-garlic crust.

687 Main St. ✆ **250/492-4019.** Reservations recommended. Main courses C$10–C$18 (US$7–US$12). AE, DC, MC, V. Mon–Sat 11am–11pm; Sun 5–11pm.

Villa Rossa Ristorante ITALIAN   Villa Rossa is one of the top Penticton options for more traditional Italian cuisine. It has an especially attractive patio shaded by grapevines, just the spot on a warm evening. The menu is varied, with classic dishes like osso bucco, chicken Marsala, and pasta joining Canadian specialties like steaks and salmon. Good wine list, too.

795 W. Westminster Ave. ✆ **250/490-9595.** www.thevillarosa.com. Reservations suggested. Main courses C$13–C$25 (US$8–US$16). AE, MC, V. Mon–Fri 11:30am–2:30pm; daily 5–10pm.

5 Kelowna

245 miles (395km) E of Vancouver

Kelowna (pop. 93,403) is the largest city in the Okanagan, and one of the fastest-growing areas in Canada. You won't have to spend much time here to understand why: The city sits astride 80-mile-long (128km) Okanagan Lake at the center of a vast fruit-, wine-, and vegetable-growing area, with lots of sun and a resort lifestyle. This is about as close to California as it gets in Canada. Kelowna is especially popular with retirees, who stream here to escape the Pacific pall of Vancouver and the winter cold of Alberta. Predictably, watersports and golf are the main leisure activities, and it's hard to imagine a better outdoor-oriented family-vacation spot.

With plenty of marinas and a beautiful beachfront park that flanks downtown, you'll have no problem finding a place to get wet. In fact, Kelowna's only problem is its popularity. The greater area now has a population of 150,000.

Tips Special Events

Kelowna gets its busy summer festival season off to a bang with the **Knox Mountain Hill Climb** (© 250/861-1990), held for nearly half a century on the second-to-last weekend in May. This motor sport race involves both cars and motorcycles, and is the longest hill-climb race in North America. The **Okanagan Wine Festival** (© 250/861-6654) is celebrated in early October in wineries and restaurants throughout the area.

Traffic is very heavy, especially on the Okanagan Lake Floating Bridge, which simply can't handle its present traffic load.

ESSENTIALS

GETTING THERE   The Kelowna airport is north of the city on Highway 97. **Air BC** (© 800/667-3721 in Canada, or 800/776-3000 in the U.S.) offers regular flights from Calgary and Vancouver, among others. **Horizon Air** (© 800/ 547-9308) offers service from Seattle. **WestJet** (© 800/538-5696; www. westjet.com) operates flights from Vancouver, Victoria, Calgary, and Edmonton.

Greyhound Canada (© 800/661-8747) travels between Vancouver and Kelowna daily. The adult fare is C$56 (US$36). Three buses per day continue on to Calgary. With the completion of the Peachland Connector to the Coquihalla Highway (Hwy. 5) in 1990, high-speed freeways linked Kelowna and the Okanagan to the Vancouver area. The 245-mile (395km) drive from Vancouver takes 4 hours. From Kelowna to Calgary, it's 386 miles (623km) over slower roads.

VISITOR INFORMATION   The **Kelowna Visitor Info Centre** is at 544 Harvey Ave. (© 800/663-4345 or 250/861-1515; www.kelownachamber.org).

GETTING AROUND   The local bus service is operated by **Kelowna Transit System** (© 250/860-8121). A one-zone fare is C$1.75 (US$1.15). For a taxi, call **Checkmate Cabs** (© 250/861-1111).

EXPLORING THE CITY

Kelowna is a big, sprawling place that has engulfed both sides of Okanagan Lake, but the sights of most interest are contained in a relatively small area. And that's good, because traffic in Kelowna can be vexing. Beware of the heavily traveled **Harvey Street** and the **Okanagan Lake Floating Bridge;** on the latter, delays of an hour are not uncommon.

Downtown is a pleasant retail area that retains a number of older buildings that now house shops, galleries, and cafes. The main commercial strip is **Bernard Street.** The showpiece of Kelowna is lovely **City Park,** which flanks downtown and the bridge's east side and has over half a mile of wide sandy beach. At the north edge is a marina where you can rent boats and recreational equipment, or sign up to learn to water-ski and parasail. Here, too, is where you board the **MV *Fintry Queen,*** which offers boat tours of the lake (see below).

Continue north through the busy marina to **Waterfront Park,** with an island band shell and promenades along the lakefront and lagoons. The **Grand Okanagan Lakefront Resort** towers above the park, and it's worth a stop to step inside the opulent lobby, or to enjoy a drink beside the pool.

Kelowna Museum   This ambitious museum touches on the history of life in the Okanagan Valley. Starting out with local fossils, moving on through the

Kelowna

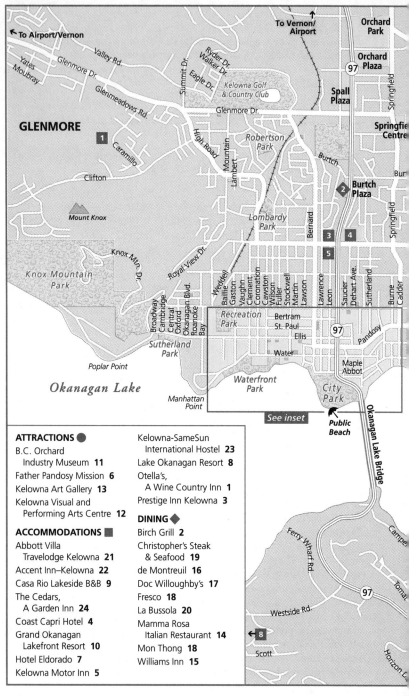

ATTRACTIONS ●

B.C. Orchard
  Industry Museum **11**
Father Pandosy Mission **6**
Kelowna Art Gallery **13**
Kelowna Visual and
  Performing Arts Centre **12**

ACCOMMODATIONS ■

Abbott Villa
  Travelodge Kelowna **21**
Accent Inn–Kelowna **22**
Casa Rio Lakeside B&B **9**
The Cedars,
  A Garden Inn **24**
Coast Capri Hotel **4**
Grand Okanagan
  Lakefront Resort **10**
Hotel Eldorado **7**
Kelowna Motor Inn **5**

Kelowna-SameSun
  International Hostel **23**
Lake Okanagan Resort **8**
Otella's,
  A Wine Country Inn **1**
Prestige Inn Kelowna **3**

DINING ◆

Birch Grill **2**
Christopher's Steak
  & Seafood **19**
de Montreuil **16**
Doc Willoughby's **17**
Fresco **18**
La Bussola **20**
Mamma Rosa
  Italian Restaurant **14**
Mon Thong **18**
Williams Inn **15**

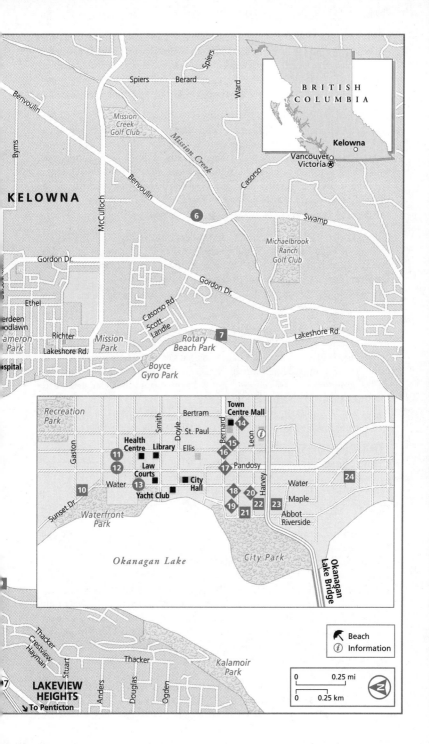

KELOWNA

BRITISH
COLUMBIA

Kelowna

Vancouver
Victoria

Benvoulin

Byms

Spiers
Berard
Spiers
Ward

Mission
Creek
Golf Club

Mission Creek

Benvoulin

McCulloch

Casorso

6

Swamp

Gordon Dr.

Michaelbrook
Ranch
Golf Club

Gordon Dr.

Ethel

Aberdeen
Woodlawn

Richter

Cameron
Park

Lakeshore Rd.

Hospital

Mission
Park

Casorso Rd
Scott
Landle

Rotary
Beach Park

7

Lakeshore Rd.

Boyce
Gyro Park

Recreation
Park

Gaston

Smith

Doyle

Bertram

St. Paul

Town
Centre Mall

14

Bernard

Leon

i

Health
Centre

Library

Ellis

11

Law
Courts

12

13

Water

10

Yacht Club

City
Hall

15

16

Pandosy

17

18

20

22

19

21

23

Harvey

Water

24

Maple

Abbot

Sunset Dr.

Waterfront
Park

Riverside

Okanagan Lake

City Park

Okanagan
Lake Bridge

Thacker

Crestview

Hayman

Stuart

Thacker

Kalamoir
Park

LAKEVIEW
HEIGHTS

Anders

Douglas

Ogden

To Penticton

Beach

ⓘ Information

| 0 | 0.25 mi |
| 0 | 0.25 km |

N

prehistoric culture of the Native Okanagans and on to the lives of the farmers and ranchers, it's all here. Eclectic only begins to describe the collection—radios, dolls, books—but everything is well curated, and you're sure to find something of interest.

470 Queensway Ave. ℂ **250/763-2417.** kmuseum@pacificcoast.net. Admission by donation. Tues–Sat 10am–5pm.

B.C. Orchard Industry Museum This museum, housed in an old apple-packing plant, tells the story of the region's apple-and-soft-fruit industry, with archival photos, equipment, and a hands-on discovery corner. Sharing space with the Orchard Museum is the **Wine Museum** (ℂ **250/868-0441**), with a few exhibits on the relatively brief history of Okanagan wine production. The shop sells a good selection of regional vintages.

1304 Ellis St. ℂ **250/763-0433.** Admission by donation. Tues–Sat 10am–5pm.

Kelowna Art Gallery Kelowna's new gallery hosts nearly 20 shows per year of work by regional, national, and international artists. The permanent collection is a good body of works by primarily British Columbian artists. The shop is a great place for unique handcrafted gifts.

1315 Water St. ℂ **250/762-2226.** www.galleries.bc.ca/kelowna. Admission by donation. Mon–Sat 10am–5pm (Thurs until 9pm); Sun 1–4pm.

Father Pandosy Mission The first non-Native person to settle in the Kelowna area was the oblate Father Pandosy, who established a mission here to convert the Native Okanagans. On the original site now stands a life-size replica of the log mission buildings, which are filled with period household items. Also on the grounds are a collection of horse-drawn wagons and carriages. A free brochure leads you on a self-guided tour.

3685 Benvoulin Rd. (at Casorso Rd.). ℂ **250/860-8369.** Admission C$2 (US$1.30). Easter to mid-Oct daily 9am–dusk. From downtown, take Richter St. south. Take a left on Cedar, then right on Casorso.

TOURING THE WINERIES

Calona Wines, 1125 Richter St., Kelowna (ℂ **250/762-3332;** wineboutique@cascadia.ca), conducts daily tours through western Canada's oldest and largest (since 1932) winery. Many antique winemaking machines are on display, alongside the state-of-the-art equipment the winery now uses.

At **Summerhill Estate Winery,** 4870 Chute Lake Rd., Kelowna (ℂ **800/667-3538** in Canada, or 250/764-8000), the shop and tasting room are open daily year-round.

An experience worth savoring even if you're not an oenophile is the **Quail's Gate Estate,** 3303 Boucherie Rd., Kelowna (ℂ **250/769-4451**), famous for its ice wines. Tours are conducted daily from mid-May to mid-October. The tasting room is in the restored log home of pioneers who arrived in the valley during the 1870s. The Old Vines Patio Restaurant is open for lunch and dinner.

The neighboring town of Westbank is home to **Mission Hill Wines,** 1730 Mission Hill Rd. (ℂ **250/768-7611;** www.missionhhillwinery.com). In July and August, tours are conducted daily; the rest of the year, on Saturday and Sunday only.

North of Kelowna is **Gray Monk Estate Winery,** 1055 Camp Rd., Okanagan Centre (ℂ **800/663-4205** or 250/766-3168; www.graymonk.com). Noted for its pinot noirs, Gray Monk boasts a patio lounge and gives winery tours daily from April 1 to October 31. The tasting room is open daily year-round.

ORGANIZED TOURS & EXCURSIONS

Built in 1948, the paddle-wheeler **MV *Fintry Queen,*** on the dock off Bernard Avenue (📞 **250/763-2780**), was once a working ferry but is now a tour boat and restaurant. Call for details on sailings and special lunch and dinner cruises.

The **Okanagan Valley Wine Train** (📞 **888/674-8725** or 250/712-9888; www.okanaganwinetrain.com) travels from Kelowna to Armstrong in vintage rail cars; a club car pours local vintages. The 6- to 7-hour excursion goes along the eastern shores of Okanagan Lake and then Kalamalka Lake before passing through the bucolic dairy country near Armstrong, where there's an optional buffet-style dinner and entertainment. The schedule and rates are rather complex; call or check the website for details.

If you want to visit the wineries themselves, contact **Okanagan Wine Country Tours** (📞 **866/689-9463** or 250/868-9463; www.okwinetours.com), which offers packages ranging from a 3-hour "Afternoon Delight" for C$35 (US$23) to the "Daytripper" for C$95 (US$62).

OUTDOOR PURSUITS

BIKING   The Kettle Valley Railway's **Myra Canyon** ⚐ route near Kelowna crosses 18 trestle bridges and passes through two tunnels that were carved out of the mountains. It's challenging, but is one of the most scenic mountain-biking routes in British Columbia. Knox Mountain Park (see "Hiking," below) also has mountain-biking trails. Guided tours are organized by **Monashee Adventure Tours Inc.** (📞 **250/762-9253**). For rentals, contact **Sports Rent,** 3000 Pandosy St. (📞 **250/861-5699**).

GOLF   There are more than a dozen courses in the area, and golf is second only to watersports as the region's recreational drawing card. The greens fees throughout the Okanagan Valley range from C$37 to C$105 (US$24 to US$68)—a good value not only for the beautiful locations but also for the quality of service you'll find at each club.

Gallagher's Canyon Golf and Country Club, 4320 McCulloch Rd. (📞 **250/861-4240**), has a Les Furber–designed 18-hole course that features one hole overlooking the precipice of a gaping canyon and another that's perched on the brink of a ravine. It also has a nine-hole course, midlength course, and double-ended learning center. **Harvest Golf Club,** 2725 Klo Rd. (📞 **250/862-3103**), is one of the finest courses in the Okanagan, a championship course in an orchard setting. The **Okanagan Golf Club** ⚐, off Highway 97 near the airport (📞 **800/898-2449** or 250/765-5955), has two 18-hole courses, the Jack Nicklaus–designed Bear Course and the Les Furber–designed Quail Course.

HIKING   The closest trails to Kelowna are in **Knox Mountain Park,** immediately north of the city. From downtown, follow Ellis Street to its terminus, where there's a parking area and trail head. The most popular trail climbs up the cactus-clad mountainside to the summit, from which you'll enjoy magnificent views of the lake and orchards.

SKIING & SNOWBOARDING   British Columbia's second-largest ski area and one of North America's snowboarding capitals, **Big White Ski Resort** ⚐, Parkinson Way, Kelowna (📞 **250/765-3101,** 250/765-SNOW for snow report, or 250/765-8888 for lodge reservations; www.bigwhite.com), is famed for its hip-deep champagne powder snow. The resort spreads over a broad mountain, featuring long, wide runs. Skiers here cruise open bowls and tree-lined glades. There's an annual average of 18 feet (5m) of fluffy powder, so it's no wonder the resort's 102 named runs are so popular. There are three high-speed quad chairs, a fixed-grip quad, a triple quad, a double chair, a T-bar, a beginner tow, and a platter lift. The resort also offers more than 15 miles (25km) of groomed cross-country ski trails, a recreational racing program, and night skiing. Adult lift tickets are C$52 (US$34). Big White is 34 miles (55km) southeast of Kelowna off Highway 33.

Only a 15-minute drive from Westbank, **Crystal Mountain Resorts Ltd.** (© **250/768-5189,** or 250/768-3753 for snow report; www.crystalresort.com) has a range of programs for all types of skiers, specializing in clinics for children, women, and seniors. This friendly, family-oriented resort has 20 runs, 80% of which are intermediate-to-novice grade. They're serviced by a double chair and two T-bars, and are equipped for day and night skiing. There's also a half pipe for snowboarders. Lift tickets start at C$29 (US$19) for adults.

Farther afield is the **Silver Star Mountain Resort** ⚐, 12 miles (20km) northeast of Vernon (© **800/663-4431** or 250/542-0224; www.silverstarmtn.com). It boasts two ski hills with 84 runs and a vertical drop of 2,500 feet (762m). The Vance Creek side offers long, rolling cruisers, and the Putnam Creek side is a little wilder with groomed and ungroomed double-blacks, glades, and bumps. For snowboarders, there's a half pipe and a terrain park. Silver Star has nine lifts, including two high-speed detachable quads. For cross-country skiers, there are 51 miles (85km) of groomed and track-set trails. Day lift tickets are C$40 (US$26) for adults.

WATERSPORTS   The marina just north of City Park has a great many outfitters that can rent you a boat, jet ski, windsurfing board, or paddle boat. If you want to call ahead, try **Dockside Marine Centre** (© **250/765-3995**), which has a wide range of boats and watercraft. To try parasailing, call **Kelowna Parasail Adventures** (© **250/868-4838**), which offers flights at C$55 (US$36).

WHERE TO STAY

Abbott Villa Travelodge Kelowna   For the money, this is one of the best places to stay in Kelowna, as it has one of the best locations downtown—right across from the City Park beaches. You'll be able to walk to the lakefront and to your favorite restaurants. The standard-issue motel units are clean and well maintained.

1627 Abbott St., Kelowna, BC V1Y 1A9. © **800/578-7878** or 250/763-7771. Fax 250/762-2402. www. travelodge.com. 53 units. High season C$119–C$129 (US$77–US$84) double. Kitchen C$10 (US$7) extra. AE, MC, V. **Amenities:** Restaurant; heated outdoor pool; Jacuzzi; sauna. *In room:* A/C, TV, coffeemaker.

Accent Inn–Kelowna   So you're heading into Kelowna on a summer weekend, and even though you're dreaming of a beachfront hotel, you didn't call 6 months ago to secure a room. Every place is absolutely booked. You're going to have to stay in a decent, basic motel, and you just hope it's clean, new, and functional. This is it.

1140 Harvey Ave., Kelowna, BC V1Y 6E7. © **800/663-0298** or 250/862-8888. Fax 250/862-8884. www. accentinns.com. 101 units. High season C$129 (US$84) double. Kitchen C$10 (US$7) extra. MC, V. **Amenities:** Restaurant; outdoor pool; Jacuzzi; sauna; exercise room. *In room:* A/C, TV, coffeemaker.

Casa Rio Lakeside B&B ⚐   This superlative B&B is like your own private resort. It sits right on the waterfront across the bridge from Kelowna, on the west shores of Okanagan Lake. The elegant three-story home rises above tiered gardens, ponds, and fountains, stepping down to 150 feet (46m) of private beachfront. The traditional B&B rooms are spacious and beautifully furnished, or you can rent the entire ground floor of the house as an enormous 1,200-square-foot suite with private entrance, kitchen, huge bathroom, and sitting

area. Guests here end up spending all of their time out on the decks, in the outdoor hot tub, or on the beach.

485 Casa Rio Dr., Kelowna, BC V1Z 3L6. ℭ **800/313-1033** or 250/769-0076. Fax 250/769-4488. www. casario.cjb.net. 3 units. High season C$125–C$160 (US$81–US$104) double. Kitchen C$40 (US$26) extra. MC, V. Call for directions. **Amenities:** Jacuzzi; free use of bikes, paddle boat, laser sailboat, and canoe. *In room:* A/C, TV, fridge, coffeemaker, hair dryer, iron.

The Cedars, A Garden Inn ✸   This English cottage–style home was built in 1906 with an eye for detail. The wainscoting, box beams, native granite fireplaces, and built-in cabinets with stained-glass panels perfectly capture an early-20th-century Canadian dream of elegance. The owners have maintained the spirit of the original home while transforming the bedrooms into a gracious contemporary vision of sumptuous fabrics and antiques. Add to that the house's location, a block from Okanagan Lake beaches in a quiet residential neighborhood, and the thoughtfulness (and culinary talents) of your hosts, and you have a memorable experience ahead of you.

278 Beach Ave., Kelowna, BC V1Y 5R8. ℭ **800/951-0769** or 250/763-1208. Fax 250/763-1109. www. cedarsinnokanagan.com. 3 units. C$125 (US$81) double. 2-night minimum stay on holiday weekends. MC, V. **Amenities:** Small outdoor pool; Jacuzzi; free bikes; laundry service. *In room:* A/C, TV/VCR, dataport, fridge, hair dryer, iron.

Coast Capri Hotel   Somewhat apart from the downtown area, the Coast Capri offers large, well-furnished rooms, most with balconies. You'll need to drive to the beaches from here, and the surrounding blocks are filled with strip malls, but if you can't get into one of the beachfront hotels yet still want high-quality lodgings, then this is your next-best choice. The Vintage Dining Room is a great old-fashioned steakhouse—probably the best place in town for an elegant dinner of prime rib or steak.

1171 Harvey Ave., Kelowna, BC V1Y 6E8. ℭ **800/663-1144** or 250/860-6060. Fax 250/762-3430. www. coasthotels.com. 185 units. High season C$145–C$170 (US$94–US$111) double. AE, MC, V. **Amenities:** Two restaurants, two bars; heated outdoor pool; Jacuzzi; fitness center. *In room:* A/C, TV, dataport.

Grand Okanagan Lakefront Resort & Conference Centre   This elegant, modern lakeshore resort sits on 25 acres (10 hectares) of beach and parkland; its atmosphere is reminiscent of Miami Beach in the 1920s. The atrium lobby has a fountain with a sculpted dolphin as its centerpiece. Guest rooms are regally outfitted with opulent furniture. This is an ideal choice for those who want to feel pampered in sophisticated surroundings while maintaining easy access to the waterfront. Guests can moor their small boats in the resort's private marina. Motorized swans and kid-sized boats offer fun for children in a protected waterway.

1310 Water St., Kelowna, BC V1Y 9P3. ℭ **800/465-4651** or 250/763-4500. Fax 250/763-4565. www.grand okanagan.com. 320 units. C$179–C$279 (US$116–US$181) double; C$290–C$499 (US$189–US$324) suite or condo. Extra person C$15 (US$10). Off-season discounts available. AE, DC, MC, V. On Hwy. 97 from Vancouver direction, cross the Okanagan Lake Bridge. At the first light, turn left onto Abbott St. At the second light, turn onto Water St. **Amenities:** Three restaurants, pub, lounge; indoor/outdoor pool; health club with spa; watersports-equipment rentals; concierge; business center; shopping arcade; salon; 24-hr. room service; laundry service; same-day dry cleaning. *In room:* A/C, TV, dataport, coffeemaker, hair dryer, iron.

Hotel Eldorado   If you like historic inns, this is one of the most charming places to stay in Kelowna. One of the city's oldest hotels (from 1926), the Eldorado was floated down the lake from its original location to its present site, on the water's edge south of downtown. It has been fully restored and is now decorated with a unique mix of antiques. The third-floor rooms with views of the lake are the largest and quietest; some have balconies. The staff can arrange boat moorage, boat rentals, and water-skiing lessons.

500 Cook Rd. (at Lakeshore Rd.), Kelowna, BC V1W 3G9. 📞 250/763-7500. Fax 250/861-4779. www.sunny okanagan.com/el. 20 units. C$139–C$179 (US$90–US$116) double. AE, DC, MC, V. Free parking. From downtown, follow Pandosy Rd. south 1 mile (1.6km); turn right on Cook Rd. **Amenities:** Restaurant, boardwalk cafe, bar; Jacuzzi. *In room:* A/C, TV.

Kelowna Motor Inn   Kelowna has a number of exclusive and wonderful lodging options, but sometimes you just need a good, clean motel room that doesn't overtax the credit card. The Kelowna Motor Inn is centrally located, offers large and simply furnished rooms, and has all the facilities you'll need for a pleasant night or two. Kitchen units are available.

1070 Harvey Ave., Kelowna, BC V1Y 8S4. 📞 800/667-6133 or 250/762-2533. Fax 250/868-3874. www. kminn.bc.ca. 50 units. High season C$75–C$105 (US$49–US$68) double. AE, MC, V. **Amenities:** Indoor pool; Jacuzzi; sauna. *In room:* A/C, TV.

Kelowna-SameSun International Hostel   If you're on a budget, this centrally located hostel-in-an-old-motel is just the ticket. You'll be close to the beach as well as downtown eats and nightlife. Facilities include private rooms, a kitchen, and a common room with TV.

245 Harvey Ave., Kelowna, BC V1Y 6C2. 📞 877/56-CARVE or 250/763-9814. Fax 250/763-9814. www. samesun.com. 67 beds. C$17 (US$11) single. MC, V. **Amenities:** Kitchen; coin-op laundry. *In room:* No phone.

Lake Okanagan Resort   The long, winding road that leads to this secluded hideaway is a sports-car driver's dream come true. And there are many more activities to keep guests occupied once they arrive at this woodsy resort with its country-club atmosphere. Located on 300 acres (122 hectares) of Okanagan Lake's hilly western shore, it offers one-, two-, three- and five-bedroom units, plus all the facilities you'd expect. Because the resort is built on a hillside, every room has a terrific view.

2751 Westside Rd., Kelowna, BC V1Z 3T1. 📞 800/663-3273 or 250/769-3511. Fax 250/769-6665. www. lakeokanagan.com. 108 units. C$189–C$219 (US$123–US$142) 1-bedroom suite; C$379 (US$246) 3-bedroom suite. Off-season discounts and packages available. AE, MC, V. Free parking. Drive 11 miles (18km) up Westside Rd. **Amenities:** Two restaurants, two bars; three outdoor pools; par-3 golf course; tennis courts; health club and spa; Jacuzzis; watersports-equipment rentals; summer children's camp; concierge; business center; salon; laundry service. *In room:* A/C, TV, dataport, kitchen, fridge, coffeemaker, hair dryer, iron.

Otella's, A Wine Country Inn 🏵   Otella's is located in the hills behind Kelowna, in a quiet, upscale neighborhood. The owners knew they didn't want a frilly B&B: Instead, they transformed this modern A-frame into a coolly elegant, sophisticated guesthouse filled with quality furniture, local art, and restrained good taste. The two nicest rooms, which share a small balcony, are on the third floor. The intriguing setting is at the end of a steep cul-de-sac against the desert hillside; the backyard incorporates ledges of rock that form a two-tiered lawn. It's favored by local quail, which stroll down for a peck at the manicured grasses. One of the owners is a professionally trained chef, so expect breakfast to be exemplary.

42 Altura Rd., Kelowna, BC V1V 1B6. 📞 888/858-8596 or 250/763-4922. Fax 250/763-4982. www.otellas. com. 3 units. High season from C$125 (US$81) double. MC, V. Free parking. **Amenities:** Laundry service. *In room:* A/C, TV, hair dryer, iron.

Prestige Inn Kelowna   One of the closest hotels to the City Park beaches, the Prestige Inn is a cornerstone of downtown Kelowna. The rooms went through a major renovation in 1999, and emerged more comfortable than ever. All units have glass-fronted balconies; suites come with canopy beds, robes,

VCRs, and double Jacuzzis. The Blue Gator Bar and Grill is one of Kelowna's premier clubs for live blues and jazz.

1675 Abbott St., Kelowna, BC V1Y 8S3. ℭ 87/PRESTIGE or 250/860-7900. Fax 250/860-7997. www. prestigeinn.com. 66 units. High season C$139–C$209 (US$90–US$136) double. AE, DISC, MC, V. **Amenities:** Restaurant, bar; indoor pool; exercise room; Jacuzzi; concierge; room service; massage; laundry service; same-day dry cleaning. *In room:* A/C, TV w/ pay movies, dataport, fridge, coffeemaker, hair dryer, iron.

CAMPING
Okanagan Lake Provincial Park (ℭ 250/494-6500), 7 miles (11km) north of Summerland and 27 miles (44km) south of Kelowna on Highway 97, has 168 campsites nestled amid 10,000 imported trees. Sites go for C$19 (US$12). Facilities include free hot showers, flush toilets, a sani-station, and a boat launch. Closer to Kelowna is **Bear Creek Provincial Park** (ℭ 250/494-6500), 6 miles (9km) north of Highway 97 on Westside Road, about 2 miles (3km) west of the Okanagan Lake Floating Bridge. The park has 80 sites for C$19 (US$12) each.

WHERE TO DINE
For the kind of hearty cooking that fulfills gastronomic stereotypes, try **Mamma Rosa Italian Restaurant,** 561 Lawrence Ave. (ℭ 250/763-4114), which serves up affordable house-made pastas and very good pizzas.

Birch Grill CONTINENTAL Its location in a strip mall along Kelowna's busiest street belies the fact that the Birch Grill is a sophisticated little bistro. The menu, which changes daily, features lots of appetizers and small plates, plus pasta dishes—like portobello ravioli with tomato cream sauce—and grilled fish and chicken. The staff is friendly and professional. The Birch Grill keeps later hours than most Kelowna eateries.

8-1470 Harvey Ave. ℭ 250/860-3103. Reservations recommended. Main courses C$12–C$18 (US$8–US$12). AE, MC, V. Mon–Fri 11:30am–2:30pm and 5–10pm; Sat 5–11pm.

Christopher's Steak & Seafood STEAKHOUSE Christopher's is a local favorite for drinks and steaks in a dark, fern-bar–like dining room. The decor and menu haven't changed much since the early years of the Reagan adminis-tration, but that's a plus if you're looking for Alberta beef served up in simple abundance. Pasta, chicken, and seafood are also offered.

242 Lawrence Ave. ℭ 250/861-3464. Reservations recommended. Main courses C$10–C$29 (US$7–US$19). AE, DC, MC, V. Sun–Thurs 4:30–10pm; Fri–Sat 4:30–11pm.

de Montreuil ★★ CONTEMPORARY CANADIAN This low-key, high-performance restaurant produces the Okanagan's most exciting cooking. The menu changes weekly, but expect everything to be fresh and filled with hearty earthiness. As an appetizer, try pan-seared goose liver with fiddleheads and morel mushroom risotto. The couscous salad is served with asparagus spears and fresh apricots, then drizzled with orange ginger dressing. For an entree, choose roast free-range chicken with red curry and coconut yogurt sauce. An impressive wine list and friendly, sophisticated staff make de Montreuil even more noteworthy.

368 Bernard Ave. ℭ 250/860-5508. Reservations recommended. Main courses C$18–C$24 (US$12–US$16). AE, DC, MC, V. Mon–Fri 11:30am–2pm; daily 5:30–10pm.

Doc Willoughby's Pub CANADIAN For a scene that's casual but on the edge of trendy, with a pub-like atmosphere but with better food, try Doc Willoughby's, in the heart of downtown. The building was once a pioneer drug-store (note the hammered-tin ceiling), but the interior has been done up in a strikingly contemporary design. This is a good spot for lunch, as the entire front of the restaurant opens to the street; you can watch the to-ing and fro-ing of tourists as you choose from salads, burgers, and sandwiches. At dinner, the eclectic menu offers lots of fish, chicken, and pasta dishes.

353 Bernard Ave. ℂ **250/868-8288.** Reservations not needed. Main courses C$8–C$15 (US$5–US$10). AE, MC, V. Mon–Thurs 11:30am–11pm; Fri–Sat 11:30am–midnight; Sun 4:30–10pm.

Fresco 🏵🏵 NEW CANADIAN This is the latest dining hot spot in Kelowna, and the first solo venture of chef/owner Rod Butters, who has worked at some of western Canada's top restaurants. The cooking focuses on fresh, relatively unfussy regional cuisine. Start with a chilled salad of citrus-marinated scallops, cucumber, radish and pepper, and move on to a main dish of baked root vegetable torte or seared Pacific tuna. Service is top-notch; the wine list celebrates the vintages of the Okanagan Valley.

1560 Water St. ℂ **250/868-8805.** Reservations recommended. Main courses C$19–C$32 (US$12–$21). Tues–Sat 5:30–10pm.

La Bussola ITALIAN La Bussola is a traditional Italian restaurant with a big local reputation. All of your favorites are here—pasta al pesto, lasagna, chicken piccata—along with an especially large selection of veal specialties. The house signature dish is grilled chicken breast with a creamy white vermouth sauce. A solid and dependable restaurant.

234 Leon Ave. ℂ **250/763-3110.** Reservations recommended. AE, MC, V. Main courses C$10–C$28 (US$7–US$18). Mon–Sat 5–10pm.

Mon Thong Thai Restaurant THAI Mon Thong has an encyclopedic menu of house specialties, making this the best Thai restaurant in the Okanagan. Almost all dishes can be made vegetarian. Choose from red, green, or yellow curries, or from signature dishes like *goong pad num prick pao,* stir-fried shrimp with fresh vegetables in fiery Thai sauce.

1530 Water St. ℂ **250/763-8600.** Reservations not needed. Main courses C$9–C$13 (US$6–US$8). MC, V. Daily 11am–2:30pm and 5–11pm.

Williams Inn CONTINENTAL The simple, rustic lines of this 1906 heritage home, on the edge of downtown, contrast nicely with the white-linen-and-crystal formality of the table service. Among the well-loved hit parade of classic dishes—escargot, lamb rack with mustard-herb crust, beef chateaubriand with béarnaise—are entrees that reflect the tastes of the region. Venison from Nicole Valley is served with local blue cheese and wine sauce, and Fraser Valley pheasant with blackberry glaze. The wine list promotes the finest vintages of the Okanagan. Expect friendly, courteous service.

526 Lawrence Ave. ℂ **250/763-5136.** Reservations required. Main courses C$12–C$28 (US$8–US$18). AE, DC, MC, V. Mon–Thurs 11am–2pm and 5:30–9pm; Fri 11am–2:30pm and 5:30–10pm; Sat 5:30–10pm; Sun 5:30–9pm.

KELOWNA AFTER DARK

The **Kelowna Visual and Performing Arts Centre,** to be completed in 2002, will include a 300-seat theater, gallery, and two restaurants. It's located on Water Street at Cawston Street, near the Grand Okanagan Resort. The **Kelowna Community Theatre,** at Water and Doyle streets (ℂ **250/763-9018**), is home to a number of performing-arts groups, including the Okanagan Symphony Orchestra and Shakespeare Kelowna.

Southeastern British Columbia & the Kootenay Valley

With the high-flying Rockies to the east and the rugged Purcell and Selkirk mountain ranges to the west, southeastern British Columbia has as much beauty and recreation to offer as anywhere else in the province. If you're looking to avoid the crowds at Banff and Jasper national parks on the Alberta side of the Rockies, try one o the smaller parks covered in this chapter.

Trenched by the mighty Kootenay and Columbia rivers, this region has a long history of mining, river transport, and ranching. However, these parts of British Columbia have yet to succumb to the resortification that characterizes much of the rest of the province and neighboring Alberta. And while that means that you may not have the ultimate dining experience here, it also means that prices are lower across the board—and you won't have to compete with tour-bus hordes while you hike the trails.

In pre-Contact Native America and the early years of western exploration, the Kootenay Valley was a major transportation corridor. Due to a curious accident of geology, the headwaters of the vast Columbia River—which flows north from Columbia Lake for 171 miles (275km) before bending south and flowing to the Pacific at Astoria, Oregon—are separated from the south-flowing Kootenay River by a low, 1¼-mile-wide (2km) berm of land called Canal Flats. The Kootenay River then zigzags down into the United States before flowing back north into Canada to join the Columbia at Castlegar, British Columbia.

Because a short portage was all that separated these two powerful rivers, Canal Flats was an important crossroads when canoes and river boats were the primary means of transport. The fact that an easily breached ridge was all that separated two major rivers caught the imagination of an early entrepreneur, William Adolph Baillie-Grohman. In the 1880s, he conceived a plan to breach Canal Flats and divert much of the Kootenay's flow into the Columbia. Unsurprisingly, he ran into opposition from people living and working on the Columbia, and had to settle for building a canal and lock system between the two rivers. Only two ships ever passed through the canal, and today this curiosity is preserved as Canal Flats Provincial Park, 27 miles (44km) north of Cranbrook, with picnic tables and a boat launch on Columbia Lake.

For advance information on southeastern British Columbia, contact **Tourism Rockies**, P.O. Box 10, Kimberley, BC V1A 2Y5 (© **250/427-4838;** www.bcrockies.com).

1 Revelstoke

254 miles (410km) W of Calgary, 350 miles (565km) NE of Vancouver

Located on the Columbia River at the foot of Mount Revelstoke National Park, Revelstoke sits in a narrow fir-cloaked valley between the Selkirk and the Monashee mountains. It's a spectacular, big-as-all-outdoors setting, and unsurprisingly, Revelstoke makes the most of the outdoor-recreation opportunities on its doorstep. Winter is high season here, as the city is a major center for heli-skiing and snowmobiling. Summer activities include rafting, hiking, and horseback riding.

The town was established in the 1880s, when the Canadian Pacific Railway pushed through. Much of the handsome downtown core was built then; most restaurants and hotels are housed in century-old buildings. For all its beauty and charm, Revelstoke is surprisingly unheralded. With a setting that rivals Banff and Jasper, Revelstoke's congenial and sleepy isolation can't last. Plan a visit before the throngs arrive.

ESSENTIALS

GETTING THERE   Revelstoke is 119 miles (192km) from Kelowna on Highway 1. It's 350 miles (565km) northwest of Vancouver and 254 miles (410km) west of Calgary. **Greyhound Canada** (© **800/661-8747** or 403/260-0877; www.greyhound.ca) operates six buses daily from Vancouver, costing C$75 (US$49) one-way. Four buses per day connect Revelstoke to Calgary, costing C$58 (US$38) one-way.

VISITOR INFORMATION   Contact the **Revelstoke Visitor Information Centre,** 204 Campbell St. (© **800/487-1493** or 250/837-5345; fax 250/837-4223; www.revelstokecc.bc.ca).

EXPLORING THE TOWN

Downtown Revelstoke (pop. 8,507) sits on a shelf of land above the confluence of the Columbia and Illecillewaet rivers. Founded in the 1880s, the town center retains a number of original storefronts and is pleasant to explore. You'll see plenty of coffeehouses, galleries, and some standout architectural jewels, like the domed **Revelstoke Courthouse,** 1123 Second St. W. **Grizzly Plaza,** near Victoria Road and Campbell Avenue, is lined with redbrick storefronts. It's the site of the Saturday farmers' market, as well as free live music from July to Labour Day, Monday through Saturday from 7 to 10pm.

Revelstoke Museum   Located in the town's original post office, this small museum contains memorabilia from Revelstoke's pioneer mining and railroading days. Upstairs is the community art gallery, with works by local and regional artists.

315 W. First St. © 250/837-3067. Admission by donation. Mid-May to Labour Day Mon–Fri 1–5pm. Labour Day to mid-May Mon, Wed, and Fri 1–4:30pm.

Revelstoke Railway Museum   It's the railroad that really put Revelstoke on the map, and this noteworthy museum—built to resemble an original Canadian Pacific Railway shop—tells the story of western Canadian rail history. Its collection of antique rolling stock includes a beautifully restored CPR steam engine from the 1940s. Other exhibits focus on the building of the first transcontinental line across Canada and the communications systems that kept the trains running safely.

Southeastern British Columbia

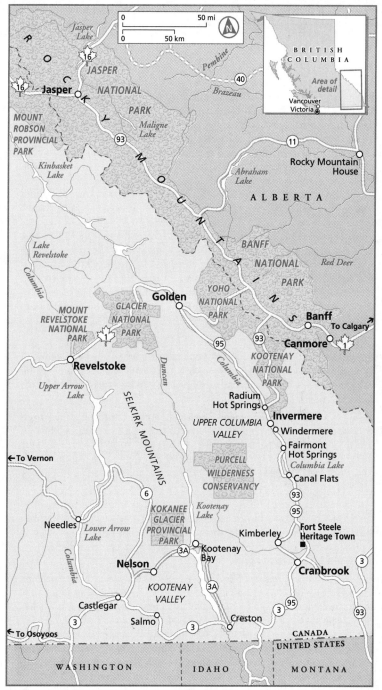

0 ____ 50 mi
0 ____ 50 km

BRITISH
COLUMBIA

Area of
detail

Vancouver
Victoria

ROCKY

Jasper
Lake

16

JASPER

16

Jasper

NATIONAL

PARK

MOUNT
ROBSON
PROVINCIAL
PARK

Kinbasket
Lake

Pembine

40

Brazeau

Maligne
Lake

93

MOUNTAINS

11

Rocky Mountain
House

Abraham
Lake

ALBERTA

Lake
Revelstoke

Columbia

MOUNT
REVELSTOKE
NATIONAL
PARK

GLACIER
NATIONAL
PARK

Golden

1

Revelstoke

Upper Arrow
Lake

Duncan

SELKIRK MOUNTAINS

BANFF

NATIONAL

PARK

Red Deer

YOHO
NATIONAL
PARK

Columbia

95

93

KOOTENAY
NATIONAL
PARK

Banff

To Calgary

Canmore

1

Radium
Hot Springs

UPPER COLUMBIA
VALLEY

PURCELL
WILDERNESS
CONSERVANCY

Invermere

Windermere

Fairmont
Hot Springs

Columbia Lake

Canal Flats

93

95

To Vernon

6

Needles

Lower Arrow
Lake

Columbia

KOKANEE
GLACIER
PROVINCIAL
PARK

Kootenay
Lake

3A

Kootenay
Bay

Nelson

KOOTENAY
VALLEY

3A

Kimberley

Fort Steele
Heritage Town

Cranbrook

3

Castlegar

3

Salmo

3

Creston

3

95

93

To Osoyoos

CANADA

UNITED STATES

WASHINGTON

IDAHO

MONTANA

263

719 Track St. W., across from downtown on Victoria Rd. ☎ 250/837-6060. www.railwaymuseum.com. Admission C$5 (US$3.25) adults, C$3 (US$1.95) seniors, C$2 (US$1.30) students, C$10 (US$7) families, free for children 5 and under. July–Labour Day daily 9am–8pm; Mar–June and Labour Day–Nov daily 9am–5pm; rest of year Mon–Fri 1–5pm.

TOURING THE DAMS

The Columbia River has the steepest descent of any large river in North America, and in terms of volume, is the continent's third-largest river, making it irresistible to hydroelectric dam builders. Two of the many electricity-generating dams on the river are near Revelstoke, and both are open for tours. **Revelstoke Dam,** 2½ miles (4km) north of Revelstoke on Highway 23, is 1,541 feet (54m) across and 574 feet (175m) high. Self-guided tours of the visitor center explain how hydroelectricity is produced and how the dams impact the local ecosystem. An elevator shoots to the top of the dam, where you get a feeling for the immensity of this structure. The visitor center is open May to mid-June, daily from 9am to 5pm, and mid-June to mid-September, daily from 8am to 8pm. Admission is free.

An 87-mile (140km) drive up Highway 23 along the shores of Revelstoke Lake takes you to **Mica Dam,** the first large dam on the Columbia—and large it is, much larger than Revelstoke Dam. More than 2,600 feet (792m) across and 656 feet (200m) high, Mica Dam forms Kinbasket Lake, which stretches for more than 100 miles (160km) and contains 14.8 trillion cubic meters of water. The visitor center is open mid-June to Labour Day, daily from 10:30am to 4:30pm. Guided tours are offered at 11am and 1:30pm.

OUTDOOR PURSUITS

Revelstoke is surrounded by rugged mountains with extremely heavy snowfalls (almost 60 ft./18m annually). The town is particularly known as a center for heli-skiing, a sport that employs helicopters to deposit expert skiers high on mountain ridges, far from lifts and ski areas.

BIKING The mountains around Revelstoke are etched with old logging roads that have been converted into mountain-bike trails; ask at the visitor center for a map. For a 4-hour guided trip that includes the magical 17-mile (27km), 5,000-foot (1,524m) descent down Mount Revelstoke, contact **Summit Cycle Tours** (☎ 888/700-3444 or 250/837-3734; www.summitcycle.com). The cost is C$69 (US$45).

GOLF **Revelstoke Golf Club** (☎ 800/991-4455 or 250/837-4276) is an 18-hole, par-72 championship course established in 1924, with narrow fairways lined with mammoth conifers and small lakes. The club—one of the oldest in British Columbia—has a driving range, clubhouse with lounge and restaurant, and pro shop. Greens fees are C$33 (US$21).

SKIING **Powder Springs Ski Area,** 4 miles (6km) south of Revelstoke on Camozzi Road (☎ 877/422-8754 or 250/837-5151), has 1,000 feet (305m) of vertical drop, with 3,500 feet (1,067m) of total runs. There are two lifts, a T-bar, and a rope tow; lift tickets are C$28 (US$18).

CMH Heli-Skiing (☎ 800/661-0252; www.cmhski.com) offers helicopter skiing to remote slopes and glaciers in the Monashee and Selkirk mountains. Three-, 4-, and 7-day packages include meals, lodging, and use of specially designed heli-skis. Prices for a week of heli-skiing range from C$4,400 to C$7,495 (US$2,860 to US$4,872). Pickup at the Calgary airport can be arranged.

The long-established **Selkirk Tangiers Heli Skiing** (© **800/663-7080;** www.selkirk-tangiers.com) offers helicopter-assisted skiing and snowboarding trips to more than 200 approved areas in the Monashee and Selkirk mountains, with some runs up to 7,200 feet (2,195m) in length. In addition, the company's Albert Canyon base, 22 miles (35km) east of Revelstoke on Highway 1, offers heli-skiing in the Selkirks. A week of midwinter skiing goes for C$6,192 (US$4,025).

Cat Powder Skiing (© **800/991-4455;** www.catpowder.com) uses Snowcats to transport skiers and snowboarders to backcountry slopes. The Snowcat takes you to the 7,500-foot (2,286m) elevation of Mount Mackenzie, where you can choose from a number of runs up to 3,500 feet (1,067m) long, including a half pipe and a terrain park. Packages include guide service, lodging, and meals; a 3-day option costs C$1,500 (US$975).

SNOWMOBILING   A detailed brochure of snowmobiling trails is available from the visitor center, or contact **Great Canadian Snowmobile Tours** (© **800/ 667-8865** or 250/837-6500; www.snowmobilerevelstoke.com) for guided trips.

WHITE-WATER RAFTING   Apex Rafting Company (© **888/232-6666** or 250/837-6376; www.apexrafting.com) offers excursions down Illecillewaet River's Albert Canyon. The trip provides thrills, but nothing too extreme. In summer, daily 3-hour trips cost C$42 (US$27) for adults and C$32 (US$21) for youths 10 to 17.

WHERE TO STAY

The **Powder Springs Inn,** 200 Third St. W. (© **800/991-4455** or 250/ 837-5151; www.catpowder.com), is a pleasant, inexpensive place to stay, particularly in summer. **Martha Creek Provincial Park,** just north of Revelstoke on Highway 23 (© **250/825-3500**), sits on Lake Revelstoke and has 28 campsites that go for C$12 (US$8) each.

The Coast Hillcrest Resort Hotel   Located on the eastern edge of Revelstoke, this brand-new hotel does its best to look like a grand mountain lodge, complete with turrets, balconies, log beams, stone walls, and a vast lobby dominated by a river-rock fireplace. The Hillcrest has the most complete facilities in Revelstoke, and its rooms are large and comfortable. Suites come with Jacuzzis. The only downside is that you'll need to drive to get to downtown Revelstoke.

2 miles (3km) east of Revelstoke on Hwy. 1 (Box 1979), Revelstoke, BC V0E 2S0. © 250/837-3322. Fax 250/ 837-3340. 75 units. C$120–C$145 (US$78–US$94) double; C$176–C$230 (US$114–US$150) suite. AE, MC, V. **Amenities:** Restaurant, lounge; Jacuzzis; sauna; exercise room; game room. *In room:* A/C, TV, coffeemaker, hair dryer, iron, safe.

Mulvehill Creek Wilderness Inn and Bed & Breakfast ✦✦   One of the most superlative inns in all of British Columbia, this inn sits in a clearing in the forest, just steps from Arrow Lake and a magnificent 300-foot (90m) waterfall. The cedar-shake-sided lodge has three queen rooms, one king room, and two units with twin beds, plus two suites (one with Jacuzzi and private deck). All rooms are beautifully decorated with locally made pine furniture and original folk art. The lounge is lined with bookcases; grab a novel and curl up by the fireplace. From the deck, look onto the organic garden, which supplies much of the produce served here; the inn's hens provide the eggs. Your hosts are happy to arrange cross-country skiing, snowshoeing, horseback-riding, biking, and fishing excursions. A couple days at Mulvehill may well be the highlight of your trip to British Columbia. Children are welcome.

4200 Hwy. 23 S. (12 miles/19km) south of Revelstoke), P.O. Box 1220, Revelstoke, BC V0E 2S0. ☎ 877/
837-8649 or 250/837-8649. www.mulvehillcreek.com. 8 units. C$95–C$135 (US$62–US$88) double; C$195
(US$127) suite. Rates include breakfast. AE, MC, V. **Amenities:** Heated outdoor pool; Jacuzzi; playground; free
canoes. *In room:* Hair dryer, no phone.

Regent Inn   The finest lodging in downtown Revelstoke, the Regent is a
refurbished heritage hotel facing historic Grizzly Plaza. The large bedrooms are
individually decorated with restrained good taste; some have private Jacuzzis.
The One Twelve Restaurant offers fine dining (see "Where to Dine," below).

112 First St. E., Revelstoke, BC V0E 2S0. ☎ 888/245-5523 or 250/837-2107. Fax 250/837-9669. www.
regentinn.com. 50 units. C$99–C$159 (US$64–US$103) double. Rates include continental breakfast. AE, DC,
MC, V. Pets accepted in limited rooms for C$10 (US$7). **Amenities:** Restaurant, lounge, pub; outdoor heated
pool; access to adjacent health club; Jacuzzi; sauna; golf course nearby. *In room:* A/C, TV, hair dryer, iron, safe.

Revelstoke Traveller's Hostel & Guest House   Located on the edge of
downtown, the hostel is in a spacious older home with oak floors and French
doors. There are tent sites in the large backyard.

400 Second St. W., Revelstoke, BC V0E 2S0. ☎ 888/663-8825 or 250/837-4050. Fax 250/837-6410. www.
hihostels.bc.ca. 26 beds. C$15–C$17 (US$10–US$11) HI members, C$19–C$21 (US$12–US$14) nonmembers.
MC, V. **Amenities:** Kitchen; TV lounge; bike rentals; computer and Internet access. *In room:* No phone.

Three Valley Lake Chateau   With its bright-red, steeply pitched, four-story
tin roof cleaved by dozens of sharply peaked gables, this huge new hotel and
entertainment complex stands out, to put it mildly. The hotel sits amid formal
gardens at the head of Three Valley Lake, a small body of water with sandy
swimming beaches. Guest rooms are quite large, most with balconies; if you're
interested, ask about the theme suites (the interior of the Cave Suite is lined
completely in native stone). The hotel's Walter Moberly Theatre hosts a nightly
revue with cowboy songs and skits. Also part of the development is Historic
Town, a collection of historic buildings that have been moved to the property to
form an ad hoc ghost town.

12 miles (19km) west of Revelstoke on Hwy. 1 (P.O. Box 860), Revelstoke, BC V0E 2S0. ☎ 888/667-2109 or
250/837-2109. Fax 250/837-5220. www.3valley.com. 200 units. C$100–C$120 (US$65–US$78) double. AE,
DC, DISC, MC, V. **Amenities:** Two dining rooms, cafeteria, lounge; indoor pool; whirlpool; coin-op laundry.
In room: A/C, TV.

Wintergreen Inn   This inn was newly built, but designed to fit in architecturally with its historic neighbors close to downtown. The comfortable guest
rooms, with hardwood floors and quality furniture, are decorated according to
themes that reflect local history and recreation. Guests share a living room with
a fireplace and complimentary coffee, tea, and wine. The host is happy to help
arrange local recreational activities.

312 Kootenay St., Revelstoke, BC V0E 2S0. ☎ 800/216-2008 or 250/837-3369. www.bbexpo.com/bc/
wintergreen.htm. 10 units. C$90 (US$59) double. Rates include full breakfast. MC, V. Pets accepted in certain
rooms. **Amenities:** Game room with TV. *In room:* A/C, hair dryer, no phone.

WHERE TO DINE

One Twelve Restaurant WESTERN CANADIAN   This handsome restaurant is Revelstoke's fine-dining option, with a good selection of steaks, seafood
(about half the menu options), and Continental cuisine. Veal is served with a wild-
mushroom sauce, and fresh New Brunswick lobster tails come with drawn butter.
Good service, an intriguing wine list, and a fireplace enhance the experience.

In the Regent Inn, 112 First St. E. ☎ 250/837-2107. www.regentinn.com. Reservations suggested. Main
courses C$12–C$26 (US$8–US$17). AE, MC, V. Mon–Sat 11:30am–2pm and 5:30–9pm.

Three Bears Bistro CASUAL DINING   The Three Bears is a convivial spot in Grizzly Plaza with sidewalk patio seating as well as deck seating in the garden. At lunch, the menu includes homemade soup, salads, wraps, and fajitas; the evening offerings shift to pasta, potpies, and paella. The bistro also has good desserts, espresso drinks, and specialty teas.

144 Mackenzie Ave. (*C*) **250/837-9575.** Reservations not accepted. Main courses C$5–C$10 (US$3.25–US$7). MC, V. July–Labour Day Mon–Sat 8:30am–10pm; Sun 11am–10pm. Labour Day–June Mon–Sat 8:30am–5pm.

2 Mount Revelstoke National Park

Just west of Glacier National Park is Mount Revelstoke National Park, a glacier-clad collection of craggy peaks in the **Selkirk Range.** Comprising only 161 square miles (417km²), Mount Revelstoke can't produce the kind of awe that its larger neighbor, Glacier National Park, can in good weather; it does, however, offer easier access to the high country and alpine meadows.

The park is flanked on the south by Highway 1, the Trans-Canada Highway. It has no services or campgrounds, but all tourist services are available in the neighboring town of Revelstoke (see above).

For information, contact **Mount Revelstoke National Park** (*C* **250/ 837-7500;** www.parkscanada.pch.gc.ca/revelstoke). Entry to the park costs C$4 (US$2.60) for adults, C$3 (US$1.95) for seniors, C$2 (US$1.30) for children 6 to 16, and C$10 (US$7) per family.

EXPLORING THE PARK

The most popular activity in the park is the drive up to the top of 6,000-foot (1,829m) **Mount Revelstoke,** with great views of the Columbia River and the peaks of Glacier Park. To reach Mount Revelstoke, take the paved Meadows in the Sky Parkway north from the town of Revelstoke and follow it 14 miles (23km) to Balsam Lake. The parkway is closed to trailers and motor coaches, as it is a very narrow mountain road with 16 steep switchbacks.

At **Balsam Lake,** at the Meadows in the Sky area, free shuttles operated by the parks department make the final ascent up to the top of Mount Revelstoke, but only after the road is clear of snow, usually from early July to late September. If the shuttle isn't running, you have a choice of several easy hiking trails around Balsam Lake that lead past rushing brooks through wildflower meadows. The **Eagle Knoll Trail** and the **Parapets** are two options that take under an hour. At the summit are longer trails, including the 3¾-mile (6km) **Eva Lake Trail.**

If you don't make the trip up to the Meadows in the Sky area, you can enjoy a short hike in the park from along Highway 1. The **Skunk Cabbage Trail** winds through a marsh that explodes with bright yellow and odiferous flowers in early summer. Another popular hike is the **Giant Cedars Trail,** a short board-walk out into a grove of old-growth cedars that are more than 1,000 years old.

3 Glacier National Park

44 miles (72km) E of Revelstoke, 50 miles (80km) W of Golden

Located amid the highest peaks of the Selkirk Mountains, Canada's Glacier National Park amply lives up to its name. More than 400 glaciers repose here, with 14% of the park's 837 square miles (2,168km²) lying under permanent snowpack. The reason that this high country is so covered with ice is the same reason that this is one of the more unpopulated places to visit in the mountain West: It snows and rains a lot here.

For information, contact **Glacier National Park** (© **250/837-7500;** www. parkscanada.pch.gc.ca/glacier). The visitor center is at Rogers Pass. There's no charge if you pass through the park on Highway 1 without stopping, but if you do stop to hike or picnic, the entry fee is C$4 (US$2.60) for adults, C$3 (US$1.95) for seniors, C$2 (US$1.30) for children, or C$10 (US$7) per family.

EXPLORING THE PARK

The primary attractions in the park are viewpoints onto craggy peaks and hiking trails leading to wildflower meadows and old-growth groves; heavy snow and rainfall lend a near–rain-forest feel to the hikes. Spring hikers and cross-country skiers should beware of avalanche conditions, a serious problem in areas with high snowfall and steep slopes. Call the park information number (© **250/837-7500**) for weather updates.

Glacier Park is crossed by the Trans-Canada Highway and the Canadian Pacific Railway tracks. Each has had to build snowsheds to protect its transportation system from the effects of heavy snows and avalanches. **Park headquarters** are just east of 4,100-foot (1,250m) Rogers Pass; stop here to watch videos and see the displays on natural and human history in the park. New exhibits focus on the role of the railroads in opening up this rugged area of Canada. You can sign up for ranger-led interpretive hikes here as well. On a typically gray and wet day, the visitor center may be the driest place to enjoy the park.

HIKING

Several easy trails leave from the park's Rogers Pass visitor center. **Abandoned Rails Trail** follows a rails-to-trails section of the old CPR track for an 1-hour round-trip with a gentle grade through a wildflower-studded basin. The **Balu Pass Trail** is a more strenuous 3-mile (5km) hike up to the base of the glaciers on 8,950-foot (2,728m) Ursus Major.

The other important trailhead is at **Illecillewaet Campground,** west of Rogers Pass along Highway 1. Seven major trails head up into the peaks from here, including the **Asulkan Valley Trail,** which follows a stream up a narrow valley to a hikers' hut. These trails require more exertion than the trails at Rogers Pass, and will take most of a day to complete.

Further down the Illecillewaet Valley are two other popular routes. **Loop Brook Trail** is a 1-hour saunter through a riparian wetland. The quarter-mile (.5km) **Rockgarden Trail** climbs up a valley wall of moss-and-lichen–covered boulders to a vista point onto 9,446-foot (2,880m) Smart Peak. Stop at the **Hemlock Grove Picnic Area** and follow the boardwalk through the old-growth hemlock forest.

The longest hike in the park is the 26-mile (42km) **Beaver Valley Trail,** which follows the Beaver River on the eastern edge of the park. This trail takes 3 days, one-way, to complete. If you plan on backcountry camping, you'll need to register at the visitor center and purchase a C$6 (US$3.90) wilderness pass.

WHERE TO STAY

Illecillewaet and **Loop Brook** campgrounds are just west of Rogers Pass off Highway 1 and along the Illecillewaet River. Both operate on a first-come, first-served basis. Facilities include flush toilets, kitchen shelters, firewood, and drinking water. Illecillewaet offers guided hikes and fireside programs as well. Rates at both campgrounds are C$13 (US$8) per night.

Mount Revelstoke & Glacier National Parks

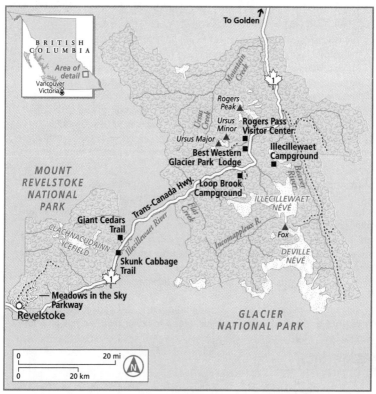

Best Western Glacier Park Lodge   This large complex is just below Rogers Pass, where Highway 1 edges over the Selkirk Range in Glacier National Park. The setting is spectacular: The glaciered faces of towering peaks crowd around a broad cirque blanketed with wildflowers and boulders, at the center of which sits this handsome lodge. Eighty-seven miles (139km) of hiking and cross-country ski trails lead out into the wilderness. Guest rooms are comfortable and nicely furnished.

Rogers Pass, BC V0E 2S0. ℂ **800/528-1234** or 250/837-2126. Fax 250/837-2130. www.glacierparklodge.ca. 50 units. C$125–C$150 (US$81–US$98) double. AE, DISC, MC, V. **Amenities:** Two restaurants, bar; heated outdoor pool; Jacuzzi; sauna; limited room service; laundry service. *In room:* TV, coffeemaker, iron.

4 Golden

83 miles (134km) W of Banff, 442 miles (713km) E of Vancouver

For more than a century, Golden (pop. 4,107) has been known primarily as a transport hub, first as a division point on the transcontinental Canadian Pacific Railway, next as the upstream steamboat terminus on the Columbia River, and then as a junction of two of Canada's busiest highway systems.

Nowadays, Golden is known for its outdoor recreation. The town sits in a breathtaking location in the trench-like Columbia River valley, between the massive Rocky Mountains and the soaring Purcell Range, within a 90-minute

> **Tips** **Special Events**
>
> The **Golden Festival of Birds and Bears** (© 800/622-4653) is held during the second week of May. Events include field trips, kids' programs, musical entertainment, and wildlife and conservation seminars. The **Golden Rodeo** brings a bit of the Wild West to the Canadian Rockies during the first weekend of August, with a pancake breakfast, street dance, barbecues, and, of course, bucking bulls and broncos, roping, and races. The rodeo grounds are a mile (1.6km) south of Golden off Highway 95. For information, contact the visitor center.

drive of five major national parks. The fact that Golden is near—and not in—the parks is in large part the reason for the area's recent phenomenal growth. Outfitters that offer heli-skiing, heli-hiking, and other recreation that isn't allowed in the national parks (for conservation reasons) choose to make Golden their base. And with park towns like nearby Banff trying to limit further development, businesses and outfitters that want a Rocky Mountain hub find Golden a convenient and congenial center.

Golden won't win any awards for charm, however. It's basically a functional little town with lots of motel rooms in a magnificent location.

Note that Golden and the other communities in this part of the Columbia Valley are in the mountain time zone, an hour earlier than the rest of British Columbia.

ESSENTIALS
GETTING THERE   Golden is at the junction of Highway 1 (the Trans-Canada Hwy.) and Highway 95. The closest airport is in Calgary. **Greyhound Canada** (© **800/661-8747** or 403/260-0877; www.greyhound.ca) links Golden to Vancouver, Banff, and Calgary, and to Cranbrook to the south. The one-way fare from Golden to Vancouver is C$94 (US$61); to Calgary, C$39 (US$25).

VISITOR INFORMATION   Contact the **Golden Visitor Info Centre,** 500 10th Ave. N. (© **800/622-4653** or 250/344-7125; fax 250/344-6688; www. goldenchamber.bc.ca).

GETTING AROUND   If you need a rental car while in Golden, contact **National,** 915 11th Ave. (© **250/344-9899**).

EXPLORING THE AREA
You could spend several days in the Golden area without realizing that the town has an older downtown core. It's a block west of busy 10th Avenue, on **Main Street.** There's not much here—just a handful of shops and cafes—but it's a pleasant break from the commercial sprawl along Highways 1 and 95. The town itself is mostly charm-free and hasn't yet developed the kind of boutique infrastructure or tourist attractions that you find in other Canadian mountain towns.

The **Golden and District Museum,** 1302 11th Ave. (© **250/344-5169**), tells the story of Golden's rail history. It also has an old log schoolhouse and blacksmith's shop. Open Monday through Friday from 10am to 6pm in May, June, and September, and daily in July and August. Admission is by donation.

Rafter J Frontier Village *Kids*   This venerable attraction is a private open-air museum housed in a re-created frontier village, complete with false-fronted stores, corrals, teepees, and the like. Guides conduct tours, pointing out Native and cowboy artifacts, while Texas longhorn cattle roam through the village. Rafter J also offers campsites for C$10 to C$15 (US$7 to US$10).

1870 Upper Donald Rd., 15 miles (24km) north of Golden (©) 250/344-3061. www.rockies.net/~rafterj. Tours C$5 (US$3.25) adults, free for children 10 and under. Mid-May to mid-Oct 9am to dusk.

OUTDOOR PURSUITS

FISHING   The Columbia River runs through town and offers fair fishing for rainbow trout and kokanee salmon. There's better fishing in the **Kinbasket Lake** section of the river, which begins just north of Golden. For guided trips in more-remote lakes and streams, contact **Kinbasket Adventures** (© 250/344-6012; www.rockies.net/~kbasket).

GOLF   **Golden Golf & Country Club** (© 866/727-7222 or 250/344-2700; www.golfcanada.com) is an 18-hole championship course along the Columbia River. Bill Newis designed the front nine holes; Les Furber took care of the back nine. The clubhouse includes a pro shop with equipment rentals. Greens fees are C$50 (US$33).

HELI-HIKING   Although based in Banff, **CMH Heli-Hiking** (© 800/661-0252 or 403/762-7100; www.cmhhike.com) offers a variety of helicopter-assisted hiking packages in the mountains west of Golden. Four-, 6-, and 8-day heli-hiking trips involve staying at remote high-country lodges accessible only by long hiking trails or by helicopter. Prices vary depending on time of year and individual lodge, but plan on a 4-day trip to cost between C$1,800 and C$2,150 (US$1,170 and US$1,398); rates include lodging, food, and helicopter transport.

Mid-June through September, **Purcell Heli-Hiking** (© 877/435-4754 or 250/344-5410; www.purcellhelicopterskiing.com) offers heli-hiking in the Purcell Mountains west of Golden. Guided day hikes go for C$245 to C$440 (US$159 to US$286), including lunch. Sightseeing tours start at C$150 (US$98).

HELI-SKIING   Golden is at the center of one of the world's best terrains for helicopter-assisted skiing. The Bugaboo, Purcell, Selkirk, and Cariboo mountains all rear up behind Golden, and since they are unencumbered with national-park status (unlike the Canadian Rockies), they're available to licensed heli-skiing operations. Banff-based **CMH Heli-Skiing** (see "Heli-Hiking,"

Moments A Bird's-Eye View

Alpenglow Aviation (© 888/244-7117 or 250/344-7117; www.rockiesair tours.com) offers a variety of flightseeing trips into the magnificent mountain ranges that ring Golden. The Glaciers & Granite Tour is a 1-hour flight over the incredible spires of the Bugaboo Mountains south of Golden (C$110/US$72 per person); the 1¼-hour Icefields & Waterfalls Tour (C$135/US$88) flies along the Continental Divide between Yoho and Banff national parks; the latter also takes in the Columbia Icefield, the largest nonpolar ice cap in the world. The Golden Airport is just west of Golden, off Fisher Road. Alpenglow also offers pickup van service anywhere in Canmore, Banff, or Lake Louise. If you happen to be in Golden on a clear day, you should definitely take advantage of these awe-inspiring air tours.

above) has eight high-country lodges in the mountain ranges near Golden. Prices vary greatly depending on the lodge and time of year, but range between C$4,400 and C$7,600 (US$2,860 and US$4,940) for 1 week. Rates include lodging, food, helicopter transport, use of specialized powder skis, and ground transport from the nearest large airport (usually Calgary).

Great Canadian Heli-Skiing (© 250/344-2326; www.greatcanadianheliski. com) offers 1-week trips in the Selkirk and Purcell mountains. Prices average C$6,100 to C$7,900 (US$3,965 to US$5,135) per week, including accommo- dations in the company's private lodge near Golden, food, skis, helicopter trans- port, and ground transport from the Calgary airport.

SKIING ✦ Kicking Horse Mountain Resort (© 866/754-5425; www. kickinghorseresort.com), is the newest ski resort in the Canadian Rockies, opened in 2001. Located 9 miles (14km) west of Golden, it features a 4,133- foot-long (1,240m) vertical drop (Canada's second longest), a gondola lift that takes skiers up above elevations of 7,700 feet (2,310m), and the Eagle's Eye, the highest-elevation restaurant in Canada. It has six lifts and over 4,000 acres (1,620 hectares) of skiable terrain. With two four-star hotels in the works, plus a variety of lodges and country inns planned for the new development, promot- ers claim that the resort is poised to become the Whistler of the Rockies.

WHITE-WATER RAFTING   The Kicking Horse River, which enters the Columbia at Golden, is one of the most exciting white-water rafting trips in Canada, with constant Class III and Class IV rapids as it tumbles down from the Continental Divide through Yoho National Park. A trip down the Kicking Horse will be a highlight of your vacation in the Rockies. Rafting trips are usu- ally offered from mid-May to mid-September.

Alpine Rafting (© 888/599-5299 or 250/344-6778; www.access-adventures. com/ab/wwr/alpnraft/alpnraft.htm) offers a daylong trip for C$80 (US$52), including a barbecue steak lunch. A gentler introduction to white water goes for C$45 (US$29) for adults and C$25 (US$16) for children.

Canadian Whitewater Adventures (© 888/577-8118 or 403/720-8745; www.canadianwhitewater.com) offers rafting trips and combination rafting/ hiking or rafting/rappelling trips. Rafting packages include Upper Canyon for C$75 (US$49), Lower Canyon for C$49 (US$32), and the Upper & Lower Combo for C$109 (US$71). The hiking package goes for C$39 (US$25), the rafting/hiking package C$99 (US$64), the rappelling package C$99 (US$64), and the rafting/rappelling package C$149 (US$97). All packages include equipment, guides, and lunch. A shuttle from Banff and Lake Louise costs C$10 (US$7).

Glacier Raft Company (© 250/344-6521; www.glacierraft.com) offers a variety of options. The easygoing scenic float day trip goes to the gentle upper valley of the Kicking Horse; it's for those who want an introduction to rafting or who don't want the thrills of white water. Cost is C$55 (US$36) for adults and C$29 (US$19) for kids 6 to 12. Two separate day trips explore the white- water sections of the Kicking Horse and cost C$89 to C$109 (US$58 to US$71). All day trips include a steak barbecue lunch.

Rocky Mountain Rafting Co. (© 888/518-7238 or 250/344-6979; www. rockymountainadventure.com) offers full-day Kicking Horse trips, including lunch, starting at C$85 (US$55). A calmer, family white-water trip in the upper valley costs C$55 (US$36). If you just want the thrills, you can choose a

Exploring the Columbia River Wetlands

South (upstream) from Golden is the Columbia River Wetlands, a 90-mile-long (144km) Wildlife Management Area that supports an incredible diversity of wildlife. More than 270 bird species have been seen in this stretch of river, marsh, and lake. The largest wetlands west of Manitoba, the Columbia River Wetlands is also a major breeding ground for the bald eagle, osprey, and great blue heron. Moose, elk, mink, and beaver make their homes here as well.

Kinbasket Adventures (℃ **250/334-6012**; www.rockies.net/~kbasket) has two different wildlife-viewing trips through the wetlands. A leisurely 2½-hour pontoon trip is C$40 (US$26) for adults and C$20 (US$13) for children 12 and under. This is suitable for all ages as well as for those with disabilities. Longer guided canoe excursions have a stronger bird-watching focus. Half-day trips are C$50 (US$33); full-day trips are C$80 (US$52), including lunch. Canoe rentals are available as well.

1½-hour trip that shoots through the longest section of continuous Class IV rapids in western Canada (C$55/US$36). Lunch is included in the full-day and family trips.

Wet 'n' Wild Adventures (℃ **800/668-9119** or 250/344-6546; www.wetnwild.bc.ca) offers Kicking Horse trips from Banff, Lake Louise, and Golden. The standard day trip is C$83 (US$54), including lunch. If you just want to shoot the rapids of the lower canyon, a half-day trip is available for C$55 (US$36). For beginners, a morning introduction to white water is C$50 (US$33) for adults and C$35 (US$23) for children 12 and under, including lunch.

Whitewater Voyageurs Ltd. (℃ **250/344-6521**; www.raftingcanada.com) has a full-day trip of continuous white-water adventure (lunch included) for C$118 (US$77). If you're really keen about rafting, consider the 2-day Kicking Horse trip, which starts gently in the upper valley. After a night of camping, be ready to shoot down the lower canyon's Class III and IV rapids. Cost is C$235 (US$153), all meals and tents provided (bring a sleeping bag). You also have the choice of floating the scenic Blaeberry River for C$55 (US$36).

HORSEBACK RIDING Located in the lovely Blaeberry River valley, **Triple C Backcountry Riding,** Goat Mountain Lodge, 236 Blaeberry Rd. (℃ **877/240-RIDE** or 250/344-6579; http://www.rockies.net/~goatmtn/TripleC.html), offers a variety of rides. The trails follow the river along the same routes traversed by Native Canadians and early frontier explorers. Full-day trips are C$75 (US$49) for adults and C$65 (US$42) for kids; 1- and 2-hour guided rides are also available. The Sundowner trip with evening cookout goes for C$55 (US$36) per adult and C$50 (US$33) per child.

WHERE TO STAY

Alpine Meadows Lodge ★ High above Golden, looking across onto the face of the Rockies, this family-owned lodge enjoys a great location—removed from the bustle of town, yet only 10 minutes to skiing, golf, and tourist services.

The lodge, which was constructed from timber felled on the property, has a central three-story great room, flanked by wraparound balconies and open staircases. A huge, two-sided stone fireplace dominates the living area. The guest rooms are light-filled and airy, with simple, unfussy decor. Outdoor recreation is literally right out the door, with paths from the lodge leading to hiking trails in neighboring federal forestland. The owner will make it easy to get you out into the wilderness or onto the fairways.

717 Elk Rd., Golden, BC V0A 1H0. (C) **888/700-4477** or 250/344-5863. Fax 250/344-5853. www.alpine meadowslodge.com. 9 units. C$99–C$109 (US$64–US$71) double. Rates include breakfast. Golf, skiing, rafting, and flightseeing packages available. MC, V. **Amenities:** Restaurant, lounge. *In room:* A/C, no phone.

Columbia Valley Lodge   This homey lodge sits on a wetlands lake beside the Columbia River, offering a relaxing place to stay for those who want to be close to nature but don't want to backpack to get to it. The flower-bedecked, Tyrolean-style inn overlooks a grassy meadow with picnic tables and play structures for the kids; a 2-minute walk leads to the lake (this is a great place for birders). The rooms are clean and basic; half have balconies.

14 miles (23km) south of Golden on Hwy. 95 (Box 2669), Golden, BC V0A 1H0. (C) **800/311-5008** or 250/348-2508. Fax 250/348-2505. www.bbcanada.com/2081.html. 12 units. C$70–C$75 (US$46–US$49) double. Extra person C$15 (US$10). Children under 6 stay free in parents' room. Rates include full breakfast. Senior, off-season, and weekly discounts available. MC, V. **Amenities:** Restaurant (Canadian/Austrian); canoe rentals. *In room:* TV.

Golden Rim Motor Inn   There are dozens of motels in Golden, but this is the pick of the litter. Standing above the precipitous Kicking Horse River valley, just half a mile east of Golden, the Golden Rim boasts sweeping views of the Rockies and the Columbia Valley. It offers standard queen-bed motel rooms, with some kitchen and Jacuzzi units available.

1416 Golden View Rd., Golden, BC V0A 1H0. (C) **877/311-2216** or 250/344-2216. Fax 250/344-6673. www.rockies.net/~goldrim. 81 units. C$98 (US$64) double. AE, MC, V. **Amenities:** Restaurant, bar; indoor pool with waterslide; Jacuzzi; sauna; coin-op laundry. *In room:* A/C, TV, dataport, hair dryer.

Hillside Lodge & Chalets   This stylish, European-style lodge with five standalone chalets sits on 60 forested acres (24 hectares) above the quiet Blaeberry River, 10 miles (16km) north of Golden. Guests stay in comfortable lodge rooms or delightful one-bedroom chalets, the latter with woodstoves, kitchenettes, decks, and handcrafted furniture. All accommodations are newly built, so you'll find everything completely shipshape.

1740 Seward Frontage Rd., Golden, BC V0A 1H0. (C) **250/344-7281.** Fax 250/344-7281. www.mistaya.com/hillside. 11 units. C$90–C$108 (US$59–US$70) lodge double; C$115–C$125 (US$75–US$81) 1-bedroom chalet. Rates include full German-style breakfast. MC, V. **Amenities:** Dining room (guests only); exercise room; sauna. *In room:* Fridge, coffeemaker, hair dryer, no phone.

Kapristo Lodge   If you're looking for a recreation-oriented vacation with homey, lodge-style accommodations, the Kapristo will prove an excellent choice. It sits high above the Columbia Valley, with sweeping views of the Purcell Mountains from the large flagstone-and-planking patio. Guest rooms are comfortably furnished with down quilts and handsome furniture; one unit has its own kitchen, fireplace, and Jacuzzi. What sets this apart from other lodges around Golden is its friendly informality and its owner's efforts to ensure that guests have a good time, whether rafting a river, riding horseback, or sunning on the deck.

1297 Campbell Rd., Golden, BC V0A 1H0. ☎ **250/344-6048**. Fax 250/344-6755. www.kapristolodge.com. 6 units. C$170–C$200 (US$111–US$130) double. Rates include breakfast. MC, V. **Amenities:** Dining room (guests only); Jacuzzi; sauna. *In room:* No phone.

Prestige Inn Golden   Easily the swankest place to stay in Golden, the Prestige Inn is newly constructed and luxurious, with excellent facilities, a variety of room types, and a good restaurant. Guest rooms are spacious and richly appointed, each with two phones and lots of extras.

1049 Trans-Canada Hwy., Golden, BC V0A 1H0. ☎ **877/737-8443** or 250/344-7990. Fax 250/344-7902. www.prestigeinn.com/golden. 82 units. C$149–C$209 (US$97–US$136) double. AE, DISC, MC, V. **Amenities:** Restaurant, bar; indoor pool; exercise room; Jacuzzi; concierge; shopping arcade; limited room service; laundry service. *In room:* A/C, TV w/ pay movies, dataport, kitchenette, fridge, coffeemaker, hair dryer, iron.

WHERE TO DINE

Cedar House PACIFIC NORTHWEST   Perched high above the Columbia Valley south of Golden, the new Cedar House has an exciting menu and one of the best views in the region. The log lodge is divided into cozy dining areas and is flanked by decks, all the better to take in the big-as-all-outdoors vista. The menu features seasonal specials and local meats and vegetables. Grilled pork tenderloin with pear, sage, and brandy cream sauce is a standout.

735 Hefti Rd., 10 min. south of Golden on Hwy 95. ☎ **250/344-4679**. Reservations recommended. Main courses C$17–C$28 (US$11–US$18). MC, V. Sun 10:30am–3:30pm; daily 5–10:30pm.

Eagle's Eye Restaurant ★★ NEW CANADIAN   Canada's highest-elevation restaurant, the Eagle's Eye towers above the new Kicking Horse Resort. Diners take the ski gondola 4,000 feet (1,200m) up to 8,033 feet (2,410m) above sea level to reach this dining room with a 360-degree view of the Rocky, Selkirk, and Purcell mountain ranges. With a panorama like this, the food needn't be good; it's excellent, however, even at this altitude (and with everything brought in by lift). The menu reflects a regional focus, with an emphasis on Alberta lamb and beef, British Columbia salmon and oysters, and seasonal specials like pistachio-crusted halibut with truffled potatoes.

Kicking Horse Resort, west of Golden on Dyke Rd. ☎ **250/344-8626**. Reservations required. Main courses C$21–C$34 (US$14–US$22). AE, MC, V. Mid-Dec to mid-Apr, mid-May to mid-June, and Labour Day to mid-Oct Mon–Thurs 10am–3:30pm, Fri–Sun 10am–9pm. Mid-June to Labour Day daily 10am–10pm. Closed mid-Oct to mid-Dec and mid-Apr to mid-May. Call to confirm opening dates.

La Cabina Ristorante ITALIAN   Golden's only in-town fine-dining option is in a historic log cabin near downtown. The menu features both traditional favorites and house specialties with the zing of *nuova cucina*. Enticing appetizers include *gamberi alla cabina,* tiger prawns sautéed with Pernod and tomatoes. The pasta selection is broad and well prepared, but the kitchen really shines with its beef, veal, chicken, and fish dishes. Pollo Cleopatra, for example, is a pan-fried chicken breast topped with shrimp and finished with a sauce of white wine, garlic, and capers.

1105 Ninth St. ☎ **250/344-2330**. Reservations recommended. Main courses C$10–C$23 (US$7–US$15). AE, MC, V. Mon–Fri 11am–2pm; daily 5–10pm.

Ricco's Family Restaurant PIZZA/CANADIAN   Ricco's is an unprepossessing little eatery with a big local reputation for its pizza. If you're traveling with a group that can't make up its mind about what to eat, Ricco's is still a good choice, as it offers a wide selection of pasta, steak, veal, and chicken dishes. Takeout and free delivery are available.

417 Ninth Ave. N. ℂ **250/344-2665.** Reservations not needed. Main courses C$7–C$13 (US$4.55–US$8). MC, V. Daily 8am–11pm.

The Timber Inn GERMAN/CONTINENTAL This country inn in the little community of Parsons contains an excellent dining room (along with handsome guest rooms). The menu offers a number of starter salads, such as the Turino with tuna and onion, plus excellent bruschetta. Moving on to the main courses, choose from schnitzel, steaks, roast lamb, and chicken. The cozy room overlooks the Columbia Valley and the Purcell Mountains. It's a lovely drive to Parsons on a long summer evening.

3483 Hwy. 95 S., 20 miles (32km) south of Golden. ℂ **250/348-2228.** Reservations recommended. Main courses C$13–C$23 (US$8–US$15). MC, V. Daily 5–9pm.

5 The Kootenay Valley: Cranbrook & Nelson

Cranbrook: 50 miles (80km) N of the U.S.–Canada border

CRANBROOK

The largest city in southeastern British Columbia, Cranbrook (pop. 18,780) exists mostly as a trade center for loggers and agriculturists. The town itself has few tourist sights, but Cranbrook is central to a number of historic and recreational areas and offers ample numbers of hotel rooms. Its setting is spectacularly dramatic: a broad forested valley that looks onto the sky-piercing Canadian Rockies and backside of the U.S. Glacier National Park.

ESSENTIALS

GETTING THERE Cranbrook is near the junction of the north-south Highway 93/95 corridor and the east-west Highway 3. **Greyhound Canada** (ℂ **800/661-8747;** www.greyhound.ca) operates buses that travel on both of these road systems. One-way service from Cranbrook to Golden costs C$28 (US$18); to Calgary, C$53 (US$34); and to Creston, C$17 (US$11). There's also daily service to Spokane, Washington. **Air BC** (ℂ **800/663-3721**) operates flights from Vancouver to the Cranbrook Airport, north of town.

VISITOR INFORMATION The **Cranbrook Visitor Info Centre** is at 2279 Cranbrook St. N. (ℂ **800/222-6174** or 250/426-5914; fax 250/426-3873; www.cranbrookchamber.com).

EXPLORING THE AREA

It's worth getting off the grim Highway 95 strip to visit the pleasant downtown area around Baker Street. As you stroll the broad, tree-lined streets, you'll see a number of heritage brick storefronts and commercial buildings. Especially impressive is the grand, turreted 1909 **Imperial Bank** building at Baker and Eighth streets.

Canadian Museum of Rail Travel ☝ Cranbrook was established as a rail division point, so it's fitting that the town is home to this fascinating museum. Devoted to the social history of rail travel, it preserves a number of historic rail cars, including several "cars of state" designed for royalty. New in 2001 is the Royal Alexandra Hall, a 3,000-square-foot oak-paneled dining room salvaged from Winnipeg's Royal Alexandra Hotel, a CPR hotel torn down in 1971. The ornate moldings, panels, and furniture were carefully numbered and stored for nearly 30 years before being reconstructed here. Other highlights include a complete set of 12 cars built in 1929 for the Canadian Pacific Railway's Trans-Canada

> **Tips** **Special Events**
>
> **Sam Steele Days** (✆ **250/426-4161**) celebrate the Wild West heritage of
> the Cranbrook area. This annual festival, held the third weekend of June,
> features an indoor rodeo, parade, barbecue, pancake breakfast, street
> dances, sports tournaments, and more.

Limited run. Rather like a traveling luxury hotel, the restored cars gleam with
brass and inlaid walnut and mahogany, a vivid testament to the craftsmanship
and taste of the early 20th century. In summer, the dining car offers tea service.

95 King St. ✆ 250/489-3918. www.trainsdeluxe.com. Admission (varies according to which tour is taken)
C$5.25–C$11.95 (US$3.40–US$8) adults, C$4.50–C$9.95 (US$2.90–US$6) seniors, C$2.25–C$6.95
(US$1.45–US$4.50) students, C$.50–C$1.95 (US$.30–US$1.25) preschoolers, C$12.95–C$29.95
(US$8–US$19) families. July–Aug daily 10am–6pm; dining car daily 10am–6pm. Sept to mid-Oct and Easter
to June daily 10am–6pm; mid-Oct to Easter Tues–Sat noon–5pm. Tours given on the half hr.

Fort Steele Heritage Town ⭐ During the 1864 gold rush, a cable ferry
stretched across a narrow section of the Kootenay River, enabling prospectors to
safely cross the turbulent waters. A small settlement sprang up, and after another
mining boom—this time for silver, lead, and zinc—Fort Steele had more than
4,000 inhabitants and was the leading town in the region, as well as the head of
steamboat navigation on the Kootenay River. But when the railroad pushed
through, it bypassed Fort Steele in favor of Cranbrook. Within 5 years, all but
150 of the citizens had left. In the 1960s, the crumbling ghost town was declared
a heritage site. Today, more than 60 restored and reconstructed buildings grace
the townsite, including a hotel, churches, saloons, and a courthouse and jail. In
summer, living-history actors give demonstrations of period skills and occupa-
tions. There's also a steam train, wagon rides, and a variety show at the Wild
Horse Theatre. The International Hotel Restaurant serves Victorian fare.

10 miles (16km) northeast of Cranbrook on Hwy. 93/95. ✆ 250/417-3351, or 250/426-7352 for recorded
information. www.fortsteele.bc.ca. Grounds, year-round daily 9:30am–5:30pm. Evening entertainment and
restaurant, late June to Labour Day Tues–Sun. Admission to grounds, May to mid-Oct C$8.50 (US$6) adults,
C$7.25 (US$5) seniors, C$5 (US$3.25) youths 13–18, C$2.25 (US$1.45) children 6–12, C$19.25 (US$13) families; free admission rest of the year. Tickets good for 2 consecutive days. Reduced 1-day evening admission
also available. Free evening admission for theater and restaurant patrons.

OUTDOOR PURSUITS

BIRD-WATCHING & HIKING   For a short leg-stretcher in a lovely natural
setting, drive just west of Cranbrook to the visitor center. It's located on the
shores of Elizabeth Lake, a small lake and marshy area where songbirds and
migrating birds stop over. Trails ring the lake.

FISHING   Eighteen area rivers, including the Elk River, St. Mary River, and
Kootenay, are often rated among the country's top 10 fly-fishing destinations.
Trophy fish are taken all season long. For lake fishing, Moyie Lake, 19 miles
(30km) south of Cranbrook, has a good stock of kokanee, rainbow, and bull
trout. **Rocky Mountain Angler** (✆ **250/489-4053;** www.geocities.com/rocky
mountainangler) offers hourly, half-day, and full-day instruction. Women-only
trips are available as well.

GOLF   Opened in 2000, the **St. Eugene Mission Golf Resort** (✆ **877/
417-3133** or 250/417-3417) is an 18-hole, Les Furber–designed course with a

links section. Greens fees are C$59 (US$38). The **Cranbrook Golf Club,** 2700 Second St. S. (© **888/211-8855** or 250/426-6462), is a long-established 18-hole course with greens fees starting at C$42 (US$27). The **Mission Hills Golf Course** (© **250/489-3009**) has 18 holes and a par-3 rating, plus a clubhouse and restaurant. Greens fees are C$18 (US$12).

KAYAKING & WHITE-WATER RAFTING Several rivers just east of Cranbrook make thrilling destinations for rafters and kayakers. **Mountain High River Adventures** (© **877/423-4555** or 250/423-4555; www.mountainhigh. bc.ca) offers daylong raft trips on the Elk River (C$75/US$49) and the Bull River (C$99/US$64). If you'd rather hit the water in an inflatable kayak, guided trips are offered for C$99 (US$64).

SKIING Fifty-seven miles (93km) east of Cranbrook, on the western face of the Rockies, is one of the best skiing and snowboarding areas in British Columbia. **Fernie Alpine Resort,** Ski Area Road, Fernie (© **250/423-4655;** www. skifernie.com), is a relatively unheralded resort that's popular with in-the-know snowboarders. Average snowfall is about 30 feet (9m), with a vertical drop of 2,811 feet (843m). There are 97 trails in five alpine bowls, with a total of more than 2,500 acres (1,013 hectares) of skiable terrain served by three quads, two triples, two T-bars, a Poma, and a handle tow with the capacity to handle 12,300 skiers per hour (but it's never *that* busy). Adult lift tickets are C$56 (US$36). Amenities include lodging (© **800/258-SNOW** for reservations), restaurants, rentals, and instruction. The resort, lodges, and lifts remain open in summer, with hiking, mountain biking, and horseback riding the main activities.

WHERE TO STAY

The **Fort Steele Resort & RV Park,** 10 miles (16km) north of Cranbrook on Highway 95 (© **250/489-4268**), has 300 sites costing from C$18 to C$26 (US$12 to US$17). It offers pull-throughs, a tenting area, hot showers, and a rentable log cabin. Trail rides are also available.

Best Western Coach House Motor Inn A well-maintained motor-court motel, the Coach House offers especially large rooms and good service. It's located on the busy Highway 95 strip north of town.

1417 Cranbrook St. N., Cranbrook, BC V1C 3S7. © **800/528-1234** or 250/426-7236. Fax 250/426-7236. bw coachhouse@cyberlink.bc.ca. 76 units. C$76 (US$49) double. Extra person C$10 (US$7). Kitchen C$6 (US$3.90) extra. Family plans available. AE, DC, DISC, MC, V. **Amenities:** Restaurant, lounge; outdoor pool; room service. *In room:* A/C, TV, dataport, coffeemaker, hair dryer, iron.

Cedar Heights B&B This modern home is situated in a residential area just minutes from downtown Cranbrook. The rooms are nicely furnished and have private entrances. Two lounges contain a fireplace, wet bar, fridge, coffee and tea service, and games. From the spacious deck, you can take in the view of the magnificent Rocky Mountains.

1200 13th St., Cranbrook, BC V1C 5V8. © **800/497-6014** or 250/426-0505. Fax 250/426-0045. www. bbcanada.com/cedarheights. 3 units. C$95–C$115 (US$62–US$75) double. Extra person C$25–C$30 (US$16–US$20). Rates include full breakfast. MC, V. Children must be 12 or older. **Amenities:** Jacuzzi; laundry service. *In room:* A/C, TV/VCR, hair dryer.

Mount Baker Hotel The only lodging in downtown Cranbrook, the Mount Baker Hotel was restored in 1999 and now shines with its former glory. For a historic hotel, the rooms are fair-size and comfortably refurbished. The friendly staff will make you feel like you're part of the family. See "Where to Dine," below, for the Corralz restaurant.

1017 Baker St., Cranbrook, BC V1C 1A6. © **888/489-3433** or 250/489-3433. Fax 250/489-3818. www.
cintek.com/mtbakerhotel. 29 units. C$58 (US$38) double; C$150 (US$98) suite. AE, DISC, MC, V. **Amenities:**
Restaurant, bar. *In room:* A/C, TV, fridge.

Nomad Motel Of the many moderately priced motels along the Highway 95
strip north of Cranbrook, the well-maintained Nomad offers the most facilities for
the money. Although it doesn't have its own restaurant, it's next door to a 24-hour
Smitty's and the Apollo steakhouse (see "Where to Dine," below). Apartment-style
family suites are available.

910 Cranbrook St. N., Cranbrook, BC V1C 3S3. © **800/863-6999** or 250/426-6266. Fax 250/426-1871. www.
nomadmotel.bc.ca. 34 units. C$52–C$79 (US$34–US$51) double. Extra person C$5–C$10 (US$3.25–US$7).
Kitchen C$6 (US$3.90) extra. Rates include continental breakfast. AE, MC, V. **Amenities:** Outdoor heated
pool; access to nearby health club; playground; business center; coin-op laundry. *In room:* A/C, TV, dataport,
kitchenette, fridge, microwave, coffeemaker.

Prestige Rocky Mountain Resort & Convention Centre By far the
poshest place to stay in Cranbrook, the Prestige resort features very large and
stylish rooms with lots of extras. There's fine dining at Delmonico's, drinks and
lighter meals at Chattanooga's Bar and Grill, and an espresso bar for your caf-
feine fix. Other perks include a spa offering aromatherapy and massage.

209 Van Horne St. S., Cranbrook, BC V1C 6R9. © **887/737-8443** or 250/417-0444. Fax 250/417-0400. www.
prestigeinn.com/cranbrook. 109 units. C$109 (US$71) double; C$129 (US$84) suite. Extra person C$20
(US$13). Off-season rates and golf/ski packages available. AE, DISC, MC, V. **Amenities:** Restaurant, bar;
indoor pool; full health club (fee); spa; Jacuzzi; room service; massage; same-day dry cleaning. *In room:* A/C,
TV w/ pay movies, fridge, coffeemaker, hair dryer, iron.

WHERE TO DINE

Apollo Ristorante & Steak House GREEK/STEAKHOUSE Ask a local to
recommend a restaurant, and Apollo is sure to be among the first choices. The
menu covers not only traditional Greek dishes, but also a broad selection of
pasta, steaks and prime rib, sandwiches, seafood, even pizza. With such a large
dining room and ambitious menu, you might suspect that quality would suffer.
But someone in the kitchen here knows how to cook, and you'll be pleased with
the hearty, slightly old-fashioned tastiness of the results.

1012 Cranbrook St. N. © **250/426-3721.** Main courses C$9–C$18 (US$6–US$12). AE, MC, V. Daily
11am–10pm.

Corralz STEAKHOUSE The dining room at the restored Mount Baker
Hotel is the best place downtown for steak, prime rib, and barbecued chicken
and ribs. The house Sasquatch Sauce is the chef's own barbecue sauce—and it
packs a wallop.

In the Mount Baker Hotel, 1017 Baker St. © **250/489-3433.** Reservations not needed. Main courses
C$13–C$23 (US$8–US$15). AE, MC, V. Daily 7am–9pm.

Heidi's Restaurant ★ CONTINENTAL The menu at this pleasantly
refined restaurant, with redbrick walls and potted plants, is dominated by the
cuisines of Germany and Italy. Appetizers range from empanadas with cumin
beef to classic escargots. Entrees include steaks from local beef, schnitzels, pastas, fresh fish, and specialties like seared duck breast with black-currant sauce
and spaetzle.

821C Baker St. © **250/426-7922.** Reservations recommended. Main courses C$11–C$23 (US$7–US$15).
AE, MC, V. Mon–Thurs 11am–2:30pm and 5–9pm; Fri–Sat 11:30am–2:30pm and 5–10pm; Sun 5–9pm.

DRIVING THE EAST SHORE OF KOOTENAY LAKE TO NELSON

Sixty-six miles (107km) southwest of Cranbrook on Highway 3 is **Creston** (pop. 4,843), an agricultural town surrounded by orchards, berry fields, and dairies. From here, you have two choices if you're driving to Nelson. You can follow Highway 3 to Salmo, 77 miles (124km), or you can drive the east shore of Kootenay Lake, cross the lake on a free car ferry from Kootenay Bay to Balfour, and then follow the West Arm of Kootenay Lake to Nelson, a distance of 69 miles (112km). We highly recommend the latter route, which connects little lakeside resorts, antiques stores, and artisans' studios—it's one of the most scenic drives in British Columbia.

Kootenay Lake is rather unusual. Trapped between the majestic Selkirk and Purcell ranges, this narrow 62-mile-long (100km) lake is fed by two major rivers from opposite ends of its valley; the lake's outflow is through its West Arm, a cleft in the Selkirks. The lake is famed for its fishing and its wildlife. The greatest concentration of ospreys in North America is along Kootenay Lake.

Driving north from Creston, follow Highway 3A along the estuarial Kootenay River valley. The valley's steep walls and flat base point to its glacial birth. Watch on the west side of the road for a **horse farm** that raises rare Norwegian fjord draft horses, the largest horse breed in the world. **Duck Lake,** a marshy body of water barely separated from Kootenay Lake, is renowned for its bass fishing. The little hamlet of Sirdar sits on the shores of Duck Lake; the **Sirdar Pub,** 8068 Hwy. 3A (© **250/866-5522**), is a good spot for home-style cooking.

Just past Duck Lake, the road drops onto the southern shores of Kootenay Lake, opening up vistas of the Selkirk Mountains. Drive through the wee burg of Sanca and then watch for the **Glass House,** 25 miles (40km) north of Creston (© **250/223-8372**). This curious landmark is a castle-like house constructed of 150,000 square glass embalming-fluid containers. Admission is C$6 (US$3.90).

Boswell is a small community of 200 with a number of venerable lakefront resorts and marinas. It's just south of **Lockhart Creek Provincial Park** (© **250/ 825-3500**), which offers forest hiking trails, access to a swimming beach, and a boat launch. Campsites go for C$12 (US$8). One of the nicer resorts here is the **Destiny Bay Resort,** 11935 Hwy. 3A (© **800/818-6633** or 250/223-8234; www.destinybay.com), with a central lodge and eight sod-roofed cottages, all with fireplaces and verandas. Cottages start at C$180 (US$117).

Be sure to stop at **Crawford Bay** (pop. 312), home to a number of unusual artisans' studios. Craftspeople at the **North Woven Broom Co.** (© **250/ 227-9245**) fashion traditional brooms from local wood and unprocessed broomcorn. At the **Kootenay Forge** (© **250/227-9466**), artist blacksmiths create functional household items using centuries-old hammer-and-forge techniques. **Weavers' Corner Handweaving Studio & Shop** (© **250/227-9655**) uses traditional looming methods to make one-of-a-kind clothing and household items. These three studios are open from mid-May to mid-October, daily from 9am to 5pm. In winter, hours are more fluid, but normally the studios are open Saturday and Sunday from 9am to 5pm.

Also at Crawford Bay is the 18-hole championship **Kokanee Springs Golf Resort** (© **800/979-7999** or 250/227-9226). One of British Columbia's top courses, it has glorious views of the lake and the glaciered face of the Selkirks. Greens fees are C$49 to C$55 (US$32 to US$36). Lessons, rentals, RV camping, dining, and lodging are available.

On the way to the ferry terminal at Kootenay Bay, you'll pass the turnoff for the **Yasodhara Ashram Retreat** (© 250/227-9224), a long-established yoga and retreat center on the shores of the lake. You can visit the Temple of Divine Light, browse the bookstore, or spend the night: Simple rooms go for C$70 to C$90 (US$46 to US$59), including meals.

The 5½-mile (9km) **Kootenay Bay–Balfour ferry** service is apparently the longest free ferry ride in the world. The 40-minute crossing offers a good chance to take in the magnificent mountain-and-fjord scenery. Ferries operate from 6am to midnight; in high season, there are 18 crossings daily.

At Balfour, turn north on Highway 31 and watch for the power poles wearing neckties. If days on the road have made you stiff and sore, **Ainsworth Hot Springs Resort,** 9 miles (15km) north of Balfour (© 800/668-1171 or 250/ 229-4212; www.hotnaturally.com), features an unusual steam-bath cave. The hot springs here were popular with the Native Ktunaxa, although the springs ran fuller after early gold miners made a mine shaft out of the cave from whence the waters flowed. The 114°F (42°C) water flows out of the cave into a large lakeside pool. You can also follow the 65-foot-long (20m) lighted cave back and soak in a waist-deep pool, with hot mineral water dripping from the cave ceiling. Single entry costs C$7 (US$4.55) for adults. The resort also offers lodge rooms from C$93 (US$60). The dining room serves three meals daily.

From Balfour, Highway 3A follows the West Arm of Kootenay Lake past more marinas and fishing resorts. **Kokanee Creek Provincial Park** (© 250/ 825-3500) is a great campground with long, sandy beaches and lots of recreational opportunities. This is also the best spot for **kokanee salmon fishing and viewing;** in late summer, guides lead tours of man-made spawning channels. To find good hiking trails, turn north from Kokanee Creek Provincial Park and follow a fair gravel road for 10 miles (16km) to **Kokanee Glacier Provincial Park.** This wilderness park contains the high country of the Slocan peaks, including 9,100-foot (2,774m) **Kokanee Peak,** draped with glaciers.

From the park entrances, Highway 3 continues along the West Arm, finally crossing over the lake to enter the lovely resort town of Nelson.

NELSON ☆☆

64 miles (102km) N of the U.S.–Canada border

Nelson (pop. 9,585) is quite possibly the most pleasant and attractive town in the British Columbian interior. The late-19th-century commercial district is still intact and still in use, with an eclectic mix of old-fashioned businesses, coffeehouses, and fancy boutiques and galleries. Nelson also offers high-quality B&Bs, hotels, and restaurants, and the setting—along a shelf of land above the West Arm of Kootenay Lake—is scenically splendid.

Nelson was born as a silver-mining town in the 1880s, and its veins proved productive and profitable. By 1900, Nelson was the third-largest city in the province, with an architecturally impressive core of Victorian and Queen Anne–style homes. Today, the gracious town center, coupled with convenient access to recreation in nearby lakes, mountains, and streams, has added to Nelson's new-found luster as an arts capital. Nelson claims to have more artists and craftspeople per capita than any other city in Canada. It certainly has an appealingly youthful, comfortably countercultural feel, and makes a great place to spend a day or two.

ESSENTIALS

GETTING THERE   Nelson is 64 miles (102km) north of the U.S.–Canada border; 151 miles (242km) north of Spokane, Washington; and 407 miles (657km) east of Vancouver. **Greyhound Canada** (© 800/661-8747; www.greyhound.ca) operates daily service from Vancouver for C$95 (US$62) one-way. **North Vancouver Air** (© 800/228-5141) offers four flights a week between Vancouver and Nelson.

VISITOR INFORMATION   Contact the **Nelson Visitor Info Centre,** 225 Hall St. (© 250/352-3433; www.discovernelson.com).

EXPLORING THE AREA

Nelson's main attractions are, in order, the city itself and what's just beyond. As an introduction to the town's wonderful Victorian architecture, stop by the visitor center for brochures on the driving and walking tours of Nelson's significant heritage buildings.

Not to be missed are the château-style **City Hall,** 502 Vernon St., and **Nelson Court House,** designed by F. M. Rattenbury, famed for his designs for the B.C. Parliament Buildings and the Empress hotel, both of which continue to dominate Victoria. Note the three-story, turreted storefront at the corner of Baker and Ward streets, and the **Mara-Barnard building,** 421–431 Baker St., once the Royal Bank of Canada building, with elaborate brickwork and bay windows.

The story of Nelson's human history is told at the **Nelson Museum,** 402 Anderson St. (© 250/352-9813), which has a number of artifacts from the Native Ktunaxa and from the silver-mining days when Nelson was one of the richest towns in Canada. There's a fascinating exhibit on the Doukhobor, a Russian Christian sect that settled along Kootenay Lake in the 1890s. Hours are Monday through Saturday from 1 to 6pm. Admission is C$2 (US$1.30) for adults, C$1 (US$.65) for seniors and students.

Nelson has a number of beautiful parks. **Gyro Park,** at Vernon and Park streets, features formal gardens, an outdoor pool, and panoramic views of Kootenay Lake and the Selkirk Mountains. **Lakeside Park,** which flanks Kootenay Lake near the base of the Nelson Bridge, offers swimming beaches, tennis courts, and a playground.

You can explore Nelson's lakefront on foot on the **Waterfront Pathway,** which winds along the shore from near the Prestige Resort to Lakeside Park. Or, in summer, hop on the restored **streetcar no. 23,** which runs from Lakeside Park to Hall Street, along the waterfront. At the turn of the 20th century, Nelson had a streetcar system and was the smallest city in Canada to boast such public transport. The system fell out of use in the 1940s, but a stretch of the track remains intact. From mid-May to Labour Day, the streetcar runs daily

---

⌜Tips A Bird's-Eye View

For a flightseeing tour of the area, contact **Nelson Mountain Air Inc.** (© 250/354-1456), which offers 1-hour floatplane tours of the Kokanee Glacier and the surrounding Selkirk Mountains for C$75 (US$49), with a minimum of two passengers. The tours begin at the floatplane base at the small Nelson airport, along the waterfront at Hall Street.

---

from noon to 6pm. Tickets are C$2 (US$1.30) for adults and C$1 (US$.65) for seniors and students.

OUTDOOR PURSUITS

FISHING   Fishing is legendary in 656-foot-deep (200m) Kootenay Lake, which has 310 miles (500km) of lakefront. For guided trips and advice, contact **Screamin' Reel Fly and Tackle,** Balfour ferry landing, 21 miles (34km) northeast of town on Highway 3A (© **250/229-5262**).

GOLF   Granite Pointe Golf Club, 1123 Richards St. W. (© **250/352-5913**), is a hilly 18-hole, par-72 course with fantastic views of Kootenay Lake. Greens fees are C$40 (US$26); rentals, a clubhouse with dining, and a driving range are available.

HIKING   Accessible right in town is a 5½-mile (9km) rails-to-trails system on the old Burlington Northern line that follows the southern edge of the town along the flanks of Toad Mountain. You can join the path at a number of places; from downtown, follow Cedar Street south to find one entry point. The closest wilderness hiking is at **Kokanee Glacier Provincial Park** (see "Driving the East Shore of Kootenay Lake to Nelson," above), 13 miles (21km) northeast of Nelson on Highway 3A, then 10 miles (16km) north on a gravel road.

KAYAKING   For rentals or a guided tour (C$89/US$58), contact **Kootenay Kayak Co.,** 579 Baker St. (© **877/229-4959** or 250/229-4959).

MOUNTAIN BIKING   The visitor center has a free map of old logging roads and rail lines that are available for biking. The Burlington Northern rails-to-trails system (see "Hiking," above) is also open to mountain bikers. For rentals and trail conditions, contact **Gerick Cycle & Sports,** 702 Baker St. (© **800/665-4441**).

SKIING   Ten miles (16km) south of Nelson off Highway 6 is the **Whitewater Ski Resort** (© **800/666-9420** or 250/354-4944; www.skiwhitewater. com), with some of British Columbia's best snow conditions. The ski area is in a natural snow-catching bowl below an escarpment of 8,300-foot (2,490m) peaks. The average snowfall is 40 feet (12m), and that snow falls as pure powder. The mountain consists of groomed runs, open bowls, glades, chutes, and tree skiing; 80% of the runs are rated either intermediate or advanced. There are two double chairs and a handle tow; the vertical drop is 1,300 feet (390m). Lift tickets cost C$37 (US$24). Facilities include a day lodge with rentals, dining, and drinks. A new Nordic Centre has 11½ miles (18km) of groomed cross-country ski trails.

WHERE TO STAY

Best Western Baker Street Inn   The Baker Street Inn stands at the end of the historic downtown area, within easy walking distance of both shopping and dining. Guest rooms are rather basic, but very clean and comfortable.

153 Baker St., Nelson, BC V1L 4H1. © **888/255-3525** or 250/352-3525. Fax 250/352/2995. www.bwbaker streetinn.com. 70 units. C$109–C$259 (US$71–US$168) double. Extra person C$20 (US$13). AE, DISC, MC, V. **Amenities:** Restaurant, lounge; Jacuzzi; exercise room; business center; coin-op laundry. *In room:* A/C, TV, dataport, fridge, microwave, coffeemaker, hair dryer.

Casa Blanca Bed & Breakfast   This exotic 1938 Art Deco mini-mansion offers spacious rooms in a great location across from Kootenay Lake. The detailing in the house is amazing: The living room boasts tropical-wood paneling, beveled-glass doors, a quartz fireplace, and inlaid hardwood floors, as well as such modern comforts as a TV, VCR, and CD player. It's an easy walk to downtown Nelson or to Kootenay Lake beaches.

724 Second St., Nelson, BC V1L 2L9. ℂ 888/354-4431 or 250/354-4431. Fax 250/354-4431. www. bbcanada.com/1941.html. 3 units (1 with private bathroom). C$70–C$100 (US$46–US$65) double. Extra person C$15 (US$10). MC, V. *In room:* A/C, no phone.

Dancing Bear Inn   The Dancing Bear is a first-rate hostel right in the thick of things downtown. The atmosphere and furnishings are more like what you'd expect to find in a B&B—a grimy backpackers' flophouse this is definitely not. The furniture is locally made from pine, beds are made up with down duvets, and paintings by area artists grace the walls. This is not your everyday hostel, and even if you're not into the hostelling scene, you'll find it a great place to meet people.

171 Baker St., Nelson, BC V1L 4H1. ℂ 250/352-7573. Fax 250/352-9818. www.dancingbearinn.com. 35 beds. C$20 (US$13) dorm bed; C$46 (US$30) private unit. Family and group rates, seasonal packages, and discounts for Hostelling International members available. MC, V. **Amenities:** Kitchen; common room with TV/VCR; computer with Internet access; laundry. *In room:* No phone.

Heritage Inn   This beautifully preserved 1898 hotel has been renovated to accommodate modern ideas of comfort while maintaining its vintage charm. For an antique hotel, the rooms are good-size and smartly furnished. You'll want to visit the Heritage Inn even if you're not staying here, just to check out the wonderful bars and lobby area.

422 Vernon St., Nelson, BC V1L 4E5. ℂ 877/568-0888 or 250/352-5331. Fax 250/352-5214. www.heritage inn.org. 43 units. C$75–C$94 (US$49–US$61) double. Extra person C$10–C$15 (US$7–US$10). Kitchen C$12 (US$8) extra. Rates include breakfast. Golf and ski packages available. AE, MC, V. **Amenities:** Two restaurants, two bars; access to nearby health club; salon; beer-and-wine store. *In room:* TV.

Inn the Garden Bed & Breakfast   This spacious B&B is perched on a hill just a block off Baker Street, with views of the lake and Kootenay Peak. The handsome painted lady–style Victorian has six rooms with a mix of private and shared bathrooms, plus a garden, patio, and deck. A separate three-bedroom cottage, with kitchen and TV/VCR, is perfect for families or groups. Rates for guests staying in the main house include full breakfast; cottage guests get the makings for breakfast plus fresh baked goods delivered to their door.

408 Victoria St., Nelson, BC V1L 4K5. ℂ 800/596-2337 or 250/352-3226. Fax 250/352-3284. www.innthe garden.com. 7 units. C$80–C$140 (US$52–US$91) double in main house; C$170 (US$111) cottage. Extra person C$15–C$25 (US$10–US$16). Rates for main house include full breakfast. Golf and ski packages available. AE, MC, V. Children accepted in cottage only.

Prestige Lakeside Resort & Convention Centre   Down on the lakeshore, the Prestige is Nelson's full-service resort, offering spacious, beautifully furnished rooms with all the services you'd expect at a luxury hotel. All units have balconies, and a number of theme rooms will spice up a special occasion.

701 Lakeside Dr., Nelson, BC V1L 6G3. ℂ 877/737-8443 or 250/352-7222. Fax 250/352-3966. www. prestigeinn.com/nelson. 101 units. C$149–C$299 (US$97–US$194) double. Extra person C$20 (US$13). Off-season rates available. AE, DC, DISC, MC, V. **Amenities:** Restaurant, coffee bar, bar; indoor pool; exercise room; spa; Jacuzzi; concierge; car-rental desk; limited room service; massage; laundry service; same-day dry cleaning. *In room:* A/C, TV w/ pay movies, dataport, fridge, coffeemaker, hair dryer, iron.

WHERE TO DINE

The restaurants at the **Prestige Resort** and the **Heritage Inn** (see "Where to Stay," above) are good, and a wander down **Baker Street** will reveal dozens of cafes, coffeehouses, and inexpensive ethnic restaurants. Don't miss the **Dominion Café,** 334 Baker St. (© **250/352-1904**), an old diner offering sandwiches, light entrees, baked goods, and a friendly, relaxed atmosphere. **Rice Bowl,** 301 Baker St. (© **250/354-4129**), serves fast-food Thai and Japanese favorites. A popular hangout, morning to night, is **Jigsaws Coffee Co.,** 503 Baker St. (© **250/352-5961**).

All Seasons Café ★★ NORTHWEST   The All Seasons is reason enough to visit Nelson. Located in a handsome heritage home a block off busy Baker Street, it isn't easy to find, but if you want to eat at British Columbia's best restaurant east of Vancouver, then persevere. To start, try the outstanding brie and asparagus flan with Italian figs and warm honey, or go for the Dungeness crab and potato latkes with fresh salsa. Main courses include a number of vegetarian and fish options. Spinach fettuccine is tossed with rosemary-infused roasted tomato sauce and topped with either hempnut balls (a surprisingly flavorful tofu creation rolled in hemp seeds) or lamb meatballs. The wine list has many Okanagan Valley selections, and the service is friendly and professional.

620 Herridge Lane. © **250/352-0101.** Reservations required. Main courses C$13–C$28 (US$8–US$18). AE, MC, V. Daily 5–10pm; Sun brunch 10am–2:30pm.

Max and Irma's Kitchen NEW ITALIAN   The focus at bright, lively Max and Irma's is the wood-fired oven. Located half a block off Baker Street, this restaurant serves very tasty, California-influenced Italian cuisine. The large menu encompasses a selection of individual pizzas, calzones, toasted panini sandwiches, and pastas.

515A Kootenay St. © **250/352-2332.** www.maxandirmaskitchen.com. Reservations not needed. Main courses C$8–C$12 (US$5–US$8). MC, V. Sun–Thurs 11am–9pm; Fri–Sat 11am–11pm.

13

Gateways to the Canadian Rockies: Calgary & Edmonton

Stretching from the Northwest Territories to the U.S. border of Montana in the south, flanked by the Rocky Mountains in the west and the province of Saskatchewan in the east, Alberta is a big, beautiful, empty chunk of North America. It has 2.5 million inhabitants, over half of whom live in Edmonton, the provincial capital, and Calgary, a former cow town grown large and wealthy with oil money.

Both Calgary and Edmonton serve as gateways to the famed Canadian Rockies that rise on their western horizons. Since both cities function as air hubs for the major national parks—there are no scheduled flights to destinations within the Canadian Rockies—and since both Calgary and Edmonton are on major east-west road systems, chances are good you'll spend some time here. (See chapter 14 for complete coverage of the Rockies.)

Culturally, Calgary and Edmonton are a beguiling mix of rural Canadian sincerity and big-city swagger and affluence. Both cities are models of modern civic pride and hospitality; in fact, an anonymous behavioral survey recently named Edmonton Canada's friendliest city.

Early settlers first came to Alberta for its wealth of furs; the Hudson's Bay Company established Edmonton House on the North Saskatchewan River in 1795. The Blackfoot, one of the West's most formidable Indian nations, maintained control of the prairies until the 1870s, when the Royal Canadian Mounted Police arrived to enforce the white man's version of law and order. The Mounties' Fort Calgary was established on the Bow River in 1875. Open-range cattle ranching prospered on the rich grasslands, and agriculture is still the basis of the rural economy. Vast oil reserves were discovered beneath the prairies in the 1960s, introducing a tremendous boom across the province.

Plan to take a day or two to explore these lively cities. Calgary has excellent museums and one of the most exciting restaurant scenes in Canada; Edmonton, dominated by its university and its capital status, has a vital arts scene and—not to be dismissed lightly—one of the largest shopping malls-cum-entertainment palaces in the world.

1 Calgary

79 miles (128km) E of Banff, 184 miles (296km) N of the U.S. border

Calgary dates back to 1875, when a detachment of the Northwest Mounted Police reached the confluence of the Bow and Elbow rivers. Gradually, the lush prairie lands drew tremendous beef herds, and Calgary grew into a cattle metropolis and meat-packing center. When World War II ended, the placid city numbered barely 100,000.

Alberta

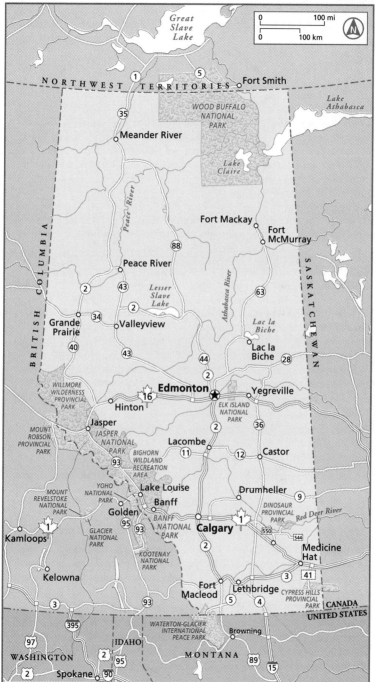

The oil boom erupted in the late 1960s, and in a single decade utterly changed the complexion of the city. The population shot up at a pace that made statisticians dizzy. Office high-rises, hotels, and shopping centers went up so fast that even locals weren't sure what was around the next corner.

The 1980s recession caused by the world's oil glut cooled Calgary's overheated growth considerably. But—at least from the visitor's angle—this enhanced the city's attractiveness. The once-ubiquitous rooftop cranes that marred its skyline have largely disappeared. However, Calgary continues to prosper. In the mid-1990s, the oil market heated up again, and Alberta's pro-business political climate tempted national companies to build their headquarters here. And in 1988, Calgary was the site of the Winter Olympics, giving it the opportunity to roll out the welcome mat on a truly international scale. The city outdid itself in hospitality, erecting a whole network of facilities, including the Canada Olympic Park west of downtown.

Calgary now has an imposing skyline with dozens of business towers topping 40 stories. Despite this, the city doesn't seem urban. With its many parks and convivial populace, Calgary retains the atmosphere of a much smaller, friendlier town.

ESSENTIALS

GETTING THERE   By Plane   Calgary International Airport is 10 miles (16km) northeast of the city. It's served by **Air Canada** (✆ **800/372-9500;** www.aircanada.ca), **Delta** (✆ **800/221-1212;** www.delta.com), **American Airlines** (✆ **800/433-7300;** www.aa.com), **United** (✆ **800/241-6522;** www.ual.com), and **KLM** (✆ **800/374-7747;** www.klm.com), plus Air BC, Horizon, and several commuter lines.

A shuttle service to and from Edmonton is run almost hourly by Air Canada and Canadian Airlines. Cab fare to downtown hotels comes to around C$25 (US$16). The **Airporter Bus** (✆ **403/531-3909**) takes you downtown for C$9 (US$6).

By Car   From the U.S. border in the south, Highway 2 runs to Calgary and continues north to Edmonton (via Red Deer). From Vancouver in the west to Regina in the east, take the Trans-Canada Highway.

By Train   The nearest VIA Rail station is in Edmonton. You can, however, take a scenic train ride between Vancouver and Calgary on the *Rocky Mountaineer,* operated by the **Great Rocky Mountaineer Railtours** (✆ **800/665-7245** or 604/606-7245; www.rockymountaineer.com). Ticket prices start at US$729 for 2 days of travel, which includes meals and overnight lodging in Kamloops.

By Bus   Greyhound Canada (✆ **800/661-8747** or 403/260-0877; www.greyhound.ca) links Calgary with most other points in Canada, including Banff and Edmonton, as well as towns in the United States. The depot is at 877 Greyhound Way SW.

VISITOR INFORMATION   The **Visitor Service Centres** at Tower Centre, Ninth Avenue SW and Centre Street, and at the airport, provide maps and information. These are run by the **Calgary Convention and Visitors Bureau,** Suite 200, 238 11th Ave. SE. Included in its telephone services is a useful, no-charge accommodations bureau (✆ **800/661-1678** or 403/263-8510; www.tourismcalgary.com).

Calgary

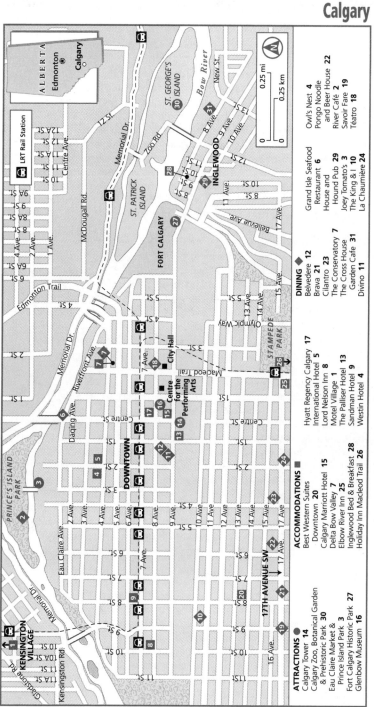

ATTRACTIONS ●

Calgary Tower **14**
Calgary Zoo, Botanical Garden & Prehistoric Park **30**
Eau Claire Market & Prince Island Park **3**
Fort Calgary Historic Park **27**
Glenbow Museum **16**

ACCOMMODATIONS ■

Best Western Suites Downtown **20**
Calgary Marriott Hotel **15**
Delta Bow Valley **7**
Elbow River Inn **25**
Inglewood Bed & Breakfast **28**
Holiday Inn Macleod Trail **26**
Hyatt Regency Calgary **17**
International Hotel **5**
Lord Nelson Inn **8**
Motel Village **1**
The Palliser Hotel **13**
Sandman Hotel **9**
Westin Hotel **4**

DINING ◆

Belvedere **12**
Brava **21**
Cilantro **23**
The Conservatory **7**
The Cross House Garden Cafe **31**
Divino **11**
Grand Isle Seafood Restaurant **6**
House and Hound Pub **29**
Joey Tomato's **3**
The King & I **10**
La Chaumière **24**
Owl's Nest **4**
Pongo Noodle and Beer House **22**
River Café **2**
Savoir Fare **19**
Téatro **18**

✐ The Calgary Stampede

Every July, Calgary puts on the biggest, wildest, woolliest western fling on earth. To call the stampede a show would be a misnomer. The whole city participates by going mildly crazy, donning western gear, whooping, hollering, dancing, and generally behaving uproariously.

Many of the organized events spill out into the streets, but most of them take place in **Stampede Park,** a show, sports, and exhibition ground south of downtown that was built for just this purpose. Portions of the park become amusement areas, whirling, spinning, and rotating with the latest rides. Other parts are set aside especially for children. Still other areas host livestock shows, a food fair, handicraft exhibitions, an art show, lectures, an international bazaar, a casino, lotteries, and entertainment on several stages.

The top attractions, though, are the rodeo events, the largest and most prestigious of their kind in North America. Cowboys from all over the world take part in such competitions as riding bucking broncos and bulls, roping calves, and wrestling steers for prize money totaling C\$1.1 million (US\$715,000). At the world-famous **Chuckwagon Race,** you'll see old-time western cook wagons thundering around the track in a fury of dust and pounding hooves. At night, the arena becomes a blaze of lights when the **Stampede Grandstand**—the largest outdoor extravaganza in the world—takes over with precision-kicking dancers, clowns, bands, and spectacles.

We should tell you right from the start that the whole city of Calgary is absolutely packed for the occasion—not just to the rafters, but way out into the surrounding countryside as well. Reserving accommodations well ahead is essential. For lodging assistance, call **Calgary's Convention and Visitors Bureau** ✆ 800/661-1678). Some downtown watering holes even take reservations for space at their bars; that should give you an idea of how busy it gets.

The same advice applies to reserving tickets for all of the park events. Tickets cost between C\$20 and C\$54 (US\$13 and US\$35), depending on the event, the seats, and whether it takes place in the afternoon or evening. Contact the **Calgary Exhibition and Stampede** (✆ 800/661-1767; fax 403/223-9736; www.calgarystampede.com).

CITY LAYOUT   Central Calgary lies between the Bow River in the north and the Elbow River to the south. The two rivers meet at the eastern end of the city, forming **St. George's Island,** which houses a park and the zoo. South of the island stands **Fort Calgary,** birthplace of the city. The Bow River makes a bend north of downtown, and in this bend nestles **Prince's Island Park** and **Eau Claire Market.** The Canadian Pacific Railway tracks run between 9th and 10th avenues. Also south of the tracks, off Macleod Drive, is **Stampede Park,** scene of Calgary's greatest annual festival. Northwest, just across the Bow River, is the **University of Calgary**'s lovely campus. The airport is just northwest of the city.

Calgary is divided into four segments: northeast (NE), southeast (SE), north-west (NW), and southwest (SW), with avenues running east–west and streets north–south. The north and south numbers begin at Centre Avenue, the east and west numbers at Centre Street—a recipe for confusion if ever there was one.

GETTING AROUND Calgary Transit System (© **403/276-1000**) operates buses and a light-rail system called the C-Train. You can transfer from light rail to buses on the same ticket. The ride costs C$1.75 (US$1.15) for adults and C$1.10 (US$.70) for children; C-Train is free in the downtown stretch between 10th Street and City Hall (buses are not). Tickets are only good for travel in one direction.

Car-rental firms include **Avis,** 211 Sixth Ave. SW (© **403/269-6166**); **Budget,** 140 Sixth Ave. SE (© **403/226-0000**); and **Hertz,** 227 Sixth Ave. SW (© **403/221-1681**). Each has a counter at the airport as well.

To summon a taxi, call **Checker Cabs** (© **403/299-9999**), **Red Top Cabs** (© **403/974-4444**), or **Yellow Cabs** (© **403/974-1111**).

The first thing a pedestrian will notice about Calgary is how long the east-west blocks are. Allow 15 minutes to walk 5 blocks. Pedestrians will also like the "Plus-15" system, a series of enclosed walkways 15 feet (4.5m) above street level that connects downtown buildings. These walkways enable you to shop in living-room comfort, regardless of weather. Watch for the little "+15" signs on streets for access points.

FAST FACTS There's an **American Express** office at 421 Seventh Ave. SW (© **403/261-5085**). The **Alberta Motor Association,** affiliated with the CAA, reciprocates with AAA; the Calgary office is at 4700 17th Ave. SW (© **403/240-5300**). The main **post office** is at 207 Ninth Ave. (© **403/974-2078**).

For medical care, go to **Foothills Hospital,** 1403 29th St. NW (© **403/670-1110**). If you need a pharmacy, look in the phone book for **Shoppers Drug Mart,** which has more than a dozen branches in Calgary, most open until midnight. The one at Chinook Centre, 6455 Macleod Trail S. (© **403/253-2424**), is open 24 hours.

EXPLORING THE CITY

Canada Olympic Park, 88 Canada Olympic Park Rd. SW (© **403/247-5452;** www.coda.ab.ca), exhibits the world's largest collection of Olympic souvenirs. Activities include summer luge rides, a mountain-bike course, and lift rides up to the ski-jump tower.

Calgary Tower Reaching 626 feet (762 steps) into the sky, this Calgary landmark is topped by an observation terrace offering unparalleled views of the city and mountains and prairies beyond. The high-speed elevator whisks you to the top in just 63 seconds. You can enjoy drinks and the panoramic vista in the cocktail lounge. The **Panorama Restaurant** (© **403/266-7171**) is the near-mandatory revolving restaurant.

Ninth Ave. and Centre St. SW. © **403/266-7171.** www.calgarytower.com. Elevator ride C$7.95 (US$5) adults, C$3 (US$1.95) children. June 15–Sept 15 daily 7:30am–11pm; Sept 16–June 14 daily 8am–10pm. LRT: First St. E.

Calgary Zoo, Botanical Garden & Prehistoric Park ☆ *Kids* Calgary's thoughtfully designed zoo lies on St. George's Island, in the Bow River. You'll particularly want to see the majestic lowland gorillas and the African warthogs.

The flora and fauna of western and northern Canada are on display in the Botanical Garden, along with an amazing tropical butterfly enclosure. The Prehistoric Park is a three-dimensional textbook of ancient dinosaur habitats populated by 22 amazingly realistic replicas. Call to inquire about special summer events, like Thursday jazz nights and free interpretive talks.

1300 Zoo Rd. NE. © **403/232-9300.** www.calgaryzoo.ab.ca. Admission C$11 (US$7) adults, C$5.50 (US$3.60) children 2–17. Off-season discounts available. Mid-May to Sept daily 9am–6pm; Oct to mid-May daily 9am–4pm. LRT: Zoo station.

Eau Claire Market & Prince's Island Park ✫✫ Calgary's most dynamic shopping, social, and dining center is Eau Claire Market, a car-free pedestrian zone north of downtown on the banks of the Bow River. This is where much of Calgary comes to eat, drink, shop, sunbathe, jog, and hang out. The market itself is a huge two-story warehouse containing fish, meat, vegetable, and fruit stalls; boutiques; innumerable casual restaurants and bars; a four-screen cinema; and the **IMAX Theatre** (© **403/974-4629**). Surrounding the market are lawns, fountains, and pathways leading to **Prince's Island Park,** a bucolic island in the Bow River, shaded by cottonwood trees and populated by hordes of Canada geese.

Near Second Ave. SW and Third St. SW. © **403/264-6450.** Free admission. Market building open 9am–9pm; shops and restaurants have varying hr. LRT: Third St. W.

Fort Calgary Historic Park ✫✫ *Kids* Fort Calgary is a public park of 40 acres (16 hectares), spread around the ruins of the original Mounted Police stronghold. At the moment, volunteers are reconstructing an exact replica of the original fort, using traditional methods and building materials. There are a number of interesting videos and docent-led displays; always in focus are the adventures and hardships of the Mounties a century ago. The rigors of their westward march and the almost unbelievable isolation they endured now seem incredible.

750 Ninth Ave. SE. © **403/290-1875.** www.fortcalgary.com. Admission C$6.50 (US$4.20) adults, C$5.50 (US$3.60) seniors and students, C$3.50 (US$2.30) youths 7–17. May to mid-Oct daily 9am–5pm. LRT: Bridgeland.

Glenbow Museum ✫✫ One of the country's finest museums, the Glenbow is a must for anyone with an interest in the history and culture of western Canada. What sets it apart from other museums chronicling the continent's Native cultures and pioneer settlement is the excellence of its interpretation. Especially notable is the third floor, with its vivid evocation of Native cultures and compelling description of western Canada's exploration and settlement. You'll enjoy the brief asides into whimsy, like the display of early washing machines.

130 Ninth Ave. SE (at First St.). © **403/268-4100.** www.glenbow.org. Admission C$10 (US$7) adults, C$7.50 (US$4.90) seniors, C$6 (US$3.90) students and children, C$30 (US$20) families. Discounted admission Thurs–Fri 5–9pm. Daily 9am–5pm (Thurs–Fri until 9pm). LRT: First St. E.

WHERE TO STAY

The **Alberta Bed & Breakfast Association** (www.bbalberta.com) and the visitor center (© **800/661-1678**) can help you secure accommodations. Reserve as far in advance as possible; Calgary is solidly booked for the Stampede.

DOWNTOWN
Expensive

Calgary Marriott Hotel The Marriott is about as central as things get in Calgary: Linked to the convention center and convenient to the Centre for the

Performing Arts and the Glenbow Museum, the hotel is also connected via sky-walk with Palliser Square, Calgary Tower, and loads of downtown shopping. Guest rooms are outfitted with niceties like windows that open and desks set up for business travelers. Yes, it's a convention hotel—but a lot nicer than the stereotype.

110 Ninth Ave. SE (at Centre St.), Calgary, AB T2G 5A6. ✆ 800/228-9290 or 403/266-7331. Fax 403/262-8442. www.marriotthotels.com. 384 units. From C$185–C$285 (US$120–US$185) double. C$189–C$259 (US$123–US$168) suite. Extra person C$20 (US$13). Weekend packages available. AE, DC, DISC, MC, V. Valet parking C$19 (US$12) per day; self-parking C$15 (US$10). **Amenities:** Restaurant, lounge; indoor pool; exercise room; Jacuzzi; sauna; concierge; business center; room service; same-day dry cleaning. *In room:* A/C, TV, dataport, microwave, fridge, coffeemaker, hair dryer, iron.

Delta Bow Valley ⭐ *Kids* The Delta is one of Calgary's finest hotels. Its focus is upscale business travel: Each corner business suite contains a printer, fax, and ergonomic desk chair. Standard rooms are spacious, equipped with all the niceties you'd expect. The Delta also goes the distance to make families welcome: In summer and on weekends, you can leave the kids at the activity center while you head out to dinner.

209 Fourth Ave. SE, Calgary, AB T2G 0C6. ✆ 403/266-1980. Fax 403/266-0007. 398 units. C$225 (US$146) double; C$245–C$299 (US$159–US$194) suite. Children under 18 stay free in parents' room; children under 6 eat free from children's menu. Weekend specials available. AE, DC, DISC, MC, V. Parking C$15 (US$10) Mon–Fri; free Sat–Sun. **Amenities:** Two restaurants, lounge; marvelous rooftop pool and deck; exercise room; Jacuzzi; sauna; children's center; concierge; business center; room service; laundry service; same-day dry cleaning. *In room:* A/C, TV, dataport, minibar, fridge, coffeemaker, hair dryer, iron.

Hyatt Regency Calgary ⭐⭐ Downtown's latest and most upscale hotel, the Hyatt is linked to the Telus Convention Centre and is convenient to shopping and arts venues. Guest rooms are large and uncrowded, even with comfy armchairs and desks. Suites are truly spacious, with most of the comforts of home. The Hyatt flanks historic Stephens Avenue, with its handsome stone storefronts that were happily preserved when the hotel was built.

700 Center St. S., Calgary, AB T2G 5P6. ✆ 800/233-1234 or 403/717-1234. Fax 403/537-4444. www.hyatt.com. 355 units. From C$180 (US$117) double; from C$404 (US$263) suite. AE, DISC, MC, V. Valet parking C$18 (US$12); self-parking C$15 (US$10). **Amenities:** Restaurant, lounge; indoor pool; health club; spa; concierge; business center; babysitting; laundry service; same-day dry cleaning. *In room:* A/C, TV, dataport, minibar, coffeemaker, hair dryer.

International Hotel ⭐ A soaring tower with breathtaking views from the upper balconies, the International is an all-suite hotel near Chinatown and Eau Claire Market. Originally constructed as an apartment building, the rooms are some of the largest in town. The downside? The elevators date from the old days; in summer, when tour buses hit, it can be exasperating to wait for them to serve guests on all 35 floors. Otherwise, this is a delightful choice if you're looking for spacious accommodations.

220 Fourth Ave. SW, Calgary, AB T2P 0H5. ✆ 800/637-7200 or 403/265-9600. Fax 403/265-6949. www.internationalhotel.ca. 247 units. C$220–C$245 (US$143–US$159) 1-bedroom suite; C$230–C$265 (US$150–US$172) 2-bedroom suite. Children under 16 stay free in parents' room. AE, DC, MC, V. Parking C$8 (US$5) per day. **Amenities:** Restaurant, bar; indoor pool; exercise room; Jacuzzi; sauna; concierge; limited room service; babysitting; same-day dry cleaning. *In room:* A/C, TV w/ pay movies, dataport, minibar, coffeemaker, hair dryer, iron.

The Palliser Hotel ⭐⭐ This is the classiest address in all of Calgary. Opened in 1914 as one of the Canadian Pacific Railway hotels, the Palliser is Calgary's landmark historic lodging. The marble lobby is the very picture of Edwardian sumptuousness. You'll feel like an Alberta Cattle King in the Rimrock Dining Room, with vaulted ceilings, a massive stone fireplace, and hand-tooled leather panels. Guest rooms are large for a hotel of this vintage—the Pacific Premier rooms would be suites at most other properties—and they preserve the period charm while incorporating modern luxuries.

133 Ninth Ave. SW, Calgary, AB T2P 2M3. ℭ 800/441-1414 or 403/262-1234. Fax 403/260-1260. www. fairmont.com. 421 units. C$178–C$299 (US$116–US$194) double; from C$299 (US$194) suite. AE, DC, DISC, MC, V. Valet parking C$18 (US$12) per day; self-parking C$15 (US$10). **Amenities:** Restaurant, bar; indoor pool; health club; spa; concierge; business center; salon; 24-hr. room service; babysitting; laundry service; same-day dry cleaning. *In room:* A/C, TV, dataport, minibar, hair dryer, iron.

Westin Hotel ★★ *Kids*   The Westin is a massive luxury block in the heart of the financial district. Despite its anonymous business-hotel exterior, the interior has a subtle western feel that's reflected in the Mission-style furniture, Navajo-look upholstery, and period photos. Beautiful barn-wood breakfronts and low-boys dispel the feeling that you're in one of the city's most modern properties. The hotel rolls out the welcome mat for kids, offering children's furniture, babysitting, and a children's menu. Special needs are anticipated, from strollers to room-service delivery of fresh diapers!

320 Fourth Ave. SW, Calgary, AB T2P 2S6. ℭ 800/937-8461 or 403/266-1611. www.westin.com. 525 units. C$99–C$299 (US$64–US$194) double; from C$349 (US$227) suite. Extra person C$20 (US$13). Family and senior rates available. AE, DC, DISC, MC, V. Parking C$14 (US$9) per day. **Amenities:** Seven restaurants (see the Owl's Nest under "Where to Dine," below), lounge; panoramic 17th-floor indoor pool; sauna; whirlpool; health club; spa; concierge; business center; 24-hr. room service; laundry service; same-day dry cleaning. *In room:* A/C, TV, dataport, coffeemaker, hair dryer.

Moderate & Inexpensive

Travelers on a budget have excellent though limited choices in downtown Calgary. Luckily, the light-rail system makes it easy to stay outside the city center yet have access to the restaurants and sights of downtown.

Best Western Suites Downtown   This all-suite hotel is an excellent value. The rooms are quite large, almost apartment-size, and fitted with quality furniture; some come with efficiency kitchens. It's located a few blocks from downtown, but near trendy 17th Avenue.

1330 Eighth St. SW, Calgary, AB T2R 1B3. ℭ 800/981-2555 or 403/228-6900. Fax 403/228-5535. www.best westernsuites.com. 123 units. C$125–C$145 (US$81–US$94) junior suite; C$165 (US$107) 1-bedroom suite; C$185 (US$120) 2-bedroom suite. Extra person C$5 (US$3.25). Senior, weekly, and monthly rates available. AE, DISC, MC, V. Free parking. **Amenities:** Restaurant; Jacuzzi; laundry. *In room:* A/C, TV, dataport, kitchenette, coffeemaker, hair dryer.

Calgary International Hostel   This is the city's most affordable lodging—but there are reasons beyond economy to stay here. The hostel is near downtown, convenient to bars and restaurants along Stephen Avenue and theaters near the performing-arts center.

520 Seventh Ave. SE, Calgary, AB T2G 0J6. ℭ 403/269-8239. Fax 403/266-6227. www.hihostels.ca. 120 beds. C$16 (US$10) members, C$20 (US$13) nonmembers. MC, V. Free parking. **Amenities:** Two family rooms; coin-op laundry; small convenience store. *In room:* No phone.

Lord Nelson Inn *Value*   One of the best deals in the city, the Lord Nelson is a modern structure with recently renovated rooms. Although on the edge of downtown, it's just a block from the free C-Train, which will put you in the center of things in 5 minutes (or you can walk in 10). Although it's not the last word in luxury, it does offer clean, perfectly pleasant motel rooms—and you don't have to pay extortionate rates for parking.

1020 Eighth Ave. SW, Calgary, AB T2P 1J3. ⓒ 800/661-6017 or 403/269-8262. Fax 403/269-4868. 57 units. C$95 (US$62) double; C$105–C$195 (US$68–US$127) suite. Extra person C$10 (US$7). Children under 18 stay free in parents' room. AE, MC, V. Free parking. **Amenities:** Restaurant, pub; Jacuzzi; laundry service. *In room:* A/C, TV, dataport, fridge.

Sandman Hotel ⓡ *Value*   This hotel on the west end of downtown is conveniently located on the free rapid-transit mall, just west of the main downtown core. The corner units feature small kitchens and great views. The Sandman boasts the most complete fitness facility of any hotel in Calgary. Its health club offers a lap pool, squash courts, and weight-training facilities.

888 Seventh Ave. SW, Calgary, AB T2P 3J3. ⓒ 800/726-3626 or 403/237-8626. Fax 403/290-1238. www. sandmanhotels.com. 301 units. C$111–C$159 (US$72–US$103) double. Children under 16 stay free in parents' room. AE, DC, DISC, MC, V. Parking C$6 (US$3.90). **Amenities:** Restaurant, bar; indoor pool; health club; spa; concierge; business center; limited room service; laundry service; same-day dry cleaning. *In room:* A/C, TV, dataport, fridge, coffeemaker, microwave, hair dryer, iron.

IN INGLEWOOD

Inglewood Bed & Breakfast ⓡ *Finds*   This is a great location: minutes from downtown, on a quiet residential street, and backed up to a park and the Bow River. The rambling modern structure was purpose built as a Queen Anne–style B&B. Guest rooms are simply but stylishly furnished with handmade pine furniture and antiques. Two turret rooms have great views over the river. The suite contains a kitchen, fireplace, and TV. Both of the owners are professional chefs, so expect an excellent breakfast.

1006 Eighth Ave. SE, Calgary, AB T2G 0M4. ⓒ 403/262-6570. www.inglewoodbedandbreakfast.com. 3 units. C$90 (US$59) double. Rates include breakfast. MC, V. *In room:* No phone.

ALONG THE MACLEOD TRAIL

This was once a cattle track, but now it's the main expressway heading south toward the U.S. border. The northern portions of the Macleod Trail are lined with inns and motels.

Elbow River Inn   This is the Macleod Trail establishment closest to downtown, located directly opposite the Stampede grounds. The only hotel on the banks of the little Elbow River, the inn has a pleasant dining room and—if you're feeling lucky—a casino. Bedrooms are simply furnished; it's a completely adequate, comfortable hostelry with near-budget rates.

1919 Macleod Trail S., Calgary, AB T2G 4S1. ⓒ 800/661-1463 or 403/269-6771. Fax 403/237-5181. www. sil-org.com. 73 units. C$79–C$129 (US$51–US$84) double. AE, DC, MC, V. Free parking. **Amenities:** Restaurant, bar, casino; limited room service. *In room:* A/C, TV, dataport, fridge, microwave.

Holiday Inn Macleod Trail   It's not exactly in the center of things, but this welcoming Holiday Inn has a light-rail station right outside, and is just a stroll away from an oasis of parkland. Downtown is a 15-minute ride away. The large, comfortably furnished rooms were completely renovated in 2001.

4206 Macleod Trail SE, Calgary, AB T2G 2R7. ⓒ 800/HOLIDAY or 403/287-2700. Fax 403/243-4721. www. calgaryholidayinn.com. 153 units. C$99–C$149 (US$64–US$97) double. Extra person C$5 (US$3.25). Senior and weekend rates available. Children 18 and under stay free in parents' room; children 11 and under eat free. AE, DC, DISC, MC, V. Free parking. **Amenities:** Restaurant, lounge; indoor pool; access to nearby health club; Jacuzzi; laundry service. *In room:* A/C, TV, dataport, coffeemaker, hair dryer.

NORTH & NORTHWEST OF DOWNTOWN

Motel Village is a triangle of more than 20 motels, restaurants, and gas stations, enclosed by Crowchild Trail, the Trans-Canada Highway, and Highway 1A. Most of the costlier establishments flank the highway; the cheaper ones lie off Crowchild Trail. If you're driving and don't want to deal with downtown traffic, simply head here to find a room.

Except during the Stampede, you'll be able to find a vacancy without reservations; on C-Train, use either Lions Park or Banff Park stops. You'll see many chain motels, including **Days Inn,** 1818 16th Ave. NW (© **800/661-9564** or 403/289-3901); **Best Western Village Park Inn,** 1804 Crowchild Trail NW (© **888/774-7716** or 403/289-4645); **Travelodge North,** 2304 16th Ave. NW (© **800/578-7878** or 403/289-0211); and **Quality Inn Motel Village,** 2359 Banff Trail NW (© **800/661-4667** or 403/289-1973).

CAMPING

The **Calgary West KOA,** on the Trans-Canada Highway West (© **403/ 288-0411**), allows tents and pets. Facilities include toilets, laundry, a dumping station, hot showers, groceries, and a pool. The price for two people is C$28 (US$18) per night; tent sites are C$25 (US$16).

WHERE TO DINE

Calgary boasts a vibrant bar-and-restaurant scene. In general, you'll find fine dining downtown; more casual bistros and restaurants tend to be along 17th Avenue.

DOWNTOWN
Expensive

Belvedere ✦✦ NEW CANADIAN   The very stylish Belvedere is one of the most impressive of Calgary's restaurants. The dining room exudes a darkly elegant, 1930s atmosphere. The menu blends traditional favorites with stand-up-and-take-notice preparations. An outstanding appetizer is trio of fois gras, which presents local pan-seared duck liver in three completely different, completely fabulous ways. For an entree, choose osso buco with fig and vanilla glaze. The bar is a sophisticated spot for a drink.

107 Eighth Ave. SW. © **403/265-9595.** Reservations recommended. Main courses C$21–C$38 (US$14–US$25). AE, DC, MC, V. Mon–Fri 11:30am–10pm; Sat 5:30–10pm.

Owl's Nest FRENCH/CONTINENTAL   One of Calgary's most wide-ranging upscale menus is found in this atmospheric dining room. Entrees range from hand-cut Alberta steaks to Continental delicacies like Dover sole with caviar. Each week, there's also a specialty menu, often featuring an ethnic cuisine. Service is excellent and the wine list is noteworthy.

In the Westin Hotel, Fourth Ave. and Third St. SW. © **403/266-1611.** Reservations required. Main courses C$20–C$30 (US$13–US$20). AE, DC, DISC, MC, V. Mon–Fri 11:30am–2pm; Mon–Sat 5:30–10:30pm.

River Café ✦✦ NEW CANADIAN   If you have one meal in Calgary, it should be here. It takes a short walk through the Eau Claire Market area, then over the footbridge to lovely Prince's Island Park in the Bow River, to reach the aptly named River Café. On a summer evening, the walk is a plus, as are the restaurant's lovely decks and excellent food. Wood-fired, free-range, and wild-gathered foods form the backbone of the menu. There's a variety of appetizers and light dishes—many vegetarian—as well as pizzalike flat breads topped with zippy cheese, vegetables, and fruit. Specialties from the grill include braised pheasant breast with mustard spaetzle, black cherry oil, and roasted apple.

Prince's Island Park. © 403/261-7670. www.river-cafe.com. Reservations recommended. Main courses C$12–C$37 (US$8–US$24). AE, MC, V. Mon–Fri 11am–11pm; Sat–Sun 10am–11pm. Closed Jan.

Téatro ☆☆ ITALIAN Located in the historic Dominion Bank building across from the Centre for the Performing Arts, Téatro offers an extensive menu featuring what's seasonally best, cooked skillfully and simply to preserve natural flavors. There's a large selection of antipasti, wood-fired pizzas, and salads; the entrees, featuring Alberta beef, veal, and seafood, are prepared with flair. The high-ceilinged dining room is dominated by columns and huge panel windows, bespeaking class and elegance. Service is excellent.

200 Eighth Ave. SE. © 403/290-1012. www.teatro-rest.com. Reservations recommended. Main courses C$12–C$40 (US$8–US$26). AE, DC, MC, V. Mon–Fri 11:30am–11pm; Sat 5pm–midnight; Sun 5–10pm.

Moderate & Inexpensive

Eau Claire Market (see "Exploring the City," earlier in this chapter) is a food-grazer's dream. Put together a picnic with fresh bread, cheese, and wine, or grab ethnic takeout and mosey on over to the park like everyone else in Calgary.

Divino ☆ CALIFORNIA/ITALIAN Divino is a great downtown option for tasty yet casual dining. Housed in a landmark building, it's both a wine bar and an intimate, bistro-style restaurant. The fare is unusual and tasty—steamed mussels in ginger-and-garlic broth, broccoli salad with toasted almonds and ginger dressing, and steak and pasta dishes.

817 First St. SW. © 403/263-5869. Reservations recommended on weekends. Main courses C$10–C$15 (US$7–US$10). AE, MC, V. Mon–Sat 11:30am–10:30pm.

Grand Isle Seafood Restaurant CANTONESE/SEAFOOD One of Chinatown's best restaurants, the Grand Isle's beautiful dining room overlooks the Bow River. Pick your entree from the saltwater tanks, then enjoy the view. Dim sum is served daily; there's a huge lunch buffet on weekdays and brunch service on weekends.

128 Second Ave. SE. © 403/269-7783. Reservations recommended on weekends. Most dishes under C$12 (US$8). AE, MC, V. Daily 10am–midnight.

Joey Tomato's ITALIAN Located in Eau Claire Market (see "Exploring the City," above), the fun, high-energy Joey Tomato's serves Italian fare to throngs of appreciative Calgarians. And no wonder it's often packed: The food is really good, the prices moderate, and there's a lively bar scene. Thin-crust pizzas come with traditional toppings or with more cosmopolitan choices. Pasta dishes are just as unorthodox, with dishes like linguini and smoked chicken, jalapeño, cilantro, and lime cream sauce.

208 Barclay Parade SW. © 403/263-6336. Reservations not accepted. Pizza and pasta C$9–C$15 (US$6–US$10). AE, MC, V. Sun–Thurs 11am–midnight; Fri–Sat 11am–1am.

The King & I THAI This restaurant was the first to introduce Thai cuisine to Calgary. Chicken, seafood, and vegetables predominate—one of the outstanding dishes is chicken filet sautéed with eggplant and peanuts in chili-bean sauce.

820 11th Ave. SW. © 403/264-7241. Main courses C$7–C$20 (US$4.55–US$13). AE, DC, ER, MC, V. Mon–Thurs 11:30am–10:30pm; Fri 11:30am–11:30pm; Sat 4:30–11:30pm; Sun 4:30–9:30pm.

SEVENTEENTH AVENUE

Seventeenth Avenue, roughly between Fourth Street SW and 10th Street SW, is home to many of Calgary's best casual restaurants and bistros. Get a feel for the scene on the deck of **Melrose Place,** 730 17th Ave. SW (✆ **403/228-3566**).

Brava ⚲★★ NEW CANADIAN   Brava offers a variety of dishes, from elegant appetizers and boutique pizzas to traditional main courses with contemporary zest. To start, try the beef carpaccio with Gorgonzola nuggets and chokecherry vinaigrette. Among the entrees, the venison schnitzel comes with lemon oregano cream; grilled salmon is served with guava barbecue sauce. Eighty wines are available by the glass.

723 17th Ave. SW. ✆ **403/228-1854.** Reservations recommended. Main courses C$15–C$21 (US$10–US$14). AE, DC, MC, V. Mon–Tues 11am–11pm; Wed–Sat 11am–midnight.

Cilantro INTERNATIONAL   Cilantro has an attractive stucco storefront, plus a garden patio with veranda bar. The food is eclectic (some would call it California cuisine). You can snack on sandwiches, pasta, or burgers (in this case, an elk burger) or have a full meal of buffalo rib-eye or grilled sea bass. The food is always excellent, and the setting casual and friendly.

338 17th Ave. SW. ✆ **403/229-1177.** Reservations recommended on weekends. Main courses C$9–C$30 (US$6–US$13). AE, DC, MC, V. Mon–Thurs 11am–11pm; Fri 11am–midnight; Sat–Sun 5–11pm.

La Chaumière ⚲ FRENCH   La Chaumière is a discreetly luxurious temple of fine dining. A meal here is an occasion to dress up. In addition to the elegant dining room, La Chaumière offers plenty of patio seating in summer. The impressively broad menu is based on classic French preparations, but features local Alberta meats and produce.

139 17th Ave. SW. ✆ **403/228-5690.** Reservations recommended. Jacket and tie required for men. Main courses C$18–C$35 (US$12–US$23). AE, DC, MC, V. Mon–Fri noon–2pm; Mon–Sat 6pm–midnight.

Pongo Noodle and Beer House FUSION   One of the hottest cocktail scenes is at Pongo, and with its late hours, this is a place that gets more popular as the evening wears on. The dining room is sleek and modern. The menu stresses "Asian comfort food": pot stickers, noodle soups, and rice bowls. The food is very flavorful, and the cocktails shaken, not stirred.

524 17th Ave. SW. ✆ **403/209-1073.** Reservations not needed. Main courses C$7–C$9 (US$4.55–US$6). AE, MC, V. Sun–Wed 11am–2am; Thurs–Sat 11am–5am.

Savoir Fare ⚲★★ NEW CANADIAN   One of 17th Avenue's most coolly elegant eateries, Savoir Fare offers a tempting selection of seasonally changing menus. Preparations mix classic techniques and nouveau ingredients. You don't have to overindulge to enjoy yourself—there's a good selection of interesting salads and sandwiches—but entrees are hard to resist: A vegetable Napoleon or a beef tenderloin crusted with pepper and ground coffee beans are sure to please.

907 17th Ave. SW. ✆ **403/245-6040.** Reservations recommended. Main courses C$13–$26 (US$8–US$17). AE, DC, MC, V. Mon–Thurs 11am–11pm; Fri–Sat 11am–midnight; Sun 11am–10pm (May–Aug 5–10pm only).

INGLEWOOD

The Cross House Garden Cafe ⚲ FRENCH   The Cross House serves upscale French cuisine in a historic home. In summer, the dining room extends into the shaded yard, where the bustle of Calgary feels far away. Grilled duck breast is served with orange and star anise sauce; lobster is accompanied by vanilla-perfumed curry sauce.

1240 Eighth Ave. SE. © **403/531-2767.** Reservations recommended. Main courses C$15–C$36 (US$10–US$23). MC, V. Mon–Sat 11:30am–2pm and 5:30–9pm; Sat 5–9pm.

Hose and Hound Pub ⊛ PUB   After a long day of shopping in Inglewood, Calgary's premier antiques district, you'll understandably think longingly of a pint and a bite to eat. This friendly pub is just the place. Besides favorites like burgers and fish-and-chips, it offers pasta, soups, and sausage specialties from Spolumbo's, local sausage-makers extraordinaire.

1030 Ninth Ave. SE. © **402/234-0508.** Reservations not needed. Main courses C$7–C$14 (US$4.55–US$9). MC, V. Mon–Thurs 11:30am–midnight; Fri–Sat 11:30pm–2am; Sun noon–midnight.

EN ROUTE TO THE ROCKIES: THE OLD WEST

If you're interested in the life of cowboys and ranchers, stop at one of the following sights. Both are short and very scenic detours on the way from Calgary to the Rocky Mountains.

Bar U Ranch National Historic Site ⊛⊛   An hour southwest of Calgary is this well-preserved and still-operating cattle ranch, celebrating traditions of the Old West. Tours of the 35 original buildings (some dating from the 1880s) are available; a video of the area's ranching history is shown in the interpretive center. Special events include displays of ranching activities and techniques; you might get to watch a branding or roundup.

P.O. Box 168, Longview. © **403/395-2212.** http://parkscanada.pch.gc.ca/parks/alberta/bar_u_ranch. Admission C$6 (US$3.90) adults, C$4.60 (US$3) seniors, C$2.90 (US$1.90) children. Late May to early Oct daily 10am–6pm. Follow Hwy. 22 south from Calgary to Longview.

Western Heritage Centre ⊛   Fifteen minutes west of Calgary in the little town of Cochrane, this center is located at the Cochrane Ranche Provincial Historic Site, which preserves Alberta's first large-scale cattle ranch, established in 1881. It commemorates traditional farm and ranch life, contains a rodeo hall of fame, and offers insights into this most western of sporting events. Special events are scheduled throughout the summer.

Box 1477, Cochrane. © **403/932-3514.** Admission C$8 (US$5) adults, C$6 (US$3.90) students and seniors, C$3.50 (US$2.30) children, C$20 (US$13) families. Late May to early Sept 9am–6pm. Follow Crowchild Trail (which becomes Hwy. 1A) out of Calgary; or from Hwy. 1 to Banff, take Hwy. 22 north to Cochrane.

2 Edmonton

176 miles (283km) N of Calgary, 224 miles (361km) E of Jasper

Edmonton, Alberta's capital, has the largest metropolitan population in the province, currently around 850,000. Located on the banks of the North Saskatchewan River, it's a sophisticated city noted for its easygoing friendliness.

Edmonton grew in spurts, following a boom-and-bust pattern as exciting as it was unreliable. During World War II, the boom came in the form of the Alaska Highway, with Edmonton as the material base and temporary home of 50,000 American troops and construction workers.

The ultimate boom, however, gushed from the ground in 1947, when a drill at Leduc, 25 miles (40km) southwest of the city, sent a fountain of crude oil soaring skyward. Some 10,000 other wells followed, all within a 100-mile (161km) radius of the city. In their wake came the petrochemical industry and the major refining and supply conglomerates. In 20 years, the population of the city quadrupled, its skyline mushroomed with glass-and-concrete office towers, a rapid-transit system was created, and a C$150-million (US$943,800) civic center rose. Edmonton had become what it is today—the oil capital of Canada.

ESSENTIALS

GETTING THERE   By Plane   Edmonton is served by most major airlines, including **Air Canada** (✆ 800/372-9500; www.aircanada.ca), which also operates more than a dozen shuttles per day to Calgary. The **Edmonton International Airport** (✆ 800/268-7134) lies 18 miles (29km) south of the city on Highway 2, about 45 minutes away. By cab, the trip costs about C$35 (US$23); by Airporter bus, C$11 (US$7).

By Car   Edmonton straddles the Yellowhead Highway, western Canada's new east-west interprovincial highway. Just west of Edmonton, the Yellowhead is linked to the Alaska Highway. The city is 320 miles (515km) north of the U.S. border, 176 miles (283km) north of Calgary.

By Train   The **VIA Rail Station** is at 104th Avenue and 100th Street (✆ 800/561-8630 or 780/422-6032). **Greyhound** buses link Edmonton to points in Canada and the United States from the depot at 10324 103rd St. (✆ 780/413-8747).

VISITOR INFORMATION   Contact **Edmonton Tourism,** 9797 Jasper Ave. NW (✆ 800/463-4667 or 780/496-8400; www.tourism.ede.org). There are also visitor centers located at City Hall and at Gateway Park, both open from 9am to 6pm, and on the Calgary Trail at the southern edge of the city, open from 9am to 9pm.

CITY LAYOUT   The winding **North Saskatchewan River** flows right through the heart of the city, dividing it into roughly equal halves. Most of this steep-banked valley has been turned into public parklands.

The street-numbering system begins at the corner of **100th Street** and **100th Avenue,** which means that downtown addresses have five digits and that suburban homes often have smaller addresses than businesses in the center of town. The main street is **Jasper Avenue** (actually 101st Ave.), running north of the river. The "A" designations for certain streets and avenues downtown add to the confusion: They're essentially old service alleys between major streets, many are now pedestrian areas with sidewalk cafes.

At 97th Street, on Jasper Avenue, rises the massive pink **Canada Place** government complex. Across the street is the **Edmonton Convention Centre,** which stair-steps down the hillside to the river.

Beneath the downtown core stretches a network of pedestrian walkways—called **Pedways**—connecting hotels, restaurants, and malls with the library, City Hall, and Citadel Theatre. These Pedways not only avoid the surface traffic, but are also climate-controlled.

At the northern approach to the High Level Bridge stand the buildings of the **Alberta Legislature.** Across the bridge, to the west, stretches the vast campus of the **University of Alberta.** Just to the east is **Old Strathcona,** a bustling neighborhood of cafes, galleries, and hip shops that's now a haven for Edmonton's more alternative population. The main arterial through Old Strathcona is **Whyte Avenue,** or 82nd Avenue. Running south from here is 104th Street, which becomes the **Calgary Trail** and leads to the airport.

West of downtown, Jasper Avenue shifts and twists to eventually become Stony Plain Road, which passes near **West Edmonton Mall,** the world's largest

Edmonton

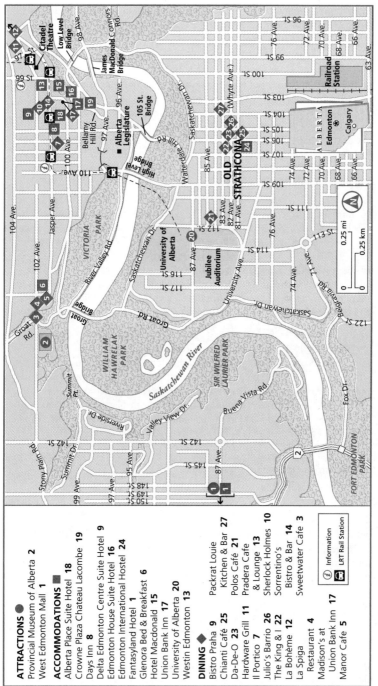

ATTRACTIONS ●
Provincial Museum of Alberta **2**
West Edmonton Mall **1**

ACCOMMODATIONS ■
Alberta Place Suite Hotel **18**
Crowne Plaza Chateau Lacombe **19**
Days Inn **8**
Delta Edmonton Centre Suite Hotel **9**
Edmonton House Suite Hotel **16**
Edmonton International Hostel **24**
Fantasyland Hotel **1**
Glenora Bed & Breakfast **6**
Hotel Macdonald **15**
Union Bank Inn **17**
University of Alberta **20**
Westin Edmonton **13**

DINING ◆
Bistro Praha **9**
Chianti Café **25**
Da-De-O **23**
Hardware Grill **11**
Il Portico **7**
Julio's Barrio **26**
The King & I **22**
La Bohème **12**
La Spiga
Restaurant **4**
Madison's at
Union Bank Inn **17**
Manor Cafe **5**

Packrat Louie
Kitchen & Bar **27**
Polos Café **21**
Pradera Cafe
& Lounge **13**
Sherlock Holmes **10**
Sorrentino's
Bistro & Bar **14**
Sweetwater Cafe **3**

(i) Information
[LRT] LRT Rail Station

shopping and entertainment center, before merging with Highway 16 on its way to Jasper National Park.

GETTING AROUND   **Edmonton Transit** (© 780/496-1611) operates the buses and the LRT (Light Rail Transit). This electric rail service connects downtown with Northlands Park to the north and the University of Alberta to the south. The LRT and buses have the same fares: C$1.75 (US$1.15) for adults and C$1.25 (US$.80) for seniors and children; a day pass goes for C$6 (US$3.90). Monday through Friday from 9am to 3pm, downtown LRT travel is free between Churchill, Central, Bay, Corona, and Grandin stations.

Car-rental agencies include **National,** 10133 100A St. NW (© 780/ 422-6097); **Budget,** 10016 106th St. (© 780/448-2000); and **Hertz,** 10815 Jasper Ave. (© 780/423-3431); all have counters at the airport as well.

Call **CO-OP Taxi** (© 780/425-2525 or 780/425-8310) if you need a cab.

FAST FACTS   There's an **American Express** office at 10180 101st St., at 102nd Avenue (© 780/421-0608). The **Alberta Motor Association,** 11220 109th St. (© 780/471-3550), affiliated with the Canadian Automobile Association, reciprocates with AAA. The main **post office** is located at 103A Avenue (at 99th Street).

The **Royal Alexandra Hospital,** 10240 Kingsway Ave. (© 780/477-4111), offers emergency care. If you need a pharmacy, **Shoppers Drug Mart** has over a dozen locations in Edmonton, including a branch at 8210 109th St. (© 780/ 433-2424). Most are open until midnight.

EXPLORING THE CITY

Fort Edmonton Park ⚡ (Kids)   Fort Edmonton Park is a complex of townscapes that reconstruct various eras of Edmonton's history. Perhaps most interesting is the old Fort Edmonton fur-trading post from the turn of the 18th century, where blacksmiths, bakers, and other docents ply their trades. On 1885 Street, you'll see Frontier Edmonton, complete with blacksmith, saloon, and Jasper House Hotel, which serves hearty pioneer meals. On 1920 Street, sip an old-fashioned ice-cream soda at Bill's confectionery. You can ride streetcar no. 1, a stagecoach, or a steam locomotive between the various streets.

On Whitemud Dr., at Fox Dr. © 780/496-8787. www.gov.edmonton.ab.ca/fort. Admission C$7.25 (US$4.70) adults, C$5.25 (US$3.40) seniors and youths, C$3.75 (US$2.45) children, C$22 (US$14) families. Mid-May to late June Mon–Fri 10am–4pm, Sat–Sun 10am–6pm; late June to early Sept daily 10am–6pm. LRT to University Station, then bus 32.

Odyssium ⚡ (Kids)   This is one of the most advanced facilities of its kind in the world. It contains, among other wonders, an IMAX theater (© 780/493-4250), the largest planetarium theater in Canada, a virtual-reality showcase, and an observatory open on clear afternoons and evenings. New exhibits include a journey through the human body (including the Gallery of the Gross!) and Mystery Avenue, where young sleuths can collect clues at a crime scene, then analyze them at a crime lab.

11211 142nd St., Coronation Park. © 780/451-3344. www.odyssium.com. Admission C$9.95 (US$7) adults, C$7.95 (US$5) seniors and youths, C$6.95 (US$4.50) children 3–12, C$38.95 (US$25) families. Summer daily 10am–9pm; winter Sun–Thurs 10am–5pm, Fri–Sat 10am–9pm. Bus: 17 or 22.

Old Strathcona ⚡⚡   This historic district contains some of the best-preserved landmarks in the city. It's best seen on foot, guided by the brochures given

Klondike Days

The gold rush that sent an army of prospectors heading for the Yukon in 1898 put Edmonton on the map. Although the actual goldfields lay 1,500 miles (2,415km) to the north, this little settlement became a giant supply store, resting place, and "recreation" ground for thousands of men who stopped here before tackling the hazards of the Klondike Trail, which led overland to Dawson City in the Yukon. Edmonton's population quickly doubled in size, and its merchants, saloonkeepers, and ladies of easy virtue grew rich in the process.

Since 1962, Edmonton has commemorated the event with one of the greatest and most colorful extravaganzas staged in Canada. **Klondike Days** are held annually in late July, with street festivities and the great Klondike Days Exposition at Northlands Park lasting 10 days.

Locals and visitors dress up in period costumes, street corners blossom with impromptu stages featuring anything from country bands to cancan girls, stagecoaches rattle through the streets, and parades and floats wind from block to block.

The 16,000-seat Coliseum holds nightly spectacles of rock, pop, variety, or western entertainment. Northlands Park turns into Klondike Village, complete with the Chilkoot Gold Mine, Silver Slipper Saloon, and gambling casino—legal for this occasion only. The Walterdale Playhouse drops serious stage endeavors for a moment and puts on hilarious melodramas with mustachioed villains to hiss and dashing heroes to cheer.

Immense "Klondike breakfasts" are served in the open air, marching bands compete in the streets, and down the North Saskatchewan River float more than 100 of the weirdest-looking home-built rafts ever seen, competing in the "World Championship Sourdough River Raft Race."

For more information on Klondike Days, call ✆ **888/800-PARK** or 780/471-7210.

out at the **Old Strathcona Foundation,** 10324 82nd Ave., 4th Floor (✆ **780/433-5866**). This is also Edmonton's hipster central, where students, artists, and the alternative community come to hang out. It's easy to spend an afternoon here, just wandering the shops, sitting at street cafes, and people-watching. Be sure to stop by the **Old Strathcona Farmers Market,** at 83rd Avenue and 103rd Street (✆ **780/439-1844**), an open-air market with fresh produce, baked goods, and local crafts. It's open Saturdays year-round, plus Tuesday and Thursday afternoons in summer.

Around 82nd Ave., between 103rd and 105th sts. Bus: 46 from downtown.

Provincial Museum of Alberta ★★ *Kids* This modern museum displays Alberta's natural and human history in three permanent galleries. The Habitat Groups show wildlife in astonishingly lifelike dioramas, sure to captivate the kids. The Aboriginal Peoples Gallery tells the 11,000-year story of Alberta's

Native inhabitants, incorporating artifacts, film, and interactive media; it's one of Canada's foremost exhibits on Native culture. The Natural History Gallery has fossils, minerals, and a live-bug room.

12845 102nd Ave. (C) **780/453-9100.** Fax 780/454-6629. www.pma.edmonton.ab.ca. Admission C$8 (US$5) adults, C$6.50 (US$4.20) seniors, C$4.50 (US$2.90) children, C$20 (US$13) families; half-price admission on Tues. Daily 9am–5pm. Bus: 1.

West Edmonton Mall You won't find many shopping malls mentioned in this book, but the West Ed Mall is something else. Although it contains 800 businesses, it's more theme park than mall, housing the world's largest indoor amusement park, including a roller coaster, bungee-jumping platform, and enclosed wave-lake, complete with beach. It has walk-through aviaries, 19 movie theaters, a lagoon with performing dolphins, and several fabulous adventure rides. Of course, you can shop here, too. On Saturdays at 2pm, you can even tour the rooms at the mall's excellent "theme" hotel, called Fantasyland. Roll your eyes all you want, but do go. You have to see the West Edmonton Mall to believe it.

8882 170th St. (C) **800/661-8890** or 780/444-5200. www.westedmontonmall.com. Bus: 10.

WHERE TO STAY
For B&Bs, try **Alberta and Pacific Bed and Breakfast** ((C) **604/944-1793;** fax 604/552-1659) or the **Alberta Bed and Breakfast Association** (www.bbalberta. com). Note that accommodations are scarce during Klondike Days.

EXPENSIVE
Delta Edmonton Centre Suite Hotel ⭐ This all-suite establishment forms part of the upscale Eaton Centre in the heart of downtown. Without having to stir out of doors, you can access 140 shops in the mall, plus movie theaters and an indoor putting green. Four other malls are connected to the hotel via Pedways. Three-quarters of the windows look into the mall, so you can stand behind the tinted one-way glass (in your pajamas, if you like) and watch the shopping action outside. If you need lots of room, or have work to do in Edmonton, these very spacious units are just the ticket.

Eaton Centre, 10222 102nd St., Edmonton, AB T5J 4C5. (C) **780/429-3900.** Fax 780/428-1566. 169 units. C$132–C$250 (US$86–US$163) standard business suite; C$218 (US$142) deluxe executive suite. Ask about summer family discounts, weekend packages, and special rates for business travelers. AE, DC, MC, V. Parking C$10 (US$7) per day; valet parking C$13 (US$8) per day. **Amenities:** Restaurant; bar; exercise room; Jacuzzi; sauna; children's center; concierge; business center; limited room service; babysitting; coin-op laundry and laundry service; same-day dry cleaning. *In room:* A/C, TV w/ pay movies, dataport, minibar, coffeemaker, hair dryer, iron.

Fairmont Hotel Macdonald ⭐⭐⭐ From the outside, with its limestone facade and gargoyles, the Mac looks like a feudal château—right down to the kilted staff. The Library Bar resembles an Edwardian gentlemen's club, and the Harvest Room offers panoramic views of the valley as well as a garden terrace for summer dining. Originally opened in 1915, the palatial Hotel Macdonald has undergone a masterwork of sensitive renovation and restoration. Signature elements like the deep tubs, brass door plates, and paneled doors were kept intact, and important additions like new plumbing were installed. Rooms are beautifully furnished with luxurious upholstery, feather duvets, and a bin for recyclables—a thoughtful touch. Even pets get special treatment: a gift bag of treats and a map of pet-friendly parks. Needless to say, there aren't many hotels like this in Edmonton, or in Canada for that matter.

10065 100th St., Edmonton, AB T5J 0N6. ℂ **800/441-1414** or 780/424-5181. Fax 780/429-6481. www. fairmont.com. 198 units. High season C$249–C$269 (US$162–US$175) deluxe standard, C$289–C$309 (US$188–US$201) premier suite, C$369–C$389 (US$240–US$253) executive suite, C$429–C$449 (US$279–US$292) specialty suite. Weekend and off-season discounts available. AE, DC, DISC, MC, V. Parking C$15 (US$10) per day. **Amenities:** Restaurant, lounge; indoor pool; health club; spa; concierge; business center; 24-hr. room service; babysitting; laundry service; same-day dry cleaning. *In room:* A/C, TV/VCR w/ pay movies, dataport, minibar, coffeemaker, hair dryer, iron.

Fantasyland Hotel ⊛ From the outside, this solemn tower at the end of the huge West Ed Mall (with all-weather access to those 800 shops and eateries) reveals little of the wildly decorated rooms found within. Fantasyland is a cross between a hotel and Las Vegas: It contains a total of 116 theme rooms decorated in nine different styles (as well as well-furnished regular rooms). Theme rooms aren't just a matter of subtle touches; these units are exceedingly clever and way over the top. Take the Truck Room: Your bed is in the back end of a real pickup, the pickup's bench seats fold down into a child's bed, and the lights on the vanity are real stoplights. In the Igloo Room, a round bed is encased in a shell that looks like ice blocks, the walls are painted with amazingly lifelike murals, and dog sleds become beds for children. The hotel offers tours of the different theme types on Saturdays at 2pm.

17700 87th Ave., Edmonton, AB T5T 4V4. ℂ **800/737-3783** or 780/444-3000. Fax 780/444-3294. www. fantasylandhotel.com. 355 units. C$175–C$305 (US$114–US$198) double. Extra person C$10 (US$7). Weekend and off-season packages available. AE, MC, V. Free parking. **Amenities:** Restaurant, bar; exercise room; concierge; 24-hr. room service; babysitting; laundry service; same-day dry-cleaning. *In room:* A/C, TV w/ pay movies, fax, dataport, fridge, coffeemaker, hair dryer, iron.

Westin Edmonton ⊛ Located in the heart of the downtown shopping and entertainment district, this modern hotel offers some of the city's largest rooms. Although the lobby is a bit austere, the guest rooms are very comfortably furnished. For an extra C$20 (US$13), business travelers can request a room with a printer and fax. See "Where to Dine," below, for a review of Pradera, one of Edmonton's most inventive establishments.

10135 100th St., Edmonton, AB T5J 0N7. ℂ **800/228-3000** or 780/426-3636. Fax 780/428-1454. www. westin.ab.ca. 413 units. From C$225 (US$146) double. AE, DC, DISC, MC, V. Parking C$14 (US$9) per day; valet parking C$17 (US$11) per day. **Amenities:** Two restaurants, lounge; indoor pool; exercise room; Jacuzzi; sauna; concierge; business center; room service; babysitting; laundry service. *In room:* A/C, TV, dataport, minibar, fridge, coffeemaker, hair dryer, iron.

MODERATE
Alberta Place Suite Hotel This downtown apartment hotel is an excellent choice for families who want full cooking facilities and extra space. It's located half a block from public transport, and is within easy walking distance of most business and government centers.

10049 103rd St., Edmonton, AB T5J 2W7. ℂ **800/661-3982** or 780/423-1565. Fax 780/426-6260. www. albertaplace.com. 86 units. C$123–C$158 (US$80–US$103) double. Extra person C$8 (US$5). Children 16 and under stay free in parents' room. AE, DC, MC, V. Free parking. **Amenities:** Indoor pool; exercise room; Jacuzzi; sauna; coin-op laundry. *In room:* A/C, TV, dataport, fridge, coffeemaker, hair dryer.

Crowne Plaza Chateau Lacombe Centrally located downtown, the Crowne Plaza, a round tower on the edge of a cliff overlooking the North Saskatchewan River, possesses some of the city's best views. The unusual design blends well with the dramatic skyline, yet it's instantly recognizable from afar—a perfect landmark. The nicely furnished rooms aren't huge, though the wedge-shaped design necessitates that they are broadest toward the windows, where you'll spend time looking over the city. Wheelchair-accessible rooms are available.

10111 Bellamy Hill, Edmonton, AB T5J 1N7. ✆ **800/661-8801** or 780/428-6611. Fax 780/425-6564. www. chateaulacombe.com. 307 units. C$139 (US$90) double, C$185–C$350 (US$120–US$228) suite. Extra person C$15 (US$10). Weekend packages available. AE, DC, MC, V. Parking C$8 (US$5) per day. **Amenities:** Revolving restaurant, lounge; exercise room; business center; room service; babysitting; laundry service. *In room:* A/C, TV, dataport, coffeemaker, hair dryer, iron.

Edmonton House Suite Hotel ✪

This is a great alternative to pricier downtown hotels: The rooms are big and well decorated, and you don't have to pay stiff parking fees. Located right above the North Saskatchewan River, the all-suite hotel has one of the best views in Edmonton. Each unit comes with a balcony and two phones. Edmonton House is within easy walking distance of most downtown office areas and public transport.

10205 100th Ave., Edmonton, AB T5J 4B5. ✆ **800/661-6562** or 780/420-4000. Fax 780/420-4008. www. edmontonhouse.com. 305 units. C$165 (US$107) 1-bedroom suite. Extra person C$15 (US$10). Weekend packages and weekly rates available. AE, DC, MC, V. Free parking. **Amenities:** Restaurant, lounge; indoor pool; exercise room; business center; room service. *In room:* TV, dataport, kitchen, fridge, coffeemaker, microwave, hair dryer, iron.

Glenora Bed & Breakfast ✪

Located in the heart of the High Street district, just west of downtown, the Glenora occupies the upper floors of a 1912 heritage boardinghouse. There's an array of room types, from simple units with shared bathrooms to suites with kitchens. All are pleasantly furnished with period antiques.

12327 102nd Ave. NW, Edmonton, AB T5N 0I8. ✆ **780/488-6766.** Fax 780/488-5168. www.glenorabnb.com. 18 units. C$70–C$140 (US$46–US$91) double. Rates include continental breakfast. AE, MC, V. **Amenities:** Restaurant and bar downstairs; access to nearby health club; coin-op laundry. *In room:* TV/VCR, dataport, mini-bar, coffeemaker, hair dryer, iron.

Union Bank Inn ✪✪

This is a wonderful choice for travelers weary of anonymous corporate hotels. The Union Bank, built in 1910, now houses an elegant restaurant and intimate boutique hotel. The owner asked Edmonton's top interior designers to each design a room. The results are charming, with each unique guest room displaying its own style, furniture, and fabrics. All units, however, have the same amenities, including fireplaces and feather duvets. Rooms vary in layout and aren't incredibly big; if you're in town with work to do, ask for one of the newer and larger units. Service is very friendly. Madison's is a great place to meet friends (see "Where to Dine," below).

10053 Jasper Ave., Edmonton, AB T5J 1S5. ✆ **780/423-3600.** Fax 780/423-4623. www.unionbankinn.com. 34 units. C$129–C$259 (US$84–US$168) double. Rates include full breakfast. AE, DC, MC, V. Free parking. **Amenities:** Restaurant, bar; exercise room; access to nearby health club; business center; room service; same-day dry cleaning. *In room:* A/C, TV, dataport, fridge, hair dryer, iron.

INEXPENSIVE

Days Inn ✪*Value* For the price, this is one of downtown's best deals. Located just 5 minutes from the city center, the motor inn offers clean, basic rooms and easy access to public transport.

10041 106th St., Edmonton, AB T5J 1G3. ✆ **800/267-2191** or 780/423-1925. Fax 780/424-5302. www.days inn.com. 76 units. C$59–C$89 (US$38–US$58) double. Children 11 and under stay free in parents' room. Senior, AAA, and corporate discounts available. AE, DC, DISC, MC, V. Free parking. **Amenities:** Restaurant, bar; limited room service; babysitting; coin-op laundry; same-day dry cleaning. *In room:* A/C, TV, dataport, coffeemaker, hair dryer, iron.

Edmonton International Hostel

This pleasant hostel is located near the university in the lively Old Strathcona neighborhood. Some family rooms are available.

10647 81st Ave. ℂ **780/988-6836.** Fax 780/988-8698. www.hihostels.ca. 88 beds. Members C$18–C$23 (US$12–US$15), nonmembers C$20–C$25 (US$13–US$16). MC, V. **Amenities:** Kitchen; coin-op laundry; bike rentals. *In room:* No phone.

University of Alberta In summer, 1,200 dormitory rooms in Lister Hall are thrown open to visitors. Most are standard bathroom-down-the-hall dorm rooms for C$30 (US$20). Available year-round are two-bed guest suites that share a bathroom with only one other suite (C$40/US$26). The university is right on the LRT line and not far from trendy Old Strathcona.

87th Ave. and 116th St. ℂ **780/492-4281.** Fax 780/492-7032. www.hfs.ualberta.ca. C$30–C$40 (US$20–US$26). MC, V. Parking C$3 (US$1.95) per day. **Amenities:** Food service nearby; coin-op laundry. *In room:* No phone.

WHERE TO DINE

Edmonton has a vigorous dining scene, with lots of hip new eateries joining traditional steak and seafood restaurants. In general, fine dining is found downtown and on High Street. Over in Old Strathcona, south of the river, are trendy cafes and bistros.

DOWNTOWN
Expensive

Hardware Grill ✦✦ NEW CANADIAN This is easily one of the city's most exciting restaurants. The building may be historic, but there's nothing antique about the dining room. Postmodern without being stark, the room is edged with glass partitions, with exposed pipes and ducts painted a smoky rose. There are as many appetizers as entrees, making it tempting to graze through a series of smaller dishes. Bison carpaccio is served with Quebec Migneron cheese, and wild-mushroom ragout spills over grilled polenta. But it's hard to resist entrees like house-made duck sausage or braised buffalo ribs with black coffee barbecue sauce.

9698 Jasper Ave. ℂ **780/423-0969.** www.hardwaregrill.com. Reservations suggested. Main courses C$24–C$37 (US$15–US$24). AE, DC, MC, V. Mon–Fri 11:30am–2pm; Mon–Thurs 5–9:30pm; Fri–Sat 5–10pm. Closed first week of July.

La Bohème FRENCH La Bohème consists of two small, lace-curtained dining rooms in a historic building northeast of downtown (at the turn of the 20th century, this structure was a luxury apartment building—the upper floors are now available as B&B accommodations). The cuisine is French, of course, as is the wine selection. There's a wide variety of appetizers and light dishes, including a number of intriguing salads. The entrees are classic preparations of lamb, chicken, and seafood. The restaurant also features daily changing vegetarian entrees. Desserts are outstanding.

6427 112th Ave. ℂ **780/474-5693.** Reservations required. Main courses C$15–C$29 (US$10–US$19). AE, MC, V. Mon–Sat 11am–3pm; Sun 11am–3:30pm; daily 5–11pm.

Madison's at Union Bank Inn ✦ NEW CANADIAN This is one of the loveliest dining rooms and casual cocktail bars in Edmonton. The formal architectural details of the original bank remain, but they share the space with modern art and avant-garde furniture. The menu is up-to-date, with grilled and roast fish and meats, pastas, and interesting salads (one special featured rose petals, baby lettuce, and shaved white chocolate). Many entrees boast an international touch, such as prawns with cilantro and tequila lime cream served over pasta.

10053 Jasper Ave. ✆ **780/423-3600.** Reservations suggested. Main courses C$14–C$27 (US$9–US$18). AE, MC, V. Mon–Thurs 7–10am, 11am–2pm, and 5–10pm; Fri 7–10am, 11am–2pm, and 5–11pm; Sat 5–11pm; Sun 5–8pm.

Pradera Cafe & Lounge ✿ INTERNATIONAL One of downtown's most inventive restaurants free-associates across several cuisines, notably French, Italian, and Canadian, to arrive at new dishes that succeed at being more than just the sum of their parts. Ostrich medallions are served with a chive and local mushroom sauce, and salmon is pan-seared with peppercorns and mustard seeds.

In the Westin Edmonton, 10135 100th St. ✆ **780/426-3636.** Reservations recommended. Main courses C$18–C$30 (US$12–US$20). AE, DC, DISC, MC, V. Mon–Fri 6:30am–2pm; Sat–Sun 7am–2pm; daily 5–11pm.

Sorrentino's Bistro and Bar ITALIAN This upscale branch of a local chain is a good addition to the downtown scene. The sophisticated dining room—flanked by the Havana Room, where Cuban cigars are available with port and single-malt Scotch—is a popular meeting place for the captains of the city's business and social life. The daily appetizer table features grilled vegetables, salads, and marinated anchovies. Entrees range from risotto to wood-fired pizza to imaginative choices like tournedos of salmon and scallops.

10162 100th St. ✆ **780/424-7500.** www.sorrentinos.com. Reservations suggested. Main courses C$23–C$35 (US$15–US$23). AE, DC, MC, V. Mon–Fri 11:30am–2:30pm and 5–11pm; Sat 5–11pm.

Moderate & Inexpensive

Bistro Praha EASTERN EUROPEAN Bistro Praha is the best of the several casual restaurants that take up the single block of 100A Street. It features a charming, wood-paneled interior and a wide selection of light dishes, convenient for a quick meal or snack. The entrees center on schnitzels, as well as a wonderful roast goose with sauerkraut. The clientele is mainly young, stylish, and cosmopolitan. Service is friendly and relaxed.

10168 100A St. ✆ **780/424-4218.** Reservations recommended on weekends. Main courses C$13–C$18 (US$8–US$12). AE, DC, ER, MC, V. Daily 11:30am–2am.

Il Portico ✿✿ ITALIAN Il Portico features traditional but updated dishes. With excellent grilled meats, pastas, and pizza, it's one of those rare restaurants where you want to try everything. Service is impeccable, and the wine list one of the best in the city: Remarkably, the staff will open any bottle on the list (except reserve bottles) if you buy a half liter. The dining room is informal but classy, and in summer there's seating in a Tuscan-style courtyard.

10012 107th St. ✆ **780/424-0707.** Reservations recommended on weekends. Main courses C$13–C$27 (US$8–US$18). AE, DC, DISC, MC, V. Mon–Fri 11:30am–2pm; Mon–Sat 5:30–11pm.

Sherlock Holmes ENGLISH This English-style pub has local and regional beers on tap (as well as Guinness) and a very good bar menu. It's housed in a charming building with a picket fence around the patio. The menu has a few traditional English dishes—fish-and-chips, steak-and-kidney pie—but there's a strong emphasis on new pub grub like chicken-breast sandwiches, beef curry, and salads. There are two other Sherlock Holmeses in Edmonton, one in the West Edmonton Mall and the other in Old Strathcona at 10341 82nd Ave.

10012 101A Ave. ✆ **780/426-7784.** www.thesherlockhomes.com. Main courses C$7–C$13 (US$4.55–US$9). AE, MC, V. Mon–Sat 11:30am–2am; Sun noon–8pm.

HIGH STREET

La Spiga Restaurant ✿ ITALIAN La Spiga, along High Street's gallery row, offers nouveau Italian cooking with an emphasis on fresh ingredients and unusual tastes and textures. The rack of lamb is marinated in fresh herbs and grappa, and the prawns and scallops are paired with a white-wine lemon sauce and served over angel-hair pasta. The dining room is casual and comfortable, and the service laid-back but astute.

10133 125th St. ☎ **780/482-3100.** Reservations recommended on weekends. Main courses C$13–C$23 (US$8–US$15). AE, DC, MC, V. Mon–Fri 11:30am–2pm; Mon–Sat 5–11pm.

Manor Cafe ⍟ INTERNATIONAL   Housed in a stately mansion overlooking a park, the Manor Cafe offers one of the most fashionable dining patios in Edmonton. The cuisine ranges from Italian pastas to a delicious Moroccan curry.

10109 125th St. ☎ **780/482-7577.** www.manorcafe.com. Reservations recommended on weekends. Main courses C$10–C$18 (US$7–US$12). AE, MC, V. Sun–Thurs 11am–11pm; Fri–Sat 11am–midnight.

Sweetwater Cafe INTERNATIONAL/SOUTHWEST   Here's a bright and lively bistro with good, inexpensive food; in summer, you can sit on the charming deck in the back, thankfully far from the roar of traffic. The food leans towards the Southwest—sandwiches are served in tortillas, and there are several types of quesadillas.

12427 102nd Ave. ☎ **780/488-1959.** Main courses C$5–C$12 (US$3.25–US$8). AE, MC, V. Mon–Thurs 11am–10pm; Fri 11am–midnight; Sat 9am–midnight; Sun 10am–5pm.

OLD STRATHCONA
Chianti Cafe ITALIAN   Chianti is a rarity among Italian restaurants: very good and very inexpensive. Pasta dishes begin at C$7 (US$4.55), and even veal and seafood specials barely top C$15 (US$10). Chianti is located in a handsomely remodeled post-office building; the restaurant isn't a secret, so it can be a fairly crowded experience.

10501 82nd Ave. ☎ **780/439-9829.** Reservations required. Main courses C$7–C$15 (US$4.55–US$10). AE, DC, DISC, MC, V. Sun–Thurs 11am–11pm; Fri–Sat 11am–midnight.

Da-De-O CAJUN/SOUTHERN   This New Orleans–style diner is authentic right down to the low-tech, juke-box-at-your-table music system. The food is top-notch, with good and goopy po' boy sandwiches, fresh oysters, and Louisiana Linguine, with crawfish and clams in basil cream. Relax in a vinyl booth, listen to Billie Holiday, and graze through some crab fritters.

10548A 82nd Ave. ☎ **780/433-0930.** Main courses C$6–C$15 (US$3.90–US$10). AE, MC, V. Mon–Wed 11:30am–11pm; Thurs–Sat 11:30am–midnight; Sun 10am–10pm.

Julio's Barrio MEXICAN   If you like Mexican food, Julio's is worth a detour—in Canada, South of the Border cooking normally takes on quite a different meaning. The food ranges from enchiladas and nachos to sizzling shrimp fajitas. The atmosphere is youthful and minimalist-hip: no kitschy piñatas or scratchy recordings of marimba bands here.

10450 82nd Ave. ☎ **780/431-0774.** Main courses C$9–C$19 (US$6–US$12). AE, MC, V. Mon–Wed 11:45am–11pm; Thurs 11:45am–midnight; Fri–Sat noon–1am; Sun noon–11pm.

The King & I ⍟ THAI   This is the place for excellent Thai food, which can be a real treat after the beef-rich cooking of western Canada. Many dishes are vegetarian, almost a novelty in Alberta. Various curries, ranging from mild to sizzling, and rice and noodle dishes are the house specialties.

8208 107th St. ☎ **780/433-2222.** Main courses C$12–C$25 (US$8–US$16). AE, MC, V. Mon–Thurs 11:30am–10:30pm; Fri 11:30am–11:30pm; Sat 4:30–11:30pm.

Tips **Summertime Special Events**

Jazz City International Music Festival (📞 **780/432-7166**; www.discover edmonton.com/JazzCity) takes over most music venues in Edmonton during the last week of June and first week of July. The **Edmonton Folk Music Festival** (📞 **780/429-1899**; www.efmf.ab.ca) is the largest of its kind in North America. Held in mid-August, it brings in musicians from around the world, from the Celtic north to Indonesia, plus major rock stars playing "unplugged." All concerts are held outdoors.

Packrat Louie Kitchen & Bar ⭐⭐ ITALIAN This popular bistro has a somewhat unlikely name, given that it's one of the best casual trattorias in Edmonton. Menu choices range from specialty pizzas to grilled meats, chicken, and pasta. Most dishes cast an eye toward light or healthy preparations. Grilled lamb chops are garnished simply with fresh tomatoes, feta, and polenta.

10335 83rd Ave. 📞 **780/433-0123.** Reservations recommended on weekends. Main courses C$8–C$21 (US$5–US$14). MC, V. Tues–Sat 11:30am–11:30pm.

Polos Café ⭐⭐ FUSION The Polo in question is Marco Polo, the first European to travel between Italy and China, and the namesake and inspiration for this exciting restaurant. The menu brings together classic Italian and Chinese cooking in a new cuisine loftily hailed as "Orie-ital." And it works: Grilled salmon comes with macadamia nut aioli, and Italian pasta and Shanghai noodles are tossed together with a variety of Sino-Italian sauces. Definitely worth a visit.

8405 112th St. 📞 **780/432-1371.** Reservations suggested. Main courses C$10–C$24 (US$7–US$16). AE, DC, MC, V. Mon–Fri 11am–2:30pm; Mon–Thurs 5–10pm; Fri–Sat 5pm–midnight.

14

The Canadian Rockies: Banff & Jasper National Parks & More

The Canadian Rockies rise to the west of the Alberta prairies and contain some of the finest mountain scenery on earth. Between them, Banff and Jasper national parks preserve much of this mountain beauty, but vast and equally spectacular regions of the Rockies (as well as portions of nearby British Columbia's Selkirk and Purcell mountain ranges, covered in chapter 12) are protected by other national and provincial parks. Because Banff and Jasper are so popular and expensive, these smaller, less thronged, but equally dramatic parks—which include Waterton Lakes, Yoho, and Kootenay national parks as well as a host of provincial parks—are excellent destinations for those travelers who are looking for wilderness adventure, and not just luxury shopping and dining in a mountain setting.

Hiking, biking, and pack trips on horseback have long pedigrees in the parks, as does superlative skiing—the winter Olympics were held in Calgary and on the eastern face of the Rockies in 1988. Outfitters throughout the region offer white-water and float trips on mighty rivers; calmer pursuits such as fishing and canoeing are also popular.

In addition, some of the country's finest and most famous hotels are in the Canadian Rockies. The incredible mountain lodges and châteaux built by early rail entrepreneurs are still in operation, offering unforgettable experiences in luxury and stunning scenery. If you're looking for a more rural holiday, head to one of the Rockies' many guest ranches, where you can saddle up, poke some doggies, and end the evening at a steak barbecue.

The Canadian Rockies boast an excellent network of paved roads, which makes exploring by car safe and easy—if slow, during the busy summer season. From Calgary, it's a stunning 1-hour drive up the Bow River to Banff on Highway 1, and driving from Edmonton to Jasper on the Yellowhead Highway (Hwy. 16) takes between 3 to 4 hours. Both these roads (which continue over the Rockies into British Columbia), along with the Icefields Parkway between Lake Louise and Jasper, remain open year-round.

1 Exploring the Canadian Rockies

Few places in the world are more dramatically beautiful than the Canadian Rockies. Banff and Jasper national parks are famous for their mountain lakes, flower-spangled meadows, spirelike peaks choked by glaciers, and abundant wildlife. Nearly the entire spine of the Rockies—from the U.S. border north for 700 miles (1,127km)—is preserved as parkland or wilderness.

That's the good news. The bad news is that lovers of solitude who come here will find themselves surrounded by increasingly larger numbers of visitors. More

The Canadian Rockies

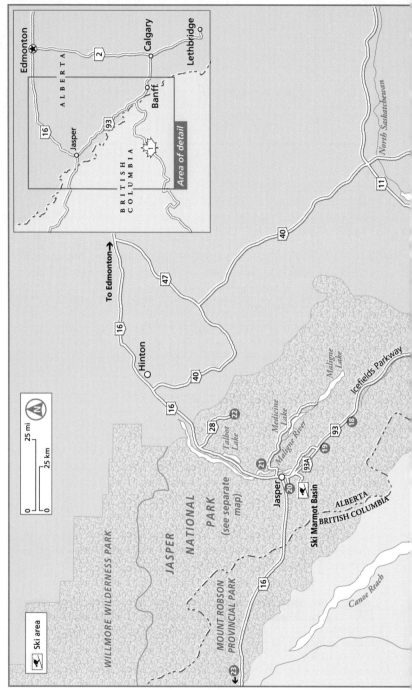

Area of detail

Edmonton
Calgary
Lethbridge
ALBERTA
Banff
Jasper
BRITISH COLUMBIA

To Edmonton →

Hinton

Talbot Lake
Medicine Lake
Maligne Lake
Maligne River
Icefields Parkway

Jasper
Ski Marmot Basin
ALBERTA
BRITISH COLUMBIA

JASPER NATIONAL PARK (see separate map)

WILLMORE WILDERNESS PARK

MOUNT ROBSON PROVINCIAL PARK

North Saskatchewan

Canoe Reach

Ski area

N

25 mi
25 km
0

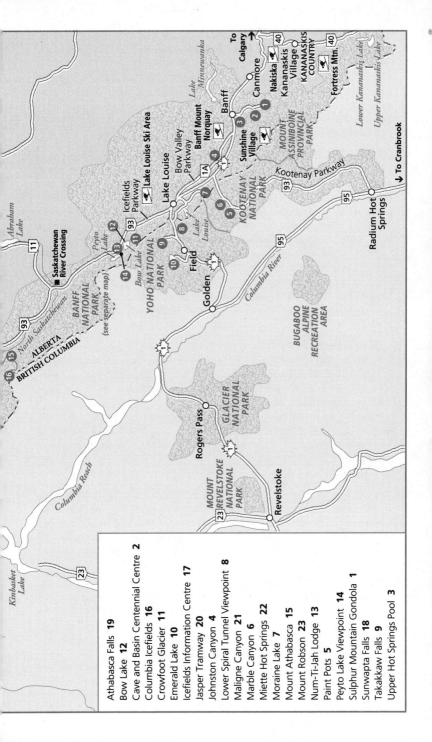

Athabasca Falls **19**
Bow Lake **12**
Cave and Basin Centennial Centre **2**
Columbia Icefields **16**
Crowfoot Glacier **11**
Emerald Lake **10**
Icefields Information Centre **17**
Jasper Tramway **20**
Johnston Canyon **4**
Lower Spiral Tunnel Viewpoint **8**
Maligne Canyon **21**
Marble Canyon **6**
Miette Hot Springs **22**
Moraine Lake **7**
Mount Athabasca **15**
Mount Robson **23**
Num-Ti-Jah Lodge **13**
Paint Pots **5**
Peyto Lake Viewpoint **14**
Sulphur Mountain Gondola **1**
Sunwapta Falls **18**
Takakkaw Falls **9**
Upper Hot Springs Pool **3**

than five million people annually make their way through Banff National Park—generally acknowledged to be Canada's single most popular destination for foreign travelers—and the numbers are shooting up astronomically. Although Draconian measures such as limiting visitors have as yet been brought up only in order to be dismissed, one thing is for certain: Advance planning is absolutely necessary if you're going to stay or eat where you want, or if you hope to evade the swarms of visitors that throng the parks during the high season, from mid-June to the end of August.

ORIENTATION

Canada's Rocky Mountain parks include Jasper and Banff, which together comprise 6,764 square miles (17,519km²); the provincial parklands of the Kananaskis Country and Mount Robson; and Yoho and Kootenay national parks, to the west in British Columbia.

The parks are traversed by one of the finest highway systems in Canada, plus innumerable nature trails leading to more remote valleys and peaks. The two "capitals," Banff and Jasper, lie 177 miles (287km) apart, connected by Highway 93, one of the most scenic routes you'll ever drive. Banff is 80 miles (128km) from Calgary via Highway 1; Jasper, 225 miles (375km) from Edmonton on Route 16, the famous Yellowhead Highway.

Entry to Banff, Jasper, Yoho, and Kootenay parks costs C$5 (US$3.25) per person per day, or C$10 (US$7) per group or family per day.

VISITOR INFORMATION

For information on the entire province of Alberta, contact **Travel Alberta** (© **800/661-8888;** www.travelalberta.com). Ask for copies of the accommodations and visitors guides, as well as the excellent *Traveler's Guide* and a road map. There's a separate guide for campers as well.

Alberta has no provincial sales tax. There's only the 7% national goods and services tax (GST), plus a 5% accommodations tax. On the other side of the Rockies, the province of British Columbia levies another 7% tax on purchases and services.

TOURS & EXCURSIONS

You'll get used to the name Brewster, associated with many things in these parts. In particular, these folks run the park system's principal tour-bus operation. **Brewster Transportation and Tours,** 100 Gopher St., Banff (© **403/762-6767;** www.brewster.ca), covers most of the outstanding scenic spots in both parks. Call for a full brochure, or ask the concierge at your hotel to arrange a trip. A couple of sample packages:

- **Banff to Jasper** (or vice versa): Some 9½ hours through unrivaled scenery, this tour takes in Lake Louise and a view of the ice field along the parkway. (The return trip requires an overnight stay, not included in the price.) In summer, the one-way fare is C$95 (US$62) for adults, C$47.50 (US$31) for children. If you don't want the tour, there's also a daily express bus between Banff and Jasper for C$59 (US$38) one-way; children pay half price.
- **Columbia Icefields:** On this 9½-hour tour from Banff, you stop at the Icefields Centre and get time off for lunch and a Snocoach ride up the glacier. Adults pay C$95 (US$62) in summer; children pay C$47.50 (US$31). The Snocoach Tour costs an extra C$28 (US$18) for adults and C$14 (US$9) for children; tickets must be purchased in advance.

Tips Avoiding the Crowds

There are lots of side roads and alternatives to the major destinations in the Canadian Rockies: After a few days of crowds and traffic, you may be looking for a blue highway. The foothills and lakes in Kananaskis Country (see section 2, below) are a good alternative to busy Banff for campers and hikers. You can also free yourself of the crowds in the Alberta national parks by heading to the British Columbian side of the mountains, where you can visit the less-thronged but equally dramatic Glacier and Mount Revelstoke national parks, in the Selkirk Mountains (see chapter 12, "Southeastern British Columbia & the Kootenay Valley").

SEASONS

The parks have two peak seasons, during which hotels charge top rates and restaurants are jammed. The first is summer, from mid-June to the end of August, when it doesn't get terribly hot—rarely above 80°F (27°C), although the sun's rays are powerful at this altitude. The other peak time is winter, the skiing season December through February; this is probably the finest skiing terrain in the entire country.

March through May is decidedly off-season: Hotels offer bargain rates and you can choose the best table in any restaurant. There's still plenty of rain in the warmer months, so don't forget to bring suitable rain gear.

ACCOMMODATIONS IN THE ROCKIES

A word about lodging in the parks: On any given day in high season, up to 50,000 people are winding through the Canadian Rockies national parks. As growth in the parks is strictly regulated, there's not an abundance of hotel rooms waiting. The result is strong competition for a limited number of very expensive rooms. Adding to the squeeze is the fact that many hotels have 80% to 90% of their rooms reserved for coach tours during the summer. In short, if you're reading this on the day you plan to arrive in Banff, Jasper, or Lake Louise and haven't yet booked your room, start worrying. Most hotels are totally booked for the season by July 1. To avoid disappointment, *reserve your room as far in advance as possible.*

Regarding prices, it seems that lodgings can ask for—and get—just about any rates they want in high season. For the most part, park hotels are well maintained, but few could justify these high prices anywhere else in the world. Knowing that, you have a few choices. You can splurge on one of the world-class hotels here, which are actually only a bit more expensive than their midrange competition. Camping is another good option, as the parks have dozens of campgrounds with varying degrees of facilities. There are also a number of hostels throughout the parks.

In the off-season, prices drop dramatically, often as much as 50%. Most hotels offer ski packages in winter, as well as other attractive getaway incentives. Ask about any special rates, especially at the larger hotels.

BED-AND-BREAKFASTS   If you're looking for a B&B, try the **Alberta Bed and Breakfast Association** (www.bbalberta.com).

HOSTELS   Hostels in the Rocky Mountain national parks are often the most affordable lodging option. Hostels aren't just for youths anymore; all **Hostelling**

International properties welcome guests of any age. To find out more about Alberta hostels, check out **www.hostellingintl.ca/alberta**.

GUEST RANCHES Alberta has been ranch country for well over a century, and the Old West lifestyle is deeply ingrained in Albertan culture. Indulge in a cowboy fantasy and spend a few days at one of the area's many historic guest ranches.

At Seebe, in the Kananaskis Country near the entrance to Banff National Park, are a couple of the oldest and most famous ranches. **Rafter Six Ranch** (℗ **403/673-3691**) has a beautiful old log lodge. The original Brewster homestead was transformed in 1923 into the **Brewster's Kananaskis Guest Ranch** ★ (℗ **403/673-3737**). The **Black Cat Guest Ranch** (℗ **800/865-8486** or 403/865-3084), near Hinton, was once a winter horse camp. At all of these, horseback riding and trail rides are the main focus, but other western activities, such as rodeos, barbecues, and country dancing, are usually on the docket. Gentler pursuits like fishing, hiking, and lolling by the hot tub are equally possible. Meals are usually served in the lodge; accommodations are either in cabins or the main lodge. A night at a guest ranch usually ranges from C$80 to C$100 (US$52 to US$65) and includes breakfast. Full bed-and-board packages are available for longer stays. There's usually an additional fee for horseback riding.

Homestays at smaller working ranches are also possible. Here you can pitch in and help your ranch-family hosts with their work, or simply relax. For a stay on a real mom-and-pop farm, obtain a list of member ranches from **Alberta Ranch & Farm Holidays** (℗ **403/625-2295;** fax 403/625-3126; www.alberta countryvacation.com).

THE GREAT OUTDOORS

Banff and Jasper national parks have long been the center of mountain recreation for Alberta. If you're staying in Banff, Jasper, or Lake Louise, you'll find that outfitters and rental operations in these centers are pretty sophisticated and professional: They make it easy and convenient to get outdoors. Most hotels will offer a concierge service that can arrange activities for you; for many, you need little or no advance registration. Shuttle buses to more distant activities are usually available as well.

You don't even have to break a sweat to enjoy the magnificent scenery—hire a horse and ride to the backcountry, or take an afternoon trail ride. Jasper, Banff, and Lake Louise have gondolas to lift travelers from valley floor to mountaintop. Bring a picnic, or plan a ridge-top hike. If you're not ready for white water,

---

Tips **Road Conditions**

Skiers should know that in winter, heavy snowfall closes some mountain roads in the Rockies. However, major passes are maintained and usually remain open to traffic. Highways 1, 3, and 16 are open year-round, though it's a good idea to call ahead to check conditions. You can inquire locally, or contact **Travel Alberta** (℗ **800/661-8888**) or the **Alberta Motor Association** (℗ **403/474-8601;** www.ama.ab.ca). If you're a member of **AAA** or **CAA,** call (℗ **800/642-3810**). If you're planning winter car travel, always carry traction devices like tire chains, plus plenty of warm clothes and a sleeping bag.

the scenic cruises on Lake Minnewanka and Maligne Lake offer a more relaxed waterborne adventure.

BACKPACKING   Backcountry trips through high mountain meadows and remote lakes provide an unforgettable experience; Banff Park alone has 1,900 miles (3,059km) of hiking trails.

BIKING   Both parks provide free maps of local mountain-bike trails; the Bow Valley Parkway between Banff and Lake Louise and Parkway 93A in Jasper Park are both good, less trafficked roads for road biking. Bike rentals are easily available nearly everywhere in the parks.

ROCK CLIMBING, ICE CLIMBING & MOUNTAINEERING   The sheer rock faces on Mount Rundle near Banff and the Pallisades near Jasper are popular with rock climbers, and the area's many waterfalls become frozen ascents for ice climbers in winter. Instruction in mountaineering skills is offered by **Yamnuska Inc. Mountain School,** based in Canmore (© **403/678-4164;** www. yamnuska.com).

SKIING   There are downhill areas at Banff, Lake Louise, Jasper, and the former Olympic site at Nakiska in the Kananaskis Country. Skiing can be superb here: The snowpack is copious, the scenery beautiful, après-ski festivities indulgent, and accommodations world-class. There's a lot of value in an Alberta ski holiday—lift tickets here are generally cheaper than at comparable ski areas in the United States.

Heli-skiing isn't allowed in the national parks, but is popular in the adjacent mountains in British Columbia. **CMH Heli-Skiing** (© **800/661-0252** or 402/762-7100; www.cmhski.com) is the leader in this increasingly popular sport, which uses helicopters to deposit skiers on virgin slopes far from the lift lines. CMH offers 7- or 10-day trips to eight different locations; prices begin at C$4,400 (US$2,860), including lodging, food, and transport from Calgary.

Cross-country skiers will find a lot to like in the Canadian Rockies. A number of snowbound mountain lodges remain open throughout the winter and serve as bases for adventurous Nordic skiers. The historic **Emerald Lake Lodge,** in Yoho National Park (© **800/663-6336** or 250/343-6321), is one of the finest.

WHITE-WATER RAFTING & CANOEING   The Rockies' many glaciers and snowfields are the source of mighty rivers. Outfitters throughout the region offer white-water rafting and canoe trips of varying lengths and difficulty—you can spend a single morning on the river, or plan a 5-day expedition. Jasper is central to a number of good white-water rivers. **Maligne Rafting Adventures Ltd.** (© **780/852-3370;** www.mra.ab.ca) has packages for rafters of all experience levels.

WILDLIFE-VIEWING   If you're thrilled by seeing animals in the wild, you've turned to the right chapter. No matter which one you choose, the Rocky Mountain national parks are all teeming with wildlife—bighorn sheep, grizzly and black bears, deer, mountain goats, moose, coyotes, lynxes, wolves, and more. See "Park Wildlife," below, for important warnings on how to handle wildlife encounters in the parks responsibly and safely.

PARK WILDLIFE

The parklands are swarming with wildlife, with some animals meandering along and across highways and hiking trails, within easy camera range. However tempting, *don't feed the animals, and don't touch them!* There is, for starters, a fine of up to C$500 (US$325) for feeding any wildlife. There's also the distinct possibility that you may end up paying more than cash for disregarding this warning.

It isn't easy to resist the blithely fearless bighorn sheep, mountain goats, elk, soft-eyed deer, and lumbering moose you meet. (You'll have very little chance of meeting the coyotes, lynx, and occasional wolves, since they give humans a wide berth.) But the stuff you feed them can kill them. Bighorns get accustomed to summer handouts of bread, candy, potato chips, and marshmallows, when they should be grazing on the high-protein vegetation that will help them survive through the winter.

Moose involve additional dangers. After being given an initial snack, they have been known to take over entire picnics, chase off picnickers, and eat up everything in sight—including the cutlery, dishes, and tablecloth.

Portions of the parks are sometimes closed to hikers and bikers during elk calving season. A mother elk can mistake your recreation for an imminent attack on her newborn, or an unsuspecting hiker could frighten a mother from her calf, separating the two for good. Pay attention to—and obey—the postings at trail heads.

Bears pose the worst problems. The parks contain two breeds: the big grizzly, standing up to 7 feet (2m) on its hind legs, and the smaller black bear, about 5 feet (1.5m) tall. The grizzly spends most of the summer in high alpine ranges, well away from tourist haunts. As one of North America's largest carnivores, its appearance and reputation are awesome enough to make visitors beat a retreat on sight. But the less formidable black bear is a born clown with tremendous audience appeal, and takes to human company like a squirrel. The black bear's cuddly looks and circus antics, plus its knack for begging and rummaging through garbage cans, tend to obscure the fact that these are wild animals: powerful, faster than a horse, and completely unpredictable.

Hiking in bear country (and virtually all parkland is bear country) necessitates certain precautions—ignore them at your own peril. Never hike alone, and never take a dog along. Dogs often yap at bears, and when the animal charges, they run toward their owners for protection, bringing the pursuer with them. Use a telephoto lens when taking pictures. Bears in the wild have a set tolerance range that, when encroached upon, may bring on an attack. Above all, never go near a cub. The mother is usually close by, and a female defending her young is the most ferocious creature you'll ever face—and possibly the last.

2 Kananaskis Country & Canmore

19 miles (31km) E of Banff, 60 miles (97km) W of Calgary

Kananaskis Country is the name given to three Alberta provincial parks on the Rocky Mountains' eastern slope, southeast of Banff National Park. Once considered only a gateway region to more glamorous Banff, the Kananaskis has developed into a recreation destination on a par with more famous resorts in the Rockies.

Located just west of the Kananaskis and just outside the eastern boundary of Banff National Park, **Canmore** is a sprawl of condominium and resort developments in a dramatic location beneath the soaring peaks of **Three Sisters Mountain.** Only 20 minutes from Banff, Canmore hasn't yet topped the list of

Canadian resort destinations, but the scenery is magnificent and the accommodations generally much less expensive and considerably less overbooked than those in Banff.

Weather is generally warmer and sunnier here, which is conducive to great golf: The championship course at Kananaskis is considered one of the best in North America.

When the 1988 Olympics were held in Calgary, the national park service wouldn't allow the alpine ski events to be held in the parks. **Nakiska,** in the Kananaskis, became the venue instead, vaulting this ski area to international prominence.

The Kananaskis offers stunning scenery without Banff's crowds and high prices. Also, because the Kananaskis Country isn't governed by national-park restrictions, there's better road access to out-of-the-way lakeside campgrounds and trail heads, which makes this a more convenient destination for family getaways (there are more than 3,000 campsites in the area!). This provincial parkland also allows "mixed use," including some traditional (though heavily regulated) ranching. Some of the best guest ranches in Alberta operate here.

The main road through the Kananaskis Country is Highway 40, which cuts south from Highway 1 at the gateway to the Rockies and follows the Kananaskis River. **Kananaskis Village,** a collection of resort hotels and shops, is the center of activities and is convenient to most recreation areas. Highway 40 eventually climbs up to 7,239-foot (2,206m) Highwood Pass, the highest pass in Alberta, before looping around to meet Highway 22 south of Calgary.

ESSENTIALS

GETTING THERE   Canmore is served by **Greyhound Canada** (© **800/ 661-8747** or 403/260-0877; www.greyhound.ca) and **Brewster** (© **403/ 762-6767;** www.brewster.ca) buses and by private shuttle services that run between Banff and Calgary; see "Getting There" under "Banff Townsite," below.

VISITOR INFORMATION   For information on Kananaskis and Canmore, contact **Kananaskis Country** (© **866/432-4322;** www.kananaskisvalley.com) or the **Barrier Lake Visitor Information Centre** (© **403/673-3985**). The province-wide **Travel Alberta Visitor Information Centre,** at the Bow Valley Trail exit off Highway 1 at Canmore (© **403/678-5277**), also has lots of information on Canmore.

EXPLORING CANMORE

You could drive past Canmore many times—indeed, you could pull off the freeway and drive down the hotel- and mall-laden Bow Valley Trail—and think you've seen all the town has to offer. In fact, the modern development that you'll glimpse from the freeway dates from the 1988 Olympics, when Canmore was the center for cross-country ski competition. Canmore has actually been around since the 1880s, when it was the headquarters for the coal mines that fueled the Canadian Pacific Railroad's transcontinental trains as they climbed up over the Rockies.

The old downtown area is on an island in the Bow River, and is reached by turning onto Main Street off Railway Avenue. Downtown is undeveloped by Banff standards, but three pleasant, pedestrian-friendly blocks are lined with shops, brewpubs, restaurants, and boutiques. The **Canmore Museum,** at Seventh Avenue and Ninth Street (© **403/678-2462**), tells the story of the community from its days as a coal-mining camp to its pinnacle as Olympic host.

OUTDOOR PURSUITS

It's the excellent access to outdoor activities that makes Canmore and the Kananaskis such a prime destination. From its offices in Kananaskis Village and in Canmore at 999 Bow Valley Trail, **Mirage Adventure Tours** (© 888/312-7238 or 403/678-4919; www.miragetours.com) represents most local outfitters. You'll find bike trips, trail rides, rafting, hiking, and sightseeing tours on offer. Mirage also rents cross-country skis and equipment.

DOWNHILL SKIING Kananaskis gained worldwide attention when it hosted the alpine ski events for the winter Olympics in 1988. At **Nakiska,** skiers can follow in the tracks of Olympians past. A second ski area, **Fortress Mountain,** is 12 miles (19km) south of Kananaskis Village. Although overshadowed by Nakiska's Olympic reputation, Fortress Mountain offers an escape from the resort crowd and features overnight accommodations in an on-site dormitory. Both areas offer terrain for every age and ability, and are open from early December to mid-April. Adult lift tickets cost C$46 (US$30) at Nakiska, C$34 (US$22) at Fortress; tickets are completely transferable between the two areas. For information, contact **Ski Nakiska** (© 800/258-7669 or 403/591-7777; www.skinakiska.com).

CROSS-COUNTRY SKIING The **Canmore Nordic Centre** ⊛, south of town off Spray Lakes Road (© 403/678-2400), was developed for the Olympic cross-country skiing competition. In winter, the center offers 44 miles (70km) of scenic cross-country trails, plus the on-site shop **Trail Sports** (© 403/678-6764), for rentals, repairs, and sales. In summer, when hikers and mountain bikers take over the trails, Trail Sports offers bike rentals, skill-building courses, and guided rides.

GOLF Kananaskis features three championship golf courses and one of Canada's premier golf resorts. **Kananaskis Country Golf Course** ⊛ boasts two 18-hole, par-72 courses set among alpine forests and streams; they feature water hazards on 20 holes, 140 sand traps, and four tee positions. Kananaskis is rated among the top courses in Canada. For information, contact **Golf Kananaskis** (© 403/591-7154; www.kananaskisgolf.com). Greens fees are C$65 (US$42).

Near Canmore, the 18-hole **Canmore Golf Course** is right along the Bow River at 2000 Eighth Ave. (© 403/678-4785). Greens fees are C$48 (US$31).

The Les Furber–designed **Golf Course at Silvertip** ⊛ (© 403/678-1600; www.silvertipresort.com), is an 18-hole, par-72 course high above Canmore, off Silvertip Drive. You'll look eye-to-eye with the Canadian Rockies here. Boasting a length of 7,300 yards, the course has sand bunkers on all holes, and water on eight. Greens fees range from C$89 to C$129 (US$58 to US$84).

HORSEBACK RIDING The Kananaskis is noted for its long-established dude ranches (see "Riding Herd at Some Noteworthy Guest Ranches," below), which offer a variety of adventures ranging from short trail rides to multi-day pack trips. **Mirage Adventure Tours** (see above) is a good clearinghouse for information.

RAFTING The Kananaskis and Bow rivers are the main draw here. In addition to half-day (C$55/US$36), full-day (C$85/US$55), and 2-day (C$229/US$149) white-water trips, there are excursions that combine a half-day of horseback riding or mountain biking with an afternoon of rafting (C$119–C$129/US$77–US$84). Contact **Mirage Adventure Tours,** above, for information.

WHERE TO STAY
IN KANANASKIS VILLAGE

The lodgings in Kananaskis Village were built for the Olympics in 1988, so all are relatively new and well maintained. There's no more than a stone's throw between them, and to a high degree, public facilities are shared among all of the hotels.

Delta Lodge at Kananaskis ⚐   This resort hotel consists of two separate buildings that face each other across a pond at the center of Kananaskis Village. The Lodge is the larger building, with a more rustic facade, a shopping arcade, and a number of drinking and dining choices. Its guest rooms are well furnished; many have balconies, some fireplaces. The Signature Club rooms are in the smaller—and quieter—of the two buildings. Rooms here are generally more spacious and even more sumptuously furnished; they include air-conditioning, dataports, deluxe continental breakfast, afternoon hors d'oeuvres, honor bar, and full concierge service.

Kananaskis Village, AB T0L 2H0. ℂ 800/268-1133 or 403/591-7711. Fax 403/591-7770. www.deltalodgeat kananaskis.ca. 321 units. High season C$225–C$330 (US$146–US$215). Ski/golf packages and discounts available. AE, DC, MC, V. Parking C$8 (US$5); valet parking C$12 (US$8). **Amenities:** Four restaurants, bar; indoor pool; golf courses nearby; tennis courts; health club; full spa with saltwater pool and whirlpool; bike rentals; concierge; tour desk; car-rental desk; business center; shopping arcade; limited room service; baby-sitting; laundry service; dry cleaning. In room: TV/VCR w/ pay movies, minibar, coffeemaker, hair dryer, iron.

Kananaskis Mountain Lodge   This handsome, wood-fronted hotel is the most affordable place to stay in Kananaskis—although that doesn't mean it's inexpensive. It offers a wide variety of room types—all renovated in 2001—including many loft units with kitchenettes that can sleep up to six. There are mountain views from practically every room.

P.O. Box 10, Kananaskis Village, AB T0L 2H0. ℂ 888/591-7501 or 403/591-7500. Fax 403/591-7633. www. kananaskismountainlodge.com. 90 units. C$110–C$230 (US$72–US$150) double; C$170–C$290 (US$111–US$189) suite. AE, DC, DISC, MC, V. Free parking. **Amenities:** Restaurant, bar; golf courses nearby; tennis courts; health club; spa; exercise room; concierge; tour desk; business center; limited room service; babysitting; laundry service; dry cleaning. In room: TV w/ pay movies, dataport, fridge, coffeemaker, hair dryer, iron.

Ribbon Creek Hostel   This is a great place for recreation-loving travelers on a budget. The hostel is located right at the Nakiska ski area, within walking distance of Kananaskis Village, and is close to 60 mountain-biking, hiking, and cross-country trails. Area outfitters offer special discounts to hostel guests. Four private family rooms are available.

At Nakiska Ski Area. ℂ 403/762-3441 for reservations, or 403/591-7333 for the hostel itself. 44 beds. C$15 (US$10) members, C$19 (US$12) nonmembers. MC, V. **Amenities:** Laundry. In room: No phone.

IN CANMORE

Much of the hotel development in Canmore dates from the 1988 Olympics, though the town is presently going through an intense period of growth. To a large degree, this is due to the restrictions on development within the national parks to the west: Hoteliers, outfitters, and other businesses designed to serve the needs of park visitors find Canmore, right on the park boundary, a much easier place to locate than Banff. As a result, Canmore is booming, and is now a destination in its own right.

The main reason to stay in Canmore is the price of hotel rooms. Rates here are between a half and a third lower than in Banff, and the small downtown area is beginning to blossom with interesting shops and good restaurants.

Riding Herd at Some Noteworthy Guest Ranches

The Brewsters were movers and shakers in the region's early days, playing a decisive role in the formation of Banff and Jasper national parks. They were also the first outfitters (and transport providers) in the parks. **Brewster's Kananaskis Guest Ranch** ★, 30 minutes east of Banff on Highway 1, P.O. Box 964, Banff, AB T0L 0C0 (© **800/691-5085** or 403/673-3737; fax 403/673-2100; www.brewsteradventures.com), the original family homestead from the 1880s, was transformed into a guest ranch in 1923. Located right on the Bow River near the mouth of the Kananaskis River, the original lodge buildings now serve as common areas. The 33 guest rooms, in chalets and cabins, are fully modern, with full bathrooms. Doubles are C$79 to C$94 (US$51 to US$61), breakfast and dinner included. Activities include horseback riding, rafting, canoeing, hiking, and more. Long-distance backcountry horseback rides are a specialty—a 2-day trip costs under C$300 (US$195)—and backcountry campsites have newly constructed cabins for sleeping accommodations.

Another old-time guest ranch with a long pedigree, **Rafter Six Ranch Resort,** P.O. Box 6, Seebe, AB T0L 1X0 (© **888/26-RANCH** or 403/673-3622; fax 403/673-3961; www.raftersix.com), is located in a meadow right on the banks of the Kananaskis River. This full-service resort accommodates guests in an especially inviting old log lodge (with restaurant, barbecue deck, and lounge), in various sizes of log cabins, and in large chalets that sleep up to six and have full kitchens. All units have private bathrooms. Doubles go for C$110 to C$250 (US$72 to US$163) in the lodge, C$125 to C$250 (US$81 to US$163) in cabins and chalets. Casual horseback and longer pack rides are offered, as well as raft and canoe trips. Seasonal special events might include rodeos, country dances, and hay or sleigh rides. Open year-round.

For a complete list of B&Bs, try the **Canmore–Bow Valley B&B Association** (www.bbcanmore.com).

Best Western Green Gables Inn   Located along Canmore's hotel strip, this pleasant Best Western features rooms with private patios or balconies; many units boast whirlpool baths and fireplaces as well.

1602 Second Ave., Canmore, AB T1W 1M8. © **800/661-2133** or 403/678-5488. Fax 403/678-2670. www. pocaterrainn.com/GreenGables/index.html. 61 units. C$159–C$199 (US$103–US$129) double. Children under 18 stay free in parents' room. AE, DISC, MC, V. **Amenities:** Restaurant, bar; exercise room; Jacuzzi. *In room:* A/C, TV, fridge, hair dryer.

Best Western Pocaterra Inn ★   One of the nicest of the hotels along the Bow Valley Trail strip is the Pocaterra Inn. All of the spacious rooms come with gas fireplaces, balconies, and lots of thoughtful niceties.

1725 Mountain Ave., Canmore, AB T1W 2W1. © **888/678-6786** or 403/678-4334. Fax 403/678-3999. www. pocaterrainn.com. 83 units. C$169–C$249 (US$110–US$162) double. Children under 18 stay free in parents' room. Rates include continental breakfast. AE, DISC, MC, V. **Amenities:** Indoor pool with waterslide; whirlpool; exercise room; sauna; coin-op laundry. *In room:* A/C, TV, dataport, fridge, coffeemaker, microwave, hair dryer.

An Eagle's View B&B   New and well designed, An Eagle's View is located in one of the recent developments high above Canmore. Views of the Three Sisters and the Bow Valley are eye-popping. Each bedroom is large and nicely furnished. Guests share a lounge with TV/VCR, a garden patio, and a sunny deck overlooking the mountains.

6 Eagle Landing, Canmore, AB T1W 2Y1. ✆ **877/609-3887** or 403/678-3264. www.aneaglesview.com. 2 units. C$100–$130 (US$65–$85) double. Rates include breakfast. AE, MC, V. *In room:* No phone.

McNeill Heritage Inn 🌲🌲   Built in 1907 as a trophy home for the manager of the local coal mine, the McNeill is a marvelous bit of historic architecture combined with modern comforts. It's located just west of downtown Canmore, literally at the end of the road on the south banks of the Bow River, perched on an outcrop of rock above the waters. The seclusion and privacy of the inn are a treat after a day out in bustling Banff or Canmore. The rambling old home's bedrooms are decorated with uncluttered, handsome simplicity. Guests share a veranda, a living room with fireplace, and a library stocked with outdoor guides. You'll find a friendly welcome and professional service, plus an excellent breakfast. This is a good choice for cross-country skiers, as it's adjacent to the Canmore Nordic Centre.

500 Three Sisters Dr., Canmore, AB T1W 2P3. ✆ **877/MCNEILL** or 403/678-4884. Fax 403/609-3450. www. mcneillinn.ab.ca. 5 units. C$125–C$185 (US$81–US$120) double. Extra person C$25 (US$16). Rates include breakfast. MC, V. **Amenities:** Laundry service. *In room:* TV/VCR, dataport, minibar, fridge, coffeemaker, hair dryer, iron.

Quality Inn Chateau Canmore 🌲   You can't miss this enormous complex along the hotel strip. Like a series of 10 four-story conjoined chalets, the all-suite Chateau Canmore offers some of the largest rooms in the area. The accommodations are decorated in rustic style; the common areas look like they belong in a log lodge. Each standard suite has a fireplace; deluxe suites add a washer/dryer. Just like home, but with a better view.

1720 Bow Valley Trail, Canmore, AB T1W 2X3. ✆ **800/261-8551** or 403/678-6699. Fax 403/678-6954. www. chateaucanmore.com. 120 units. C$169 (US$110) standard suite; from C$189 (US$123) deluxe suite. AE, DISC, MC, V. **Amenities:** Dining room, lounge; indoor pool; health club; spa; limited room service. *In room:* AC, TV, dataport, fridge, microwave, hair dryer.

Radisson Hotel and Conference Centre Canmore   This vast complex is Canmore's largest hotel and also serves as the town's convention center. With all of the services offered here, it's almost a self-contained community. Guests stay in standard units in the main building, all with balconies, or in luxury lodge rooms, most with kitchenettes.

511 Bow Valley Trail, Canmore, AB T1W 1N7. ✆ **800/333-3333** or 403/678-3625. Fax 403/678-3765. www. radisson.com/canmoreca. 224 units. C$139–C$179 (US$90–US$116) double. AE, MC, V. **Amenities:** Restaurant, bar; indoor pool; exercise room; Jacuzzi; sauna; car-rental desk; limited room service; babysitting; laundry service; same-day dry cleaning. *In room:* A/C, TV w/ pay movies, dataport, coffeemaker, hair dryer, iron.

CAMPING

Kananaskis is a major camping destination for families. There's a concentration of campgrounds at **Upper and Lower Kananaskis Lakes,** some 20 miles (32km) south of Kananaskis Village. A few campgrounds are scattered nearer to Kananaskis Village, around **Barrier Lake** and **Ribbon Creek.** For a full-service campground with RV hookups, go to **Mount Kidd RV Park** (✆ **403/591-7700**), just south of the Kananaskis golf course.

WHERE TO DINE

The dining rooms at both **Rafter Six Ranch Resort** and **Brewster's Kananaskis Guest Ranch** (see "Riding Herd at Some Noteworthy Guest Ranches," above) are open to nonguests with reservations. A popular pub with good food is the **Rose and Crown,** 749 Railway Ave., in Canmore (© **403/678-5168**).

Sherwood House CANADIAN   This handsome log restaurant on the busiest corner of downtown Canmore (which isn't *that* busy) is a longtime favorite. The well-executed menu, which offers everything from pizza and pasta to prime Angus steaks, has something for everyone, but what makes this one of Canmore's favorite gathering spots is the wonderful landscaped deck. In summer, there's no better place to spend the afternoon. In winter, you'll enjoy the traditional lodge building with its cozy fireplace.

Main St. and Eighth Ave. © 403/678-5211. Reservations recommended. Main courses C$13–C$29 (US$8–US$19). AE, MC, V. Daily 7am–10pm.

Sinclair's ☆☆ NEW CANADIAN   Right downtown in a converted heritage home, Sinclair's is the most ambitious of the new restaurants in Canmore. The menu is very broad, offering an excellent selection of appetizers and small plates. There are also a number of individual pizzas and pasta dishes for lighter appetites. The entrees, however, are hard to resist. Seared pancetta-wrapped salmon served with a warm horseradish lemon lentil salad, broiled marinated lamb chops with chili-glazed applesauce and wild-mushroom polenta tortilla— there's nothing ordinary about the food at Sinclair's.

637 Main St., Canmore. © 403/678-5370. Reservations recommended. Main courses C$12–C$20 (US$8–US$13). AE, MC, V. Daily 11am–10pm.

Zona's Late Night Bistro INTERNATIONAL   Come to this friendly hangout if you don't want to spend a fortune, but still seek sophisticated food with some zip. The menu trots the globe: Moroccan pomegranate-molasses lamb curry, coconut lime chicken lasagna, and *salmonkepita* (phyllo-wrapped salmon, spinach, and cheese). You can also choose from a number of tapas and wraps, plus ample vegetarian options.

710 Ninth St. © 403/609-2000. Reservations not accepted. Main courses C$10–C$14 (US$7–US$9). MC, V. Daily 11:30pm–midnight.

3 Banff National Park

Banff Townsite: 80 miles (129km) W of Calgary

Banff is the oldest national park in Canada, founded as a modest 10-square-mile (26km²) reserve by Canada's first prime minister, Sir John A. Macdonald, in 1885. The park is now 2,564 square miles (6,641km²) of incredibly dramatic mountain landscape, glaciers, lakes, and rushing rivers. The park's two towns, **Lake Louise** and **Banff,** are both splendid counterpoints to the surrounding wilderness, with historic hotels, fine restaurants, and a lively nightlife scene.

If there's a downside to all this sophisticated beauty, it's that Banff is very, very popular—it's generally considered Canada's number-one tourist destination. About five million people visit Banff yearly, with the vast majority squeezing in during June, July, and August.

Happily, the wilderness invites visitors to get away from the crowds and congestion of the developed sites. Banff National Park is blessed with a great many

Banff Townsite & Banff National Park

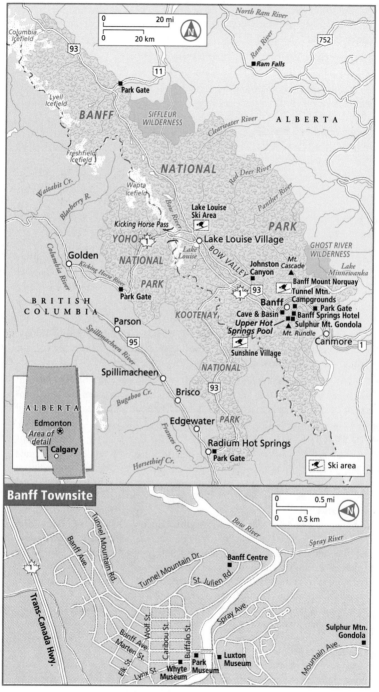

outfitters who make it easy to get on a raft, bike, or horse and find a little mountain solitude. Or consider visiting the park outside of the summer season, when
prices are lower, the locals friendlier, and the scenery just as stunning.

OUTDOOR PURSUITS IN THE PARK

There are lots of great recreational activities available in Banff National Park, so
don't just spend your vacation shopping the boutiques on Banff Avenue. Most
day trips require little advance booking—a day is usually plenty—and the easiest way to find a quick adventure is to simply ask your hotel concierge to set one
up for you. Multi-day rafting and horseback trips do require advance booking,
as spots are limited. There are many more outfitters in Banff than the ones listed
below, but the offerings and prices that follow are typical of what's available.

BIKING   The most popular cycling adventure in the Canadian Rockies is the
178-mile (287km) trip between Banff and Jasper along the Icefields Parkway,
one of the world's most magnificent mountain roads. If you're fit and ready for
a high-elevation ride, but don't want to bother with the logistics yourself, consider signing on with an outfitter. The **Great Canadian Adventure Company**
(© 888/285-1676 or 780/414-1676; www.adventures.com/gasnet/bik.htm)
offers 6-day supported trips starting at C$725 (US$471). Hardier types can also
do the 3-day stretch between Lake Louise and Jasper, overnighting at the numerous and charming hostels along the way. For an easy day trip, simply rent a bike
in Banff or Lake Louise and pedal along the Bow Valley Parkway—Highway
1A—between Banff and Lake Louise.

FISHING   **Banff Fishing Unlimited** (© 403/762-4936; www.banff-fishing.
com) offers a number of fly-fishing expeditions on the Bow River as well as lake
fishing at Lake Minnewanka.

GOLF   The **Banff Springs Golf Course** ⚑ (© 403/762-6801) rolls out
along the Bow River beneath towering mountain peaks. One of the most venerable courses in Canada, it offers 27 holes of excellent golf. Although associated
with the resort hotel, the course is open to the public.

HIKING   One of the great virtues of Banff is that many of its most scenic
areas are easily accessible by day hikes. The park has more than 80 maintained
trails, ranging from interpretive nature strolls to long-distance expeditions
(you'll need a permit if you're planning on camping in the backcountry). For a
good listing of popular hikes, pick up the free *Banff/Lake Louise Drives and
Walks* brochure.

   One of the best day hikes is up **Johnston Canyon** ⚑, 15 miles (24km) north
of Banff on Highway 1A. This relatively easy hike up a limestone canyon passes
seven waterfalls before reaching a series of jade-green springs known as the
Inkpots. Part of the fun of this trail is the narrowness of the canyon—the walls
are more than 100 feet (30m) high, but only 18 feet (5m) across; the path skirts
the cliff face, tunnels through walls, and winds across wooden footbridges for
more than a mile (1.6km). The waterfalls plunge down through the canyon,
soaking hikers with spray; watch for black swifts diving in the mist. The hike
through the canyon to Upper Falls takes 1½ hours; all the way to the Inkpots will
take at least 4 hours.

   It's also easy to strike out from Banff Townsite and find any number of satisfying short hikes. Setting off on foot can be as simple as following the paths

> **Tips A Bird's-Eye View**
>
> If you'd like to see the beautiful scenery of the Canadian Rockies from the air, contact **Alpine Helicopters** (© **403/678-4802**), which operates out of Canmore. This company's flights over the Rockies start at C$130 (US$85). See also the section on Golden in chapter 12, "Southeastern British Columbia & the Kootenay Valley," for details on **Alpenglow Aviation** (© **888/ 244-7117** or 250/344-7117), which offers a variety of flightseeing trips.

along both sides of the **Bow River.** From the west end of the Bow River Bridge, trails lead east to Bow Falls, past the Banff Springs Hotel to the Upper Hot Springs. Another popular hike just beyond town is the **Fenlands Trail,** which begins past the train station and makes a loop through marshland wildlife habitat near the Vermillion Lakes.

Two longer trails leave from the Cave and Basin Centennial Centre. The **Sundance Trail** follows the Bow River for nearly 3 miles (5km) past beaver dams and wetlands, ending at the entrance to Sundance Canyon. Keen hikers can continue up the canyon another 1½ miles (2.4km) to make a loop past Sundance Falls. The **Marsh Loop** winds 1½ miles (2.4km) past the Bow River and marshy lakes.

Parks Canada offers several guided hikes daily. Ask at the Banff visitor center to find out what options are available. Some walks are free; others (like the popular evening **Wildlife Research Walks**) charge a small fee; all require preregistration. For information and preregistration, call © **403/762-9818.**

HORSEBACK RIDING Warner Guiding and Outfitting (© **800/ 661-8352** or 403/762-4551; www.horseback.com) offers multi-day trail rides, starting at C$475 (US$309) for a 3-day lodge-to-lodge trip and peaking at C$958 (US$623) for a 6-day backcountry tenting trip. Shorter day rides are also offered from two stables near the town. A morning ride with brunch goes for C$67 (US$44). Operating out of Lake Louise, **Timberline Tours** (© **888/ 858-3388** or 403/522-3743) offers day trips to some of the area's more prominent beauty sites, starting at C$45 (US$29) for 90 minutes; 3- to 10-day pack trips are also offered.

RAFTING & CANOEING   Family float trips on the Bow River are popular diversions, available from **Canadian Rockies Rafting Company** (© **877/ 226-7625** or 403/678-6535; www.teluxplanet.net/public/canrock). The 1½-hour trips are C$40 (US$26) for adults and C$28 (US$18) for children, with free pickup at Banff and Canmore hotels.

For serious white water, the closest option is the **Kicking Horse River** ⭐, past Lake Louise just over the Continental Divide near Field, British Columbia. **Hydra River Guides** (© **800/644-8888** or 403/762-4554; www.raftbanff.com) offers a 3-hour run down the Kicking Horse through Grade IV rapids. Trips go for C$85 (US$55), which includes gear, lunch, and transport.

SKIING   Banff National Park has three ski areas, which together have formed a partnership for booking and promotional purposes. For information on all of the following, contact **Ski Banff/Lake Louise** (© **403/762-4561;** fax 403/ 762-8185; www.skibanfflakelouise.com).

Banff Mount Norquay (© 403/762-4421) are twin runs just above the town of Banff. They cater to family skiing and offer day care, instruction, and night skiing. Rates start at C$47 (US$31) for adults.

Skiers must ski or take a gondola to the main lifts at **Sunshine Village** (© 403/762-6500) and the Sunshine Inn, a ski-in/ski-out hotel. Sunshine, located 15 minutes west of Banff off Highway 1, receives more snow than any ski area in the Canadian Rockies (more than 30 ft./9m per year!) and boasts the fastest high-speed quad lifts in the world. Lift tickets start at C$60 (US$39) for adults.

Lake Louise Ski Area (© 800/258-SNOW or 403/552-3555) is the largest in Canada, with 40 miles (64km) of trails. With 11 lifts, management guarantees no long lines on major lifts, or your money back! Snowmaking machines keep the lifts running from November to early May. Rates are C$59 (US$38) for adults.

A special pass for Banff Mount Norquay, Sunshine Village, and Lake Louise Ski Area allows skiers unlimited access to all three resorts (and free rides on shuttles between the ski areas). Passes for 3 days cost C$175 (US$114) for adults and C$64 (US$42) for children.

BANFF TOWNSITE

Few towns in the world boast as beautiful a setting as Banff. The mighty Bow River courses right through town, and massive mountain blocks rear up right on Banff's outskirts. Mount Rundle, a finlike mountain that somehow got tipped over on its side, parades off to the south. Mount Cascade rises up immediately north of downtown. In every direction, still more craggy peaks fill the sky.

This is a stunning, totally unlikely place for a town, and Banff has been trading on its beauty for more than a century. The Banff Springs Hotel was built in 1888 as a destination resort by the Canadian Pacific Railroad. As outdoor-recreation enthusiasts began to frequent the area for its scenery, hot springs, and access to fishing, hunting, climbing, and other activities, the little town of Banff grew up to service their needs.

Although the setting hasn't changed since the early days of the park, the town certainly has. Today, the streets of Banff are lined with exclusive boutiques; trendy cafes spill out onto the sidewalks; and bus after bus filled with tourists chokes the streets. Japanese, English, French, and German visitors are very much in evidence. There's a vital and cosmopolitan feel to the town; just don't come here expecting a bucolic alpine village—Banff in summer is a very busy place.

ESSENTIALS

GETTING THERE   The Trans-Canada Highway takes you right to Banff's main street. **Greyhound Canada** (© 800/661-8747 or 403/260-0877; www.greyhound.ca) operates buses that pass through Banff on the way from Calgary to Vancouver. One-way fare between Banff and Calgary is C$20 (US$13).

The closest **VIA Rail** train service is at Jasper, 178 miles (287km) north. **Brewster Transport** (© 403/762-6767) offers an express bus between the two park centers five times weekly for C$59 (US$38) one-way.

If you're flying into Calgary and heading straight to Banff, call and reserve a seat on the **Banff Airporter** (© 403/762-3330; www.banffairporter.com). A one-way ticket costs C$22 (US$14).

VISITOR INFORMATION   The **Banff Information Centre,** 224 Banff Ave. (© 403/762-0270; fax 403/762-8545; www.banfflakelouise.com), houses both the **Banff Tourism Bureau** and a national-park information center. The center is open daily June 15 to October 15 9am to 9pm, the rest of the year 9am to 5pm. For information on the national park, go to **www.parkscanada.pch. gc.ca/banff**.

ORIENTATION   Getting your bearings is easy. The bus depot is located at the corner of Gopher and Lynx streets. The main street—**Banff Avenue**—starts at the southern end of town at the Bow River and runs north until it's swallowed by the Trans-Canada Highway. Along this broad, bright, and bustling thoroughfare, you'll find most of Banff's hotels, restaurants, stores, and nightspots.

Just beyond the river stands the park administration building amid a beautifully landscaped garden. Here the road splits: **Banff Springs Hotel** and the **Banff Gondola** are to the left; to the right are the **Cave and Basin Hot Springs,** Banff National Park's original site. At the northwestern edge of town is the old railroad station, and a little farther northwest the road branches off to Lake Louise and Jasper. In the opposite direction, northeast, is the highway going to Calgary.

GETTING AROUND   Banff offers local bus service along two routes designed to pass through downtown and by most hotels. Service on the summer-only **Banff Bus** (✆ 403/760-8294) is pretty informal, but there's generally a bus every half hour. One route runs from the Banff Springs Hotel down Banff Avenue to the northern end of town; the other runs between the train station and the Banff Hostel on Tunnel Mountain; the fare is C$1 (US$.65). For a taxi, call **Banff Taxi and Limousine** (✆ 403/762-4444). For a rental car, try **National,** at Caribou and Lynx streets (✆ 403/762-2688), or **Banff Rent A Car,** 204 Lynx St. (✆ 403/762-3352), for a less expensive but reliable vehicle. Avis, Budget, and Hertz also have offices in Banff.

EXPLORING THE AREA
Banff Gondola ✵   Apart from helicopter excursions (see "A Bird's-Eye View," above), the best way to get an overall view of Banff's landscape is this high-wire act (formerly the Sulphur Mountain Gondola). In 8 minutes, the enclosed gondolas lift you 2,292 feet (688m) from the valley floor up to the top of Sulphur Mountain, at 7,486 feet (2,246m). Trails lead out along the mountain ridges. At the upper terminal are two restaurants, a snack bar, and gift shop. Lines can be very long in summer; try to go as early as possible.

4 miles (6km) southeast of town, on Mountain Ave. ✆ 403/762-5438. www.banffgondola.com. Admission C$19 (US$12) adults, C$9.50 (US$6) children. May–Labour Day daily 7:30am–9pm; off-season, check website for complex schedule.

Banff Park Museum   Housed in a lovely wood-lined building dating from the 1910s, this museum beside the Bow River Bridge is largely a paean to taxidermy, but there's a lot to learn here about the wildlife of the park and how the various ecosystems interrelate. The real pleasure, though, is the rustic, lodge-style building, now preserved as a national historic site.

Banff Ave. and Buffalo St. ✆ 403/762-1558. Admission C$3 (US$1.95) adults, C$2 (US$1.30) seniors, C$1.50 (US$1) children 6–16. Summer daily 10am–6pm.

Cave and Basin National Historic Site ✵   Although most people now associate Banff with skiing or hiking, in the early days of the park, travelers streamed in to visit the curative hot springs. In fact, it was the discovery of the hot springs, now preserved at this historic site, that spurred the creation of the

---

> ### *Tips* Special Events
>
> The **Banff Centre,** St. Julien Road (℗ **800/413-8368** or 403/762-6300; www.
> banffcentre.ab.ca), is devoted to the arts in the widest sense. June
> through August, it hosts the **Banff Arts Festival** ⚘, offering a stimulating
> mixture of drama, opera, jazz, ballet, classical and pop music, and the
> visual arts. Highlights include the International String Quartet Competi-
> tion, with 10 world-class quartets vying for a cash prize and a national
> tour, and the Digital Playgrounds series, which brings performance artists
> to the stage. In November, the center is home to the **Festival of Mountain
> Films.** Find out what's currently on by getting the program at the visitor
> center or by checking out the center's website.

---

national park in 1888. During the 1910s, these hot mineral waters, which rise
in a limestone cave, were piped into a rather grand natatorium. Although the
Cave and Basin springs are no longer open for swimming or soaking, the old
pool area and the original cave have been preserved; interpretive displays and
films round out the experience.

1 mile (1.6km) west of Banff (turn right at the west end of the Bow River Bridge). ℗ **403/762-1566.** Admission C$2.50 (US$1.60) adults, C$2 (US$1.30) seniors, C$1.50 (US$1) children 6–18. Daily 9am–6pm.

Lake Minnewanka Boat Tours   These popular scenic and wildlife-viewing
trips in glassed-in motor cruisers take place on Lake Minnewanka, a glacial lake
wedged between two mountain ranges. The 1½-hour trips are among the excursions that nearly every visitor to Banff ends up taking, so unless you want to be
part of a huge throng, try to go early in the day. Reservations are suggested. In
high season, there are five sailings a day; buses depart from the Banff bus station
and from most hotels to meet these departures.

15 miles (24km) north of Banff. ℗ **403/762-3473.** Fax 403/762-2800. www.lakemineenwankaboattours.com.
Tickets C$28 (US$18) adults, C$12 (US$8) children. Mid-May to early Oct daily. Call for departure times.

Luxton Museum of the Plains Indian   Housed in a log fort south of the
Bow River, just across the bridge from downtown Banff, this museum is devoted
to the Native history of the Canadian Rockies and Northern Plains. It offers
realistic dioramas, a sun-dance exhibit, artifacts, and ornaments.

1 Birch Ave. ℗ **403/762-2388.** Admission C$8 (US$5) adults, C$4 (US$2.60) seniors and students, C$2.50
(US$1.60) children. Daily 9am–7pm.

Whyte Museum of the Canadian Rockies   Part art gallery, part local-his-
tory museum, this is the only museum in North America that exhibits and inter-
prets the history and culture of the Canadian Rockies. Two furnished heritage
homes on the grounds are open in summer. Interpretive programs and tours are
offered year-round. The Elizabeth Rummel Tea Room, open from mid-May to
mid-October, serves light lunches, desserts, and coffee.

111 Bear St. ℗ **403/762-2291.** Admission C$6 (US$3.90) adults, C$3.50 (US$2.30) seniors and students,
C$15 (US$10) families. Daily 10am–5pm.

Upper Hot Springs Pool   If visiting the Cave and Basin makes you long for
a soak in mountain hot springs, then drive up Mountain Avenue to this spa. In
addition to the swimming pool filled with hot, sulfurous waters, you'll find a

restaurant, snack bar, and home spa boutique. If you're looking more for a cure than a splash, try the adjacent **Upper Hot Springs Spa** (✆ **403/760-2500**), with a steam room, massage, plunge pools, and aromatherapy treatments.

At the top of Mountain Ave., 3 miles (5km) west of Banff. ✆ **403/762-1515.** Pool admission C$7.50 (US$4.90) adults, C$6.50 (US$4.20) seniors and children, C$21.50 (US$14) families. Spa treatments from C$32 (US$21). Sun–Thurs 10am–10pm, Fri–Sat 10am–11pm.

SHOPPING
The degree to which you like the town of Banff will depend largely upon your taste for shopping. **Banff Avenue** is increasingly an open-air boutique mall, with throngs of shoppers milling around. Of course, you would expect to find excellent outdoor-gear and sporting-goods stores here, as well as the usual T-shirt and gift emporiums. What's more surprising are the boutiques devoted to Paris and New York designers, the upscale jewelry stores, and the high-end galleries. What's most surprising of all is that many visitors seem to actually prefer to while away their time in this masterpiece of nature called Banff by shopping for English soaps or Italian shoes. There are no secrets to shopping here: Arcade after arcade opens onto Banff Avenue, where you'll find everything you need. Quality and prices are both quite high.

WHERE TO STAY
All prices listed below are for high season, which normally runs from mid-May to mid-October; nearly all hotels have a complex rate schedule with discounts for late fall, holidays, winter, and spring. Call for information on these reduced off-season rates, as well as ski and other packages. If you're having trouble finding affordable lodgings in Banff, try properties in Canmore, located 20 minutes away (see "Kananaskis Country & Canmore," above).

Very Expensive
Banff Park Lodge Resort Hotel and Conference Centre ✹   A handsome cedar-and-oak structure with a cosmopolitan air, the Banff Park Lodge is a quiet 1½ blocks off the town's main street, near the Bow River. Calm and sophisticated are the key words here: All of the rooms are soundproofed, and wild, après-ski cavorting isn't the norm, or even much encouraged. The lodge will feel like a tranquil retreat after a day in antic Banff. Standard rooms are spacious and exceptionally well furnished; all come with balconies. Most suites have jetted tubs and fireplaces. With its abundant ground-floor rooms and wide hallways, this lodging is ideal for travelers with disabilities or mobility concerns.

222 Lynx St., Banff, AB T0L 0C0. ✆ **800/661-9266** or 403/762-4433. Fax 403/762-3553. www.banffpark lodge.com. 211 units. C$259 (US$168) double. From C$379 (US$246) suite. Extra person C$10–C$15 (US$7–US$10). Children 16 and under stay free in parents' room. Off-season and ski packages available. AE, DC, MC, V. **Amenities:** Two restaurants, bar; indoor pool; access to nearby health club; exercise room; spa; Jacuzzi; concierge; tour/activities desk; business center; shopping arcade; salon; limited room service; babysitting; laundry service; same-day dry cleaning. *In room:* A/C, TV, dataport, fridge, coffeemaker, hair dryer.

Banff Springs Hotel ✹   Standing north of Bow River Falls like a Scottish baronial fortress, the Banff Springs is one of the most famous hotels in North America. Founded in 1888 as an opulent destination resort by the Canadian Pacific Railroad, this stone castle of a hotel is still the best address in Banff—especially so after the renovation of all guest rooms (the most recent upgrade devoted C$32,000/US$20,800 to each room!). This venerable lodging doesn't offer the largest rooms in Banff, but the amenities are superlative: Expect sumptuous linens, fancy toiletries, real art, and quality furniture. With the views, the spa, and the near pageantry of service, this is still the most amazing resort in an area blessed with beautiful accommodations. The Springs maintains a staff of 1,200 and stages such events as medieval banquets for convention groups.

405 Spray Ave. (P.O. Box 960), Banff, AB T0L 0C0. ☎ **800/441-1414** or 403/762-2211. Fax 403/762-5755. www.fairmont.com. 770 units. C$255–C$627 (US$166–US$408) double; C$457–C$1,007 (US$297–US$655) suite. Rates include full breakfast, service charges, and valet parking. AE, DC, DISC, MC, V. Valet parking C$20 (US$13); self-parking C$7 (US$4.55). **Amenities:** 15 restaurants and eateries, three lounges; Olympic-size pool; the famed Banff Springs golf course (one of the most scenic in the world); four tennis courts; Solace Spa (with mineral baths, beauty treatments, fitness training, and lifestyle programs); Jacuzzi; bike rentals; concierge; tour/activities desk; business center; shopping arcade; 24-hr. room service; babysitting; laundry service; same-day dry cleaning. *In room:* A/C, TV/VCR w/ pay movies and video games, dataport, coffeemaker, hair dryer, iron.

Buffalo Mountain Lodge 🏔🏔

The most handsome of the properties on Tunnel Mountain, a mile (1.6km) northeast of Banff, this is the perfect choice if you'd rather avoid the frenetic pace of downtown and yet remain central to restaurants and activities. Its quiet location and beautiful lodge make this a good alternative to equally priced hotels in the heart of town. The lodge building itself is an enormous log cabin, right out of your fantasies. The lobby is supported by massive rafters and filled with Navajo-style carpets. A fieldstone fireplace dominates the interior, separating the dining room (see "Where to Dine," below) from the lounge.

Accommodations are scattered around the forested 8-acre (3-hectare) property. They range from one-bedroom apartments with kitchens to exceptionally handsome rooms in brand-new buildings. The nicest are the Premier units, which feature slate-floored bathrooms with both claw-foot tubs and slate-walled showers. The pine-and-twig furniture lends a rustic look to the otherwise sophisticated decor. All units have fireplaces (wood is stacked near your door), balconies or patios, and beds made up with feather duvets. These are some of the most attractive rooms in Banff.

1 mile (1.6km) northeast of Banff on Tunnel Mountain Rd., P.O. Box 1326, Banff, AB T0L 0C0. ☎ **800/ 661-1367** or 403/762-2400. Fax 403/760-4492. www.crmr.com. 108 units. C$255 (US$166) double; C$325 (US$211) 1-bedroom apt. AE, MC, V. **Amenities:** Two restaurants (see Buffalo Mountain Lodge Dining Room under "Where to Dine," below), lounge; exercise room; Jacuzzi; steam room; laundry service; same-day dry cleaning. *In room:* TV, dataport, coffeemaker, hair dryer, iron.

Rimrock Resort Hotel

If you seek modern luxury and great views, this is your hotel. The stunning Rimrock drops nine floors from its roadside lobby entrance down a steep mountain slope, affording tremendous vistas from nearly all of its rooms. Aiming for the same quality of architecture and majesty of scale as venerable older lodges, the Rimrock offers a massive glass-fronted lobby that's lined with cherry wood, tiled with unpolished marble, and filled with inviting chairs and Oriental rugs. The limestone fireplace, open on two sides, is so large that staff members step inside it to ready the kindling. Guest rooms are large and well appointed; some have balconies. The suites are truly large, with balconies and wet bars.

Mountain Ave., 3 miles (5km) south of Banff, P.O. Box 1110, Banff, AB T0L 0C0. ☎ **800/661-1587** or 403/ 762-3356. Fax 403/762-1842. www.rimrockresort.com. 366 units. C$255–C$355 (US$166–US$231) double; C$375–C$1,200 (US$244–US$780) suite. AE, DC, DISC, MC, V. Valet parking C$10 (US$7); free self-parking in heated garage. **Amenities:** Two restaurants (see Ristorante Classico under "Where to Dine," below), two bars; pool; well-equipped health club (with squash court, aerobics, beauty treatments, and massage); Jacuzzi; concierge; tour/activities desk; business center; shopping arcade; 24-hr. room service; babysitting; laundry service; same-day dry cleaning. *In room:* A/C, TV w/ pay movies and video games, dataport, minibar, coffeemaker, hair dryer, iron.

Expensive

Banff Caribou Lodge   The Caribou, with its gabled roof, outdoor patio, and wooden balconies, has a western-lodge look that blends well with the landscape. The interior is equally impressive, especially the vast lobby with slate floor, peeled-log woodwork, and stone fireplace. The finely furnished bedrooms continue the theme with rustic pine chairs and beds decked out with snug down comforters; some units have balconies. The lodge is long on service and friendliness. Although it's not in the absolute center of town (about 10 min. on foot), a free shuttle ferries guests to destinations throughout Banff.

521 Banff Ave., Banff, AB T0L 0C0. (℡ 800/563-8764 or 403/762-5887. Fax 403/762-5918. 207 units. www. bestofbanff.com. C$220–C$235 (US$143–US$153) double; C$300–C$350 (US$195–US$228) suite. Children under 16 stay free in parents' room. AE, DC, DISC, MC, V. Free heated parking. **Amenities:** Restaurant, bar; exercise room; Jacuzzi; sauna; concierge; limited room service. *In room:* TV w/ pay movies, dataport, coffeemaker, hair dryer, iron.

Brewster's Mountain Lodge (★) (*Value*)   For the comfort, convenience, and moderate (by Banff standards) prices, this is one of the top picks right in the heart of Banff. The handsome hotel is operated by the Brewster family, who dominate much of the local recreation, guest-ranching, and transportation scene. The modern hotel does its best to look rustic: peeled-log posts and beams fill the lobby, and pine furniture and paneling grace the spacious guest rooms. Wheelchair-accessible units are available. Although there's no fine-dining restaurant in the hotel, you'll find plenty adjacent in central Banff. The Brewster affiliation makes it simple to take advantage of adventure packages involving horseback riding and hiking.

208 Caribou St., Banff, AB T0L 0C0. (℡ 888/762-2900 or 403/762-2900. Fax 403/762-2970. www.brewster adventures.com. 73 units. C$179–C$199 (US$116–US$129) double. AE, MC, V. Self-parking C$4 (US$2.60). **Amenities:** Coffee shop; Jacuzzi; sauna; car-rental desk; same-day dry cleaning. *In room:* TV/VCR, dataport, hair dryer, iron.

Ptarmigan Inn   This pine-green hotel on the edge of downtown has a few advantages over most of the other lodgings along busy Banff Avenue. For one, the rooms are set well back from the street, minimizing road noise. It's also a good choice for families: Some rooms have sleeping areas divided by the bathroom, offering a little privacy for everyone. Accommodations are outfitted with rustic-looking pine furnishings and down comforters. Half of the rooms have balconies; 16 units (the least expensive) look into the lodge-like central atrium.

337 Banff Ave., Banff, AB T0L 0C0. (℡ 800/661-8310 or 403/762-2207. Fax 403/762-3577. www.bestof banff.com. 166 units. C$220–C$235 (US$143–US$153) double; C$250 (US$163) suite. Children under 16 stay free in parents' room. AE, DC, DISC, MC, V. Free heated parking. **Amenities:** Restaurant, bar; exercise room; Jacuzzi; sauna; concierge; limited room service. *In room:* TV w/ pay movies, dataport, coffeemaker, hair dryer, iron.

Thea's House (★)   The most upscale and elegant bed-and-breakfast in Banff, Thea's is a modern home that was designed as a B&B. Just a couple minutes' walk from downtown, this striking log-and-stone structure boasts 25-foot (8m) ceilings, exquisite artwork, and discreet service. Guest rooms are beautifully outfitted, with vaulted pine ceilings, fir floors, fireplaces, rustic pine and antique furniture, CD players, and private balconies. "Elegant Alpine" is how Thea's describes itself, and you'll have no trouble imagining yourself in a fairy-tale mountain lodge. A perfect spot for a romantic getaway.

138 Otter St. (Box 1237), Banff, T0L 0C0. (℡ 403/762-2499. Fax 403/762-2496. www.theashouse.com. 3 units. C$225–C$245 (US$146–US$159) double. Rates include full breakfast. MC, V. **Amenities:** Complimentary passes to health club; bike rentals. *In room:* TV, hair dryer, iron.

Traveller's Inn   A 5-minute walk from downtown, this well-maintained motel offers reasonably good value for the dollar—remember, this is Banff. Rooms are quite large and pleasantly decorated. Some are divided into two sleeping areas by the bathroom, a great configuration for families or groups. All units have balconies or patio access.

401 Banff Ave., Banff, AB T0L 0C0. ☎ **800/661-0227** or 403/762-4401. Fax 403/762-5905. www.banff travellersinn.com. 89 units. C$200 (US$130) double. AE MC, V. **Amenities:** Breakfast restaurant (boxed lunches available); Jacuzzi; sauna; coin-op laundry and laundry service. *In room:* TV, coffeemaker.

Moderate

Bed & Breakfast on Mountain Lane   Reserve early if you want a shot at this pleasant ground-floor suite in a quiet neighborhood between park headquarters and the Banff Springs Hotel. It has a fireplace, queen bed, and sofa bed, and opens onto the backyard (with patio, swing, and slides). Kids are welcome. Your hostess will bring down a basket of fresh-baked muffins and rolls in the morning.

104 Mountain Lane (Box 12), Banff, AB T0L 0C0. ☎ **403/762-2009.** Fax 403/762-8043. www.standish-banff.com. 1 suite. C$140 (US$91). No credit cards. *In room:* TV/VCR, dataport, kitchen, fridge, coffeemaker, hair dryer, iron.

Blue Mountain Lodge   This rambling place east of downtown began its life in 1908 as a boardinghouse. As you might expect in an older building constructed at the edge of the wilderness, the bedrooms were never exactly palatial to begin with—and when the rooms were redesigned to include private bathrooms, they got even smaller. That's the bad news. The good news is that the lodge is full of charm and funny nooks and crannies. Those small rooms just mean that you'll be spending time with new friends in the lounge and common kitchen. Sound familiar? The owner admits that guests refer to the Blue Mountain Lodge as an upscale hostel, and it's an accurate characterization. Whatever you call it, it's one of the friendliest lodgings in Banff. Many guests are avid outdoorsy types, making this a great place to stay if you're on your own and would appreciate meeting other people to hike with.

137 Muskrat St. (Box 2763), Banff, AB T0L 0C0. ☎ **403/762-5134.** Fax 403/762-8081. www.bluemtnlodge. com. 10 units. C$85–C$110 (US$55–C$72) double. Extra person C$10 (US$7). Rates include continental breakfast and afternoon beverages and cookies. Extended-stay discounts available. MC, V. **Amenities:** Internet access; laundry; ski storage. *In room:* TV, no phone.

Dynasty Inn   One of the newest accommodations in Banff, the Dynasty is a handsome, lodge-like structure about a mile (1.6km) from downtown. Like most of the other hotels along the Banff Avenue strip, the illusion of the lodge ends at the lobby—the guest rooms are comfortable, nicely furnished, and identical to corporate hotel rooms across North America, except that some have balconies and fireplaces. The Banff Bus stops right outside, with frequent service to the city center.

P.O. Box 1018, 501 Banff Ave., Banff, AB T0L 0C0. ☎ **800/667-1464** or 403/762-8844. Fax 403/762-4418. www.banffdynastyinn.com. 99 units. C$189 (US$123) double. Extra person C$15 (US$10). Children under 12 stay free in parents' room. Early-bird specials available. AE, MC, V. **Amenities:** Breakfast-only coffee shop; Jacuzzi; sauna. *In room:* A/C, TV, hair dryer.

Eleanor's House   One of the most comfortable B&Bs in Banff, Eleanor's is a large home on the south side of the Bow River, an easy walk from downtown. The lounge has a western feel to it, complete with stuffed game heads; each bedroom reflects the lives of the owners: a childhood on the prairies and a career as a park ranger. The rooms are quite large and have nice mountain views. There's a separate entrance for guests.

125 Kootenay Ave., Box 1553, Banff, AB T0L 0C0. ✆ **403/760-2457**. Fax 403/762-3852. www.bbeleanor.com. 2 units. C$160 (US$104) double. Rates include full breakfast and evening drinks. MC, V. Closed mid-Oct to mid-Apr. Children must be 16 or older. Free off-street parking. **Amenities:** Access to Internet and fax; bike and ski storage. *In room:* Hair dryer.

Homestead Inn *(Value* One of the best deals in Banff is the Homestead Inn, only a block from all the action on Banff Avenue. Though the amenities are modest compared to upscale alternatives, the rooms are tastefully furnished. Factor in the free downtown parking, and this well-maintained older motel seems all the more enticing.

217 Lynx St., Banff, AB T0L 0C0. ✆ **800/661-1021** or 403/762-4471. Fax 403/762-8877. www.homestead innbanff.com. 27 units. C$149 (US$97) double. Extra person C$10 (US$7). Children under 12 stay free in parents' room. AE, MC, V. **Amenities:** Restaurant. *In room:* TV, hair dryer.

King Edward Hotel Youthful travelers—and others who don't mind the bustle—will like the newly remodeled King Edward, one of Banff's originals, dating from 1904. The accommodations are basic but clean. Best of all is the location, in the heart of town and immediately next door to the epicenter of Banff nightlife. Budget travelers who aren't into the hostel scene will find a lot to like here.

137 Banff Ave., Banff, AB T0L 0C0. ✆ **800/344-4232** or 403/762-2202. Fax 403/762-0876. 21 units. C$129–C$159 (US$84–US$103) double. AE, MC, V. Limited free parking. **Amenities:** Restaurants and bars on ground floor. *In room:* TV, coffeemaker.

Mountain Home Bed & Breakfast *✦* If you're looking for a bit of historic charm coupled with modern comforts, this B&B may be it. It was originally built as a tourist lodge in the 1940s, then served as a private home before being restored and turned back into a guesthouse. The decor manages to be evocative without being too fussy. Bedrooms are nicely outfitted with quality furniture and antiques. Especially nice is the cozy Rundle Room, with its own slate fireplace. Downtown is just a 2-minute walk away.

129 Muskrat St. (P.O. Box 272), Banff, AB T0L 0C0. ✆ **403/762-3889**. Fax 403/762-3254. www.mountain homebb.com. 3 units. C$150 (US$98) double. Extra person $20 (US$13). Rates include full breakfast. MC, V. *In room:* TV/VCR w/ pay movies, dataport, hair dryer, iron.

Pension Tannenhof *(Value* This rambling home, in a quiet neighborhood an 8-minute stroll from downtown, has a curious story. Built during World War II by a Calgary businessman with 10 children, the structure is the result of an elaborate adaptation of two preexisting cabins. During the war, no new construction was allowed, so the owner "remodeled" by building around the cabins, eventually tearing them down from the inside. The rooms have a mix of en suite and private bathrooms; most units are quite large and simply furnished. In a separate chalet are two king suites, each with fireplace and jetted tub. Pension Tannenhof is an excellent choice for clean, unfussy accommodations.

121 Cave Ave. (P.O. Box 1914), Banff, AB T0L 0C0. ✆ **877/999-5011** or 403/762-4636. Fax 403/762-5660. www.pensiontannenhof.com. 10 units. C$95–C$180 (US$62–US$117) double. Extra person C$20 (US$13). Rates include full breakfast. AE, MC, V. **Amenities:** Jacuzzi; sauna; coin-op laundry; use of "the world's oldest barbecue"—made of dinosaur bones. *In room:* TV, no phone.

Red Carpet Inn *(Value* The handsome brick Red Carpet Inn is well maintained and more than adequately furnished. There's no restaurant on site, but there is an excellent one right next door. The entire facility is shipshape—just the thing if you don't want to spend a fortune.

425 Banff Ave., Banff, AB T0L 0C0. ✆ **800/563-4609** or 403/762-4184. Fax 403/762-4894. 52 units. C$125–C$150 (US$81–US$98) double. AE, MC, V. **Amenities:** Jacuzzi (winter only). *In room:* A/C, TV, dataport, fridge, coffeemaker, hair dryer, iron.

Rocky Mountain B&B   A former boardinghouse converted into a B&B, this pleasant and rambling inn offers comfortable, clean, and cozy rooms just a few minutes from downtown. Accommodations have a mix of private and shared bathrooms; four units have kitchenettes. Families are welcome.

223 Otter St. (Box 2528), Banff, AB T0L 0C0. ✆ and fax **403/762-4811.** www.bbcanada.com/3120.html. 10 units. From C$95 (US$62) double. Extra person C$15 (US$10). Rates include breakfast. MC, V. Closed Dec–Apr. *In room:* TV, no phone.

Woodside Cottage   If you'd like a private room but you're on a budget, this charming B&B unit—a main-floor suite with two twin beds, bathroom, and library—might be just the place. The Woodside is a heritage bungalow with a stone-columned porch just a couple minutes' stroll from downtown. Children are welcome.

132 Otter St. (Box 227), Banff, AB T0L 0C0. ✆ **403/762-2441.** 1 unit. C$85 (US$55). Rates include continental breakfast. No credit cards. *In room:* TV, fridge, no phone.

Inexpensive

Banff International Hostel   With a mix of two-, four-, and six-bed rooms, this new hostel is the most pleasant budget lodging in Banff. Couple and family rooms are available. Facilities include a recreation room, kitchen, and lounge with fireplace. Reserve at least a month in advance for summer stays.

Tunnel Mountain Rd., 1 mile (1.6km) northeast of Banff (P.O. Box 1358), Banff, AB T0L 0C0. ✆ **403/762-4122.** Fax 403/762-3441. www.hostellingintl.ca/alberta. 214 beds. C$21.50 (US$14) members, C$25 (US$16) nonmembers. MC, V. **Amenities:** Restaurant (see Cafe Alpenglow under "Where to Dine," below); access to health club across the street; bike rentals; activities desk; coin-op laundry. *In room:* No phone.

Banff Y Mountain Lodge (YWCA) *Value*   The YWCA is a bright, modern building with good amenities, just across the Bow River Bridge from downtown. The Y accommodates singles, couples, and family groups in private or dorm rooms. Some units have private bathrooms.

102 Spray Ave., (P.O. Box 520), Banff, AB T0L 0C0. ✆ **800/813-4138** or 403/762-3560. Fax 403/760-3202. www.ymountainlodge.com. 53 beds, 7 private units. C$20–C$22 (US$13–US$14) bunk in dorm (sleeping bag required); C$55–C$99 (US$36–US$64) double. MC, V. Free parking. **Amenities:** Restaurant; common room with TV; coin-op laundry. *In room:* No phone.

CAMPING

Banff National Park offers hundreds of campsites within easy commuting distance of Banff. The closest are the three **Tunnel Mountain campgrounds** 🐾, just past the youth hostel west of town. Two are for RVs only and have both partial and full hookups (C$22/US$14); the third has showers and is usually reserved for tenters (C$16/US$10). For information, call the park's visitor center (✆ **403/762-1500**). Campsites within the park cannot be reserved in advance.

WHERE TO DINE

Food is generally good in Banff, although you pay handsomely for what you get. The difference in price between a simply okay meal in a theme restaurant and a nice meal in a classy dining room can be quite small. Service is often indifferent, as many restaurant staff members have become used to waiting on the in-and-out-in-a-hurry tour-bus crowds. An abundance of eateries line **Banff Avenue,** and most hotels have at least one dining room. The following recommendations are just the beginning of what's available in a very concentrated area.

Expensive

Buffalo Mountain Lodge ★★ NEW CANADIAN   One of the most pleasing restaurants in Banff, the dining room at the Buffalo Mountain Lodge occupies half of the lodge's soaring, three-story lobby, set in a quiet wooded location just outside town. As satisfying as all this is to the eye and the spirit, the food here is even more notable. The chef brings together the best of regional ingredients—Alberta beef, lamb, pheasant, venison, trout, and British Columbia salmon—and prepares each in a seasonally changing, contemporary style. The fireplace-dominated bar is a lovely place for an intimate cocktail.

1 mile (1.6km) west of Banff on Tunnel Mountain Rd. ℂ **403/762-2400.** www.crmr.com. Reservations recommended on weekends. Main courses C$19–C$33 (US$12–US$21). AE, DC, MC, V. Daily 6–10pm.

Grizzly House FONDUE   Grizzly House has nothing to do with bears except a rustic log-cabin atmosphere. The specialty here is fondue—from cheese to hot chocolate, and everything in between, including rattlesnake, frogs' legs, alligator, and buffalo fondue. Steaks and game dishes are the Grizzly's other specialty. The setting is frontier Banff, not the Swiss shtick you might expect from a fondue palace, and the fare excellent.

207 Banff Ave. ℂ **403/762-4055.** Reservations appreciated. A la carte fondue for two C$30–C$48 (US$19–US$31). AE, MC, V. Daily 11:30am–midnight.

Ristorante Classico INTERNATIONAL   This dining room boasts the best views in Banff and a four-star rating that will appeal to the serious gastronome. The artfully prepared dishes, which feature fresh seafood, veal, fowl, and up-to-the-minute ingredients, are almost as impressive as the view. The cuisine invokes the classic traditions of France and Italy, while optimizing the regional ingredients of Canada. Unusual combinations include rosehip and lavender smoked Atlantic salmon, macadamia-crusted lamb rack on sweet pepper and peach couscous, and loin of Arctic caribou with candied endive and sour cherry pan juices.

In the Rimrock Resort Hotel, 3 miles (5km) south of Banff on Mountain Ave. ℂ **403/762-3356.** Reservations required. Three-course table d'hôte C$75 (US$49). AE, DC, DISC, MC, V. Tues–Sun 6–10pm.

Saltlik ★ STEAK   While most eateries in Banff are content to evoke mountain lodges or Swiss chalets, this new entry is all urban chic: minimalist steel, concrete, and glass. The concept works, due in no small part to the glass walls that open to let in the incongruously natural beauty of the mountains. Steaks and meats are the specialty, with a handful of grilled fish, rotisserie chicken, and seafood entrees to round out the menu. Very stylish and upscale, the Saltlik is the restaurant of the moment in Banff.

221 Bear St. ℂ **403/760-2467.** Reservations recommended. Main courses C$12–C$25 (US$8–US$16). MC, V. Daily 11am–11pm.

Moderate

Balkan Restaurant GREEK   You'll find this airy blue-and-white dining room up a flight of stairs, with windows overlooking the street below. The fare consists of reliable Hellenic favorites served with a flourish; pastas and steaks are available as well. The Greek platter for two consists of a small mountain of beef souvlaki, ribs, moussaka, lamb chops, tomatoes, and salad. If you're dining alone, you can't do better than the *lagos stifado* (rabbit stew) with onions and red wine.

120 Banff Ave. © **403/762-3454.** Main courses C$9–C$21 (US$6–US$14). AE, MC, V. Daily 11am–11pm.

Coyotes Deli & Grill ★ SOUTHWEST/MEDITERRANEAN   One of the few places in Banff where you can find lighter, healthier food, Coyotes' offers a broad selection of vegetarian options, as well as fresh fish, grilled meats, and ethnic dishes prepared with an eye to spices and full flavors. There's also a deli, where you can get the makings for a picnic and head to the park. This is a very popular place, so go early or make reservations if you don't want to stand in line.

206 Caribou St. © **403/762-3963.** Reservations recommended. Main courses C$14–C$22 (US$9–US$14). AE, DC, MC, V. Daily 7:30am–11pm.

Giorgio's Trattoria ITALIAN   Giorgio's is a cozy eatery dimly lit by low-hanging lamps. Divided into a counter section and table area, it serves authentic old-country specialties at eminently reasonable prices. Wonderful rolls—a delicacy in themselves—come with your meal. Don't miss the *gnocchi alla piemontese* (potato dumplings in meat sauce).

219 Banff Ave. © **403/762-5114.** Reservations accepted for groups of 8 or more. Pastas C$12–C$15 (US$8–US$10); pizzas C$12–C$17 (US$8–US$11). MC, V. Daily 4:30–10pm.

Magpie & Stump Restaurant & Cantina ★ MEXICAN   The false-fronted Magpie & Stump doesn't really match up architecturally with the rest of smart downtown Banff—and neither does the food nor atmosphere, thank goodness. The Mexican and Tex Mex fare is done up with style and heft: Someone in the kitchen sure knows how to handle a tortilla. This isn't high cuisine, just well-prepared favorites like enchiladas, tacos, and the like. The interior looks like a cozy English pub, except for the buffalo heads and cactus plants everywhere—along with a lot of Southwest kitsch. The Cantina is a good place for a lively late-night drink.

203 Caribou St. © **403/762-4067.** Reservations accepted for groups of 10 or more. Main courses C$8–C$18 (US$5–US$12). AE, MC, V. Daily noon–2am.

Melissa's Restaurant and Bar CANADIAN   Banff's original hostelries weren't all as grand as the Banff Springs Hotel. There was also the Homestead Inn, established in the 1910s, with its much-loved restaurant, Melissa's. The original hotel has been replaced with a more modern structure, but the old log cabin that houses Melissa's remains. Old-fashioned Canadian dishes still dominate the menu. Breakfasts are famed, especially the apple hot cakes. Lunch and dinner feature burgers, sandwiches, local trout, and steaks.

218 Lynx St. © **403/762-5511.** Reservations recommended. Main courses C$8–C$25 (US$5–US$16). AE, MC, V. Daily 7:30am–9:30pm.

St. James Gate Irish Pub IRISH   The St. James Gate is owned by Guinness, a company that knows a thing or two about Irish pubs. Newly created to resemble a traditional draught house, the pub offers an extensive menu of bar meals to accompany its beers and ales. Halibut-fish-and-chips is a specialty, as are traditional meat pies and sandwiches. This is a lively place, and you never know when a table full of dislocated Finnians will break into a heartfelt ballad or two.

207 Wolf St. © **403/762-9355.** Reservations not accepted. Main courses C$10–C$17 (US$7–US$11). MC, V. Food service Mon–Fri 11am–2pm; Sat–Sun 10am–2pm.

Inexpensive

If you're really on a budget, you'll probably get used to the deli case at **Safeway,** at Martin and Elk streets, as even inexpensive food is costly here. **Evelyn's Coffee Bar,** 201 Banff Ave. (✆ **403/762-0352**), has great home-baked muffins and rolls. The **Jump Start Coffee and Sandwich Place,** 206 Buffalo St. (✆ **403/762-0332**), offers sandwiches, soup, salads, pastries, and picnics to go. For all-day and all-night pizza, head to **Aardvark Pizza,** 304a Caribou St. (✆ **403/762-5500**), open daily to 4am.

Bruno's Cafe and Grill CANADIAN   Bruno's serves burgers, pizza, wraps, and hearty Canadian-style entrees—all best washed down with locally brewed beer. This cozy and casual joint is open late, a rarity in Banff.

304 Caribou St. ✆ **403/762-8115.** Reservations not accepted. Main courses C$8–C$15 (US$5–US$10). MC, V. Daily 7am–1pm.

Cafe Alpenglow INTERNATIONAL   You don't usually associate hostels with good food, but the Banff International Hostel is different than most. This little cafe features wraps, sandwiches, soups, and other healthy food with youthful flair; it's got a patio and a liquor license, too.

In the Banff International Hostel, 1 mile (1.6km) northeast on Tunnel Mountain Road. ✆ **403/762-4122.** Reservations not accepted. Main courses C$6–C$10 (US$4–US$7). AE, V. Daily 7am–9pm.

BANFF AFTER DARK

Most of Banff's larger hotels and restaurants offer some form of nightly entertainment. However, for a more lively selection, head to downtown's Banff Avenue.

Aurora   It took the ultra-cool cocktail lounge format a while to reach Banff, but here it is. Dance to DJ-spun rock while sipping something delicious in a martini glass. 110 Banff Ave. ✆ **403/760-5300.**

The Barbary Coast   Popular with foreign visitors, this is a California-style bar and restaurant that features live music among the potted plants. The offerings range from 1980s cover bands to light jazz. 119 Banff Ave. ✆ **403/762-4616.**

Outabounds   Banff's most popular dance club is in the basement of the old King Eddy Hotel. DJs spin while young white-water guides chat and dance with impressionable young tourists. 137 Banff Ave. ✆ **403/762-8434.**

Rose and Crown Pub   This venerable pub used to be the only place to hear live music in Banff. It's still one of the best. Bands range from Celtic to folk to rock. In summer, sit at the rooftop bar and watch the stars. 202 Banff Ave. ✆ **403/762-2121.**

Wild Bill's Saloon   One of the best Banff nightspots is this legendary saloon, where you can watch tourists in cowboy hats learning to line dance. Alt-rock bands dominate on Monday and Tuesday; Wednesday through Saturday, it's all country rock, all the time. 203 Banff Ave. ✆ **403/762-0333.**

LAKE LOUISE

Deep-green Lake Louise, 35 miles (56km) northwest of Banff and surrounded by snowcapped mountains, is one of the most famed beauty spots in a park renowned for its scenery. The village in the valley below the lake has developed into a resort destination in its own right. Lake Louise boasts the largest ski area in Canada and easy hiking access to the remote high country along the Continental Divide.

The lake may be spectacular, but probably as many people wind up the road to Lake Louise to see its most famous resort, the **Chateau Lake Louise.** Built by the Canadian Pacific Railroad, the Chateau is, along with the Banff Springs Hotel, one of the most celebrated hotels in Canada. More than just a lodging, this storybook castle—perched a mile (1.6km) high in the Rockies—is the center of recreation, dining, shopping, and entertainment for the Lake Louise area.

In case you were wondering, there's a reason the water in Lake Louise is so green: The stream water that tumbles into the lake is filled with minerals, ground by the glaciers that hang above the lake. Sunlight refracts off the glacial "flour," creating vivid colors. You'll want to at least stroll around the shore and gawk at the glaciers and the massive Chateau. The gentle **Lakeshore Trail** follows the northern shore to the end of Lake Louise. If you're looking for more exercise and even better views, continue on the trail as it begins to climb. Now called the **Plain of Six Glaciers Trail** ☆, it passes a teahouse (3 miles/5km from the Chateau and open in summer only) on its way to a tremendous viewpoint over Victoria Glacier and Lake Louise.

The **Lake Louise Summer Sightseeing Lift** (© **403/522-3555**) offers a 10-minute ride up to the Whitehorn Lodge, midway up the Lake Louise Ski Area. From here, the views of Lake Louise and the mountains along the Continental Divide are magnificent. Hikers can follow one of many trails into alpine meadows, or join a free naturalist-led walk to explore the delicate ecosystem. The restaurant at the Whitehorn Lodge is much better than you'd expect at a ski area, and specially priced ride-and-dine tickets are available for those who would like to have a meal at 7,000 feet (2,100m); the Canadian barbecue buffet is especially fun. The round-trip costs C$16.95 (US$11) for adults, C$14.95 (US$10) for seniors and students, and C$8.95 (US$6) for children 6 to 15. The lift operates from early June to mid-September.

To many visitors, **Moraine Lake** ☆☆ is even more beautiful than Lake Louise, its more famous twin. Ten spirelike peaks, each over 10,000 feet (3,000m) high, rise precipitously from the shores of this tiny gem-blue lake. It's an unforgettable sight, and definitely worth the short 8-mile (13km) drive from Lake Louise. A trail follows the lake's north shore to the mountain cliffs. There's a lodge offering meals. If the panorama looks familiar, you might recognize it from the back of a Canadian $20 bill.

WHERE TO STAY

Deer Lodge ☆   The Chateau Lake Louise isn't the only historic lodge here. Built in the 1920s, the original Deer Lodge was a teahouse for the early mountaineers who came to the area to hike (the original tearoom is now the Mount Fairview Dining Room, offering Northwest cuisine). Although Lake Louise itself is a short stroll away, the charming Deer Lodge features a sense of privacy and solitude that the busy Chateau can't offer. Choose from cozy rooms in the original lodge, larger rooms in the newer Tower Wing, and Heritage Rooms, the largest rooms in the newest wing. All have feather duvets and handsome mountain-style furniture. If you're looking for a quiet Rockies getaway, choose this over the Chateau.

109 Lake Louise Dr., Lake Louise (P.O. Box 1598), Banff, AB T0L 0C0. © **800/661-1595** or 403/522-3747. Fax 403/522-4222. www.crmr.com. 73 units. C$150–C$220 (US$98–US$143) double. AE, MC, V. **Amenities:** Restaurant, lounge; rooftop Jacuzzi; sauna; coin-op laundry; dry cleaning. *In room:* TV.

Fairmont Chateau Lake Louise ⓐ The Chateau Lake Louise is one of the best-loved hotels in North America. If you want to splurge on only one place in the Canadian Rockies, make it this one—you won't be sorry. The massive, formal structure is blue-roofed and turreted, furnished with Edwardian sumptuousness and alpine charm. Built in stages over the course of a century by the Canadian Pacific Railroad, the entire hotel was remodeled in 1990, and now stays open year-round. The cavernous grand lobby and other common areas overlook the Chateau's gardens and the deep blue-green lake in its glacier-hung cirque. The guest rooms' marble bathrooms, crystal barware, and down duvets are indicative of the luxury you can expect here. The Chateau can sometimes feel like Grand Central Terminal—so many guests and so many visitors crowding into the place—but the rooms are truly sumptuous and the service highly professional.

Lake Louise, AB T0L 1E0. ⓒ 800/441-1414 or 403/522-3511. Fax 403/522-3834. www.fairmont.com. 513 units. High season C$587–C$787 (US$382–US$512) double; C$790–C$979 (US$514–US$636) suite. (Rates vary depending on whether you want a view of the lake or mountains.) Off-season rates and packages available. Children under 17 stay free in parents' room. AE, DC, DISC, MC, V. Parking C$9 (US$6) per day. **Amenities:** Nine restaurants and eateries in high season (see Walliser Stube Wine Bar under "Where to Dine," below), two bars; indoor pool; health club; Jacuzzi; sauna; exercise room; bike and canoe rentals; concierge; tour desk; business center; shopping arcade; salon; 24-hr. room service; massage; babysitting; laundry service; same-day dry cleaning. *In room:* A/C, TV, dataport, minibar, coffeemaker, hair dryer, iron.

Lake Louise Inn The Lake Louise Inn stands in a wooded 8-acre (3-hectare) estate at the base of the moraine, a 7-minute drive from the fabled lake. The inn consists of five different buildings with five different room types. The superior queen and executive rooms in Building Five are the nicest, with pine-railed balconies and sitting areas. For families, the superior lofts can sleep up to eight, with two bathrooms, a kitchen, two bedrooms, and a sofa bed.

210 Village Rd. (P.O. Box 209), Lake Louise, AB T0L 1E0. ⓒ 800/661-9237 or 403/522-3791. Fax 403/522-2018. www.lakelouiseinn.com. 232 units. High season C$165–C$375 (US$107–US$244) double. AE, DC, MC, V. Free parking. **Amenities:** Restaurant, bar; pool; Jacuzzi; sauna; business center; coin-op laundry. *In room:* TV, dataport, fridge, coffeemaker, microwave, hair dryer.

Moraine Lake Lodge The only place to stay at beautiful Moraine Lake is this handsome lakeside lodge. The original building contains eight basic rooms. The newer Wenkchemna Wing has six rooms with fireplaces; cabins feature sunken seating areas with fireplaces. One suite has a fireplace, Jacuzzi, king bed, and views over the lake. All units are simply but nicely furnished with pine furniture. Room rates include use of canoes and naturalist presentations.

8 miles (13km) south of Lake Louise at Moraine Lake (Box 70), Banff, AB T0L 0C0. ⓒ 403/522-3733. Fax 403/522-3719. www.morainelake.com. 33 units. C$395–C$450 (US$257–US$293) double; C$500 (US$325) suite; C$490 (US$319) cabin. AE, MC, V. **Amenities:** Restaurant (Northwest), bar; canoe rentals; concierge. *In room:* Hair dryer, no phone.

Post Hotel ⓐⓐ This wonderful log hotel with a distinctive red roof began its life in 1942 as a humble ski lodge. New owners completely rebuilt the old lodge, transforming it into one of the most luxurious getaways in the Canadian Rockies (and one of only two Relais & Châteaux properties in western Canada). The public rooms are lovely, from the renowned dining room (preserved intact from the original hotel) to the two-story, wood-paneled library (complete with rolling track ladders and river-stone fireplace).

Accommodations are beautifully furnished with rustic pine pieces and rich upholstery. Most units have stone fireplaces, balconies, and whirlpool tubs. Due to the rambling nature of the property, there are a bewildering 14 different layouts available. Families will like the "N" rooms, as each has a loft, fireplace, and balcony. The "F" units are fantastic, featuring a huge tiled bathroom with both shower and Jacuzzi, balcony, and sitting area with river-stone fireplace. Hospitality and service here are top-notch.

P.O. Box 69, Lake Louise, AB T0L 1E0. © **800/661-1586** or 403/522-3989. Fax 403/522-3966. www.post hotel.com. 98 units. High season C$340–C$374 (US$221–US$243) double; C$450–C$600 (US$293–US$390) suite; C$475–C$660 (US$309–US$429) cabin. AE, MC, V. Closed Nov. **Amenities:** Restaurant (see Post Hotel Dining Room under "Where to Dine," below), two bars; indoor pool; Jacuzzi; sauna; massage; babysitting; laundry service; dry cleaning. *In room:* TV/VCR, hair dryer, iron.

WHERE TO DINE
Lake Louise Station PIZZA/STEAK   This handsome log building served as the Lake Louise train station for nearly a century, before rail service ceased in the 1980s. Guests now dine in the old waiting room, or enjoy a quiet drink in the old lobby. Two dining cars beside the station are open for fine dining in the evening. Excellent steaks and grilled meats are the specialties here.

200 Sentinel Rd. © **403/522-2600.** Reservations recommended on weekends. Pizzas C$15 (US$10); steaks and seafood C$14–C$22 (US$9–US$14). AE, MC, V. Daily 11:30am–midnight.

Post Hotel Dining Room ⟡⟡ INTERNATIONAL   Let's face it: Your trip through the Canadian Rockies is costing you a *lot* more than you planned. But don't start economizing on food just yet, because the Post Hotel offers some of the finest dining in western Canada, earning the highly prized endorsement of the Relais & Châteaux organization. The rustic room features wood beams and windows looking out onto glaciered peaks. The menu focuses on full-flavored meat and fish preparations. You might try Pacific marlin carpaccio with heirloom tomato tartar and three mustard sauces, or buffalo striploin with blackberry maple syrup butter and corn fritters. Service is excellent, as is the very impressive wine list.

In the Post Hotel, Lake Louise. © **403/522-3989.** www.posthotel.com. Reservations required. Main courses C$30–C$42 (US$20–US$27). AE, MC, V. Daily 7–11am, 11:30am–2pm, and 5–10pm.

Walliser Stube Wine Bar ⟡ SWISS   Although the Chateau Lake Louise operates four major restaurants, including the formal Edelweiss Room, the most fun and relaxing place to eat is the Walliser Stube, which serves excellent Swiss-style food and some of the best fondue ever. The back dining room is called the Library, and is indeed lined with tall and imposing wood cases and rolling ladders. Happily, the cases are filled with wine, not books. A meal here is an entire evening's worth of eating and drinking, as the best foods—a variety of fondues and raclettes—make for convivial and communal dining experiences. The cheese fondue is fabulous; forget the stringy glutinous experience you had in the 1970s and give it another chance. It's all great fun in a great atmosphere—go with friends and you'll have a blast.

In the Chateau Lake Louise, Lake Louise. © **403/522-1817.** Reservations required. Main courses C$17.50–C$29 (US$11–US$19); fondues for two C$33–C$45 (US$21–US$29). AE, DISC, MC, V. Daily 5–11:30pm.

THE ICEFIELDS PARKWAY ⟡⟡⟡
Between Lake Louise and Jasper winds one of the most spectacular mountain roads in the world. Called the Icefields Parkway, the road climbs through three deep river valleys, beneath soaring mountains, and past dozens of peaks shrouded with permanent snowfields. Capping this 178-mile (287km) route is

the **Columbia Icefields,** a massive dome of glacial ice and snow straddling the top of the continent. From this mighty cache of ice—the largest nonpolar ice cap in the world—flow the Columbia, Athabasca, and North Saskatchewan rivers.

Although you can drive the Icefields Parkway in 3 hours, leave enough time to stop at eerily green lakes, hike to a waterfall, and take an excursion up onto the Columbia Icefields. There's a good chance that you'll see wildlife: ambling bighorn sheep, mountain goats, elk with huge shovel antlers, and mama bears with cubs—all guaranteed to halt traffic and set cameras clicking.

After Lake Louise, the highway divides: Highway 1 continues west toward Golden, British Columbia; Highway 93 (the Icefields Parkway) continues north along the Bow River. **Bow Lake,** the river's source, glimmers below enormous **Crowfoot Glacier.** On the shores of Bow Lake, **Num-Ti-Jah Lodge** is a good place to stop for a bite to eat.

The road mounts Bow Summit and drops into the North Saskatchewan River drainage. Stop at the **Peyto Lake Viewpoint** and hike up a short but steep trail to glimpse this startling blue-green body of water. The North Saskatchewan River collects its tributaries at the little community of Saskatchewan River Crossing; thousands of miles later, the Bow and Saskatchewan rivers will join and flow east through Lake Winnipeg to Hudson Bay.

The parkway then begins to climb in earnest toward the Sunwapta Pass. Here, in the shadows of 11,450-foot (3,490m) **Mount Athabasca,** the icy tendrils of the **Columbia Icefields** come into view. However impressive these glaciers may seem from the road, they're nothing compared to the massive amounts of centuries-old ice and snow hidden by mountain peaks; the Columbia Icefields cover nearly 200 square miles (518km²) and are more than 2,500 feet (762m) thick. From the parkway, the closest fingers of the ice field are Athabasca Glacier, which fills the horizon to the west of the **Columbia Icefields Centre (© 780/ 852-7032),** a lodge with a restaurant open from 8am to 10pm and double rooms starting at C$185 (US$120). The **Icefields Information Centre,** beside the lodge (© **780/852-7030),** is open May 1 to June 14, daily 9am to 5pm; June 15 to September 7, daily 9am to 6pm; and September 8 to October 15, daily 9am to 5pm; closed October 15 to May 1.

From the **Brewster Snocoach Tours ticket office (© 403/762-6735),** specially designed buses with balloon tires take visitors out onto the face of the glacier. The 90-minute excursion includes a chance to hike the surface of Athabasca Glacier. The cost is C$28 (US$18) for adults and C$14 (US$9) for children. If you don't have time for the tour, you can drive to the toe of the glacier and walk up onto its surface. Use extreme caution when on the glacier; tumbling into a crevasse can result in broken limbs or even death.

From the Columbia Icefields, the parkway descends steeply into the Athabasca River drainage. From the parking area for **Sunwapta Falls,** travelers can choose to crowd around the chain-link fence and peer at the turbulent falls, or take the half-hour hike to equally impressive but less crowded Lower Sunwapta Falls. **Athabasca Falls,** farther north along the parkway, is another mustsee. Here, the wide and powerful Athabasca River constricts into a roaring torrent before dropping 82 feet (25m) into a narrow canyon. A mist-covered bridge crosses the chasm just beyond the falls; a series of trails lead to more viewpoints. The parkway continues along the Athabasca River, through a landscape of meadows and lakes, before entering the Jasper Townsite.

Facilities are few along the parkway. Hikers and bikers will be pleased to know that there are rustic **hostels** at Mosquito Creek, Rampart Creek, Hilda Creek, Beauty Creek, Athabasca Falls, and Mount Edith Cavell. Reservations for all Icefields Parkway hostels can be made by calling ✆ **403/439-3215**. A **shuttle** runs between the Calgary International Hostel and hostels in Banff, Lake Louise, and along the Icefields Parkway to Jasper. You must have reservations at the destination hostel to use the service. Call ✆ **403/283-5551** for more information.

4 Jasper National Park

Jasper Townsite: 178 miles (287km) NW of Banff

Jasper, now Canada's largest mountain park, was established in 1907, although it already boasted a "guesthouse" of sorts in the 1840s. A visiting painter described it as "composed of two rooms of about 14 and 15 feet square. One of them is used by all comers and goers, Indians, voyageurs and traders, men, women, and children being huddled together indiscriminately, the other room being devoted to the exclusive occupation of Colin Fraser (postmaster) and his family, consisting of a Cree squaw and nine interesting half-breed children."

Things have changed.

Slightly less busy than Banff to the south, Jasper National Park attracts a much more outdoors-oriented crowd, with hiking, biking, climbing, horseback riding, and rafting the main activities. Sure, there's shopping and fine dining in Jasper, but it's not the focus of activity as it is in Banff. Travelers seem a bit more determined and rugged-looking, as if they've just stumbled in from a long-distance hiking trail or off the face of a rock.

OUTDOOR PURSUITS IN THE PARK

The **Jasper Adventure Centre,** 604 Connaught Dr. (✆ **800/565-7547** in western Canada, or 780/852-5595; www.jasperadventurecentre.com), is a clearinghouse of local outfitters. Rafting and canoeing trips, horseback rides, guided hikes, and other activities can be arranged out of this office, which is open June through September, daily from 9am to 9pm.

Mountain bikes, canoes and rafts, tents, fishing gear, and skis are available for rent from **On-Line Sport and Tackle,** 600 Patricia St. (✆ **780/852-3630**). Snowboards, cross-country ski equipment, and more bikes are available from **Freewheel Cycle,** 618 Patricia St. (✆ **780/852-3898**).

FISHING Currie's Guiding Ltd. (✆ **780/852-5650;** curries@telusplanet.net) conducts fishing trips to beautiful Maligne Lake; the cost is C$149 (US$97) per person (minimum two persons) for an 8-hour day, including tackle, bait, boat, and lunch. Patricia and Pyramid lakes, north of Jasper, are more convenient to Jasper-based anglers who fancy trying their luck at trout fishing.

GOLF The 18-hole course at **Jasper Park Lodge** ⛳ (✆ **780/852-6090**), east of Jasper Townsite, is one of the most challenging courses in the Rockies, with 73 sand traps and other, more natural hazards—like visiting wildlife. *Score Magazine* ranked this the best golf course in Alberta.

HIKING Long-distance hikers will find an abundance of backcountry trails around Jasper, reaching into some of the most spectacular scenery in the Canadian Rockies. Day hikers have fewer, but still good, choices. The visitor center's brochure *Day Hikers' Guide to Jasper National Park* (C$1/US$.65) details dozens

Jasper Townsite & Jasper National Park

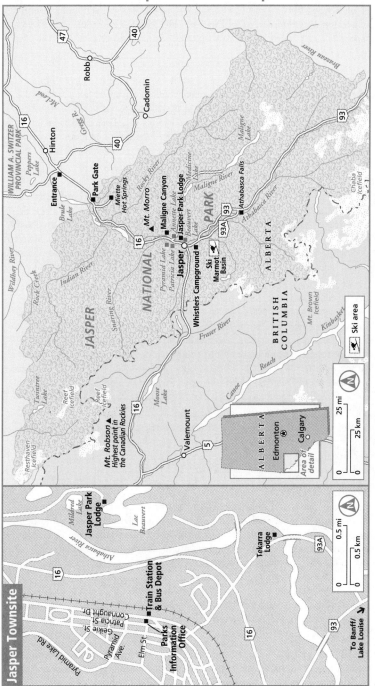

of hikes. Several outfitters lead guided hikes; contact **Jasper Park Lodge Mountaineering and Interpretive Hiking** (© 780/852-3301) or **Walk and Talks Jasper** (© 780/852-4945; www.walksntalks.com) for a selection of half- and full-day hikes.

The complex of trails around **Maligne Canyon** ★ makes a good choice for a group, as there are a number of access points (across six different footbridges). The less keen can make the loop back and meet fellow hikers (after getting the car) farther down the canyon. Trails ring parklike Beauvert and Annette lakes (the latter is wheelchair accessible), both near Jasper Park Lodge. Likewise, Pyramid and Patricia lakes just north of town have loop trails but more of a backcountry atmosphere.

HORSEBACK RIDING   One of the most exhilarating experiences the park can offer is trail riding. Guides take your riding prowess (or lack of it) into account and select trails slow enough to keep you mounted. The horses used are steady, reliable animals not given to sudden antics. For a short ride, call **Pyramid Stables** (© 780/852-7433), which offers 1- to 3-hour trips around Pyramid and Patricia lakes. **Skyline Trail Rides** (© 888/582-7787 or 780/852-4215; www.skylinetrail.com/skyline) offers a number of short day trips costing roughly C$25 (US$16) per hour, as well as 3- to 4-day trips to a remote, albeit modernized, lodge. Sleigh rides are offered in winter.

RAFTING   Jasper is the jumping-off point for float and white-water trips down several rivers. A raft trip is a good option for that inevitable drizzly day, as you're going to get wet anyway. The mild rapids (Class II to III) of the Athabasca River make a good introductory trip; wilder runs down the Maligne River (Class III) will appeal to those needing something to brag about. Jasper is loaded with rafting outfitters; ask your hotel concierge for assistance, or call **Maligne River Adventures** (© 780/852-3370; www.mra.ab.ca), which offers trips down both rivers, as well as a 3-day wilderness trip on the Kakwa River (Class IV-plus).

SKIING   Jasper's downhill ski area is **Ski Marmot Basin,** 12 miles (19km) west of Jasper on Highway 93 (© 780/852-3816; www.skimarmot.com). Marmot is generally underrated as a ski resort; it doesn't get the crowds of Banff, nor does it get the infamous Chinook winds. The resort has 52 runs and seven lifts, and rarely any lines. Lift tickets start at C$44 (US$29).

JASPER TOWNSITE

Jasper isn't Banff, and to listen to most residents of Jasper, that's just fine with them. Born as a railroad division point, Jasper Townsite lacks its southern neighbor's glitz and slightly precious air of an internationalized alpine fantasyland. Instead, it gives off a lived-in, community-oriented feel that's largely lacking in Banff. The streets are thronged with avid young hikers and mountain bikers rather than the shopping hordes.

However, development is rapidly approaching: New nightclubs, restaurants, and shops geared toward tourists are springing up along Patricia Street, and that sound you hear in the distance is the thunder of tour buses.

ESSENTIALS
GETTING THERE   Jasper is on the Yellowhead Highway System, linking it with Vancouver, Prince George, and Edmonton—and is therefore an important transportation hub. The town is 178 miles (287km) northwest of Banff.

Tips **Organized Tours of the Park**

Some of the principle outfitters and guides also offer transportation to outlying park beauty spots. Organized tours of the park's major sites—notably the Athabasca snowfields (C$83/US$54) and a Maligne Lake cruise (C$63/US$41)—are offered by **Brewster** (© 780/852-3332; www.brewster.ca) and **Maligne Tours** (© 780/852-3370; www.malignelake.com). **Beyond the Beaten Path** (© 780/852-5650; www.jasperbeyondthebeatenpath.com) also offers excursions to these popular destinations, as well as trips to Miette Hot Springs (C$45/US$29) and more intimate sightseeing, photography, wildlife-viewing, and picnic options. In addition, the company offers a shuttle service for hikers and rafting parties.

VIA Rail connects Jasper to Vancouver and Edmonton with three trains weekly; the station (© **780/852-4102**) is at the town center, along Connaught Street. Also headquartered at the train station is the **Greyhound** bus station (© **780/852-3926**) and **Brewster Transportation** (© **780/852-3332**), which offers express service to Banff, as well as a large number of sightseeing excursions.

VISITOR INFORMATION   For information on the townsite, contact **Jasper Tourism and Commerce** (© **780/852-3858;** fax 780/852-4932; www.jasper canadianrockies.com). For information on the park, contact **Jasper National Park** (© **780/852-6176;** http://parkscanada.pch.gc.ca/jasper).

ORIENTATION   Jasper Townsite is much smaller than Banff. The main street, **Connaught Drive,** runs alongside the Canadian National Railway tracks, and is the address of the majority of Jasper's hotels. **Patricia Street,** a block west, is quickly becoming the boutique street, with new shops and cafes springing up. Right in the center of town, surrounded by delightful shady gardens, is the **park information office** (© **780/852-6146**). The post office is at the corner of Patricia and Elm streets. At the northern end of Connaught and Geike streets, a quarter mile (.5km) from downtown, is another complex of hotels.

GETTING AROUND   For a rental car, contact **National,** 607 Connaught Dr. (© **780/852-1117**). For a **taxi,** call © **780/852-5558** or 780/852-3600.

EXPLORING THE AREA

Just northeast of Jasper, off the Jasper Park Lodge access road, the Maligne River drops from its high mountain valley to cut an astounding canyon into a steep limestone face on its way to meet the Athabasca River. The chasm of **Maligne Canyon** is up to 150 feet (46m) deep at points, yet only 10 feet (3m) across. A sometimes-steep trail follows the canyon down the mountainside, bridging the gorge six times. In summer, a teahouse operates at the top of the canyon.

An incredibly blue mountain lake buttressed by a ring of high-flying peaks, **Maligne Lake** is 45 minutes east of Jasper, and is one of the park's great beauty spots. Maligne is the largest glacier-fed lake in the Rockies, and the second largest in the world. Droves of tour buses go to the "hidden lake," and the area is a popular destination for hikers, anglers, trail riders, and rafters. No matter what else they do, most visitors take a boat cruise to **Spirit Island,** at the head of the lake. The 90-minute cruise leaves from below the **Maligne Lake Lodge,** an attractive summer-only facility with a restaurant and bar (but no lodging). Cruise tickets cost C$35 (US$23) for adults, C$29 (US$19) for seniors, and C$17.50 (US$11) for kids.

Maligne Lake waters are alive with rainbow and eastern brook trout, and the **Maligne Lake Boathouse** is stocked with licenses, tackle, bait, and boats. Guided fishing trips include equipment, lunch, and hotel transportation, with half-day excursions starting at C$185 (US$120). You can rent a boat, canoe, or sea kayak to ply the waters. Morning and afternoon horseback rides up the Bald Hills depart from the Chalet at Maligne Lake; the cost is C$55 (US$36).

All facilities at Maligne Lake, including lake cruises, fishing, trail rides, and a white-water raft outfitter that offers trips down three park rivers, are operated by **Maligne Tours** (www.malignelake.com). Offices are located at the lake, next to the lodge; in Jasper at 626 Connaught Dr. (© **780/852-3370**); and at the Jasper Park Lodge (© **780/852-4779**). Maligne Tours also operates a shuttle bus between Jasper and the lake.

Downstream from Maligne Lake, the Maligne River flows into **Medicine Lake.** This large body of water appears regularly every spring, grows 5 miles (8km) long and 60 feet (18m) deep, and then vanishes in fall, leaving only a dry gravel bed through the winter. The reason for this annual wonder is a system of underground drainage caves. The local Indians believed that spirits were responsible for the lake's annual disappearance, hence the name.

Jasper Tramway   Canada's longest and highest aerial tramway tour starts at the foot of Whistler's Mountain, 4 miles (6km) south of Jasper off Highway 93. Each car takes 30 passengers and hoists them 1¼ miles (2km) up to the summit (7,400 ft./2,220m) in a breathtaking sky ride. At the upper terminal, you'll step out into alpine tundra and a wonderful picnic area carpeted with mountain grass. Combo tickets that include meals at the Treeline Restaurant are available.

© **780/852-3093.** www.jaspertramway.com. Tickets C$17.75 (US$12) adults, C$9 (US$6) children. June–Labour Day daily 8:30am–10pm; call for off-season schedule. Closed mid-Oct to Apr.

Miette Hot Springs   The hot mineral water pools are only one reason to make the side trip to Miette Hot Springs. The drive is also one of the best wildlife-viewing routes in the park: Watch for elk, deer, coyotes, and moose. The springs can be enjoyed in a beautiful swimming pool or two soaker pools, surrounded by forest and an imposing mountain backdrop. Campgrounds and an attractive lodge with refreshments are nearby.

37 miles (60km) northeast of Jasper off Hwy. 16. © **780/866-3939.** Admission C$6 (US$3.90) adults, C$5 (US$3.25) children and seniors, C$17 (US$11) families. June 22–Sept 9 daily 8:30am–10:30pm; May 11–June 21 and Sept 10–Oct 8 daily 10:30am–9pm.

SHOPPING

Weather can be unpredictable in Jasper. If it's raining, you can while away an afternoon in the town's shops and boutiques. The arcade at the Jasper Park Lodge, called the **Beauvert Promenade,** has a number of excellent clothing and gift shops. In Jasper itself, Patricia Street contains most of the high-quality choices. A number of galleries feature Inuit and Native arts and crafts: Check out **Our Native Land,** 601 Patricia St. (© **780/852-5592**).

WHERE TO STAY

As in Banff, there's a marked difference in rates between high season and the rest of the year, so if you can avoid the June-through-September crush, you may save up to 50%. All prices listed below are for high season; call for off-season rates. Reserve well in advance. **Rocky Mountain Reservations** (© **877/902-9455** or 780/852-9455; fax 780/852-9425; www.rockymountainreservations.com) offers a free booking service for Jasper accommodations and activities. If you find the prices too astronomical in Jasper, or just can't find a room, consider staying east of the park near Hinton (see below).

Very Expensive

Fairmont Jasper Park Lodge   Jasper's most exclusive lodging, the Jasper Park Lodge was built by the Canadian Pacific Railroad and has an air of luxury and gentility, but with a more woodsy feel—sort of like an upscale summer camp. The hotel's wooded, elk-inhabited grounds are located along Lac Beauvert, about 5 miles (8km) east of Jasper proper. The central lodge's lofty great room offers huge fireplaces to snuggle by. Accommodations are extremely comfortable, though a bit hard to characterize, as there are a wide variety of cabins, lodge rooms, chalets, and cottages available—all from different eras, all set amid the forest. It's a good idea to call and find out what suits your budget and needs. Groups can opt for one of the wonderful housekeeping cabins, some of which have up to eight bedrooms.

P.O. Box 40, Jasper, AB T0E 1E0. © **800/465-7547** in Alberta, 800/441-1414 elsewhere in North America, or 780/852-3301. Fax 780/852-5107. www.fairmont.com. 446 units. C$159–C$499 (US$103–US$324) double; C$299–C$749 (US$194–US$487) suite; from C$1,850 (US$1,203) cabin. AE, DC, DISC, MC, V. Free parking. **Amenities:** Five restaurants, including the four-star Edith Cavell Dining Room and the Moose's Nook Dining Room (see "Where to Dine," below), four lounges; heated outdoor pool; one of Canada's finest golf courses; tennis courts; health club; spa; canoe, paddle-boat, and bike rentals; horseback riding; children's center; concierge; tour desk; business center; shopping arcade; 24 hr. room service; babysitting; laundry service; same-day dry cleaning. *In room:* TV w/ pay movies, dataport, minibar, coffeemaker, hair dryer, iron.

Royal Canadian Lodge   Usually considered Jasper Townsite's best hotel, the Royal Canadian Lodge is a refined three-story lodging with some of the best staff and service in town. The grounds are beautifully landscaped. Guest rooms come with all the amenities you'd expect at a four-star property. If anything, they're a tad overdecorated—considering the dramatic views from every window, you don't need the slightly boudoir-y upholstery and wall coverings.

96 Geikie St., Jasper, AB T0E 1E0. © **800/661-1225** or 780/852-5644. Fax 780/852-4860. www.charlton resorts.com. 119 units. C$315 (US$205) double; C$390–C$415 (US$254–US$270) suite. AE, DC, DISC, MC, V. Parking C$5 (US$3.25) per day. **Amenities:** Restaurant (see Beauvallon Dining Room under "Where to Dine," below), bar; indoor pool; Jacuzzi; concierge; room service; babysitting; laundry service; same-day dry cleaning. *In room:* A/C, TV, dataport, coffeemaker, hair dryer.

Expensive

Amethyst Lodge   If you're sick of the faux-alpine look prevalent in the Canadian Rockies, then you may be ready for the Amethyst Lodge, a comfortable and unabashed motor inn. The Amethyst is more central to downtown Jasper than most lodgings. Half of the guest rooms have balconies. Afternoon tea is served daily in the lounge.

200 Connaught Dr. (P.O. Box 1200), Jasper, AB T0E 1E0. © **888/852-7737** or 780/852-3394. Fax 780/ 852-5198. www.mtn-park-lodges.com. 97 units. C$202 (US$131) double. AE, DC, MC, V. **Amenities:** Restaurant, lounge; Jacuzzi; coin-op laundry; dry cleaning. *In room:* A/C, TV, dataport, hair dryer.

Jasper Inn Alpine Resort   The Jasper Inn, on the northern end of town but set back off the main road, is one of the nicest lodgings in town. Rooms are available in four different buildings and in many configurations. If you're looking for good value, ignore the standard units (which are perfectly nice, mind you); instead, fork over C$10 (US$7) more and reserve a spacious suite with fireplace and kitchen. Even nicer are the rooms in the separate Maligne Suites building, which come with marble-and-granite bathrooms, fireplaces, Jacuzzis, and balconies. Two-bedroom chalet-style rooms can sleep up to seven.

98 Geikie St. (P.O. Box 879), Jasper, AB T0E 1E0. ☎ 800/661-1933 or 780/852-4461. Fax 780/852-5916. www.jasperinn.com. 143 units. C$212–C$218 (US$138–US$142) double; C$225–C$413 (US$146–US$268) suite. Extra person C$10 (US$7). Children 16 and under stay free in parents' room. AE, DC, MC, V. Free parking. **Amenities:** Restaurant; small indoor pool; Jacuzzi; sauna; babysitting; coin-op laundry and laundry service. *In room:* TV, dataport, fridge, microwave, hair dryer.

Lobstick Lodge *(Kids)*   The Lobstick Lodge is a longtime favorite for the discerning traveler with an eye to value, with the largest standard units in Jasper. Even more impressive are the huge kitchen units, which come with a full-size fridge, four-burner stove, and microwave, plus double and twin beds and a sofa bed. These are perfect for families and go fast—reserve early.

96 Geikie St. (P.O. Box 1200), Jasper, AB T0E 1E0. ☎ 888/852-7737 or 780/852-4431. Fax 780/852-4142. www.mtn-park-lodges.com. 139 units. C$202 (US$131) double; C$215 (US$140) kitchen unit. Children under 15 stay free in parents' room. AE, DC, MC, V. Free parking. **Amenities:** Restaurant, lounge; indoor pool; Jacuzzis. *In room:* TV, dataport, coffeemaker, hair dryer.

Marmot Lodge   At the northern end of Jasper's main street, the Marmot Lodge offers pleasant rooms, decorated with a Native American theme, in three different buildings. One building contains kitchen units with fireplaces, popular with families. The building facing the street offers smaller, less expensive rooms; the third building features very large deluxe units. All are comfortable according to a relaxing, unfussy aesthetic that's restful after a day of sightseeing.

86 Connaught Dr., Jasper, AB T0E 1E0. ☎ 800/661-6521 or 780/852-4471. Fax 780/852-3280. 107 units. C$183–C$205 (US$119–US$133) double; C$217–C$227 (US$141–US$148) kitchen unit. Children under 15 stay free in parents' room. AE, DC, MC, V. **Amenities:** Restaurant, lounge; indoor pool; Jacuzzi; sauna. *In room:* TV w/ pay movies, coffeemaker, hair dryer.

Sawridge Hotel Jasper *(R)*   The three-story lobby of this hotel is large and airy, opening onto a central atrium lit with skylights. One-bedroom units face this atrium; other rooms overlook the town and offer balconies as well. The entire hotel has recently been redecorated with a casual rustic theme. The Sawridge, on the northern edge of Jasper, is unique in that it's owned by the Sawridge Cree Indian Band.

82 Connaught Dr., Jasper, AB T0E 1E0. ☎ 800/661-6427 or 780/852-5111. Fax 780/852-5942. 154 units. C$219–C$259 (US$142–US$168) double; C$300–C$390 (US$195–US$254) suite. AE, MC, V. **Amenities:** Restaurant, lounge; indoor pool; Jacuzzi; spa; sauna; massage; business center; coin-op laundry and laundry service. *In room:* A/C, TV, dataport, coffeemaker, fridge, hair dryer.

Moderate

In high season, it seems that nearly half the dwellings in Jasper let B&B-style rooms; contact **Jasper Home Accommodation Association,** P.O. Box 758, Jasper, AB T0E 1E0, for a full list. B&Bs listed with the visitor center have little signs in front; if you arrive early enough in the day, you can comb the streets looking for a likely suspect. Note that B&Bs here are much less grand than those in Banff, and less expensive as well. Rates are C$50 to C$75 (US$33 to US$49) at most homes. You'll need to pay cash for most. There's no central booking agency in Jasper, so contact your host directly.

Athabasca Hotel *(Value)*   This hotel's lobby is like a hunting lodge, with a stone fireplace and trophy heads of deer and elk. A gray-stone corner building with a homey, old-fashioned air, the Athabasca was built in 1929. Each guest room offers a mountain view, although only half have private bathrooms; the furnishings are simple and tasteful. The place is really quite pleasant—it's the very image of venerable Canadian charm—and one of the few good values in Jasper.

510 Patricia St., Jasper, AB T0E 1E0. ✆ **877/542-8422** or 780/852-3386. Fax 780/852-4955. www.athabasca hotel.com. 61 units (39 with private bathroom). C$145 (US$94) double with private bathroom; C$89 (US$58) double with shared bathroom. AE, DC, MC, V. **Amenities:** Restaurant, coffee shop, two bars; concierge; limited room service. *In room:* TV, dataport, hair dryer.

Becker's Chalets 🐾   This attractive log-cabin resort offers a variety of lodging options in freestanding chalets, set in a glade of trees along the Athabasca River. While the resort dates from the 1940s and retains the feel of an old-fashioned mountain retreat, most of the chalets have been built in the last 10 years, and thus are thoroughly modernized. Accommodations come with river-stone fireplaces and kitchens. The dining room here is one of Jasper's best.

Hwy. 95, 3 miles (5km) south of Jasper (P.O. Box 579), Jasper, AB T0E 1E0. ✆ **780/852-3779.** Fax 780/ 852-7202. www.beckerchalets.com. 118 chalets. C$85–C$155 (US$55–US$101) 1-bedroom cabin; C$145–C$215 (US$94nd]US$140) 2-bedroom cabin; C$185–C$350 (US$120–US$228) 3-bedroom cabin. AE, MC, V. **Amenities:** Restaurant (see Becker's Gourmet Restaurant under "Where to Dine," below); babysitting; coin-op laundry; playground. *In room:* TV, coffeemaker, fridge, hair dryer, no phone.

Tekarra Lodge 🐾   Just east of Jasper, this log-cabin resort is situated above the confluence of the Miette and Athabasca rivers. Accommodations are in the lodge or in cabins that can sleep from two to seven people. The cabins are rustic-looking and nicely furnished, but it's the location that really sets Tekarra apart. Just far enough from the bustle of Jasper, off a quiet road in the forest, it offers the kind of charm that you dream of in a mountain-cabin resort. One of Jasper's best restaurants is located in the lodge, making this a great place for a family seeking solitude yet access to good food.

1 mile (1.6km) east of Jasper off Hwy. 93A (P.O. Box 669), Jasper AB T0E 1E0. ✆ **888/404-4540** or 780/ 852-3058. Fax 780/852-4636. www.tekarralodge.com. 52 units. C$154 (US$100) lodge unit; C$154–C$214 (US$100–US$139) cabin double. 2-night minimum stay for cabins in summer. Extra person C$10 (US$7). Rates for lodge units include continental breakfast. AE, DC, MC, V. **Amenities:** Restaurant, bar; bike rentals; coin-op laundry. *In room:* Coffeemaker, hair dryer, no phone.

Inexpensive

Two **Hostelling International** hostels, both reachable at P.O. Box 387, Jasper, AB T0E 1E0 (✆ **780/852-3215;** www.hihostels.ca/alberta), are the best alternatives for the budget traveler. Advance reservations are strongly advised in summer. The 80-bed **Jasper International Hostel,** on Skytram Road 4 miles (6km) west of Jasper, charges C$18 (US$12) for members and C$23 (US$15) for nonmembers. The closest hostel to Jasper, it's open year-round. Two family rooms are available. The **Maligne Canyon Hostel,** off Maligne Lake Road 11 miles (18km) east of Jasper, sleeps 24; rates are C$13 (US$8) for members and C$18 (US$12) for nonmembers. This convenient hostel is just above the astonishing Maligne Canyon.

In & Around Hinton

Just east of the park gate in and near Hinton are a number of options that offer quality accommodations at significantly lower prices than you'll find in Jasper. Downtown Jasper is a 30- to 45-minute drive away from the choices listed below.

A Local Guest Ranch

The venerable **Black Cat Guest Ranch,** 35 miles (56km) northeast of Jasper, P.O. Box 6267, Hinton, AB T7V 1X6 (© **800/859-6840** or 780/865-3084; fax 780/865-1924; www.blackcatranch.ab.ca), was established in 1935 by the Brewsters. This wilderness retreat boasts a superb mountain setting just outside the park boundaries in the foothills. The rustic lodge, built in 1978, offers 16 unfussy units, each with private bathroom and an unspoiled view of the crags in Jasper Park. Rates of C$170 (US$111) double include three family-style meals. Activities include hiking, horseback riding (C$20/US$13 per hr. for guided trips), canoe rentals, murder-mystery weekends, and fishing. The ranch staff will meet your train or bus at Hinton.

Hinton has a number of motels with standard rooms. The **Best Western Motor Inn,** 828 Carmichael Lane (© **800/220-7870** in Canada, or 780/865-7777), has 42 rooms, most with kitchenettes. The **Black Bear Inn,** 571 Gregg Ave. (© **888/817-2888** or 780/817-2000), features an exercise room, hot tub, and restaurant. The **Crestwood Hotel,** 678 Carmichael Lane (© **800/262-9428** or 780/865-4001), has a pool and restaurant. Doubles at these motels cost between C$89 and C$105 (US$58 and US$68).

Mountain Splendour Bed & Breakfast   This modern home offers spacious bedrooms with English-theme decor. The largest is the English Garden Suite, with a private deck, fireplace, and large bathroom with Jacuzzi, separate shower, and cathedral ceilings. Guests can watch TV in the airy living room, which has picture windows framing a view of Jasper Park.

P.O. Box 6544, 17 Folding Mountain Village, Jasper East, AB T7V 1X8. © 780/866-2116. Fax 780/866-2117. 3 units. C$105–C$150 (US$68–US$98) double. Rates include breakfast. MC, V. **Amenities:** Jacuzzi. *In room:* TV, hair dryer, iron, no phone.

Overlander Mountain Lodge ☆   The Overlander is a historic lodge on the edge of Jasper Park. The original lodge building houses a rustic and evocative dining room featuring good Northwest cuisine, along with cozy guest rooms with queen or twin beds. A newer wing offers rooms with gas fireplaces and jetted tubs. The fourplex cabins have sitting rooms and separate bedrooms. Most of the chalets contain a fireplace or wood-burning stove, kitchen, washer/dryer, and patio. Accommodations throughout are handsomely furnished with rustic furniture. This property offers excellent value and makes a charming base for exploring the park.

Half a mile (1km) from Jasper Park East Gate (Box 6118), Hinton, AB T7V 1X5. © 780/866-2330. Fax 780/866-2332. www.overlandermountainlodge.com. 29 units. C$165–C$185 (US$107–US$120) lodge unit; C$125 (US$81) cabin unit; C$275 (US$179) 2-bedroom chalet; C$325 (US$211) 4-bedroom chalet. AE, MC, V. **Amenities:** Restaurant, lounge. *In room:* Coffeemaker, hair dryer, no phone.

Suite Dreams B&B   A modern home built as a B&B, Suite Dreams offers comfortable rooms with lots of natural light in a quiet, forested setting. Each unit is decorated according to a horticultural theme. The spacious living room has a fireplace, TV, and VCR, and the backyard features 100 yards of golf greens. The hostess is happy to make specialty breakfasts for guests with dietary restrictions.

Box 6145 (Lot 3134 Maskuta Estates), Hinton, AB T7V 1X5. © 780/865-8855. Fax 780/865-2199. www. suitedream.com. 3 units. From C$80 (US$52) double. Extra person C$20 (US$13). Rates include full breakfast. MC, V. *In room:* TV, no phone.

Wyndswept Bed & Breakfast   This B&B has a hostess who will make you feel like family. Guest rooms come with robes, handmade soaps, kettles, and other extras. The suite measures 1,200 square feet and has a kitchen, large bathroom, and sitting area. Breakfast is delicious and substantial—there's even a dessert course. Chances are good you'll see wildlife while here: Bears, coyotes, wolves, and deer have all been spotted from the deck.

2½ miles (4km) east of Jasper Park gates (Box 2683), Hinton, AB T7V 1Y2. © 780/866-3950. Fax 780/866-3951. www.wyndswept.com. 3 units. C$95 (US$62) double. Extra person C$35 (US$23). MC, V. **Amenities:** Access to computer and fax. *In room:* A/C, TV, dataport, coffeemaker, hair dryer, iron.

CAMPING

There are 10 campgrounds in Jasper National Park. You'll need a special permit to camp anywhere in the park outside the regular campgrounds; contact the park information office (© **780/852-6176**). The campgrounds range from completely unserviced sites to those providing water, power, sewer connections, laundry facilities, gas, and groceries. The closest to Jasper Townsite is the **Whistlers,** up the road toward the gondola, providing a total of some 700 campsites.

WHERE TO DINE
Expensive

Beauvallon Dining Room NEW CANADIAN   Offering one of the most ambitious menus in Jasper, the Beauvallon specializes in innovative yet classic European preparations of unusual and highly Canadian ingredients. Pan-seared caribou loin is served with ice wine–marinated figs; salmon cordon bleu comes wrapped in calamari bacon and stuffed with Boursin cheese. Local duck, beef, and pork also receive inventive treatment, and there are always vegetarian dishes. Service is excellent, and the dining room is cozy. The wine list is extensive and well priced.

In the Royal Canadian Lodge, 96 Geike St. © 780/852-5644. www.charltonresorts.com. Reservations recommended. Main courses C$20–C$40 (US$13–US$26); table d'hôte C$44 (US$29); Sun brunch C$18 (US$12) adults, C$14 (US$9) seniors and youths. AE, DC, MC, V. Daily 6:30am–1pm and 5:30–10:30pm.

Becker's Gourmet Restaurant FRENCH/CANADIAN   Although the name's not very elegant, it's highly descriptive. This inventive restaurant serves what could only be termed gourmet food, observing the mandate to serve what's fresh and local without turning the menu into a list of endangered game animals. Samples include four-nut crusted lamb chops, chèvre Mornay sauce and dill on grilled chicken breast, and grilled venison loin with Saskatoonberry compote. The dining room is an intimate log-and-glass affair that overlooks the Athabasca River.

At Becker's Chalets, Hwy. 93, 3 miles (5km) south of Jasper. © 780/852-3779. Reservations required. Main courses C$12–C$25 (US$8–US$16). MC, V. Daily 8am–2pm and 5:30–10pm.

Moose's Nook Grill Room CANADIAN   This atmospheric restaurant off the great room of the Jasper Park Lodge features "Canadiana" specialties. With equal parts tradition and innovation, the Moose's Nook offers hearty presentations of native meats, fish, and game. Pheasant breast is grilled and served with a compote of local Saskatoonberry; buffalo steak is prepared with a wild-mushroom, shallot, and whiskey sauce. Lighter appetites will enjoy the vegetarian cabbage rolls.

In the Fairmont Jasper Park Lodge, 5 miles (8km) east of Jasper. ✆ **780/852-6052.** Reservations recommended. Main courses C$18–C$33 (US$12–US$21). AE, DISC, MC, V. Daily 6–10pm.

Moderate

Andy's Bistro ⚡ CONTINENTAL/CANADIAN   This resourceful little restaurant's dining room looks like a wine cellar, and indeed the wine list is noteworthy. The food is classic Continental with a sprinkling of New World specialties thrown in for spice. Starters feature baked brie jubilee—with sour cherry sauce—and black olive toast. Main courses range from pork tenderloin Calvados (with sautéed apples) to ostrich schnitzel with white zinfandel and stoneground mustard sauce. Though the menu might seem high-brow, the atmosphere is casual and friendly—one communal table for 10 is saved for first-come, first served diners.

606 Patricia St. ✆ **780/852-4559.** Reservations recommended. Main courses C$17–C$29 (US$11–US$19). MC, V. Mid-May to mid-Oct daily 5–11pm; mid-Oct to mid-May Tues–Sat 5–11pm.

Denjiro Japanese Restaurant JAPANESE   Denjiro's is a slice of Japan, complete with sushi bar, karaoke lounge, intimate ozashiki tables, shoeless patrons, and service that's both fast and impeccable. The place has a studied simplicity that goes well with the traditional fare: sukiyaki, sashimi, tempura, and teriyaki.

410 Connaught Dr. ✆ **780/852-3780.** Most items C$8–C$19 (US$5–US$12). AE, MC, V. Mid-May to mid-Oct daily noon–10pm; mid-Oct to mid-May 5pm–10pm.

Fiddle River Seafood ⚡ SEAFOOD   This rustic-looking retreat has panoramic windows facing the Jasper rail station and the mountains beyond. Its specialty is fresh fish, though a number of pasta dishes and red-meat entrees will complicate your decision-making process. The 8 to 10 daily seafood specials may include oysters and several preparations of Pacific salmon, such as pan-seared steelhead salmon filet with a honey, lime, and tarragon butter sauce.

620 Connaught Dr. ✆ **780/852-3032.** Reservations required. Main courses C$15–C$28 (US$10–US$18). AE, MC, V. Daily 5pm–midnight.

Something Else INTERNATIONAL/PIZZA   Something Else is accurately named: Folded together here are a good Greek restaurant, pizza parlor, quality Canadian-style eatery, and Creole bistro. In short, if you're with a group that can't decide where to eat, this is the place to go. Prime Alberta steaks, fiery Louisiana jambalaya, Greek saganaki and moussaka, an array of 21 pizzas—no matter what you choose, it's all well prepared.

621 Patricia St. ✆ **780/852-3850.** Reservations not needed. Main courses C$12–C$23 (US$8–US$15). AE, DC, MC, V. Daily 11am–11pm.

Tekarra Lodge Restaurant STEAK/INTERNATIONAL   This local favorite offers excellent Greek-influenced food, as well as steaks and other intriguing dishes like pan-seared chicken with roast grapes. Lighter dishes such as stir-fries and pastas are also available. The charming lodge dining room is one of Jasper's hidden gems; the service is friendly, and the fireplace-dominated room intimate.

Hwy. 93A, 1 mile (1.6km) east of Jasper (call for directions). ℰ 780/852-3058. Reservations recommended on weekends. Main courses C$13–C$23 (US$8–US$15). AE, DC, MC, V. Daily 5–11pm.

Inexpensive

For sandwiches, soups, desserts, and coffee, go to **Soft Rock Cafe,** in the Connaught Square Mall, 622 Connaught Dr. (ℰ **780/852-5850**). You can check your e-mail at one of its computers. Another casual spot is **Spooner's Coffee Bar,** upstairs at 610 Patricia St. (ℰ **780/852-4046**), with a juice bar, coffee drinks, burritos, sandwiches, and other deli items.

Jasper Pizza Place PIZZA   One of Jasper's most popular eateries, the Pizza Place agreeably combines the features of an upscale boutique pizzeria with a traditional Canadian bar. The pizzas are baked in a wood-fired oven, and come in some very unusual—some would say unlikely—combinations. If you're not quite ready for the escargot pizza, perhaps the smoked salmon, caper, and black-olive version will please. The bar side of things is lively, with pool tables and a crowd of summer resort workers on display.

402 Connaught Dr. ℰ 780/852-3225. Reservations not accepted. Pizzas C$7–C$13 (US$4.55–US$8). MC, V. Daily 11am–11pm.

Mountain Foods Café *Value* DELI   This small deli and cafeteria is bright and friendly, and just the antidote to the stodgy food pervasive in much of the park. Most meals are light and healthful—salads, soups, wraps, melts, and breakfast scrambles. The deli case is filled with items available to go. Beer and wine are served.

606 Connaught Dr. ℰ 780/852-4050. Reservations not accepted. Main courses C$5–C$10 (US$3.25–US$7). MC, V. Daily 8am–10pm.

JASPER AFTER DARK

Nearly all of Jasper's nightlife can be found in the bars and lounges of the hotels, motels, and inns.

D'ed Dog Bar and Grill   This straightforward party scene is where young river and hiking guides gather to compare exploits by shouting above the din of country rock. 404 Connaught Dr. ℰ 780/852-3351.

Downstream Bar   You may think of most basement bars as dank and airless, but this lively billiards club has one advantage over most Canadian bars: It's smoke-free. It's also a friendly place for a late-evening drink, and you won't feel out of place if you're not 25 and totally tan. 620 Conaught Dr. ℰ 780/852-9449.

O'Shea's   This party den at the Athabasca Hotel is usually just called the Atha'B, or simply The B. It caters to a young clientele with its changing lineup of Top 40 bands, dance floor, and movies shown on the large-screen TV. In action Monday through Saturday until 2am. In the Athabasca Hotel, 510 Patricia St. ℰ 780/852-3386.

Pete's Night Club   Jasper's hottest club for music, Pete's presents live alternative and blues bands. Upstairs at 614 Patricia St. ℰ 780/852-6262.

Tent City   It's a little bit anomalous—Jasper's most exclusive and expensive hotel containing one of the town's most popular 20-something hangouts. In the bowels of the Jasper Park Lodge, you'll find this youthful gathering place, with billiards, loud music, and a preponderance of the JPL's 650 employees. In the Fairmont Jasper Park Lodge, 5 miles (8km) east of Jasper. ℰ 780/852-3301.

5 British Columbia's Rockies: Mount Robson Provincial Park & Yoho & Kootenay National Parks

MOUNT ROBSON PROVINCIAL PARK

15 miles (24km) W of Jasper

The highlight of this beautiful park, just west of Jasper National Park along the Yellowhead Highway, is 12,972-foot (3,954m) Mount Robson, the highest peak in the Canadian Rockies. This massive sentinel fills the sky from most vantage points, making it a certainty that you'll easily run through a roll of film if the weather's good.

The mighty Fraser River rises in the park, offering a challenging white-water adventure for experienced rafters. A number of Jasper-area outfitters offer trips down the Fraser; see "Outdoor Pursuits in the Park" under "Jasper National Park," above.

Two- to 4-hour park tours are offered by **Mount Robson Adventure Holidays** (*©* **250/566-4386;** fax 250/556-4351). For C$45 (US$29), visitors can choose a guided nature tour by raft, canoe, or van. Longer hiking or backpacking excursions are also available.

For additional information on the park, call *©* **250/566-4325** or go to www.mountrobson.com.

YOHO NATIONAL PARK

East gate is 37 miles (60km) W of Banff, west gate is 12 miles (20km) E of Golden

Located just east of Golden on the western slopes of the Rockies in British Columbia, Yoho National Park preserves some of the most famous rocks in Canada, as well as a historic rail line and the nation's second-highest waterfall. The park is essentially the drainage of the Kicking Horse River—famed for its white-water rafting—and is traversed by the Trans-Canada Highway.

The first white exploration of this area was by scouts looking for a pass over the Rockies that would be suitable for the Canadian Pacific's transcontinental run. Kicking Horse Pass, at 5,333 feet (1,626m), was surveyed, and the railroad began its service in 1884. However, the grade down the aptly named Big Hill, on the west side of the pass, was precipitous. The steepest rail line in North America, it descended the mountain at a 4½% grade. The first train to attempt the descent lost control and crashed, killing three men. In 1909, after decades of accidents, the Canadian Pacific solved its problem by curling two spiral rail tunnels into the mountains facing Big Hill. Together, the two tunnels are more than 6,100 feet (1,859m) long. At the Lower Spiral Tunnel Viewpoint, interpretive displays explain this engineering feat, and you can still watch trains enter and emerge from the tunnels.

ESSENTIALS

The service center for Yoho National Park is the little town of **Field,** with a half dozen modest accommodations and a few casual restaurants. The park's **visitor center** is just off Highway 1 near the entrance to town. For advance information, contact **Yoho National Park** (*©* **250/343-6324;** www.parkscanada.pch.gc.ca/yoho).

The daily entrance fee is C$5 (US$3.25) for adults, C$4 (US$2.60) for seniors, and C$2.50 (US$1.60) for children 6 to 16. The pass is good for entry at all of the four contiguous Rocky Mountain national parks.

EXPLORING THE PARK

Eight miles (13km) from the Kicking Horse Pass, turn north onto Yoho Valley Road to find some of the park's most scenic areas. Past another viewpoint of the Spiral Tunnels, continue 8 miles (13km) to **Takakkaw Falls** ⟨, Canada's second highest, which cascades 1,248 feet (380m) in two drops. A short trail leads from the road's end to a picnic area, where views of this waterfall are even more eye-popping.

Another impressive waterfall is **Wapta Falls,** on the rushing Kicking Horse River. The falls is reached by an easy 1½-mile (2.4km) hike near the park's western entrance.

The Kicking Horse River descends between Mount Field and Mount Stephen, famous in paleontological circles for the **Burgess Shale,** fossil-rich deposits from the Cambrian era that were the subject of Stephen Jay Gould's 1988 best-seller, *A Wonderful Life.* Interpretive displays on these fossil digs, which have produced organisms that seem to challenge some established evolutionary tenets, are found at the visitor center in Field. If you're interested enough to face a 12-mile (19km) round-trip hike, you can join a guided excursion to the quarries (see "Hiking," below).

Emerald Lake, a jewel-toned lake in a glacial cirque, is one of the park's most popular stops. Hiking trails ring the lake; the destination is popular for cross-country skiing as well. The **Emerald Lake Lodge** ⟨ (© **250/343-6321**) is open for meals and lodging year-round (see "Where to Stay," below). In summer, this is a very busy place, but it's worth the drive.

Lake O'Hara is another beautiful mountain lake nestled below the soaring peaks of the Continental Divide. To protect the fragile alpine ecosystem, access to the lake is restricted. Although you can hike into the lake basin—8 miles (13km) one-way—most people reserve a seat on the bus that travels the gravel road leading to the lake, four times per day. Reservations are essential, and in high season difficult to obtain. The buses run mid-June through September; tickets are C$12 (US$8), and the reservation fee another C$10 (US$7). For reservations, call © **250/343-6433.** Check out www.worldweb.com/parks canada-yoho/oharae.html for the most recent information on this area; the restrictions and options are fairly complex. Lake O'Hara is very popular with backcountry hikers, as the wilderness **campground** here serves as a hub for a great many trails. Sitting on the shores is **Lake O'Hara Lodge** (© **250/ 343-6418;** www.lakeohara.com), a rustic resort with 23 cabins starting at C$280 (US$182).

HIKING

The trails that lead out from Emerald Lake are among the most popular in the park. The **Emerald Lake Trail** is a 3¼-mile (5.2km), all-abilities nature loop that leads from the parking area to the bridge at the back of the lake. At the end of the lake, it connects to the **Emerald Basin Trail,** a 5.3-mile (8.6km) round-trip hike ending dramatically in a natural amphitheater of hanging glaciers and avalanche paths. The Emerald Lake circuit alone will take 1 to 2 hours; the Emerald Basin Trail is a half-day hike taking from 3 to 4 hours.

The **Yoho Glacier Moraine Trail** is a half-day hike, 5 miles (8.2km) in length, that passes by Laughing Falls en route to Twin Falls, the most popular destination in the valley. Energetic folks can continue to the top of **Twin Falls,** then over the **Whaleback Trail** for some of the most incredible views of glaciers in the park. Before you take this route, ask the staff at the visitor center in Field if the bridge is in. Returning to Takakkaw Falls via the Whaleback and Laughing falls is a 12.4-mile (20km) circuit.

Heading up to the **Burgess Shale** formations is limited to guided hikes. The exquisitely preserved fossils discovered here were like none seen before, and even today are still reshaping our understanding of early evolution of modern animal life. The **Yoho–Burgess Shale Foundation** (© 800/343-3006; www.burgess-shale.bc.ca) offers educational earth-science hikes from July to mid-September. The Burgess Shale Hike is 12.4 miles (20km) round-trip, a moderately difficult 10-hour trek. The cost is C$45 (US$29) per adult and C$25 (US$16) per child. The Mount Stephen Fossil Beds hike is a moderately difficult 3.7 miles (6km), lasting about 6 hours. The cost is C$25 (US$16) per adult and C$15 (US$10) per child. Other options include a special hike for seniors and the Mary Vaux Interpretive Hike. Call ahead for reservations.

WHERE TO STAY & DINE
The Emerald Lake Lodge 𝒜   The Emerald Lake Lodge sits at the base of a placid aquamarine lake beneath towering cliff-faced mountains. The lake was discovered in 1882, when the Canadian Pacific Railway pushed over Kicking Horse Pass; by 1902, the railway had built a lodge on the lakeshore. The original lodge has expanded since then, but retains a marvelous sense of woodsy venerability and rustic charm. The main lodge houses a formal dining room, a bar, and conference facilities. Guest accommodations are in 24 newly built, cabin-style buildings, designed to harmonize with the historic lodge. Each unit features a fieldstone fireplace, bent-willow chairs, down comforters, and a balcony. There's fine dining in the elegant restaurant and lighter cuisine at Cilantro. The lounge features an oak bar salvaged from an 1890s Yukon saloon.

Box 10, Field, BC V0A 1G0. © 800/663-6336 or 250/343-6321. www.crmr.com. 85 units. C$325–C$650 (US$211–US$423) double. Extra person C$25 (US$16). Children 12 and under stay free in parents' room. Off-season rates available. AE, DC, MC, V. **Amenities:** Two restaurants, lounge; Jacuzzi; sauna; canoe and cross-country ski rentals; horseback riding. *In room:* TV, dataport, hair dryer.

CAMPING
There are five campgrounds in Yoho National Park. East of Field, sites go for C$13 (US$8) at Monarch and C$18 (US$12) at Kicking Horse. Near the park's western gate, Chancellor Peak charges C$12 (US$8) per site, and Hoodoo Creek C$14 (US$9). There's also a walk-in campground near Takakkaw Falls, where sites are C$13 (US$8).

KOOTENAY NATIONAL PARK & RADIUM HOT SPRINGS
Radium Hot Springs is 65 miles (105km) SE of Golden; Vermillion Pass is 23 miles (38km) SW of Banff

Kootenay National Park, just west of Banff on the western slopes of the Canadian Rockies, preserves the valleys of the Kootenay and Vermillion rivers. The park contains prime wildlife habitats and a number of hiking trails. Although Kootenay's scenery is as grand as anywhere else in the Rockies, its trails are considerably less crowded than those in the neighboring parks.

ESSENTIALS
Kootenay National Park is linked to the other Canadian Rockies parks by Highway 93, which departs from Highway 1 at Castle Junction to climb over the Vermillion Pass and descend to **Radium Hot Springs,** the park's western entrance. The town of Radium Hot Springs sits at the junction of Highways 93 and 95.

Not an especially attractive place, it nonetheless offers ample motel rooms along the stretch of Highway 93 just before the park gates.

For information on the town, contact **Radium Hot Springs Visitor Information Centre,** Unit #4, Radium Plaza, 7685 Main St. W. (℃ **800/347-9704** or 250/347-9331; www.radiumhotsprings.com). For information on the park, contact **Kootenay National Park** (℃ **250/347-9505;** fax 250/347-9980; www.worldweb.com/ParksCanada-Kootenay).

The entry fee is C$5 (US$3.25) for adults, C$4 (US$2.60) for seniors, and C$2.50 (US$1.60) for children. The pass is good at all of the four contiguous Rocky Mountain national parks.

EXPLORING THE PARK & RADIUM HOT SPRINGS
Kootenay National Park is on the west side of the Continental Divide, just west of Banff. Kootenay has the fewest facilities of the four major Rocky Mountain national parks, and day-hiking options are limited. The drive through the park on Highway 93 does offer spectacular scenery.

Much of the area around **Vermillion Pass,** the eastern entrance to the park, was burned in a massive forest fire in 1968; from the parking area at the pass, the interpretive 15-minute Fireweed Trail leads into the still-devastated forest, describing the process of revegetation.

Four miles (7km) into the park is another dramatic stop. **Marble Canyon** is a narrow 200-foot-deep (61m) chasm cut through a formation of limestone. A short trail winds over and through the canyon, bridging the canyon in several places. Just 5 minutes down the road are the **Paint Pots.** Here, cold spring water surfaces in an iron-rich deposit of red and yellow clay, forming intense colored pools.

The highway leaves the Vermillion River valley and climbs up to a viewpoint above the **Hector Gorge,** into which the river flows before meeting the Kootenay River. From here, look out for mountain goats, which can often be seen on the rocky cliffs of Mount Wardle to the north.

The highway passes through one of these narrow limestone canyons after it mounts Sinclair Pass and descends toward Radium Hot Springs. Called **Sinclair Canyon,** the chasm is about 6 miles (10km) long, and in places is scarcely wide enough to accommodate the roadbed.

Radium Hot Springs Pool (℃ **250/347-9485**), a long-established hot springs spa and resort, sits at the mouth of Sinclair Canyon. It's open from mid-May to mid-October, daily from 9am to 11pm, and mid-October to mid-May, daily from noon to 9pm. Day passes are C$6 (US$3.90) for adults, C$5 (US$3.25) for seniors and children, C$17 (US$11) per family. Also here is the **Radium Hot Springs Massage Clinic** (℃ **250/347-9714**).

There's not much to delay you in the town of Radium Hot Springs unless you need an inexpensive motel room. The town does boast two new championship 18-hole golf courses, the **Springs Course,** along the Columbia just west of town, and the **Resort Course,** south of Radium. Both are operated by **Radium Golf Resort** (℃ **250/347-9311**), which offers restaurants, clubhouses, pro shops, and luxury accommodations.

WHERE TO STAY
The Chalet Europe ✦ One of the few places to stay in Radium that doesn't have busy Highway 93 as its front yard, the Chalet is perched high above the

Columbia Valley, just above the entrance to Kootenay Park. Each suite has a galley kitchen and private balcony with superlative views of the Rockies and Columbia Valley.

5063 Madsen Rd., Radium Hot Springs, BC V0A 1M0. ℂ 888/428-9998 or 250/347-9305. Fax 250/347-9316. www.chaleteurope.com. 17 units. C$99–C$139 (US$64–US$90) double. Extra person C$10 (US$7). AE, DISC, MC, V. **Amenities:** Exercise room; Jacuzzi; sauna; coin-op laundry. *In room:* A/C, TV, dataport, kitchenette, fridge, coffeemaker, microwave, hair dryer.

Gables Motel   One of the many motels that line the entry road to Kootenay National Park, the Gables is an attractive place with Bavarian-style balconies, lots of flower boxes, and good-size rooms.

5028 Hwy. 93, Radium Hot Springs, BC V0A 1M0. ℂ 250/347-9866. Fax 250/347-0042. www.radiumhot springs.com/gables. 17 units. C$79 (US$51) double. AE, MC, V. **Amenities:** Jacuzzi. *In room:* A/C, TV, fridge, coffeemaker.

Motel Tyrol   Like most other businesses in Radium Hot Springs, Motel Tyrol does its best to look like an emanation from the Alps. Well maintained, with colorful flowers and landscaping, it offers great value for the money. Consider what a motel like this would cost if it were in Banff!

East on Hwy. 93 (P.O. Box 312), Radium Hot Springs, BC V0A 1M0. ℂ 888/881-1188 or 250/347-9402. www.moteltyrol.com. 22 units. C$55–C$79 (US$36–US$51) double. Kitchen C$10 (US$7) extra. AE, MC, V. **Amenities:** Outdoor pool; Jacuzzi. *In room:* TV.

WHERE TO DINE

In addition to the following restaurants, consider stopping in for a beer and a light meal at **Horsethief Creek Pub & Eatery,** 7538 Main St. (ℂ **250/347-6400**).

Back Country Jack's CANADIAN   Jack's is a lively bar and restaurant that stresses a mountain-man theme; its woodsy dining room is filled with items from the mining and lumbering past. The menu ranges from sandwiches and ribs to steaks and seafood. One unusual taste treat is a grilled New York strip steak with the house-special cranberry sauce.

7555 W. Main St. ℂ 250/347-0097. Reservations not needed. Main courses C$8–C$25 (US$5–US$16). MC, V. Daily 11am–10pm.

Old Salzburg Restaurant AUSTRIAN   This is one of the most authentic-looking of Radium's ersatz Alpine structures, flanked by filigreed balconies, gables, and flowerpots. The menu features six varieties of schnitzel, but thankfully also contains a broad selection of other Austrian and Continental dishes. *Jagerrostbraten* is grilled beef loin in red wine, bacon, mushroom, and cranberry sauce. Homemade sausages, fish, and steaks round out the menu.

4943 Hwy. 93. ℂ 250/347-6553. Reservations recommended. Main courses C$13–C$22 (US$8–US$14). AE, MC, V. Daily 11am–10pm.

6 Waterton Lakes National Park

159 miles (264km) S of Calgary

In the southwestern corner of the province, Waterton Lakes National Park is linked with Glacier National Park in neighboring Montana; together these two beautiful tracts of wilderness comprise Waterton-Glacier International Peace Park. Once the hunting ground of the Blackfoot, 203-square-mile (526km²) Waterton Park contains superb mountain, prairie, and lake scenery and is home to abundant wildlife.

The transition from plains to mountains in Waterton and Glacier parks is abrupt: The formations that now rise above the prairie were once under the primal Pacific Ocean, but when the North American continent collided with the Pacific ocean floor, wedges of the ocean's basement rock broke along deep horizontal faults, cutting these rock layers free from their geologic moorings. The continued impact of the continental and ocean-floor tectonic plates gouged these free-floating rock blocks up out of the bowl they were formed in and pushed them eastward onto the top of younger rock. Under continued pressure from the elevating mass of the Rockies, the Waterton formations slid east almost 35 miles (56km) over the prairies. Almost 3 miles (5km) high, the rock block of Waterton Park—an overthrust in geological terms—is a late arrival, literally sitting on top of the plains.

During the last ice age, the park was filled with glaciers, which deepened and straightened river valleys. Those peaks that remained above the ice were carved into distinctive finlike ridges. The park's famous lakes also date from the ice ages; all three of the Waterton Lakes nestle in glacial basins.

ESSENTIALS

Waterton Park is 159 miles (264km) south of Calgary and 78 miles (130km) west of Lethbridge. From Waterton, it's 62 miles (100km) south across the U.S.–Canada border to St. Mary, at the entrance to Montana's Glacier National Park. **Greyhound Canada** (© **800/661-8747;** www.greyhound.ca) runs buses to Waterton Townsite from late June to Labour Day. Once in Waterton, you can make use of Glacier Park's minivan service, linking Waterton to Glacier National Park to the south. For information, call © **406/226-9311.**

For information, contact **Waterton Park Chamber of Commerce and Visitors Association** (© **403/859-5133** in summer, or 403/859-2224 in winter). Online, check out **www.parkscanada.pch.gc.ca/waterton** and **www.discover waterton.com.**

The park entry fee is C$4 (US$2.60) for adults, C$3 (US$1.95) for seniors, and C$2 (US$1.30) for children.

EXPLORING THE PARK

The main entrance road leads to **Waterton Townsite,** the park's only commercial center, with a number of hotels and restaurants. Akimina Parkway goes from the townsite to **Cameron Lake,** glimmering beneath the crags of the Continental Divide. You can rent canoes at the small visitor center; this is a great spot for a picnic. Red Rock Parkway follows Blackiston Creek past the park's highest peaks to **Red Rock Canyon.** From here, three trails lead up deep canyons to waterfalls.

The most popular activity in the park is the **International Shoreline Cruise** (© **403/859-2362**), which leaves from the townsite and sails Upper Waterton Lake past looming peaks to the ranger station at Goat Haunt, Montana, in Glacier Park. These tour boats leave five times daily; the cruise usually takes 2 hours. The price is C$22 (US$14) for adults, C$12 (US$8) for youths 13 to 17, and C$8 (US$5) for children 4 to 12.

OUTDOOR PURSUITS

BIKING   Unusual in a national park, mountain biking is allowed on a number of trails. Cameron Lake is a good trail head, offering three different options. Two short but steep trails climb up to Wall and Forum lakes; the Akimina Creek

Trail follows an old forestry road 9 miles (14km) up Akimina Creek. For rentals, contact **Pat's Cycle Rental** (☎ **403/859-2266**).

GOLF The **Waterton Park Golf Course** ⚐ (☎ **403/859-2114**) is one of the oldest courses in Alberta. An original Stanley Thompson design (he designed the famed courses at Banff and Jasper), hazards include incredible Rocky Mountain vistas and meandering elk, bear, and moose. Greens fees are C$30 (US$20) for 18 holes.

HIKING A 2-mile (3km) loop trail rings the peninsula that holds Waterton Townsite and links to long-distance trails. **Cameron Falls,** just above the Evergreen Avenue Bridge, is a good place to pick up the trail. From the Red Rock Canyon Trailhead, follow the main trail a mile up the canyon to see rust-red cliffs. From the same trail head, turn south and follow Blackiston Creek to Blackiston Falls, a short half-mile (1km) leg-stretcher.

The most famous day hike is to **Crypt Lake.** This 10.6-mile (17km) round-trip is moderately strenuous, but worth the effort for those in shape. The hike begins with a boat ride to the trail head, then a steep climb past four waterfalls up the side of Vimy Ride. The trail drops down onto snow-ringed Crypt Lake, right on the international border. The International Shoreline Cruise to Goat Haunt (see above) makes eight stops daily at the trail head.

Long-distance hiking trails skirt the edge of Upper Waterton Lake and link to the trail system in Glacier National Park.

HORSEBACK RIDING **Alpine Stables,** across from the golf course on Entrance Road (☎ **403/859-2462**), offers a variety of guided rides on more than 155 miles (250km) of trails.

WHERE TO STAY

All lodgings in the park are in Waterton Townsite, a tiny settlement beside Waterton Lake. No matter where you stay, you won't be more than a 5-minute stroll from the lake.

Aspen Village Inn ⚐ Aspen Village offers motel rooms in the Wildflower building, suites in the Aspen building, and duplex cottages. The suites are the newest, and can accommodate up to eight persons each. The entire complex, located 2 blocks from the lake, is hung with flower boxes and is well maintained.

P.O. Box 100, Waterton Lake, AB T0K 2M0. ☎ **403/859-2255.** Fax 403/859-2033. www.aspenvillageinn.com. 51 units. C$132–C$162 (US$86–US$105) double. Extra person $10 (US$7). Children under 16 stay free in parents' room. AE, DISC, MC, V. Closed mid-Oct to Apr. **Amenities:** Jacuzzi; playground; barbecue and picnic area. *In room:* TV, dataport, iron, coffeemaker, hair dryer.

Crandell Mountain Lodge A Bavarian guesthouse look-alike, the Crandell is one of the original lodges in the park. It has the feel of a charming country inn, with individually decorated rooms ranging from small units under the eaves to suites with kitchens and fireplaces. Two wheelchair-accessible units are available as well. The inn is noted for its friendly staff.

P.O. Box 114, Waterton Lake, AB T0K 2M0. ☎ and fax **403/859-2288.** www.crandellmountainlodge.com. 17 units. C$129–C$199 (US$84–US$129) double. Extra person C$10 (US$7). DC, MC, V. *In room:* TV, fridge, coffeemaker, hair dryer.

Kilmorey Lodge Beloved by oft-returning guests, the Kilmorey is a rambling old lodge from the park's heyday. One of the few lodgings that has direct lake views, it offers small but elegantly appointed rooms. Expect down comforters, antiques, squeaky floors, and loads of character. The Lamp Post is one of Waterton's most acclaimed restaurants (see "Where to Dine," below).

P.O. Box 100, Waterton Park, AB T0K 2M0. *©* **888/859-8669** or 403/859-2334. Fax 403/859-2342. www. kilmoreylodge.com. 23 units. C$98–C$194 (US$64–US$126) double. Extra person C$20 (US$13). Children under 16 stay free in parents' room. AE, DC, DISC, MC, V. **Amenities:** Restaurant, outdoor cafe, bar. *In room:* Hair dryer, no phone.

Prince of Wales Hotel *Overrated*   Built in 1927 by the Great Northern Railway, this beautiful mountain lodge, perched on a bluff above Upper Waterton Lake, is reminiscent of the historic resorts in Banff. Rooms have been renovated, though many are historically authentic in that they're rather small. Operated by the same dilatory consortium that manages the historic lodges in Glacier National Park in Montana, the Prince of Wales is in need of some serious reinvestment (at these prices, you don't expect water-stained acoustic ceiling tile in the lobby bar). You'll want to at least visit this landmark for the view and perhaps for a meal at the Garden Court (see "Where to Dine," below). Historic-monument status aside, however, there are better places to stay.

P.O. Box 33, Waterton Lakes National Park, AB T0K 2M0. *©* **403/859-2231.** Fax: 403/859-2630. In off-season, contact 1225 N. Central Ave., Phoenix, AZ 85077. *©* **602/207-6000.** www.glacierparkinc.com/site/ prince.cfm. 86 units. C$289–C$329 (US$188–US$214) double. Extra person C$15 (US$10). Children under 12 stay free in parents' room. MC, V. Closed Sept 27–May 13. **Amenities:** Restaurant, tearoom, lounge.

Waterton Glacier Suites   These attractive suites are some of the nicest accommodations in Waterton, particularly if you're able to step up and pay for a top-end loft unit. Most expensive are town house–style suites with two bathrooms and a two-person Jacuzzi. All units are attractively furnished, with both fireplaces and balconies.

P.O. Box 51, Waterton Park, AB T0K 2M0. *©* **403/859-2004.** Fax 403/859-2118. www.watertonsuites.com. 26 units. C$159–C$259 (US$103–US$168) double. Extra person C$10 (US$7). AE, MC, V. **Amenities:** Jacuzzi. *In room:* A/C, TV, dataport, fridge, coffeemaker, microwave, hair dryer.

Waterton Lakes Lodge *⚬*   This new and classy complex sits on 4 acres (1.6 hectares) in the heart of Waterton Townsite. Nine lodge-like buildings contain everything from standard rooms with queen beds to deluxe units with a gas fireplace, two-person shower, jetted tub, kitchenette, and sofa bed. All are appointed with handsome pine furniture.

P.O. Box 4, Waterton Park, AB T0K 2M0. *©* **888/98-LODGE** or 403/859-2150. Fax 403/859-2229. www. watertonlakeslodge.com. 80 units. C$160–C$265 (US$104–US$172) double. Extra person C$15 (US$10). Off-season rates available. AE, MC, V. **Amenities:** Two restaurants, bar; pool; health club; spa; cross-country ski rentals; coin-op laundry. *In room:* TV, dataport, fridge, coffeemaker, hair dryer.

WHERE TO DINE

Garden Court PACIFIC NORTHWEST   This elegant dining room overlooks stunning Waterton Lake, with the towering peaks of Glacier National Park incising the southern horizon. By and large, the food is up to the challenge of competing with the vista. Appetizers include baked brie with sliced apples, crostini, and cranberry coulis; and scallops in chives, mushrooms, and cream in a puff-pastry shell. Entrees range from prime rib to the house specialty Princess chicken, a spinach-and-feta-stuffed breast with a pine-nut crust, served with Saskatoonberry and onion chutney.

In Prince of Wales Hotel. *©* **403/859-2231.** Reservations required. Main courses C$18–C$30 (US$12–US$20). MC, V. May 14–Sept 26 daily 6:30–9:30am, 11:30am–2pm, and 5–9pm.

Kootenai Brown Dining Room CANADIAN   The only restaurant in Waterton that's directly on the lake, the food at Kootenai Brown doesn't try to interfere with the view. The dining room has seen some hard use, but the steaks here are good. The menu is centered on classic western-style cooking, though a few international and fancy dishes appear, like chicken tandoori or stuffed trout with mushroom duxelle. The Bayshore complex also contains the Koffee Shop (serving up soup, salads, and sandwiches) and a lounge offering a late-night menu of pizza and burgers.

In the Bayshore Inn, Waterton Ave. ℂ **403/859-2211.** Reservations suggested. Main courses C$15–C$22 (US$10–US$14). Breakfast buffet C$8.95 (US$6). AE, DISC, MC, V. Apr 1–Oct 15 daily 7–10am, 11am–2:30pm, and 5–9pm.

Lamp Post Dining Room NORTHWEST   This dining room has a big regional reputation, and while the food is well prepared and the ambience pleasant, some of the preparations are a little sketchy. The menu stresses its "mix of cultures," but the most successful dishes are those featuring local beef, regional game and fish, and wild mushrooms and berries. As an appetizer, try the wild-boar paté. Filet mignon comes with Dijon-mustard glaze; poached salmon is served with a cucumber-and-yogurt sauce. The wine list is extensive, and the service prompt despite the busyness of the room.

In the Kilmorey Lodge. ℂ **403/859-2334.** Reservations required. Main courses C$14–C$28 (US$9–US$18). AE, DISC, MC, V. Daily 7:30–10pm.

Little Italian Café ITALIAN   This cafe on Waterton's main street is a pleasant place for relatively inexpensive Italian food. Breakfasts feature dishes like eggs Florentine; lunch brings grilled focaccia sandwiches. At night, the menu tilts toward pasta—with more than 20 choices—plus classic preparations of chicken, veal, and beef. The patio is a marvelous spot to people-watch.

Waterton Ave. ℂ **403/859-0003.** Reservations not accepted. Main courses C$7–C$18 (US$4.55–US$12). MC, V. Daily 8am–10pm.

Appendix:
British Columbia & the Canadian
Rockies in Depth

The more you know about British Columbia and the Canadian Rockies, the more you're likely to enjoy and appreciate everything the region has to offer. The pages that follow include a brief history, a range of highly recommended books, a primer on the unique cuisine of the area, and more.

1 British Columbia & the Canadian Rockies Today

Canada's westernmost region has a lot to offer travelers, including dramatic landscapes, a vibrant arts culture, and unparalleled access to outdoor recreation. British Columbia and the Canadian Rockies, which stretch across the provincial border into Alberta, are obviously part of Canada, and have a thoroughly Canadian infrastructure and political system. However, these two giant provinces—British Columbia covers 366,255 square miles (948,600 km²), Alberta 255,285 square miles (661,188km²)—are separated from the nation's capital, Ottawa, and the political and cultural centers of eastern Canada by thousands of miles of farmland.

Much closer is the northwestern tier of the United States. Although British Columbia and Alberta are definitely part of Canada, they are much closer in spirit to the Pacific Northwest states than to, say, Quebec or Nova Scotia. The states of Washington, Oregon, Idaho, and Montana share their northern neighbors' climate, economies, and cultural histories. These regions of Canada and the United States have more in common with each other than with the rest of their respective countries—a reality that seems to please everyone in both the Canadian and the American Pacific Northwest.

There's another cultural overlay at work here, not quite at odds with the above observation, but simultaneously true: In the United States, the westering urge—that uniquely North American drive to keep moving west toward unspecified freedom and opportunity—was diffused across a dozen or so states, each of which developed its own culture and institutions. In Canada, there were just British Columbia and Alberta to absorb all the hopes, idealism, and pragmatism of 150 years' worth of western migration.

British Columbia is often called the California of Canada, with Canada's most temperate climate, a vibrant film industry, a visible and powerful gay and lesbian community, and a soft-focus New Age patina. However, British Columbia is also the Idaho of Canada, the Washington State of Canada, and, incidentally, the Asia of Canada. In terms of cultural diversity and competing interests, there's a lot going on here.

Likewise, the Alberta of prosperous Edmonton and Calgary may seem like an oil- and agriculture-fueled monoculture, but dozens of its rural communities began as colonies of religious refugees whose stories have a lot in common with the Mormons of Utah. And with its nouveau-riche wealth and well-rehearsed swagger, Alberta is more like Texas than anywhere else on earth.

As if these factors weren't enough to explain the schizoid nature of the two westernmost provinces, the populace is further divided by highly politicized environmental issues. Although Canadians in general seem more environmentally conscious than Americans, that doesn't mean that individual Canadians want to lose their salmon-fishing jobs to some vague international treaty, or that they want to close down the mine that's employed their families for generations just because of a little mud in the river. Environmental issues—especially those surrounding logging, agriculture, mining, and fishing—are especially contentious, often pitting urban and rural residents against each other.

It's easy to think of Canada as North America's Scandinavia—well ordered, stable, and culturally just a little sleepy. In fact, during your own travels across British Columbia and the Rocky Mountains, you'll likely find this corner of Canada a fascinating amalgam of cultures, histories, and conflicting interests.

2 History 101

NATIVE WESTERN CANADA

According to generally accepted theories, the Native peoples of North America arrived on this continent about 15,000 to 20,000 years ago from Asia, crossing a land bridge that spanned the Bering Strait. At the time, much of western Canada was covered with vast glaciers. Successive waves of these peoples moved south down either the coast or a glacier-free corridor that ran along the east face of the Rockies. As the climate warmed and the glaciers receded, the Native peoples moved north, following ice-age game animals like the woolly mammoth.

The ancestors of the tribes and bands that now live on the prairies of Alberta didn't make their year-round homes here in the pre-Contact era. The early plains Indians wintered in the lake and forest country around present-day Manitoba, where they practiced forms of basic agriculture. In summer and fall, hunting parties headed to the prairies of Alberta and Saskatchewan in search of buffalo. The move to a year-round homeland on the Great Plains was a comparatively recent event, caused by Native displacement as the eastern half of North America became increasingly dominated by European colonists.

Dateline

- 1670 Hudson's Bay Company is established by English King Charles II.
- 1741 Danish sailor Vitus Bering explores northern Pacific coast for Russia.
- 1759 English defeat French at Montreal's Plains of Abraham, ending the French and Indian War; British take control of Upper and Lower Canada.
- 1774 Spaniard Juan Perez sails up British Columbian coast from Mexico, landing in the Queen Charlottes and on Vancouver Island; the first European to explore the coast, he claims all of the Pacific coast for Spain.
- 1776 American colonies declare their independence from Britain; Canada remains royalist.
- 1778 Capt. James Cook of England lands at Nootka Sound, on Vancouver Island, and trades for otter furs on his way to China, establishing the beginning of the Northwest/China trade triangle. Establishes British claim to Northwest.
- 1778 North West Company establishes Fort Chipewyan on Lake Athabasca, the first European settlement in Alberta.
- 1792 Nootka Accord settles British/Spanish dispute over the Northwest coast; Spain renounces claims to the northern coast.

continues

Thus, a number of linguistically and culturally unrelated tribes were forced onto the prairies at the same time, competing for food and shelter.

The Natives of the prairies relied on the buffalo for almost all their needs. The hide provided teepee coverings and leather for moccasins; the flesh was eaten fresh in season and preserved for later consumption; and the bones were used to create a number of tools.

The Native Indians along the Northwest coast had a very different culture and lifestyle, and in all likelihood migrated to the continent much later than the Plains Indians. Living at the verge of the Pacific or along the region's mighty rivers, these early people settled in wooden longhouses in year-round villages, fished for salmon and shellfish, and used the canoe as the primary means of transport. The Pacific Northwest coast was one of the most heavily populated areas in Native America, and an extensive trading network developed. Because the temperate coastal climate and abundant wildlife made this a relatively hospitable place to live, the tribes were reasonably well off, and the arts—carving and weaving in particular—flourished. Villages were organized according to clans, and elaborately carved totem poles portrayed ritual clan myths.

EUROPEAN   EXPLORATION

The first known contact between Europeans and the Natives of western Canada came in the last half of the 18th century, as the Pacific Northwest coast became a prize in the colonial dreams of distant nations. Russia, Britain, Spain, and the United States each would assert a claim over parts of what would become British Columbia and Alberta.

In 1774, the Spanish explorer Juan Perez landed on the Queen Charlotte Islands and then on the western shores of Vancouver Island, at Nootka

- 1793 British fur trader Alexander Mackenzie arrives in Bella Coola, becoming the first European to traverse North America.

- 1794 Rocky Mountain House, a North West Company trading post, opens at the juncture of the Peace and Moberly rivers, becoming the first permanent European settlement in British Columbia.

- 1795 Hudson's Bay Company establishes Edmonton House on the banks of the North Saskatchewan River.

- 1804–06 Americans Lewis and Clark journey up the Missouri River and down the Columbia River to the Pacific, then Spanish territory. The journey reveals a great wealth of furs in the Northwest, piquing American settlement interest.

- 1808 Fur trader Simon Fraser floats the Fraser River from the Rocky Mountains to the site of present-day Vancouver.

- 1811 David Thompson floats the entire length of the Columbia River, arriving at the Pacific to find an already-established American trading post, Fort Astoria.

- 1812 Outbreak of War of 1812; British take control of Fort Astoria.

- 1818 Treaty of Ghent ends War of 1812; Spain renounces claim in Pacific Northwest; United States and Britain agree to "joint occupancy" of Pacific Northwest.

- 1821 Hudson's Bay Company and North West Company merge.

- 1825 Hudson's Bay Company's Fort Vancouver is established near present-day Portland, becoming the administrative center over nearly all of the Pacific Northwest.

- 1841 Act of Union creates the United Provinces of Canada.

- 1843 Settlers in Oregon decide to set up American-style government, and British withdraw to north of the Columbia River; Fort Victoria is established on Vancouver Island.

- 1846 U.S.–Canada boundary is established at 49th Parallel.

- 1849 Vancouver Island becomes British colony.

continues

Sound. England's James Cook made a pass along the Pacific Northwest coast, spending a couple weeks at Nootka Sound in 1778, where the crew traded trinkets for sea-otter pelts. Later in the same journey, when Cook visited China, he discovered that the Chinese were willing to pay a high price for otter furs.

Thus was born the Chinese trade triangle that would dominate British economic interests in the northern Pacific for 30 years. Ships entered the waters of the Pacific Northwest, traded cloth and trinkets with Natives for pelts of sea otters, and then set sail for China, where the skins were traded for tea and luxury items. After the ships returned to London, the Asian goods were sold.

Since the Spanish and the English had competing claims over the Pacific Northwest coast, these nations sent envoys to the region—the Spaniard Don Juan Francisco de la Bodega y Quadra and the British Captain George Vancouver—to further explore the territory and resolve who controlled it. The expeditions led by these explorers resulted in a complete mapping of the region, though the ownership of the territory wasn't resolved until 1793, when Spain renounced its claims.

Fur traders also first explored the interior of British Columbia and the Alberta prairies. Two British fur-trading companies, the Hudson's Bay Company (HBC) and the North West Company, began to expand from their bases along the Great Lakes and Hudson's Bay, following mighty prairie rivers to the Rockies. Seeking to gain advantage over the Hudson's Bay Company, the upstart North West Company sent traders and explorers farther inland to open new trading posts and to find routes to the Pacific. Alexander Mackenzie became the first white man to cross the continent when he followed the Peace River across northern Alberta and British

- **1858** Fraser River gold rush begins; the B.C. mainland becomes colony of New Caledonia.
- **1859** First wine grapes are planted along Lake Okanagan by Catholic missionary Father Pandosy.
- **1862** Gold is discovered at Barkerville, beginning the Cariboo gold rush.
- **1866** Colonies of Vancouver Island and New Caledonia combine to form colony of British Columbia.
- **1867** Britain grants further independence to the new Dominion of Canada.
- **1871** British Columbia agrees to join the Dominion of Canada and not the United States, as long as Canada builds the transcontinental railroad.
- **1872** The Dominion Lands Acts, Canada's Homestead Act, opens the prairies to farmers and ranchers.
- **1874** Royal Canadian Mounted Police (RCMP) ride west to establish order on prairies of Ruperts Land (Alberta and Saskatchewan).
- **1875** RCMP establish Fort Calgary at the confluence of the Bow and Elbow rivers.
- **1877** Blackfoot chief Crowfoot signs treaty relegating the tribe, the largest and most powerful of the Canadian Plains tribes, to reservations.
- **1883** Canadian Pacific Railroad reaches Calgary.
- **1885** Canadian Pacific Railroad is completed, and the first train steams from Montreal to Burrard Inlet, on the Pacific near Vancouver; Banff National Park, Canada's first, is proclaimed by Prime Minister John Macdonald.
- **1886** Vancouver, a rail siding near a popular tavern named Gassy's, is established.
- **1896** Gold is discovered in the Yukon; Edmonton becomes a major outfitting center for overland journey to the Klondike.
- **1904** Butchart Gardens opens to the public.
- **1905** Alberta becomes a province.
- **1914** Grand Trunk Railroad reaches from Winnipeg to Prince Rupert, becoming Canada's second transcontinental railroad.

continues

Columbia, crossing the Rockies and the Fraser River Plateau to reach Bella Coola, on the Pacific, in 1793.

Simon Fraser followed much of Mackenzie's route in 1808, though he floated down the Fraser River to its mouth near present-day Vancouver. Another fur trader and explorer was David Thompson, who crossed the Rockies and established Kootenay House trading post on the upper Columbia River. In 1811, Thompson journeyed to the mouth of the Columbia, where he found Fort Astoria, an American fur-trading post, already in place. Competing American and British interests would dominate events in the Pacific Northwest for the next 2 decades.

By the 1820s, seasonal fur-trading forts were established along the major rivers of the region. Cities like Edmonton, Kamloops, Prince George, and Hope all had their beginnings as trading posts. Each of the forts was given an assortment of trade goods to induce the local Indians to trap beaver, otter, fox, and wolf. Although the fur companies generally treated the Native populations with respect and fairness, there were tragic and unintentional consequences to the relationships that developed. While blankets, beads, and cloth were popular with the Natives, nothing was as effective as whiskey: Thousands of gallons of alcohol passed from the trading posts to the Natives, corrupting traditional culture and creating a cycle of dependence that enriched the traders while poisoning the Indians. The white traders also unwittingly introduced European diseases to the Natives, who had little or no resistance to such deadly scourges as smallpox and measles.

The Louisiana Purchase, which gave the U.S. control of all the territory along the Missouri River up to the 49th parallel and to the Continental Divide, and the Lewis and Clark

- **1914** First ski resort opens at Whistler.
- **1914–18** In World War I, 60,000 Canadian troops die and another 173,000 are wounded.
- **1923** British Columbia restricts immigration by Japanese and Chinese.
- **1930s** The depression and mass unemployment hit Canada. Prairie farms and ranches are especially hard hit; social unrest rocks Vancouver.
- **1935** Social Credit Party forms in response to the Great Depression; becomes leading political party in much of western Canada until 1980s.
- **1939** Canada declares war on Germany.
- **1945** World War II ends; 42,000 Canadians die in the war, another 54,000 are wounded.
- **1947** Native Canadians are granted right to vote in provincial elections; first major oil reserves are discovered in Alberta.
- **1960** Native Canadians are granted right to vote in federal elections.
- **1967** "Vive le Quebec Libre": de Gaulle visits Quebec, spurring Quebec secessionism.
- **1968** The Official Languages Bill declares French and English the two official languages of Canada.
- **1972** Canada bans whaling off the Pacific Coast.
- **1988** Calgary hosts winter Olympic Games.
- **1989** Canada–U.S. Free Trade Agreement eliminates all tariffs on goods of national origin moving between the two countries.
- **1993** Environmentalists, loggers, and law enforcement clash near Clayoquot Sound; 800 logging protesters are arrested.
- **1995** Quebec votes narrowly to remain in Canada.
- **1997** Britain hands over Hong Kong to mainland Chinese. Major emigration of Hong Kong Chinese to Vancouver area precedes the repatriation; Port Hardy fishermen and -women blockade Alaska Marine Highway ferry in protest of Alaskan fishing practices.

continues

Expedition of 1804–1806 gave the Americans a toe-hold in the Pacific Northwest. As part of the settlement of the War of 1812, the Pacific Northwest—which included all of today's Oregon, Washington, and much of British Columbia—was open to both British and American exploitation, though neither country was allowed to set up governmental institutions. In fact, Britain had effective control of this entire area through its proxies in the Hudson's Bay Company, which had quasi-governmental powers over its traders and over relations with the Native peoples, which included pretty much everyone who lived in the region.

- 1999 Nunavut becomes a standalone territory, splitting off from the Northwest Territories; the first new territory in over a century.
- 2000 Jean Chretien is re-elected for a third consecutive term, defeating Stockwell Day of the right-wing Canadian Alliance Party.

B.C. CONSOLIDATES & JOINS CANADA   From its headquarters at Fort Vancouver, on the north banks of the Columbia River near Portland, Oregon, the Hudson's Bay Company held sway over the river's huge drainage, which extended far into present-day Canada. However, with the advent of the Oregon Trail and settlement in what would become the state of Oregon, the HBC's control over this vast territory began to slip. In 1843, the Oregon settlers voted by a slim majority to form a government based on the American model. The HBC and Britain withdrew to the north of the Columbia River, which included most of Washington and British Columbia.

The U.S.–Canada boundary dispute became increasingly antagonistic. The popular slogan of the U.S. 1844 presidential campaign was "54/40 or fight," which urged the United States to occupy all of the Northwest up to the present Alaskan border. Finally, in 1846, the British and the Americans agreed to the present border along the 49th parallel. The HBC headquarters withdrew to Fort Victoria on Vancouver Island; many British citizens moved north as well. In order to better protect its interests and citizens, Vancouver Island became a crown colony in 1849—just in case the Americans grew more expansionist-minded. However, population in the Victoria area—then the only settled area of what would become British Columbia—was still small: In 1854, the population counted only 250 white people.

Then, in 1858, gold-rush fever struck this remote area of the British Empire. The discovery of gold along the Fraser River and in 1862 in the Cariboo Mountains brought in a flood of people. By far the vast majority of the estimated 100,000 who streamed into the area were Americans who came north from the by-now-spent California goldfields. Fearing domination of mainland Canada by the United States, Britain named the mainland a new colony, New Caledonia, in 1858. In 1866, the two colonies—Vancouver Island and the mainland—merged as the British colony of British Columbia.

As population and trade increased, the need for greater political organization grew. As a colony, British Columbia had little local control, and was largely governed by edict from London. In order for British Columbia to have greater freedom and self-determination, the growing colony had two choices: join the prosperous United States to the south, with which it shared many historic and commercial ties, or join the new Dominion of Canada far to the east. After Ottawa promised to build a railroad to link eastern and western Canada, B.C. delegates voted in 1871 to join Canada as the province of British Columbia.

THE RAILROADS LINK CANADA   Meanwhile, the rule of the HBC over the inland territory known as Ruperts Land relaxed as profits from trapping decreased, and in 1869, the Crown bought back the rights to the entire area. The border between the United States and Canada in the prairie regions was hazy at best, lawless at worst. Although selling whiskey to Native people was illegal, in the no-man's-land between Montana and Canada, trade in alcohol was rife.

In response to uprisings and border incursions, the Canadian government created a new national police force, the Royal Canadian Mounted Police. In 1873, a contingent of Mounties began their journey across the Great Plains, establishing Fort Macleod (1874) in southern Alberta along with three other frontier forts, including Fort Calgary at the confluence of the Bow and Elbow rivers. The Mounties succeeded in stopping the illegal whiskey trade and creating conditions favorable for settlement. By 1875, there were 600 residents at Fort Calgary, lured by reports of vast and fertile grasslands.

However, for the prairies and the interior of Canada to support an agrarian economy, these remote areas needed to be linked to the rest of Canada. In 1879, the Canadian Pacific Railroad reached Winnipeg, and in 1883 arrived at Banff. Finding a route over the Rockies proved a major challenge: The grades were very steep, the construction season short, and much of the rail bed had to be hacked out of rock.

Canada's transcontinental railway needed a mainland coastal terminus in British Columbia, as the new province's population center and capital, Victoria, was on an island. Railroad engineers set their sites on the sheltered Burrard Inlet, then a sparse settlement of saloons, lumber mills, and farms. The first train arrived from Montreal in 1886, stopping at a thrown-together, brand-new town called Vancouver. A year later, the first ship docked from China, and Vancouver began its boom as a trading center and transportation hub.

All along the railroad's transcontinental reach, towns, farms, and other industries sprang up for the first time. In Alberta, huge ranches sprawled along the face of the Rockies, and Calgary boomed as a cow town. The railroads also brought foreign immigration. Entire communities of central and eastern European farmers appeared on the prairies overnight, the result of the railroads' extensive promotional campaign in places like the Ukraine. Other settlers came to western Canada seeking religious tolerance; many small towns on the prairies began as utopian colonies for Hutterites, Mennonites, and Doukhobors. Alberta became a province in 1905, and in 1914 the Grand Trunk Railroad, Canada's second transcontinental railroad, opened up the more northerly prairies, linking Saskatoon and Edmonton to Prince George and Prince Rupert. By 1920, Alberta was Canada's leading agricultural exporter.

All this development demanded lumber for construction, and in Canada, lumber—then as now—meant British Columbia. In return for building the transcontinental railroad, the CPR was granted vast tracts of land along its route. As the demand for lumber skyrocketed, these ancient forests met the saw.

As the population, industry, logging, farming, and shipping all increased in western Canada, it was not just the local ecosystem that took a hit. The Natives had at first reasonably cooperative relations with the HBC trappers and traders. Although European diseases wiped out enormous numbers of Indians, these early whites did little to overtly disturb the traditional life and culture of the Natives.

That awaited the arrival of agriculture, town settlements, and Christian missionaries. After the HBC lost its long-standing role in Indian relations, authority was wielded by a federal agency in Ottawa. The Natives received no compensation for the land deeded over to the CPR, and increased contact with the whites who were flooding the region simply increased contact with alcohol, trade goods, and disease. The key social and religious ritual of the coastal Indians—the potlatch, a feast and gift-giving ceremony—was banned in 1884 by the provincial government under the influence of Episcopal missionaries. The massive buffalo herds of the open prairies were slaughtered to near-extinction in the 1860s and 1870s, leaving the once proud Plains Indians little choice but to accept confinement on reservations.

THE 20TH CENTURY   The building of the Panama Canal, which was completed in 1914, meant easier access to markets in Europe and along North America's east coast, bringing about a boom for the western Canadian economy. As big business grew, so did big unions. In Vancouver in the 1910s, workers organized into labor unions to protest working conditions and pay rates. A number of strikes hit key industries, and in several instances resulted in armed confrontations between union members and soldiers. However, one area where the unions, the government, and business could all agree was racism: The growing Chinese and Japanese populations were a problem they felt only punitive legislation and violence could solve. Large numbers of Chinese had moved to the province and were instrumental in building the CPR; they were also important members of hard-rock mining communities and ran small businesses such as laundries. Japanese settlers came slightly later, establishing truck farms and becoming the area's principal commercial fishermen. On several occasions, Vancouver's Chinatown and Little Tokyo were the scene of white mob violence, and in the 1920s, British Columbia passed legislation that effectively closed its borders to nonwhite immigration.

The period of the World Wars was turbulent on many fronts. Settlers with British roots returned to Europe to fight the Germans in World War I, dying in great numbers and destabilizing the communities they left behind. Following the war, Canada experienced an economic downturn, which led to further industrial unrest and unemployment. After a brief recovery, the Wall Street crash of 1929 brought severe economic depression and hardship. Vancouver, with its comparatively mild climate, became a kind of magnet for young Canadian men—hungry, desperate, and out of work. The city, however, held no easy answers for these problems, and soon the streets were filled with demonstrations and riots. Vancouver was in the grip of wide-spread poverty.

Anti-German riots took hold of the city streets; German-owned businesses were burned. The war years were also hard times for nonwhite immigrants. In 1941, Japanese-Canadians were removed from their land and their fishing boats and interned by the government on farms and work camps in inland British Columbia, Alberta, and Saskatchewan.

Prosperity returned only with the advent of World War II: the unemployed enlisting as foot soldiers against the Axis nations, and the shipbuilding and armaments-manufacturing industries bolstering the region's traditional farming, ranching, and lumbering.

Alberta's wild oil boom began in 1947, when drillers struck black gold near Leduc and a period of tremendous economic growth ensued. By the 1960s, Alberta was supplying most of Canada's crude oil and natural gas. In the 1970s, as oil-producing nations joined together to form the Organization of Petroleum Exporting Countries (OPEC) and oil shortages hit North America, Alberta was left holding the hose. The value of the province's petroleum resources tripled almost overnight; by the end of the 1970s, its value had quadrupled again, allowing for a period of nearly unlimited building and infrastructure development. Calgary morphed from a sleepy ranchers' town into a brand-new city of soaring office towers, the financial and business center of Canada's oil industry. Edmonton, the capital of Alberta, boomed as the center of oil technology and refining.

Since the war years, British Columbia generally boomed economically as well, especially under the leadership of the Social Credit Party, supposedly the party of small business. Father and son premiers, W. A. C. and Bill Bennett, effectively ruled the Social Credit Party and the province from 1952 until 1986. With close ties between government ministers and the resources they oversaw, business—especially manufacturing, mining, and logging—certainly boomed, but along with prosperity came significant governmental scandals, opportunistic financial shenanigans, and major resource mismanagement. Social Credit Premier Bill Vander Zalm was forced to resign in 1991. Reform-minded governments have been in place in Victoria since, although Chicago-style corruption still seems rampant in both government and business.

The 1990s saw a vast influx of Hong Kong Chinese to the Vancouver area, the result of fears accompanying the British hand-over of Hong Kong to the mainland Chinese in 1997. Unlike earlier migrations of Chinese to North America, these Hong Kong Chinese were middle- and upper-class merchants and business leaders. Real-estate prices shot through the roof, and entire neighborhoods became Chinese enclaves. Currently, Vancouver has the world's largest Chinese population outside of Asia.

Asians are not the only people bolstering western Canada's fast-growing population. Canada has relatively open immigration laws, resulting in a steady flow of newcomers from the Middle East, the Indian subcontinent, and Europe. Additionally, many young Canadians from the economically depressed eastern provinces see a brighter future in the west. With their strong economies and big-as-all-outdoors setting, Vancouver, Edmonton, and Calgary serve as magnets for many seeking new lives and opportunities.

3 A Taste of British Columbia & the Canadian Rockies

Western Canada is home to an excellent and evolving regional cuisine that relies on local produce, farm-raised game, grass-fed beef and lamb, and fresh-caught fish and shellfish. These high-quality ingredients are matched with inventive sauces and accompaniments, often based on native berries and wild mushrooms. In attempting to capture what the French call the *terroir,* or the native taste of the Northwest, chefs from Edmonton and Calgary to Victoria and Vancouver are producing a delicious school of cooking with distinctive regional characteristics.

One of the hallmarks of Northwest cuisine is freshness. In places like Vancouver Island, chefs meet fishing boats to select the finest of the day's catch. The lower Fraser Valley and the interior of British Columbia are filled with small specialty farms and orchards. Visit Vancouver's Granville Island Market or stop at a roadside farmer's stand to have a look at the incredible bounty of the land.

Cooks in the Northwest are also very particular about where the food comes from. Menus often tell you exactly what farm grew your asparagus, what ranch your beef was raised on, which orchard harvested your peaches, and what bay your oysters came from. To capture the distinct flavor of the Northwest—its *terroir*—means using only those products that swam in the waters or grew in or on the soil of the Northwest.

Once you've assembled your extra-fresh, locally produced foodstuffs, you need to cook it according to some kind of esthetic. This is where Northwest cooks get inventive. While many chefs marry the region's superior meat, fish, and produce to traditional French or Italian techniques, other cooks turn elsewhere for inspiration. One popular school of Northwest cooking looks west across the Pacific to Asia. Pacific Rim or Pan Pacific cuisine, as this style of cooking is often called, matches the North American Pacific coast's excellent fish and seafood with the flavors of Pacific Asia. The results can be subtle—the delicate taste of lemon grass or nori—or intense, with lashings of red curry or wasabi. However, don't expect Pacific Rim cuisine to follow the rules of Asian cooking: One memorable meal at Calgary's Belvedere restaurant (see chapter 13) matched grilled Pacific salmon with a sauce of Japanese seaweed and reduced red wine, served with heirloom potato cakes.

Other attempts to find the authentic roots of Northwest cooking look back to frontier times or to Native American techniques. There's no better way to experience salmon than at a traditional salmon bake at a Native village—most First Nations communities have an annual festival open to the general public—and many restaurants replicate this method by baking salmon on a cedar plank. Several restaurants in Vancouver and on Vancouver Island specialize in full Northwest Native feasts.

FRUITS OF THE FIELD & FOREST   Although there's nothing exotic about the varieties of vegetables available in western Canada, what will seem remarkable to visitors from distant urban areas is the freshness and quality of the produce here. Many fine restaurants contract directly with small, often organic, farms to make daily deliveries. Heirloom varieties—old-fashioned strains that are often full of flavor but don't ship or keep well—are frequently highlighted.

Fruit trees do particularly well in the hot central valleys of British Columbia, and apples, peaches, apricots, plums, and pears do more than grace the fruit basket. One of the hallmarks of Northwest cuisine is its mixing of fruit with savory meat and chicken dishes. And as long as the chef is slicing apricots to go with sautéed chicken and thyme, he might as well chop up a few hazelnuts (filberts) to toss in: These nuts thrive in the Pacific Northwest.

Berries of all kinds do well in the milder coastal regions. Cranberries grow in low-lying coastal plains. The blueberry, along with its wild cousin, the huckleberry, are both used in all manner of cooking, from breads to savory chutneys. In Alberta, another wild cousin, the Saskatoonberry, appears on menus to validate regional cooking aspirations. The astringent wild chokecherry, once used to make pemmican (a sort of Native American energy bar), is also finding its way into fine-dining restaurants.

Wild mushrooms grow throughout western Canada, and harvesting the chanterelles, morels, porcinis, and myriad other varieties is big business. Expect to find forest mushrooms in pasta, alongside a steak, in savory bread puddings, or braised with fish.

MEATS & SEAFOOD   Easily the most iconic of the Northwest's staples is the salmon. For thousands of years, the Native people have followed the cycles of the salmon, netting or spearing the fish, then smoking and preserving it for later use. The delicious and abundant salmon became the mainstay of settlers and early European residents as well. Although salmon fishing is now highly restricted and some salmon species are endangered, salmon is still very available and easily the most popular fish in the region. Expect to find a salmon dish on practically every fine-dining menu in the Northwest.

However, there are other fish in the sea. The fisheries along Vancouver Island and the Pacific Coast are rich in bottom fish like sole, flounder, and halibut, which grows to enormous size here. Fresh-caught rock and black cod are also delectable, and the Pacific has plentiful tuna, especially ahi and albacore.

Although shellfish and seafood are abundant in the Pacific, it is only recently that many of the varieties have appeared on the dinner table. Oysters grow in a number of bays on Vancouver Island, and while wild mussels blanket rocks the length of the coast, only a few sea farms grow mussels commercially. Fanny Bay, north of Qualicum Beach on Vancouver Island, is noted for both its oysters and its mussels. Another Northwest shellfish delicacy is the razor clam, a long, thin bivalve with a nutty and rich flavor. Shrimp of all sizes thrive off the coast of British Columbia, and one of the clichés of Northwest cooking is the unstinting use of local shrimp on nearly everything, from pizza to polenta. Local squid and octopus are beginning to appear on menus, while sea urchin—abundant along the coast—is harvested mostly for export to Japan.

Both British Columbia and Alberta have excellent ranch-raised beef and lamb. Steaks are a staple throughout the region, as is prime rib. You'll see lamb on menus more often in western Canada than in many areas of the United States. Game meats are increasingly popular, especially in restaurants dedicated to Northwest cuisine. Buffalo and venison are offered frequently enough to no longer seem unusual, and farm-raised pheasant is easily available. You'll look harder to find meats like caribou or elk, however. Savor it when you can.

FRUITS OF THE VINEYARDS   British Columbia wines remain one of western Canada's greatest secrets. Scarcely anyone outside of the region has ever heard of these wines, yet many are delicious and, while not exactly cheap, still less expensive than comparable wines from California. There are wineries on Vancouver and Saturna islands and in the Fraser Valley, but the real center of British Columbia's winemaking is the Okanagan Valley. In this hot and arid climate, noble grapes like cabernet sauvignon, merlot, and chardonnay thrive when irrigated. You'll also find more unusual varietals, like Gewürztraminer and sangiovese. More than three dozen wineries in the Okanagan Valley are open for tastings; when combined with excellent restaurants in Kelowna and Penticton, this region becomes a great vacation choice for the serious gastronome.

DINING IN RESTAURANTS   Canadians enjoy eating out, and you'll find excellent restaurants throughout British Columbia and Alberta. Many of the establishments recommended in this guide serve Northwest regional cuisine, the qualities of which are outlined above.

However, there is also a wealth of other kinds of restaurants available. If you're a meat eater, it's worth visiting a traditional steakhouse in Calgary or Edmonton. In many smaller centers, Greek restaurants double as the local steakhouse. Don't be surprised when you see a sign for, say, Dimitri's Steakhouse; both the steaks and the souvlaki will probably be excellent.

> **Fun Fact** **British Columbia in Television & Film**
>
> British Columbia is one of the centers of film in Canada, and many Canadian features are set in Vancouver. Numerous Hollywood films have also been shot in the province: *Legends of the Fall, Little Women, Jumanji,* and *Rambo: First Blood* give an idea of the range of films done here. The most noted recent production in the Vancouver area is television's *The X-Files,* which for its first 4 years was shot in and around the city (Vancouver doubles as many American cities, notably Washington, D.C.).

Vancouver is one of the most ethnically diverse places on earth, and the selection of restaurants is mind-boggling. You'll find some of the best Chinese food this side of Hong Kong, as well as the cooking of Russia, Mongolia, Ghana, and Sri Lanka, along with every other country and ethnic group in between.

Several Canadian chain restaurants are handy to know about. White Spot restaurants serve basic but good-quality North American cooking. Often open 24 hours, these are good places for an eggs-and-hash-browns breakfast. Tim Horton's is the place to go for coffee and donuts, plus light snacks. Earl's serves a wide menu and frequently has a lively bar scene. Expect grilled ribs and chicken, steaks, and gourmet burgers. The Keg is another western Canadian favorite, and is a bit more sedate than Earl's, with more of a steakhouse atmosphere.

4 Recommended Reading

In addition to the specialized volumes listed below, we recommend two excellent books as adjuncts to this guide, especially if you're on a road trip. The *Big New B.C. Travel Guide* is published by *Beautiful British Columbia Magazine*—an arm of the provincial tourism office—and is an amazing kilometer-by-kilometer guide to the natural and human history of the province, along with all sorts of curious facts and insights. The *Canadian Rockies Superguide,* by Graeme Pole (Altitude Publishing), has a similarly encyclopedic approach to western Alberta and eastern British Columbia, with lots of history and nature writing, accompanied by attractive photos. It's also a good source of information on hikes and other outdoor adventures.

CANADIAN HISTORY   A basic primer on the country's complex history is *The Penguin History of Canada,* by Kenneth McNaught. *The Canadians,* by Andrew H. Malcolm (St. Martin's Press), is an insightful and highly readable rumination on what it is to be Canadian, written by the former *New York Times* Canada bureau chief.

Peter C. Newman has produced an intriguing history of the Hudson's Bay Company, *Caesars of the Wilderness,* beginning with the early fur-trading days. *The Great Adventure,* by David Cruise and Alison Griffiths (St. Martin's Press), tells the story of the Mounties and their role in the subduing of the Canadian west.

For a specific history of British Columbia, try *British Columbia: An Illustrated History,* by Geoffrey Molyneux (Polestar Books), or *The West Beyond the West: A History of British Columbia,* by Jean Borman (University of Toronto Press). Review Vancouver's past with *Vancouver: A History in Photographs,* by Aynsley Wyse and Dana Wyse (Altitude Publishing).

Alberta: A History in Photographs, by Faye Reinebert Holt (Altitude Publishing), is a good introduction to the history of that province, though the engaging *Alberta History Along the Highway: A Traveler's Guide to the Fascinating Facts, Intriguing Incidents and Lively Legends in Alberta's Remarkable Past,* by Ted Stone (Orca Books), is the book you'll want to take along in the car (the same author has a companion volume on British Columbia).

To learn about Canada's Native peoples, read *Native Peoples and Cultures of Canada,* by Alan D. McMillan (Douglas & McIntyre), which includes both history and current issues. The classic book on Canada's indigenous peoples, *The Indians of Canada* (University of Toronto Press), was written in 1932 by Diamond Jenness. The author's life is an amazing story in its own right, as he spent years living with various indigenous peoples across the country.

NATURAL HISTORY   Two good general guides to the natural world in western Canada are the Audubon Society's *Pacific Coast,* by Evelyn McConnaghey, and *Western Forests,* by Stephen Whitney (both published by Knopf).

British Columbia: A Natural History, by Richard Cannings (Douglas & McIntyre), is an in-depth guide to the province's plants, animals, and geography. *Plants and Animals of the Pacific Northwest: An Illustrated Guide to the Natural History of Western Oregon, Washington, and British Columbia,* by Eugene N. Kozloff (University of Washington Press), is another good general resource.

For information on the natural history of Alberta's southern prairies, pick up *From Grasslands to Rockland: An Explorers Guide to the Ecosystems of Southernmost Alberta,* by Peter Douglas Elias (Rocky Mountain Books).

Bird-watchers might want to dig up a copy of *Familiar Birds of the Northwest,* by Harry B. Nehls (Audubon Society of Portland).

Read about the natural history of extinct wildlife in *A Wonderful Life: The Burgess Shale and the Nature of History,* by Stephen Jay Gould (Norton), which details the discovery and scientific ramifications of the fossil beds found in Yoho National Park.

OUTDOOR PURSUITS   Edward Weber's *Diving and Snorkeling Guide to the Pacific Northwest* (Pisces) is a good place to start if you're planning a diving holiday in the Northwest.

Mountain Bike Adventures in Southwest British Columbia, by Greg Maurer and Tomas Vrba (Mountaineers), is just one of a cascade of books on off-road biking in western Canada.

A good hiking guide to western British Columbia is *Don't Waste Your Time in the B.C. Coast Mountains: An Opinionated Hiking Guide to Help you Get the Most from this Magnificent Wilderness,* by Kathy Copeland. *A Guide to Climbing and Hiking in Southwestern British Columbia,* by Bruce Fairley, also includes Vancouver Island.

Hiking Alberta, by Will Harmon (Falcon), covers 75 hikes along the eastern face of the Rockies. Chris Dawson's *Due North of Montana: A Guide to Flyfishing in Alberta* (Johnson Books) will point you toward favorite fishing holes.

FICTION & MEMOIR   Alice Munro's short fiction captures the soul of what it is to be Canadian in brief, though often wrenching, prose. Some of the stories in *The Love of a Good Woman* take place in Vancouver. Another good selection of short stories as well as poetry is *Fresh Tracks: Writing the Western Landscape* (Pamela Banting, editor), a collection of writings by western Canadian authors.

The frontier-era conflicts in southern Alberta form the backdrop for the award-winning *The Englishman's Boy,* by Guy Vanderhaeghe, an atmospheric western with a story that travels from Fort Macleod to Hollywood.

Richard P. Hobson Jr. writes of his experiences as a modern-day cowboy on the grasslands of central British Columbia in an acclaimed series of memoirs titled *Grass Beyond the Mountains: Discovering the Last Great Cattle Frontier on the North American Continent, The Rancher Takes a Wife,* and *Nothing Too Good for a Cowboy.*

Vancouver and southwestern British Columbia are home to a number of noted international authors. *Generation X* chronicler Douglas Coupland lives here, as does Jane Rule, author of *Desert of the Heart.* Science-fiction writer William Gibson's dark vision of the cyber-future attracts a large young audience. W. P. Kinsella (*Shoeless Joe*) and mystery writer Laurali R. Wright also make their homes here. Wright's Karl Alberg mystery series usually takes place in and around Vancouver.

Index

See also Accommodations and Restaurant indexes, below.

ACCOMMODATIONS

RESTAURANTS

FROMMER'S® COMPLETE TRAVEL GUIDES

Alaska
Alaska Cruises & Ports of Call
Amsterdam
Argentina & Chile
Arizona
Atlanta
Australia
Austria
Bahamas
Barcelona, Madrid & Seville
Beijing
Belgium, Holland & Luxembourg
Bermuda
Boston
British Columbia & the Canadian
    Rockies
Budapest & the Best of Hungary
California
Canada
Cancún, Cozumel & the Yucatán
Cape Cod, Nantucket &
    Martha's Vineyard
Caribbean
Caribbean Cruises & Ports of Call
Caribbean Ports of Call
Carolinas & Georgia
Chicago
China
Colorado
Costa Rica
Denmark
Denver, Boulder & Colorado Springs
England
Europe
European Cruises & Ports of Call
Florida
France

Germany
Great Britain
Greece
Greek Islands
Hawaii
Hong Kong
Honolulu, Waikiki & Oahu
Ireland
Israel
Italy
Jamaica
Japan
Las Vegas
London
Los Angeles
Maryland & Delaware
Maui
Mexico
Montana & Wyoming
Montréal & Québec City
Munich & the Bavarian Alps
Nashville & Memphis
Nepal
New England
New Mexico
New Orleans
New York City
New Zealand
Nova Scotia, New Brunswick &
    Prince Edward Island
Oregon
Paris
Philadelphia & the Amish Country
Portugal
Prague & the Best of the Czech
    Republic
Provence & the Riviera

Puerto Rico
Rome
San Antonio & Austin
San Diego
San Francisco
Santa Fe, Taos & Albuquerque
Scandinavia
Scotland
Seattle & Portland
Shanghai
Singapore & Malaysia
South Africa
South America
Southeast Asia
South Florida
South Pacific
Spain
Sweden
Switzerland
Texas
Thailand
Tokyo
Toronto
Tuscany & Umbria
USA
Utah
Vancouver & Victoria
Vermont, New Hampshire
    & Maine
Vienna & the Danube Valley
Virgin Islands
Virginia
Walt Disney World & Orlando
Washington, D.C.
Washington State

FROMMER'S® DOLLAR-A-DAY GUIDES

Australia from $50 a Day
California from $70 a Day
Caribbean from $70 a Day
England from $75 a Day
Europe from $70 a Day

Florida from $70 a Day
Hawaii from $80 a Day
Ireland from $60 a Day
Italy from $70 a Day
London from $85 a Day

New York from $90 a Day
Paris from $80 a Day
San Francisco from $70 a Day
Washington, D.C., from $80
    a Day

FROMMER'S® PORTABLE GUIDES

Acapulco, Ixtapa & Zihuatanejo
Amsterdam
Aruba
Australia's Great Barrier Reef
Bahamas
Baja & Los Cabos
Berlin
Big Island of Hawaii
Boston
California Wine Country
Cancún
Charleston & Savannah
Chicago
Disneyland

Dublin
Florence
Frankfurt
Hong Kong
Houston
Las Vegas
London
Los Angeles
Maine Coast
Maui
Miami
New Orleans
New York City
Paris

Phoenix & Scottsdale
Portland
Puerto Rico
Puerto Vallarta, Manzanillo &
    Guadalajara
San Diego
San Francisco
Seattle
Sydney
Tampa & St. Petersburg
Vancouver
Venice
Virgin Islands
Washington, D.C.

FROMMER'S® NATIONAL PARK GUIDES

Family Vacations in the National
    Parks
Grand Canyon

National Parks of the American
    West
Rocky Mountain
Yellowstone & Grand Teton

Yosemite & Sequoia/
    Kings Canyon
Zion & Bryce Canyon

FROMMER'S® MEMORABLE WALKS

Chicago
London

New York
Paris

San Francisco

FROMMER'S® GREAT OUTDOOR GUIDES

Arizona & New Mexico
New England

Northern California
Southern New England

Vermont & New Hampshire

SUZY GERSHMAN'S BORN TO SHOP GUIDES

Born to Shop: France
Born to Shop: Hong Kong,
  Shanghai & Beijing

Born to Shop: Italy
Born to Shop: London

Born to Shop: New York
Born to Shop: Paris

FROMMER'S® IRREVERENT GUIDES

Amsterdam
Boston
Chicago
Las Vegas
London

Los Angeles
Manhattan
New Orleans
Paris
Rome

San Francisco
Seattle & Portland
Vancouver
Walt Disney World
Washington, D.C.

FROMMER'S® BEST-LOVED DRIVING TOURS

Britain
California
Florida
France

Germany
Ireland
Italy

New England
Scotland
Spain

HANGING OUT™ GUIDES

Hanging Out in England
Hanging Out in Europe

Hanging Out in France
Hanging Out in Ireland

Hanging Out in Italy
Hanging Out in Spain

THE UNOFFICIAL GUIDES®

Bed & Breakfasts and Country
  Inns in:
    California
    New England
    Northwest
    Rockies
    Southeast
Beyond Disney
Branson, Missouri
California with Kids
Chicago
Cruises
Disneyland

Florida with Kids
Golf Vacations in the
  Eastern U.S.
The Great Smoky &
  Blue Ridge Mountains
Hawaii
Inside Disney
Las Vegas
London
Mid-Atlantic with Kids
Mini Las Vegas
Mini-Mickey
New England & New York
  with Kids

New Orleans
New York City
Paris
San Francisco
Skiing in the West
Southeast with Kids
Walt Disney World
Walt Disney World for
  Grown-ups
Walt Disney World for Kids
Washington, D.C.
World's Best Diving Vacations

SPECIAL-INTEREST TITLES

Frommer's Adventure Guide to Australia & New
  Zealand
Frommer's Adventure Guide to Central America
Frommer's Adventure Guide to India & Pakistan
Frommer's Adventure Guide to South America
Frommer's Adventure Guide to Southeast Asia
Frommer's Adventure Guide to Southern Africa
Frommer's Britain's Best Bed & Breakfasts and
  Country Inns
Frommer's France's Best Bed & Breakfasts and
  Country Inns
Frommer's Italy's Best Bed & Breakfasts and Country
  Inns
Frommer's Caribbean Hideaways

Frommer's Exploring America by RV
Frommer's Gay & Lesbian Europe
Frommer's The Moon
Frommer's New York City with Kids
Frommer's Road Atlas Britain
Frommer's Road Atlas Europe
Frommer's Washington, D.C., with Kids
Frommer's What the Airlines Never Tell You
Israel Past & Present
The New York Times' Guide to Unforgettable
  Weekends
Places Rated Almanac
Retirement Places Rated

Wickedly honest guides for sophisticated travelers—and those who want to be.